THIS ITEM 2 WEEKS ONLY
NO RENEWALS

DATE DUE

01-31-01 IC: 4595792		

Theory of
Incomplete Markets

Volume 1

Theory of
Incomplete Markets

Volume 1

Michael Magill

Martine Quinzii

The MIT Press
Cambridge, Massachusetts
London, England

LaTeX composition in Computer Modern fonts: Arthur Ogawa
Illustrations: David Niergarth

This book was printed and bound in the United States of America.

Library of Congress Cataloging-in-Publication Data
Magill, Michael, J. P.
   Theory of incomplete markets / Michael J. P. Magill, Martine Quinzii
    v. < 1,   >; cm.
   Includes bibliographical references and index.
   ISBN 0-262-13324-5 (hc: alk. paper)
   1. Equilibrium (Economics) 2. Uncertainty. 1. Quinzii, Martine. II. Title
HB145.M34 1996
339.5—dc20   95-26219
CIP

This book is dedicated to

the founders of modern equilibrium theory

KENNETH ARROW   GERARD DEBREU

LIONEL MCKENZIE   ROY RADNER

and to

the memory of their predecessors

IRVING FISHER

LEON WALRAS

to whom

the subject owes its origin

Foreword

Uncertainty and Expectation
are the Joys of Life

Love for Love, W. Congreve

When I was asked to write a foreword for *Theory of Incomplete Markets*, I felt very honored since at that time I had already read various versions of the manuscript, and it was clear to me that the final product would become a splendid book (a rational expectation). Yet why did Martine and Michael ask me, having made no scientific contribution to the field? Surely, they knew that I am an ardent admirer and respectful supporter of General Equilibrium Theory. Also they must have felt my active and lasting interest in their research during the last ten years. Indeed, during every BOWO from 1988 to 1992 the "theory of incomplete markets" was always a central theme of the Bonn-Workshop. I immensely enjoyed following closely the impressive annual progress in this research area and the exchange of ideas, opinions and often heated arguments.

When I read Debreu's *Theory of Value* thirty years ago, I was enthusiastic about General Equilibrium Theory until I came to chapter 7: Uncertainty. The treatment of time and uncertainty was not entirely convincing—at least from a descriptive point of view. Time and uncertainty was treated in an amazingly simple way. This simplicity was achieved by postulating a highly idealized market structure, the Arrow-Debreu complete system of contingent contracts. But invoking this hypothesis dispenses with the modelling of expectations of what the future has in store—and gone are the joys of life.

Theory of Incomplete Markets (the present book and the forthcoming volume 2) is an essential extension of Debreu's chapter 7; it offers a more realistic and richer modelling of time and uncertainty. This important new development has its origin in the well-known fundamental contributions by K. Arrow (1953) and R. Radner (1972). In Radner's treatment of time and uncertainty, economic agents trade sequentially on spot markets and are unable to make more than limited contractual commitments into the future to coordinate their activities and share their risks.

During the academic year 1985/86, G. Debreu organized a one-year work-shop on Mathematical Economics at the Mathematical Sciences Research Institute at Berkeley. I remember when at one of the weekly seminars D. Duffie and W. Shafer presented their paper, "Equilibrium in incomplete markets—A basic model of generic existence". In essence, they showed how a difficulty in Radner's model, pointed out by O. Hart (1975) by some well-chosen examples, could be resolved. Due to this development there was enthusiasm again among a small group of mathematical economists. General Equilibrium Theory with Incomplete Markets became an active field of research. Martine and Michael, among others, have made outstanding contributions to this new and important development.

The present book is the first part of the contemporary story of Incomplete Markets. This is a splendid book. It contains the most recent research and still is eminently readable by any economist who is willing to invest some effort. Even though Martine and Michael do not sidestep the unescapable technical problems, the message of the book can still be understood and appreciated by readers who do not place great value on the technical skills of mathematical economists. The sections entitled *Motivation and Summary* and *Historical Remarks* are masterpieces. They give deep insight into the subject and suggest new directions for research.

No economist should miss the chance to read *Theory of Incomplete Markets*.

Werner Hildenbrand
Bonn, February 1995

Theory of

Incomplete Markets

Contents

3 Two-Period Security Pricing 137

Preface

The paradox is now fully established that the utmost abstractions are
the true weapons with which to control our thought of concrete fact.

Science and the Modern World, (1925) A. N. Whitehead

Every now and then new concepts and techniques emerge which lead to a
fresh way of looking at old problems: hitherto disjoint or disconnected subfields come together to form part of a coherent whole. Economists have long
been interested in the relationship between the real, financial, and monetary
sectors of an economy. Traditionally the analysis of the real sector was the
purview of equilibrium theory and microeconomics (price theory), financial
markets were the subject of finance, while monetary theory formed part of
macroeconomics. The object of this book is to show that the newly emerging
theory of incomplete markets provides a useful framework for unifying these
subfields and for clarifying the mutual dependence between real, financial and
monetary phenomena.

Since mutual dependence is the subject of equilibrium theory it is natural
that the model draws heavily on traditional equilibrium theory: the new element is the recognition that given the imperfections in their knowledge and
their motivation by self-interest, agents are obliged to trade sequentially and
are unwilling or unable to make more than limited contractual commitments
into the future to co-ordinate their activities and share their risks. In short,
agents trade in a sequence economy with incomplete markets.

The theory we outline has taken a long time to emerge. It took more than
a century to pass from Walras (1874), through Irving Fisher (1930), Arrow-
Debreu-McKenzie (1950's) and Radner (1972), to where we stand now. The
immediate cause for writing this book was a stimulating series of developments in the 1980's, in which we were involved, along with a small group of
researchers. These results attracted the curiosity and attention of economists—
it became clear that the elements of a new theory of markets was emerging that
could retain the coherence and generality of the traditional general equilibrium
model, but in which the types of markets and contracts modelled were much

closer to those observed in the real world. In addition it was found that when nominal contracts were introduced, monetary policy was non-neutral. All this created a sense of excitement since an equilibrium model was emerging which, although based on rational expectations, had distinctly Keynesian features.

High points in the collective effort for advancing this newly emerging field were a memorable series of Summer Workshops on Incomplete Markets organized by Mordecai Kurz and Werner Hildenbrand—the IMSSS Workshops in 1987 and 1989 at Stanford University and the BOWO Workshops held annually between 1988 and 1992 at the University of Bonn. We, and our fellow researchers in the field, owe much to the stimulus and initiative of Mordecai and Werner who believed in the field at an early stage and provided a forum in which ideas, techniques and often heated arguments were exchanged.

Part of the syndrome of work on the frontiers of any field of modern economics is that to an outsider, ideas seem couched in language which is esoteric, and hidden by technique which is forbidding; it is rarely clear how much of this inaccessibility is to be attributed to the inherent difficulty of the problems treated or rather is simply a reflection of the immaturity of the field. It takes time to make ideas simple and to appreciate where their most natural domain of application lies. This book seeks to circumvent these difficulties by making the ideas accessible to as wide an audience of economists as possible. Following the tradition first introduced by Irving Fisher (1930) in his *Theory of Interest*, we begin with the simplest version of the general model—a one-good, two-period exchange economy—and build up progressively from there, extending the analysis to the multiperiod setting, to an economy with production and finally to an economy with nominal contracts and money. For simplicity all the formal results of this first volume are derived in the setting of a one-good economy, although the multicommodity model is introduced and discussed whenever this serves to better appreciate the ideas.

The Introduction provides an intuitive discussion of the ideas which lie behind the primitive assumptions of the model. Each chapter that follows is written with the same structure. An initial section—entitled *Motivation and Summary*—seeks to summarize the main ideas in a language which is as far as possible non-technical, while the final section—entitled *Historical Remarks*—rather than being a conventional list of references, seeks to place the development of the ideas in their historical perspective: thus the beginning and end are non-technical and should be accessible to everyone. The central part of each chapter is largely self-contained. Primitive concepts are expressed as axioms, assumptions, or definitions, and results are expressed as propositions or theorems. Whenever mathematical concepts and techniques beyond standard calculus and linear algebra are required to express the ideas, they are motivated and introduced at the beginning of the central core of the chapter, or if they are more technical in the *Appendix*. Stating results as propositions leads to clarity of exposition, but brings with it an inevitable conciseness. To have the best of both worlds, we compensate this by an extended economic discussion of the content and implications of the propositions. Believing the maxim that a good picture is worth a thousand words, we draw at every stage on the reader's geometric intuition: the key idea behind almost every proof can be understood by means of a carefully chosen figure. One of the best ways of developing a facility for using the model is to do the *Exercises* at the end of each chapter. Each exercise is preceded by a statement of the idea that it seeks to illustrate.

This book can be used as textbook for an introductory course on the theory of incomplete markets for first or second year graduate students and even for advanced undergraduates who are sufficiently well prepared. It can also be used to complement first and second year courses in microeconomics, macroeconomics, and the theory of finance by a selective choice of material from different chapters. Since sections rather than chapters have been chosen as the basic units, this leaves ample flexibility for a selective use of the book. A reader familiar with Hal Varian's *Microeconomic Analysis* and Andreu Mas-Colell, Michael Whinston, and Jerry Green's *Microeconomic Theory* will be well prepared to master the material. Earlier drafts have been used for a number of years to teach advanced undergraduates and first year graduates at the University of Bonn, for first year graduates at the University of Paris (I, II and IX), the University of Copenhagen, and Stanford University, and for second year graduates at the University of Southern California and the University of California, Davis. Earlier drafts have circulated widely since 1989; we are grateful to the many students at these and other institutions for their constructive criticisms.

When this book was originally planned, Wayne Shafer was part of the team that set itself the task of writing down the gospel of Incomplete Markets. The hazards of academic life have sent Wayne far from California and reduced the team to the two remaining authors. We hope, however, that the benefits from our past collaboration with Wayne have sufficiently penetrated to this final draft, so as to minimize the evident loss for the reader.

Research is as much a social as an individual activity, and in this regard we have been most fortunate with the co-authors and researchers with whom we have worked, interacted and exchanged ideas over the years: in addition to our special debt to Wayne Shafer, we owe special thanks to Jacques Drèze, John Geanakoplos, Andreu Mas-Colell, Don Brown, David Cass, Darrel Duffie, Thorsten Hens, Heracles Polemarchakis, Jan Werner, Mike Woodford and Charles Wilson. We are also grateful to Ken Arrow, Gerard Debreu, Lionel McKenzie, and Roy Radner for the example they set, and for their personal encouragement in this project.

Financial support from the National Science Foundation over many years and from the Gottfried-Wilhelm-Leibniz-Förderpreis has played a crucial role in making this research possible: without their support much of this research would never have taken place.

More recently we have drawn on the patience of our colleagues who kindly read and criticized a seemingly unending sequence of drafts: our thanks go to Richard Day, Vai-Lam Mui, Andy Neumeyer, and Peter Rosendorff at the University of Southern California and to Louis Makowski, Klaus Nehring, John Roemer, Kevin Salyer, Steve Sheffrin, and Joaquim Silvestre at the University of California, Davis.

The actual production of the manuscript would have been unthinkable without the exceptional skill and lightning speed of Sena Schlessinger who became an expert with TEX to fulfill our exponentially growing needs and who never complained of creating a new directory for yet another revised version. Finally our thanks to the staff at the MIT Press and especially to Terry Vaughn for shepherding the manuscript to its final form and in the process proving that his patience with incorrigible authors knows no end.

Despite all our efforts at simplification this still remains a book of theory, and abstract theory is sometimes perceived as drawing us away from reality: hence its occasional bad press and bad reputation. But this is simply an error in the perception of the role of science. In the pages that follow Simon's concept of bounded rationality will help us understand the role and structure of social institutions composed of human beings: but it can also help us understand the role of abstract thought in modern science. For the human mind has a limited capacity to understand the complexity of the real world: it needs to build a simplified model of reality. To paraphrase Whitehead, abstract theory is the instrument by which we acquire our understanding of concrete facts.

Los Angeles   Michael Magill
June 20, 1994   Martine Quinzii

1
INTRODUCTION

Perhaps the reader feels that this general, philosophical disquisition on the behavior of mankind is somewhat remote from the economic theory under discussion. But I think not. I accuse the classical economic theory of being itself one of these pretty, polite techniques which tries to deal with the present by abstracting from the fact that we know very little about the future. I daresay that a classical economist would readily admit this. But, even so, I think he has overlooked the precise nature of the difference which his abstraction makes between theory and practice, and the character of the fallacies into which he is likely to be led.

Quarterly Journal of Economics, (1937), J.M. Keynes

The capacity of the human mind for formulating and solving complex problems is very small compared with the size of the problems whose solution is required for objectively rational behavior in the real world.

Models of Man, (1957), H.A. Simon

1. MAIN THEMES

Some fifty years ago two far-reaching but apparently unrelated contributions set in motion a radical transformation of the way economists think about their subject, ushering in the era of *modern economics*. The new vision of the functioning of an economy offered by Keynes in his *General Theory of Employment, Interest and Money* (1936) and the principle of *bounded rationality* elaborated by Simon (1947, 1957) in a long series of studies on the nature of human decision making, have this in common, that they seek a new foundation for economics based on an explicit recognition of the limited ability of human beings to cope with, and hence make decisions in, a complex environment of time and uncertainty. Studying the consequences of these imperfections for the organization and functioning of an economy constitutes a large part of the agenda of modern economics. This book focuses on consequences of these imperfections for a general equilibrium model of an economy: we argue that when agents have only limited knowledge and ability to cope with the uncertainties presented by the future, they trade sequentially and use a system of contracts which involve only limited commitments into the future. Our main objective is to study the qualitative properties of the equilibria of an economy with such a sequential and incomplete market structure.

Classical economics sought to explain the way markets co-ordinate the activities of many distinct individuals each acting independently in their own self-interest. An elegant synthesis of two hundred years of classical thought was achieved by general equilibrium theory, often referred to as *Arrow-Debreu-McKenzie theory*.[1] The essential message of this theory is that when there are markets and associated prices for all goods and services in the economy, no externalities or public goods and no informational asymmetries or market power,[2] then competitive markets allocate resources efficiently.

Since economic activity (production, exchange and consumption) inevitably takes place over time and since many activities connected with the future involve significant degrees of uncertainty, a realistic analysis of a market economy must explicitly take into account the unfolding of time and uncertainty. In such a setting, the key hypothesis of the *Arrow-Debreu model*[3] is that at some initial date there is a market for each good produced or consumed in every possible future contingency—in short, that there is a complete set of contingent markets. If economic agents had full knowledge of all possible future events, had unlimited powers to calculate the relative benefits accruing from different courses of action, and if in addition the society could costlessly monitor and enforce the commitments and actions of agents, then, in such an ideal society, we might expect to observe this structure of complete contingent markets. If all future generations had stand-in representatives at the initial date, then such a system of comprehensive contractual agreements would dispose, at one stroke, of all future economic problems: agents and their descendants would automatically carry out their production and consumption activities, planned and co-ordinated in advance, watching the future unfold down one of its pre-ordained paths. Such an extreme idealized description of a market economy is of course an overstatement of the classical theory, however in spirit it conveys its basic message, namely that markets can be relied upon to solve the economic problem of resource allocation, and that except for the provision of

---

[1]The first formalized general equilibrium model was due to Walras (1874), who laid out a rich descriptive model of a market economy, complete with capital goods and money. A stripped down version of this model, which is basically the model of modern general equilibrium theory, was subjected to a deeper normative analysis by Pareto (1896–97, 1909) who introduced the criterion of Pareto efficiency and proved local versions of the First and Second Welfare Theorems. The model acquired its modern abstract axiomatic form in the 1950s with the papers of Arrow (1951), Debreu (1952, 1959), Arrow-Debreu (1954) and McKenzie (1954, 1955, 1959). The development of the abstract theory in the 1950s was made possible by the earlier contributions of Wald (1933, 1934, 1936), von Neumann (1937) and Nash (1950).

[2]In particular there are no increasing returns to scale—firms are small relative to the market.

[3]While the general equilibrium theory developed in the 1950s is referred to as the Arrow-Debreu-McKenzie model, when this theory is applied to an economy with uncertainty and complete contingent markets it is typically referred to as the Arrow-Debreu model, since Arrow (1953) for the two-period model and Debreu (1959) for the multiperiod model, first explicitly introduced this market structure.

public goods or the resolution of problems arising from externalities, there is no need for government intervention.

The faith of classical economists in an orderly, rational and predictable world which was so characteristic of the 18th and 19th centuries began to be seriously questioned at the beginning of the 20th century. The turmoil forced on the economies of Europe by the First World War, the subsequent hyperinflations and the massive unemployment of the Great Depression cast serious doubts in the minds of many economists on the validity of the classical paradigm. The breaking point occurred with the publication of Keynes' *General Theory* which in essence offered a new paradigm, differing in crucial ways from that of classical economic theory. He argued that imperfections, having their origin in the unpredictability of—and hence the limited ability of agents to cope with—the uncertain future, lead to missing markets, rigidities in prices and a process of decision-making by agents which is based more on simple rules of thumb and the collective psychology of the market than a rational, systematic evaluation of possible future scenarios. The overall effect of these imperfections is that modern economies exhibit an intrinsic instability that can lead to major co-ordination failures characterized by prolonged periods of unemployment.

If much of the economics profession was seduced by the impressionist picture of a capitalist economy sketched by Keynes, it has proved much harder to reformulate economic theory so as to take into account these imperfections in a rigorous and coherent way, based on a consistent theory of the behavior of agents under uncertainty. As frequently happens in science, progress came from the study of a seemingly unrelated problem. Simon (1947, 1957) was interested in understanding the nature of organizations: he argued that the hierarchical structure and division of tasks characteristic of organizations can only be understood if agents are recognized to be what he called boundedly rational. In contrast to the intuitive and broadly sketched ideas of Keynes, Simon developed a more systematic and precise analysis of the limited ability of human beings to process information and compute optimal strategies in a complex environment—an analysis with close connections to his simultaneous work on artificial intelligence (Simon 1969, 1979a).

Keynes attached considerable weight to the idea that when agents face substantial uncertainty they are reluctant to make more than limited contractual commitments into the future: as a result markets which might otherwise be active in matching future demand and supply are missing.[4] We will argue at more length in the next section that one consequence of the limited capacity of agents to foresee future events and to calculate the relative benefits of different courses of action, combined with the possibility of opportunistic behavior which arises in a world where information regarding the characteristics and actions

---

[4]See Keynes (1936, ch. 16, p. 210–211).

of other agents is at best costly and perhaps impossible to acquire, is that the ideal structure of markets in which everything is traded out in advance would involve prohibitively large "transactions costs". The market structure that we observe in the real world, which is better adapted to a society in which agents are opportunistic, have limited capacity to cope with uncertainty and in which the enforcement of contracts is costly, consists of a sequential system of spot markets for the exchange of goods and services combined with contractual markets involving limited commitments into the future. Thus a great deal of realism is gained if this type of market structure is incorporated into a general equilibrium model in place of the idealized system of complete contingent markets.

When agents enter into contracts which involve commitments in the future, they need to form expectations about the possible future circumstances in which they may find themselves. To the extent that agents know that contracts are enforced, they must limit their contractual commitments to those they are confident they can meet: the requirement that contracts are fulfilled is almost tantamount to the requirement that agents' expectations are fulfilled. Since boundedly rational agents are limited in their ability to foresee what the future has in store, they have to restrict the contracts they use to those whose provisions are simple (i.e. depend only on broadly defined events) and whose consequences for the parties involved can be predicted with relative accuracy. While it is often argued that bounded rationality implies that agents will typically make errors in their expectations, our argument is rather that bounded rationality implies that agents will restrict their trading to a simplified structure of contracts relative to which they are less likely to make errors in their expectations, or in the theoretical limit, no error at all. These ideas are developed at greater length in Section 3 where we explain why macroeconomists and economists studying financial markets were led to switch from the assumption of adaptive expectations, widely used in the post-war period, to the hypothesis of rational expectations, finding it a more fruitful assumption on which to base a theory of sequence economies.

Model of Sequence Economy

These considerations lead us to study a general equilibrium model in which agents trade on a sequence of markets in which there are limited forward trades, and in which the decisions of agents are based on expectations which are fulfilled in equilibrium. The resulting model retains the simplicity, coherence and generality which are the hallmarks of the Arrow-Debreu construction, while moving the nature of the markets, contracts and constraints on agent participation into closer conformity with the actual structure of markets observed in the real world. A sequence of spot markets constitutes the basic set of markets on which goods and services are exchanged; the transactions on these markets are monitored using money as the medium of exchange.[5] On top of this initial level of markets is a sequence of contractual markets which permit commitments to be made that stretch to more or less extended periods into the future. While these commitments can take a variety of forms, they typically involve either the promise to deliver goods and services (real contracts) or the delivery of amounts of money (nominal contracts). This collection of contracts is part of the institutional data of the model and when there is only a limited set of such contracts, markets are said to be incomplete.

This model poses the problem of resource allocation in a more general setting than the traditional general equilibrium (GE) model; furthermore it provides a natural bridge between several subfields of economics—principally microeconomics, the theory of financial markets and macroeconomics. It is our belief that we are still only at the beginning of exploiting its potential for formalizing and studying many issues of macroeconomics and that it will prove to have fruitful connections with many other subfields of economics such as international trade and finance, public finance, money and banking. It is for this reason we have gone to great lengths to decompose the general model into a sequence of simpler submodels of progressively greater generality, developing the basic insights that can be derived at each stage, and choosing just those mathematical techniques which seem best adapted to exploit the structure of the model and reveal its basic insights.

Following the example set many years ago by Irving Fisher in his *Theory of Interest* (1930), we devote the first volume to the one-good model: simplifying the structure of the general model by omitting the spot markets, focuses attention on the financial markets. As we shall see, the resulting finance economy has a surprisingly rich structure. Furthermore, gaining insight and experience by analyzing the finance economy is an excellent preliminary step to understanding the general model: techniques and intuition can be developed gradually before more advanced techniques are introduced which are needed to handle the general model (in the second volume).

Equilibrium Analysis

The method of analysis of an equilibrium model developed in the *Arrow-Debreu-McKenzie theory* focuses on three questions: existence, determinacy and optimality of equilibrium. Establishing existence of an equilibrium ensures that the various components of the model fit together in a meaningful way, namely that the model has a coherent structure. The importance

---

[5]This is explicitly modelled in Chapter 7: in Chapters 2–6 it is assumed that accounts are kept in the numeraire good.

of determinacy, namely the local uniqueness of equilibria, is often underestimated: it provides a measure of the ability of the model to predict the outcome of economic activity and it is a *sine qua non* for comparative statics, namely the analysis of how an equilibrium changes when certain basic parameters of the model are altered. Studying the optimality properties of an equilibrium is crucial since it evaluates the efficiency of the underlying market structure as a mechanism for allocating resources.

This is the method of analysis that we adopt in Chapters 2 and 4 to study the two-period and multiperiod models. While proving existence of an equilibrium is one of the best ways of understanding the internal structure of a model, economists who are primarily interested in the use of the model in specific contexts, or in its qualitative predictions, may consider the proof of existence an abstract exercise without immediate payoff. Since our goal is not to discourage but rather to seduce the reader, we deal only briefly with the question of existence. The proof of existence established for the one-good two-period model permits the introduction in a simple setting of geometric methods which (as shown in the second volume) lead to a clean and direct proof of existence for the general model. In Chapter 4 the one-good multiperiod model is used to illustrate why an equilibrium may not exist in the general model. In this case the difficulty comes from the capital value terms: when there are many periods a long-lived security yields a current dividend and can in addition be sold for the capital value of its remaining dividend stream. We construct an example in which these capital value terms lead to discontinuities in agents' demands in such a way that no equilibrium exists. Thus as soon as there are more than two periods (or more than one good) an equilibrium can only be shown to exist for most economies. The methods which have been developed to deal with this problem will be explained in the second volume.

Since the overall objective of this volume is to take the analysis as far as possible without introducing the more sophisticated techniques of equilibrium theory, the problem of determinacy is not systematically studied. However in Chapter 7, where nominal contracts are introduced, the problem cannot be avoided: such contracts introduce a new element into the story which can only be understood by studying the determinacy of equilibrium. We show (intuitively) that when nominal contracts are introduced, the standard concept of equilibrium leads to an indeterminate outcome. This is a clear manifestation that something is missing in the standard model: the missing element will come as no surprise to a macroeconomist—it is no less than an explicit modelling of the monetary side of the economy.

When markets are incomplete, agents' activities are not well co-ordinated in an equilibrium. Establishing this property—which was for a long time a Folk Theorem—leads us to introduce some techniques that play an important role in the analysis of the model: for an economy with a sequential structure, many properties while true for "most" are not true for "all" economies. The key idea is to introduce a parametrized family of economies where the parameters are chosen from the exogenous data which defines an economy (the initial resources, preferences, technology and structure of contracts). The mathematical argument draws on techniques of differential topology known as *Transversality Theory* which provide a precise abstract way of asserting that a certain property (defined by a system of equations) holds for most parameter values. These ideas are explained in Chapter 2 and are used to prove that for most economies with incomplete markets, agents' marginal rates of substitution are not equalized in equilibrium—as a result the equilibrium is Pareto inefficient. Since this property and the way in which it is established play such an important role throughout the theory of incomplete markets, we have taken great care to explain both the mathematical and the economic ideas which underlie this type of proof.

The concept of Pareto optimality is not the appropriate criterion for judging the efficiency of an incomplete system of competitive markets. The appropriate notion is a less demanding criterion of constrained efficiency which defines the optimality of the markets relative to the limited ability of agents to redistribute their income across future contingencies. An equilibrium is always constrained efficient in the one-good two-period model: it might be inferred from this that with rational expectations, competitive markets allocate resources as efficiently as can be expected given the limited market structure. However as soon as there are more than two periods or more than one good this efficiency property typically ceases to hold. The source of the inefficiency lies in the failure of the competitive mechanism to take into account the feedback between the distribution of income that emerges from trading on the financial markets and the future prices of the securities (or in the multigood model, the future spot prices). While the presence of this feedback, or pecuniary externality, suggests a potential role for the government for improving the allocation of resources, in most cases substantial information would be required by the government to achieve such an improvement.

Pricing of Financial Contracts

Broadly speaking the contracts which are commonly traded in an economy fall into two categories: those which are used for organizing (co-ordinating) production activity over time and those which are used for transferring (redistributing) income over time and across contingencies. The first category includes all the supply and delivery contracts signed between firms, between firms and government and between firms and individuals, as well as all the labor contracts between firms and employees. The second category includes the many different types of insurance contracts, lending contracts (bonds), equity contracts and a variety of futures and option contracts. The sequential model studied in this book has sufficient flexibility to incorporate both categories of contracts. However the contracts about which we know the most in a competitive setting are the financial contracts (the second category) and the development of this theory has been one of the success stories of modern economics.

Chapters 3 and 5 tell an important part of this story from a perspective somewhat different from that usually taken in the finance literature. On a purely personal note, these chapters emerged from the difficulties we had in properly understanding the finance literature: from the perspective of equilibrium theory, it seemed hard to accept the idea that a message on risk pricing is general when it is based on models with assumptions as specific as those of the famous Capital Asset Pricing Model (CAPM) or the complete markets and additively separable utilities of representative agent pricing. Thus we studied how the basic message could be expressed in a general model in which markets are incomplete. The result is Chapter 3 which shows that in any two-period equilibrium model the risk value of a security (the excess of its price over the discounted expected value of its dividends) is equal to the covariance of its dividend stream with a reference security that we call the *ideal security* (at equilibrium): this ideal security offers (from the point of view of all agents at equilibrium) the best trade-off between risk reduction and increase in the mean among all income streams lying in the marketed subspace. Under the assumptions usually adopted in finance, the ideal security is a decreasing function of aggregate output.

Chapter 5 studies what is popularly referred to as the random walk property of security prices: roughly speaking the idea is that if agents only have access to publicly available information, then no agent can expect to make abnormal profit by attempting to predict the future dividends of securities better than the market: in short, contrary to Wall Street lore, neither technical nor fundamental analysis can yield abnormal profit. In the finance literature the formalization of this idea, known as the *efficient markets hypothesis*, is usually restricted to the case where agents are risk neutral and is expressed by the martingale property of security prices. On the other hand Harrison-Kreps (1979) showed that any no-arbitrage price process has the property that under an appropriate change of measure on the state space each security price can be expressed as the conditional expectation of its future dividends: this important result is normally presented as a powerful mathematical tool for pricing derivative securities, and the fact that it has a significant economic interpretation is not mentioned. In Chapter 5 we show that this property leads to the most natural way of expressing the efficient markets hypothesis in any financial market equilibrium, in the general case where agents are risk averse.

Firms and Financing of Production

If the dividing line between classical and modern economics lies in the recognition of the far-reaching consequences of the limited knowledge and limited capacity of human beings to cope with an uncertain future, then nowhere are these difficulties present in more concentrated form than in the organizations designed to co-ordinate productive activities of agents, known as firms. It is the fact that agents are limited both in their physical and in their mental abilities that leads to the need for specialization: specialization in turn leads to the need for organization, that is, the co-ordination of agents' activities. Thus production and organization are dual activities of a firm: production can not take place without organization and organization is not an objective in its own right—it is there to co-ordinate the activity of production. In practice, production takes time and time invariably brings with it uncertainty. If the same activity could always be repeated then organization and production would be relatively straightforward: it is uncertainty about the future, coupled with constantly changing conditions that accounts for most of the significant difficulties faced by a firm.

Our analysis of the firm in Chapter 6 captures only a limited aspect of this story, concentrating on the relation between scale, organizational structure and financing of the three principal types of firms, the sole proprietorship, the partnership and the corporation. When the efficient scale of a firm is sufficiently small it is typically financed (owned) and managed by a single entrepreneur: a theory of the sole proprietorship is, at least to a first approximation, relatively straightforward. When the scale of operation required for efficient production becomes sufficiently large, a single entrepreneur will typically find it difficult, if not impossible, to finance the required initial investment, even with access to borrowed funds: for the unavoidable risks involved in a typical investment project limit the extent to which it can be financed by debt. The risks must be shared by several and sometimes a large number of individuals: the partnership and corporation are the two legal entities that society has designed which make it possible to provide the initial capital and share the risks involved in large scale productive ventures. Joint ownership leads however to a problem of collective decision making as soon as shareholders differ in their objectives for the firm, and it is on the resolution of this problem that much of the attention of Chapter 6 is focused.

Nominal Contracts and Money

The final chapter studies the relation between nominal contracts, monetary policy and inflation and brings the analysis close to issues at the heart of macroeconomics. A significant proportion of contracts in a modern economy are nominal, that is, their payoffs are expressed as amounts of money. Such contracts cannot however be meaningfully studied without an explicit modelling of the monetary side of the economy: for the main risks associated with such contracts arise from the variability of inflation. This property underlies the idea, recurrent in monetary theory but rarely formalized, that the presence of nominal contracts is the main reason why monetary policy affects economic activity. Chapter 7 presents a stylized model in which money is used as a medium of exchange and in which the money supply leads through a classical quantity theory equation to the determination of the price level. The model is tailored to study the following question: under what conditions does perfectly anticipated monetary policy have an effect on the real side of the economy? We find that four conditions are indispensable: the presence of nonindexed nominal contracts, incomplete markets, heterogeneous agents and a variable monetary policy. The last condition is crucial with rational expectations, since the average level of inflation is automatically taken into account in the prices of the nominal contracts and has no effect: only the variability of inflation affects the real equilibrium outcome.[6] This result should be of interest to monetary theorists since it characterizes the conditions under which money is more than a "veil", so that monetary theory becomes a worthwhile field of study.

2. BOUNDED RATIONALITY, OPPORTUNISM AND STRUCTURE OF MARKETS

An actual market economy like that of the United States, Great Britain or Japan is not an abstract entity—it consists of a people with customs and legal institutions, organizations like firms, local, state and federal governments and a private and social capital structure consisting of factories, buildings, roads and communications which have been inherited from the past, in which the customs, laws and organizations have evolved by a process of trial and error over many centuries. The theory of market economies attempts to sort out those key concepts that enable us to understand how this complex of people, institutions and organizations interact.

At the present time we have no general theory which explains the functioning of a society: social science is divided into different branches such as the principles of *government* or *politics* (decision making for the community as a whole), the principles of *law* (framing rules for the conduct of individuals and organizations) and the principles of *economics* (the study of the commercial activities of individuals and organizations). Specialization, reinforced by

---

[6]This is a slight exaggeration since the model studied in Chapter 7 does not take into account the seignorage tax imposed by inflation on agents' money balances.

tradition, led to the perception of these fields as separate domains. Modern developments however are making it clear that deep logical connections, in essence a common set of basic principles, underlie these fields. This is exciting since it suggests the development of a more universal theory of the behavior of individuals and organizations in society, namely a social science founded on a common set of principles.

The method of analysis which at the current time gives the broadest scope for understanding the role of different customs, institutions and market structures and the reason why some forms of social and economic organization are more likely to emerge than others, is provided by the *New Institutional Economics.* This theory, associated in particular with the work of Williamson (1975, 1985), can be viewed as a synthesis of three basic ideas previously introduced in the economic literature: bounded rationality, transactions costs and opportunism. Hayek (1945) and Simon (1947, 1957) emphasized that an explicit recognition of the limited ability of agents to process large amounts of information and to calculate alternative outcomes in a complex environment is essential to understanding the role of markets and economic organizations. Coase (1937) recognized the importance of explaining why some economic activities take place through firms rather than markets and showed how an explanation could be based on the idea of transaction costs. The much more recent literature analyzing the role of incentives, moral hazard and adverse selection in inducing different types of market failure, led to the recognition of the role of opportunistic behavior of agents in explaining the malfunctioning of certain markets.[1] It is the merit of Williamson to have identified the origin of transactions costs more precisely than Coase, showing that they arise from bounded rationality and opportunism of agents: on the basis of these transactions costs he shows that certain types of economic activity are less costly when undertaken as activities internal to a firm rather than as external transactions on markets. The idea of economizing on the transactions costs induced by bounded rationality and opportunism has proved to have extensive explanatory power in the theory of industrial organization. Our object here is to show how this type of analysis can help to explain why one type of market structure is likely to provide a cheaper way than another for carrying out economic activity in an environment of uncertainty.[2]

---

[1] Arrow's paper (1963) was one of the first to recognize the role of asymmetric information in the malfunctioning of markets. The well-known paper Arrow (1969) laid out a broad agenda for a theory of market failure. The formalized literature on moral hazard (unobservable actions) began with Spence-Zeckhauser (1971) and Ross (1973), while the literature on adverse selection (unobservable characteristics) originates with the well-known papers of Akerlof (1970) and Rothschild-Stiglitz (1976).

[2] Since the transactions costs arguments are derived from basic (universal) attributes of human beings, we must expect that they will be applicable in every area of social science.

Contracts

Economics studies mutually beneficial exchange between the individuals in a society. If the real world were static, all transactions would have to take place at the same moment: the goods and services one agent offers being exchanged at the same moment of time for those he is to receive from others. The real world however is dynamic and only a small part of economic activity is of this kind: most mutually beneficial exchange takes place over time. One party renders a good or service in the present in exchange for the *promise* by another to render some good or service in the future. For such an arrangement to work, the agent who performs in the present must have confidence that the other party will perform the promised service in the future. The basic way of organizing these intertemporal exchanges is through the use of contracts. A *contract* is a reciprocal agreement between two (or more) parties to perform and/or receive the transfer of some specified goods, services or income under specified contingencies from some initial date (its *date of issue*) until some terminal date (its *date of maturity*). Contracts enable agents to carry out mutually beneficial exchange of goods, services or income and to co-ordinate their production activities. A *trading system* is an institutional framework (customs, laws, property rights) supported by a (possibly imperfect) system of monitoring and enforcement within which agents make contractual commitments for carrying out economic activity. The two trading systems we want to compare are the following:

  (i) a complete system of Arrow-Debreu contracts at date 0 for all future date-events;

  (ii) a system of spot contracts in conjunction with a limited set of forward contracts, with the problem of monitoring partially resolved by the use of money.

A proper comparison of the relative desirability of these two trading systems would require a complete analysis of both the benefits and the costs associated with each system. Such an analysis is at the moment much too ambitious: we will confine ourselves to the simpler objective of indicating why the transactions costs associated with (ii) are likely to be much smaller than those associated with (i). Implicit in the argument is the idea that since (ii) is closer to the trading system observed in the real world, presumably its net benefits are greater than those of (i).

Axioms on Economic Agents

The transactions cost literature is based on the idea that economic behavior can be explained on the basis of two axioms regarding the knowledge and motives of economic agents.

Axiom 1: *Every agent is boundedly rational.*

Axiom 2: *Every agent acts in his self-interest.*[3]

An agent is *boundedly rational* if time and effort on his part are necessary to gain access to and process information, create a mental image of possible future outcomes, carry out the necessary calculations to obtain a solution to a decision problem, and if the agent is limited in the amount of time and effort he can devote to such activities. This definition of bounded rationality is more encompassing than the definitions which are often adopted, especially in the formalized literature.[4] We take bounded rationality to involve three types of limitations

  (i) limitations on the *knowledge* that an agent has of his environment—which includes the characteristics and actions of other agents;
 (ii) limitations on the ability of an agent to *envision* (imagine) what the future may have in store;
(iii) limitations on the ability of an agent to *calculate* optimal strategies in a complex decision problem.

The asymmetric information and search literature are concerned with the first type of limitation. The incomplete contracts literature focuses on the second type of limitation and its consequences for the design and enforcement of contractual agreements: long-term contracts typically involve unforeseen contingencies in which the mutual obligations of parties (including third parties) may not be fully specified.[5] Formalizations in game theory have focused on (iii), by modelling this limitation as the limited calculating capacity (memory) of a computer programmed to find an optimal strategy.[6] Some economists do not include (i) and (ii) in their definition of bounded rationality, focusing instead on the limited computational abilities of agents. Following Williamson, we shall find it convenient to adopt the broad definition that includes (i)–(iii). Thus Axiom 1 expresses the fact that agents are limited in their ability to understand and observe all aspects of the environment around them, to sort out all the possible contingencies which might arise in the future and to compute optimal strategies in a complex problem with uncertain outcomes. Ultimately this axiom has its origin in the limitations of the "wiring" of the human mind

---

[3] *Throughout this book the pronouns "his", "he" and "him" are used in a generic sense encompassing both sexes.*

[4] The hardest problem with developing a formalized theory is to find the appropriate workable definition of bounded rationality.

[5] See for example Hart (1987).

[6] See for example Binmore (1992), Rubinstein (1986), Abreu-Rubinstein (1988). Their approach is based on a modification of the idea of a Turing machine, one of the earliest ways of formalizing the idea of artificial intelligence.

which works like a serial processor, only capable of performing one task at a time, and in the limitations of time and energy that the human being has available to devote to the solution of decision problems: all the operations of observation, search, imagination and computation draw on the same limited resources of the human mind.

Self-interest has long been accepted as a basic axiom of economic theory: indeed it was the fundamental innovation of the classical economists, beginning with Adam Smith (1776), to have introduced this axiom as the key hypothesis of economics. This step served to transform economics into an organized, scientific discipline and led to the most important discovery of classical economics: if agents' activities are fully channeled through markets, then individual actions chosen on the basis of self-interest lead to a social optimum. The classical economists however provided no explicit description of the way economic activity takes place over time; an explicit recognition of the fact that economic activity over time is organized through contracts and that self-interested behavior may create difficulties for the functioning of a system based on contractual commitments is of much more recent origin. For contracts involve promises to deliver goods, services or income in the future and self-interest raises the possibility that agents may try to renege on their commitments: the problem of fulfillment of contracts is compounded when there is difficulty in observing the actions of agents or fully specifying agents' obligations in all contingencies. Thus in a world of time and uncertainty, self-interest translates into the possibility of opportunistic behavior: an agent is said to be *opportunistic* if the choice of his actions is based exclusively on his self-interest and is not influenced by a desire to respect social norms. An opportunistic agent does not honor contractual commitments if it is not in his interest to do so and whenever possible exploits to his advantage the nonobservability of his actions or characteristics.

Transaction Costs and Types of Contracts

For an economy in which the behavior of agents is characterized by these two axioms, the costs of administering economic activity via a system of contracts are of two types: social and individual. Since opportunistic agents will not honor their contractual commitments if it is not in their interest to do so, there must be a mechanism in the economy—the *legal system*—which gives agents the incentive to honor their commitments. Such a system is composed of a monitoring system which identifies whether the circumstances under which an agent must make delivery have occurred and an enforcement system which penalizes agents if they should decide to renege. An additional function of the legal system is to resolve disputes arising from the incompleteness of contracts: for the bounded rationality of agents means that they find it difficult, if not impossible, to imagine all possible contingencies that could arise during the life of a contract: should a contingency arise which had not been explicitly taken into account in the provisions of the contract, then the legal system may have to be called upon to determine where the responsibilities lie. Thus the costs of the legal system consist of the costs of monitoring and enforcing contracts (arising from opportunistic behavior) and the costs of resolving disputes due to the incompleteness of contracts (arising from bounded rationality).

For an individual agent the costs are two-fold. First the costs of time and effort involved in assessing future contingencies, searching for alternatives, gathering information and then writing, negotiating and itemizing possibly detailed actions in complex contracts over more or less extended periods into the future: all these are *ex ante* costs arising before the contracts come into effect. After a contract has been signed there are *ex post* costs arising from possible opportunistic behavior on the part of the contracting parties which can involve bargaining and negotiation or litigation costs, and in the extreme case, costs arising from default or bankruptcy.

Contracts whose enforcement is ensured by the legal system are often called *explicit contracts*. There is another important class of contracts whose provisions are not explicitly written out in a legally enforceable document: rather the terms represent a reciprocal understanding between two parties about the goods they are to exchange or the services they are to perform over some period into the future. Such contracts are called *implicit contracts*: they arise when two parties are involved in a long-term relationship and the mechanism which prevents either party from reneging on the contract is the loss of reputation. Such contracts often appear in conjunction with an existing explicit contract and serve to extend the mutually beneficial provisions of this contract.[7]

---

[7]Some caution is needed here since the distinction is not so clear cut in the law: many implicit contracts are also enforceable by law even though the reputation effect is their primary enforcement mechanism. For a systematic analysis of American (English) contract law, see Atiyah (1989), Farnsworth (1990), Posner (1992) and Cooter-Ulen (1988). For a comparison of contract law in different legal systems (e.g. the French and German Civil Codes) see Zweigert-Kötz (1992). The emergence of contract law essentially paralleled the development of commerce: in England, France (Napoleon's famous Code Civil (1804)), and elsewhere, the most significant developments occurred during the Industrial Revolution—although it should be remembered that the skeleton of most European contract law can be traced to the sophisticated written Roman law (see *Institutionum* and *Digesta* of Justinian (533)), which was one of the really significant contributions of the Roman Empire to modern civilization. Contract law provides the organizational equivalent of social physical capital; it bonds the long-term commitments between individuals in a community and, by making the future (actions of agents) more predictable, permits the development of an elaborate system of commerce. On a historical note, it should be recognized that the young field of economics only became a subject in its own right when it learned to separate itself from the much older field of law—and this separation lasted for some two hundred years. What is surprising is that it has taken so long for economists to recognize the fundamental importance of law and above all of contracts for a proper understanding of the functioning of an economy.

An Arrow-Debreu system of contracts assumes that at some initial date agents make complete and detailed commitments on their actions and mutual obligations over the indefinite future. Once it is recognized that the actors in the economy are boundedly rational and opportunistic (Axioms 1 and 2) and that monitoring and enforcement are costly in both resources and time, then such a system of contracts reveals itself to be an inflexible and highly expensive trading system to operate. Even the most stylized description of a modern economy must recognize that it is characterized by extensive specialization, a huge array of commodities which are produced and distributed to a large number of spatially dispersed agents: the technology and goods are constantly changing and the necessity of finding appropriate employment in these changing circumstances forces agents to become mobile and ready to search for new employment opportunities. The explicit writing of a complete system of contingent contracts would require the agents to envision (and agree on) all possible advances in technology, all the possible characteristics of goods available in the future, all possible national laws, international treaties and political developments affecting the production and distribution of goods, all possible employment patterns for all agents in all economies in the world for all future time. A complete itemization of all possible events at each date, for an extended period into the future would involve far more contingencies than any individual (or computer) could possibly calculate or envision. The individual costs of time and effort involved in the use of contingent contracts become prohibitive; this is not to speak of the social costs of monitoring and enforcing such complicated contracts using boundedly rational agents.

Observed Structure of Contracts

The limited ability of agents to calculate and envision the future calls for a trading system that is not a giant once for all commitment at some initial date with highly complex long-term contracts, but rather involves a more flexible system of repeated sequential trading using much simpler short-term contracts that allow agents to make commitments as information unfolds. The simplest type of contract is the *spot contract* for which the maturity date and date of issue coincide. The use of such a system of contracts essentially eliminates the problem of reneging and greatly reduces the foresight and planning required by the agents: they have full flexibility to buy and sell goods on current markets as information regarding their resources and needs unfold. Given that in the real world the large number of agents and commodities are widely dispersed there still remains the problem of monitoring the accountability of agents who buy and sell the commodities on the spot markets at widely dispersed locations. If *money* is introduced to serve as a unit of account and a medium of exchange and if agents sell goods in exchange for money then the problem of monitoring the accountability of agents in their spot market transactions is essentially resolved.

Once money has been introduced as a medium of exchange it can also be used as a store of value. In this latter role however, money only provides agents with a limited ability to redistribute income over time: purchasing power can only be carried forward in time. Although it introduces the possibility of reneging (and thus transactions costs) agents have found it beneficial to extend their ability to redistribute income over time by introducing a variety of loan contracts which permit agents to borrow and lend. While bounded rationality implies that consumers are on the whole not prepared to make detailed forward contractual commitments with respect to *goods*, they do make extensive commitments to assure themselves of a (relatively) uniform *income* stream over time. The financial system is essentially a giant borrowing and lending machine which transfers funds under given contingencies between lenders (savers) and borrowers (spenders). For some contracts the emphasis is more on the temporal redistribution of income, as with equity contracts or standard borrowing and lending contracts such as bonds and mortgages, while for others the emphasis is more on the redistribution of income across contingencies, as with insurance contracts.

Unlike the situation faced by consumers, the need to assure continuity of the production process obliges firms to make extensive contractual commitments for the delivery of goods and services: such contracts are the principal way by which a firm co-ordinates its production activity with those of other firms, assuring it of a steady "throughput" in Chandler's phrase.[8] Every firm has suppliers with whom it makes contracts to ensure a steady supply of inputs; similarly, every firm makes sales contracts with other firms, wholesalers or retailers to whom it delivers its finished product or service. The internal organization and physical operation of the production activities of a firm require trained, experienced and predictable employees (executives, managers and workers) with a high level of morale, whose ongoing participation is (more or less effectively) assured by an extensive system of labor contracts. Reflecting the fact that the relation between an employee and a firm is normally a long-term relationship, labor contracts typically consist of two parts: the first, the *implicit* contract, is a general understanding of the nature of the possible tasks, the performance criteria, and the promotion, layoff and wage policies that can be expected over the course of a typical career in the firm; the second, the *explicit* contract is a specific (legal) committment specifying the job classification and wage payment over a short period into the future, typically between one and three years. The labor contracts in conjunction with the equity contracts are the principal forward commitments which bind the interests

---

[8]See Chandler (1990).

of consumers and firms, assuring firms of a steady supply of labor services, and consumers (except in periods of recession) a reasonably steady and predictable source of income from their salaries and from the dividends distributed by the firms.

Like most other social institutions, the structure of contracts in a modern economy, which was briefly described above, has emerged by a selection process which tends to minimize both the social costs of enforcement and monitoring and the individual costs arising from bounded rationality. The limited ability of agents to calculate, monitor and enforce means that the contracts which are most widely used in practice have terms of delivery which are simple to describe and easy to verify (even by third parties), to such an extent that many of these contracts are written on standard legal forms: furthermore these contracts are essentially self-enforcing. Even with standardized contracts however the costs are never completely eliminated.

The simplest contracts are those whose terms of delivery depend only on time and are independent of states. This is the case for most loans and for futures contracts. For these contracts self-enforceability is partially assured by the use of collateral for loans, and margin requirements for futures contracts. The transactions costs which remain lead to the formation of financial intermediaries which perform the task of monitoring and enforcing the contracts: lending institutions gather information to check the bona fide nature of collateral, while futures exchanges monitor the margin payments of traders.

Most other state dependent contracts such as equity and insurance have delivery terms which are in principle simple to describe. Thus equity contracts which permit agents to undertake substantial investment projects by sharing the associated risks, entitle shareholders to a proportion of the firms' profits based on their share in the investment. Roughly speaking, enforcement is assured by giving shareholders the ultimate rights to control over the corporations. However, as was already noted by Adam Smith[9] there may be a loss in the efficiency with which the firm is managed due to the bounded rationality of shareholders: typically the shareholders of a large corporation do not have the time or the expertise to monitor the activities of managers and to assess the quality of their performance, thus leaving room for opportunistic behavior by the managers.

Insurance contracts promise delivery of income to agents when some specified circumstances occur (death in the case of life insurance, sickness in the case of health insurance and so on): these contracts allow agents to protect their income streams against major catastrophes. The functioning of the insurance market is based on the property that independent risks which are

---

[9]See Adam Smith (1776, Book V, Chapter 1). For a further discussion see J.S. Mill (1848, Book I, ch. 9).

unpredictable at the individual level become relatively predictable at the aggregate level through the operation of the law of large numbers. It is clear from the sheer magnitude of insurance contracts sold annually (life, health, fire, automobile and marine insurance to mention only a few) that they represent one of the most significant types of risk sharing contracts in an economy. Insurance contracts are however of all financial contracts perhaps the most exposed to the difficulties created by opportunistic behavior of agents. The practical problems posed by moral hazard and adverse selection were recognized from the earliest times when the sale of insurance contracts began to be organized and the first insurance institutions emerged. It is no coincidence that these concepts were first introduced and studied in the insurance literature: economists have only much more recently begun a systematic study of the consequences of these two types of opportunistic behavior for the design of contracts and the functioning of markets.

For an insurance market to function, it must be possible to accurately assess the probability of the contingencies under which compensation is to be made. This is necessary to correctly price the insurance contracts but is rendered difficult by the possibility of opportunistic behavior on the part of agents. For some types of insurance the probability cannot be correctly assessed without acquiring information on private characteristics of agents which it may not be in their self interest to reveal: this is the problem of *adverse selection*. Furthermore in some cases the probability may be influenced by unobservable actions of the agents. The availability of insurance coverage may reduce the incentives of agents to take appropriate precaution with respect to the insured hazard, thereby increasing its probability of occurrence: this is the problem of *moral hazard*.[10] These two difficulties set limits to the extent to which risk sharing can be achieved by insurance contracts. Qualitatively the difficulties posed by adverse selection seem less serious than those posed by moral hazard. For adverse selection leads to the problem of gathering information on agents' characteristics in order to categorize agents into appropriate risk classes. But moral hazard poses a more fundamental problem: when uncertain outcomes are in addition influenced by unobservable actions of the agents, then risk sharing must remain incomplete to provide agents with appropriate incentives.

All the contracts that we have discussed above fall far short of anything like a complete system of Arrow-Debreu contracts. The simplification for consumers of using a dual system of spot markets for goods and forward contracts for income significantly economizes on computation costs relative to those that would be incurred with a complete system of forward contracts for goods. Such

---

[10]The typical way of inducing agents to take appropriate precautionary action in insurance contracts is to have a *deductible* which forces the insuree to pay a part of the costs if there is an accident.

a dual system permits consumers to split their planning problem for the future into a *financial problem* of allocating income (expenditure), and a sequence of *commodity problems* for spending income on current spot markets as the date-events arrive. In practice individuals concentrate most of their planning effort on the financial problem, letting the sequence of commodity problems resolve themselves as the time and place arrive. However the gains from such a system which are so evident for consumers are much less evident when viewed from the perspective of firms: production in general takes time so that managers of firms need to make detailed forward plans for the supply of commodities without the benefit of forward commitments to buy on the part of consumers. Indeed Keynes argued that many of the imperfections in the functioning of a modern economy have their origin in missing contracts for the forward delivery of goods, which permit co-ordination failure to arise between the production and consumption sectors of the economy.[11]

Co-ordination Failure

At the heart of the problem of misallocation lies the fact that bounded rationality makes consumers unwilling or unable to make detailed forward commitments for the purchase of goods from firms. It is likely that a significant part of the business cycle could be resolved if individuals were prepared to make such forward commitments and could do so without error. For firms could then make appropriate investment plans and periodic over-and under-investment would be avoided. The unwillingness and inability of consumers to make forward commitments for the purchase of goods makes it unfeasible for firms to offer detailed forward commitments for the purchase of labor services. Thus just as firms periodically face a lack of demand for their goods, so individuals periodically face a lack of demand for their labor services.

To some extent the government seeks to attenuate these difficulties by offering limited unemployment insurance for individuals, and programs of government spending to increase demand for the output of firms. Apart from the standard insurable hazards of death, health, and property mentioned above, the risk of unemployment is the most serious hazard threatening the income stream of an individual. Since there is a large unobservable component of effort and initiative involved in the effective labor service that an individual offers both when employed and when searching for new employment, moral hazard limits the extent to which government (or any other institution) can offer insurance against the risk of unemployment. Thus unemployment insurance will most likely always remain incomplete.

---

[11]Keynes (1936, ch. 16, pp. 210–211).

3. RATIONAL EXPECTATIONS

In a sequence economy, present actions have future consequences: to make reasonable decisions in the present, agents must make the effort to envision what the future has in store. The axiom of bounded rationality implies that this effort is costly: time and energy must be expended to acquire updated information about the current environment, mental resources must be harnessed to envision possible future scenarios and to calculate as widely as possible the consequences for the future of the presently available information. In his characteristically intuitive manner, Keynes was acutely aware of these costs and basically founded the *General Theory* on the idea that when agents are faced with substantial uncertainty they are reluctant or unable to form reasonable expectations about the future.[1]

> It would be foolish in forming our expectations, to attach great weight to matters which are very uncertain. It is reasonable, therefore, to be guided to a considerable degree by the facts about which we feel somewhat confident, even though they may be less decisively relevant to the issue than other facts about which our knowledge is vague and scanty. For this reason the facts of the existing situation enter, in a sense disproportionately, into the formation of our long-term expectations; our usual practice being to take the existing situation and to project it into the future, modified only to the extent that we have more or less definite reasons for expecting a change.[2]

In the early postwar period it seemed natural to Keynes' successors to adopt his theory of expectation formation in their attempt to formalize the *General Theory*, a collective effort which led to the new field of macroeconomics. Keynes' idea that agents "take the existing situation and ... project it into the future" led to the hypothesis of adaptive expectations: agents are said to have *adaptive expectations* if they use a specific rule for transforming the past and current values of a variable (price, income or output) into a forecast of its future value. However the assumption that agents blindly follow an adaptive expectations rule runs into serious conceptual difficulties, since it leads to models in which agents fail to exploit obvious profit opportunities. This point, which has been much discussed in the setting of macromodels, is perhaps most

---

[1] The clearest statement that Keynes viewed the foundation for the General Theory to hinge on the way agents make decisions in the face of substantial uncertainty may be found in his famous QJE article (Keynes (1937)). The difficulties of adequately describing the way agents behave in the face of a very uncertain future is a topic that runs through all his academic writings and can be traced to his earliest major publication *A Treatise on Probability* (1921): this in turn was an attempt to answer questions posed by his Cambridge mentor G.E. Moore (1903) in his *Principia Ethica* (Chapter V, Ethics in Relation to Conduct).

[2] Keynes (1936, p.148).

simply illustrated in the setting of a commodity futures market, for on such a market expectations play an especially important role.

Example of Futures Market

Suppose agents can buy or sell contracts which promise to deliver a definite quantity of a given commodity (say 5,000 bushels of wheat) at a definite date in the future (say the harvest time). Since agents have the choice of buying or selling the commodity in advance using the futures contract or waiting to trade on the spot market at the harvest time, the price of the futures contract must reflect the expectations of agents regarding the likely future spot price at the delivery date. Suppose the contract is traded at regular time intervals between its date of issue (spring) until its date of maturity (fall). If all agents have adaptive expectations then at each date the futures price will be an average of past and current spot prices of wheat and will remain essentially unchanged until the harvest time.

Suppose now that we introduce a collection of wealthy agents, less boundedly rational than the others, who can construct in their minds a model of the spot market at harvest time with a downward sloping demand curve and a vertical supply curve. From experience they know that demand does not vary very much over time and can be deduced from past observations. Suppose they enquire regularly during the course of the year into the weather conditions prevailing in the different wheat growing regions and know from experience how these weather conditions translate into wheat supplies at harvest time. Based on the (weather) information at each date they can make their best estimate of the future spot price: this is just the conditional expectation of the future spot price given current information. Using a trading strategy of buying (selling) whenever the futures price is below (above) the expected spot price, these agents will make "huge" expected profits: furthermore these expected gains of the rational informed agents will be exactly the expected losses of the boundedly rational uninformed agents. Surely the agents following the adaptive expectations rule will one day wake up to the fact that their bounded rationality is getting rather expensive.

The presence of the rational informed agents greatly changes the stochastic behavior of the futures price. It goes from being an unchanged, biased estimator of the future spot price at each date prior to the harvest, which changes discontinuously to the spot price at harvest time, to being at each instant the (unbiased) best predictor of the future spot price conditional on current information. The presence of the rational informed agents transforms the futures price into what Holbrook Working has called a *reliably anticipatory price*.[3]

---

[3]See Working (1949, 1958). The theory of informational efficiency of speculative prices, which was first proposed by Holbrook Working, is explained in a more general setting in Chapter 5.

The hypothesis that agents behave like the informed agents in the above example, constructing in their minds a model of the underlying economic environment and using all the appropriate information available at each date, has come to be known, following Muth (1961), as the *rational expectations hypothesis*:

> I would like to suggest that expectations, since they are informed predictions of future events, are essentially the same as the predictions of the relevant economic theory... We call such expectations "rational" ... The hypothesis can be rephrased a little more precisely as follows: that expectations ... (or, more generally, the subjective probability distribution of outcomes) tend to be distributed, for the same information set, about the prediction of the theory (the objective probability distribution of outcomes).

The hypothesis of rational expectations is essentially an equilibrium concept: it depends both on individual behavior (how agents form their expectations and make their decisions) and on market clearing (the determination of prices). It assumes that agents make informed predictions of future prices i.e. predictions based on a correct model of the economy. The subsequent market clearing prices that arise from the decisions based on these expectations confirm their predictions. A rational expectations equilibrium is essentially the only equilibrium concept which is consistent in the sense that agents' expectations are self-fulfilling.[4]

Consistency with Axioms on Economic Agents

But is the concept of rational expectations consistent with the two basic axioms of bounded rationality and self-interest which characterize the knowledge and behavior of agents? There is clearly a tension between the forces induced by these two axioms: self-interest induces agents to focus on the *gains* from informed predictions (obtained by exploiting arbitrage opportunities), while bounded rationality obliges them to incur *costs* in coming up with informed predictions. Thus it would seem that rational expectations should serve as a useful concept in circumstances where the gains from prediction greatly outweigh the costs. It is surely no accident that the areas of economics in which rational expectations has been felt to provide a good first approximation, are precisely those in which there is most money at stake for those willing to make intelligent forecasts. It was in the fast moving arena of commodity futures markets, where new information spills rapidly into changed futures prices, that Holbrook Working (1949) first introduced the concept of a *reliably anticipatory price*. This concept, which was formalized by Samuelson (1965) as the

---

[4]An early discussion of self-fulfilling forecasts is due to Merton (1948). The first formalization of a self-fulfilling forecast as an equilibrium phenomenon (a fixed point) is due to Grundberg-Modigliani (1954) and Simon (1954).

martingale property, then spread to the finance literature on equity markets as the *efficient markets hypothesis* (Fama (1970)). At about the same time, Lucas (1972) introduced the concept into macroeconomics using the terminology of *rational expectations* proposed by Muth. His analysis was an extension of Friedman's (1968) argument on the long-run neutrality of monetary policy: once agents have experienced inflation and understand that the government is attempting to exploit the Phillips curve, they come to anticipate future inflation in a way that prevents monetary policy from having further effects. The rational expectations school[5] argued that a natural way of constructing a monetary model which captures this phenomenon is to assume that agents in the private sector make use of their information regarding the government's monetary policy in forming their expectations of future inflation. When agents negotiate nominal contracts extending into the future (unindexed bonds, labor and rental contracts, supply contracts between firms etc...) predicting future inflation is essential for predicting the real value of their contractual commitments: there is too much at stake for agents to permit themselves to make systematic errors in their anticipations of future inflation. The assertion (Lucas (1976), Sargent-Wallace (1975)) that agents alter both their expectations and their actions when the government changes its monetary policy—possibly nullifying the effect of the policy change—presented a radical challenge to the then accepted macroeconomic theory.

Critics of the hypothesis of rational expectations argue that once it is recognized that agents are boundedly rational, it is unreasonable to use a concept of equilibrium which seems to call for such extensive powers of prescience on the part of agents: an economic system is extremely complex and the computation of future equilibrium outcomes in all possible contingencies certainly far exceeds the calculating powers of any available computer or the most sophisticated human brain. This criticism is entirely valid if the model is used to describe situations where agents face new and unfamiliar events, so that they cannot draw on past experience and intuition to help them make their decisions. The hypothesis of rational expectations is only applicable to a stable world where similar types of events occur regularly, so that agents can through experience develop a reliable intuition for the values of the relevant variables in most circumstances. It is well known, and has been extensively documented,[6] that even though human beings can at any given moment only handle a limited number of pieces of information, when they find themselves in familiar situations where they can draw on past experience, the intuition they have developed permits them to solve problems of great complexity. The studies of the behavior of chess players reported by Simon and Chase (1973a,

---

[5] See Lucas (1972) and Lucas-Sargent (1978, 1981).
[6] See Simon (1979a, 1983)

1973b) show that a chess master does not have a greater capacity for calculating alternative forward moves than an ordinary player, but is distinguished by an ability to draw on extensive experience and intuition to "see" the "right" moves which deserve consideration and to which to apply his limited powers of computation. In this sense the agents of a model with rational expectations should be viewed as experienced masters in the economic game in which they are all participants.[7] Thus the principal justification for using the hypothesis of rational expectations is that, when agents can draw on experience and intuition, to a first approximation, they behave relative to their (possibly simplified) environment like fully rational agents.

Common Knowledge of Rationality

So far we have examined the hypothesis of rational expectations from the perspective of an *individual* agent: in the interactive environment of markets, the hypothesis of rational expectations carries with it an additional *social* element that must be present to make it into a consistent concept of equilibrium. An agent can only be confident that he should behave in a rational way if he believes that other agents are simultaneously behaving rationally. In more precise language, rationality must be *common knowledge*: each agent must know (believe) that every other agent is rational, that every other agent knows that all other agents are rational, and knows that every other agent knows every other agent is rational and so on.... For if some agents believe that some other agents "send" demands or supplies to the markets which are not made on a rational basis, then there is no reason for them to believe that the prices will establish themselves at those values which would clear supply and demand of rational agents. But then there is no longer any reason to act as if the prices were going to be those predicted by the "relevant economic theory" and the hypothesis of rational expectations falls apart. Speculative episodes on

---

[7] When an agent has been operating for some time in a stable environment where similar types of events occur regularly, he accumulates substantial intuition about the way the environment functions and how "good" decisions should be made i.e. how to wisely interpret the current new information. If we think of this latter knowledge as being stored in the subconscious, then a great deal of intuition about the right way to apply the agent's limited calculating power is stored in the subconscious (the 50,000 moves familiar to a grand master in chess). The conscious or front part of the mind, which carries out the calculations, has a very limited ability to make "good" decisions, unless it is aided by accumulated experience stored in the subconscious. This is why in most jobs agents need to acquire *experience* before they become reliable decision makers: architects, engineers, physicians, lawyers, entrepreneurs, salesmen... need to serve a period of apprenticeship before they are accepted as good decision makers in their profession. It is the fundamental reason why there is specialization of tasks. Accumulated experience is however a reliable guide for decision making only when the environment is stable: only in such an environment can the hypothesis of rational expectations serve as a useful first approximation.

financial markets provide excellent examples of the violation of the assumption of common knowledge of rationality.

Speculative Bubbles

On financial markets, the hypothesis of rational expectations implies that the price of a security is equal to its *fundamental value*, namely the present value of its future dividend stream (see Chapters 2–5). Several centuries of observation of the prices of securities and other long-lived assets, have made it abundantly clear that there are periods, so-called speculative booms, when the prices of some securities (assets) far exceed even the most exaggerated forecast of the present value of their future dividends. Historically, the most striking examples of *speculative bubbles*[8] are the Tulipmania of 1637 in Holland, the Mississippi venture and the South Sea Bubble of 1720, and in this century the famous stock market boom and crash of 1929: milder versions of such speculative manias hit most capital markets intermittently.

How can we explain the breakdown of rational expectations during such episodes? The crucial characteristic of these markets is their liquidity: a long-lived security or capital good (a tulip bulb) can be purchased for two quite distinct reasons. The first is to purchase the asset for "keeps", that is to receive the future stream of dividends that it offers; the second is to purchase the asset with a view to subsequent resale with the prospect of a capital gain. When an agent purchases an asset for keeps, he will never accept to pay more for it than the present value of its future dividend stream; but when an agent buys an asset for subsequent resale, what matters in assessing its value is what other agents will be ready to pay for it later. If agents can assess the asset's future dividends (with reasonable precision) and have good grounds to believe that all other agents can make a similar assessment (a plausible assumption in a familiar setting) then they have no reason to believe that the price of the asset at any future date will differ from the value of its remaining dividend stream:[9] they will thus not accept paying more for it to-day than the present value of its future dividends, even when they purchase with a view to subsequent resale.

Speculative bubbles can normally be traced to some new and unfamiliar event, an innovation or new discovery whose consequences may be far-reaching but whose likelihood of success is difficult to assess (the appearance of fashion-

---

[8] An asset is said to have a *speculative bubble* when its price exceeds its fundamental value.

[9] For a finite-lived asset the argument proceeds by backward induction (see Chapter 4): at each stage no agent has a reason to believe that any agent will pay more for it than the value of its remaining dividends. For an infinite-lived asset the proof is more delicate (it requires a transversality argument) and there are some exceptions (securities in zero net supply or models with overlapping generations): see Magill-Quinzii (1993) and Santos-Woodford (1993). However none of these exceptions can justify the speculative phenomena mentioned above.

able new varieties of tulips, the creation of a new trade monopoly, significant changes in techniques of production or organization of publicly traded companies): this event puts agents on unfamiliar terrain and (when a fad or fashion develops) draws new agents into the capital markets who are unfamiliar with the functioning of these markets. Agents now have no accumulated experience to draw on in assessing future values and they know that other agents face the same difficulties: it is no longer rational for agents to believe that price of a security should be equal its fundamental value: common knowledge of rationality disappears and with it the hypothesis of rational expectations.

If a consistent theoretical explanation of speculative episodes is out of reach of current economic theory—which is based on the assumption of common knowledge of rationality—these episodes, which are well documented, seem to follow a similar pattern.[10] Aware of the potential of the innovation or the new discovery (or more generally a new phenomenon that has occurred) to create possibly far-reaching gains in the future, knowledgeable (professional) investors enter the market and begin to drive up prices. As the prices rise, the optimism of these initial investors in the success of the new venture is reinforced by their apparent unanimity. This process continues for a while, creating an initial phase of gradually rising prices.

When the rise in prices has continued for a sufficient time to give the impression of being an ongoing process, the information that the market has acquired an upward inertia spreads among a broader segment of investors. Eager to exploit the newly discovered potential for capital gains and recognizing that the greatest gains are made by those who enter early, new investors precipitate themselves onto the market. The more investors are attracted to the market, the more the price rises and the more expectations of rising prices become self-fulfilling. Agents' expectations of rising prices begin to feed on themselves and gradually become disconnected from the rational valuation made by an agent buying for "keeps". It is during this phase that the assumption of common knowledge of rationality breaks down: agents recognize that there are other agents in the market who are not pricing the asset by its fundamental value, but rather are basing their valuation on the continued upward inertia of the market.

After this process has continued for a while—the length of this phase can vary greatly depending on the potential pool of investors—an increasing number of agents (in general the professionals) begin to have doubts about the continued upward inertia of the market: as they progressively place themselves on the selling side of the market and as the number of buyers dwindles, the process of rising prices gradually comes to an end. As soon as there is a general perception that the market has lost its upward inertia, no agent has a reason to be a buyer.

---

[10]See for example Mackay (1841) and Galbraith (1993).

The bubble bursts and as all agents seek to get out of the market, the price comes tumbling down, until it settles once again to a level which corresponds approximately with agents' perceptions of its fundamental value.

Laboratory Experiments

If one way of studying speculative phenomena is to observe them in action on actual markets, a recently explored alternative is to duplicate (at least the elements of) real world capital market trading in experimental laboratory settings: this approach, with all the advantages attendant to controlled experiments, promises to greatly enhance our understanding of the trading behavior of agents on such markets. One sequence of experiments, reported by Vernon Smith *et al.* (1988), has shown that speculative bubbles can arise even in settings where the traded asset is finitely lived and the distribution of its dividends is common knowledge: bubbles however arose in only some of the experiments. The crucial element which seems to determine whether or not a bubble occurs is the perception that agents have of the trading behavior of others: if there are some traders who believe that there are others who are prepared to "ride a bubble" then they can readily be tempted into paying more for an asset than its fundamental value, in the expectation of selling for a higher price. The experiments showed, however, that the more the traders on the market are experienced, the smaller the propensity of the market to develop a speculative bubble. The experimental findings are broadly consistent with the assertions that we made earlier about the circumstances under which the hypothesis of rational expectations is applicable: a model of capital market equilibrium based on rational expectations provides a useful first approximation of market outcomes when investors are experienced and are trading in a familiar setting. However capital markets are fragile since the outcome depends crucially on agents' perceptions of the trading behavior of other agents. To use an analogy drawn from crowd psychology, when a fire occurs in a crowded theatre one of two outcomes can occur: either the participants exit in an orderly way or they panic. The first outcome is more likely when the participants are experienced (by fire drills or familiarity with crowd situations), but there is still a small chance that even they can panic.

4.   THE EQUILIBRIUM MODEL

In economics, as in every branch of science, three levels or types of theory can be distinguished. The first level, which may be called *intuitive theory*, is based on a few simple concepts which lead by direct and intuitive arguments to qualitative propositions which may have considerable breadth of application. Most economic theory begins at this level and most of our broader conceptual

understanding of economics has its roots in this category. The chief weakness
of intuitive theory arises from the element of vagueness in the underlying concepts, with the result that precise conditions under which qualitative results
hold can often not be established beyond question. This makes it difficult (and
perhaps impossible) to develop a coherent and sophisticated theory in which
the concepts and results fit together in a watertight manner.

The second level is *formal theory*: at this stage a new level of precision enters
the analysis since concepts are defined precisely by means of variables which
satisfy certain relations. These relations are used to establish further properties using intuitive mathematical arguments. Formal theory is an important
intermediate stage in the development of a theory: the new level of mathematical precision leads not only to more precise predictions but also to clearer
propositions.

The third level is *abstract (mathematical) theory*: this is the final level of abstraction where primitive concepts are expressed as *axioms* (or *assumptions*),
derived concepts are given a precise meaning through *definitions* and the qualitative results of the theory are stated in precise *theorems* whose validity is
established by rigorous mathematical *proofs*. The advantage of abstract theory
is that it insists on complete clarity at each stage of the argument: in axioms, in
definitions, in theorems and in proofs. Thus, in principle, there is no ambiguity
in any part of the argument. Theory is placed on firm foundations and results
once established can be used as building blocks for subsequent extensions of
the theory.

In general, as a science advances in the clarity and simplicity of its concepts,
the more it is amenable to precise mathematical formulation. The principal
advantage of reaching the third level is that it becomes much clearer exactly
what the theory is or is not capable of explaining. There is however a cost to
this precision: while the theorems which are obtained in an abstract mathematical theory are more precise, they are also typically based on more restrictive
assumptions than the less precise qualitative results that are established using intuitive theory. Exactly because it is less precise, intuitive theory often
enables us to link broader areas of the subject with qualitative results that
can provide an important guide to the appropriate way to develop formal and
abstract theory. The three levels are thus complementary ways of developing
economic theory.

The previous sections have been expressed in the language of intuitive theory; the rest of the book is abstract theory. It studies the properties of an
equilibrium model of a sequence economy. Five basic ingredients are needed to
construct such a model:

(1) *Time-uncertainty setting*; a description of the way time and uncertainty
     are modelled and the associated commodity space.
(2) *Real side of the economy*; a description of the real characteristics of the

economy, namely the goods, the agents, resources and preferences, and the available technology.

(3) *Market structure*; a description of the contracts, markets and more generally the trading arrangements to which agents have access.

(4) *Behavior of agents*; a description of the way agents, given their characteristics and the market structure, make their decisions.

(5) *Concept of equilibrium*; given (1)–(4) the model is closed with a concept of equilibrium which describes the conditions under which agents' decisions are mutually consistent.

Implicit Bounded Rationality

We have argued that a realistic description of (3) consists of a system of spot markets for goods combined with a limited set of contracts and money. The intuitive arguments of Section 2 showed that this market structure has its origin in characteristic imperfections of human beings who find themselves trading in an environment of time and uncertainty. To formalize this argument (4) should therefore reflect these attributes of bounded rationality and opportunism. A consistent general equilibrium model which explicitly incorporates these imperfections seems—at least currently—to be beyond the reach of formal economic theory: as yet there is no operational way of formalizing bounded rationality. This would involve an explicit modelling of the costs that agents incur to reach an informed and rational decision; this in turn would require a much more detailed description of the process of decision making than most economic models can handle at the moment. Opportunistic behavior has recently been extensively studied in simple and specialized partial equilibrium models, but has not yet been shown to be extendable to a general equilibrium setting. At this time, we thus find ourselves obliged to step back to a more classical description of rational agents who are symmetrically informed and take actions in the setting of an economy in which there are no unobservable characteristics or variables that can induce opportunistic behavior. Every economic model involves striking a compromise between realism (completeness of description) on the one hand and tractability of analysis on the other. The compromise which is adopted here is to model the consequences of bounded rationality and the possibility of opportunistic behavior implicitly through the incomplete market structure: agents are then assumed to behave rationally with respect to this market structure.[1] With this in mind, let us examine in more detail the com-

---

[1]The modelling of an agent assumes *explicit bounded rationality* if the costs of processing information and making decisions are explicitly included in the model: the modelling assumes *implicit bounded rationality* if such costs are not included (so that agents have unlimited powers of calculation) but instead certain restrictions or limitations on transactions (for example restrictions on types of contracts) are included as surrogate statements of the consequences

ponents (1)–(5) of the equilibrium model that form the basis for the analysis in this book.

Time-uncertainty Setting

The way time and uncertainty are modelled is based on the description of random phenomena in probability theory. The simplest description of a stochastic process involves three components:

  (i) the description of an *event-tree*;
 (ii) a *function* defined on the event-tree;
(iii) the assignment of *probabilities* to events.

An event-tree is a description of the alternative outcomes (nodes) that can arise at successive moments of time ($t = 0, 1, \ldots, T$). If only a finite number of outcomes is possible at each date and if only a finite number of dates is considered, then at the final date there are a finite number of terminal nodes (see Figure 4.1). With each terminal node we can associate a path through the event-tree; the finite number of terminal nodes thus represents the finite number of possible paths or ways in which uncertainty can evolve over time. A (vector-valued) *stochastic process* is a (vector-valued) function defined on the

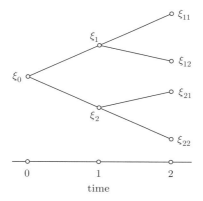

Figure 4.1   Event-tree

of the agents' bounded rationality. Implicit bounded rationality amounts to shrinking the opportunity sets available to agents and hypothesizing that agents are unboundedly rational on the reduced opportunity sets: this provides a first approximation to bounded rationality along the lines suggested by Simon (1957, p. 198): "The first consequence of the principle of bounded rationality is that the intended rationality of an actor requires him to construct a simplified model of the real situation in order to deal with it. He behaves rationally with respect to this model." As Selten (1990, 1991) has rightly complained, very few models assume explicit bounded rationality: the papers listed in footnote 6 of Section 2 are among the few pioneers in this direction. In this book agents are taken to be implicitly boundedly rational.

event-tree (i.e. a vector assigned to each node in the tree). The actions of the agents and the prices associated with the commodities and the contracts will be stochastic processes.

In probability theory the third component in the description of a stochastic process involves an assignment of probabilities to the terminal nodes of the tree—thus each possible path through the tree is assigned an objective probability. In much of the analysis that follows an explicit assignment of objective probabilities is not required (except in Chapters 3 and 5). Loosely speaking, while there are no objective probabilities specified in the model, subjective probabilities are implicit in the preferences of the agents.

Describing an economy with uncertainty via an event-tree amounts to collapsing the complexities of the real world into a rather organized and comfortable description of the way agents perceive uncertainty about the future. Agents are assumed to be capable of correctly envisioning all the possible scenarios that can arise in the future.[2] Thus they agree on the future events which are possible and nothing completely unforeseen can arise. The future in essence appears like some glorified coin tossing experiment in which only a finite number of outcomes can arise at each stage; no unforeseen branches ever appear in the tree.

In Section 2 we argued that the bounded rationality of agents would make it difficult for them to enumerate all possible nodes for society's event-tree if it stretches far into the future, since there is a very large number of contingencies that can arise. For this reason (among others) Keynes was convinced that a quite different approach to the modelling of time and uncertainty would be required (see Keynes (1921, 1937)). For the moment however, a more satisfactory description of the time-uncertainty setting has not yet been found. Despite its defects, the analytical insights obtained using this approach seem to justify its adoption at least as a first approximation.

Real Side of the Economy

The economy has a finite number of goods and a finite number of consumers and firms. Real economic activity is decomposed into the *production* and *distribution* of goods. For an initial analysis it is convenient to assume that production decisions are fixed, restricting attention to the problem of distribution of goods: this is the focus of study in an *exchange economy*. The simultaneous analysis of the activities of production and distribution is undertaken in a *production economy*.

The goods are assumed to be perishable, perfectly divisible and to have qual-

---

[2]In this volume the analysis is restricted to models over a finite horizon: in the second volume we show how the analysis can be extended to an infinite horizon i.e. an open ended future.

itative characteristics which are known to all agents. In an exchange economy each consumer has an initial endowment of the goods which is a stochastic process: thus at each node in the event-tree each agent has an exogenously given initial endowment of the goods. As a thought process we can imagine each consumer as owning a farm, for which all production decisions have been made in advance and from which a sequence of harvests of commodities is forthcoming at the beginning of each period.

Each agent has a *preference ordering* for commodities across the event-tree which expresses the relative desirability of the goods at the different nodes of the tree. The preference ordering is taken to satisfy the classical axioms for a rational agent: it is complete, transitive, continuous, and monotone and has convex preferred sets. In view of the importance we have attached to the phenomenon of bounded rationality, it is the assumption of *completeness* which is perhaps the most unrealistic in a complex environment of time and uncertainty: for completeness implies that an agent is capable of comparing all present and future bundles and thus understands what his preferences and needs will be in the future. But a boundedly rational agent faced with a highly complex environment of uncertainty is likely to feel very uncertain about the future and may not be capable of envisioning with much precision what his future needs and preferences will be. An explicit recognition of the bounded rationality of agents would thus seem to require that the completeness axiom be dropped. Generalizations of the model in this direction have recently been explored and are certainly worth pursuing.[3] However, since the analytical treatment of the model with incomplete preferences requires a good understanding of the behavior of the model with complete preferences, it seems wise to begin with the more tractable case where preference orderings are complete.

The convexity of agents' preferences plays an important role in the analysis: underlying this assumption are the ideas of diminishing rates of substitution between goods and risk aversion. This assumption is natural since the model focuses attention on risk sharing between agents in an environment of uncertainty. In an exchange economy each agent's harvest is random, that is, it fluctuates across the nodes of the event-tree. If some other agent has a different random harvest over time, then presumably the agents can somehow exchange commodities via a system of markets, the sharing of risks acting to their mutual benefit: this is the focus of analysis in an exchange economy.

In a production economy a finite collection of firms is added to this structure. In a modern economy there are three types of firms: sole proprietorships, partnerships and corporations. The analysis of financial markets typically concentrates on the case where the firms are corporations, since trading the equity contracts of these firms is an important way of sharing the risks of production.

---

[3]See Bewley (1986) and Epstein-Wang (1994).

A corporation is a firm whose ownership is divided among a collection of shareholders and whose control is under the joint supervision of a Manager and a Board of Directors. Such firms are complex decision making units whose hierarchical and organizational structure has been the subject of extensive study. We do not attempt to analyze the way in which information, transactions costs and incentives can help to explain the organizational structure of such firms and the range of their activities (i.e. which goods are inputs and outputs). From our perspective firms are viewed as decision making units that use certain commodities which they purchase on an array of markets to produce other commodities which are also sold on markets. The production possibilities which express the way certain goods can be produced by using other goods as inputs are summarized in a *technology set* which is taken as exogenously given. Certain restrictions are imposed on these sets, the strongest of which is the assumption of convexity, which eliminates the possibility of increasing returns to scale. In a stochastic production economy we seek to understand how the production and investment decisions of firms which determine the supply of current and future goods are influenced by the risk sharing possibilities offered by the system of markets.

Market Structure

Traditional general equilibrium theory studies an economy without time or uncertainty: the allocation of resources is achieved by a system of spot markets for current delivery. Arrow and Debreu showed that the analysis for a static economy could be extended to a stochastic economy by introducing a market structure consisting of a system of contingent contracts: for each good and for each date-event (node) in the future there is a contract which promises to deliver one unit of the specified good at the given node and nothing otherwise, and all these contracts are traded at the initial date. In the transition from a timeless-riskless economy to a stochastic economy, the Arrow-Debreu markets are transformed from markets for the current delivery of real goods to a refined class of contingent contracts for the future delivery of goods. The merit of the Arrow-Debreu concept is that it introduces an idealized market structure for a stochastic economy through which resources can be allocated with the same efficiency as in a standard static economy: it constitutes a canonical system of markets against which the imperfections or incompleteness of other market structures can be measured. However such markets are not used to allocate resources in a world with time and uncertainty, since the behavioral imperfections of agents make them unfeasible.

Our analysis will focus on a market structure which is closer to that observed in the real world. Commodities are traded on spot markets; this trading takes place sequentially and involves current delivery and payment for goods. Contracts, less refined than the Arrow-Debreu system, permit agents to co-ordinate their activities and to achieve a limited redistribution of income across date-events. Two types of contracts are distinguished. *Real* contracts call for the delivery of the spot market value of specified vectors of goods at future date-events: equity and futures contracts are of this form. *Nominal* contracts call for the delivery of specified amounts of a unit of account (dollars) at future date-events: bonds are contracts of this type.

Behavior of Agents

As we explained above, to keep the analysis tractable, each consumer's preference ordering is taken to satisfy the classical assumptions for a rational agent. Given his preference ordering, his anticipated future endowments and his anticipations of future spot and security prices across the event-tree, each agent calculates the consumption and portfolio decision (at each date-event) which generates the most preferred consumption stream across the event-tree. In the same way firms choose a production plan and a financial policy which maximizes the present value of their future profit.

Two types of variables enter into a consumer's or firm's maximization problem: *decision variables* which agents must choose and *anticipated variables* whose values they must assess in order to make an appropriate choice of the decision variables. In a sequential market structure, the decision variables consist of *current* consumption or production of goods and agents' portfolios of securities. Under the Arrow-Debreu system of contingent contracts, since all trade takes place simultaneously, *all* variables which enter an agent's maximization problem are decision variables: at the initial date an agent decides on his consumption or production plan for the entire future. If there are many goods, if the horizon extends far into the future and if the number of traded securities is small relative to the number of contingencies that can occur at each date-event, then the number of decision variables which have to be chosen at each date-event in a sequential market structure is much smaller than in a contingent market structure, although the values of many future variables need to be anticipated. Thus the sequential structure is better adapted to boundedly rational agents only if the cost of assessing the values of anticipated variables is smaller than the cost of choosing the correct values of decision variables. This seems to be a reasonable assumption. In practice the optimality of a decision which has future consequences can normally be adequately assessed without making detailed calculations of all future actions. For example for a consumer, the optimality of an income transfer from the present to some future date (say his retirement) rarely depends on a detailed assessment of the way that future income will be spent. As Simon (1957) pointed out, boundedly rational agents construct simplified models in order to reduce the complexity of the problems that they have to solve to a manageable size. A maximization problem, which involves anticipating what future actions will be, can be simplified by reducing the anticipated variables which are taken into account to those which are most directly relevant. However, it is not possible to simplify a problem in which all variables are decision variables, since the values of all these variables must be determined simultaneously.

Concept of Equilibrium

The model with the components (1)–(4) needs to be closed by introducing an appropriate concept of equilibrium which makes precise the sense in which agents' decisions and expectations are required to be compatible. The minimal condition is that the agents' trading decisions in the *current* markets for goods and contracts are compatible i.e. that these markets clear. The additional restriction imposed on the compatibility of expectations and anticipated variables is the feature that distinguishes one intertemporal model from another.[4] In this book we study the outcome of a model in which individual agents make decisions based on expectations regarding future prices of goods and contracts and these decisions and expectations are taken to be collectively compatible. Viewed from date 0 this means that not only do current markets clear, but also the anticipated demands and supplies for goods and contracts at each future date-event. If at the initial date agents base their decisions on correct anticipations regarding future prices, then the actual course of prices which unfold will coincide with those anticipations: the model thus predicts what happens at the initial date and in the future. We are thus led to the concept which Radner (1972) called an equilibrium of plans, prices and price expectations and which, for brevity, we call a *correct expectations equilibrium*. Note that this concept permits agents to hold different probability assessments regarding future events: in the case where all agents hold common probability assessments the concept reduces to the equilibrium referred to in macroeconomics as a *rational expectations equilibrium*.

The problem of finding such an equilibrium can be reduced to the following mathematical problem. Agents' current and anticipated demands for goods and contracts are functions of the current and anticipated prices: the equality of demand and supply leads to a system of equations with as many unknowns (prices) as equations (demand equals supply for each good and each contract

---

[4]The two main concepts of equilibrium which have been studied in a general equilibrium framework are the concept of a *temporary equilibrium*, in which no restriction is imposed on the expectations or the anticipated variables of agents, and the concept of a *correct expectations equilibrium* which is adopted here. The concept of a temporary equilibrium is the abstract general equilibrium version of the models with *adaptive expectations* which have been studied in macroeconomics.

at each date-event), a solution of which is an equilibrium price vector. The equilibrium consumption, production and portfolio vectors of the agents can then be deduced from the equilibrium price vector.

5.   REAL AND FINANCIAL SECTORS OF THE ECONOMY

The allocation of resources in a correct expectations equilibrium is the combined outcome of real markets which allocate goods and financial markets which redistribute income among the agents. It has been traditional in economic theory to conduct separate analyses of the activities of the real and financial sectors of the economy: the analysis of demand and supply for goods on real markets is the subject of *price theory*, while the analysis of income flows on financial markets is the subject of the *theory of finance*. When financial markets are incomplete, the two sectors can not be treated independently: production and consumption decisions depend on the risk sharing possibilities offered by the financial sector, while agents' financial decisions in turn depend on the consumption needs and investment opportunities created by the real sector. The simultaneous analysis of the real and financial sectors of the economy is however rather complicated and—provided due care is taken to understand what is involved—there is much to be gained by first studying the functioning of the financial markets, taking certain data from the real sector as fixed. This leads to a simplified model of an economy which we call a *finance economy*. Analyzing the properties of such a finance economy is the objective of this first volume. A more complete analysis of the feedback between the real and financial sectors is the subject of the second volume.

Simplifying the functioning of an economy by reducing it to a finance economy is a useful expository device for two reasons. First, qualitative properties of the financial sector—the risk sharing it achieves, the risk premia and informational efficiency of security prices—can be analyzed in the simplest setting and in the most direct way. Second, many of the techniques and concepts needed for the analysis of the general model can be progressively introduced and made familiar in the setting of this simpler model.

Simple Version of General Model

The object of this section is to show how a finance economy is generated from an equilibrium of the overall economy when the spot prices of the goods are fixed at their equilibrium values. This can be done by considering the simplest version of the general model with real and financial sectors, namely a two-period exchange economy. The time-uncertainty setting is described by an event-tree consisting of an initial date $(t = 0)$ and $S \geq 1$ states of nature at the second date $(t = 1)$. For convenience we often refer to date $t = 0$ as state $s = 0$, so that in total there are $S + 1$ states. Since there are L commodities available in each state $(s = 0, 1, \ldots, S)$ the commodity space is $\mathbb{R}^{L(S+1)}$. Each consumer i $(i = 1, \ldots, I)$ has an initial endowment of the L goods at date 0 and correctly anticipates his endowment ω_s^i in state s at date 1. Agent i is thus endowed with a vector of initial resources

$$\omega^i = (\omega_0^i, \omega_1^i, \ldots, \omega_S^i), \quad i = 1, \ldots, I$$

which lies in the non-negative orthant of the commodity space. The preference ordering of agent i is represented by a utility function

$$u^i : \mathbb{R}_+^{L(S+1)} \longrightarrow \mathbb{R}, \quad i = 1, \ldots, I$$

which is defined over consumption streams

$$x^i = (x_0^i, x_1^i, \ldots, x_S^i), \quad i = 1, \ldots, I$$

which lie in the non-negative orthant $\mathbb{R}_+^{L(S+1)}$. In each state s there are spot markets for each of the L goods and these give rise to a vector of spot prices for state s, $p_s = (p_{s1}, \ldots, p_{sL})$. We let

$$p = (p_0, p_1, \ldots, p_S)$$

denote the vector of *spot prices*. There are J financial contracts. The jth contract can be purchased for the price q_j at date 0 and delivers the payoff V_s^j in state s at date 1. We let

$$q = (q_1, \ldots, q_J)$$

denote the vector of *security prices*. It is useful to summarize the date 1 payoffs of the J securities in the matrix

$$V = \begin{bmatrix} V_1^1 & \cdots & V_1^J \\ \vdots & \ddots & \vdots \\ V_S^1 & \cdots & V_S^J \end{bmatrix}$$

where $V_s = (V_s^1, \ldots, V_s^J)$ denotes the sth row. Let

$$z^i = (z_1^i, \ldots, z_J^i), \quad i = 1, \ldots, I$$

denote the number of units of each of the J securities purchased by agent i: we call this the *portfolio* of financial contracts purchased by agent i.

At date 0 the agent sells his initial endowment vector (his vector of farm outputs) ω_0^i on the current spot markets on which the vector of spot prices is p_0: this gives him a date 0 income $p_0 \omega_0^i = \sum_{l=1}^L p_{0l} \omega_{0l}^i$. The purchase of a portfolio of the J securities z^i involves an expenditure $qz^i = \sum_{j=1}^{J} q_j z_j^i$. The income which is left can be spent on the purchase of a vector of consumption x_0^i on the date 0 spot markets at the spot prices p_0: the consumption expenditure $p_0 x_0^i = \sum_{l=1}^{L} p_{0l} x_{0l}^i$ must thus satisfy

$$p_0 x_0^i = p_0 \omega_0^i - qz^i \tag{1}$$

In state s the agent will sell his harvest ω_s^i at the current spot price p_s to obtain the income $p_s \omega_s^i = \sum_{l=1}^{L} p_{sl} \omega_{sl}^i$. The purchase of the portfolio z^i at date 0 yields the contract income $V_s z^i = \sum_{j=1}^{J} V_s^j z_j^i$ in state s. The harvest and the contract income will be spent on the purchase of a vector of consumption x_s^i at the current spot price p_s: the consumption expenditure $p_s x_s = \sum_{l=1}^{L} p_{sl} x_{sl}$ must thus satisfy

$$p_s x_s^i = p_s \omega_s^i + V_s z^i, \quad s = 1, \ldots, S \tag{2}$$

Since the choice of a portfolio z^i at date 0 determines the contract income $V_s z^i, (s = 1, \ldots, S)$ and since the "usefulness" of this future income can only be judged by the future consumption that it permits, at date 0 the agent must anticipate his future consumption x_s^i $(s = 1, \ldots, S)$. Since the budget equations (2) must be satisfied, to do this he must correctly anticipate his harvest (ω_s^i), the security payoffs (V_s) and the vector of spot prices (p_s) in each of the states at date 1. The date 0 consumption-portfolio choice (x_0^i, z^i) and the anticipated date 1 consumption stream $(x_1^i, \ldots, x_S^i)$ are viewed as a pair $(x^i, z^i) = (x_0^i, x_1^i, \ldots, x_S^i, z^i) \in \mathbb{R}_+^{L(S+1)} \times \mathbb{R}^J$ which maximize the utility $u^i(x^i)$ of agent i subject to his date 0 and date 1 budget constraints, (1) and (2).

A *correct expectations equilibrium* for this two-period exchange economy consists of consumption and portfolio choices for each of the I consumers

$$(\bar{x}, \bar{z}) = (\bar{x}^1, \ldots, \bar{x}^I, \bar{z}^1, \ldots, \bar{z}^I)$$

spot prices for the goods at date 0 and prices for the financial contracts

$$(\bar{p}_0, \bar{q})$$

and spot prices for the goods in each state at date 1

$$(\bar{p}_1, \ldots, \bar{p}_S)$$

which are correctly anticipated by all agents such that the following four conditions are satisfied:

(i) $(\bar{x}^i, \bar{z}^i)$ maximizes the utility function $u^i(x^i)$ subject to the budget constraints (1) and (2) with $(p, q) = (\bar{p}, \bar{q})$, $i = 1, \ldots, I$

(ii) The spot market for each of the L goods clears for each date-event

$$\sum_{i=1}^{I} \bar{x}_{sl}^i = \sum_{i=1}^{I} \omega_{sl}^i, \quad s = 0, 1, \ldots, S, \quad l = 1, \ldots, L$$

(iii) The market for each security clears

$$\sum_{i=1}^{I} \bar{z}_j^i = 0, \quad j = 1, \ldots, J$$

(iv) A system of monetary equations determines the levels of the spot prices

$$\bar{p}_s \sum_{i=1}^{I} \bar{x}_s^i = M_s, \quad s = 0, 1, \ldots, S \tag{3}$$

where M_s is the total amount of money available for transactions in state s.

(i) expresses the rational maximizing behavior of the agents on the markets. (ii) and (iii) are the usual market clearing conditions which express the compatibility of both the anticipations and the actions of the agents. (iv) is a system of monetary equations whose role is to determine the levels of the spot prices. This merits a separate explanation.

The prices $(\bar{p}, \bar{q})$ and the payoffs (V_s^j) of the financial contracts are measured in units of account (dollars). The payoffs (V_s^j) are homogeneous functions of the spot prices (p_s) when the contract promises to deliver the value under the current spot prices of a specified bundle of goods (*real* contracts). The payoffs (V_s^j) are independent of the spot prices if the contract is expressed directly in units of account (*nominal* contracts). In order for the purchasing power of the nominal contract payoffs (V_s^j) to be well-defined, agents must be able to correctly anticipate future spot price levels. While many other normalization rules (for example $p_{s1} = 1$, $s = 0, 1, \ldots, S$) can be chosen in place of (3) to determine the price levels, from an economic point of view it is more natural to relate price levels to the quantity of money available for transactions (see Chapter 7). With the monetary equations (3), the assumption that agents correctly anticipate future price levels amounts to assuming that they correctly anticipate the current and future money supply $M = (M_0, M_1, \ldots, M_S)$. When the contracts are real, the budget equations (1) and (2) are homogeneous of degree 1 in the prices: if the spot prices in some state are doubled then the contract payoffs in this state are doubled. In this case the equilibrium is independent of the money supply M so that for all practical purposes the monetary equations (iv) can be omitted. When the contracts are nominal, price levels will in general matter: doubling the spot prices in some state halves the purchasing power of the nominal contract payoffs. In this case when the financial markets are incomplete, the equilibrium is in general influenced by the money supply, so that money enters the economy in a way which is not neutral. This non-neutrality of money in the presence of incomplete markets appears to us to be an interesting aspect of this model of the real and financial markets.

Decomposition into Real and Financial Problems

The consumer's maximum problem in (i)

$$\max_{(x^i,z^i)\in\mathbb{R}_+^{L(S+1)}\times\mathbb{R}^J}\left\{u^i(x^i)\ \middle|\ \begin{array}{l} p_0(x_0^i-\omega_0^i)=-qz^i \\ p_s(x_s^i-\omega_s^i)=V_sz^i, \quad s=1,\ldots,S \end{array}\right\} \tag{4}$$

can be decomposed into a goods allocation and an income allocation problem as follows. Given the current and anticipated spot prices $p = (p_0, p_1, \ldots, p_S)$ and a profile of income across the event-tree

$$m^i = (m_0^i, m_1^i, \ldots, m_S^i)$$

agent i determines his optimal consumption stream[1]

$$x^i(p, m^i) = \arg\max_{x^i\in\mathbb{R}_+^{L(S+1)}} \left\{u^i(x^i)\ |\ p_sx_s^i = m_s^i, \quad s = 0, \ldots, S\right\} \tag{5}$$

which induces an *indirect utility function* for income

$$\widetilde{u}^i(m^i; p) = u^i\left(x^i(p, m^i)\right) \tag{6}$$

Given the prices (p, q) of the goods and the financial contracts, the optimal portfolio $z^i(p, q)$ of agent i is the solution of the maximum problem

$$z^i(p, q) = \arg\max_{z^i\in\mathbb{R}^J}\widetilde{u}^i(p_0\omega_0^i - qz^i, p_1\omega_1^i + V_1z^i, \ldots, p_S\omega_S^i + V_Sz^i; p) \tag{7}$$

The optimal portfolio choice $z^i(p, q)$ induces an income stream $m^i(p, q)$ defined by

$$m_0^i(p, q) = p_0\omega_0^i - qz^i(p, q)$$
$$m_s^i(p, q) = p_s\omega_s^i + V_sz^i(p, q), \quad s = 1, \ldots, S$$

Agent i's demand f^i for the goods as a function of the prices (p, q) is given by

$$f^i(p, q) = x^i\left(p, m^i(p, q)\right)$$

---

[1]The conditions under which the functions in (5) and (7) are well-defined will be specified later.

Thus agent i's solution $\left(f^i(p,q), z^i(p,q)\right)$ of (4) has been obtained as the solution of the goods problem (5) and the portfolio problem (7).

The equilibrium conditions (ii)–(iv) can be expressed as a system of equations

$$\sum_{i=1}^{I} \left(f^i(p,q) - \omega^i\right) = 0 \tag{8}$$

$$\sum_{i=1}^{I} z^i(p,q) = 0 \tag{9}$$

$$p_s \sum f_s^i(p,q) - M_s = 0, \quad s = 0, \ldots, S \tag{10}$$

for determining equilibrium prices $(\bar{p}, \bar{q})$, given a monetary policy

$$M = (M_0, M_1, \ldots, M_S)$$

Finance submodel

Let $\mathscr{E}(u, \omega, V)$ denote an exchange economy in which $u = (u^1, \ldots, u^I)$ and $\omega = (\omega^1, \ldots, \omega^I)$ are the utility functions and the endowments characterizing the I agents and V denotes the matrix of date 1 payoffs of the financial contracts. Suppose $(\bar{p}, \bar{q})$ is an equilibrium vector of spot prices and security prices for $\mathscr{E}(u, \omega, V)$, namely a solution of the system of equations (8)–(10). For each agent let

$$\widetilde{u}^i(\,\cdot\,; \bar{p}) : \mathbb{R}_+^{S+1} \longrightarrow \mathbb{R}, \quad i = 1, \ldots, I \tag{11}$$

denote the induced utility function over income streams defined by (6) with $p = \bar{p}$ and let

$$\widetilde{\omega}^i = \left(\widetilde{\omega}_s^i\right)_{s=0}^{S} = \left(\bar{p}_s \omega_s^i\right)_{s=0}^{S}, \quad i = 1, \ldots, I \tag{12}$$

denote the value of his initial resources (his initial income stream) under the spot prices $\bar{p}$. Recalling that for some contracts (real contracts) the payoffs V_s^j depend on the spot prices $\bar{p}_s$, we define

$$\widetilde{V} = V(\bar{p}) \tag{13}$$

as the matrix of date 1 payoffs of the financial contracts under the equilibrium spot prices $\bar{p}$. Let $\widetilde{u} = (\widetilde{u}^1, \ldots, \widetilde{u}^I)$ and $\widetilde{\omega} = (\widetilde{\omega}^1, \ldots, \widetilde{\omega}^I)$, then $\mathscr{E}_{\bar{p}}(\widetilde{u}, \widetilde{\omega}, \widetilde{V})$ will be called the *finance economy* induced by the equilibrium vector of spot prices $\bar{p}$. We sometimes also refer to such an economy as an *income model* since agents begin with an initial stream of income $(\widetilde{\omega}^i)$ and have utility functions

$(\widetilde{u}^i)$ defined over income streams. An income model $\mathscr{E}_{\bar{p}}(\widetilde{u}, \widetilde{\omega}, \widetilde{V})$ is thus a sub-model of the financial markets for the original economy $\mathscr{E}(u, \omega, V)$ induced by an equilibrium vector of spot prices $\bar{p}$. It is clear that only the equilibrium price $q^* = \bar{q}$ for $\mathscr{E}_{\bar{p}}(\widetilde{u}, \widetilde{\omega}, \widetilde{V})$ will generate an equilibrium $(\bar{p}, q^*)$ of the original economy $\mathscr{E}(u, \omega, V)$.

As a pedagogical device, or simply as a thought experiment, an income model can also be viewed as a special case of the general model with only *one good* ($L = 1$). This latter interpretation is convenient when we want to view the model as an instructive but special case of the general model. Some caution is needed to ensure that an appropriate interpretation is given to the model, namely whether it is to be interpreted as an income model or as a model with one good. In sections which deal with qualitative properties of security prices such as no-arbitrage, the risk pricing of securities (Chapter 3) or the martingale property (Chapter 5), the income interpretation is more natural. When we discuss problems of existence or constrained optimality of equilibrium the model may be viewed as a one-good model—although even in this case, the income interpretation is instructive (see Section 12).

Except in the special case of separable homothetic preferences, which is described below, there is a feedback between financial markets and goods markets which makes it impossible to split the equilibrium problem into disjoint problems of determination of spot prices for goods and prices for financial contracts. Because of this feedback, the results on optimality of equilibrium are also different in an income model, in which relative prices for goods are fixed, from those in a general multigood model, in which all prices are determined simultaneously.

Separable-homothetic preferences

While for most economies $\mathscr{E}(u, \omega, V)$ an equilibrium vector of prices $(\bar{p}, \bar{q})$ which clears both the spot markets and the financial markets can only be obtained by a simultaneous analysis of these markets, there is a special but instructive class of economies in which the equilibrium vector of spot prices can be obtained independently of, and hence before, an equilibrium analysis of the financial markets is carried out.

The idea is the following. If we want equilibrium prices on the spot markets to be independent of equilibrium on the financial markets, then the aggregate spot market demand for the L goods in each state s should depend only on the incomes of the agents in this state (and not on their incomes in other states) and should be independent of the distribution of income among agents in this state. The following definition gives conditions on agents' preferences which ensure that these two properties hold.

5.1 Definition: We say that the exchange economy $\mathscr{E}(u, \omega, V)$ has *separable-homothetic preferences* if the utility functions $u^1, \ldots, u^I$ are weakly separable across the states and identically homothetic within the states, namely if there exist I functions

$$U^i : \mathbb{R}^{S+1} \longrightarrow \mathbb{R}, \quad i = 1, \ldots, I$$

which are smooth, strictly quasi-concave and strictly monotonic, and $S + 1$ functions

$$v_s : \mathbb{R}_+^L \longrightarrow \mathbb{R}, \quad s = 0, 1, \ldots, S$$

which are smooth, strictly concave, strictly monotonic, and homogeneous of degree one, such that

$$u^i(x^i) = U^i \left(v_0(x_0^i), v_1(x_1^i), \ldots, v_S(x_S^i) \right), \quad i = 1, \ldots, I$$

Suppose agent i's income stream across the states $m^i = (m_0^i, m_1^i, \ldots, m_S^i)$ is given. By the separability of his utility function u^i his commodity choice problem (5) breaks up into $S + 1$ separate choice problems generating the demand functions

$$\xi_s(p_s, m_s^i) = \arg \max_{x_s^i \in \mathbb{R}_+^L} \left\{ v_s(x_s^i) \mid p_s x_s^i = m_s^i \right\}, \quad s = 0, 1, \ldots, S$$

Since $v_s(\cdot)$ is homothetic $\xi_s(p_s, m_s^i) = m_s^i \xi_s(p_s, 1)$ and the equilibrium spot prices in state s satisfy

$$\sum_{i=1}^I m_s^i \xi_s(p_s, 1) = \xi_s(p_s, p_s \sum_{i=1}^I \omega_s^i) = \sum_{i=1}^I \omega_s^i, \quad s = 0, 1, \ldots, S$$

Thus the spot prices must be proportional to the gradient[2] $\nabla v_s(w_s)$ of v_s at the aggregate endowment $w_s = \sum_{i=1}^I \omega_s^i$. Using the monetary equations (10) gives the equilibrium spot prices

$$\bar{p}_s = \left(\frac{\nabla v_s(w_s)}{v_s(w_s)} \right) M_s, \quad s = 0, 1, \ldots, S \tag{14}$$

Note that these spot prices are independent of what happens on the financial markets and are thus independent of the security structure.

Given the vector of spot prices $\bar{p}$ defined by (14), the prices of the financial contracts are the equilibrium prices of the finance economy $\mathscr{E}_{\bar{p}}(\tilde{u}, \tilde{\omega}, \tilde{V})$ where $(\tilde{u}, \tilde{\omega}, \tilde{V})$ are given by (11)–(13). It is clear that as soon as we give up either the assumption that agents' preferences are separable across the states or the assumption that they are identical and homothetic within each state, a feedback

---

[2] For a reader who wants to check the definition of a gradient, see the subsection *Differentiability and First-Order Conditions* of Section 7.

is induced between the financial markets and the spot markets which makes it essential to look for a simultaneous equilibrium on these markets: a failure to properly take into account this feedback can lead to incorrect statements.

The income model studied in this volume is essentially a modern version of the model of financial market equilibrium studied with such clarity by Irving Fisher in his *Theory of Interest* (1930). Fisher was concerned with the intertemporal price of income, namely intertemporal interest rates in an idealized economy with no uncertainty and with complete loan markets. He showed that the intertemporal structure of interest rates depends on agents' rates of impatience on the one hand and on the investment opportunities available to individuals on the other. The analysis of the finance model can be viewed as an extension of Irving Fisher's theory to a world with uncertainty in which financial contracts are traded which are more general than loans and in which the structure of the markets is incomplete.

2
TWO-PERIOD FINANCE ECONOMY

MOTIVATION AND SUMMARY

The objective of this book is to analyze a general model of a sequence economy in which the task of guiding the economic activities of agents is divided between two types of markets, *spot markets* for commodities and *financial markets* for income. This specialization of tasks by the two types of markets represents a deep and far-reaching method for resolving the complex problem of decision making faced by a community in a time-uncertainty setting.

The focus of this first volume is on understanding the role and functioning of the financial markets and this chapter begins the analysis by considering the simplest two-period model. The key to the simplicity of this model is that it abstracts from all the complicating elements of the general model except two, which are taken as primitive for each agent, namely his preference ordering and an exogenously given income stream. The preference ordering represents the agent's attitude toward consumption today versus consumption in the future (his impatience) as well as his attitude towards the variability of an uncertain consumption stream in the future (his risk aversion). The characteristic of the income streams of the agents is that they typically are not evenly distributed over time or across the uncertain states of nature. A financial contract is a claim to an income stream—hence the logic of the financial markets: by exchanging such claims agents change the shapes of their income streams, obtaining a more even consumption across time and the uncertain contingencies.

The two-period model drastically simplifies the future—it just consists of a finite number of states $\{1, \ldots, S\}$ at the second date. The chapter begins by studying the ideal or reference model (the Arrow-Debreu model) in which, for each state, there is a claim which promises to pay one unit of income in the specified state. Trading in these *primitive* claims leads to equilibrium prices $(\pi_s, \ s = 1, \ldots, S)$ which are the present values at date 0 of one unit of income in each state at date 1. Since agents in solving their maximum problems are led to equalize their marginal rates of substitution with these prices, the equilibrium allocation is Pareto optimal (Section 7).

A more general class of financial contracts is then introduced, in which each contract is a *composite* claim (it promises to deliver income in several states at date 1) and where there may not be enough securities to span all the states at date 1. Two ideas (results) are studied which are crucial to all the analysis that follows:

(i) the characterization and consequences of *absence of arbitrage* on the financial markets

(ii) the definition and consequences of *incomplete financial markets*.

The financial securities must always be appropriately priced in the minimal sense that they do not offer arbitrage opportunities: it must not be possible to purchase a portfolio of securities which gives a positive return at zero cost—for any agent would want to hold an infinite amount of such a portfolio. The idea is simple but has an important consequence: it implies the existence of present-value prices $(\pi_s, s = 1, \ldots, S)$ for income in the states at date 1 such that the price of each security is equal to the discounted value of its future dividend stream (i.e. the price of a composite security is the sum of the prices of its primitive components). This result (obtained in Section 9) is extremely general and is basic to all the theory of finance.

When there are no arbitrage opportunities on the financial markets an agent's portfolio choice problem has a solution. Purchasing one unit of a security incurs a cost at date 0 equal to its price and generates an income stream at date 1 given by its dividend stream. The income transfers generated by forming all possible portfolios of the securities form a subspace $\langle W \rangle$ which we call the *market subspace*. For agent i, the choice of a portfolio (z^i) is simply a way of achieving an income transfer (τ^i) lying in the market subspace. The first-order conditions for the agent's financial market maximum problem assert that the optimal income transfer $\bar{\tau}^i$ is the point where the agent's indifference surface is tangent to the market subspace: at this point his gradient (present value) vector is orthogonal to the market subspace $(\bar{\pi}^i \in \langle W \rangle^{\perp})$.

The financial markets are said to be *complete* when the market subspace $\langle W \rangle$ has maximal dimension S; they are said to be *incomplete* when its dimension is less that S, and in this case agents are actually constrained in the income transfers that they can achieve. The dual side of the story is that when financial markets are complete there is a unique vector of present value (or state) prices π that supports the market subspace $(\pi \in \langle W \rangle^{\perp})$. Thus all agents' (normalized) gradient vectors coincide $(\bar{\pi}^i = \pi)$ and the equilibrium is Pareto optimal. The financial market equilibrium is essentially an Arrow-Debreu equilibrium.

When the financial markets are incomplete the subspace of state prices $\langle W \rangle^{\perp}$ has at least dimension 2: there is thus room for the agents' present-value vectors to differ. In Section 11 it is shown that when markets are incomplete, in an equilibrium any two agents' present-value vectors are typically distinct $(\bar{\pi}^i \neq \bar{\pi}^j)$: the equilibrium allocation is thus not Pareto optimal.

The reader should not be discouraged by the fact that Section 7 begins with an existence proof—on the whole we will not spend much time in this volume on technical questions of existence. There are however several reasons for establishing the existence of an equilibrium in this very simple setting. First, experience shows that going carefully through the steps of an existence proof is one of the most effective ways of understanding the structure and functioning of a model: one is obliged to check the role that each assumption plays in ensuring that there is an equilibrium. Second, the method presented in Section 7 adapts itself readily to the proof of existence of a financial market equilibrium and perhaps most importantly extends in a natural way to the existence proofs for the general model in Volume 2.

6. CHARACTERISTICS OF THE FINANCE ECONOMY

In Section 4 it was briefly explained how the time-uncertainty setting can be described by an event-tree. The simplest event-tree which allows for both time and uncertainty has two periods ($t = 0, 1$) and S alternative possible outcomes (states of nature) at date 1. The states will be written $s = 1, \ldots, S$ and it is often convenient to include date $t = 0$ as state $s = 0$, so that there are a total of $S + 1$ states. Consider the simplest economy with a single good and a finite number of consumers ($i = 1, \ldots, I$). Since there is a single good in each state, the *commodity space* is $\mathbb{R}^n$ with $n = S + 1$. Let $X^i \subset \mathbb{R}^n$ denote the *consumption set* of agent i: in all of Volume 1 (except Section 17) the consumption set is the non-negative orthant of the commodity space, $X^i = \mathbb{R}_+^n$. Agent i has a *preference ordering* defined on the consumption set which is complete, transitive and continuous and can thus be represented by a utility function

$$u^i : \mathbb{R}_+^n \longrightarrow \mathbb{R}$$

It is convenient to single out three sets of assumptions on the utility functions:

Assumption $\mathcal{U}''$ (Strong Monotonicity):
   (i) $u^i : \mathbb{R}_+^n \longrightarrow \mathbb{R}$ is continuous on $\mathbb{R}_+^n$.
   (ii) For any $x, x' \in \mathbb{R}_+^n$ with $x \geq x'$ and $x \neq x'$, $u^i(x) > u^i(x')$.

Assumption $\mathcal{U}'$ (Strong Monotonicity and Strict Quasi-concavity): u^i satisfies Assumption $\mathcal{U}''$ and is strictly quasi-concave i.e. for all $x, x' \in \mathbb{R}_+^n$ and $0 < \lambda < 1$, $u^i(\lambda x + (1 - \lambda)x') > \min(u^i(x), u^i(x'))$.

The consequences of the absence of arbitrage opportunities on the financial markets (Section 9) are most naturally analyzed using Assumption $\mathcal{U}''$. Assumption $\mathcal{U}'$ is used when we want to work with a continuous demand function, as in the equilibrium existence Theorems 7.4 and 10.5. When a differentiable demand function is needed (for example to prove Theorem 11.6) the following stronger Assumption $\mathscr{U}$ is invoked. Let $\mathbb{R}^n_{++}$ denote the positive orthant of the commodity space

$$\mathbb{R}^n_{++} = \left\{ x = (x_1, \ldots, x_n) \in \mathbb{R}^n \mid x_j > 0, \quad j = 1, \ldots, n \right\}$$

The function u^i is said to be $\mathcal{C}^k$ on $\mathbb{R}^n_{++}$ if all k^{th} order partial derivatives of u^i are continuous: if this property holds for all $k = 1, 2, \ldots$ then u^i is said to be $\mathcal{C}^\infty$ or *smooth* on $\mathbb{R}^n_{++}$. If u^i is $\mathcal{C}^k$ for any finite k then it can be approximated arbitrarily closely by a smooth function. Since there is no significant gain of generality from assuming that u^i has some finite order of differentiability and since it is cumbersome to keep track of the exact order of differentiability of all functional relations (for example first-order relations) derived from u^i, in the analysis that follows it is typically assumed that u^i is smooth on $\mathbb{R}^n_{++}$. The following assumption is essentially a differentiable version of $\mathscr{U}'$ and will play a key role in almost all the analysis of this book.

Assumption $\mathscr{U}$ (Smooth Preferences):

(i) $u^i : \mathbb{R}^n_+ \longrightarrow \mathbb{R}$ is continuous on $\mathbb{R}^n_+$ and $\mathcal{C}^\infty$ on $\mathbb{R}^n_{++}$.

(ii) $U^i(x) = \left\{ x' \in \mathbb{R}^n_+ \mid u^i(x') \geq u^i(x) \right\} \subset \mathbb{R}^n_{++}, \ \forall\, x \in \mathbb{R}^n_{++}$.

(iii) For each $x \in \mathbb{R}^n_{++}$, $\left(\frac{\partial u^i(x)}{\partial x_1}, \ldots, \frac{\partial u^i(x)}{\partial x_n} \right) \in \mathbb{R}^n_{++}$.

(iv) For each $x \in \mathbb{R}^n_{++}$, $\sum_{j=1}^n \sum_{k=1}^n h_j h_k \frac{\partial^2 u^i(x)}{\partial x_j \partial x_k} < 0$ for all $h \in \mathbb{R}^n$, $h \neq 0$, such that $\sum_{j=1}^n h_j \frac{\partial u^i(x)}{\partial x_j} = 0$.

Assumption $\mathscr{U}$ was introduced by Debreu (1972) to obtain a differentiable demand function for goods in the standard *general equilibrium* (GE) model; it plays the same role in the analysis of the financial market model. (ii) asserts that any indifference curve passing through a positive consumption bundle does not intersect the boundary of the non-negative orthant: this prevents the solution of the agent's maximizing problem from occurring at the boundary of the consumption set. (iii) is the assumption of strong monotonicity (for the differentiable case). (iv) expresses the fact that for each positive vector of consumption x, the quadratic form of the second derivative of u^i (which can be written as $h^T D^2 u^i(x) h$) is negative definite when restricted to the tangent hyperplane to the indifference surface through x (which can be written as $\left\{ h \in \mathbb{R}^n \mid \nabla u^i(x) h = 0 \right\}$). This family of local conditions (for all $x \in \mathbb{R}^n_{++}$) implies the global property that u^i is strictly quasi-concave on $\mathbb{R}^n_{++}$. Moreover, for each $x \in \mathbb{R}^n_{++}$, it implies the local property that the gradient ($\nabla u^i(x)$) to the indifference surface through x always changes direction for *any* local displacement (from x) on the indifference surface, so that the surface is not locally flat in any direction. This curvature property of the indifference surfaces will be proved in Section 11 (see Lemma 11.7 and the remark which follows). For a further analysis of the curvature properties implied by (iv) see Mas-Colell (1985, Chapter 2). A utility function satisfying Assumption $\mathcal{U}$ is sometimes called *differentiably strictly quasi-concave*. In the GE model the strict quasi-concavity of u^i implies that agent i has a well-defined demand function and the curvature property implies that this function is differentiable. Lemma 11.5 will establish the equivalent properties for the model with financial markets.

When an agent chooses a consumption stream

$$x^i = (x_0^i, x_1^i, \ldots, x_S^i)$$

he makes a choice of consumption to-day (x_0^i) versus consumption in the future $(x_1^i, \ldots, x_S^i)$, as well as a choice over the relative amounts of consumption in the different states at date 1. The study of the nature and properties of preference orderings over intertemporal and risky consumption streams is a subject in itself that we do not attempt to cover. Two properties are considered typical for preference orderings over such consumption streams. The first is the property of *impatience*: intuitively it means that agents prefer consumption to-day to consumption in the future. The second is the property of *risk aversion* which expresses the idea that agents always prefer the expected value of a random consumption stream for sure to the random consumption stream itself.[1] The simplest class of utility functions exhibiting these properties are the so-called additively-separable utility functions

$$u^i(x_0^i, x_1^i, \ldots, x_S^i) = v^i(x_0^i) + \delta_i \sum_{s=1}^{S} \rho_s v^i(x_s) \qquad (1)$$

where v^i is a real-valued, increasing, concave function defined on $\mathbb{R}_+$. The parameter δ_i, which satisfies $0 < \delta_i < 1$, indicates how the agent discounts the utility of future consumption and $\rho = (\rho_1, \ldots, \rho_S)$ denotes the probabilities of the states at date 1. The utility of a consumption stream is the sum of the utility of date 0 consumption plus the discounted expected utility of consumption at date 1. The vector ρ can either represent a vector of *objective* (commonly agreed upon) probabilities or a vector of *subjective* probabilities, in which case it can

---

[1]The most intuitive and extensive discussion of the psychological, social and institutional factors which influence the nature of intertemporal preferences still remains the classical account of Rae (1834): his ideas were formalized by Irving Fisher (1930). The modern literature on non-additively separable (recursive) preferences originates with Koopmans (1960). Modulo Bernouilli's perceptive discussion of expected utility (1738), the modern literature on preference orderings over risky consumption streams begins with von Neumann-Morgenstern (1944, Chapter I, Section 3) and has become very extensive: a good discussion may be found in Kreps (1988) and Karni-Schmeidler (1991).

be indexed by the agent, $\rho^i = (\rho_1^i, \ldots, \rho_S^i)$. While some of the results derived in Chapter 3 are based on the assumption that agents' utility functions have the specific functional form (6.1), the results of this chapter only require the weaker assumptions of continuity, monotonicity, and quasi-concavity. The assumption of strict quasi-concavity, which implies that for a given date 0 consumption, a convex combination of two date 1 consumption streams is strictly preferred, is a general way of expressing the property of risk aversion without using expected utility.

The other characteristic of an agent is his *initial endowment*

$$\omega^i = (\omega_0^i, \omega_1^i, \ldots, \omega_S^i)$$

of the good (or income) in each state. The characteristics of consumer i are thus summarized by the pair (u^i, ω^i), $i = 1, \ldots, I$. Let

$$(u, \omega) = (u^1, \ldots, u^I, \omega^1, \ldots, \omega^I)$$

denote the vector of characteristics of the I agents and let $\mathscr{E}(u, \omega)$ denote the associated *finance (exchange) economy*. Our object is to study the problem of resource allocation for the economy $\mathscr{E}(u, \omega)$.

6.1 Definition: An *allocation* $x = (x^1, \ldots, x^I)$ for the economy $\mathscr{E}(u, \omega)$ consists of a consumption stream $x^i \in \mathbb{R}^n$ for each agent $i = 1, \ldots, I$. An allocation $x = (x^1, \ldots, x^I)$ is *feasible* if

$$\text{(i)}\quad x^i \in \mathbb{R}_+^n, \quad i = 1, \ldots I \qquad \text{(ii)}\quad \sum_{i=1}^{I}(x^i - \omega^i) \leq 0$$

Let F denote the *set of feasible allocations*

$$F = \left\{ x \in \mathbb{R}_+^{nI} \;\middle|\; \sum_{i=1}^{I}(x^i - \omega^i) \leq 0 \right\}$$

Note that the feasible set F depends only on the *aggregate endowment*

$$w = \sum_{i=1}^{I} \omega^i$$

and not on the distribution of endowments among the agents. In the simplest interpretation of an exchange economy the vector ω^i is the (exogenously given) output of the firm (or farm) belonging to agent i, so that w is often called the *aggregate output* of the economy. The feasible allocations which are of special interest are those which cannot be improved upon in the sense introduced by Pareto (1897).

6.2 Definition: An allocation $\bar{x} = (\bar{x}^1, \ldots, \bar{x}^I)$ is a *Pareto optimum* if

(i) $\bar{x} \in F$

(ii) there does not exist $x = (x^1, \ldots, x^I) \in F$ such that $u^i(x^i) \geq u^i(\bar{x}^i)$, $i = 1, \ldots, I$ with a strict inequality for at least one i.

7. CONTINGENT MARKET EQUILIBRIUM

We are interested in studying the qualitative properties of the allocations that arise when *different market structures* are adjoined to the basic exchange economy $\mathscr{E}(u, \omega)$. Two such market structures will be studied: a system of *contingent markets* and a system of *financial markets*.

When agents trade on a system of markets they sell some commodities (or contracts) from which they obtain an income and purchase others for which they incur an expenditure. Exchange on markets is based on the idea that each agent can buy and sell as he wishes provided he satisfies the condition of *accountability* that the value of the commodities (contracts) that he withdraws from the market does not exceed the value of the commodities (contracts) that he offers to the market. Clearly some organized method must be devised for *keeping the accounts* and the standard way of doing this is to measure the prices of all goods (or contracts) in a unit of account. In the simple two-period model with one good all trading commitments are made at date 0, so that accountability only has to be checked at date 0. It is assumed that there is a costless monitoring mechanism which ensures that agents do not renege on their contractual commitments at date 1—in short, there is no default. Thus only a unit of account at date 0 is required and π_0 denotes the number of units of account that must be paid for one unit of the good at date 1.

The static GE model has a market for each good and all the goods are traded simultaneously. As Arrow (1953) and Debreu (1959, Chapter 7) observed, by suitably extending the notion of the commodity traded, the GE model can be generalized to a setting with time and uncertainty. In the one-good model the extended notion of a commodity is a contract calling for the future delivery of the good contingent on the occurrence of a particular state of nature.

7.1 Definition: A *contingent contract* for state s $(s = 0, 1, \ldots, S)$ is a promise to deliver one unit of the (single) good in state s and nothing otherwise. Its price π_s, payable at date 0, is measured in units of account at date 0.

If there is a complete set of such contingent contracts $(s = 0, 1, \ldots, S)$ at date 0, then each agent i can sell his endowment $\omega^i = (\omega_0^i, \omega_1^i, \ldots, \omega_S^i)$ obtaining the *income* (measured in units of account at date 0)

$$\pi_0 \omega_0^i + \pi_1 \omega_1^i + \cdots + \pi_S \omega_S^i, \quad i = 1, \ldots, I$$

and can then purchase on the *contingent markets* any consumption stream $x^i = (x_0^i, x_1^i, \ldots, x_S^i)$ satisfying

$$\sum_{s=0}^{S} \pi_s x_s^i \leq \sum_{s=0}^{S} \pi_s \omega_s^i$$

Since the preferences of the agents are always assumed to be monotonic, an agent will always fully spend his income. There is thus no loss of generality in defining the budget set of agent i by

$$B(\pi, \omega^i) = \left\{ x^i \in \mathbb{R}_+^n \;\middle|\; \sum_{s=0}^{S} \pi_s x_s^i = \sum_{s=0}^{S} \pi_s \omega_s^i \right\} \tag{1}$$

where $\pi = (\pi_0, \pi_1, \ldots, \pi_S)$ is the vector of *contingent market prices*. Using the standard *inner product* notation, for $\pi \in \mathbb{R}^n$, $\omega^i \in \mathbb{R}^n$, $\pi \omega^i = \sum_{s=0}^{S} \pi_s \omega_s^i$, $B(\pi, \omega^i)$ can be written more compactly as

$$B(\pi, \omega^i) = \left\{ x^i \in \mathbb{R}_+^n \;\middle|\; \pi(x^i - \omega^i) = 0 \right\}$$

$B(\pi, \omega^i)$ is called the *contingent market budget set* of agent i. This leads to the following concept of equilibrium.

7.2 Definition: A *contingent market (CM) equilibrium* for the economy $\mathscr{E}(u, \omega)$ with one good is a pair consisting of an allocation and a vector of prices $(\bar{x}, \bar{\pi}) \in \mathbb{R}_+^{nI} \times \mathbb{R}_+^n$ such that

(i) $\bar{x}^i \in \arg \max \left\{ u^i(x^i) \;\middle|\; x^i \in B(\bar{\pi}, \omega^i) \right\}, \quad i = 1, \ldots, I$

(ii) $\displaystyle\sum_{i=1}^{I} (\bar{x}^i - \omega^i) = 0$

where *arg max* means the set of arguments or variables which maximize $u^i(x^i)$ over $B(\bar{\pi}, \omega^i)$.

Absence of Free Contracts

A contingent market equilibrium is a competitive equilibrium in which agents are price takers: each agent can buy as much as he wants of the contingent contract s without affecting its price π_s. Since the agent's preferences are strictly monotone the price of the contract must be positive in each state if the agent's maximum problem is to have a solution: in such an economy there are *no free contracts in an equilibrium*. More precisely the following property holds:

7.3 Proposition (Absence of Free Contracts on Contingent Markets): *Let the utility functions satisfy Assumption $\mathscr{U}''$, then the following conditions are equivalent:*

(i) *The problem* $\max \left\{ u^i(x^i) \mid x^i \in B(\bar{\pi}, \omega^i) \right\}$ *has a solution.*
(ii) $\bar{\pi} \in \mathbb{R}_{++}^n$.
(iii) $B(\bar{\pi}, \omega^i)$ *is compact.*

PROOF: Let us show that (i) $\Rightarrow$ (ii) $\Rightarrow$ (iii) $\Rightarrow$ (i).

(i) $\Rightarrow$ (ii) Suppose $\pi_s = 0$ for some s. Then by monotonicity, agent i's demand for good s is unbounded and (i) has no solution.

(ii) $\Rightarrow$ (iii) Let $m^i = \sum_{s=0}^{S} \bar{\pi}_s \omega_s^i$ denote agent i's income. Then $x^i \in B(\bar{\pi}, \omega^i)$ implies $0 \le x_s^i \le m^i / \bar{\pi}_s$, $s = 0, 1, \ldots, S$, so that $B(\bar{\pi}, \omega^i)$ is bounded. Since the map which takes x^i into $\bar{\pi} x^i$ is continuous, $B(\bar{\pi}, \omega^i)$ is closed and hence compact.

(iii) $\Rightarrow$ (i) A continuous function on a compact set attains a maximum. $\square$

Existence of CM Equilibrium

An equilibrium defines the *outcome* of a trading process when agents behave as postulated in the trading environment described by the model. It is useful for predicting the consequence of such trading only if it has a well-defined outcome i.e. if it can be shown that an equilibrium exists (at least for a broad class of characteristics). Showing that a contingent market equilibrium exists depends on being able to simultaneously solve two interrelated problems:

(a) taking prices $\bar{\pi}$ as fixed, each consumer must find the utility maximizing demand vector $\bar{x}^i$: this generates an aggregate demand $\sum_{i=1}^{I} \bar{x}^i$:
(b) prices $\bar{\pi}$ must be found such that this aggregate demand exactly coincides with the total available supply $\sum_{i=1}^{I} \omega^i$.

Proposition 7.3 shows that (a) has a solution for all $\bar{\pi} \in \mathbb{R}_{++}^n$. It is a much deeper problem to establish that a price vector $\bar{\pi} \in \mathbb{R}_{++}^n$ can be found that solves (b), given the solution to (a).

In the theorem that follows Assumption $\mathscr{U}'$ is invoked to permit the use of demand functions (as opposed to correspondences) in proving the existence of equilibrium. This assumption is stronger than necessary (quasi-concavity of the utility functions would suffice) but the objective is to exhibit a proof of existence of equilibrium which is simple and extends in a natural way to the general model studied in Volume 2.

7.4 Theorem (Existence of CM Equilibrium):   *Let Assumption $\mathscr{U}'$ hold. If $\sum_{i=1}^{I} \omega^i \in \mathbb{R}_{++}^n$, then the exchange economy $\mathscr{E}(u, \omega)$ has a contingent market equilibrium.*

PROOF: Let us sketch the key ideas behind the proof, since they give useful insights into properties of the standard GE model. As we shall see in Section 10, only minor modifications of these ideas are required to establish existence of an equilibrium for the one-good two-period model with financial markets. Indeed the underlying vector-field argument will carry over in an elegant way to the general multiperiod multigood model.

It follows from the strict quasi-concavity of agent i's utility function that his maximum problem leads to a *demand function* $f^i : \mathbb{R}_{++}^n \longrightarrow \mathbb{R}^n$

$$f^i(\pi) = \arg \max \left\{ u^i(x^i) \mid x^i \in B(\pi, \omega^i) \right\}, \quad i = 1, \ldots, I$$

If the *aggregate excess demand* function $Z : \mathbb{R}_{++}^n \longrightarrow \mathbb{R}^n$ is defined by

$$Z(\pi) = \sum_{i=1}^{I} (f^i(\pi) - \omega^i)$$

then the pair $(\bar{x}, \bar{\pi})$ is a contingent market equilibrium if and only if it satisfies

$$\bar{x} = (f^1(\bar{\pi}), \ldots, f^I(\bar{\pi}))$$
$$Z(\bar{\pi}) = 0 \tag{2}$$

(2) is simply the assertion that a vector of prices $\bar{\pi}$ must be found such that total demand at these prices is equated with the total supply of the good in each state $s = 0, \ldots, S$. If there are a large number of states it is not at all obvious that such a system of prices exists. *What must be established therefore is that the system of equations* (2) *has a solution.* What is the information available for deducing such a result?

Using Assumption $\mathscr{U}'$, standard arguments show that the individual demand functions f^i have the following properties:[1]

(i) $f^i(\pi) \geq 0$ for all $\pi \in \mathbb{R}_{++}^n$
(ii) f^i is continuous on $\mathbb{R}_{++}^n$

---

[1](i), (iii) and (iv) are immediate. (iii) simply reflects the fact that while doubling prices makes any given consumption stream twice as expensive, it is affordable since the doubling of prices has doubled the agent's income from the sale of his endowment. Proving (ii) and (v) is more subtle: the proof is based on the property of sequential compactness; every bounded infinite sequence in $\mathbb{R}^n$ has a convergent subsequence. The details are familiar from a good course on microeconomics, for example (Hildenbrand and Kirman (1988, Chapter 3)). (v) essentially means that when some goods become very inexpensive, an agent demands very large amounts of them.

(iii) $f^i(\alpha\pi) = f^i(\pi)$ for all $\alpha > 0$, for all $\pi \in \mathbb{R}^n_{++}$

(iv) $\pi f^i(\pi) = \pi\omega^i$ for all $\pi \in \mathbb{R}^n_{++}$

(v) If $\pi^\nu \in \mathbb{R}^n_{++}$ is such that $\pi^\nu \to \pi \in \partial\mathbb{R}^n_{++}$ and if $\pi\omega^i > 0$, then $\|f^i(\pi^\nu)\| \to \infty$ as $\nu \to \infty$, where $\|x\| = (\sum_{s=0}^{S} x_s^2)^{1/2}$ is the *norm* of the vector x in $\mathbb{R}^{S+1}$ and $\partial\mathbb{R}^n_{++}$ is the *boundary* of the positive orthant.

The aggregate excess demand then has the induced properties:

(i)′ $Z(\pi) \geq -w$ for all $\pi \in \mathbb{R}^n_{++}$ (*bounded below*)

(ii)′ Z is continuous on $\mathbb{R}^n_{++}$ (*continuity*)

(iii)′ $Z(\alpha\pi) = Z(\pi)$ for all $\alpha > 0$, for all $\pi \in \mathbb{R}^n_{++}$ (*homogeneity*)

(iv)′ $\pi Z(\pi) = 0$ for all $\pi \in \mathbb{R}^n_{++}$ (*Walras' Law*)

(v)′ If $\pi^\nu \in \mathbb{R}^n_{++}$ is such that $\pi^\nu \to \pi \in \partial\mathbb{R}^n_{++}, \pi \neq 0$, then $\|Z(\pi^\nu)\| \to \infty$ as $\nu \to \infty$ (*boundary behavior*).

Property (iii)′ is a characteristic property of the standard general equilibrium model: each individual's demand and hence aggregate excess demand depends only on *relative* prices. Thus any normalization of prices can be chosen to make the price level determinate. For the economic interpretation of the model the most natural normalization is obtained by setting $\pi_0 = 1$ so that the unit of account at date 0 is one unit of the good. For the mathematical proof of existence which is given here a more convenient normalization is $\sum_{s=0}^{S} \pi_s^2 = 1$, which amounts to replacing any vector of prices on the ray OA in Figure 7.1

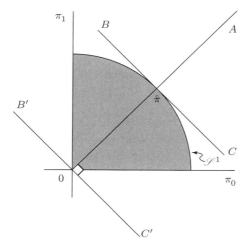

Figure 7.1 Normalization of prices to unit sphere when $n = 2$: the tangent hyperplane (BC) to the sphere at $\hat{\pi}$ and the tangent space $(B'C')$.

by the point $\hat{\pi}$ lying on the unit sphere (circle). The $(n-1)$-dimensional unit sphere in $\mathbb{R}^n$ (where $n = S + 1$) is defined by

$$\mathscr{S}^{n-1} = \left\{ \pi \in \mathbb{R}^n \ \middle|\ \sum_{j=1}^{n} \pi_j^2 = 1 \right\}$$

and the non-negative and positive unit spheres are defined by

$$\mathscr{S}_+^{n-1} = \mathscr{S}^{n-1} \cap \mathbb{R}_+^n, \quad \mathscr{S}_{++}^{n-1} = \mathscr{S}^{n-1} \cap \mathbb{R}_{++}^n$$

The sphere is just the level surface $g(\pi) = 1$ of the function $g(\pi_1, \ldots, \pi_n) = \sum_{j=1}^{n} \pi_j^2$. The equation for the *tangent hyperplane*[2] at a point $\hat{\pi}$ in $\mathscr{S}^{n-1}$ is given by

$$\nabla g(\hat{\pi})(\pi - \hat{\pi}) = 0 \iff \hat{\pi}(\pi - \hat{\pi}) = 0 \iff \hat{\pi}\pi = 1$$

where $\nabla g(\hat{\pi}) = (\partial g(\hat{\pi})/\partial \pi_1, \ldots, \partial g(\hat{\pi})/\partial \pi_n)$ denotes the vector of partial derivatives (the gradient) of g at $\hat{\pi}$. Translating this hyperplane (BC in Figure 7.1) parallel to itself so that it passes through the origin (to $B'C'$) gives the *tangent space* at $\hat{\pi}$

$$T_{\hat{\pi}}\mathscr{S}^{n-1} = \{ z \in \mathbb{R}^n \mid \hat{\pi}z = 0 \}$$

which consists of all vectors in $\mathbb{R}^n$ which are at right angles to $\hat{\pi}$. Walras' Law (iv)' implies that aggregate excess demand $Z(\hat{\pi})$ lies in the tangent space $T_{\hat{\pi}}\mathscr{S}^{n-1}$.

A map $v : \mathscr{S}^{n-1} \longrightarrow \mathbb{R}^n$ such that $v(\pi) \in T_{\pi}\mathscr{S}^{n-1}$ for all $\pi \in \mathscr{S}^{n-1}$ is called a *vector field*[3] on the unit sphere $\mathscr{S}^{n-1}$. Thus Walras' Law implies that the aggregate excess demand function $Z : \mathscr{S}_{++}^{n-1} \longrightarrow \mathbb{R}^n$ defines a vector field on the positive unit sphere. A vector field v on the non-negative unit sphere is said to be *inward pointing* on the boundary $\partial \mathscr{S}_+^{n-1}$ if $v_j(\pi) \geq 0$ for all $\pi \in \partial \mathscr{S}_+^{n-1}$ with $\pi_j = 0$, since the vector $v(\pi)$ located at π points towards the interior of $\mathscr{S}_+^{n-1}$. Z itself is not defined on the boundary $\partial \mathscr{S}_+^{n-1}$, since excess demand is infinite with zero prices. More precisely, condition (v)' (combined with (i)') implies that when the price of one good tends to zero then the excess demand for this good becomes arbitrarily large ($\pi_j \to 0$ implies $Z_j \to \infty$). When the prices of several goods tend simultaneously to zero, the excess demand for each of the goods may not tend to infinity, however the excess demand for at least one of these goods will tend to infinity. This behavior of Z when some of the prices go to zero implies that Z can be modified near the boundary $\partial \mathscr{S}_+^{n-1}$ so as to obtain a vector field $\widetilde{Z}$ which is defined on all of $\mathscr{S}_+^{n-1}$, has the same

---

[2]The derivation of the equation for the tangent hyperplane is explained in the case of an indifference surface on page 61.

[3]The concept of a vector field is explained in more detail in the appendix to this chapter.

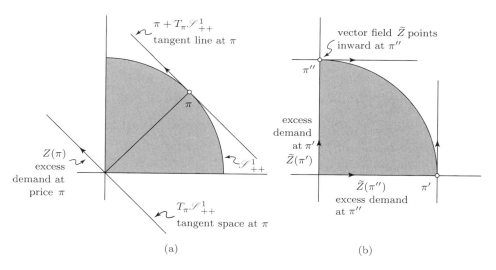

Figure 7.2 (a) Excess demand as a vector field on $\mathscr{S}^1_{++}$ when $n = 2$; (b) Inward-pointing property of $\widetilde{Z}(\pi)$.

zeros as Z (i.e. $\widetilde{Z}(\pi) = 0$ if and only if $Z(\pi) = 0$) and is inward pointing on the boundary ($\pi_j = 0$ implies $\widetilde{Z}_j(\pi) > 0$). This property of $\widetilde{Z}$ is shown in Figure 7.2(b) for the case $n = 2$: at $\pi' = (1,0)$, $\widetilde{Z}_0(\pi') > 0$ and at $\pi'' = (0,1)$, $\widetilde{Z}_1(\pi'') > 0$.

The exact construction of this equivalent vector field $\widetilde{Z}$ is given in the appendix: $\widetilde{Z}$ is the same as Z except in a small neighborhood of $\partial \mathscr{S}^{n-1}_+$ (which does not contain any zero of Z). The existence of an equilibrium price vector then follows from the property that every continuous inward-pointing vector field on the non-negative unit sphere has a zero. □

7.5 Theorem (Inward-Pointing Vector Field Theorem): *If $v : \mathscr{S}^{n-1}_+ \longrightarrow \mathbb{R}^n$ is a continuous inward-pointing vector field on the non-negative unit sphere $\mathscr{S}^{n-1}_+$, then there exists $\bar{\pi} \in \mathscr{S}^{n-1}_+$ such that $v(\bar{\pi}) = 0$.*

PROOF: The proof will be given in Volume 2. □

This theorem is very remarkable: it asserts that solely on the basis of information about the behavior of a vector field on the boundary of a region, we can deduce a property of the vector field on the interior of that region—namely that there is a zero (for a further explanation, see the appendix).

Pareto Optimality of CM Equilibrium

The Arrow-Debreu system of contingent markets constitutes an ideal market system in two senses. First, it leads to equilibrium equations that are of canonical simplicity for mathematical analysis; in the sequel we will find that more complex concepts of equilibrium are most easily studied when transformed into constrained versions of the Arrow-Debreu concept of equilibrium. Second, from an economic point of view, it constitutes an ideal mechanism in that it leads to Pareto optimal allocations. The reason why these properties hold is that, with this market structure, *all agents face a single budget constraint induced by a common vector of prices* $\bar{\pi}$.

7.6 Theorem (Pareto Optimality of CM Equilibrium): *Let $\mathscr{E}(u, \omega)$ be an economy satisfying Assumption $\mathscr{U}''$. If $(\bar{x}, \bar{\pi})$ is a contingent market equilibrium, then the allocation $\bar{x}$ is a Pareto optimum.*

PROOF: Suppose $\bar{x}$ is not a Pareto optimum, then there exists $x \in F$ such that $u^i(x^i) \geq u^i(\bar{x}^i)$, $i = 1, \ldots, I$ with $u^j(x^j) > u^j(\bar{x}^j)$ for some j. Since $\bar{x}^j$ is optimal for agent j in $B(\bar{\pi}, \omega^j)$, $x^j \notin B(\bar{\pi}, \omega^j)$ or equivalently $\bar{\pi}x^j > \bar{\pi}\omega^j$. For $i \neq j$, $\bar{\pi}x^i \geq \bar{\pi}\omega^i$ since u^i is monotonic (local non-satiation is sufficient to obtain this property). Thus

$$\bar{\pi} \sum_{i=1}^{I} x^i > \bar{\pi} \sum_{i=1}^{I} \omega^i$$

which contradicts $x \in F$. $\square$

Differentiability and First-Order Conditions

Over the last fifty years the calculus approach to general equilibrium theory has been successively in and out of vogue depending on the aspect of the theory to which attention was being directed at the time. The refinement and extension of the methods of comparative statics in the 1940s (Hicks (1939), Samuelson (1947)) was based on calculus and differentiability. One of the messages of the Arrow-Debreu theory developed in the 1950s (Debreu (1959)) was that calculus and differentiability are not required to prove the existence of an equilibrium and the two Welfare Theorems. These results can be obtained using a set theoretic approach based on convexity of agents' preferred sets and firms' production sets. Subsequently when attention was directed to analyzing the qualitative properties of equilibria (stability of the tatonnement process and finiteness of the number of equilibria) it was found convenient to reintroduce assumptions of differentiability. Of particular importance was Debreu's paper (1970) on the local uniqueness of equilibria which, for the first time, revealed the power of the analytical tools of differential topology. The analysis of the Arrow-Debreu model using the methods of differential topology was extensively developed in the 1970s: the results of this research are summarized in Dierker (1974), Mas-Collel (1985) and Balasko (1988). In this book the differentiable approach is used for two reasons: first, the analysis is often more intuitive using differentiability; second, it permits us to draw on techniques of differential topology to establish a number of important properties of the model with financial markets.

When the assumption of differentiability is introduced, qualitative results are sometimes easier to understand. A good example is provided by Theorem 7.6: while differentiability is not required to obtain this result, if we strengthen the assumption on agents' utility functions by requiring that they be differentiable (replace $\mathcal{U}''$ by $\mathcal{U}$) then a proof of Theorem 7.6 can be given which reveals more clearly why a contingent market equilibrium leads to a Pareto optimum.

If $u^i : \mathbb{R}^{S+1}_{++} \longrightarrow \mathbb{R}$ is differentiable, let $\nabla u^i(x^i)$ denote the vector of partial derivatives at $x^i \in \mathbb{R}^{S+1}_{++}$

$$\nabla u^i(x^i) = \left(\frac{\partial u^i(x^i)}{\partial x^i_0}, \frac{\partial u^i(x^i)}{\partial x^i_1}, \dots, \frac{\partial u^i(x^i)}{\partial x^i_S} \right)$$

This vector is called the *gradient* of u^i at x^i. For $\bar{x}^i \in \mathbb{R}^{S+1}_{++}$ let

$$I^i_{\bar{x}^i} = \left\{ x^i \in \mathbb{R}^{S+1}_+ \;\middle|\; u^i(x^i) = u^i(\bar{x}^i) \right\}$$

denote agent i's indifference surface through $\bar{x}^i$. The hyperplane which best approximates $I^i_{\bar{x}^i}$ in a neighborhood of $\bar{x}^i$ is called the *tangent hyperplane* to $I^i_{\bar{x}^i}$ at $\bar{x}^i$ and is denoted by $\mathcal{T}_{\bar{x}^i}\left(I^i_{\bar{x}^i}\right)$. Since the Taylor expansion of u^i at $\bar{x}^i$ is given by

$$u^i(x^i) = u^i(\bar{x}^i) + \nabla u^i(\bar{x}^i)(x^i - \bar{x}^i) + \mathrm{o}\|x^i - \bar{x}^i\|$$

to terms of first order (where $\mathrm{o}\|x^i - \bar{x}^i\|$ is the standard notation for terms of order greater than one), $u^i(x^i) = u^i(\bar{x}^i)$ if and only if $\nabla u^i(\bar{x}^i)(x^i - \bar{x}^i) = 0$. Thus the tangent hyperplane at $\bar{x}^i$ is given by

$$\mathcal{T}_{\bar{x}^i}\left(I^i_{\bar{x}^i}\right) = \left\{ x^i \in \mathbb{R}^{S+1} \;\middle|\; \nabla u^i(\bar{x}^i)(x^i - \bar{x}^i) = 0 \right\} \tag{3}$$

and the gradient is orthogonal to the tangent hyperplane to the indifference surface (see Figure 7.3). Intuitively while the tangent hyperplane gives the directions of local indifference, the gradient points in the direction that is most preferred by agent i (this is made precise in Section 14, see Proposition 14.18).

The tangent hyperplane $\mathcal{T}_{\bar{x}^i}(I^i_{\bar{x}^i})$ passes through the point $\bar{x}^i$. The (unique) hyperplane parallel to $\mathcal{T}_{\bar{x}^i}(I^i_{\bar{x}^i})$ which passes through the *origin* is a linear

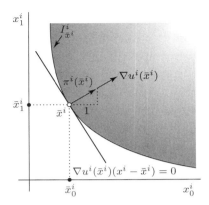

Figure 7.3 The gradient $\nabla u^i(\bar{x}^i)$ is orthogonal to the tangent hyperplane to the indifference surface $I_{\bar{x}^i}^i$. $\pi^i(\bar{x}^i)$ is the normalized gradient at $\bar{x}^i$.

subspace of $\mathbb{R}^{S+1}$ which is called the *tangent space* to $I_{\bar{x}^i}^i$ at $\bar{x}^i$ and is denoted by $T_{\bar{x}^i}(I_{\bar{x}^i})$. Thus

$$T_{\bar{x}^i}(I_{\bar{x}^i}) = \left\{ h \in \mathbb{R}^{S+1} \mid \nabla u^i(\bar{x}^i)h = 0 \right\}$$

While the magnitude of the gradient depends on the utility function chosen to represent the agent's preference ordering, its direction depends only on the indifference surface and hence only on the preference ordering. Thus all that matters as far as preferences are concerned is the direction in which the gradient points, and a convenient way of focusing on this direction is to choose a normalization. For the purposes of this book the normalization which has the most natural economic interpretation is obtained by setting the co-ordinate at date 0 equal to 1. This amounts to dividing the marginal utility of income in each state by the marginal utility of income at date 0. The resulting vector

$$\pi^i(\bar{x}^i) = \frac{1}{\lambda_0^i(\bar{x}^i)} \nabla u^i(\bar{x}^i) \quad \text{where} \quad \lambda_0^i(\bar{x}^i) = \frac{\partial u^i(\bar{x}^i)}{\partial x_0^i} \tag{4}$$

is called the *normalized gradient* of agent i at $\bar{x}^i$. The components $\pi_s^i(\bar{x}^i) = \frac{\partial u^i(\bar{x}^i)}{\partial x_s^i} / \frac{\partial u(\bar{x}^i)}{\partial x_0^i}$ of this vector are the marginal rates of substitution between consumption in state s ($s = 0, 1, \ldots, S$) and consumption at date 0; they indicate the number of units of income (or the good) at date 0 that agent i is prepared to give up to obtain an additional unit of income in state s i.e. the present value at date 0 of one unit of income in state s. Thus $\pi^i(\bar{x}^i)$ is also called the *present-value vector* of agent i at $\bar{x}^i$.

For any vector $y = (y_0, y_1, \ldots, y_S) \in \mathbb{R}^{S+1}$ we let $y_{\mathbf{1}}$ denote the vector of date 1 components

$$y_{\mathbf{1}} = (y_1, \ldots, y_S)$$

so that y can be written in date 0 and date 1 components as

$$y = (y_0, y_{\mathbf{1}}).$$

The first-order conditions which are necessary and sufficient for a Pareto optimal allocation can then be stated as follows.

7.7 Proposition (Characterization of Pareto Optimality): *Let $\mathscr{E}(u, \omega)$ be an economy satisfying Assumption $\mathscr{U}$. An allocation $\bar{x} = (\bar{x}^1, \ldots, \bar{x}^I)$ is Pareto optimal if and only if (i) $\bar{x} \in F$ and (ii) there exists $\bar{\pi}_{\mathbf{1}} \in \mathbb{R}^S$ such that*

$$\pi_{\mathbf{1}}^1(\bar{x}^1) = \cdots = \pi_{\mathbf{1}}^I(\bar{x}^I) = \bar{\pi}_{\mathbf{1}} \tag{5}$$

PROOF: $\bar{x}$ is Pareto optimal if and only if there exist $(\bar{v}^2, \ldots, \bar{v}^I) \in \mathbb{R}^{I-1}$ such that

$$\bar{x} = \arg \max_{x \in \mathbb{R}_+^{nI}} \left\{ u^1(x^1) \;\middle|\; \begin{array}{l} u^i(x^i) \geq \bar{v}^i, \quad i = 2, \ldots, I \\ \displaystyle\sum_{i=1}^{I} (x^i - \omega^i) \leq 0 \end{array} \right\} \tag{6}$$

Note that if $\bar{v}^i \leq u^i(0)$, then the strict monotonicity of u^i implies that $\bar{x}^i = 0$ and agent i can be omitted. If $\bar{v}^i > u^i(0)$, then by the continuity of u^i there exists $x^i \in \mathbb{R}_{++}^n$ such that $\bar{v}^i > u^i(x^i)$ and by Assumption $\mathscr{U}$(ii), $\bar{x}^i \in \mathbb{R}_{++}^n$. Thus we may without loss of generality assume that $\bar{x}$ is an interior maximum of (6). The first-order conditions for this maximum problem can be written as: there exist vectors

$$\bar{\alpha} = (\bar{\alpha}_1, \ldots \bar{\alpha}_I) \in \mathbb{R}_{++}^I, \quad \bar{\pi} = (1, \bar{\pi}_{\mathbf{1}}) \in \mathbb{R}^{S+1}$$

such that

$$\bar{\alpha}_i \nabla u^i(x^i) = \bar{\pi}, \quad i = 1, \ldots, I \tag{7}$$

Dividing by the date 0 component, (7) implies

$$\pi_{\mathbf{1}}^i(x^i) = \bar{\pi}_{\mathbf{1}}, \quad i = 1, \ldots, I$$

so that a Pareto optimal allocation must satisfy (5). Conversely if $\bar{x} \in F$ and $\bar{v}^i = u^i(\bar{x}^i)$, $i = 2, \ldots, I$ then $\bar{x}$ satisfies the constraints in (6). If in addition (5) holds then the first-order conditions (7) are satisfied with $\bar{\alpha}_i = 1/\frac{\partial u^i(\bar{x}^i)}{\partial x_0^i}$,

$(i = 1, \ldots, I)$. Since $u^1(\cdot)$ is quasi-concave and the constraint set is convex, $\bar{x}$ is Pareto optimal.[4] $\square$

Proposition 7.7 is perhaps the most familiar proposition in economics. For an allocation $(\bar{x}^1, \ldots, \bar{x}^I)$ to be Pareto optimal the agents' gradients

$$\left(\nabla u^1(\bar{x}^1), \ldots, \nabla u^I(\bar{x}^I) \right)$$

must all point in the same direction or equivalently their normalized gradients must be equalized $\pi^1(\bar{x}^1) = \cdots = \pi^I(\bar{x}^I) = \bar{\pi}$: the common vector $\bar{\pi}$ is the vector of prices imputed to the $S+1$ goods (or income) across the states of nature at the Pareto optimum. The equality of the agents' normalized gradients can also be expressed as the condition that the marginal rates of substitution of all agents between all pairs of goods are equalized. If this condition is not satisfied then a (small) reallocation of the goods between the agents can be found which is preferred by all agents (i.e. the reallocation is a Pareto improvement).

Conversely if at an allocation the agents' gradients all point in the same direction, then the allocation is Pareto optimal. Trading on contingent markets ensures that this condition is satisfied as we shall now show.

ALTERNATIVE PROOF OF THEOREM 7.6 (*with Assumption $\mathcal{U}$*):   Let $(\bar{x}, \bar{\pi})$ be a contingent market equilibrium, where $\bar{\pi}$ is normalized so that $\bar{\pi} = (1, \bar{\pi}_1)$. Then $\bar{x}^i$ is a solution of agent i's maximum problem

$$\bar{x}^i = \arg \max_{x^i \in \mathbb{R}^n_+} \left\{ u^i(x^i) \mid \bar{\pi}(x^i - \omega^i) = 0 \right\} \tag{8}$$

If $\omega^i = 0$ then $\bar{x}^i = 0$. If $\omega^i \neq 0$, $\omega^i \in \mathbb{R}^n_+$ then $\bar{\pi}\omega^i > 0$ and the first-order conditions for the problem (8) are: there exists $\bar{\lambda}_0^i > 0$ such that

$$\nabla u^i(x^i) = \bar{\lambda}_0^i \bar{\pi} \tag{9}$$

For $x^i \in \mathbb{R}^n_{++}$ this is equivalent to

$$\pi_1^i(x^i) = \bar{\pi}_1 \tag{10}$$

Since $\bar{x} \in F$ and (10) is satisfied at $\bar{x}^i$ for $i = 1, \ldots, I$, by Theorem 7.7 $\bar{x}$ is a Pareto optimum. $\square$

A geometric interpretation of Theorem 7.6 is shown in Figure 7.4 for the

---

[4] A maximum problem $\max \{ f(x) \mid x \in K \}$ is said to be *convex* if $f(\cdot)$ is quasi-concave and K is convex. For a convex maximum problem the first-order conditions are necessary and sufficient for a maximum, modulo a technical condition which will always be satisfied for the maximum problems considered in this book (see Simon-Blume (1994)). The first-order conditions thus characterize the solutions of the maximum problem.

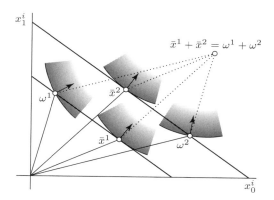

Figure 7.4 Contingent Market Equilibrium. Two agents begin with initial endowments ω^1, ω^2 at which their normalized gradients are distinct: $\left(\pi^1(\omega^1) \neq \pi^2(\omega^2)\right)$. Trading on contingent markets leads to an equilibrium $(\bar{x}^1, \bar{x}^2, \bar{\pi})$ at which their normalized gradients are equalized $\pi^1(\bar{x}^1) = \pi^2(\bar{x}^2) = \bar{\pi}$.

case $n = I = 2$.

The calculus approach has the merit of showing how individuals in *seeking their own self-interest* are led to a consumption vector at which their gradients $\nabla u^i(\bar{x}^i)$ are proportional to the vector of prices $\bar{\pi}$. Since all agents face the same vector of prices $\bar{\pi}$ their gradients $\nabla u^i(\bar{x}^i)$ all point in the same direction and this ensures the Pareto optimality of the equilibrium allocation $\bar{x}$: *thus individual self-interest* (8) *leads to maximum social welfare* (6) *when agents trade under a common vector of prices $\bar{\pi}$ established on competitive markets.* In this simplified context of exchange on competitive markets this formalizes precisely Adam Smith's notion of the operation of the invisible hand $(\bar{\pi})$.

8. FINANCIAL MARKET EQUILIBRIUM

A contingent contract which promises to deliver *income* in a specific contingency can be used to model an insurance contract if the states of nature include individual specific contingencies such as fire, theft, automobile accident, illness or death, occurring to specific individuals. Note that such risks are typically well-defined *physical* risks that are (to an important extent) beyond the control of the individuals concerned. In the real world such insurance contracts are among the most common and important of financial contracts that individuals can purchase to insure themselves against uncertain contingencies. In the contingent market model of the previous section it was assumed that such contracts cover all contingencies that can affect the economy and are the only type of financial contract which is traded. As we mentioned in Section 3 the problems of adverse selection and moral hazard (opportunism) and the difficulty of defining ahead of time all contingencies that can arise (bounded rationality) limit the extent of such insurance contracts. There is a broad class of *economic* risks that affect individuals, subgroups of individuals or firms which depend in an important way on actions taken by the economic agents involved and which are not covered by state specific insurance contracts. Such risks are covered by a different class of financial contracts, which includes the equity contracts of firms. Our object is to extend the definition of financial contracts so as to be able to include these and the earlier state specific contingent contracts. This broader class of financial contracts also includes loan contracts, whose objective is to facilitate the transfer of income over time, although they may also be exposed to the risk of default.

8.1 Definition: *Financial contract j $(j = 1, \ldots, J)$ is a promise to deliver $V_s^j \in \mathbb{R}$ units of the good (or income) in state s for $s = 1, \ldots, S$. Its price q_j, payable at date 0, is measured in the unit of account at date 0.*

Our object is to model financial contracts which are traded on markets: such contracts have objectively stated conditions which are the same for all buyers and sellers (the quantities V_s^j in the above definition). Bilateral contracts between agents or firms—recently studied in the literature[1] on incomplete contracts—do not enter this framework. We have in mind financial contracts such as bonds, equity of firms, futures contracts, options and insurance, which are bought and sold on large organized financial markets such as the Chicago Board of Trade and the New York Stock Exchange or are traded through financial intermediaries such as banks, savings and loan institutions and insurance companies. The cost of using the one-good two-period model is that it is not possible to distinguish precisely between all these types of contracts: for example, since there is only one good there is only one futures contract and it coincides with a riskless bond; secondary contracts such as options are not realistically modelled in the two-period framework. The canonical examples of contracts studied in the finance model are bonds and equity. In keeping with the terminology used in the finance literature such contracts will often be called *financial securities.*

Example (Riskless Bond): If security j is the riskless bond then

$$V_s^j = 1, \quad s = 1, \ldots, S$$

---

[1]See Hart (1987) and Hart-Holmstrom (1987).

and its price $q_j = 1/(1+r)$ defines the *riskless rate of interest* r. For the riskless bond it is natural to assume that each lender is matched with a borrower so that this security is in zero net supply. □

Example (Equity Contracts): If security j is the equity contract of firm j then

$$V_s^j = y_s^j, \quad s = 1, \ldots, S$$

where y_s^j is the output (profit) of firm j in state s. To interpret such contracts in the finance model it should be recalled that the one-good model is viewed as a special case of the general model in which the spot price vector is frozen at an equilibrium value. In addition, in an exchange economy, production plans of firms are taken as exogenously given. Equity contracts are in positive net supply: "initial" shareholders sell their ownership shares in the firm to "new" shareholders on the date 0 stock market. However, as will be shown in Section 16 (Bond-Equity Economy), a simple change of variable permits equity contracts to be modelled as securities which are in zero net supply. □

In all the analysis that follows standard idealized assumptions are made: the markets on which the financial contracts are traded are *competitive*, so that agents believe that they can buy and sell as many contracts as they want without affecting their prices. In addition each contract can be purchased and sold in *perfectly divisible* amounts and *no transactions costs* are involved in such purchases and sales. The contracts are assumed to be *perfectly monitored* and enforced so that agents never renege on their contracts: this can be viewed as a limit case in which the penalties are so high that no agent attempts to default on his contractual committments. Alternatively, if there are circumstances in which a debt will not be repaid, the circumstances (states) are known in advance and verifiable and are thus built into the provisions of the contract. For example, if a firm is to go bankrupt in certain states then the provisions of its debt and equity contracts take this into account.

The exogenously given date 1 payoffs of the J securities can be conveniently brought together in $S \times J$ matrix

$$V = \begin{bmatrix} V_1^1 & \cdots & V_1^J \\ \vdots & \ddots & \vdots \\ V_S^1 & \cdots & V_S^J \end{bmatrix} \tag{1}$$

An exchange economy consisting of I agents with characteristics $(u, \omega) = (u^1, \ldots, u^I, \omega^1, \ldots, \omega^I)$, who trade J securities with date 1 payoffs given by the matrix V in (1), is denoted by $\mathcal{E}(u, \omega, V)$. Note that with S contingent contracts the matrix V is the $S \times S$ identity matrix I_S, so that $\mathcal{E}(u, \omega, I_S)$ denotes the contingent market economy studied in the previous section.

Let $q = (q_1, \ldots, q_J)$ denote the vector of *security prices* where q_j is expressed in the unit of account at date 0 for $j = 1, \ldots, J$. In most of the analysis that follows it is natural to choose the unit of account to be one unit of the good at date 0 ($\pi_0 = 1$). Let $z^i = (z_1^i, \ldots, z_J^i) \in \mathbb{R}^J$ denote the ith agent's *portfolio* giving the number of units of each of the J securities purchased (if $z_j^i > 0$) or sold (if $z_j^i < 0$) by agent i. If buying and selling these J securities is the only trading opportunity available to agent i then his budget set is given by

$$\mathbb{B}(q, \omega^i, V) = \left\{ x^i \in \mathbb{R}_+^n \;\middle|\; \begin{array}{ll} x_0^i = \omega_0^i - q_1 z_1^i - \cdots - q_J z_J^i, & z^i \in \mathbb{R}^J \\ x_s^i = \omega_s^i + V_s^1 z_1^i + \cdots + V_s^J z_J^i, & s = 1, \ldots, S \end{array} \right\}$$

If W denotes the combined date 0-date 1 *matrix of security payoffs*

$$W = W(q, V) = \begin{bmatrix} -q \\ V \end{bmatrix} = \begin{bmatrix} -q_1 & \cdots & -q_J \\ V_1^1 & \cdots & V_1^J \\ \vdots & \ddots & \vdots \\ V_S^1 & \cdots & V_S^J \end{bmatrix} \tag{2}$$

then the budget set can be written using matrix notation[2] as

$$\mathbb{B}(q, \omega^i, V) = \left\{ x^i \in \mathbb{R}_+^n \;\middle|\; x^i - \omega^i = W z^i, \quad z^i \in \mathbb{R}^J \right\} \tag{3}$$

$\mathbb{B}(q, \omega^i, V)$ is called agent i's *financial market budget set*. Agent i now decides on a pair consisting of a vector of consumption x^i and a portfolio z^i and the pair (x^i, z^i) is called the *action* of agent i. When agent i chooses a portfolio z^i such that $x^i - \omega^i = W z^i$, z^i is said to *finance* x^i; the notation

$$(x^i; z^i) \in \mathbb{B}(q, \omega^i, V) \tag{4}$$

is used to denote a consumption-portfolio pair $(x^i, z^i) \in \mathbb{B}(q, \omega^i, V) \times \mathbb{R}^J$ such that z^i finances x^i. Thus (4) is equivalent to

$$x^i \in \mathbb{B}(q, \omega^i, V), \quad x^i - \omega^i = W z^i, \quad z^i \in \mathbb{R}^J \tag{5}$$

If $\bar{x}^i$ is a consumption vector which maximizes agent i's utility $u^i(x^i)$ over the budget set $\mathbb{B}(q, \omega^i, V)$ and if $\bar{z}^i$ is a portfolio which finances $\bar{x}^i$ then we write

$$(\bar{x}^i; \bar{z}^i) \in \arg\max \left\{ u^i(x^i) \;\middle|\; (x^i; z^i) \in \mathbb{B}(q, \omega^i, V) \right\}$$

---

[2] A clean vector-matrix notation which avoids unnecessary use of the transpose operation is obtained by adopting a convention which distinguishes vectors which are *quantities* from those those which are *prices* (elements of the dual space). Throughout this book, quantity vectors (consumption vectors, portfolios, production plans) are taken to be *column* vectors, while price vectors (state price vectors, security prices, utility gradients) are taken to be *row* vectors.

this being a shorthand expression for "$\bar{x}^i$ is one of the arguments which maximizes utility over the budget set and $\bar{z}^i$ finances $\bar{x}^i$". The concept of a perfectly competitive equilibrium for the I agents trading on this system of J financial markets is then defined as follows.

8.2 Definition: *A financial market (FM) equilibrium* for the finance economy $\mathscr{E}(u, \omega, V)$ is a pair consisting of actions and prices $((\bar{x}, \bar{z}), \bar{q}) \in \mathbb{R}_+^{nI} \times \mathbb{R}^{JI} \times \mathbb{R}^J$ such that

(i) $(\bar{x}^i; \bar{z}^i) \in \arg\max \left\{ u^i(x^i) \mid (x^i; z^i) \in \mathbb{B}(\bar{q}, \omega^i, V) \right\}$, $i = 1, \ldots, I$

(ii) $\sum_{i=1}^I \bar{z}^i = 0$

Note that the market-clearing equations $\sum_{i=1}^I \bar{z}^i = 0$ for the financial contracts imply that the allocation $\bar{x}$ is feasible,

$$\sum_{i=1}^I (\bar{x}^i - \omega^i) = 0$$

This latter equation means that in a one-good model when the financial markets clear, the demand for the good induced by the agents' portfolio choices equals its supply in each state. Thus the implied spot market for the good clears in each state.

9. ABSENCE OF ARBITRAGE

Proposition 7.3 implies that there are no free contracts in a contingent market equilibrium. This result is a consequence of the form of the contingent market budget set $B(\bar{\pi}, \omega^i)$ in (7.1) and the fact that each agent's preferences are strictly monotone. The same property holds in a financial market equilibrium: but since in the financial market budget set (8.3) the net purchases of the good, $x^i - \omega^i$, are obtained *indirectly* through investment in a portfolio of securities z^i with payoff matrix W, the condition is more subtle.

The idea of *no free goods* is simple: it means you cannot get something for nothing. The generalization of this concept is *absence of arbitrage*: *in an environment where investment opportunities have constant returns to scale, there are no arbitrage opportunities if there does not exist an investment strategy which gives a positive payoff in at least one state with non-negative payoffs in all remaining states.* Since there are constant returns to scale to investment in (competitive) financial markets, an investment strategy with an arbitrage opportunity can create an arbitrarily large payoff in some state with no corresponding sacrifice in any other state: but this is essentially like having a good with a zero price—in such a situation there is no solution to a consumer's maximum problem and hence no equilibrium. Since the investment opportunities on the financial markets are characterized by the matrix $W(q, V)$, this leads to the following definition. (Recall that a vector y in $\mathbb{R}^{S+1}$ is said to be *semi-positive* (written $y > 0$) if it is non-negative but not zero; it thus has at least one component which is strictly positive $(y > 0 \iff y \in \mathbb{R}_+^{S+1}, y \neq 0)$.)

9.1 Definition: Given (q, V) there are *no arbitrage opportunities* on the financial markets if there does not exist a portfolio which generates a semi-positive income stream (i.e. there does not exist $z \in \mathbb{R}^J$ such that $Wz > 0$).

It is often useful to interpret the condition in Definition 9.1 as a restriction on the security price vectors q, which can be associated with a given payoff matrix V.

9.2 Definition: q is a vector of *no-arbitrage security prices* (relative to V) if given (q, V) there are no arbitrage opportunities on the financial markets.

Geometric Interpretation of No-Arbitrage

In Section 5 we pointed out that the finance model can be interpreted in one of two ways:

(a) as a *one-good* version of the general model
(b) as an *income* model.

The interpretation (a) is useful for exploring the formal structure of the finance model and its relation with the general model in the second volume. But in order to explore the economic role of financial markets it is much better to use the interpretation (b), viewing the finance model as an income model. Thus in this section the latter interpretation is adopted.

Trading on the financial markets enables agents to redistribute their income across the $S+1$ states (recall that date 0 is interpreted as state 0). Thus agent i by purchasing the portfolio of securities

$$z^i = (z_1^i, \ldots, z_J^i) \in \mathbb{R}^J$$

induces a vector of *income transfers* across the states

$$\tau^i \in \mathbb{R}^{S+1}, \quad \tau^i = Wz^i$$

The set of all possible income transfers that can be obtained in this way is the subspace of $\mathbb{R}^{S+1}$ generated by the J columns of the matrix W, which is denoted by $\langle W \rangle$. This subspace, which summarizes the opportunities offered by the financial markets,

$$\langle W \rangle = \{ \tau \in \mathbb{R}^{S+1} \mid \tau = Wz, \quad z \in \mathbb{R}^J \} \tag{1}$$

will be called the *subspace of income transfers* or the *market subspace*. The absence of arbitrage opportunities on the financial markets can then be expressed as the geometric property that the market subspace has only one point in common with the non-negative orthant $\mathbb{R}_+^{S+1}$, namely the zero vector. This expresses the condition that income cannot be obtained in some state without giving it up in another. The absence of arbitrage can thus be written mathematically as

$$\langle W \rangle \cap \mathbb{R}_+^{S+1} = \{0\} \tag{2}$$

Example: Consider the simplest case where there is no uncertainty ($S = 1$) and one security ($J = 1$) which is a bond ($V_1^1 = 1$). Then W is the 2×1 matrix

$$W = \begin{bmatrix} -q_1 \\ 1 \end{bmatrix}$$

and $\langle W \rangle$ is the line through the origin (the one-dimensional subspace of $\mathbb{R}^2$) generated by the vector $(-q_1, 1)$. It is clear from Figure 9.1 that if the no-arbitrage condition (2) is to be satisfied then the bond price q_1 must be positive: if a security pays one unit of income date $t = 1$ then it must cost something at date $t = 0$. It is also clear from Figure 9.1 that when this condition is satisfied,

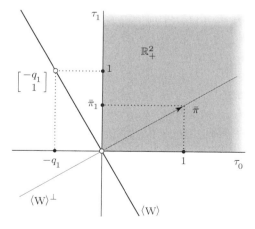

Figure 9.1 Geometric interpretation of absence of arbitrage opportunities when $S = 1$: since the bond pays one unit at date 1 its price q_1 must be positive at date 0.

there is a vector $\bar{\pi} = (\bar{\pi}_0, \bar{\pi}_1) \in \mathbb{R}^2_{++}$ (written as a row vector) which is at right angles to the (column) vector W

$$\bar{\pi}W = 0 \qquad\qquad (3)$$

If $\bar{\pi}$ is written in the normalized form $\bar{\pi} = (1, \pi_1)$ then condition (3) reduces to $q_1 = \bar{\pi}_1$. This is a most natural condition: for $\bar{\pi} = (1, \bar{\pi}_1)$ is a vector of state prices, with $\bar{\pi}_1$ denoting the value at date 0 of one unit of income at date 1. (3) thus asserts that the value of a bond (q_1) is the present value $(\bar{\pi}_1)$ at date 0 of one unit of income at date 1. $\square$

In the above example the requirement that the market subspace $\langle W \rangle$ have no point in common with the semi-positive orthant $\mathbb{R}^{S+1}_+ \setminus \{0\}$ (the *space of free lunches*) is readily seen to imply that there is a strictly positive vector of state prices $\bar{\pi} \in \mathbb{R}^{S+1}_{++}$ which is at right angles to the market subspace. We will now show that this is a general property which has an interesting geometric and economic interpretation.

The collection of all vectors $\pi \in \mathbb{R}^{S+1}$ that are orthogonal (at right angles) to each of the column vectors of the matrix W is called the subspace *orthogonal* to $\langle W \rangle$ and is denoted by $\langle W \rangle^\perp$. The reader can easily check that each vector π in $\langle W \rangle^\perp$ is orthogonal to every vector in $\langle W \rangle$. Thus

$$\langle W \rangle^\perp = \left\{ \pi \in \mathbb{R}^{S+1} \mid \pi W = 0 \right\} = \left\{ \pi \in \mathbb{R}^{S+1} \mid \pi\tau = 0, \quad \forall \tau \in \langle W \rangle \right\} \quad (4)$$

By convention the prices $\pi \in \langle W \rangle^\perp$ are written as row vectors, while the quantities (income transfers) $\tau \in \langle W \rangle$ are written as column vectors. The space $\langle W \rangle^\perp$ will be called the *space of state prices* or the *space of present-value vectors*. When the latter interpretation of π as a present-value vector is adopted it is natural to normalize the price vector $\pi = (\pi_0, \pi_1, \ldots, \pi_S)$ so that $\pi_0 = 1$: then the price π_s $(s = 1, \ldots, S)$ can be interpreted as the *present value (at date 0) of one unit of income in state s*. The existence of a positive vector of state prices at right angles to the market subspace can be expressed geometrically as the condition

$$\langle W \rangle^\perp \cap \mathbb{R}^{S+1}_{++} \neq \emptyset \qquad\qquad (5)$$

where $\emptyset$ denotes the empty set. Our objective is thus to show that (2) (no-arbitrage) implies (5) (existence of positive state prices): in fact Theorem 9.3 below shows that the converse is also true so that (2) and (5) are equivalent properties.

If agents have strongly monotone preferences then (2) must hold if each agent is to have a solution to his maximum problem

$$\max \left\{ u^i(x^i) \mid x^i \in \mathbb{B}(\bar{q}, \omega^i, V) \right\} \tag{6}$$

on a system of financial markets. Theorem 9.3 shows that the converse is also true, so that (2) is equivalent to (6) having a solution. Finally (6) has a solution if and only if the financial market budget set $\mathbb{B}(q, \omega^i, V)$ is compact. The no-free-lunch theorem which generalizes Proposition 7.3 to the setting of financial markets can thus be expressed as follows. (Recall that in this chapter $n = S + 1$).

9.3 Theorem (Absence of Arbitrage on Financial Markets): *If the utility functions satisfy Assumption $\mathscr{U}''$ then the following conditions are equivalent:*

(i) *The problem* $\max \left\{ u^i(x^i) \mid x^i \in \mathbb{B}(\bar{q}, \omega^i, V) \right\}$ *has a solution.*
(ii) *There are no arbitrage opportunities on the financial markets.*
(iii) *There is a vector of positive state prices* $\bar{\pi} \in \mathbb{R}^n_{++}$ *such that* $\bar{\pi} W(\bar{q}, V) = 0.$
(iv) *The financial market budget set* $\mathbb{B}(\bar{q}, \omega^i, V)$ *is compact.*

PROOF: Let us show that (i) $\Rightarrow$ (ii) $\Rightarrow$ (iii) $\Rightarrow$ (iv) $\Rightarrow$ (i).

(i) $\Rightarrow$ (ii) Let $\bar{x}^i \in \arg\max \left\{ u^i(x^i) \mid x^i \in \mathbb{B}(\bar{q}, \omega^i, V) \right\}$ with $\bar{x}^i = \omega^i + W\bar{z}^i$. If there exists $z^i \in \mathbb{R}^J$ such that $Wz^i > 0$ then $x^i = \omega^i + W\bar{z}^i + Wz^i > \bar{x}^i$. By Assumption $\mathscr{U}''$, u^i is strongly monotone so that $u^i(x^i) > u^i(\bar{x}^i)$, contradicting the optimality of $\bar{x}^i$.

(ii) $\Rightarrow$ (iii) Let $\Delta = \left\{ \tau \in \mathbb{R}^{S+1}_+ \mid \sum_{s=0}^S \tau_s = 1 \right\}$ denote the non-negative simplex in $\mathbb{R}^{S+1}$. Absence of arbitrage on the financial markets is equivalent to $\langle W \rangle \cap \left(\mathbb{R}^{S+1}_+ \setminus \{0\} \right) = \emptyset$ which implies that $\langle W \rangle \cap \Delta = \emptyset$. Since $\langle W \rangle$ and Δ are convex sets, the following separation theorem for convex sets applies:

9.4 Theorem (Strict Separation of Convex Sets): *Let X be a finite-dimensional vector space, and let K and M be non-empty convex subsets of X with $K \cap M = \emptyset$. If K is compact and M is closed, then there exists $\pi \in X$, $\pi \neq 0$, such that*

$$\sup_{\tau \in M} \pi\tau < \inf_{\tau \in K} \pi\tau$$

PROOF: The proof is given in the appendix (Theorem A2.6). $\square$

Let $X = \mathbb{R}^{S+1}$, $K = \Delta$, $M = \langle W \rangle$, then by Theorem 9.4 there exists $\bar{\pi} \in \mathbb{R}^{S+1}$ such that

$$\sup_{\tau \in \langle W \rangle} \bar{\pi}\tau < \inf_{\tau \in \Delta} \bar{\pi}\tau \tag{7}$$

We need to show that $\bar{\pi} \in \mathbb{R}_{++}^{S+1}$. Suppose $\bar{\pi}_\sigma \leq 0$ for some state σ. Consider $\widetilde{\tau} \in \Delta$ such that $\widetilde{\tau}_\sigma = 1$, $\widetilde{\tau}_s = 0$, $s \neq \sigma$. Then $\bar{\pi}\widetilde{\tau} \leq 0$ so that $\sup_{\tau \in \langle W \rangle} \bar{\pi}\tau < 0$, contradicting $\bar{\pi}\tau = 0$ for $\tau = 0$. It remains to show that $\bar{\pi} \in \langle W \rangle^\perp$ or equivalently that $\bar{\pi}\tau = 0$, $\forall \tau \in \langle W \rangle$. Suppose there exists $\widetilde{\tau} \in \langle W \rangle$ such that $\bar{\pi}\widetilde{\tau} \neq 0$. Since $\langle W \rangle$ is a subspace, there exists $\alpha \in \mathbb{R}$ such that $\alpha\widetilde{\tau} \in \langle W \rangle$ and $\bar{\pi}(\alpha\widetilde{\tau}) > \min_{\tau \in \Delta} \bar{\pi}\tau$ which contradicts (7).

(iii) $\Rightarrow$ (iv) Since $\bar{\pi} \in \mathbb{R}_{++}^{S+1}$, by Proposition 7.3 the contingent market budget set $B(\bar{\pi}, \omega^i)$ is compact. For any $x^i \in \mathbb{B}(\bar{q}, \omega^i, V)$ there exists $z^i \in \mathbb{R}^J$ such that $x^i - \omega^i = Wz^i$. Since $\bar{\pi}W = 0$, $\bar{\pi}(x^i - \omega^i) = 0$ so that $x^i \in B(\bar{\pi}, \omega^i)$. Thus $\mathbb{B}(\bar{q}, \omega^i, V) \subset B(\bar{\pi}, \omega^i)$. Clearly $\mathbb{B}(\bar{q}, \omega^i, V)$ is closed. Since a closed subset of a compact set is compact, $\mathbb{B}(\bar{q}, \omega^i, V)$ is compact.

(iv) $\Rightarrow$ (i) A continuous function on a compact set attains a maximum. $\square$

Remarks on Theorem 9.3

This is the fundamental theorem on the pricing of financial securities. First, it asserts that an agent with monotone preferences has a solution to his maximum problem if and only if there are no arbitrage opportunities on the financial markets. Thus a precondition for a vector of security prices to be an equilibrium price is that it be a no-arbitrage vector of security prices. Absence of arbitrage opportunities is however a more primitive concept than that of a financial market equilibrium since it is independent of the precise characteristics of the agents (their preferences and initial resources (u, ω)) and depends only on the payoff structure V of the financial securities.

Recall that a vector of state prices $\pi \in \mathbb{R}^{S+1}$ defines a hyperplane H_π in the space $\mathbb{R}^{S+1}$

$$H_\pi = \left\{ \tau \in \mathbb{R}^{S+1} \mid \pi\tau = 0 \right\}$$

If a subset $C \subset \mathbb{R}^{S+1}$ is contained in the half-space

$$H_\pi^- = \left\{ \tau \in \mathbb{R}^{S+1} \mid \pi\tau \leq 0 \right\}$$

and if C has a point in common with H_π (i.e. if $C \subset H_\pi^-$ and $C \cap H_\pi \neq \emptyset$) then H_π is said to be a *supporting hyperplane* to C. Let $D \subset \mathbb{R}^{S+1}$ denote a second subset. If $C \cap D = \emptyset$ and if $C \subset H_\pi^-$ and $D \subset H_\pi^+$ where

$$H_\pi^+ = \left\{ \tau \in \mathbb{R}^{S+1} \mid \pi\tau \geq 0 \right\}$$

then the hyperplane H_π is said to *separate* C and D.

Theorem 9.3 asserts that the absence of arbitrage opportunities on the financial markets is equivalent to the existence of a positive vector of state prices $\bar{\pi} \in \mathbb{R}_{++}^{S+1}$ which defines a supporting hyperplane $H_{\bar{\pi}}$ to the market subspace $\langle W \rangle$. The hyperplane $H_{\bar{\pi}}$ separates the market subspace $\langle W \rangle$ from the *space of free lunches* $\mathbb{R}^{S+1}_+ \setminus \{0\}$ so that

$$\langle W \rangle \subset H^-_{\bar{\pi}} \quad \text{and} \quad \mathbb{R}^{S+1}_+ \setminus \{0\} \subset H^+_{\bar{\pi}}$$

For each security j the vector of state prices $\bar{\pi}$ defines a profit on the investment activity which consists in purchasing one unit of security j for the price q_j at date 0 and obtaining the income V^j_s at date 1 if state s occurs ($s = 1, \ldots, S$). If $W^j = (-\bar{q}_j, V^j_1, \ldots, V^j_S)$ denotes the jth column of the matrix W, then the equality

$$\bar{\pi} W^j = 0, \quad j = 1, \ldots, J \tag{8}$$

implies that there is *zero profit* on a one-unit investment in each security j ($j = 1, \ldots, J$). Thus the theorem asserts that no-arbitrage is equivalent to the existence of a positive vector of state prices under which investment in every security makes a zero profit.

The equivalence result ((ii) $\iff$ (iii)) first appeared explicitly in *activity analysis*:[1] if we let the columns $W^j (j = 1, \ldots, J)$ denote activities, then the choice of a portfolio ($z \in \mathbb{R}^J$) is equivalent to the choice of an activity vector ($\xi \in \mathbb{R}^J$)—except that in activity analysis each component ξ_j of ξ is required to be non-negative. *The absence of arbitrage is equivalent to the requirement that it is not possible to produce any good in positive amount without using some other good as an input*—a condition that Koopmans (1951) called the *impossibility of the land of Cockaigne*. As Koopmans points out, the supporting price property first appeared in the remarkable paper of von Neumann (1937) which analyzed equilibrium in an activity analysis model of an expanding economy.

The parallel with activity analysis is not trivial. In this model a financial security creates a special type of investment opportunity, characterized by the fact that it has *constant returns to scale*. The price-taking (competitive) assumption means that no investor envisions operating at a scale that will alter the columns of the matrix W. In more complicated settings where the security structure is endogenous (for example in the model of Chapter 6 where firms choose their production plans and hence influence the payoff streams of their equity contracts) it is the fact that the security structure is linear for investors on the financial markets which ensures that the model retains a simple and tractable mathematical structure.

---

[1] *Activity analysis* is the analysis of production with a finite number of techniques (activities) operated under constant returns to scale (see Koopmans (1951)).

Security Pricing

The zero profit condition (8) can be written as

$$\bar{\pi}_0 \bar{q} = \bar{\pi}_1 V$$

or with $\bar{\pi} = (\bar{\pi}_0, \bar{\pi}_1)$ normalized so that $\bar{\pi}_0 = 1$, as

$$\bar{q} = \bar{\pi}_1 V \iff \bar{q}_j = \sum_{s=1}^{S} \bar{\pi}_s V_s^j, \quad j = 1, \ldots, J \tag{9}$$

As explained above, with this normalization, $\bar{\pi}_s$ denotes the present value (at date 0) of one unit of income in state s. Thus (9) asserts that *the price q_j of security j is the present value of its future income stream V_s^j, $s = 1, \ldots, S$.*

The scope of the pricing formula (9) can be expanded so as to obtain a pricing formula for any income stream which can be obtained by forming a portfolio of the J basic securities. The choice of a portfolio $z = (z_1, \ldots, z_J) \in \mathbb{R}^J$ leads to the date 1 income stream

$$y = \sum_{j=1}^{J} V^j z_j$$

where $V^j = (V_1^j, \ldots, V_S^j)$ is the jth column of the payoff matrix V (defined in (8.1)). The set of all possible portfolios $z \in \mathbb{R}^J$ generates the subspace of $\mathbb{R}^S$ spanned by the columns of V, which is denoted by $\langle V \rangle$:

$$\langle V \rangle = \left\{ y \in \mathbb{R}^S \,\middle|\, y = \sum_{j=1}^{J} V^j z_j, \quad z \in \mathbb{R}^J \right\}$$
$$= \left\{ y \in \mathbb{R}^S \,\middle|\, y = Vz, \quad z \in \mathbb{R}^J \right\}$$

Thus $\langle V \rangle$ is the subspace consisting of all possible date 1 income streams that can be obtained by investing in the J basic securities.

9.5 Definition: The subspace $\langle V \rangle \subset \mathbb{R}^S$ generated by the columns of the payoff matrix V is called the *marketed subspace.*

For any income stream y lying in the marketed subspace $\langle V \rangle$ there exists a portfolio $z \in \mathbb{R}^J$ such that $y = Vz$. We define the cost of y as the cost of the portfolio z.

9.6 Definition: If $q = (q_1, \ldots, q_J)$ is a vector of prices for the J basic securities then the *cost* $c_q(y)$ of an income stream y lying in the marketed subspace $\langle V \rangle$ is defined by

$$c_q(y) = qz \quad \text{for any} \quad z \in \mathbb{R}^J \quad \text{such that} \quad y = Vz \tag{10}$$

If $\bar{\pi} \in \mathbb{R}^{S+1}$ is a vector of present value prices induced by a no-arbitrage security price vector $\bar{q} \in \mathbb{R}^J$ (so that (9) holds) then for any $y \in \langle V \rangle$

$$c_{\bar{q}}(y) = \bar{q}z = \sum_{j=1}^{J} \sum_{s=1}^{S} \bar{\pi}_s V_s^j z_j = \sum_{s=1}^{S} \bar{\pi}_s y_s \tag{11}$$

so that *the cost $c_{\bar{q}}(y)$ of the income stream y is equal to its present value.* All the pricing formulae of the theory of finance can essentially be traced to (11).

First-Order Conditions

Theorem 9.3 asserts that the maximum problem (6) of agent i has a solution if $\bar{q}$ is a no-arbitrage security price. Let us examine the first-order conditions for a maximum when the utility function u^i satisfies Assumption $\mathcal{U}$. Let $V_s = (V_s^1, \ldots, V_s^J)$ denote row s of the matrix V for $s = 1, \ldots, S$. Agent i's maximum problem can be written as

$$\max_{(x^i, z^i) \in \mathbb{R}_+^{S+1} \times \mathbb{R}^J} \left\{ u^i(x^i) \,\middle|\, \begin{array}{l} x_0^i - \omega_0^i = -\bar{q}z^i \\ x_s^i - \omega_s^i = V_s z^i, \quad s = 1, \ldots, S \end{array} \right\} \tag{12}$$

Let $\lambda^i = (\lambda_0^i, \lambda_1^i, \ldots, \lambda_S^i)$ denote the vector of Lagrange multipliers induced by the $S+1$ budget constraints. Forming the Lagrangean

$$L^i(x^i, z^i, \lambda^i) = u^i(x^i) - \lambda_0^i(x_0^i - \omega_0^i + qz^i) - \sum_{s=1}^{S} \lambda_s^i(x_s^i - \omega_s^i - V_s z^i)$$

the first-order conditions, which are necessary and sufficient for $(\bar{x}^i, \bar{z}^i)$ to be a solution of (12), are that there exist $\bar{\lambda}^i \in \mathbb{R}_{++}^{S+1}$ such that

$$\nabla L^i(\bar{x}^i, \bar{z}^i, \bar{\lambda}^i) = 0$$

which is equivalent to

$$\nabla u^i(\bar{x}^i) = \bar{\lambda}^i \tag{13}$$

$$-\bar{\lambda}_0^i \bar{q} + \sum_{s=1}^{S} \bar{\lambda}_s^i V_s = 0 \tag{14}$$

$$\bar{x}_0^i - \omega_0^i = -\bar{q}\bar{z}^i, \quad \bar{x}_s^i - \omega_s^i = V_s \bar{z}^i, \quad s = 1, \ldots, S \tag{15}$$

The $S+1$ budget equations in (12) express the accountability of agent i in each of the $S+1$ states. The vector of Lagrange multipliers associated with the problem (12) of maximizing utility subject to these $S+1$ budget constraints is the vector of marginal utilities of income. In this chapter the convention has been adopted that accounts in each state are kept in units of the good (the payoffs of the securities in each state at date 1 are expressed in units of the good and the normalization $\pi_0 = 1$ implies that the unit of account at date 0 is the unit of the good). (13) then simply asserts[2] that the vector of marginal utilities of income $(\bar{\lambda}^i)$ is equal to the vector of marginal utilities of the good $(\nabla u^i(\bar{x}^i))$. Dividing both sides of (13) by the marginal utility of the good (income) at date 0 and recalling the definition of the present-value vector $\pi^i(\bar{x}^i)$ introduced in Section 7 (equation 7.4), (13) is equivalent to

$$\bar{\pi}^i = \pi^i(\bar{x}^i) \quad \text{with} \quad \bar{\pi}^i = \left(\frac{1}{\bar{\lambda}_0^i}\right)\bar{\lambda}^i$$

which asserts that the normalized vector of multipliers $(\bar{\pi}^i)$ is equal to the present-value vector $(\pi^i(\bar{x}^i))$ of agent i at $\bar{x}^i$. (14) can then be written in component form as

$$\bar{q}_j = \sum_{s=1}^{S} \bar{\pi}_s^i V_s^j, \quad j = 1, \ldots, J \tag{16}$$

(16) asserts that agent i invests in each asset j in such a way that the marginal cost of an additional unit of the security $(\bar{q}_j)$ is equal to its marginal benefit, the present value for agent i of its future stream of dividends $\sum_{s=1}^{S} \bar{\pi}_s^i V_s^j$. (16) can also be written more succinctly as

$$\bar{\pi}^i W = 0 \tag{17}$$

and the budget equations (15) can be expressed in more condensed form as

$$\bar{x}^i - \omega^i = W \bar{z}^i \tag{18}$$

Finally if we introduce the *net trade vector* $\tau^i = x^i - \omega^i$ of agent i (which is also, in this one-good model, his vector of income transfers) then the first-order conditions for agent i can be written as

$$\bar{\tau}^i \in \langle W \rangle, \quad \bar{\pi}^i \in \langle W \rangle^{\perp} \tag{19}$$

---

[2]This property is not true in a model with many goods.

$\bar{\tau}^i \in \langle W \rangle$ is just the condition that agent i chooses a net trade in his opportunity set (the market subspace). $\bar{\pi}^i \in \langle W \rangle^{\perp}$ implies that

$$\langle W \rangle \subset T_{\bar{x}^i}\left(I^i_{\bar{x}^i}\right)$$

since the tangent space $T_{\bar{x}^i}(I_{\bar{x}^i})$ is the hyperplane orthogonal to the (normalized) gradient of u^i at $\bar{x}^i$ (see Section 7). This inclusion is readily interpreted: when agent i is at his preferred net trade no marginal change can further increase his utility since all the changes in his opportunity set (those in $\langle W \rangle$) are contained in the tangent space to his indifference surface. Note that the inclusion of $\langle W \rangle$ in the tangent space is strict if the dimension of $\langle W \rangle$ is less than S. Since $x^i = \omega^i + \tau^i$, the preferences of agent i over consumption streams x^i induce preferences on net trade vectors τ^i. (19) asserts that in the net trade space *agent i is at his most preferred net trade vector in the market subspace when his indifference surface through this point is tangent to the market subspace.*

The geometric interpretation of (19) is shown in Figure 9.2 for the simplest case $S = J = 1$. The heavily drawn axes are the co-ordinates for the space of net trades i.e. the vectors $\tau^i = (\tau^i_0, \tau^i_1) \in \mathbb{R}^2$. $\langle W \rangle$ is the 1-dimensional subspace of feasible net trades and $\langle W \rangle^{\perp}$ is the 1-dimensional orthogonal subspace.

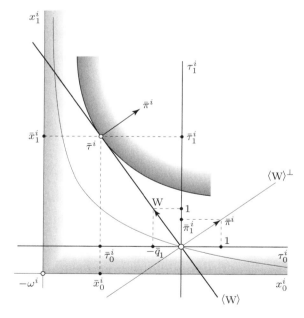

Figure 9.2   Agent i is at a maximum at the net trade vector $\bar{\tau}^i \in \langle W \rangle$ when his indifference curve through $\bar{\tau}^i$ is tangent to the market subspace. At such a point his gradient $\bar{\pi}^i$ lies in the orthogonal subspace $\langle W \rangle^{\perp}$.

Agent i's indifference curves are drawn with respect to the consumption axes i.e. the axes which pass through the point $-\omega^i$ in the net trade space.

Geometric Interpretation of FM Equilibrium

So far we have only given a geometric interpretation of how an individual agent i chooses his optimal net trade vector $\bar{\tau}^i$ when faced with a given market subspace $\langle W(q) \rangle$. Having shown how an individual's maximum problem can be solved geometrically, let us study the geometric interpretation of an equilibrium suggested by the formulation (19). By Theorem 9.3 an agent's net trade function

$$\tau^i(q) = \arg \max \left\{ u^i(\omega^i + \tau^i) \mid \tau^i \in \langle W(q) \rangle \right\}, \quad i = 1, \dots, I$$

is well-defined if and only if the security price q lies in the set of no-arbitrage security prices

$$Q = \left\{ q \in \mathbb{R}^J \mid q = \pi_1 V, \quad \pi_1 \in \mathbb{R}^S_{++} \right\}$$

Varying the security price $q \in Q$ rotates the market subspace $\langle W(q) \rangle$ in the space of net trades $\mathbb{R}^{S+1}$. For each subspace $\langle W(q) \rangle$ offered by the market, agents respond by choosing their net trade vectors $\left(\tau^1(q), \dots, \tau^I(q) \right)$: each vector $\tau^i(q)$ is located at the point of the subspace $\langle W(q) \rangle$ where agent i's indifference surface is tangent to the market subspace. An equilibrium security price $\bar{q} \in Q$ has the property that the net trade vectors $\left(\tau^1(\bar{q}), \dots, \tau^I(\bar{q}) \right)$ are *balanced* in the subspace $\langle W(\bar{q}) \rangle$ in the sense that $\sum_{i=1}^{I} \tau^i(\bar{q}) = 0$. *Finding an equilibrium security price thus amounts rotating the market subspace by varying $q \in Q$ until a balanced market subspace is found.* The steps for establishing the existence of an equilibrium security price are outlined in Exercises 7 and 8. An example of a balanced market subspace is shown in Figure 10.1 for a case where markets are *complete* and in Figure 11.4 for a case where markets are *incomplete*: in the former case the agents' gradients $(\bar{\pi}^1, \bar{\pi}^2)$ coincide, in the latter case they are distinct.

Complete and Incomplete Markets

A linear space can be decomposed into a direct sum of a linear subspace and its orthogonal complement (see Proposition 14.10). Thus the space of net trades $\mathbb{R}^{S+1}$ can be decomposed into a direct sum of the market subspace $\langle W \rangle$ and its orthogonal complement $\langle W \rangle^{\perp}$

$$\mathbb{R}^{S+1} = \langle W \rangle \oplus \langle W \rangle^{\perp} \tag{20}$$

If the market subspace offers no arbitrage opportunities then it has a (positive) vector of supporting prices i.e. there exists $\bar{\pi} \in \langle W \rangle^{\perp}$. Since (20) implies

$$S + 1 = \dim \langle W \rangle + \dim \langle W \rangle^{\perp} \tag{21}$$

whenever the market subspace $\langle W \rangle$ offers no arbitrage opportunities

$$\dim \langle W \rangle \leq (S + 1) - 1 = S$$

Thus S is the maximal dimension of the market subspace. The "best" trading opportunities that financial markets can offer arise when the maximal dimension is attained. This leads to the following definition.

9.7 Definition: Let the market subspace $\langle W(q, V) \rangle$ be arbitrage free. If the market subspace has maximal dimension then the (financial) markets are said to be *complete*: if it is of less than maximal dimension then the markets are *incomplete*.

Definition 9.7 is based on a complete description of the financial markets in that it involves both the vector of security prices (q) and the exogenously given security payoff matrix (V). However the one-good two-period model of this chapter has a special property: *the dimension of the market subspace $\langle W(q, V) \rangle$ is independent of the no-arbitrage security price q*. This property permits the completeness or incompleteness of $\langle W(q, V) \rangle$ to be checked directly from the date 1 payoff matrix V.

9.8 Proposition (Characterization of Completeness):   *In a two-period finance economy $\mathscr{E}(u, \omega, V)$, the financial markets are complete for any vector of no-arbitrage security prices q if and only if rank $V = S$.*

PROOF: If q is a no-arbitrage security price then there exists $\pi \in \mathbb{R}^{S+1}$ such that $q = \sum_{s=1}^{S} \pi_s V_s$. This implies that the first row of the matrix $W = [-q, V]^T$ is a linear combination of the rows (V_s, $s = 1, \ldots, S$) of V. Thus rank $W =$ rank V. $\square$

Thus for a (one-good) two-period economy the completeness of the financial markets can be defined by the condition rank $V = S$. However in an economy with more than two periods (Chapter 4) the dimension of the market subspace can vary as the security price q is changed; if there is more than one good (Volume 2) then the dimension of the market subspace can change when the spot prices vary. In such economies the dimension of $\langle W \rangle$ cannot be deduced directly from the security payoffs but depends in addition on the prices of the commodities and the securities. Definition 9.7 has the advantage of being applicable without change to these more general economies.

The behavior of agents which is stated in condensed form in equation (19), shows that each agent i's *net trade vector* $\bar{\tau}^i$ lies in the market subspace $\langle W \rangle$, while his *present-value vector* $\bar{\pi}^i$ lies in the orthogonal subspace $\langle W \rangle^\perp$. The pair of equations (19) and (20) summarize the essential property of an economy with financial markets which drives most of the results in the remainder of this book. For (20) implies that the greater (smaller) the dimension of the market subspace, the smaller (greater) the space of present-value vectors. In short, the greater the opportunities for income transfer, the smaller the (potential) differences of opinion among agents about the present value of a stream of date 1 income.

When the markets are complete

$$\dim \langle W \rangle = S, \quad \dim \langle W \rangle^\perp = 1$$

There is thus a unique present-value vector $\bar{\pi}$ (with $\bar{\pi}_0 = 1$) lying in the orthogonal subspace $\langle W \rangle^\perp$ so that in a financial market equilibrium the present-value vectors of all agents coincide

$$\bar{\pi}^1 = \cdots = \bar{\pi}^I = \bar{\pi}$$

This property leads to the equivalence between financial market equilibrium and contingent market equilibrium allocations when markets are complete (Theorem 10.6 below).

When markets are incomplete

$$\dim \langle W \rangle = J < S, \quad \dim \langle W \rangle^\perp = S - J + 1 > 1$$

In this case trading on the financial markets no longer forces agents' present-value vectors ($\bar{\pi}^i$) into equality. In fact, typically in a financial market equilibrium with incomplete markets the agents' present-value vectors are distinct (Theorem 11.6 below): many of the results that we establish for economies with incomplete financial markets are attributable to this property.

10. NO-ARBITRAGE EQUILIBRIUM

Two approaches can be used to study a financial market equilibrium. The first is the direct approach based on security prices; the second is an indirect approach based on state prices. The first approach[1] is useful for analyzing

---

[1] The main steps for the proof of existence of a financial market equilibrium based on the direct approach are given in Exercises 7 and 8.

qualitative properties of an equilibrium, but encounters difficulties for establishing existence of an equilibrium as soon as the economy has more than two periods. For in such an economy the dimension of the market subspace $\langle W(q) \rangle$ can change when the security price q changes and this leads to discontinuities in the security demand functions. The second approach, which at first seems less intuitive, is in fact more versatile and can be extended to cover the general model of Volume 2. It involves transforming the concept of a financial market equilibrium into the concept of a *no-arbitrage equilibrium* which is a constrained Arrow-Debreu equilibrium. This transformation permits techniques developed for analyzing the traditional Arrow-Debreu model to be transferred to the model with incomplete markets.

The idea behind a no-arbitrage equilibrium is to exploit the no-arbitrage equation

$$q = \pi_1 V$$

so as to reformulate the concept of a financial market equilibrium in terms of the new variables $\pi = (1, \pi_1)$. Under this change of variables, demand functions for securities as functions of q are replaced by demand functions for goods as functions of the state prices π.

Agent i's budget set with a system of financial markets is given by

$$\mathbb{B}(q, \omega^i, V) = \left\{ x^i \in \mathbb{R}_+^n \; \middle| \; \begin{array}{ll} x_0^i - \omega_0^i = -qz^i, & z^i \in \mathbb{R}^J \\ x_s^i - \omega_s^i = V_s z^i, & s = 1, \ldots, S \end{array} \right\} \tag{1}$$

If $q = \pi_1 V$ then the date 0 budget constraint gives

$$x_0^i - \omega_0^i = -qz^i = -\pi_1 V z^i = -\sum_{s=1}^{S} \pi_s V_s z^i \tag{2}$$

In view of the date 1 budget constraints

$$x_s^i - \omega_s^i = V_s z^i, \quad s = 1, \ldots, S \tag{3}$$

(2) can be written as

$$\sum_{s=0}^{S} \pi_s (x_s^i - \omega_s^i) = 0 \iff \pi(x^i - \omega^i) = 0 \tag{4}$$

Thus if $q = \pi_1 V$ then the date 0 budget constraint in $\mathbb{B}(q, \omega^i, V)$ reduces to the contingent market budget constraint (4).

Let $(x_1^i - \omega_1^i) = (x_1^i - \omega_1^i, \ldots, x_S^i - \omega_S^i)$ denote agent i's vector of date 1 net trades. Then the date 1 budget constraints can be written as

$$x_1^i - \omega_1^i = V z^i \tag{5}$$

Since agent i is free to choose any portfolio $z^i \in \mathbb{R}^J$, (5) implies that the date 1 net trade vector $x_1^i - \omega_1^i$ must lie in the subspace $\langle V \rangle$ spanned by the columns of V. Thus the date 1 budget equations can be expressed without explicit reference to the portfolio variables z^i by writing them in the form

$$x_1^i - \omega_1^i \in \langle V \rangle \tag{6}$$

Thus if we define the budget set

$$\mathscr{B}(\pi, \omega^i, V) = \left\{ x^i \in \mathbb{R}_+^n \ \middle| \ \begin{array}{l} \pi(x^i - \omega^i) = 0 \\ x_1^i - \omega_1^i \in \langle V \rangle \end{array} \right\} \tag{7}$$

which depends on the state prices π, then whenever $q = \pi_1 V$

$$\mathscr{B}(\pi, \omega^i, V) = \mathbb{B}(q, \omega^i, V) \tag{8}$$

so that the budget sets (1) and (7) coincide. The budget set (7) can be viewed as a constrained Arrow-Debreu budget set under the price system π: in addition to the standard budget constraint (4), the agent is constrained to choose a vector of date 1 net trades which lies in the marketed subspace $\langle V \rangle$.

The no-arbitrage equation thus yields a parametric way of defining agents' budget sets in which the security price variables q are replaced by the state price variables π. Requiring that each agent maximize utility over the budget (7) and that demand equals supply for the good in each state, leads to the concept of a no-arbitrage equilibrium.

10.1 Definition: A *no-arbitrage equilibrium* for the finance economy $\mathscr{E}(u, \omega, V)$ is a pair consisting of an allocation and a vector of prices $(\bar{x}, \bar{\pi}) \in \mathbb{R}_+^{nI} \times \mathbb{R}_+^n$ such that

(i) $\bar{x}^i \in \arg\max \left\{ u^i(x^i) \ \middle| \ x^i \in \mathscr{B}(\bar{\pi}, \omega^i, V) \right\}$, $i = 1, \ldots, I$
(ii) $\sum_{i=1}^I (\bar{x}^i - \omega^i) = 0$

REMARK. The equality of the budget sets (8) implies that if $(\bar{x}, \bar{\pi})$ is a no-arbitrage equilibrium with $\bar{\pi} = (1, \bar{\pi}_1)$ then $((\bar{x}, \bar{z}), \bar{q})$ is a financial market equilibrium if $\bar{q} = \bar{\pi}_1 V$ and $\bar{z} = (\bar{z}^1, \ldots, \bar{z}^I)$ is such that $\bar{x}_1^i - \omega_1^i = V\bar{z}^i$, $i = 2, \ldots, I$ and $\bar{z}^1 = -\sum_{i=2}^I \bar{z}^i$. Conversely, if $((\bar{x}, \bar{z}), \bar{q})$ is a financial market equilibrium then by Theorem 9.3 there exists a vector of state prices $\bar{\pi} = (1, \bar{\pi}_1)$ such that $\bar{q} = \bar{\pi}_1 V$ and $(\bar{x}, \bar{\pi})$ is a no-arbitrage equilibrium.

When the markets are incomplete ($\dim \langle V \rangle = J < S$) there are many state prices associated with a no-arbitrage equilibrium allocation $\bar{x}$: for if $(\bar{x}, \bar{\pi})$

is a no-arbitrage equilibrium with $\bar{\pi} = (1, \bar{\pi}_1)$, then $(\bar{x}, \pi)$ is a no-arbitrage equilibrium for any $\pi = (1, \pi_1)$ with π_1 lying in the set

$$R(\bar{\pi}_1) = \{ \pi_1 \in \mathbb{R}_{++}^S \mid \pi_1 V = \bar{\pi}_1 V \}$$

This follows at once from (8) which implies

$$\mathscr{B}(\pi, \omega^i, V) = \mathscr{B}(\bar{\pi}, \omega^i, V), \quad \forall \pi = (1, \pi_1) \quad \text{with} \quad \pi_1 \in R(\bar{\pi}_1)$$

If rank $V = J$, then $\dim R(\bar{\pi}_1) = S - J$, since $R(\bar{\pi}_1)$ is defined by a set of J independent equations in S unknowns. Thus the dimension of the indeterminacy in the state prices is $S - J$.

This freedom of choice in the state prices permits a particular state price vector to be chosen from the set $R(\bar{\pi}_1)$ in a way that proves very convenient for later analysis. The no-arbitrage equilibrium $(\bar{x}, \bar{\pi})$ corresponds to a financial market equilibrium $((\bar{x}, \bar{z}), \bar{q})$ with $\bar{q} = \bar{\pi}_1 V$ and $\bar{z} = (\bar{z}^1, \ldots, \bar{z}^I)$ such that $\bar{x}_1^i - \omega_1^i = V \bar{z}^i$, $i = 1, \ldots, I$. By virtue of the first-order conditions (9.16) for agent i, in a financial market equilibrium

$$\bar{\pi}_1^i V = \bar{q} \Rightarrow \bar{\pi}_1^i \in R(\bar{\pi}_1), \quad i = 1, \ldots, I$$

The present-value vector $\bar{\pi}_1^i$ of any agent can thus be chosen to represent the set $R(\bar{\pi}_1)$. For convenience we choose $\bar{\pi}_1 = \bar{\pi}_1^1$. This amounts to omitting the date 1 budget constraints $x_1^1 - \omega_1^1 \in \langle V \rangle$ from agent 1's no-arbitrage budget set, which then reduces to the contingent market budget set $B(\bar{\pi}_1, \omega^1)$. This leads to the following very useful concept of equilibrium.

10.2 Definition: A *normalized no-arbitrage (NA) equilibrium* for the finance economy $\mathscr{E}(u, \omega, V)$ is a pair consisting of an allocation and a vector of prices $(\bar{x}, \bar{\pi}) \in \mathbb{R}_+^{nI} \times \mathbb{R}_+^n$ such that

(i) $\bar{x}^1 \in \arg \max \{ u^1(x^1) \mid x^1 \in B(\bar{\pi}, \omega^1) \}$
$\bar{x}^i \in \arg \max \{ u^i(x^i) \mid x^i \in \mathscr{B}(\bar{\pi}, \omega^i, V) \}$, $i = 2, \ldots, I$
(ii) $\sum_{i=1}^I (\bar{x}^i - \omega^i) = 0$

The following proposition asserts that analyzing financial market (FM) equilibria is equivalent to analyzing normalized no-arbitrage (NA) equilibria.

10.3 Proposition (Equivalence of FM and NA Equilibria): Let $\mathscr{E}(u, \omega, V)$ be *a one-good economy satisfying Assumption $\mathscr{U}$.*

(i) *If $((\bar{x}, \bar{z}), \bar{q})$ is an FM equilibrium and if $\bar{\pi}^1$ is agent 1's present-value vector, then $(\bar{x}, \bar{\pi}^1)$ is an NA equilibrium.*

(ii) *If $(\bar{x}, \bar{\pi})$ is an NA equilibrium with $\bar{\pi} = (1, \bar{\pi}_1)$, then there exist portfolios $\bar{z} = (\bar{z}^1, \ldots, \bar{z}^I)$ and security prices $\bar{q} = \bar{\pi}_1 V$ such that $((\bar{x}, \bar{z}), \bar{q})$ is an FM equilibrium.*

PROOF: (i) Let $\bar{\pi}^1 = \pi^1(\bar{x}^1)$ denote the present vector of agent 1 at the FM equilibrium $((\bar{x}, \bar{z}), \bar{q})$. Since $\bar{x}^1 - \omega^1 = W\bar{z}^1$ and $\bar{\pi}^1 W = 0$ (by 9.19), then $\bar{\pi}^1(\bar{x}^1 - \omega^1) = 0$ so that $\bar{x}^1 \in B(\bar{\pi}^1, \omega^1)$. Since $\pi^1(\bar{x}^1) = \bar{\pi}^1$, the first-order conditions for maximizing $u^1(x^1)$ over $B(\bar{\pi}^1, \omega^1)$ are satisfied at $\bar{x}^1$. By (8), $\mathscr{B}(\bar{\pi}^1, \omega^i, V) = \mathbb{B}(\bar{q}, \omega^i, V)$ so that for each agent $i = 2, \ldots, I$, maximizing over the NA budget set $\mathscr{B}(\bar{\pi}^1, \omega^i, V)$ leads to the same optimal choice $\bar{x}^i$. Since $\bar{x}$ is feasible, $(\bar{x}, \bar{\pi}^1)$ is an NA equilibrium.

(ii) Let $(\bar{x}, \bar{\pi})$ be an NA equilibrium with $\bar{\pi} = (1, \bar{\pi}_1)$. Then $\bar{\pi}^1 = \pi^1(\bar{x}^1) = \bar{\pi}$. Define $\bar{q} = \bar{\pi}_1 V$, $\bar{z}^i$ as a solution of $\bar{x}_1^i - \omega_1^i = V z^i$, $i = 2, \ldots, I$, and let $\bar{z}^1 = -\sum_{i=2}^{I} \bar{z}^i$. Then $\sum_{i=1}^{I}(\bar{x}_1^i - \omega_1^i) = 0$ implies $\bar{x}_1^1 - \omega_1^1 = V\bar{z}^1$. Thus agent 1 satisfies the first-order conditions (9.13)–(9.15) and $(\bar{x}^1, \bar{z}^1)$ is utility maximizing over the budget set $\mathbb{B}(\bar{q}, \omega^1, V)$. For all other agents $(i = 2, \ldots, I)$, (8) implies $\mathbb{B}(\bar{q}, \omega^i, V) = \mathscr{B}(\bar{\pi}^1, \omega^i, V)$ so that $\bar{x}^i$ is the utility maximizing choice over the FM budget set $\mathbb{B}(\bar{q}, \omega^i, V)$. Since $\bar{x}$ is feasible and $\sum_{i=1}^{I} \bar{z}^i = 0$, $((\bar{x}, \bar{z}), \bar{q})$ is an FM equilibrium. $\square$

It will become particularly clear in the second volume that the concept of a normalized no-arbitrage equilibrium provides a remarkably powerful tool for analyzing financial market equilibria. This is in essence because it transforms the concept of an FM equilibrium into a form that captures much of the simplicity of the Arrow-Debreu concept of equilibrium, as is clear in the proof of the following proposition.

10.4 Proposition (Existence of NA Equilibrium): *Let the economy $\mathscr{E}(u, \omega, V)$ satisfy Assumption $\mathscr{U}'$. If $\omega^i \in \mathbb{R}_{++}^n$, $i = 1, \ldots, I$, then there exists a vector of state prices $\bar{\pi} \in \mathbb{R}_{++}^n$ and an allocation $\bar{x}$ such that $(\bar{x}, \bar{\pi})$ is a normalized no-arbitrage equilibrium.*

PROOF: Consider the demand functions $f^1 : \mathbb{R}_{++}^n \longrightarrow \mathbb{R}^n$, $f_V^i : \mathbb{R}_{++}^n \longrightarrow \mathbb{R}^n$, $i = 2, \ldots, I$ defined by

$$f^1(\pi) = \arg\max \left\{ u^1(x^1) \mid x^1 \in B(\pi, w^1) \right\}$$
$$f_V^i(\pi) = \arg\max \left\{ u^i(x^i) \mid x^i \in \mathscr{B}(\pi, \omega^i, V) \right\}, \quad i = 2, \ldots, I$$

The contingent market demand function $f^1(\pi)$ of agent 1 has the properties (i)–(v) in the proof of Theorem 7.4. It is easy to check that the demand functions $f_V^i(\pi)$ of the remaining agents $(i = 2, \ldots, I)$ have the properties (i)–(iv) (see

Exercise 6). Thus the *aggregate excess demand function* $Z_V : \mathbb{R}^n_{++} \longrightarrow \mathbb{R}^n$ defined by

$$Z_V(\pi) = f^1(\pi) - \omega^1 + \sum_{i=2}^{I} \left(f^i_V(\pi) - \omega^i \right)$$

has the properties (i)′–(v)′ in the proof of Theorem 7.4, where the boundary property (v)′ is inherited from the boundary behavior of f^1 (property (v)). These five properties imply that Z_V defines a continuous vector field on the positive unit sphere $\mathscr{S}^{n-1}_{++}$ which is equivalent to (i.e. has the same zeros as) a vector field $\widetilde{Z}_V$ on $\mathscr{S}^{n-1}_+$ which points inwards on the boundary $\partial \mathscr{S}^{n-1}_+$. Using Theorem 7.5 we deduce that there exists $\bar{\pi} \in \mathscr{S}^{n-1}_{++}$ such that $Z_V(\bar{\pi}) = 0$. □

10.5 Theorem (Existence of FM Equilibrium): *Let $\mathscr{E}(u, \omega, V)$ be a one-good economy satisfying Assumption $\mathscr{U}$. If $\omega^i \in \mathbb{R}^n_{++}$, $i = 1, \ldots, I$ then there exists a financial market equilibrium $((\bar{x}, \bar{z}), \bar{q})$.*

PROOF: This follows from Proposition 10.4 and Proposition 10.3 (ii). □

REMARK. Proposition 10.3 on the equivalence of FM and NA equilibria can be established without the differentiability assumption on preferences (i.e. replacing $\mathscr{U}$ by $\mathscr{U}'$). In order to do this, the present-value vectors of the agents which are defined as normalized gradients under Assumption $\mathscr{U}$ must be defined as normalized subgradients (of convex analysis) under Assumption $\mathscr{U}'$ (see the section *Subgradients* in the appendix to Chapter 6). Then Theorem 10.5 holds under the weaker Assumption $\mathscr{U}'$. For the sake of simplicity we initially avoid the use of convex analysis, adopting instead the assumption of differentiability. The same remark applies to Theorem 10.6 below.

A no-arbitrage equilibrium is a constrained contingent market equilibrium. If the marketed subspace $\langle V \rangle$ is all of $\mathbb{R}^S$ then the date 1 constraints in the no-arbitrage budget sets disappear and a no-arbitrage equilibrium reduces to a contingent market equilibrium.

10.6 Theorem (FM-CM Equivalence with Complete Markets): *Let $\mathscr{E}(u, \omega, V)$ be a one-good economy satisfying Assumption $\mathscr{U}$ and let the financial markets be complete ($\langle V \rangle = \mathbb{R}^S$).*

(i) *If $((\bar{x}, \bar{z}), \bar{q})$ is a financial market equilibrium, then $(\bar{x}, \bar{\pi})$ is a contingent market equilibrium where $\bar{\pi} = (1, \bar{\pi}_1) \in \mathbb{R}^{S+1}_{++}$ is the unique vector of state prices satisfying $\bar{q} = \bar{\pi}_1 V$.*

(ii) *If $(\bar{x}, \bar{\pi})$ is a contingent market equilibrium with $\bar{\pi} = (1, \bar{\pi}_1)$ then there exist portfolios $\bar{z} = (\bar{z}^1, \ldots, \bar{z}^I)$ and a vector of security prices $\bar{q} = \bar{\pi}_1 V$ such that $((\bar{x}, \bar{z}), \bar{q})$ is a financial market equilibrium.*

PROOF: When $\langle V \rangle = \mathbb{R}^S$, $\mathscr{B}(\pi, \omega^i, V) = B(\pi, \omega^i)$. The result then follows from Proposition 10.3. □

A geometric interpretation of Theorem 10.6 is shown in Figure 10.1 for the case $S = J = 1$. The heavily drawn axes are the co-ordinates for the space of net trades, $\tau^i = (\tau_0^i, \tau_1^i) \in \mathbb{R}^2$. The budget set $\mathbb{B}(\bar{q}, \omega^1, V)$ is the segment $[a, b]$ on $\langle W \rangle$, while the budget set $\mathbb{B}(\bar{q}, \omega^2, V)$ is the segment $[a', b']$. In the net trade variables $\tau^i = x^i - \omega^i$ the equilibrium is given by $(\bar{\tau}^1, \bar{\tau}^2)$ where

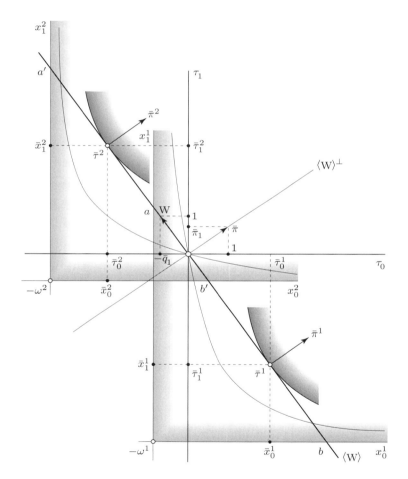

Figure 10.1 Equivalence of financial market equilibrium and contingent market equilibrium when markets are complete with $S = J = 1 = V_1^1$. Since $\bar{\pi}W = 0$ (i.e. $\bar{\pi}_1 = \bar{q}$) and $\dim \langle W \rangle = 1$, the budget sets in the FM and CM equilibrium are the same: the segment $[a, b]$ for agent 1 and $[a', b']$ for agent 2. For the equilibrium in this figure, since $\bar{q}_1 < 1$ the rate of interest is positive.

$\bar{\tau}^1 + \bar{\tau}^2 = 0$. It is clear that since $\dim \langle W \rangle = 1$, the markets are complete. The unique vector $\bar{\pi} = (1, \bar{\pi}_1) \in \langle W \rangle^{\perp}$ defines the two contingent market budget sets $B(\bar{\pi}, \omega^1)$ and $B(\bar{\pi}, \omega^2)$, which are the segments $[a, b]$ and $[a', b']$.

11.   A BASIC PROPERTY OF INCOMPLETE MARKETS

Arrow-Debreu equilibrium theory is based on the system of contingent markets. In the framework of a finance economy this means that there are markets for income in each state so that agents can transfer income as they want across the states at the state prices $\bar{\pi}_s$, $s = 1, \ldots, S$. Trading on such a system of markets under the common system of prices $\bar{\pi}$ forces the agents' (normalized) gradient vectors $\pi^i(\bar{x}^i)$ into equality and this in turn leads to Pareto optimality. Theorem 10.6 shows that a similar result holds with a system of financial markets if these markets are complete. This property arises from the fact that when markets are complete the trading subspace $\langle W \rangle$ is of maximal dimension or equivalently that the subspace of state prices $\langle W \rangle^{\perp}$ is of minimal dimension

$$\dim \langle W \rangle = S \iff \dim \langle W \rangle^{\perp} = 1$$

When agents have only a limited ability to redistribute their income across the states then markets are incomplete. The limited ability of agents to trade income makes it possible for agents to have different opinions on the value of income at date 1. Agents' gradient vectors $\pi^i(\bar{x}^i)$ can now differ in a financial market equilibrium. More formally, since the dimension of the trading subspace $\langle W \rangle$ has been reduced, the dimension of the subspace of state prices $\langle W \rangle^{\perp}$ has been increased

$$\dim \langle W \rangle < S \iff \dim \langle W \rangle^{\perp} > 1 \tag{1}$$

Thus the first-order conditions for each agent in a financial market equilibrium given by (9.19)

$$\bar{\tau}^i \in \langle W \rangle, \quad \bar{\pi}^i \in \langle W \rangle^{\perp} \tag{2}$$

no longer imply equality of the agents' present-value vectors $\pi^i(\bar{x}^i)$.

(1) and (2) do not however imply that the vectors $\bar{\pi}^i$ are distinct: we may have overlooked some property which could imply that these vectors coincide. It is easy to construct an example of an economy in which the vectors $\bar{\pi}^i$ are distinct at an equilibrium: it suffices to consider an economy with two agents and no financial markets ($V = 0$), such that $\pi^1(\omega^1) \neq \pi^2(\omega^2)$ at the initial endowment vector and hence at the no-trade FM equilibrium $(\bar{x}^1, \bar{x}^2) = (\omega^1, \omega^2)$. Note that there also exist vectors of initial endowments (ω^1, ω^2) which are Pareto optimal, so that $\pi^1(\omega^1) = \pi^2(\omega^2)$. Thus for an economy with incomplete financial markets, both cases—coincidence or distinctness of the π^i vectors—

are possible. The question is: *which of these two situations is typical?* In the above example, if the pair of initial endowments are chosen at random, then endowments for which $\pi^1(\omega^1) \neq \pi^2(\omega^2)$ are much more likely to be obtained than Pareto optimal endowments. For this economy with two agents and no financial securities it can thus be argued that the typical situation is $\bar{\pi}^1 \neq \bar{\pi}^2$ at an equilibrium.

Can the insight offered by this simple example be extended to more general situations? To answer this question we need a framework that permits the argument in the above example to be made both rigorous and general, that is, a framework in which it can be proved that certain properties of an equilibrium are typical (i.e. hold for most economies).

Mathematical Approach

There is a well developed mathematical approach for formalizing problems of this kind which consists in embedding the particular problem into a family of parametrized problems. By the use of a technique which is explained shortly, the parameter space for the problem can be split up into two disjoint sets, the first consisting of the parameter values where the desired property is known to be satisfied and the second consisting of parameter values where it may or may not hold. If it can be proved that the second set is an exceptional set in the parameter space, then the desired property will have been shown to be typical.

The formal procedure can be described as follows. Suppose the phenomenon under consideration (in our case a financial market equilibrium) can be described as a solution of a system of J equations in J unknowns q (the vector of security prices) where q must lie in an open subset $Q \subset \mathbb{R}^J$. Suppose that there is a natural vector of parameters ω that can be introduced, where ω must lie in the *parameter space* Ω which is an open subset of a finite-dimensional space $\mathbb{R}^K$. Let $f : Q \times \Omega \longrightarrow \mathbb{R}^J$ denote the function whose zeros define the basic phenomenon (equilibrium) for each parameter value $\omega \in \Omega$

$$f(q, \omega) = 0 \tag{E}$$

We want to know whether a solution of (E) has a certain property (P): in our case (P) is the property $\bar{\pi}^i \neq \bar{\pi}^j$, $\forall\, i \neq j$. Let (P′) denote the statement that (P) is not satisfied: in our case (P′) is equivalent to $\bar{\pi}^i - \bar{\pi}^j = 0$ for some $i \neq j$. Suppose (P′) can be described by a system of $N \geq 1$ equations

$$g(q, \omega) = 0 \tag{P′}$$

where $g : Q \times \Omega \longrightarrow \mathbb{R}^N$. Thus while the basic phenomenon (equilibrium) is described by a system of J equations in J unknowns (E), the requirement that the phenomenon fails to exhibit the desired property (P) leads to a system of $J + N$ equations in J unknowns (E, P'). The crucial point is that the conditions (P') introduce no new unknowns, but add N new equations.

Define the function

$$h = (f, g) : Q \times \Omega \longrightarrow \mathbb{R}^J \times \mathbb{R}^N \tag{3}$$

then the pair of equations (E) and (P') can be written as

$$h(q, \omega) = 0 \tag{E,P'}$$

Suppose it is known that for every parameter value $\omega \in \Omega$, the system of equations (E) has a solution. If we can establish the existence of a set of parameter values $\Omega^* \subset \Omega$, with the property that its complement $\Omega \setminus \Omega^*$ is an "exceptional" set, such that for all $\omega \in \Omega^*$ the system of equations (E, P') has no solutions, then we will have proved that *for most parameter values ($\omega \in \Omega^*$) the property* (P) *is satisfied by any solution of* (E).

Sets of Measure Zero

To carry out this procedure we need to formalize the idea that a subset $C \subset \mathbb{R}^n$ is *exceptional*. This is expressed by saying that a set C is exceptional if, when points are drawn at random from $\mathbb{R}^n$, the probability of choosing a point in C is zero. The probability that a point drawn at random will lie in a set C depends on the "size" or *measure* of C as a subset of $\mathbb{R}^n$: the measure of a set is given by its length in $\mathbb{R}^1$, its area in $\mathbb{R}^2$ and its volume in $\mathbb{R}^3$. This concept is easily generalized to the simplest sets in $\mathbb{R}^n$ which are cubes.

11.1 Definition: Let $a, b \in \mathbb{R}^n$ with $a_i < b_i$, $i = 1, \ldots, n$. The *cube* $C(a, b)$ generated by (a, b) is defined by

$$C(a, b) = \{x \in \mathbb{R}^n \mid a_i < x_i < b_i, \quad i = 1, \ldots, n\}$$

and its *measure* $\mu(C(a, b))$ is defined by

$$\mu(C(a, b)) = \prod_{i=1}^{n} (b_i - a_i)$$

A set $C \subset \mathbb{R}^n$ is "exceptional" if it can be covered by (contained in) a countable collection of cubes of arbitrarily small measure. More precisely

11.2 Definition: A subset $C \subset \mathbb{R}^n$ is of *measure zero* if for every $\epsilon > 0$ there exists a countable collection of cubes $(C_\epsilon^i)_{i=1}^{\infty}$ such that

$$\text{(i)} \quad C \subset \bigcup_{i=1}^{\infty} C_\epsilon^i \qquad \text{(ii)} \quad \sum_{i=1}^{\infty} \mu(C_\epsilon^i) \leq \epsilon$$

A set is said to be of *full measure* if its complement is a set of measure zero. It follows from the definition that a finite or countable union of sets of measure zero is a set of measure zero.

Example: A point is a set of measure zero in $\mathbb{R}^1$; a line (or curve) is a set of measure zero in $\mathbb{R}^2$; a plane (or surface) is a set of measure zero in $\mathbb{R}^3$. More generally $\mathbb{R}^{n-1}$ (or an $(n-1)$-dimensional surface) is a set of measure zero in $\mathbb{R}^n$. To prove this property, let C^i $(i = 1, 2, \ldots)$ be cubes in $\mathbb{R}^{n-1}$ whose sides have unit length such that $\mathbb{R}^{n-1} = \bigcup_{i=1}^{\infty} C^i$ (i.e. cubes covering $\mathbb{R}^{n-1}$). For every $\epsilon > 0$ and $i = 1, 2, \ldots$, consider the sequence of cubes in $\mathbb{R}^n$ defined by

$$C_\epsilon^i = C^i \times \left(-\frac{\epsilon}{2^{i+1}}, \frac{\epsilon}{2^{i+1}} \right) \supset C^i \times \{0\}, \quad i = 1, 2, \ldots$$

Then $\mathbb{R}^{n-1} \times \{0\} \subset \bigcup_{i=1}^{\infty} C_\epsilon^i$ and $\sum_{i=1}^{\infty} \mu\left(C_\epsilon^i\right) = \sum_{i=1}^{\infty} \epsilon/2^i = \epsilon$ so that $\mathbb{R}^{n-1}$ is a set of measure zero in $\mathbb{R}^n$. $\square$

Parametric System of Equations

Let $h : Q \times \Omega \longrightarrow \mathbb{R}^M$ denote the function defined in (3) with $M = J + N$. If h is *differentiable* on $Q \times \Omega$ and if $(\bar{q}, \bar{\omega}) \in Q \times \Omega$ then $\left[D_{q,\omega} h(\bar{q}, \bar{\omega}) \right]$ denotes the $M \times (J + K)$ matrix of partial derivatives (the *Jacobian*) of h evaluated at $(\bar{q}, \bar{\omega})$

$$\left[D_{q,\omega} h(\bar{q}, \bar{\omega}) \right] = \begin{bmatrix} \dfrac{\partial h^1(\bar{q}, \bar{\omega})}{\partial q_1} & \cdots & \dfrac{\partial h^1(\bar{q}, \bar{\omega})}{\partial q_J} & \dfrac{\partial h^1(\bar{q}, \bar{\omega})}{\partial \omega_1} & \cdots & \dfrac{\partial h^1(\bar{q}, \bar{\omega})}{\partial \omega_K} \\ \vdots & \ddots & \vdots & \vdots & \ddots & \vdots \\ \dfrac{\partial h^M(\bar{q}, \bar{\omega})}{\partial q_1} & \cdots & \dfrac{\partial h^M(\bar{q}, \bar{\omega})}{\partial q_J} & \dfrac{\partial h^M(\bar{q}, \bar{\omega})}{\partial \omega_1} & \cdots & \dfrac{\partial h^M(\bar{q}, \bar{\omega})}{\partial \omega_K} \end{bmatrix}$$

and $\left[D_q h(\bar{q}, \bar{\omega}) \right]$ (resp. $[D_\omega h(\bar{q}, \bar{\omega})]$) denotes the $M \times J$ (resp. $M \times K$) sub-matrix of partial derivatives with respect to q (resp. ω). We can now state the theorem which gives conditions under which a parametric system of equations with more equations than unknowns (such as (E,P$'$)) typically has no solution. This theorem belongs to a family of Transversality Theorems which are derived from one of the important results of Differential Topology known as Sard's Theorem. These transversality results are treated in more detail in Volume 2: our object at this stage is simply to introduce the reader to a certain type of argument which is extensively used in the study of the general model.

11.3 Theorem (Non-existence of Solutions to Parametric Systems of Equations with More Equations than Unknowns):   *Let $Q \subset \mathbb{R}^J$, $\Omega \subset \mathbb{R}^K$ be open sets and let $h : Q \times \Omega \longrightarrow \mathbb{R}^M$ be a smooth function. If*

(i) $J < M$

(ii) for all $(\bar{q}, \bar{\omega}) \in Q \times \Omega$ such that $h(\bar{q}, \bar{\omega}) = 0$

$$\text{rank}\left[D_{q,\omega} h(\bar{q}, \bar{\omega})\right] = M \tag{4}$$

then there exists a set $\Omega^* \subset \Omega$, with $\Omega \setminus \Omega^*$ a set of measure zero, such that

$$\{q \in Q \mid h(q, \omega) = 0\} = \emptyset, \quad \forall \omega \in \Omega^*.$$

PROOF: The proof is given in Volume 2. □

REMARK. The rank condition (4) can be expressed as follows: at every solution $(\bar{q}, \bar{\omega})$ of the system of equations $h(q, \omega) = 0$, the equations can be *locally controlled* in the sense that for any $dy \in \mathbb{R}^M$ there exists[1] $(dq, d\omega) \in \mathbb{R}^J \times \mathbb{R}^K$ such that

$$dh = \left[D_{q,\omega} h(\bar{q}, \bar{\omega})\right] (dq, d\omega)^T = dy \tag{5}$$

In many applications of Theorem 11.3 there are sufficiently many parameters to be able to solve (5) by an appropriate choice of $d\omega$, setting $dq = 0$.

The idea behind Theorem 11.3 can be expressed intuitively as follows. Condition (i) expresses the fact that the system of equations

$$h^i(q, \omega) = 0, \quad i = 1, \ldots, M \tag{6}$$

has more equations (M) than unknowns (J). In the $(J + K)$-dimensional space $Q \times \Omega$ each of the equations in (6) defines a $(J + K - 1)$-dimensional surface. Since at any point $(\bar{q}, \bar{\omega})$ where these M surfaces intersect, the M gradients

$$\left\{\nabla h^1(\bar{q}, \bar{\omega}), \ldots, \nabla h^M(\bar{q}, \bar{\omega})\right\}$$

are linearly independent (by condition (4)), the surface in $Q \times \Omega$ defined by (6) is of dimension $J + K - M$. Notice that, since $J < M$, when this surface is projected onto the parameter space Ω, a surface of at most dimension $J - M + K < K$ is obtained. But this means that the parameter values for which there exists a $q \in Q$ such that $h(q, \omega) = 0$ are exceptional.

A geometric interpretation of Theorem 11.3 for the case $J = K = 1, M = 2$, $Q = \Omega = (0, \infty)$ is shown in Figure 11.1(a). There is a system of two equations in one unknown q with one parameter ω

$$\begin{aligned} h^1(q, \omega) &= 0 \\ h^2(q, \omega) &= 0 \end{aligned} \tag{7}$$

---

[1] dq, being the change in a price vector, is written as a row vector: for notational simplicity the change in the vector of parameters $d\omega$ is also written as a row vector. T denotes the transpose operator, so that $(dq, d\omega)^T$ is a column vector.

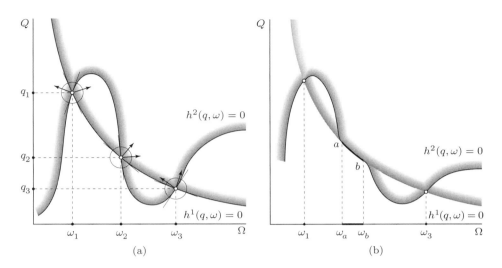

(a)   (b)

Figure 11.1   (a) If two curves in $\mathbb{R}^2$ intersect without being tangent then they intersect at points. (b) If they are tangent they can meet along a common segment $[\,a, b\,]$.

Each equation in (7) defines a one-dimensional surface (i.e. a curve) in $Q \times \Omega = R_{++}^2$. Since at any of the points

$$\{(q_1, \omega_1), (q_2, \omega_2), (q_3, \omega_3)\} \tag{8}$$

where these two curves intersect the gradients

$$\left\{\nabla h^1(q_j, \omega_j),\ \nabla h^2(q_j, \omega_j)\right\}, \quad j = 1, 2, 3 \tag{9}$$

are linearly independent, the "surface" defined by (7) is zero-dimensional: when this "surface" is projected onto the parameter space Ω, the set

$$\Omega^* = \{\omega_1, \omega_2, \omega_3\}$$

is obtained, consisting of the parameter values for which there is a value of the variable q satisfying (7). Ω^* is clearly a set of measure zero in $\Omega = (0, \infty)$.

There is an alternative way of understanding the intuition underlying the condition that the gradients in (9) corresponding to the points in (8) be linearly independent. Take one of these points, say (q_j, ω_j) and consider a small change $d\omega$ in the parameter. The linear independence of the two gradients ∇h^1 and ∇h^2 at (q_j, ω_j) implies that the dq value (say dq^1) which lies on the tangent line $dh^1 = \nabla h^1(q_j, \omega_j)(dq^1, d\omega)^T = 0$ is different from the dq value (say dq^2) which lies on the tangent line $dh^2 = \nabla h^2(q_j, \omega_j)(dq^2, d\omega)^T = 0$. At any point (q_j, ω_j) at which the two curves intersect, a small change $d\omega$ will pull them apart.

The role played by the rank condition (4) in Theorem 11.3 should now be clear. For suppose as in Figure 11.1(b) that there are points (q, ω) satisfying (6) or (7) (the points on the segment $[a, b]$) at each of which the gradients $\{\nabla h^1(q, \omega), \nabla h^2(q, \omega)\}$ are linearly dependent. These points constitute a one-dimensional curve $[a, b]$ in $\mathbb{R}^2_{++}$ which, when projected onto the parameter space $\Omega = (0, \infty)$, gives the interval $[\omega_a, \omega_b]$. In this case $\Omega^* = \{\omega_1, [\omega_a, \omega_b], \omega_3\}$ is not a set of measure zero in Ω.

Security Demand Functions

To apply the procedure explained above, a parametrized family of economies must be chosen. Since the finance economy $\mathscr{E}(u, \omega, V)$ is characterized by the utility functions $u = (u^1, \ldots, u^I)$ of the agents, their endowments $\omega = (\omega^1, \ldots, \omega^I)$ and the security structure V, there are a number of different parametrizations that can be chosen. To prove the main result of this section it is sufficient to consider the family of economies obtained by fixing a profile of utility functions $u = (u^1, \ldots, u^I)$ and the security structure V, and allowing the agents' endowments to vary in the open set $\mathbb{R}^{nI}_{++}$. The economy $\mathscr{E}(u, \omega, V)$ is thus thought of as being parametrized by

$$\omega \in \Omega = \mathbb{R}^{nI}_{++}$$

We want to analyze an equilibrium of the economy $\mathscr{E}(u, \omega, V)$. As explained in Section 10 there are two ways in which this can be done: the first reduces an equilibrium to a system of equations in the security prices; the second, based on the concept of a no-arbitrage equilibrium, leads to a system of equations in the state prices. The analysis of this section will be based on the security price representation.

Agent i's maximum problem in a financial market equilibrium is given by

$$\max \left\{ u^i(x^i) \mid x^i - \omega^i = W(q)z^i, \quad z^i \in \mathbb{R}^J \right\} \quad \text{with} \quad W(q) = \begin{bmatrix} -q \\ V \end{bmatrix} \quad (10)$$

The matrix of income transfers W is expressed as a function of q only, since V is taken as fixed. By Theorem 9.3 the problem (10) has a solution if and only if q is a no-arbitrage security price. Thus q must lie in the *set of no-arbitrage security prices*

$$Q = \left\{ q \in \mathbb{R}^J \mid q = \pi_1 V, \quad \pi_1 \in \mathbb{R}^S_{++} \right\} \quad (11)$$

Q is the cone spanned by the rows of the matrix V.

With strict quasi-concavity of u^i there is a unique commodity bundle x^i which is the solution to (10) for a given vector of security prices q. Since there are J securities, if rank $W(q) = J$ then there is a unique portfolio $z^i \in \mathbb{R}^J$

generating x^i. If there are redundant securities ($\Longleftrightarrow$ rank $W(q) = J' < J$) then there are many portfolios $z^i \in \mathbb{R}^J$ generating the same vector x^i. To obtain a well-defined demand function for securities it suffices to pick any J' securities that generate $\langle W(q) \rangle$ as the basic securities. Thus it may be assumed without loss of generality that rank $W(q) = J$ ($\Longleftrightarrow$ rank $V = J$). The security demand function of agent i, $\tilde{z}^i : Q \times \Omega \longrightarrow \mathbb{R}^J$, is then well-defined

$$\tilde{z}^i(q, \omega^i) = \arg \max_{z^i \in \mathbb{R}^J} u^i \left(\omega^i + W(q)z^i \right), \quad i = 1, \dots, I \tag{12}$$

To apply Theorem 11.3 the following properties need to be established:

(1) The set Q defined by (11) is an open subset of $\mathbb{R}^J$
(2) The function $\tilde{z}^i$ defined by (12) is a smooth function on $Q \times \Omega$.

11.4 Lemma: *If* rank $V = J$ *then* Q *is an open subset of* $\mathbb{R}^J$.

PROOF: This follows from the fact that the image of an open set under a surjective linear map is open. This property is proved in the appendix to this chapter (see Proposition A2.7). □

11.5 Lemma: *If* rank $V = J$ *and* u^i *satisfies Assumption $\mathscr{U}$, then the security demand function* $\tilde{z}^i : Q \times \Omega \longrightarrow \mathbb{R}^J$ *is a smooth function,* $i = 1, \dots, I$.

PROOF: The first-order conditions for the problem (12) are

$$\nabla u^i(\omega^i + Wz^i)W = 0 \tag{13}$$

where the gradient ∇u^i as a vector of (personal) state prices is taken to be a row vector. These equations implicitly define $\tilde{z}^i(q, \omega)$. Thus by the Implicit Function Theorem $\tilde{z}^i$ is a smooth function if the matrix

$$W^T \left[D^2 u^i(\omega^i + Wz^i) \right] W$$

is nonsingular whenever (13) is satisfied, where $\left[D^2 u^i(x^i) \right]$ denotes the $(S+1) \times (S+1)$ matrix of second partial derivatives (the Hessian matrix) of u^i at x^i. Suppose the matrix were singular when (13) is satisfied. Then there would exist $\xi \in \mathbb{R}^J$, $\xi \neq 0$ such that

$$\xi^T W^T \left[D^2 u^i \right] W\xi = 0 \quad \text{and} \quad \nabla u^i W\xi = 0$$

contradicting Assumption $\mathscr{U}$(iv). □

Distinctness of Present-Value Vectors

It can now be proved that the present-value vectors of the agents are typically distinct in an equilibrium with incomplete markets.

11.6 Theorem (Basic Property of Incomplete Markets):   *Let $\mathscr{E}(u,\omega,V)$ be a family of economies parametrized by the agents' endowments $\omega \in \Omega$, in which*

(i) *there are at least two agents ($I \geq 2$)*
(ii) $u = (u^1,\ldots,u^I)$ *satisfies Assumption $\mathscr{U}$*
(iii) *the financial markets are incomplete ($\operatorname{rank} V = J < S$).*

Then there exists a set of full measure $\Omega^* \subset \Omega$ such that, if $\omega \in \Omega^*$, the present-value vectors of all agents are distinct

$$\pi^i(\bar{x}^i) \neq \pi^j(\bar{x}^j), \quad \forall\, i \neq j$$

in each financial market equilibrium $((\bar{x},\bar{z}),\bar{q})$ of the economy $\mathscr{E}(u,\omega,V)$.

PROOF: Let $f : Q \times \Omega \longrightarrow \mathbb{R}^J$, defined by

$$f(q,\omega^1,\ldots,\omega^I) = \sum_{i=1}^I \bar{z}^i(q,\omega^i)$$

denote the *aggregate excess demand* for the J securities. $\bar{q} \in Q$ is an *equilibrium price* if and only if

$$f(\bar{q},\omega^1,\ldots,\omega^I) = 0 \tag{14}$$

Let $\tilde{x}^i : Q \times \Omega \longrightarrow \mathbb{R}^n_+$, defined by

$$\tilde{x}^i(q,\omega^i) = \omega^i + W(q)\tilde{z}^i(q,\omega^i), \quad i = 1,\ldots,I$$

denote agent i's optimal consumption bundle. Define $\tilde{\pi}^i_1 : Q \times \Omega \longrightarrow \mathbb{R}^S$ by

$$\tilde{\pi}^i_1(q,\omega^i) = \pi^i_1(\tilde{x}^i(q,\omega^i)), \quad i = 1,\ldots,I$$

For any pair i, j with $i \neq j$, we want to show that the system of equations

$$\begin{aligned}
f(q,\omega^1,\ldots,\omega^I) &= 0 \\
\tilde{\pi}^i_1(q,\omega^i) - \tilde{\pi}^j_1(q,\omega^j) &= 0
\end{aligned} \tag{15}$$

has no solution for almost all endowments $\omega \in \Omega$. Proving that (15) typically has no solution can be simplified as follows. The fact that the security markets are incomplete ($\langle V \rangle \neq \mathbb{R}^S$) implies $\langle V \rangle^\perp \neq \{0\}$. Thus there exists

$\pi_1 \in \langle V \rangle^\perp, \pi_1 \neq 0$ so that $\pi_{\bar{s}} \neq 0$ for some $\bar{s} \in \{1, \ldots, S\}$. It thus suffices to prove that the system of equations

$$f(q, \omega^1, \ldots, \omega^I) = 0$$
$$\tilde{\pi}_{\bar{s}}^i(q, \omega^i) - \tilde{\pi}_{\bar{s}}^j(q, \omega^j) = 0 \tag{16}$$

has no solution for almost all endowments $\omega \in \Omega$.

Defining the function

$$h : Q \times \Omega \longrightarrow \mathbb{R}^{J+1} \quad \text{by} \quad h = (f, \tilde{\pi}_{\bar{s}}^i - \tilde{\pi}_{\bar{s}}^j)$$

the problem reduces to showing that

$$h(q, \omega) = 0 \tag{17}$$

has no solution for all $\omega \in \Omega_{ij}^* \subset \Omega$, where Ω_{ij}^* is a set of full measure. To obtain this result it suffices to apply Theorem 11.3 with $K = nI$, $M = J + 1$.

It thus remains to check that condition (4) in Theorem 11.3 is satisfied or equivalently that, if $(\bar{q}, \bar{\omega})$ satisfies (17), then for each $dy \in \mathbb{R}^{J+1}$ there exists $(dq, d\omega) \in \mathbb{R}^J \times \mathbb{R}^{nI}$ such that

$$\left[D_{q,\omega} h(\bar{q}, \bar{\omega}) \right] (dq, d\omega)^T = dy$$

namely that the linear transformation $\left[D_{q,\omega} h(\bar{q}, \bar{\omega}) \right]$ is surjective. Let $e^1 = (1, \ldots, 0), \ldots, e^{J+1} = (0, \ldots, 1)$ denote the standard basis for $\mathbb{R}^{J+1}$. Then it suffices to show that for each e^j there exists $(dq, d\omega)$ such that

$$\left[D_{q,\omega} h(\bar{q}, \bar{\omega}) \right] (dq, d\omega)^T = e^j \tag{18}$$

namely that each equation $(j = 1, \ldots, J + 1)$ can be *locally controlled* independently of the others.

Let $(\bar{q}, \bar{\omega}) \in Q \times \Omega$ be a solution to (17) and let $(\bar{x}^i, \bar{z}^i) = (\tilde{x}^i(\bar{q}, \bar{\omega}^i), \tilde{z}^i(\bar{q}, \bar{\omega}^i))$, $i = 1, \ldots, I$. Let us show that we can solve (18) for $j = 1, \ldots, J$. *How can we induce a one-unit increase in the demand for security j?* Since one unit of security j generates the stream of income $(V_1^j, \ldots, V_S^j)$ across the states at date 1 but requires the sacrifice of $\bar{q}_j$ units at date 0, if the endowment of agent 1 is changed by

$$d\omega^1 = (\bar{q}_j, -V_1^j, \ldots, -V_S^j) \in \langle W \rangle$$

then the optimal response of agent 1 will be to purchase one more unit of security j: his consumption will be unchanged provided the equilibrium price $\bar{q}$ is not changed, and

$$\bar{x}^1 \in \mathbb{B}(\bar{q}, \bar{\omega}^1 + d\omega^1), \quad \pi_1^1(\bar{x}^1) V = \bar{q}$$

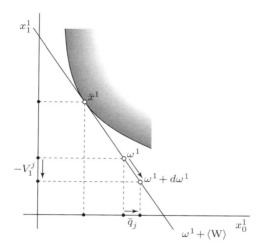

Figure 11.2 Agent 1 responds to the endowment change $d\omega^1 = (\bar{q}_j, -V_1^j) \in \langle W \rangle$ by purchasing one more unit of security j.

namely the first-order conditions for a maximum still hold (see Figure 11.2). If we set $d\omega^i = 0$, $i = 2, \ldots, I$ and $dq = 0$ then $d\tilde{z}^i = 0$, $i = 2, \ldots, I$ and $\pi_{\bar{s}}^i(\bar{x}^i)$, $\pi_{\bar{s}}^j(\bar{x}^j)$ are unchanged. Thus the jth equation has been controlled as required by (18), all other equations remaining unchanged.

How can we induce a one-unit increase in the $(J+1)^{\text{st}}$ equation in (16)? First, by the choice of $\bar{s}$, there exists $d\pi_1 \in \langle V \rangle^\perp$ such that $d\pi_{\bar{s}} = 1$. The idea is to show that by making an appropriate change in the initial endowment ω^i, agent i can be induced to change consumption $\bar{x}^i \longrightarrow \bar{x}^i + dx^i$ in such a way that his (date 1) present-value vector changes from $\bar{\pi}_1^i = \pi_1^i(\bar{x}^i)$ to $\bar{\pi}_1^i + d\pi_1$. This can be achieved if there exists dx^i such that

$$\pi_1^i(\bar{x}^i + dx^i) = \bar{\pi}_1^i + d\pi_1 \qquad (19)$$

(19) involves inducing a change in the direction of the gradient $\nabla u^i(x^i)$ so that the normalized gradient π^i makes the change

$$\bar{\pi}^i = (1, \bar{\pi}_1^i) \longrightarrow \bar{\pi}^i + d\pi = (1, \bar{\pi}_1^i + d\pi_1)$$

This local controllability of the direction of the gradient along agent i's indifference surface is precisely the property guaranteed by Assumption $\mathscr{U}$(iv) on the curvature of the indifference surfaces. A geometric interpretation is shown in Figure 11.3. A formal statement of this property is given by the following lemma: the idea of the proof is simple, but involves some calculations, which are given in the appendix.

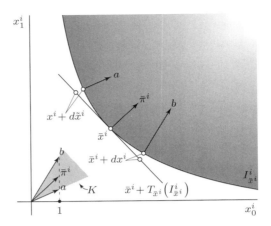

Figure 11.3   An indifference curve of a utility function satisfying $\mathscr{U}$ with $S = 1$. At $\bar{x}^i$ the normalized gradient is $\bar{\pi}^i$. For any normalized vector in a small cone K around $\bar{\pi}^i$, there exists a consumption vector $\bar{x}^i + dx^i$ on the indifference curve $I_{\bar{x}^i}^i$ with this vector as normalized gradient. Furthermore, for any two distinct consumption vectors close to $\bar{x}^i$ on $I_{\bar{x}^i}^i$, the normalized gradients are distinct.

11.7 Lemma (Local Controllability of Present-Value Vector π^i):   *Let u^i : $\mathbb{R}_+^{S+1} \longrightarrow \mathbb{R}$ be a utility function satisfying Assumption $\mathscr{U}$ and let $\bar{x}^i \in \mathbb{R}_{++}^{S+1}$. The linear map $D_{x^i} \pi_1^i(\bar{x}^i) : T_{\bar{x}^i}\left(I_{\bar{x}^i}^i\right) \longrightarrow \mathbb{R}^S$ is surjective i.e. for any $d\pi_1 \in \mathbb{R}^S$ there exists a change in consumption dx^i in the tangent space $T_{\bar{x}^i}\left(I_{\bar{x}^i}^i\right)$ such that to terms of first order*

$$\pi_1^i(\bar{x}^i + dx^i) = \pi_1^i(\bar{x}^i) + d\pi_1$$

PROOF: (see Appendix A2.8).   □

REMARK. Since $\dim T_{\bar{x}^i}\left(I_{\bar{x}^i}^i\right) = \dim \mathbb{R}^S = S$, the linear map $D_{x^i}\pi_1^i(\bar{x}^i)$ being surjective is also injective when restricted to the tangent space $T_{\bar{x}^i}\left(I_{\bar{x}^i}^i\right)$. Thus if $dx^i \in T_{\bar{x}^i}\left(I_{\bar{x}^i}^i\right)$ and $dx^i \neq 0$ then $\pi^i(\bar{x}^i + dx^i) \neq \pi^i(\bar{x}^i)$. This proves the comment made in Section 6 following Assumption $\mathscr{U}$: $\mathscr{U}$(iv) *implies that the gradient always changes direction for any local displacement from $\bar{x}^i$ on the indifference surface $I_{\bar{x}^i}^i$, so that the indifference surface is not locally flat.*

Thus by Lemma 11.7 for $d\pi_1 \in \langle V \rangle^\perp$ such that $d\pi_{\bar{s}} = 1$ there exists $dx^i \in \mathbb{R}^{S+1}$ such that (19) holds. Let us show that

$$dq = 0, \quad d\omega^i = dx^i, \quad d\omega^j = 0, \quad j \neq i \tag{20}$$

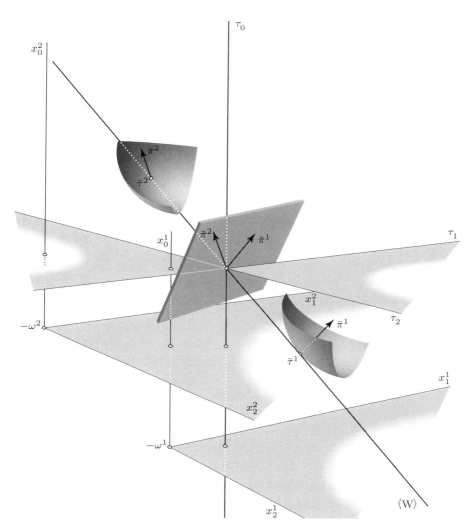

Figure 11.4 Geometric interpretation of Theorem 11.6. At an FM equilibrium with incomplete markets $(\bar{\tau}^1, \bar{\pi}^1)$ and $(\bar{\tau}^2, \bar{\pi}^2)$ lie in $\langle W \rangle \times \langle W \rangle^\perp$ but $\bar{\pi}^1 \neq \bar{\pi}^2$.

leads to the required one-unit increase in the $(J+1)^{\mathrm{st}}$ equation and leaves all other equations unchanged. Since $d\pi_1 \in \langle V \rangle^\perp \iff d\pi_1 V = 0$, it follows that the first-order conditions for agent i

$$\pi_1^i(\bar{x}^i + dx^i)V = (\pi_1^i(\bar{x}^i) + d\pi_1)V = \pi_1^i(\bar{x}^i)V = \bar{q}$$

are satisfied.

Since $\bar{x}^i + dx^i \in \mathbb{B}(\bar{q}, \bar{\omega}^i + d\omega^i)$, $\bar{x}^i + dx^i$ is the optimal consumption of agent i. Since $\pi_s^j(\bar{x}^j)$ is unchanged, the $(J+1)^{\text{st}}$ equation has been increased by one unit. It is clear from (20) that $dz^j = 0$, $j = 1, \ldots, I$ so that $df = 0$, implying that the first J equations in (16) are unchanged. Thus we have shown that condition (ii) in Theorem 11.3 holds. It follows that there exists a set of full measure Ω_{ij}^* such that (17) has no solution for $\omega \in \Omega_{ij}^*$. Repeating the argument for all i, j with $i < j$ and forming the set $\Omega^* = \bigcap_{i<j} \Omega_{ij}^*$ completes the proof. $\square$

A geometric interpretation of Theorem 11.6 for the case of two agents ($I = 2$), two states of nature at date 1 ($S = 2$) and one financial security ($J = 1$) is shown in Figure 11.4. For simplicity we have drawn only the trading subspace $\langle W \rangle$, the equilibrium net trades $(\bar{\tau}^1, \bar{\tau}^2)$ of the two agents and the associated present-value vectors $(\bar{\pi}^1, \bar{\pi}^2)$, which lie in $\langle W \rangle^{\perp}$.

Inefficiency of FM Equilibrium

By Proposition 7.7, equality of the agents' normalized gradients

$$\pi^1(\bar{x}^1) = \cdots = \pi^I(\bar{x}^I)$$

is a necessary and sufficient condition for Pareto optimality of a feasible allocation $\bar{x} = (\bar{x}^1, \ldots, \bar{x}^I)$. An immediate consequence of the distinctness of agents' normalized gradients when markets are incomplete is the Pareto inefficiency of every financial market equilibrium for most economies.

11.8 Corollary (Pareto Inefficiency with Incomplete Markets): *Let $\mathcal{E}(u, \omega, V)$ be a family of economies satisfying the assumptions of Theorem 11.6. Then there exists a set of full measure $\Omega^* \subset \Omega$, such that if $\omega \in \Omega^*$ then for each financial market equilibrium $((\bar{x}, \bar{z}), \bar{q})$ of the economy $\mathcal{E}(u, \omega, V)$ the allocation $\bar{x}$ is Pareto inefficient.*

PROOF: Follows immediately from Proposition 7.7 and Theorems 11.6. $\square$

The traditional justification of a system of markets as a mechanism for allocating resources is that it leads to Pareto optimality. When markets are incomplete this is no longer a valid justification. But perhaps the criterion of Pareto optimality is too demanding. *Is there not some less demanding criterion with respect to which the system of financial markets does a good job of allocating risks?*

12. CONSTRAINED PARETO OPTIMALITY

In this section we will show that there is a restricted sense in which equilibria with incomplete markets are efficient if

  (i) the security structure V is *fixed* (exogenously given)
  (ii) there is only *one* good.
 (iii) there are only *two* periods.

As we shall see later when either (i), (ii), or (iii) are not satisfied the arguments of this section break down: in Section 25 it is shown that when there are three or more periods then FM equilibria are typically constrained inefficient. The constrained inefficiency of incomplete markets equilibria poses some important problems which are studied in greater depth in Volume 2. But let us start by examining the simpler world where (i)–(iii) are satisfied.

When there are less instruments (J) than risks at date 1 that need to be allocated (S), trading in the J instruments cannot be expected to equalize agents' rates of substitution among the S risks as required by Proposition (7.7). Since each agent's consumption at date 1 is given by

$$x_1^i = \omega_1^i + V z^i, \quad i = 1, \ldots, I \tag{1}$$

and since each agent is not free to choose x_1^i directly but must instead choose the portfolio $z^i \in \mathbb{R}^J$, it is clear that agent i has only limited control over consumption x_1^i at date 1. Saying that a financial market equilibrium $((\bar{x}, \bar{z}), \bar{q})$ is not Pareto optimal amounts to saying that a planner who can directly choose the vectors of consumption $\bar{x}^i$, $i = 1, \ldots, I$ of all agents—and hence can *directly choose their date 1 consumption vectors* x_1^i, $i = 1, \ldots, I$—can improve on the allocation $\bar{x} = (\bar{x}^1, \ldots, \bar{x}^I)$. But this is certainly not surprising since the planner has not been constrained, as in (1), to date 1 consumption vectors x_1^i obtained by *assigning a portfolio of securities* z^i *to each agent* $i = 1, \ldots, I$. If we accept the idea that even the planner can only distribute goods at date 1 by assigning portfolios of securities to the agents (so that financial instruments are the only mechanism for redistributing risks at date 1) then the set of feasible allocations F (Definition 6.1) to which the planner has access must be modified.

12.1 Definition: An allocation $x = (x^1, \ldots, x^I)$ is *V-feasible* if

$$\text{(i)} \quad x \in F \quad \text{(ii)} \quad x_1^i - \omega_1^i \in \langle V \rangle, \quad i = 1, \ldots, I$$

We let F_V denote the *set of V-feasible allocations* so that

$$F_V = \left\{ x \in F \mid x_1^i - \omega_1^i \in \langle V \rangle, \quad i = 1, \ldots, I \right\}$$

12.2 Definition: An allocation $\bar{x} = (\bar{x}^1, \ldots, \bar{x}^I)$ is *constrained Pareto optimal (relative to V)* if (i) $\bar{x} \in F_V$ (ii) there does not exist $x = (x^1, \ldots, x^I) \in F_V$ such that $u^i(x^i) \geq u^i(\bar{x}^i)$, $i = 1, \ldots, I$ with strict inequality for at least one i; for brevity we also write: $\bar{x}$ is CPO.

The next theorem shows that competitive financial markets are efficient as a mechanism for redistributing income indirectly via portfolios of exogenously given securities—at least in the one-good two-period exchange model in which there is no spillover effect between the income distribution induced by security trading and prices on other markets.

12.3 Theorem (Constrained Pareto Optimality of FM Equilibrium): *Let $\mathscr{E}(u, \omega, V)$ be an economy satisfying Assumption $\mathscr{U}''$. If $((\bar{x}, \bar{z}), \bar{q})$ is a financial market equilibrium then the allocation $\bar{x}$ is constrained Pareto optimal relative to V.*

PROOF: Suppose $\bar{x}$ is not a CPO, then there exists $x \in F_V$ such that $u^i(x^i) \geq u^i(\bar{x}^i)$, $i = 1, \ldots, I$ with $u^j(x^j) > u^j(\bar{x}^j)$ for some j. Since $x \in F_V$, there exist $z^i \in \mathbb{R}^J$ such that $x_{\mathbf{1}}^i = \omega_{\mathbf{1}}^i + Vz^i$, $i = 1, \ldots, I$ and $\sum_{i=1}^I \left(x_{\mathbf{1}}^i - \omega_{\mathbf{1}}^i \right) \leq 0$ implies $V \sum_{i=1}^I z^i \leq 0$. Since $\bar{q}$ is a no-arbitrage price, $\bar{q} \sum_{i=1}^I z^i \leq 0$. $u^j(x^j) > u^j(\bar{x}^j)$ implies $x^j \notin \mathbb{B}(\bar{q}, \omega^j)$ so that $x_0^j > \omega_0^j - \bar{q}z^j$. By monotonicity of agents' preferences $u^i(x^i) \geq u^i(\bar{x}^i)$ implies $x_0^i \geq \omega_0^i - \bar{q}z^i$ for $i \neq j$. Summing these inequalities gives $\sum_{i=1}^I x_0^i > \sum_{i=1}^I \omega_0^i - \bar{q} \sum_{i=1}^I z^i \geq \sum_{i=1}^I \omega_0^i$, which contradicts the feasibility of x. $\square$

First-Order Conditions

Economic intuition suggests that trading on the system of financial markets under a common vector of prices $\bar{q}$ should lead to the equalization of certain rates of substitution among agents in the economy. This property is not directly revealed by the proof of Theorem 12.3. Under the assumption of smooth preferences (Assumption $\mathscr{U}$) the first-order conditions which characterize constrained Pareto optimality reveal the restricted sense in which there is equalization of agents' rates of substitution in a financial market equilibrium.

12.4 Proposition (Characterization of Constrained Pareto Optimality): *Let the utility functions of the agents satisfy Assumption $\mathscr{U}$. An allocation $\bar{x} = (\bar{x}^1, \ldots, \bar{x}^I)$ is constrained Pareto optimal if and only if (i) $\bar{x} \in F_V$ (ii) there exists $\bar{q} \in \mathbb{R}^J$ such that the agents' present-value vectors $\pi^i(\bar{x}^i)$, $i = 1, \ldots, I$ satisfy*

$$\pi_{\mathbf{1}}^1(\bar{x}^1)V = \cdots = \pi_{\mathbf{1}}^I(\bar{x}^I)V = \bar{q} \qquad (2)$$

PROOF: Without loss of generality V can be assumed to be of maximal rank J (redundant securities can be neglected). It is easy to show that if V is injective, $\bar{x}$ is CPO relative to V if and only if there exist $(\bar{v}^2, \ldots, \bar{v}^I) \in \mathbb{R}^{I-1}$ such that

$$\bar{x} = \arg \max \left\{ u^1(x^1) \; \middle| \; \begin{array}{l} u^i(x^i) \geq \bar{v}^i, \quad i = 2, \ldots, I \\ x_1^i = \omega_1^i + Vz^i, \quad z^i \in \mathbb{R}^J, \quad i = 1, \ldots, I \\ \sum_{i=1}^I (x_0^i - \omega_0^i) = 0, \quad \sum_{i=1}^I z^i = 0 \end{array} \right\} \tag{3}$$

The first-order conditions for this maximum problem can be written as: there exist vectors

$$\bar{\alpha} = (\bar{\alpha}^1, \ldots, \bar{\alpha}^I) \in \mathbb{R}_{++}^I, \quad \bar{\pi}^i = (1, \bar{\pi}_1^i) \in \mathbb{R}_{++}^{S+1}, \quad i = 1, \ldots, I, \quad \bar{q} \in \mathbb{R}^J$$

such that

$$\bar{\alpha}^i \nabla u^i(x^i) = \bar{\pi}^i, \quad \bar{\pi}_1^i V = \bar{q}, \quad i = 1, \ldots, I$$

Thus a CPO allocation satisfies (2). Conversely if $\bar{x} \in F_V$ and $\bar{v}^i = u^i(\bar{x}^i)$, $i = 2, \ldots, I$ then $\bar{x}$ satisfies the constraints in (3). If in addition (2) holds, then the first-order conditions are satisfied with $\bar{\alpha}_i = 1/\frac{\partial u^i(\bar{x}^i)}{\partial x_0^i}$, $\bar{\pi}^i = \pi^i(\bar{x}^i)$, $i = 1, \ldots, I$. Since $u^1(\cdot)$ is quasi-concave and the constraint set is convex, $\bar{x}$ is CPO. □

Just as Proposition 7.7, which characterized Pareto optimality by equality of agents' normalized gradients, led to an intuitive calculus proof of the Pareto optimality of a contingent market equilibrium, so Proposition 12.4, which characterizes constrained Pareto optimality leads to a calculus proof of the constrained Pareto optimality of a financial market equilibrium.

ALTERNATIVE PROOF OF THEOREM 12.3 (*with Assumption* $\mathscr{U}$): Let $((\bar{x}, \bar{z}), \bar{q})$ be an FM equilibrium of $\mathscr{E}(u, \omega, V)$. Since $\bar{x} \in F$ and $\bar{z}^i$ finances $\bar{x}^i$ ($i = 1, \ldots, I$), $\bar{x} \in F_V$ and since the first-order conditions for the optimal choice of portfolio by agent i, $\bar{q} = \pi_1^i(\bar{x}^i)V$ (equation (9.16)) for each agent $i = 1, \ldots, I$, imply that (2) is satisfied, the result follows. □

The most direct way in which Proposition 12.4 can be interpreted as an equalization of marginal rates of substitution is obtained by defining the agents' utility functions for date 0 consumption (x_0^i) and portfolios (z^i)

$$v^i : \mathbb{R}_+ \times \mathbb{R}^J \longrightarrow \mathbb{R}, \quad v^i(x_0^i, z^i) = u^i(x_0^i, \omega_1^i + Vz^i), \quad i = 1, \ldots, I$$

and the normalized *portfolio gradients*

$$q^i = \frac{1}{\lambda_0^i} \nabla_1 v^i, \quad i = 1, \dots, I$$

where

$$\lambda_0^i = \frac{\partial v^i}{\partial x_0^i}, \quad \nabla_1 v^i = \left(\frac{\partial v^i}{\partial z_1^i}, \dots, \frac{\partial v^i}{\partial z_J^i} \right)$$

q_j^i denotes agent i's marginal rate of substitution between security j and date 0 consumption. The first-order conditions for both a constrained Pareto optimum and a financial market equilibrium can then be expressed as follows.

12.5 Corollary (Portfolio Gradients Equalized):   *Under the assumptions of Proposition 12.4, if $\bar{x} = (\bar{x}^1, \dots, \bar{x}^I)$ is a constrained Pareto optimum with associated portfolios $\bar{z} = (\bar{z}^1, \dots, \bar{z}^I)$, then the agents' normalized portfolio gradients $\bar{q}^i$ at $(\bar{x}_0^i, \bar{z}^i)$ are equalized i.e. there exists a vector $\bar{q} \in \mathbb{R}^J$ such that*

$$\bar{q}^1 = \cdots = \bar{q}^I = \bar{q} \tag{4}$$

PROOF: Given the relation between the partial derivatives of v^i and u^i,

$$\frac{1}{\lambda_0^i} \frac{\partial v^i}{\partial z_j^i} = \frac{1}{\lambda_0^i} \sum_{s=1}^{S} \frac{\partial u^i}{\partial x_s^i} V_s^j, \quad j = 1, \dots, J, \quad i = 1, \dots, I$$

(4) is an immediate consequence of (2). □

Thus by defining agents' induced utility functions v^i for portfolios, we see that trading on financial markets under a common vector of prices $\bar{q}$ drives the agents' portfolio gradients $(\bar{q}^i)$ into equality with the vector of security prices. Of course when markets are incomplete $(J < S)$ the co-ordination achieved by trading in securities is imperfect since it fails to drive the agents' present-value vectors $(\bar{\pi}^i)$ into equality.

There is however a restricted sense in which co-ordination is achieved among the $\bar{\pi}^i$ vectors of the agents. To see this, write the present-value vectors in their normalized form $\bar{\pi}^i = (1, \bar{\pi}_1^i)$, $i = 1, \dots, I$. The marketed subspace $\langle V \rangle$ leads to a natural direct sum decomposition of the space of date 1 income streams $\mathbb{R}^S$:

$$\mathbb{R}^S = \langle V \rangle \oplus \langle V \rangle^{\perp}$$

This implies that any vector $\pi_1^i \in \mathbb{R}^S$ has a unique decomposition as a sum of two vectors

$$\bar{\pi}_1^i = \bar{\pi}_V^i + \bar{\pi}_{V\perp}^i, \quad \bar{\pi}_V^i \in \langle V \rangle, \quad \bar{\pi}_{V\perp}^i \in \langle V \rangle^{\perp} \tag{5}$$

where $\bar{\pi}_V^i$ is the projection of π_1^i onto $\langle V \rangle$ and $\bar{\pi}_{V\perp}^i$ is the projection of $\bar{\pi}_1^i$

onto $\langle V \rangle^{\perp}$. Let us show that the differences in the $\bar{\pi}_1^i$ vectors asserted by Theorem 11.6 arise entirely from differences in the components $\bar{\pi}_{V^{\perp}}^i$, while Proposition 12.4 implies that the components $\bar{\pi}_V^i$ are all equal.

12.6 Corollary (Projections of Valuation Vectors Equalized):   *Under the assumptions of Proposition 12.4, if $\bar{x} = (\bar{x}^1, \ldots, \bar{x}^I)$ is a constrained Pareto optimum, then the projections $\bar{\pi}_V^i$ of the agents' present-value vectors at $\bar{x}^i$ $(i = 1, \ldots, I)$ onto the marketed subspace $\langle V \rangle$ are equalized i.e. there exists a vector $\bar{\pi}_V \in \langle V \rangle$ such that*

$$\bar{\pi}_V^1 = \cdots = \bar{\pi}_V^I = \bar{\pi}_V \tag{6}$$

PROOF: Let $\bar{q}$ be the security price associated with the CPO allocation $\bar{x}$ satisfying

$$\bar{\pi}_1^i V = \bar{q} \quad \text{with} \quad \bar{\pi}_1^i = \pi_1^i(\bar{x}^i), \quad i = 1, \ldots, I$$

Using the decomposition (5) gives

$$\bar{\pi}_1^i V = \bar{\pi}_V^i V = \bar{q}, \quad i = 1, \ldots, I$$

since $\bar{\pi}_{V^{\perp}}^i V = 0$. Thus

$$\left(\bar{\pi}_V^i - \bar{\pi}_V^j \right) V = 0, \quad i, j = 1, \ldots, I$$

so that $\bar{\pi}_V^i - \bar{\pi}_V^j \in \langle V \rangle \cap \langle V \rangle^{\perp} = \{0\}$, $i, j = 1, \ldots, I$, which completes the proof. □

Equality (4) asserts that all agents have the same (marginal) valuations for the J basic securities (in terms of the date 0 income they are ready to sacrifice to obtain an additional unit of a basic security). Since these J securities span the marketed subspace and since marginal valuations are linear, all agents have the same (marginal) valuations for all income streams in the marketed subspace $\langle V \rangle$. Finally, since an agent's valuation of an income stream in the subspace $\langle V \rangle$ is determined by the projection $\bar{\pi}_V^i$ of his present-value vector $\bar{\pi}_1^i$ onto $\langle V \rangle$, all these projections must be equal (the assertion of (6)). Corollaries 12.5 and 12.6 are thus equivalent ways of expressing the marginal conditions which characterize a CPO—namely that (marginal) valuations of income streams in the marketed subspace are equalized.

13.   ABSTRACT APPROACH: ADJOINT EQUATIONS

In this section we present an abstract and succinct way of bringing together the principal results of this chapter. The idea is to exploit the fact that the behavioral equations for the agents in a financial market equilibrium can be expressed by a pair of adjoint equations.

The operation by which a portfolio $z \in \mathbb{R}^J$ induces a vector of date 1 income transfers $\tau_1 \in \mathbb{R}^S$ is a linear transformation

$$\mathscr{V} : \mathbb{R}^J \longrightarrow \mathbb{R}^S$$

which is represented in the standard bases of $\mathbb{R}^J$ and $\mathbb{R}^S$ by the matrix V. The linear transformation $\mathscr{V}$ induces an *adjoint* transformation

$$\mathscr{V}^* : \mathbb{R}^S \longrightarrow \mathbb{R}^J$$

which associates with a state price vector $\pi_1 \in \mathbb{R}^S$ a security price vector $q \in \mathbb{R}^J$. $\mathscr{V}^*$ is defined as follows. Let

$$[\ ,\ ]_S : \mathbb{R}^S \times \mathbb{R}^S \longrightarrow \mathbb{R} \quad \text{and} \quad [\ ,\ ]_J : \mathbb{R}^J \times \mathbb{R}^J \longrightarrow \mathbb{R}$$

denote the standard inner product on $\mathbb{R}^S$ and $\mathbb{R}^J$ respectively. Given the linear transformation $\mathscr{V}$, every vector $\pi_1 \in \mathbb{R}^S$ induces a linear functional on $\mathbb{R}^J$

$$z \longmapsto [\pi_1, \mathscr{V}(z)]_S , \quad \forall z \in \mathbb{R}^J$$

By the inner product representation theorem (see Theorem 14.15) there exists a unique vector $q \in \mathbb{R}^J$ such that

$$[\pi_1, \mathscr{V}(z)]_S = [q, z]_J , \quad \forall z \in \mathbb{R}^J$$

Thus we have associated with each vector $\pi_1 \in \mathbb{R}^S$ a vector $q \in \mathbb{R}^J$. This map defines a linear transformation $\mathscr{V}^* : \mathbb{R}^S \longrightarrow \mathbb{R}^J$, $q = \mathscr{V}^*(\pi_1)$ called the *adjoint* of $\mathscr{V}$. $\mathscr{V}^*$ is thus defined by the relation

$$[\pi_1, \mathscr{V}(z)]_S = [\mathscr{V}^*(\pi_1), z]_J , \quad \forall z \in \mathbb{R}^J, \quad \forall \pi_1 \in \mathbb{R}^S$$

The matrix which represents $\mathscr{V}^*$ in the standard bases for $\mathbb{R}^S$ and $\mathbb{R}^J$ is the *transpose* V^T of V obtained by transposing the rows of V into columns of V^T,

$$V^T = \begin{bmatrix} V_1^1 & \cdots & V_S^1 \\ \vdots & \ddots & \vdots \\ V_1^J & \cdots & V_S^J \end{bmatrix}$$

REMARK. Since every state price vector $\pi_1 \in \mathbb{R}^S$ induces a linear functional on $\mathbb{R}^S$

$$y \longmapsto [\pi_1, y]_S, \quad \forall\, y \in \mathbb{R}^S$$

and since by the inner product representation theorem (Theorem 14.15) every linear functional on $\mathbb{R}^S$ can be represented in this way, every price vector $\pi_1 \in \mathbb{R}^S$ can be viewed as an element of the *dual space* $\mathbb{R}^{S*}$ (the space of linear functionals on $\mathbb{R}^S$). In the same way every security price vector $q \in \mathbb{R}^J$ induces a linear functional on $\mathbb{R}^J$

$$z \longmapsto [q, z]_J, \quad \forall\, z \in \mathbb{R}^J$$

and every price vector $q \in \mathbb{R}^J$ can be viewed as an element of the *dual space* $\mathbb{R}^{J*}$ (the space of linear functionals on $\mathbb{R}^J$). Thus the adjoint transformation $\mathscr{V}^*$ can be viewed as a linear map between the dual spaces

$$\mathscr{V}^* : \mathbb{R}^{S*} \longrightarrow \mathbb{R}^{J*}$$

which associates with each state price vector, a vector of security prices. The relation between the quantity spaces $(\mathbb{R}^J, \mathbb{R}^S)$, the price spaces $(\mathbb{R}^{J*}, \mathbb{R}^{S*})$ and the pair of adjoint transformations $(\mathscr{V}, \mathscr{V}^*)$ is shown in Figure 13.1.

Many of the properties studied in Sections 9–11 are a consequence of the following relation between the linear transformation $\mathscr{V}$ and its adjoint $\mathscr{V}^*$. Since the above remark shows that a finite-dimensional vector space $\mathbb{R}^S$ (or $\mathbb{R}^J$) can be identified with its dual $\mathbb{R}^{S*}$ (or $\mathbb{R}^{J*}$), to simplify notation we revert to the standard convention of omitting the star when referring to a dual space.

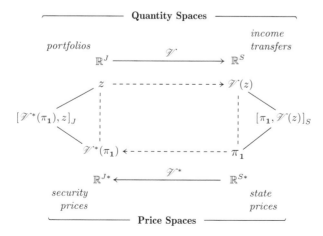

Figure 13.1 The adjoint transformations.

13.1 Proposition (Properties of $\mathscr{V}$ and $\mathscr{V}^*$):   *Let $\mathscr{V}$ and $\mathscr{V}^*$ be a pair of adjoint transformations, $\mathscr{V} : \mathbb{R}^J \longrightarrow \mathbb{R}^S$, $\mathscr{V}^* : \mathbb{R}^S \longrightarrow \mathbb{R}^J$. Then*

(i) *$\mathscr{V}$ is injective $\Longleftrightarrow$ $\mathscr{V}^*$ is surjective*
(ii) *$\mathscr{V}$ is surjective $\Longleftrightarrow$ $\mathscr{V}^*$ is injective.*

PROOF: The equality

$$[\mathscr{V}^*(\pi_1), z]_J = [\pi_1, \mathscr{V}(z)]_S, \quad \forall z \in \mathbb{R}^J, \quad \forall \pi_1 \in \mathbb{R}^S$$

implies that $(\mathscr{V}^*)^* = \mathscr{V}$. Thus property (ii) follows from property (i) when $\mathscr{V}$ is replaced by $\mathscr{V}^*$ and $\mathscr{V}^*$ by $\mathscr{V}^{**} = \mathscr{V}$. It thus suffices to prove (i).

A linear transformation $\mathscr{V} : \mathbb{R}^J \longrightarrow \mathbb{R}^S$ has two natural sets associated with it in the domain and the range. The *kernel* (or *null space*) of $\mathscr{V}$, denoted by ker $\mathscr{V}$, is the subset of the domain defined by

$$\ker \mathscr{V} = \left\{ z \in \mathbb{R}^J \mid \mathscr{V}(z) = 0 \right\}$$

The *image* of $\mathscr{V}$, denoted by Im $\mathscr{V}$, is the subset of the range defined by

$$\text{Im } \mathscr{V} = \left\{ \tau_1 \in \mathbb{R}^S \mid \tau_1 = \mathscr{V}(z), \quad z \in \mathbb{R}^J \right\}$$

Both of these sets are linear subspaces. $\mathscr{V}$ is injective if and only if ker $\mathscr{V} = \{0\}$ and surjective if and only if Im $\mathscr{V} = \mathbb{R}^S$.

Property (i) follows from the following relation between the kernel of $\mathscr{V}$ and the image of $\mathscr{V}^*$

$$\ker \mathscr{V} = (\text{Im } \mathscr{V}^*)^\perp \tag{1}$$

$\mathscr{V}$ is injective $\Longleftrightarrow$ ker $\mathscr{V} = \{0\} \Longleftrightarrow (\text{Im } \mathscr{V}^*)^\perp = \{0\} \Longleftrightarrow \text{Im } \mathscr{V}^* = \mathbb{R}^J \Longleftrightarrow$ $\mathscr{V}^*$ is surjective.

(1) is readily established: $z \in \ker \mathscr{V} \Longleftrightarrow \mathscr{V}(z) = 0 \Longleftrightarrow [\pi_1, \mathscr{V}(z)]_S = 0,$ $\forall \pi_1 \in \mathbb{R}^S \Longleftrightarrow [\mathscr{V}^*(\pi_1), z]_J = 0, \ \forall \pi_1 \in \mathbb{R}^S \Longleftrightarrow z \in (\text{Im } \mathscr{V}^*)^\perp. \ \square$

The behavioral equations (9.19) of agent i in a financial market equilibrium lead to the pair of equations

$$\bar{\tau}_1^i = V \bar{z}^i \tag{2}$$
$$\bar{q}^T = V^T \bar{\pi}_1^{iT} \tag{3}$$

where the latter equation is equivalent to $\bar{q} = \bar{\pi}_1^i V$. (2) and (3) constitute a pair of adjoint equations

$$\bar{\tau}_1^i = \mathscr{V}(\bar{z}^i) \tag{2$'$}$$
$$\bar{q} = \mathscr{V}^*(\bar{\pi}_1^i) \tag{3$'$}$$

$\mathcal{V}$ *injective* implies that, for any date 1 income stream τ_1 lying in the marketed subspace $\mathrm{Im}\,\mathcal{V} = \langle V \rangle$, there is a unique portfolio $z \in \mathbb{R}^J$ generating this income stream: $\tau_1 = \mathcal{V}(z)$. As shown in Section 11, this condition is necessary to obtain well-defined demand functions for the securities. In economic terms assuming that $\mathcal{V}$ is injective is not a restrictive condition: the injectivity of $\mathcal{V}$ is equivalent to the property that the payoffs on the J basic securities, which form the starting point of the analysis, are linearly independent; thus the injectivity of $\mathcal{V}$ amounts to assuming that none of the J basic securities, whose payoffs are given by the J columns of the matrix V, is redundant—a condition which can always be satisfied by a suitable initial choice of basic securities.

If in addition $\mathcal{V}$ is surjective (so that $J = \mathrm{rank}\, V = S$) then $\mathcal{V}$ is both injective and surjective and is hence an isomorphism of $\mathbb{R}^S$; thus every date 1 income stream $\tau_1 \in \mathbb{R}^S$ has associated with it a unique portfolio $z \in \mathbb{R}^J$ and conversely. In this case the financial markets are complete and agents are not constrained in their ability to redistribute income across the states at date 1. By Proposition 13.1, $\mathcal{V}^*$ is also an isomorphism of $\mathbb{R}^S$: every security price $q \in \mathbb{R}^J$ has associated with it a unique state price $\pi_1 \in \mathbb{R}^S$ and conversely. This latter property accounts for the equalization of agents' present-value vectors and leads to the Pareto optimality of any financial market equilibrium when markets are complete.

If $\mathcal{V}$ is not surjective so that $J = \mathrm{rank}\, V < S$, then agents are constrained to date 1 income streams which lie in a strict subspace $\mathrm{Im}\,\mathcal{V}$ of $\mathbb{R}^S$. In this case the financial markets are incomplete. By Proposition 13.1 (ii), $\mathcal{V}^*$ is not injective: thus equation (3′) does not imply equalization of the present-value vectors of the agents. This leads to the Pareto inefficiency of any financial market equilibrium for most economies. The requirement that there be no arbitrage opportunities in an FM equilibrium implies that we are only interested in a subset Q of security prices $q \in \mathbb{R}^J$—those that lie in the image of the set of strictly positive state prices $\mathbb{R}^S_{++}$ under $\mathcal{V}^*$. The injectivity of $\mathcal{V}$ implies that $\mathcal{V}^*$ is surjective (by Proposition 13.1(i)). The surjectivity of $\mathcal{V}^*$ ensures that the set of no-arbitrage security prices Q is an open subset of $\mathbb{R}^J$—a property which is essential for the local analysis of equilibria in the proof of Theorem 11.6.

When markets are incomplete, FM equilibrium allocations are typically inefficient. Such allocations are however constrained efficient—that is, they are efficient relative to reallocations lying in the marketed subspace $\mathrm{Im}\,\mathcal{V} = \langle V \rangle$. By Proposition 12.4, the condition which characterizes constrained Pareto optimality can be expressed in terms of the adjoint operator $\mathcal{V}^*$ as

$$\mathcal{V}^*(\bar{\pi}_1^1) = \cdots = \mathcal{V}^*(\bar{\pi}_1^I) \tag{4}$$

As shown in Corollary 12.6, (4) implies that the present-value vectors $\bar{\pi}_1^i$ of agents coincide when projected onto the marketed subspace $\operatorname{Im} \mathscr{V} = \langle V \rangle$.

An abstract approach which explains this property can be presented as follows. When a linear map is not an isomorphism, there is a canonical way of restricting the domain and the range so as to induce an isomorphism. The original map can be recovered by composing the isomorphism with an appropriate embedding and projection.

Let us show how this approach can be applied to the two maps $\mathscr{V}$ and $\mathscr{V}^*$. *When the financial markets are incomplete, $\mathscr{V}$ is injective but not surjective.* It is clear that by restricting the range of $\mathscr{V}$ to its image ($\operatorname{Im} \mathscr{V} = \langle V \rangle$), we obtain a map $\widetilde{\mathscr{V}} : \mathbb{R}^J \longrightarrow \operatorname{Im} \mathscr{V}$ which is an isomorphism. To recover the map $\mathscr{V}$ from $\widetilde{\mathscr{V}}$ it suffices to compose $\widetilde{\mathscr{V}}$ with the natural embedding ι of $\operatorname{Im} \mathscr{V}$ into $\mathbb{R}^S$:

$$\mathbb{R}^J \xrightarrow{\ \widetilde{\mathscr{V}}\ } \operatorname{Im} \mathscr{V} \xrightarrow{\ \iota\ } \mathbb{R}^S \tag{5}$$

When the financial markets are incomplete, $\mathscr{V}^*$ is surjective but not injective. $\mathscr{V}^*$ can be made injective by placing elements of $\mathbb{R}^S$ which have the same image under $\mathscr{V}^*$ into an equivalence class. This leads to a map $\widetilde{\mathscr{V}}^*$ whose domain is the collection of equivalence classes (the *quotient space*) induced in this way. Since $\mathscr{V}^*$ is a linear map, two elements of $\mathbb{R}^S$ have the same image under $\mathscr{V}^*$ if their difference lies in the kernel of $\mathscr{V}^*$. Thus the equivalence relation defined by

$$\pi_1 \simeq \pi_1' \quad \text{if and only if} \quad \mathscr{V}^*(\pi_1) = \mathscr{V}^*(\pi_1')$$

is the same as the equivalence relation defined by

$$\pi_1 \simeq \pi_1' \quad \text{if and only if} \quad \pi_1 - \pi_1' \in \ker \mathscr{V}^* \tag{6}$$

For $\pi_1 \in \mathbb{R}^S$ let $\phi(\pi_1) = \{\pi_1' \in \mathbb{R}^S \mid \pi_1' \simeq \pi_1\}$ denote the equivalence class defined by the equivalence relation (6). Then ϕ defines the projection of $\mathbb{R}^S$ onto the *quotient space* $\mathbb{R}^S / \ker \mathscr{V}^*$. To recover the map $\mathscr{V}^*$ from the map $\widetilde{\mathscr{V}}^*$ it suffices to compose ϕ and $\widetilde{\mathscr{V}}^*$:

$$\mathbb{R}^J \xleftarrow{\ \widetilde{\mathscr{V}}^*\ } \mathbb{R}^S / \ker \mathscr{V}^* \xleftarrow{\ \phi\ } \mathbb{R}^S \tag{7}$$

Consider the orthogonal decomposition of $\mathbb{R}^S$

$$\mathbb{R}^S = \ker \mathscr{V}^* \oplus (\ker \mathscr{V}^*)^\perp$$

This decomposition induces a map which is the orthogonal projection of $\mathbb{R}^S$ onto $(\ker \mathscr{V}^*)^\perp$ (the reader unfamiliar with this map should consult Section 14). Under this map the subspace $\ker \mathscr{V}^*$ is collapsed to the vector 0. Since every element of $\ker \mathscr{V}^*$ is identified with 0, projecting $\mathbb{R}^S$ onto $(\ker \mathscr{V}^*)^\perp$ is equivalent to the forming the quotient space $\mathbb{R}^S/\ker \mathscr{V}^*$. Thus we obtain the isomorphism

$$\mathbb{R}^S/\ker \mathscr{V}^* \cong (\ker \mathscr{V}^*)^\perp \tag{8}$$

(5), (7) and (8) can be combined to give the diagram

$$
\begin{array}{ccc}
& \mathscr{V} & \\
\mathbb{R}^J \xrightarrow{\ \widetilde{\mathscr{V}}\ } & \operatorname{Im}\mathscr{V} & \xrightarrow{\ \iota\ } \mathbb{R}^S \\
& \Big\downarrow \text{Id} & \\
\mathbb{R}^J \xleftarrow{\ \widetilde{\mathscr{V}^*}\ } & \mathbb{R}^S/\ker \mathscr{V}^* & \xleftarrow{\ \phi\ } \mathbb{R}^S \\
& \mathscr{V}^* &
\end{array}
\tag{9}
$$

Since $\mathscr{V}$ and $\mathscr{V}^*$ are adjoint maps

$$(\ker \mathscr{V}^*)^\perp = \operatorname{Im}\mathscr{V}$$

Thus ϕ can be identified with the projection of $\mathbb{R}^S$ onto $\operatorname{Im}\mathscr{V}$.

Corollary 12.6 follows from the construction summarized in (9). Equation (3′) implies that in a financial market equilibrium all the present-value vectors $(\bar{\pi}_1^i,\ i = 1, \ldots, I)$ of the agents have the same image under $\mathscr{V}^*$. Thus the vectors $(\bar{\pi}_1^i,\ i = 1, \ldots, I)$ all lie in the same equivalence class of $\mathbb{R}^S/\ker \mathscr{V}^*$. Equivalently, since $\widetilde{\mathscr{V}^*}$ is an isomorphism, given $\bar{q}$ there exists a unique vector $\bar{\pi}_V \in (\ker \mathscr{V}^*)^\perp = \operatorname{Im}\mathscr{V}$ such that

$$\phi(\bar{\pi}_1^i) = \bar{\pi}_V, \quad i = 1, \ldots, I$$

Thus (3′) implies that each of the present-value vectors $\bar{\pi}_1^i$ ($i = 1, \ldots, I$) when projected onto the marketed subspace $\operatorname{Im}\mathscr{V}$, gives the same vector $\bar{\pi}_V$.

APPENDIX

Vector Field in $\mathbb{R}^n$

The simplest notion of a vector field is obtained by considering a vector-valued function $v : \mathbb{R}^n \longrightarrow \mathbb{R}^n$ which assigns to each vector $x = (x_1, \ldots, x_n) \in \mathbb{R}^n$, the vector

$$v(x) = (v_1(x_1, \ldots, x_n), \ldots, v_n(x_1, \ldots, x_n)) \in \mathbb{R}^n$$

When $n = 2$ such a vector-valued function can be visualized by associating with each vector x in the plane the vector $v(x)$ as shown in Figure A2.1(a). A useful way of studying a vector field v is to consider the flow induced by v in $\mathbb{R}^n$, that is, the paths $x(t) = x(t; x_0)$ in $\mathbb{R}^n$ which satisfy $\dot{x} = \frac{dx(t)}{dt} = v(x)$ and $x(0) = x_0$ with $x_0 \in \mathbb{R}^n$. The path $\{x(t; x_0), t \geq 0\}$ is the curve in $\mathbb{R}^n$ obtained by starting at x_0 when $t = 0$ and moving with velocity $\dot{x} = v(x)$ at each point x of the path (see Figure A2.1(b)). A *zero* of the vector field v is a point $\bar{x}$ in $\mathbb{R}^n$ such that $v(\bar{x}) = 0$: such a point is also called a *stationary point* or an *equilibrium point* of the flow $\dot{x} = v(x)$, since any path starting at $x_0 = \bar{x}$ remains indefinitely at $\bar{x}$ (i.e. $x(t; \bar{x}) = \bar{x}$, for all $t \geq 0$).

Continuous vector fields have some remarkable properties which express the idea that there is a global logic to the way the individual vectors of the field fit together. One instance of such a global logic is the following. Suppose a continuous vector field is defined on some bounded region of $\mathbb{R}^n$ such as the disc of radius r, $D^n = \left\{ x \in \mathbb{R}^n \mid \sum_{j=1}^n x_j^2 \leq r^2 \right\}$ and suppose that all that is known about f is its behavior on the *boundary of the disc*, $\partial D^n = \left\{ x \in \mathbb{R}^n \mid \sum_{j=1}^n x_j^2 = r^2 \right\}$. Is it possible, knowing only the boundary behavior of v, to deduce that there is a zero of v inside the disc? There is a very intuitive boundary condition which gives just such a result, which can be expressed as follows: *if v is a continuous vector field on the disc D^n which sat-*

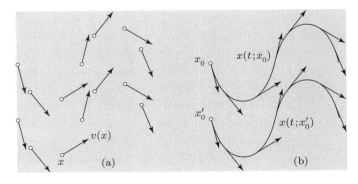

Figure A2.1 (a) A vector field v in $\mathbb{R}^2$: (b) the flow induced by v.

isfies $v(x)x \leq 0$ *for each* x *on the boundary* ∂D^n *then there exists an* $\bar{x}$ *in* D^n *such that* $v(\bar{x}) = 0$. This theorem (often referred to as Kronecker's theorem) is the analogue for a vector field on the disc of Theorem 7.5. The condition $v(x)x < 0$ implies that $v(x)$ makes an obtuse angle with x and thus points inward at the boundary point x: a vector field which satisfies this condition (with the weak inequality) at each boundary point is said to be *inward pointing* (see Figure A2.2). When $n = 1$, $D^1 = [-r, r]$ and the strict inward-pointing condition reduces to $v(-r) > 0$ and $v(r) < 0$, so that the theorem is just the Intermediate Value Theorem.

Vector Field on a Surface in $\mathbb{R}^n$

A more subtle notion of a vector field is obtained by considering a vector field on a surface in $\mathbb{R}^n$. Let M be a smooth $(n-1)$-dimensional surface in $\mathbb{R}^n$—this is a notion which will be made precise in Volume 2—but here we can think of it geometrically as a surface which (like the sphere $\mathscr{S}^{n-1}$) can be approximated at each point $x \in M$ by an $(n-1)$-dimensional *tangent hyperplane* $\mathcal{T}_x M$. This tangent hyperplane is the translation to x of an $(n-1)$-dimensional linear subspace (hyperplane passing through the origin) which is called the *tangent space* at x and is denoted by $T_x M$: thus $\mathcal{T}_x M = x + T_x M$ (see Figure A2.3). For example when M is the $(n-1)$-dimensional sphere $\mathscr{S}^{n-1} = \{x \in \mathbb{R}^n \mid \sum_{j=1}^{n} x_j^2 = r^2\}$ of radius r then the tangent space at $x \in \mathscr{S}^{n-1}$ is the $(n-1)$-dimensional subspace orthogonal to x, $T_x \mathscr{S}^{n-1} = \{z \in \mathbb{R}^n \mid xz = 0\}$ and the tangent hyperplane is the translation to x of $T_x \mathscr{S}^{n-1}$.

A *vector field* on M is a map $v : M \longrightarrow \mathbb{R}^n$ such that $v(x) \in T_x M$ for each $x \in M$. It is usually "visualized" by locating the vector $v(x)$ in the tangent hyperplane $\mathcal{T}_x M$. As in the previous case of a vector field in $\mathbb{R}^n$, the vector field v induces a flow—in this case a flow which stays on the surface M. A

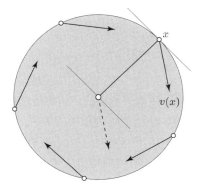

Figure A2.2   Inward-pointing condition for vector field on the disc D^2.

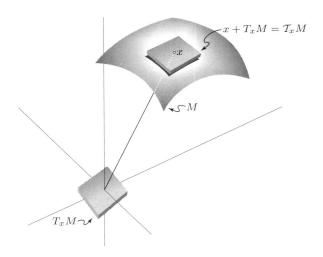

Figure A2.3   Tangent hyperplane $\mathcal{T}_x M$ and tangent space $T_x M$ at $x \in M$.

path $x(t; x_0)$ starting at x_0 in M and satisfying $\dot{x} = dx(t)/dt = v(x)$ stays on M since the velocity vector $\dot{x}$ is tangent to M at x.

In Section 7 it was shown that the aggregate excess demand function $Z(\pi)$ for a system of contingent markets with price vector π defines a continuous vector field on the positive (unit) sphere $\mathscr{S}_{++}^{n-1}$. The boundary behavior of excess demand when prices tend to zero implies that the vector field is inward pointing at the boundary $\partial \mathscr{S}_{+}^{n-1}$; more accurately, there is an equivalent vector field $\widetilde{Z}$ constructed in the next subsection, which has the same zeros as Z and is inward pointing on the boundary. For the present discussion we commit the slight abuse of assimilating Z and $\widetilde{Z}$ and consider Z as (strictly) inward pointing i.e. $Z_j(\pi) > 0$ if $\pi_j = 0$. Figure A2.4(a) shows the boundary behavior of an inward-pointing vector field Z on $\mathscr{S}_{+}^2$ ($n = 3$): at A, $\pi_0 = 0$ and $Z_0 > 0$; at B, $\pi_1 = 0$ and $Z_1 > 0$; at C, $\pi_2 = 0$ and $Z_2 > 0$; at D, $\pi_0 = \pi_1 = 0$ and $Z_0 > 0$, $Z_1 > 0$.

Theorem 7.5 asserts that *a continuous vector field on the non-negative sphere $\mathscr{S}_{+}^{n-1}$ which points inward at the boundary has a zero on the interior of $\mathscr{S}_{+}^{n-1}$*. This theorem is essentially equivalent to Kronecker's theorem on the disc stated above. The geometric intuition is clear: the non-negative sphere $\mathscr{S}_{+}^{n-1}$ in $\mathbb{R}^n$ can be projected onto $\mathbb{R}^{n-1}$ and then stretched out so as to coincide with the $(n-1)$-dimensional disc D^{n-1}; in the process the inward-pointing vector field v on $\mathscr{S}_{+}^{n-1}$ is transformed into an inward-pointing vector field v' on D^{n-1}. The reason for posing the existence problem on the non-negative sphere is that if the prices are normalized to be on the sphere, then Walras' Law implies directly that the aggregate excess demand function defines a vector field on

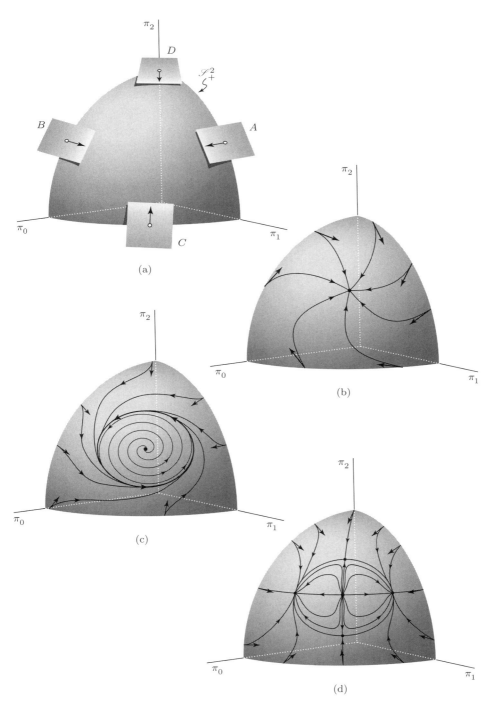

Figure A2.4 (a) Inward-pointing vectors at the boundary of $\mathscr{S}_+^2$: (b)–(d) flows associated with inward-pointing vector fields on $\mathscr{S}_+^2$.

$\mathscr{S}_+^{n-1}$: there is no need to transform the excess demand function into some appropriate map whose zero gives an equilibrium.

These two inward-pointing vector field theorems (on the non-negative sphere or on the disc) are in turn equivalent to *Brouwer's fixed-point theorem*. Brouwer's theorem asserts that *a continuous map ϕ from a compact convex subset of $\mathbb{R}^n$ (for example the disc D^n) into itself, has a fixed point*. To see the intuition for the relation between the fixed-point property and the existence of a zero for an inward-pointing vector field, note that if ϕ is a map from the disc D^n into itself then $v(x) = \phi(x) - x$ defines an inward-pointing vector field on D^n: the fixed points of ϕ are the zeros of v.

We have seen that when $n = 2$, the inward-pointing vector field theorem is equivalent to the Intermediate Value Theorem, but this might suggest that the result is rather obvious. The case $n = 3$ gives a much better feel for its subtlety. Imagine following the flow $\dot{\pi} = Z(\pi)$ induced by the vector field Z on the two-dimensional non-negative sphere $\mathscr{S}_+^2$ shown in Figure A2.4. At first sight it would seem that Figure A2.4(b) explains the result: a flow which flows inward across the boundary of $\mathscr{S}_+^2$ must "disappear" somewhere and this happens at a point $\bar{\pi}$ where $Z(\bar{\pi}) = 0$. This nice behavior of the flow (illustrated in A2.4(b)) is however far from being the only one possible. Inward-pointing flows on $\mathscr{S}_+^2$ (or equivalently on D^2) have been the subject of extensive analysis, and Figures A2.4(c) and (d) depict prototypes of more complicated behavior. As illustrated in (c), the flow can "disappear" into a closed orbit: however it can be shown that the region inside a closed orbit always contains an equilibrium point. (d) shows a typical example with multiple equilibria. In higher dimensions the behavior of flows is much more complicated; Theorem 7.5 asserts that all flows on $\mathscr{S}_+^{n-1}$ which flow inward across the boundary—no matter how complicated their limit sets—always have at least one equilibrium point.[1]

Studying the flow $\dot{\pi} = Z(\pi)$ induced by an economy's aggregate excess demand function gives more than just a physical representation of excess demand as a vector field. It can be used as an approach to *computing equilibria* once the excess demand function of an economy is known. The approach is based on a classical procedure for adjusting prices: beginning with some initial vector of prices $\pi(0)$, the prices of goods for which demand exceeds supply are increased $(Z_j > 0 \Rightarrow d\pi_j/dt > 0)$ while the prices of goods for which demand falls short of supply are decreased $(Z_j < 0 \Rightarrow d\pi_j/dt < 0)$, the increase or decrease in

---

[1] An interesting way of appreciating what is involved in Theorem 7.5 is to prove it when $n = 3$ using *dynamical systems* arguments, the so-called Poincaré-Bendixon techniques. The first step is to show that a limit set of a flow which flows inward across the boundary $\partial\mathscr{S}_+^2$ is either a closed orbit or the union of equilibrium points and paths which converge to equilibrium points as $t \to \pm\infty$. An additional argument then shows that a closed orbit has the property that its enclosed region always contains an equilibrium point (see Hirsch-Smale (1974, Chapter 11)).

price being proportional to the magnitude of excess demand. This approach works nicely in cases such as (b) and (d) in Figure A2.4, but calls for much more ingenuity in cases such as (c).

Constructing the Equivalent Vector Field $\widetilde{Z}$

We now show how to construct the vector field $\widetilde{Z}$ referred to in the proof of Theorem 7.4. $\widetilde{Z}$ has the same zeros as Z, is defined on all of $\mathscr{S}_{+}^{n-1}$ and points inward on the boundary. It is constructed by first finding a subset K of $\mathscr{S}_{+}^{n-1}$ (defined by (1) below) which contains all the zeros of Z. A continuous function α is then defined which (roughly speaking) has weight 1 on K and is zero outside an open set containing K (see (2)). $\widetilde{Z}$ (defined by (4)) is then constructed by taking a weighted combination of the original vector field Z and a simple vector field Z^* (defined by (3)) which points inward at the boundary, the weights being given by the function α.

A2.1. Proposition (Inward-Pointing Vector Field Equivalent to Z):   *If $Z :$ $\mathscr{S}_{++}^{n-1} \longrightarrow \mathbb{R}^n$ is an aggregate excess demand function satisfying properties* (i)′–(v)′ *in the proof of Theorem 7.4, then there exists a continuous inward-pointing vector field $\widetilde{Z} : \mathscr{S}_{+}^{n-1} \longrightarrow \mathbb{R}^n$ having the same zeros as Z,*

$$\widetilde{Z}(\pi) = 0 \quad \Longleftrightarrow \quad Z(\pi) = 0$$

PROOF: It is convenient to index the goods $j = 1, \ldots, n$ rather than $s = 0, 1, \ldots, S$. Consider the sets

$$N_j = \left\{ \pi \in \mathscr{S}_{++}^{n-1} \;\middle|\; Z_j(\pi) > 0, \quad \pi_j < \frac{1}{\sqrt{n}} \right\}$$

From the definition of N_j, Z cannot have a zero in N_j, so the zeros of Z must lie in the set

$$K = \mathscr{S}_{++}^{n-1} \setminus \cup_{j=1}^{n} N_j \tag{1}$$

Let us show that K is closed as a subset of $\mathscr{S}_{+}^{n-1}$. Let $\pi^\nu \in K$ be a sequence such that $\pi^\nu \to \pi$. If $\pi \in \partial \mathscr{S}_{+}^{n-1}$, let $J = \left\{ j \in \{1, \ldots, n\} \;\middle|\; \pi_j = 0 \right\}$. For ν sufficiently large, $\pi_j^\nu < 1/n$ for $j \in J$ and since $\pi^\nu \notin \cup_{j=1}^{n} N_j$, $Z_j(\pi^\nu) \leq 0$, $j \in J$. But then $\| Z(\pi^\nu) \|$ cannot tend to infinity since $Z_j(\pi^\nu)$ is bounded below by (i)′ for all $j = 1, \ldots, n$ and for $j \notin J$ is bounded above by Walras' Law (iv)′, contradicting the boundary behavior (v)′. Thus $\pi \in \mathscr{S}_{++}^{n-1}$. Since π^ν does not belong to $\cup_{j=1}^{n} N_j$ which is open, π cannot belong to this set either so that $\pi \in K$ and K is closed.

Let U be an open neighborhood of K in $\mathscr{S}_{++}^{n-1}$ such that $K \subset U \subset \bar{U} \subset \mathscr{S}_{++}^{n-1}$. By a classical construction (given for completeness in A2.2) there exists a continuous function $\alpha : \mathscr{S}_{+}^{n-1} \longrightarrow [0,1]$ such that

$$\alpha(\pi) = \begin{cases} 1 & \text{if } \pi \in K \\ 0 & \text{if } \pi \notin U \end{cases} \tag{2}$$

Let $\pi^* = (1/\sqrt{n}, \dots, 1/\sqrt{n}) \in \mathscr{S}_{++}^{n-1}$ and define the vector field Z^* on $\mathscr{S}_{+}^{n-1}$ by

$$Z^*(\pi) = \frac{\pi^*}{\pi^* \pi} - \pi \tag{3}$$

Z^* is inward pointing on the boundary $\partial \mathscr{S}_{+}^{n-1}$ since $\pi_j = 0$ implies $Z_j^*(\pi) = \pi_j^*/(\pi^* \pi) > 0$. It follows that the vector field $\widetilde{Z}$ on $\mathscr{S}_{+}^{n-1}$ defined by

$$\widetilde{Z}(\pi) = \alpha(\pi) Z(\pi) + (1 - \alpha(\pi)) Z^*(\pi) \tag{4}$$

(with the convention $\alpha(\pi) Z(\pi) = 0$ if $\pi \in \partial \mathscr{S}_{+}^{n-1}$) is continuous and is inward pointing on the boundary $\partial \mathscr{S}_{+}^{n-1}$. It remains to show that $\widetilde{Z}(\pi) = 0$ if and only if $Z(\pi) = 0$. Suppose $Z(\pi) = 0$. Then $\pi \in K \Rightarrow \alpha(\pi) = 1 \Rightarrow \widetilde{Z}(\pi) = 0$. Conversely suppose $\widetilde{Z}(\pi) = 0$, then three cases are possible: (a) $\pi \in K$, (b) $\pi \in N_j$ for some j, (c) $\pi \in \partial \mathscr{S}_{+}^{n-1}$. (a) $\Rightarrow \alpha(\pi) = 1 \Rightarrow Z(\pi) = 0$. Let us show that (b) is impossible. $\pi \in N_j \Rightarrow Z_j(\pi) > 0$, $\pi_j < 1/\sqrt{n}$ so that $\alpha_j(\pi) Z_j(\pi) \geq 0$. Since $\pi, \pi^* \in \mathscr{S}_{+}^{n-1}$, $\pi \pi^* \leq 1$ so that $Z_j^*(\pi) = (1/(\pi^* \pi)) 1/\sqrt{n} - \pi_j > 0$. Thus $\pi \in N_j \Rightarrow \widetilde{Z}_j(\pi) > 0$. (c) is also impossible since $\pi \in \partial \mathscr{S}_{+}^{n-1} \Rightarrow \pi_j = 0$ for some $j \Rightarrow Z_j^*(\pi) > 0 \Rightarrow \widetilde{Z}_j(\pi) > 0$, a contradiction. $\square$

A2.2 Construction of function α: We now show how to construct the function α in (2). For any $x = (x_1, \dots, x_n) \in \mathbb{R}^n$ let $\hat{x} = (x_1, \dots, x_{n-1})$ be the vector in $\mathbb{R}^{n-1}$ which omits the last component of x. The map which assigns to each vector $x \in \mathbb{R}^n$ the vector $\hat{x} \in \mathbb{R}^{n-1}$, when restricted to $\mathscr{S}_{+}^{n-1}$ defines a projection $\Pi : \mathscr{S}_{+}^{n-1} \longrightarrow \mathbb{R}^{n-1}$

$$\Pi(x) = \hat{x} = (x_1, \dots, x_{n-1}), \quad \forall x \in \mathscr{S}_{+}^{n-1}$$

The image of $\mathscr{S}_{+}^{n-1}$ under Π is the positive part of the closed $(n-1)$-dimensional unit ball

$$\Pi(\mathscr{S}_{+}^{n-1}) = \left\{ y \in \mathbb{R}_{+}^{n-1} \mid \|y\| \leq 1 \right\} = B_{+}^{n-1}(0,1)$$

and the map $\phi : B_{+}^{n-1}(0,1) \longrightarrow \mathscr{S}_{+}^{n-1}$ defined by

$$\phi(y_1, \dots, y_{n-1}) = (y_1, \dots, y_{n-1}, 1 - y_1^2 - \dots - y_{n-1}^2)$$

is the inverse of Π. $\Pi(K) = E$ is compact and $\Pi(U)$ is open in $B_+^{n-1}(0,1)$ and in $\mathbb{R}^{n-1}$ and $F = B_+^{n-1}(0,1) \setminus \Pi(U)$ is closed in $B_+^{n-1}(0,1)$ and in $\mathbb{R}^{n-1}$. If we can prove that there exists a continuous function $\epsilon : \mathbb{R}^{n-1} \longrightarrow \mathbb{R}$ with the property

$$\epsilon(y) = \begin{cases} 1 & \text{if } y \in E \\ 0 & \text{if } y \in F \end{cases} \tag{5}$$

then the composite map $\alpha = \epsilon \circ \Pi : \mathscr{S}_+^{n-1} \longrightarrow [0,1]$

$$\alpha(x) = \epsilon\left(\Pi(x)\right), \quad \forall x \in \mathscr{S}_+^{n-1}$$

is continuous and satisfies (2). The existence of the required function α is thus a consequence of the following lemma.

A2.3 Lemma: *Let E and F be subsets of $\mathbb{R}^{n-1}$ with E compact, F closed and $E \cap F = \emptyset$. Then there exists a continuous function $\epsilon : \mathbb{R}^{n-1} \longrightarrow [0,1]$ satisfying (5).*

PROOF: For all $a, b, \in, \mathbb{R}$ with $0 \leq a < b$, consider the piecewise linear function $f_{ab} : \mathbb{R}_+ \longrightarrow [0,1]$ defined by

$$f_{ab}(t) = \begin{cases} 1, & \text{if } t \in [0,a] \\ 1 - \dfrac{t-a}{b-a}, & \text{if } t \in [a,b] \\ 0, & \text{if } t \in [b, \infty) \end{cases}$$

Let $B(\bar{y}, a)$ and $B(\bar{y}, b)$ denote concentric balls in $\mathbb{R}^{n-1}$ of radius $0 < a < b$ centered at $\bar{y}$. Then the function $\psi : \mathbb{R}^{n-1} \longrightarrow [0,1]$ defined by

$$\psi(y) = f_{ab}(\|y - \bar{y}\|), \quad \forall y \in \mathbb{R}^{n-1}$$

is continuous and satisfies $\psi(y) = 1$, $\forall y \in B(\bar{y}, a)$, and $\psi(y) = 0$, $\forall y \notin B(\bar{y}, b)$.

Since E is compact it can be covered by a finite number of open balls B_k, $k = 1, \ldots, m$. Since the complement of F is open, B_k can be chosen so that $B_k \cap F = \emptyset$, $k = 1, \ldots, m$. Furthermore, by the property of an open covering, for each $k = 1, \ldots, m$ there exists a ball $\widetilde{B}_k$ of slightly smaller radius and the same center as B_k such that $E \subset \bigcup_{k=1}^m \widetilde{B}_k$. By the construction given above, there exist functions $\psi_k : \mathbb{R}^{n-1} \longrightarrow [0,1]$, $k = 1, \ldots, m$ which are continuous and satisfy $\psi_k(y) = 1$, $\forall y \in \widetilde{B}_k$ and $\psi_k(y) = 0$, $\forall y \notin B_k$. The function $\epsilon : \mathbb{R}^{n-1} \longrightarrow [0,1]$ defined by

$$\epsilon(y) = 1 - \prod_{k=1}^m \left(1 - \psi_k(y)\right)$$

is continuous and satisfies (5). $\square$

Separation of Convex Sets

The most basic result of convex analysis is the theorem which asserts that disjoint convex sets can be separated by a hyperplane. Under the stronger hypothesis that one of the sets is compact and the other closed, the separation is strict. This latter property is the assertion of Theorem 9.4; the former and more general property will be used in Chapter 6. It is convenient to prove both results simultaneously using the following two lemmas.

A2.4 Lemma (Projection on Convex Set): *Let C be a nonempty closed subset of $\mathbb{R}^n$. If $x \notin C$, then there exists a vector $y \in C$ which is closest to x*

$$\|x - y\| = \min\{\|z - x\| \mid z \in C\}$$

If in addition C is convex, then the vector y is unique. y is called the projection of x onto C and is denoted by $y = \Pi_C(x)$.

PROOF: Pick any $z \in C$ and consider the ball $B(x, a)$ of radius $a = \|z - x\|$ around x. Since $C \cap B(x, a)$ is compact, the distance function $d_x(y) = \|y - x\|$ attains a minimum and it is clearly sufficient to consider d_x restricted to this set.

Suppose that C is convex and there exists $y' \in C$ with $\|x - y'\| = \|x - y\|$ and $y \neq y'$ then

$$\|y - x\|^2 = \left\|y - \tfrac{1}{2}(y + y')\right\|^2 + \left\|x - \tfrac{1}{2}(y + y')\right\|^2 > \left\|x - \tfrac{1}{2}(y + y')\right\|^2 \quad (6)$$

(see Figure A2.5) contradicting the fact that y is closest to x. $\square$

A2.5 Lemma (Separation of Point and Convex Set):   *Let C be a nonempty closed convex subset of $\mathbb{R}^n$ and let $x \notin C$, y denoting the projection of x onto C. The hyperplane H_π^y orthogonal to $\pi = x - y$ which passes through y strictly separates x and C, namely*

$$\left.\begin{array}{l} \pi(z - y) \leq 0, \quad \forall z \in C \\ \pi(x - y) > 0 \end{array}\right\} \iff \pi z \leq \pi y < \pi x, \quad \forall z \in C$$

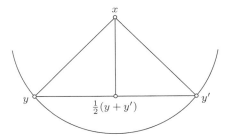

Figure A2.5   Geometric interpretation of inequality (6).

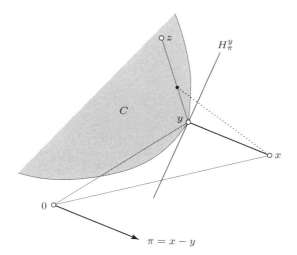

Figure A2.6   The hyperplane H_π^y orthogonal to π which passes through y separates x from the convex set C.

PROOF: For all $z \in C$, consider the function $\phi_z : [0, 1] \longrightarrow \mathbb{R}$ defined by

$$\phi_z(t) = \| x - (tz + (1 - t)y) \|^2$$

Since y is the projection of x onto C, ϕ_z attains its minimum on $[0, 1]$ at $t = 0$ so that $\phi_z'(0) \geq 0$, $\forall z \in C$. Since

$$\phi_z(t) = \| (x - y) + t(y - z) \|^2 = \| x - y \|^2 + 2t(x - y)(y - z) + t^2 \| y - z \|^2$$

$\phi_z'(0) = 2(x - y)(y - z)$. Thus $\pi(y - z) \geq 0$. Since $x \notin C$, $\pi(x - y) = \| x - y \|^2 > 0$ and the proof is complete. $\square$

A2.6 Theorem (Separation of Disjoint Convex Sets):

(i) *If K and M are non-empty convex subsets of $\mathbb{R}^n$ with $K \cap M = \emptyset$, then there exists $\pi \in \mathbb{R}^n$, $\pi \neq 0$, such that*

$$\sup_{x \in M} \pi x \leq \inf_{x' \in K} \pi x' \qquad (7)$$

(ii) *If in addition K is compact and M is closed, then*

$$\sup_{x \in M} \pi x < \inf_{x' \in K} \pi x' \qquad (8)$$

PROOF: The set $C = M - K = \{y \in \mathbb{R}^n \mid y = x - x', x \in M, x' \in K\}$ is non-empty and convex and $K \cap M = \emptyset$ implies $0 \notin C$. There are two cases to consider.

(a) $0 \notin \overline{C}$. By Lemma A2.5 there exists $\pi \in \mathbb{R}^n$, $\pi \neq 0$ such that $\pi z > \pi 0$, $\forall z \in \overline{C}$ and thus in particular for all $z \in C$, which implies (8). If K is compact and M is closed then $C = \overline{C}$ and thus (8) holds.

(b) $0 \in \overline{C}$. Let $\{e^1, \ldots, e^m\}$ be a maximal collection of linearly independent vectors in C. Then for all $x \in C$, $\{x, e^1, \ldots, e^m\}$ are linearly dependent so that $x = \sum_{i=1}^m \lambda_i e^i$. Let us show that for all $\alpha > 0$, $-\alpha \sum_{i=1}^m e^i \notin \overline{C}$. For suppose there exists $\alpha > 0$ such that $-\alpha \sum_{i=1}^m e^i \in \overline{C}$, then there exists a sequence $x^\nu = \sum_{i=1}^m \lambda_i^\nu e^i \in C$ such that $x^\nu \to -\alpha \sum_{i=1}^m e^i$. Since $\{e^1, \ldots, e^m\}$ are linearly independent, $\lambda_i^\nu \to -\alpha$, $i = 1, \ldots, m$, so that for sufficiently large ν, $\lambda_i^\nu < 0$, $i = 1, \ldots, m$. By the convexity of C

$$
0 = \left(\frac{1}{1 - \sum_{i=1}^m \lambda_i^\nu} \right) x^\nu - \sum_{i=1}^m \left(\frac{\lambda_i^\nu}{1 - \sum_{i=1}^m \lambda_i^\nu} \right) e^i \in C
$$

contradicting $0 \notin C$. Thus for all $k \in \mathbb{N}$, $-\frac{1}{k} \sum_{i=1}^m e^i \notin \overline{C}$. By Lemma A2.5 there exist $\pi_k \in \mathbb{R}^n$, which can be chosen with $\|\pi_k\| = 1$, such that

$$
\pi_k z < \pi_k \left(-\frac{1}{k} \sum_{i=1}^m e^i \right), \quad \forall z \in \overline{C}
$$

Picking a subsequence such that $\pi_k \to \pi$ and restricting the inequality to elements of C gives

$$
\pi z \leq 0, \quad \forall z \in C \Longleftrightarrow \pi x \leq \pi x', \quad \forall x \in M, \quad \forall x' \in K
$$

which proves (7). $\square$

Linear Surjective Maps

A2.7 Proposition (Open Property of Surjective Linear Map): *If $L : \mathbb{R}^S \longrightarrow \mathbb{R}^J$ is a surjective linear transformation, then for every open set $U \subset \mathbb{R}^S$ the image $L(U)$ is an open subset of $\mathbb{R}^J$.*

PROOF: Let $B^J(z, \epsilon)$ denote a ball in $\mathbb{R}^J$ of radius $\epsilon > 0$ around $z \in \mathbb{R}^J$ and let $B^S(y, \eta)$ denote a ball in $\mathbb{R}^S$ of radius $\eta > 0$ around $y \in \mathbb{R}^S$. Let $U \subset \mathbb{R}^S$ be an open set in $\mathbb{R}^S$ and let $\bar{z} \in L(U)$. We want to show that there exists $\epsilon > 0$ such that $B^J(\bar{z}, \epsilon) \subset L(U)$.

Since $\bar{z} \in L(U)$ there exists $\bar{y} \in U$ such that $L(\bar{y}) = \bar{z}$ and since U is open there exists $\eta > 0$ such that $B^S(\bar{y}, \eta) \subset U$. $\mathbb{R}^S$ can be written as

$$\mathbb{R}^S = \bigcup_{\lambda \geq 0} \lambda B^S(0, \eta)$$

The surjectivity of L implies

$$\mathbb{R}^J = L(\mathbb{R}^S) = L\left(\bigcup_{\lambda \geq 0} \lambda B^S(0, \eta)\right) = \bigcup_{\lambda \geq 0} L\left(\lambda B^S(0, \eta)\right)$$

By linearity of L

$$\mathbb{R}^J = \bigcup_{\lambda \geq 0} \lambda L\left(B^S(0, \eta)\right)$$

Thus there exists $\bar{\lambda} > 0$ such that

$$B^J(0, 1) \subset \bar{\lambda} L\left(B^S(0, \eta)\right)$$

which is equivalent to

$$B^J(0, \frac{1}{\bar{\lambda}}) \subset L\left(B^S(0, \eta)\right)$$

Let $\epsilon = 1/\bar{\lambda}$ then

$$B^J(\bar{z}, \epsilon) = \bar{z} + B^J(0, \epsilon) \subset L(\bar{y}) + L\left(B^S(0, \eta)\right) = L\left(B^S(\bar{y}, \eta)\right) \subset L(U) \;\square$$

Local Controllability of Gradients

A2.8 Lemma (Local Controllability of π^i):   *Let $u^i : \mathbb{R}^{S+1}_+ \longrightarrow \mathbb{R}$ be a utility function satisfying Assumption $\mathcal{U}$ and let $\bar{x}^i \in \mathbb{R}^{S+1}_{++}$. The linear map $D_{x^i}\pi^i_1(\bar{x}^i) : T_{\bar{x}^i}(I^i_{\bar{x}^i}) \longrightarrow \mathbb{R}^S$ is surjective i.e for any $d\pi_1 \in \mathbb{R}^S$ there exists a change in consumption dx^i in the tangent space $T_{\bar{x}^i}(I^i_{\bar{x}^i})$ such that to terms of first order*

$$\pi^i_1(\bar{x}^i + dx^i) = \pi^i_1(\bar{x}^i) + d\pi_1$$

PROOF: Define $\lambda^i(x^i) = \nabla u^i(x^i)$ and $\bar{\lambda}^i = \nabla u^i(\bar{x}^i)$. Then

$$\pi^i(x^i) = \frac{\lambda^i(x^i)}{\lambda^i_0(x^i)}$$

and $\pi^i(x^i) = \left(1, \pi^i_1(x^i)\right)$. Let $d\pi^i_1$ denote the differential of the map π^i_1 at $\bar{x}^i$, then $d\pi^i_1 : \mathbb{R}^{S+1} \longrightarrow \mathbb{R}^S$ so that $d\pi^i_1$ is defined on all of $\mathbb{R}^{S+1}$. The lemma asserts that this map is surjective when restricted to the subspace $T_{\bar{x}^i}(I_{\bar{x}^i}^i)$. Let $d\lambda^i = (d\lambda_0^i, d\lambda_1^i)$ denote the differential of λ^i at $\bar{x}^i$, then

$$dπ_1^i = \frac{1}{\left(\bar{\lambda}_0^i\right)^2} \left(\bar{\lambda}_0^i d\lambda_1^i - d\lambda_0^i \bar{\lambda}_1^i\right) \tag{9}$$

A change dx^i in consumption induces a change $d\lambda^i = (d\lambda_0^i, d\lambda_1^i, \ldots, d\lambda_S^i)$ in the gradient given by

$$d\lambda_s^i = \sum_{\sigma=0}^{S} \frac{\partial^2 u^i(\bar{x}^i)}{\partial x_s^i \partial x_\sigma^i} dx_\sigma^i, \quad s = 0, 1, \ldots, S \tag{10}$$

Let $dπ_1$ denote the change in the present-value vector of agent i that we want to induce by an appropriate change dx^i in his consumption restricted to lie in the tangent space $T_{\bar{x}^i}(I_{\bar{x}^i}^i)$. Let us show that if there exists a solution $(dx^i, d\lambda_0)$ of the system of linear equations

$$\begin{bmatrix} D^2 u^i(\bar{x}^i) & -\dfrac{\nabla u^i(\bar{x}^i)^T}{\bar{\lambda}_0^i} \\[2ex] -\dfrac{\nabla u^i(\bar{x}^i)}{\bar{\lambda}_0^i} & 0 \end{bmatrix} \begin{bmatrix} dx^i \\[2ex] d\lambda_0 \end{bmatrix} = \begin{bmatrix} 0 \\[1ex] \bar{\lambda}_0^i dπ_1 \\[2ex] 0 \end{bmatrix} \tag{11}$$

then dx^i lies in the tangent space $T_{\bar{x}^i}(I_{\bar{x}^i}^i)$ and the induced change in the normalized gradient of agent i is

$$dπ_1^i = dπ_1$$

so that the proof of the lemma is complete. Now the date 0 component of (11) is

$$\sum_{\sigma=0}^{S} \frac{\partial^2 u^i(\bar{x}^i)}{\partial x_0^i \partial x_\sigma^i} dx_\sigma^i - \left(\frac{1}{\bar{\lambda}_0^i}\right) \frac{\partial u^i(\bar{x}^i)}{\partial x_0^i} d\lambda_0 = 0 \Longleftrightarrow d\lambda_0^i = d\lambda_0$$

by virtue of (10). The state s component of (11) is

$$\sum_{\sigma=0}^{S} \frac{\partial^2 u^i(\bar{x}^i)}{\partial x_s^i \partial x_\sigma^i} dx_\sigma^i - \left(\frac{1}{\bar{\lambda}_0^i}\right) \frac{\partial u^i(\bar{x}^i)}{\partial x_s^i} d\lambda_0 = \bar{\lambda}_0^i dπ_s, \quad s = 1, \ldots, S$$

which by (9), (10) and $d\lambda_0^i = d\lambda_0$, is equivalent to

$$d\lambda_1^i - \left(\frac{1}{\bar{\lambda}_0^i}\right) \bar{\lambda}_1^i d\lambda_0^i = \bar{\lambda}_0^i dπ_1 \Longleftrightarrow dπ_1^i = dπ_1$$

The last equation in (11) ensures that dx^i lies in the tangent space $T_{\bar{x}^i}(I_{\bar{x}^i}^i)$ to the indifference surface at $\bar{x}^i$.

To complete the proof it suffices to show that the system of equations (11) has a solution for any $d\pi_1 \in \mathbb{R}^S$. Suppose the matrix in (11) is not invertible, then there exist $(dx^i, d\lambda_0) \neq 0$ such that

$$D^2 u^i(\bar{x}^i) dx^i - \frac{\nabla u^i(\bar{x}^i)^T}{\bar{\lambda}_0^i} d\lambda_0 = 0 \tag{12}$$

$$\nabla u^i(\bar{x}^i) dx^i = 0 \tag{13}$$

Since $\nabla u^i(\bar{x}^i) \in \mathbb{R}_{++}^{S+1}$ implies $dx^i \neq 0$, premultiplying (12) by $(dx^i)^T$ and using (13) implies that there exists $dx^i \in \mathbb{R}^{S+1}$, $dx^i \neq 0$ such that

$$(dx^i)^T D^2 u^i(\bar{x}^i) dx^i = 0 \quad \text{and} \quad \nabla u^i(\bar{x}^i) dx^i = 0$$

which contradicts Assumption $\mathscr{U}$(iv). Thus the matrix in (11) is invertible and (11) has a solution $(dx^i, d\lambda_0)$ for any $d\pi_1 \in \mathbb{R}^S$. $\square$

EXERCISES

1. *Interest rate and impatience.*

The oldest financial contract (other than money) is the instrument which permits agents to borrow and lend. In the idealized setting where agents do not default, this is the *riskless bond*: its price defines the *rate of interest*. There are two groups of characteristics which determine the equilibrium rate of interest: the first is the profile of agents' initial income streams and their *impatience* to consume today rather than in the future; the second is the *productivity* of investment (capital). This exercise studies how the first group of characteristics combine to determine the equilibrium rate of interest. This constitutes what Irving Fisher in his *Theory of Interest* (1930) called the first approximation to the rate of interest. The reader will find it rewarding to read Chapters IV and V of the *Theory of Interest* when doing the exercise that follows. This exercise is continued in Exercise 1 at the end of Chapter 6 where it is shown, in the setting of a production economy, how the productivity of capital combines with the impatience of agents to determine the rate of interest.

Consider a simple two-period economy without uncertainty. There are two (types of) agents ($i = a, b$) with utility functions

$$u^i(x_0^i, x_1^i) = v^i(x_0^i) + \delta_i v^i(x_1^i)$$

where $v^i(\xi) = \log \xi$ and $0 < \delta_i \leq 1$. There is a single security: a bond which pays one unit of income at date 1. If q denotes its price then the *rate of interest* r is defined by $q = 1/(1+r)$. Let $\omega^i = (\omega_0^i, \omega_1^i)$ denote agent i's initial income stream.

(a) Find the equilibrium bond price (rate of interest) as a function of the parameters $(\omega_0^i, \omega_1^i, \delta_i)$ as well as each agent's consumption-portfolio plan $(\bar{x}^i, \bar{z}^i)$.

(b) Agent i's *rate of impatience* $r^i(x^i)$ at the consumption stream $x^i = (x_0^i, x_1^i)$ is defined by

$$r^i(x^i) = \frac{\dfrac{\partial u^i(x^i)}{\partial x_0^i} - \dfrac{\partial u^i(x^i)}{\partial x_1^i}}{\dfrac{\partial u^i(x^i)}{\partial x_1^i}}$$

Explain in precise terms what $r^i(x^i)$ measures in terms of the compensation that agent i requires at date 1 to give up consumption today.

(c) Find the expression for $r^i(x^i)$ for the utility function given above and explain in intuitive terms how $r^i(x^i)$ varies when x_0^i, x_1^i and δ_i change. Is the behavior of $r^i(x^i)$ along the diagonal $x_0^i = x_1^i$ plausible? (See Fisher (1930, Chapter X, Section 8).) This is a crucial defect of this class of additively separable utility functions.

(d) What is the relation between $r^i(x^i)$ and the rate of interest at equilibrium? Explain the intuition.

(e) Show what happens to the equilibrium rate of interest when (i) the date 1 incomes (ω_1^a, ω_1^b) are increased and (ii) the pure impatience factors (δ_a, δ_b) decrease. Give an intuitive explanation using the results in (c) and (d).

(f) Suppose $\delta_a = \delta_b = 1$, $\omega^a = (10{,}000, 100{,}000)$, $\omega^b = (100{,}000, 10{,}000)$. Draw a figure (reasonably accurately) (similar to Figure 10.1) exhibiting the equilibrium with the financial market subspace in the net trade space (τ_0, τ_1).

(g) Which agent is more impatient at his initial income profile? Why does it make sense that he borrows while the other agent lends?

(h) For the same economy find the Arrow-Debreu (contingent market) equilibrium $(\bar{x}, \bar{\pi})$ with $\bar{\pi} = (1, \bar{\pi}_1)$. Interpret the equilibrium geometrically using the figure drawn in (f).

(i) Prove Theorem 10.6 directly for the general two-period economy $\mathscr{E}(u, \omega, V)$ when there is no uncertainty and the only security is the bond.

2. *No-arbitrage.*

This exercise is a simple computational exercise designed to familiarize the reader with the property of no-arbitrage and its consequences.

Consider a two-period economy with $S = 3$ states of nature at date 1. Suppose there are $J = 2$ securities with date 1 payoffs

$$V^1 = (10, -20, 60)^T, \quad V^2 = (20, 30, 10)^T$$

(a) Find the set Q of all prices $q = (q_1, q_2)$ which are arbitrage free. Show that Q is an open cone.

(b) For each $q \in Q$ find all state price vectors $\pi_1 = (\pi_1, \pi_2, \pi_3)$ such that $q = \pi_1 V$.

(c) Consider a vector of security prices which offers arbitrage opportunities: exhibit a portfolio $z = (z_1, z_2)$ which gets something for nothing i.e. such that $W(q)z > 0$.

3. *No-arbitrage and compactness of the budget set.*

In the proof of Proposition 9.3 it was shown that if a security price vector q offers no arbitrage opportunities, then the budget set $\mathbb{B}(q, \omega^i, V)$ is compact since it is contained in the contingent market budget set $B(\pi, \omega^i)$, for any positive state price vector satisfying $\pi_0 q = \pi_1 V$. It is instructive to show directly, without making use of the compactness of $B(\pi, \omega^i)$, that the no-arbitrage condition on q implies that $\mathbb{B}(q, \omega^i, V)$ is bounded. The explicit bounds on the portfolios are useful in some analytical arguments.

Let $\mathscr{E}(u, \omega, V)$ be a two-period one-good economy with I agents and J financial securities. Assume without loss of generality that the payoff matrix V is of maximum rank J. Let $q = (q_1, \ldots, q_J)$ be a vector of security prices which does not admit any arbitrage opportunity.

(a) Show that the function $\ell : \mathbb{R}^J \longrightarrow \mathbb{R}$ defined by $\ell(z) = \min\{-qz, V_1 z, \ldots, V_S z\}$ is continuous, linear homogeneous and satisfies $\ell(z) < 0$ for all $z \in \mathbb{R}^J$, $z \neq 0$.

(b) Define ℓ^* by $\ell^* = \max\{\ell(z) \mid \|z\| = 1\}$ (where $\| \ \|$ denotes the Euclidean norm of $\mathbb{R}^J$). Show that $\ell^* < 0$.

(c) Let $\omega^i \in \mathbb{R}_+^{S+1}$ be the endowment stream of agent i and let

$$M^i = \max\{\omega_0^i, \omega_1^i, \ldots, \omega_S^i\}$$

Show that $(x^i; z^i) \in \mathbb{B}(q, \omega^i, V) \Rightarrow \ell(z^i) \geq -M^i$.

(d) Deduce from (a)–(c) that $(x^i; z^i) \in \mathbb{B}(q, \omega^i) \Rightarrow \|z^i\| \leq -M^i/\ell^*$ and that $\mathbb{B}(q, \omega^i, V)$ is bounded.

4. *Financial market equilibrium with complete or incomplete markets.*

This is a computational exercise designed to familiarize the reader with the concept of a financial market equilibrium.

Consider a two-period economy with $S = 2$, states of nature at date 1. Suppose there are $I = 2$ agents with utility functions

$$u^1(x) = \log x_0 + \frac{1}{2}\left(\frac{1}{2}\log x_1 + \frac{1}{2}\log x_2\right)$$

$$u^2(x) = \log x_0 + \frac{1}{3}\left(\frac{1}{2}\log x_1 + \frac{1}{2}\log x_2\right)$$

and endowments $\omega^1 = (19/8, 1, 3)$, $\omega^2 = (21/8, 5, 3)$.

(a) Suppose there are two securities traded at date 0: the riskless bond and a security which pays 1 unit in state 1 and nothing in state 2. Find the financial market equilibrium. (Hint: the computation can be kept short if you are clever). What is the rate of interest? Give a careful economic interpretation of the portfolio strategy adopted by each agent.

(b) Suppose that only the riskless bond is traded at date 0. Find the FM equilibrium for this incomplete market economy and compare the equilibrium allocation with that in (a). Comment on the differences. (Hint: it is not possible to avoid some tedious computation but the numbers are chosen so that you can find the equilibrium without help of a computer).

5. *Inward-pointing vector field on the non-negative sphere S_+^1.*
(a) Use the Intermediate Value Theorem to prove Theorem 7.5 for the case $n = 2$.
(b) For the case $n = 2$ show that Theorem 7.5 is equivalent to Brouwer's Theorem.

6. *Constrained demand function.*
Prove that the constrained demand function

$$f_V^i(\pi) = \arg\max \left\{ u^i(x^i) \mid x^i \in \mathscr{B}(\pi, \omega^i, V) \right\}$$

(where $\mathscr{B}(\pi, \omega^i, V)$ is defined by equation 7 in Section 10) has the properties (i)–(iv) in the proof of Theorem 7.4. If you try to prove (v), where do you find a difficulty?

7. *Alternative proof of existence of an FM equilibrium.*

In the text, the existence of an FM equilibrium was proved by transforming the concept of equilibrium to a normalized no-arbitrage equilibrium (Proposition 10.4 and Theorem 10.5). Here is a direct proof (see Hens (1991)) which requires some more work. (The proof of the boundary behavior of the excess demand for portfolios in question 8(c) is not easy). It is convenient to begin by showing that formally the model that we study is a special case of a model in which agents take their portfolio decisions before the period in which they consume.

Consider an economy $\mathscr{E}(u, \omega, V)$ with I agents as described in Chapter 2. Consider also an *artificial economy* $\widetilde{\mathscr{E}}(u, \omega, \widetilde{V})$ with two periods, $S + 1$ states of nature in the second period denoted by $s = 0, \ldots, S$, no consumption and no endowments in the first period, and endowments and utility of consumption in the second period given by u^i and ω^i for all $i = 1, \ldots, I$. The artificial economy has $J + 1$ securities whose payoffs in the second period are given by the matrix

$$\widetilde{V} = \begin{bmatrix} 1 & 0 & \cdots & 0 \\ 0 & & & \\ \vdots & & V & \\ 0 & & & \end{bmatrix}$$

Let $\tilde{q} = (\tilde{q}_0, \tilde{q}_1, \ldots, \tilde{q}_J)$ denote the prices of the securities in the economy $\widetilde{\mathscr{E}}$ and let $(\tilde{z}_0^i, \tilde{z}_1^i, \ldots, \tilde{z}_J^i)$ be the portfolio of agent i. In the economy $\widetilde{\mathscr{E}}$, agent i has the budget set

$$\mathbb{B}(\tilde{q}, \widetilde{V}) = \left\{ x^i \in \mathbb{R}^{S+1} \; \middle| \; \begin{array}{l} \tilde{q} z^i \leq 0, \quad z^i \in \mathbb{R}^{J+1} \\ x^i - \omega^i = \widetilde{V} z^i \end{array} \right\}$$

(a) Show that the maximum problem of agent i in $\widetilde{\mathscr{E}}$, $\max \left\{ u^i(x^i) \mid x^i \in \mathbb{B}(\tilde{q}, \widetilde{V}) \right\}$ decomposes the choice of agent i into two components: (i) the total saving or debt at date 0 $(\tilde{z}_0^i)$ and (ii) the composition of the portfolio $(\tilde{z}_1^i, \ldots, \tilde{z}_J^i)$ which has the chosen value $-\tilde{q}_0 \tilde{z}_0^i$.

(b) Show that if $(\bar{x}, \tilde{z}, \tilde{q})$ is an equilibrium of $\widetilde{\mathscr{E}}(u, \omega, \widetilde{V})$, then $\tilde{q}_0 > 0$ and $(\bar{x}, \bar{z}, \bar{q})$ with $\bar{z}_j^i = \tilde{z}_j^i$, $i = 1, \ldots, I$, $j = 1, \ldots, J$ and $\bar{q}_j = \tilde{q}_j / \tilde{q}_0$, $j = 1, \ldots, J$ is an equilibrium for the original economy $\mathscr{E}(u, \omega, V)$.

8. *Proof of existence (continued)*

To prove existence of an equilibrium for $\mathscr{E}(u, \omega, V)$ it is thus sufficient to prove that $\widetilde{\mathscr{E}}(u, \omega, \widetilde{V})$ has an equilibrium. Assume

- u^i satisfies Assumption $\mathscr{U}'$ for $i = 1, \ldots, I$
- $\omega^i \gg 0$ for $i = 1, \ldots, I$
- rank $V = J$

To simplify notation omit the tilde on the security prices and the portfolios. Let

$$Q = \left\{ q \in \mathbb{R}^{J+1} \mid q = \pi \widetilde{V}, \quad \pi \in \mathbb{R}_{++}^{S+1} \right\}$$

denote the set of no-arbitrage security prices for $\widetilde{\mathscr{E}}$ and let

$$\overline{Q} = \left\{ q \in \mathbb{R}^{J+1} \mid q = \pi \widetilde{V}, \quad \pi \in \mathbb{R}_+^{S+1} \right\}$$

denote its closure.

(a) Show that if $q \in Q$ then agent i's problem

$$\max \left\{ u^i(x^i) \mid x^i \in \mathbb{B}(q, \widetilde{V}) \right\}$$

has a unique solution $(x^i(q); z^i(q))$ where $z^i(q)$ finances $x^i(q)$. Define the aggregate excess demand for securities

$$Z(q) = \sum_{i=1}^{I} z^i(q)$$

(b) Show that Z is continuous on Q.

(c) Show that if $\bar{q} \neq 0$ belongs to $\overline{Q} \setminus Q$ and (q^ν) is a sequence converging to $\bar{q}$ with $q^\nu \in Q$ then $\| z^i(q^\nu) \| \to \infty$ as $\nu \to \infty$.

(d) Normalize the prices q by $q_0^2 + \cdots + q_J^2 = 1$ so that $q \in \mathscr{S}^J$, the J-dimensional unit sphere in $\mathbb{R}^{J+1}$. Then $Z(q)$ defines a vector field on $Q \cap \mathscr{S}^J$, which, although topologically equivalent to the positive sphere, does not coincide with it. The following theorem is a variant of the Inward-Pointing Vector Field Theorem.

Theorem: Let $\overline{Q} \in \mathbb{R}^{J+1}$ be a closed convex cone which is not a linear space (i.e. $0 \notin \text{int}\,\overline{Q}$). Let Q denote the interior of $\overline{Q}$, and let $\widehat{Q} = Q \cap \mathscr{S}^J$. If $Z : \widehat{Q} \longrightarrow \mathbb{R}^{J+1}$ is a continuous function which satisfies $qZ(q) = 0$, $\forall q \in \widehat{Q}$ and the property (BB) (boundary behavior) below, then there exists $q^* \in \widehat{Q}$ such that $Z(q^*) = 0$.

(BB) if $q^\nu \to \bar{q}$ with $\bar{q} \in \partial \widehat{Q}$ and $q^\nu \in \widehat{Q}$ for all $\nu > 0$, there exists $\hat{q} \in \widehat{Q}$ such that, for ν sufficiently large, $\hat{q} Z(q^\nu) > 0$.

Draw a figure to convince yourself that (BB) is an inward-pointing condition for the vector field Z. Use this theorem to prove the existence of an equilibrium vector of security prices $q^* \in \mathbb{R}^{J+1}$.

9. *Diversification of portfolios*

This exercise is an application of the methods explained in Section 11 to prove that a property is typical at an equilibrium.

Let $\mathscr{E}(u, \omega, V)$ be a two-period economy satisfying Assumption $\mathscr{U}$ and let rank $V = J$. Use the method shown in Section 11 to prove that typically (i.e. except if ω is chosen in a set of measure zero in the endowment space $\Omega = \mathbb{R}_{++}^{(S+1)I}$) every financial market equilibrium $((\bar{x}, \bar{z}), \bar{q})$ of $\mathscr{E}(u, \omega, V)$ satisfies $\bar{z}_j^i \neq 0$, $i = 1, \dots, I$, $j = 1, \dots, J$. What does this property tell you about diversification of agents' equilibrium portfolios?

HISTORICAL REMARKS

The finance model studied in Chapters 2 and 3 can be viewed as the fusion of two distinct traditions in the economic literature: the general equilibrium tradition which dates back to Walras' *Eléments d'Economie Politique Pure* (1874) and the finance tradition which originates with Irving Fisher's (1906, 1907, 1930) studies of the theory of capital and the rate of interest. These two branches of the economic literature have focused on somewhat different properties of the underlying model. In the general equilibrium approach which is presented in Chapter 2, the focus is on the allocations—the conditions under which an equilibrium exists and its welfare (constrained Pareto optimal) properties. In the finance approach which is presented in Chapter 3, the focus is on the equilibrium prices of the securities and their relation to the risk characteristics of their payoff streams. We shall concentrate here on the historical development of the general equilibrium model with time and uncertainty, postponing the contributions of the finance literature to the risk pricing of securities to the end of Chapter 3. Since general equilibrium models typically involve more than one good, to place the model of this chapter in its proper perspective, it will be convenient to include historical developments on the multigood model.

Walras (1874) conceived his general equilibrium model as a genuine intertemporal model, that is, time and capital were to play an essential role. In the end, analytical difficulties forced him to confine his attention to a special equilibrium, namely a steady state in which all prices remain unchanged and the sole price linking adjoining periods is the rate of interest. From a practical point of view this is essentially a two-period model without uncertainty. For a long time no serious attempts were made to extend Walras' analysis to permit the explicit presence of uncertainty. In his *Value and Capital* (1939) Hicks severely criticized the steady state analysis of Walras (and the classical economists) as a highly deceptive way of analyzing the intertemporal equilibrium of an economy. While in Parts III and IV of *Value and Capital* Hicks supplied a perceptive verbal account of what would now be called a *rational expectations* (or more precisely, a *correct expectations*) *equilibrium* and the more general *temporary equilibrium*, he offered no mathematical extension of Walras' model to include uncertainty.

The first and decisive step towards the introduction of uncertainty into general equilibrium was made in the classic paper of Arrow (1953). The underlying idea was simple and powerful: it amounted to introducing the approach of probability theory into equilibrium analysis—namely, the idea that a random variable is a function defined on states of nature. Just as equilibrium can be extended over time by viewing the same commodity at different dates as distinct commodities, so equilibrium can be extended to uncertainty by viewing the same commodity deliverable in different states as distinct commodities (contracts). This simple idea permits the standard general equilibrium model to be extended to a setting with time and uncertainty and leads to the concept of a *contingent market equilibrium*, presented for the two-period one-good model in Section 7 and which will be studied in full generality in the second volume.

In the same paper Arrow made an astute observation which proved to have far-reaching consequences: he noted that it was not necessary to trade the complete set of contingent contracts for goods (one for each good in each state) at the initial date to obtain a Pareto optimal allocation of resources, since the same allocation could be obtained by a simpler market structure involving financial securities and spot markets. The financial securities considered by Arrow were *elementary securities* which promise to deliver one unit of account if state s occurs and nothing otherwise. This insight into the division of tasks between financial markets for redistributing income and spot markets for allocating goods was an important contribution which cannot however be appreciated in the one-good model of this chapter since, in the absence of spot markets, the contingent contracts for goods coincide with the contingent contracts for income. The relation between these two concepts of equilibrium for the multigood model will be explored in the second volume.

More realistic financial securities—in particular bonds and equity contracts of firms—were considered in the finance literature which emerged in the 1950s and were progressively introduced into the general equilibrium literature. Diamond (1967) was the first to explicitly model incomplete markets in a one-good two-period model of a production economy in which the shares of firms are traded on a stock market. He recognized that the concept of Pareto optimality is no longer a useful criterion for judging the efficacy of a system of markets when the markets are incomplete and introduced the concept of *constrained optimality* which is studied in Section 12 in the simpler context of an exchange economy. Due to the special assumption on the technology sets of firms (multiplicative uncertainty), the production model of Diamond exhibited both constrained efficiency and unanimity of shareholders regarding the production plans that should be chosen by firms. It was subsequently recognized that without this special assumption neither of these properties hold. This led to active discussions in the 1970s on the problem of the objective function of the firm when markets are incomplete. The contributions on this subject will be reviewed in Chapter 6 which deals with a production economy.

Diamond's paper was the first of a series of papers in the early 1970s on equilibrium in sequence economies in which agents have limited ability to transfer income across adjoining date-events. In such a sequential setting agents must form expectations regarding future prices and payoffs of financial securities. Two approaches have been adopted for closing such a model with an equilibrium concept. The first is motivated by the idea that agents, being boundedly rational, have difficulty in correctly anticipating future variables. This leads to the concept of a *temporary equilibrium* in which agents have exogenously given rules for forming their expectations as functions of current and past variables—which (in Section 3) we called adaptive expectations—and only current markets are required to clear, no condition being imposed on future spot markets since agents' expectations are not required to be self-fulfilling: this concept was first formalized by Stigum (1969a,b) and Grandmont (1970, 1974). A temporary equilibrium analysis of financial markets in two-period economies in which agents have different expectations about the future returns on securities was provided by Green (1973) for the case of futures contracts in a multigood model and by Hart (1974) for a general security structure in a one-good (income) model. The main conclusion of these papers—and more generally of the temporary equilibrium literature—is that an equilibrium exists provided agents do not hold too different expectations (a minimum consensus or overlap in their expectations is needed) regarding future payoffs. The concept of no-arbitrage is also a necessary condition for equilibrium in these papers, although it is expressed in a different form from that in Section 9, since these papers describe security payoffs using probability distributions rather than as functions of a finite set of states of nature, and since the prices of the securities must not permit arbitrage among agents holding different expectations.

The second approach to sequence economies is motivated by the idea that agents do not make systematic mistakes—in short that they correctly anticipate future variables. This leads to the concept of equilibrium which we called a *correct expectations equilibrium* in which markets clear at each date-event and anticipated prices are the equilibrium prices at future date-events (Section 5). This equilibrium concept, which was implicit in Arrow's paper (1953), was first explicitly introduced by Radner (1972) for a T-period economy with spot markets and an incomplete set of commodity futures contracts at each date-event. To contrast the equilibrium concept from that in temporary equilibrium, Radner referred to it as an equilibrium of plans, prices and price expectations. This is the concept of equilibrium on which the analysis of this book is based. It should be noted that Hahn (1971b, 1973b) used the same concept of equilibrium in a model without uncertainty in which transactions costs give a role for sequential spot markets and the use of money. In the case of an exchange economy Radner showed that an equilibrium exists if short sales constraints are imposed on agents' portfolios. For a stock market production economy Radner encountered difficulties in proving that an equilibrium exists—difficulties which are linked to the choice of objective functions for firms when markets are incomplete—a topic which will be discussed in Chapter 6.

In a paper which did much to stimulate the development of the theory of incomplete markets, Hart (1975) revealed by means of well-chosen examples a number of conceptual difficulties with the equilibrium model introduced by Radner, even for the case of an exchange economy. In particular, as far as the existence of an equilibrium is concerned, he showed that an equilibrium may depend crucially on the arbitrary bounds imposed on agents' portfolios, since without the bounds an equilibrium may not exist. In a multigood model where the payoffs on securities (such as futures contracts) depend on the spot prices of commodities at subsequent date-events, variations in these spot prices can cause the rank of the payoff matrix (the matrix V in this chapter) to change. If there are no bounds on agents' portfolios, such changes in rank induce discontinuities in the agents' demand functions which can lead to nonexistence of an equilibrium. Hart argued convincingly that imposing bounds on agents' portfolios is an *ad hoc* assumption which does not lead to a satisfactory model. As a result, in the ensuing literature on Radner's incomplete markets model, two different strategies have been adopted for avoiding the problem of discontinuities in agents' portfolio demands. The first (and simplest) is to restrict attention to those securities for which the payoff matrix cannot change rank: in a two-period model this amounts to restricting the analysis to securities which pay off either in units of account (Cass (1984), Werner (1985)) or in a numeraire commodity (Geanakoplos-Polemarchakis (1986)). The second approach is to work directly with a model that permits general security structures and involves showing that the economies for which an equilibrium fails to exist are exceptional and can thus typically be disregarded. This is the approach which will be followed in the second volume and is based on the contributions of Duffie-Shafer (1985), Husseini-Lasry-Magill (1990), Hirsch-Magill-Mas-Colell (1990) and Geanakoplos-Shafer (1990). The proof of existence in each of these papers when specialized to the one-good case provides a proof of existence for the model studied in this chapter. The proof given in Section 10 is the one-good version of Hirsch-Magill-Mas-Colell (1990).

All of the above papers use the characterization of no-arbitrage prices (Theorem 9.3) to restrict the set of candidate equilibrium prices and all of them (with the exception of Werner (1985) and Geanakoplos-Polemarchakis (1986)) use the notion of a normalized no-arbitrage equilibrium defined in Section 10. The idea of using state prices to obtain an equivalent representation of an agent's budget set was first exploited by Fischer (1972) in order to obtain comparative static Slutsky equations for the demand for assets. The concept of a no-arbitrage equilibrium as an equivalent representation of a financial market equilibrium seems to have first appeared in Cass (1984) and Magill-Shafer (1985).

An interesting link between temporary equilibrium models and the models with correct expectations is provided by Werner's paper (1987). His model covers the temporary equilibrium models of Green (1973), Hart (1974) and Hammond (1983) but is restricted, in the case of correct expectations, to the one-good two-period model. When agents hold different expectations regarding the future payoffs of securities, no-arbitrage prices become agent specific. Werner shows that an equilibrium exists if the intersection of the agents' sets of no-arbitrage prices is non-empty: for most preference orderings this condition is also necessary.

The idea of no-arbitrage which was introduced in Section 9 appears naturally as soon as financial contracts are introduced. When expressed in its simplest form—*under conditions of free exchange equivalent commodities (contracts) sell at the same price*—it is surely no exaggeration to call it one of the oldest and most basic principles of economics. It has long been used as a method for establishing relations between the prices of various commodities or contracts. Early formal discussions were provided by Cournot (1838, Chapters 3 and 10) and Irving Fisher (1896). As Samuelson (1957) argued in a suggestive paper, when the idea of *spatial* price relations—the differences in the prices of the same commodity at different centres must be related to the cost of transport between the two centres—is applied to a model with *intertemporal* price relations—price differences are related to the temporal carrying costs (interest and risk charges)—we are led to the beginnings of a theory of speculative prices. Strictly speaking, this is a topic that we shall address at greater length in Chapters 3 and 5. Except for rather straightforward applications of these ideas (for example, the ratio of the spot to the forward exchange rate between two currencies must equal the ratio of their interest rates) the abstract study of price relations was long ignored by economists. The contributions of Modigliani-Miller (1958) and Black-Scholes (1973) changed all this in a radical way: no-arbitrage once again became a familiar type of argument. Ross (1976, 1978a) seems to have been the first to recognize the general principle underlying no-arbitrage arguments which is embodied in Theorem 9.3 ((ii) $\iff$ (iii)).

For a long time the Pareto inefficiency of equilibrium allocations when markets are incomplete was regarded as a Folk Theorem. The intuition was simply that barring unusual initial circumstances, such as starting at a Pareto optimum, with an insufficient number of markets to trade on, agents' marginal rates of substitution will not be equalized by trade. Formal proofs are however recent, since as shown in Section 11 this property is only generic[1], and establishing the result requires techniques from differential topology. As we mentioned in Section 7 these techniques were introduced in the 1970s for studying qualitative properties of the standard general equilibrium model—they have turned out to be crucial for studying the model with incomplete markets since many of its properties (including existence of equilibrium in the general model) are only generic. Three proofs of the generic inefficiency of equilibrium allocations can be found in the literature, associated with three different parametrizations of the underlying economies—in Geanakoplos-Polemarchakis (1986), in Duffie-Shafer (1986b) and in Geanakoplos-Magill-Quinzii-Drèze (1990). The proof given in Section 11 is adapted from the third paper: we have omitted the proof that the set of economies with inefficient equilibrium allocations is open (see Volume 2).

As mentioned in Section 12, the property of constrained optimality of equilibrium allocations is satisfied for all characteristics of the economy only in the special case of a one-good, two-period economy. As we shall see in Chapter 4 and in the second volume, when there are two or more periods and/or two or more goods there is a precise sense in which equilibrium allocations are generically constrained inefficient.

---

[1]A property is said to be *generic* if it holds on an open set of full measure.

3

TWO-PERIOD SECURITY PRICING

MOTIVATION AND SUMMARY

Security markets enable the members of a community to share their risks. By buying and selling securities, individuals can reduce and even eliminate many of the risks they face and are rewarded for sharing the unavoidable risks (arising from fluctuations in economic activity) faced by the society as a whole. It would seem natural therefore that the price of a security should reflect how well its income stream is adapted to meet the needs of the individuals in the community, taking into account the services offered by other securities in the market. The object of this chapter is to explain how the needs of the agents combine with the services offered by the securities to explain their equilibrium prices.

In Chapter 2 we showed that an agent faced with market prices $\bar{q} = (\bar{q}_1, \ldots, \bar{q}_J)$ for the J basic securities has chosen his optimal consumption-portfolio plan $(\bar{x}^i, \bar{z}^i)$ when the equilibrium price of each security is equal to the present value of its income stream to agent i

$$\bar{q}_j = \sum_{s=1}^{S} \pi_s^i(\bar{x}^i) V_s^j, \quad j = 1, \ldots, J \tag{1}$$

Furthermore in an equilibrium this relation holds for each of the agents $i = 1, \ldots, I$. The services offered by the jth security consist of the income stream $(V_1^j, \ldots, V_S^j)$, while the needs of agent i at his *equilibrium consumption* $\bar{x}^i$ are expressed by the present-value vector $\pi^i(\bar{x}^i)$ whose components indicate how much agent i values an additional unit of income in each state, in terms of the consumption at date 0 that the agent is prepared to forego. As we showed in Section 9, the pricing equation (1) can be extended from the J basic securities to a pricing relation for all income streams in the marketed subspace by setting the price $c_{\bar{q}}(y)$ of an income stream y equal to the cost $\bar{q}z$ of the portfolio which generates it $(y = Vz)$. Thus (1) induces the pricing relation

$$c_{\bar{q}}(y) = \sum_{s=1}^{S} \pi_s^i(\bar{x}^i)y_s, \quad \forall\, y \in \langle V \rangle \tag{2}$$

Implicit in relation (1) is the assumption that all agents have *correct* (and hence common) *anticipations* regarding the date 1 dividend streams V^j of the basic securities. If in addition it is assumed that all agents agree on the probabilities of occurrence of the states of nature at date 1, so that agents have *rational expectations*, then the pricing equation (1) can be written in a more intuitive form. For the introduction of objective probabilities of the states permits this equation to be expressed in terms of statistical measures involving the means, variances and covariances of the dividend streams of the securities and appropriately adjusted present-value vectors of the agents.

The transformation of the pricing equation (1), or its equivalent (2), to a form which exploits the probability setting of the model is the subject of Section 15. To gain an intuition for the formula which is derived, note first that (2) is a marginal valuation which can be expressed equivalently, using the differential of agent i's utility function, as

$$du_{\bar{x}^i}^i(-c_{\bar{q}}(y), y) = 0$$

$c_{\bar{q}}(y)$ is the date 0 income that agent i is prepared to forego to obtain the income stream y. More precisely, agent i is indifferent between the new consumption stream $(\bar{x}_0^i - c_{\bar{q}}(y), \bar{x}_1^i + y)$ and the original consumption stream $(\bar{x}_0^i, \bar{x}_1^i)$, provided y is sufficiently small. Since the states at date 1 have objective probabilities, the income stream y is a random variable which can be decomposed into its *certain part* $\hat{y}$ (its mean) and its *purely random part* $\tilde{y}$ (the centered variable)

$$y = \hat{y} + \tilde{y}, \quad E(y) = E(\hat{y}), \quad \text{var}(\hat{y}) = 0 = E(\tilde{y})$$

At the new date 1 consumption stream $\bar{x}_1^i + \hat{y} + \tilde{y}$ that the agent obtains, the mean $\hat{y}$ offers more (or less) consumption uniformly in each state, while the random component $\tilde{y}$ alters the risk characteristics of the consumption stream relative to $\bar{x}_1^i$. *The date 0 income that the agent is prepared to forego to obtain the income stream y must thus be explained by the needs of the agent for these two types of services.* These needs can be found by solving the agent's *local mean-variance problem*

$$\max\left\{ du_{\bar{x}^i}^i(h_0, h_1) \;\middle|\; \begin{array}{c} |h_0|^2 + (E(h_1))^2 + \text{var}(h_1) = k^2 \\ h_1 \in \langle V \rangle \end{array} \right\} \tag{3}$$

at the equilibrium consumption $\bar{x}^i$. In this problem the agent chooses the optimal increment to his consumption stream $\bar{x}^i \to \bar{x}^i + h$ subject to the condition that the *magnitude* of the increment h is small (k^2) and that the date 1 component h_1 lies in the marketed subspace. The limited magnitude of the increment h forces the agent to make an optimal trade-off between increasing *date* 0 *consumption* (h_0), increasing the *mean* $(\widehat{h}_1)$ at date 1 and reducing the *risk* of date 1 consumption $(\widetilde{h}_1)$. Since the problem is homogeneous in k, the way the agent solves the trade-off involved in the mean-variance problem (3) is summarized by the security $\gamma^i(\bar{x}^i) = h_1^*(k)/h_0^*(k)$ which is independent of k. We call this security the *ideal security* of agent i at $\bar{x}^i$ in the marketed subspace. The certain part $\widehat{\gamma}^i$ of γ^i summarizes the agent's *time preference*, while the random part $\widetilde{\gamma}^i$ summarizes the agent's *risk preference*.

In an equilibrium the ideal securities of all agents coincide

$$\gamma^1(\bar{x}^1) = \cdots = \gamma^I(\bar{x}^I) = \gamma$$

and the common vector is called the *ideal security* in the marketed subspace at the equilibrium. Since this security expresses the common way that all agents value marginal changes about their equilibrium consumption, it explains the logic that underlies the equilibrium prices of the securities in the following way. For each security $y \in \langle V \rangle$ its market value satisfies

$$c_{\bar{q}}(y) = E(\gamma)E(y) + \mathrm{cov}(\gamma, y) \tag{4}$$

Since γ (like all securities) can be decomposed into a certain part $\widehat{\gamma}$ which expresses the *equilibrium time preference* of the agents $(\widehat{\gamma} = \widehat{\gamma}^i)$ and its random part $\widetilde{\gamma}$ which expresses the *equilibrium risk preference* of the agents $(\widetilde{\gamma} = \widetilde{\gamma}^i)$, the pricing formula (4) can be written as

$$c_{\bar{q}}(y) = E(\widehat{\gamma})E(\widehat{y}) + \mathrm{cov}(\widetilde{\gamma}, \widetilde{y}) \tag{5}$$

The market value of a security y thus decomposes into the value of its certain part $\widehat{y}$ and the value of its risky part $\widetilde{y}$. If the riskless bond is traded in the market $((1, \ldots, 1) \in \langle V \rangle)$ then the equilibrium interest rate $\bar{r}$ is well-defined and satisfies $1/(1+\bar{r}) = E(\widehat{\gamma})$. Thus (5) becomes

$$c_{\bar{q}}(y) = \frac{E(\widehat{y})}{1 + \bar{r}} + \mathrm{cov}(\widetilde{\gamma}, \widetilde{y}) \tag{6}$$

The first term is the discounted value of the expected income stream and the second term is the *covariance value*, which is positive if $\mathrm{cov}(\widetilde{\gamma}, \widetilde{y}) > 0$ ($\widetilde{y}$ offers risk reducing services) and negative if $\mathrm{cov}(\widetilde{\gamma}, \widetilde{y}) < 0$ ($\widetilde{y}$ increases the agents' risks).

The mathematical concepts needed to establish these results are explained in Section 14. The basic idea is to show how well-known properties of the standard inner product $[x, y] = \sum_{s=1}^{S} x_s y_s$ on $\mathbb{R}^S$ extend to a *probability-induced inner product* $[\![x, y]\!]_\rho = \sum_{s=1}^{S} \rho_s x_s y_s$ where $(\rho_1, \ldots, \rho_S)$ is the vector of probabilities of the states. The new geometry on $\mathbb{R}^S$ induced by this probability inner product is well adapted to analyzing the properties (in particular the risk pricing) of income streams, since, in this geometry, lengths and angles capture the statistical properties of income streams summarized in their means, variances and covariances.

When stronger assumptions are made regarding agents' preferences, endowments and/or the security structure, then a more precise understanding can be obtained about the way risks in the economy are shared and how the non-diversifiable risks are priced at equilibrium. In the models considered in Sections 16 and 17 agents are assumed to be *risk-averse in a precise sense*: they either have state independent *additively separable* utility functions (Section 16) or they have *mean-variance* preferences (Section 17). In addition it is either assumed that the financial markets are *complete* or that the contracts which exist are *well-adapted* to the risks that individuals face ($\omega^i \in \langle V \rangle$). Under these conditions it is shown that the equilibrium consumption of each agent is an increasing function of the aggregate output: thus the ideal security of each agent is related to aggregate output.

Broadly speaking there are two kinds of risks in an economy: *individual risks* and *aggregate risks*: the individual risks are those faced by consumers or individual firms; the aggregate risks are those that remain when the consumers' individual endowments and the outputs of firms are summed to form *aggregate output*. Trading on the financial markets enables individuals to get rid of, or at least to reduce, their individual risks— and under the assumptions made in Sections 16 and 17 this trading actually enables them to completely eliminate their individual risks. The only risks which are left in equilibrium are the aggregate risks due to the fluctuations of aggregate output which cannot be diversified away by the financial markets. What the markets do is allocate the holding of these risks (for example through equity ownership on the stock market) among the consumers, rewarding the agents with risk premia for holding the more risky securities.

In the finance literature, portfolio theory and the analysis of the equilibrium risk pricing of securities is usually carried out under the special assumptions of Sections 16 and 17. As we indicated above these models are interesting since they lead to clear-cut results which have strong intuitive appeal. However the restrictive nature of the hypotheses made could cast doubt on the generality of the results. The purpose of this chapter, and more especially of Section 15, is to isolate the qualitative properties which survive in the abstract setting of the general model. Even if the financial markets are incomplete and agents cannot entirely eliminate their individual risks, the price of a security always depends on how well adapted its dividend stream is to the needs of the agents implied by the profiles of their equilibrium consumption. There is always an ideal security (common to all agents in the economy) which summarizes the component of the aggregate risks in the marketed subspace which cannot be diversified away and with respect to which risk premia can be computed.

14. INNER PRODUCT, DIFFERENTIAL AND GRADIENT

A much richer geometry is obtained for the space $\mathbb{R}^S$, when it is considered as a space of random variables on S states of nature, if an inner product is used which weights the states by their probabilities. In this new geometry, lengths and angles capture the average properties of random variables summarized in their means, variances and covariances. The *standard* geometry of $\mathbb{R}^S$ is induced by the *standard* (unweighted) inner product $[x, y] = \sum_{s=1}^{S} x_s y_s$ which was used in Chapter 2. To understand how alternative geometries can be introduced on $\mathbb{R}^S$, it is best to use the abstract axiomatic definition of an inner product, which extracts the essential properties needed to do geometry. Changing inner products amounts to changing the formulae by which the lengths of vectors and the angles between pairs of vectors are calculated.

14.1 Definition: An *inner product* $[\![\, , \,]\!] : \mathbb{R}^S \times \mathbb{R}^S \longrightarrow \mathbb{R}$ is a real-valued function with the following properties:

(i) (symmetric): $[\![x, y]\!] = [\![y, x]\!]$, $\forall\, x, y \in \mathbb{R}^S$
(ii) (bilinear): $[\![\alpha x + \beta x', y]\!] = \alpha\, [\![x, y]\!] + \beta\, [\![x', y]\!]$, $\forall\, x, x', y \in \mathbb{R}^S$, $\forall\, \alpha, \beta \in \mathbb{R}$
(iii) (positive): $[\![x, x]\!] > 0$, $\forall\, x \in \mathbb{R}^S, x \neq 0$.

Let $\{e_1, \ldots, e_S\}$ be the standard basis for $\mathbb{R}^S$ where $e_s = (0, \ldots, 1, \ldots, 0)$, $s = 1, \ldots, S$. For any $x \in \mathbb{R}^S$ with $x = \sum_{s=1}^{S} x_s e_s$ we use the standard convention that x is identified with the *column vector* with components x_s, $s = 1, \ldots, S$.

14.2 Proposition (Matrix Representation of Inner Product): *If $[\![\, , \,]\!]$ is an inner product on $\mathbb{R}^S$, then there exists a unique $S \times S$ symmetric positive definite matrix $[\rho]$ such that*

$$[\![x, y]\!] = x^T [\rho]\, y, \quad \forall\, x, y \in \mathbb{R}^S \tag{1}$$

Conversely for any $S \times S$ symmetric positive definite matrix $[\rho]$

$$[\![x, y]\!] = x^T [\rho]\, y, \quad \forall\, x, y \in \mathbb{R}^S$$

defines an inner product on $\mathbb{R}^S$.

PROOF: ($\Longrightarrow$) Let $\{e_1, \ldots, e_S\}$ be the standard basis of $\mathbb{R}^S$. Define $\rho_{s\sigma} = [\![e_s, e_\sigma]\!]$ and $[\rho] = [\rho_{s\sigma}]_{s,\sigma=1,\ldots,S}$. By symmetry of $[\![\, , \,]\!]$, $[\rho]$ is symmetric. By bilinearity, $[\![x, y]\!] = \sum_{s=1}^{S} \sum_{s=1}^{S} x_s [\![e_s, e_\sigma]\!] y_\sigma = x^T [\rho]\, y$ and by positivity of $[\![\, , \,]\!]$, $[\rho]$ is positive definite. $[\rho]$ is unique, since (1) implies $\rho_{s\sigma} = [\![e_s, e_\sigma]\!]$, $s, \sigma = 1, \ldots, S$. The proof of the converse is immediate. $\square$

We will identify an inner product on $\mathbb{R}^S$ by the matrix $[\rho]$ which represents it in the standard basis of $\mathbb{R}^S$ and write $[\![\, , \,]\!]_\rho$.

14.3 Example: If $[\rho] = I$, where

$$I = \begin{bmatrix} 1 & \cdots & 0 \\ \vdots & \ddots & \vdots \\ 0 & \cdots & 1 \end{bmatrix}$$

is the $S \times S$ identity matrix, then $[\![x, y]\!]_{\rho} = \sum_{s=1}^{S} x_s y_s$ is the *standard inner product*. It is convenient to use the simpler notation $[\,,\,]$ to denote this inner product instead of $[\![\,,\,]\!]_{I}$. $\square$

14.4 Example: If $[\rho]$ denotes the diagonal matrix of probabilities defined by

$$[\rho] = \begin{bmatrix} \rho_1 & \cdots & 0 \\ \vdots & \ddots & \vdots \\ 0 & \cdots & \rho_S \end{bmatrix}$$

with $\rho_s > 0$ denoting the probability of state s, for $s = 1, \ldots, S$, then $[\![x, y]\!]_{\rho} = \sum_{s=1}^{S} \rho_s x_s y_s$. We call this the *probability inner product* on $\mathbb{R}^S$. $\square$

14.5 Definition: A *norm* on $\mathbb{R}^S$ is a real-valued function $\|\ \| : \mathbb{R}^S \longrightarrow \mathbb{R}$ with the following properties:

   (i) (positive): $\|x\| > 0$ if $x \neq 0$ and $\|x\| = 0$ if $x = 0$
   (ii) (homogeneous): $\|\alpha x\| = |\alpha|\,\|x\|$, $\forall\,\alpha \in \mathbb{R}$, $\forall\,x \in \mathbb{R}^S$
   (i) (triangle inequality): $\|x + y\| \leq \|x\| + \|y\|$, $\forall\,x, y \in \mathbb{R}^S$

   An inner product $[\![\,,\,]\!]_{\rho}$ induces a *norm* on $\mathbb{R}^S$ defined by

$$\|x\|_{\rho} = \left([\![x, x]\!]_{\rho} \right)^{\frac{1}{2}}$$

It is clear from the properties of $[\![\,,\,]\!]_{\rho}$ that $\|\ \|_{\rho}$ satisfies (i) and (ii) in Definition 14.5. The triangle inequality is readily deduced from the following property relating the inner product to the norm.

14.6 Proposition (Cauchy-Schwartz Inequality):

$$\left| [\![x, y]\!]_{\rho} \right| \leq \|x\|_{\rho}\,\|y\|_{\rho}, \quad \forall\,x, y \in \mathbb{R}^S$$

with equality if and only if x and y are collinear.

PROOF: $p(t) = \|tx + y\|_{\rho}^2 = t^2\,\|x\|_{\rho}^2 + 2t\,[\![x, y]\!]_{\rho} + \|y\|_{\rho}^2$ is a second order polynomial which is non-negative for all $t \in \mathbb{R}$. Its discriminant must thus be non-positive. If x and y are linearly independent (collinear) then $p(\cdot)$ has no root (a unique root) and the discriminant is negative (zero). Thus $[\![x, y]\!]_{\rho}^2 < \|x\|_{\rho}^2\,\|y\|_{\rho}^2$

if x and y are linearly independent and $[\![x,y]\!]_\rho^2 = \|x\|_\rho^2 \|y\|_\rho^2$ if x and y are collinear. $\square$

The norm $\|\ \|_\rho$ associated with inner product $[\![\ ,\ ]\!]_\rho$ assigns a *length* $\|x\|_\rho$ to every vector $x \in \mathbb{R}^S$ and induces a measure of *distance* $\|x - y\|_\rho$ between any pair of vectors in $\mathbb{R}^S$. The inner product $[\![x,y]\!]_\rho$ of two vectors measures the *angle* between these vectors. More precisely, since by the Cauchy-Schwartz inequality we have

$$-1 \le \frac{[\![x,y]\!]_\rho}{\|x\|_\rho \|y\|_\rho} \le 1, \quad \forall\, x, y \in \mathbb{R}^S, \quad x \neq 0, \quad y \neq 0$$

for each pair of non-zero vectors $x, y \in \mathbb{R}^S$, it follows that there exists a unique number $\theta_{x,y}^\rho \in [0, \pi]$ such that

$$\cos \theta_{x,y}^\rho = \frac{[\![x,y]\!]_\rho}{\|x\|_\rho \|y\|_\rho}$$

$\theta_{x,y}^\rho$ measures the *angle* between x and y in the geometry induced by the positive definite form ρ. If x is a positive (negative) multiple of y then $\theta_{x,y}^\rho = 0$ (π) for any choice of inner product. Any other angle $\theta_{x,y}^\rho \in (0, \pi)$, in particular a right angle ($\theta_{x,y}^\rho = \pi/2$), depends on the choice of inner product.

14.7 Definition: Let $[\![\ ,\ ]\!]_\rho$ be an inner product on $\mathbb{R}^S$. If $x, y \in \mathbb{R}^S$ and $[\![x,y]\!]_\rho = 0$ then x and y are said to be *ρ-orthogonal*: we write $x \perp\!\!\!\perp y$. If M is a subset of $\mathbb{R}^S$, then $M^{\perp\!\!\!\perp} = \{y \in \mathbb{R}^S \mid y \perp\!\!\!\perp x,\ \forall\, x \in M\}$ is called the ρ-orthogonal set.

It is easy to check that for any subset M, the set $M^{\perp\!\!\!\perp}$ is a linear subspace of $\mathbb{R}^S$. If M is a linear subspace then M and $M^{\perp\!\!\!\perp}$ lead to a useful decomposition of the space.

14.8 Definition: Two subspaces M and M' of $\mathbb{R}^S$ are said to be *complementary* subspaces or to induce a *direct sum* decomposition of $\mathbb{R}^S$ if for any $x \in \mathbb{R}^S$ there exist unique vectors $x^* \in M$ and $x' \in M'$ such that $x = x^* + x'$: we write $\mathbb{R}^S = M \oplus M'$.

14.9 Proposition (Characterization of Complementary Subspaces): *M and M' are complementary subspaces of $\mathbb{R}^S$ if and only if*

(i) $M \cap M' = \{0\}$
(ii) $\dim M + \dim M' = S$

PROOF: ($\Longrightarrow$) If $x \in M \cap M'$, then x can be written as $x = x + 0$, $x \in M$, $0 \in M'$ or $x = 0 + x$, $0 \in M$, $x \in M'$. The decomposition is unique only if $x = 0$. Thus $M \cap M' = \{0\}$. Let $\{m_1, \dots, m_k\}$ be a basis for M and $\{m'_{k+1}, \dots, m'_n\}$ a basis for M'. Since any vector $x \in \mathbb{R}^S$ can be written as $x = x^* + x'$ with x^* a linear combination of $\{m_1, \dots, m_k\}$ and x' a linear combination of $\{m'_{k+1}, \dots, m'_n\}$ the vectors $\{m_1, \dots, m_k, m'_{k+1}, \dots, m'_n\}$ span $\mathbb{R}^S$. $M \cap M' = \{0\}$ implies that the vectors are linearly independent and thus form a basis for $\mathbb{R}^S$. Thus $n = S$.

($\Longleftarrow$) Let $\{m_1, \dots, m_k\}$ be a basis for M and $\{m_{k+1}, \dots, m_S\}$ a basis for M'. $M \cap M' = \{0\}$ implies that the vectors are linearly independent and hence form a basis for $\mathbb{R}^S$. Thus $\mathbb{R}^S = M \oplus M'$. $\square$

14.10 Proposition (Orthogonal Decomposition):   *If M is a linear subspace then $\mathbb{R}^S$ can be decomposed into the direct sum*

$$\mathbb{R}^S = M \oplus M^\perp$$

PROOF: If $x \in M \cap M^\perp$, then $x \perp\!\!\!\perp x \implies [\![x, x]\!]_\rho = 0 \implies x = 0$. Thus, $M \cap M^\perp = \{0\}$. Let $\{m_1, \dots, m_k\}$ be a basis for M and let $[m]$ denote the $S \times k$ matrix whose columns are the co-ordinates of $m_1, \dots, m_k$ in the standard basis of $\mathbb{R}^S$. Then

$$M^\perp = \left\{ x \in \mathbb{R}^S \mid x \perp\!\!\!\perp m_j, \quad j = 1, \dots, k \right\}$$
$$= \left\{ x \in \mathbb{R}^S \mid [m]^T [\rho] x = 0 \right\}$$

Since $[\rho]$ is nonsingular, $\operatorname{rank} [m]^T [\rho] = k$, and

$$\dim M^\perp = \dim \ker [m]^T [\rho] = S - k$$

Thus by Proposition 14.9, $\mathbb{R}^S = M \oplus M^\perp$. $\square$

14.11 Definition: Let $x \in \mathbb{R}^S$ and let M be a linear subspace. If $x = x^* + x'$ with $x^* \in M$ and $x' \in M^\perp$, then x^* is called the *ρ-orthogonal projection of x onto M* (see Figure 14.1). The following proposition is a convenient restatement of this property.

14.12 Proposition (ρ-Orthogonal Projection):   *Let $x \in \mathbb{R}^S$ and let M be a linear subspace, then $x^* \in M$ is the ρ-orthogonal projection of x onto M if and only if*

$$[\![x - x^*, \xi]\!]_\rho = 0, \quad \forall \xi \in M \iff [\![x, \xi]\!]_\rho = [\![x^*, \xi]\!]_\rho, \quad \forall \xi \in M$$

ρ-orthogonal projections appear naturally in problems of quadratic optimization, since the operation of ρ-projection provides the solution of a quadratic

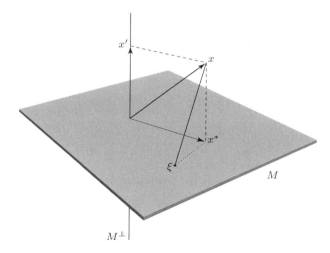

Figure 14.1 Orthogonal Projection. The figure is drawn with the standard inner product. x^* is the orthogonal projection of x onto M. The distance from x to x^* is smaller than the distance from x to ξ for any other $\xi \in M$.

extremum problem. The ρ-projection x^* of x is the vector in M which best approximates (lies closest to) x in the ρ-norm. This property follows from the well-known Theorem of Pythagoras, which asserts that in a rectangular triangle, the square of the hypotenuse is the sum of squares of the sides.

14.13 Proposition (Pythagoras): *If $x, y \in \mathbb{R}^S$ and $x \perp\!\!\!\perp y$ then*

$$\|x + y\|_\rho^2 = \|x\|_\rho^2 + \|y\|_\rho^2$$

PROOF: $\|x + y\|_\rho^2 = [\![x + y, x + y]\!]_\rho = \|x\|_\rho^2 + 2[\![x, y]\!]_\rho + \|y\|_\rho^2 = \|x\|_\rho^2 + \|y\|_\rho^2$ □

14.14 Proposition (Projection as Best Approximation): *Let $x \in \mathbb{R}^S$ and let M be a linear subspace. x^* is the ρ-orthogonal projection of x onto M if and only if*

$$x^* = \arg\min_{\xi \in M} \|x - \xi\|_\rho$$

PROOF: Let x^* be the ρ-orthogonal projection of x onto M and let x^{**} be the solution of the minimum distance problem $x^{**} = \arg\min_{\xi \in M} \|x - \xi\|_\rho$. Since $x^* - x^{**} \in M$, by Proposition 14.12, $(x - x^*) \perp\!\!\!\perp (x^* - x^{**})$ and by Pythagoras Theorem

$$\|x - x^{**}\|_\rho^2 = \|x - x^*\|_\rho^2 + \|x^* - x^{**}\|_\rho^2$$

If $x^* \neq x^{**}$, then x^* is closer to x than x^{**}, contradicting the definition of x^{**}. □

Representation of a Linear Functional

A real-valued linear function on $\mathbb{R}^S$ is called a *linear functional*. It is easy to check that the collection of all linear functionals on $\mathbb{R}^S$ (written $\mathbb{R}^{S*}$) is a vector space. $\mathbb{R}^{S*}$ is called the *dual space* of $\mathbb{R}^S$. In economic terms, $\mathbb{R}^{S*}$ is the space of (linear) *valuation* functions on $\mathbb{R}^S$. An important property of finite-dimensional vector spaces is that they are *self-dual*: $\mathbb{R}^S$ can be identified with its dual space $\mathbb{R}^{S*}$. The identification can be achieved using any inner product. If γ is a fixed vector in $\mathbb{R}^S$, then by the linearity of the inner product, the map $y \longmapsto [\![\gamma, y]\!]_\rho$ defines a linear functional on $\mathbb{R}^S$. The next theorem shows that the converse is also true: *any linear functional on $\mathbb{R}^S$ can be represented as an inner product with a fixed vector of $\mathbb{R}^S$*. This is a theorem of great importance on which all the results of this chapter hinge. In economic terms, it means that any (linear) valuation can be represented by a vector of prices in $\mathbb{R}^S$. If the linear functional is only defined on a *linear subspace* M, then, in order to be unique, the representation must be made with a fixed vector in M.

14.15 Theorem (Inner Product Representation of Linear Functional): *If M is a linear subspace of $\mathbb{R}^S$ and $\ell : M \longrightarrow \mathbb{R}$ is a linear functional defined on M, then there exists a unique vector $\gamma \in M$ such that*

$$\ell(y) = [\![\gamma, y]\!]_\rho, \quad \forall y \in M$$

PROOF: Either $\ell(y) = 0$, $\forall y \in M$, in which case we set $\gamma = 0$, or $\ell(y) \neq 0$ for some $y \in M$, and $\mathrm{Im}(\ell) = \mathbb{R}$. Thus $\dim M - \dim(\ker \ell) = 1$. If $(\ker \ell)^\perp$ denotes the ρ-orthogonal complement of $\ker \ell$ in M, then by Proposition 14.9, $\dim(\ker \ell)^\perp = 1$. Let $\widehat{\gamma} \in M$ be a basis for $(\ker \ell)^\perp$. By Proposition 14.10, for any $y \in M$, $y = y^* + \lambda\widehat{\gamma}$, where $y^* \in \ker \ell$ and

$$[\![\widehat{\gamma}, y]\!]_\rho = [\![\widehat{\gamma}, y^*]\!]_\rho + \lambda[\![\widehat{\gamma}, \widehat{\gamma}]\!]_\rho = \lambda[\![\widehat{\gamma}, \widehat{\gamma}]\!]_\rho \implies \lambda = \frac{[\![\widehat{\gamma}, y]\!]_\rho}{\|\widehat{\gamma}\|_\rho^2}$$

so that for all $y \in M$

$$\ell(y) = \ell(y^* + \lambda\widehat{\gamma}) = \lambda\ell(\widehat{\gamma}) = \frac{[\![\widehat{\gamma}, y]\!]_\rho\, \ell(\widehat{\gamma})}{\|\widehat{\gamma}\|_\rho^2} = [\![\gamma, y]\!]_\rho \text{ with } \gamma = \frac{\widehat{\gamma}\ell(\widehat{\gamma})}{\|\widehat{\gamma}\|_\rho^2}$$

The uniqueness of γ follows from $[\![\gamma, y]\!]_\rho = [\![\gamma', y]\!]_\rho$, for all $y \in M$ so that $[\![\gamma - \gamma', y]\!]_\rho = 0$, $\forall y \in M$. Letting $y = \gamma - \gamma'$ gives $\|\gamma - \gamma'\|_\rho^2 = 0$, so that $\gamma = \gamma'$. $\square$

Differential and Gradient

Let $f : \mathcal{U} \longrightarrow \mathbb{R}$ be a real-valued differentiable function defined on an open set $\mathcal{U} \subset \mathbb{R}^S$. The Representation Theorem 14.15 can be applied to the linear function (the differential) which approximates f at a point $x \in \mathcal{U}$. Recall first what it means for a real-valued function to be differentiable.

14.16 Definition: $f : \mathcal{U} \longrightarrow \mathbb{R}$ is *differentiable* at $x \in \mathcal{U}$ if there exist

(i) a linear function $\ell_x : \mathbb{R}^S \longrightarrow \mathbb{R}$
(ii) a function $\epsilon_x : \mathbb{R}^S \longrightarrow \mathbb{R}$, satisfying $\lim_{\|h\|_\rho \to 0} \epsilon_x(h) = 0$

such that

$$f(x + h) - f(x) = \ell_x(h) + \epsilon_x(h)\,\|h\|_\rho, \quad \forall h \in \mathbb{R}^S \text{ with } x + h \in \mathcal{U}$$

ℓ_x is called the *differential* of f at x and is written df_x. f is said to be *differentiable* if it is differentiable at every $x \in \mathcal{U}$.

When f is differentiable at x, *the differential df_x is unique.*[1] By a well-known theorem of analysis,[2] all norms on $\mathbb{R}^S$ are equivalent; *thus the differential df_x does not depend on the norm $\|\ \|_\rho$ chosen.* However, *the choice of the inner product (and norm) on $\mathbb{R}^S$ does affect the representation of the linear function df_x as an inner product.* Furthermore, if the increments h in the vector x are restricted to a linear subspace M, then the differential induces a linear map on M which can be represented by a vector in M. The representation of the differential df_x as an inner product thus depends both on the choice of the ρ-norm and the choice of the linear subspace M.

14.17 Proposition (Inner Product Representation of Differential): *Let $[\![\ ,\ ]\!]_\rho : \mathbb{R}^S \times \mathbb{R}^S \longrightarrow \mathbb{R}$ be an inner product, represented by a positive definite form ρ, and let M be a linear subspace of $\mathbb{R}^S$. If $f : \mathcal{U} \longrightarrow \mathbb{R}$ is differentiable at $x \in \mathcal{U}$, then there exists a vector $\gamma_M^\rho \in M$ such that*

$$df_x(h) = [\![\gamma_M^\rho, h]\!]_\rho, \quad \forall h \in M$$

γ_M^ρ is called the (ρ, M)-gradient of f at x and is written $\nabla_M^\rho f(x)$.

PROOF: The result follows by applying the Inner Product Representation Theorem 14.15 to the restriction of ℓ_x to M. □

---

[1]Suppose $f(x + h) - f(x) = \ell_x(h) + \epsilon_x(h)\,\|h\|_\rho = \ell'_x(h) + \epsilon'_x(h)\,\|h\|_\rho$ with ℓ_x and ℓ'_x linear functions on $\mathbb{R}^S$ and $\lim_{\|h\|_\rho \to 0} \epsilon_x(h) = \lim_{\|h\|_\rho \to 0} \epsilon'_x(h) = 0$. Let $v \in \mathbb{R}^S$ be such that $\|v\|_\rho = 1$ and $h = \lambda v$. Then $\lambda\ell_x(v) - \lambda\ell'_x(v) = |\lambda|\,(\epsilon_x(\lambda v) - \epsilon'_x(\lambda v)) \iff \ell_x(v) - \ell'_x(v) = \epsilon_x(\lambda v) - \epsilon'_x(\lambda v), \forall \lambda > 0$ which implies $\ell_x(v) = \ell'_x(v)$ when $\lambda \to 0$.
[2]See for example Fleming (1965, p. 30).

The (ρ, M) gradient of a function f has an interesting extremal property: intuitively it points in the direction of maximum increase of f. More precisely, if the ρ-norm measures the *cost* of increments h in the variable x, then $\nabla^\rho_M f(x)$ is the direction in M for which the function f attains the greatest increase for all increments h of the same cost $\|h\|_\rho = 1$.

14.18 Proposition (Maximum Property of (ρ, M)-Gradient):

$$\frac{\nabla^\rho_M f(x)}{\|\nabla^\rho_M f(x)\|_\rho} = \arg\max\left\{ df_x(h) \ \Big| \ h \in M, \quad \|h\|_\rho = 1 \right\}$$

PROOF: By Propositions 14.17 and 14.6

$$df_x(h) = [\![\gamma^\rho_M, h]\!]_\rho \leq \|\gamma^\rho_M\|_\rho \|h\|_\rho = \|\gamma^\rho_M\|_\rho$$

When h points (does not point) in the direction of γ^ρ_M, then the equality (strict inequality) holds. Thus $df_x(h)$ attains its maximum at $h^* = \gamma^\rho_M / \|\gamma^\rho_M\|_\rho$. □

Probability Inner Product

Let $\mathbf{S} = \{1, \ldots, S\}$ be a finite set of states of nature with vector of probabilities $\rho = (\rho_1, \ldots, \rho_S)$. A vector in $\mathbb{R}^S$ defines a *random variable* on the *probability space*[3] $(\mathbf{S}, \mathscr{S}, \rho)$, where $\mathscr{S}$ is the field of subsets of $\mathbf{S}$ and $\rho(\sigma) = \sum_{s \in \sigma} \rho_s$ is the probability of an event $\sigma \in \mathscr{S}$.

Given a random variable $y : \mathbf{S} \longrightarrow \mathbb{R}$, it is useful to have an average measure of its behavior across the states of nature. The simplest and most natural average is the *mean* (or *expectation*)

$$E(y) = \sum_{s=1}^{S} \rho_s y_s$$

The *variance* of y

$$\mathrm{var}(y) = \sum_{s=1}^{S} \rho_s \left(y_s - E(y) \right)^2$$

measures the error involved in using the mean to approximate y.

Given a pair of random variables $\gamma, y : \mathbf{S} \longrightarrow \mathbb{R}$, a useful average measure of their joint fluctuation (comovement) across the states of nature is given by their *covariance*

$$\mathrm{cov}(\gamma, y) = E\left((\gamma - E(\gamma))(y - E(y)) \right) = \sum_{s=1}^{S} \rho_s \left(\gamma_s - E(\gamma) \right)\left(y_s - E(y) \right)$$

---

[3]For the definition of a *probability space* see Section 26.

The covariance measures the extent to which γ and y are simultaneously above (below) their means. The covariance (variance) can be written as

$$\text{cov}(\gamma, y) = E(\gamma y) - E(\gamma)E(y) \tag{2}$$
$$\text{var}(y) = \text{cov}(y, y) = E(y^2) - (E(y))^2 \tag{3}$$

Given the probability space $(\mathbf{S}, \mathscr{S}, \rho)$, the *probability inner product* $[\![\,,\,]\!]_\rho : \mathbb{R}^S \times \mathbb{R}^S \longrightarrow \mathbb{R}$ is defined by

$$[\![\gamma, y]\!]_\rho = E(\gamma y) = \sum_{s=1}^S \rho_s \gamma_s y_s = \gamma^T [\rho] y, \quad \forall \gamma, y \in \mathbb{R}^S \tag{4}$$

where $[\rho]$ denotes the positive definite diagonal matrix

$$[\rho] = \begin{bmatrix} \rho_1 & \cdots & 0 \\ \vdots & \ddots & \vdots \\ 0 & \cdots & \rho_S \end{bmatrix}$$

induced by the vector of probabilities $\rho = (\rho_1, \ldots, \rho_S)$. The *probability-norm* $\|\,\|_\rho : \mathbb{R}^S \longrightarrow \mathbb{R}$, induced by the inner product (4), is defined by

$$\|y\|_\rho = \left(E(y^2)\right)^{\frac{1}{2}} = \left(\sum_{s=1}^S \rho_s y_s^2\right)^{\frac{1}{2}}, \quad \forall y \in \mathbb{R}^S \tag{5}$$

In view of (2) and (3), the inner product and norm can be written as

$$[\![\gamma, y]\!]_\rho = E(\gamma)E(y) + \text{cov}(\gamma, y) \tag{6}$$
$$\|y\|_\rho = \left((E(y))^2 + \text{var}(y)\right)^{\frac{1}{2}} \tag{7}$$

Every *certain (non-random)* variable $y \in \mathbb{R}^S$ can be written as $y = \alpha \mathbb{1}$ for some $\alpha \in \mathbb{R}$, where $\mathbb{1} = (1, \ldots, 1)$. Let

$$\langle \mathbb{1} \rangle = \left\{ y \in \mathbb{R}^S \mid y = \alpha \mathbb{1}, \quad \alpha \in \mathbb{R} \right\} = \left\{ y \in \mathbb{R}^S \mid \text{var}(y) = 0 \right\}$$

be the one-dimensional subspace of $\mathbb{R}^S$ consisting of all non-random variables. Its ρ-orthogonal complement $\langle \mathbb{1} \rangle^\perp$ consists of all *purely random (centered)* variables

$$\langle \mathbb{1} \rangle^\perp = \left\{ y \in \mathbb{R}^S \mid [\![\mathbb{1}, y]\!]_\rho = 0 \right\} = \left\{ y \in \mathbb{R}^S \mid E(y) = 0 \right\}$$

The probability inner product thus induces an orthogonal decomposition of the space of random variables $\mathbb{R}^S = \langle \mathbb{1} \rangle \oplus \langle \mathbb{1} \rangle^{\perp}$. Every random variable $y \in \mathbb{R}^S$ is decomposed into a *certain part* $\widehat{y}$ and a *purely random part* $\widetilde{y}$

$$y = \widehat{y} + \widetilde{y}, \quad \widehat{y} = E(y)\mathbb{1} \in \langle \mathbb{1} \rangle, \quad \widetilde{y} = y - E(y)\mathbb{1} \in \langle \mathbb{1} \rangle^{\perp} \tag{8}$$

It is straightforward to see that the certain part $\widehat{y}$ is the best approximation of y by a constant function in the ρ-norm.[4] The contributions $(E(y))^2$ and $\mathrm{var}(y)$ in (7), are the contributions of the certain part and the random part to the norm of y.

The orthogonal decomposition of $\mathbb{R}^S$ implies that the inner product (6) can be written as

$$[\![\gamma, y]\!]_{\rho} = [\![\widehat{\gamma}, \widehat{y}]\!]_{\rho} + [\![\widetilde{\gamma}, \widetilde{y}]\!]_{\rho} = E(\widehat{\gamma})E(\widehat{y}) + \mathrm{cov}(\widetilde{\gamma}, \widetilde{y}) \tag{9}$$

Since $[\![\widehat{\gamma}, \widetilde{y}]\!]_{\rho} = [\![\widetilde{\gamma}, \widehat{y}]\!]_{\rho} = 0$. Thus the inner product of a pair of random variables decomposes into the sum of the inner products of their certain and purely random components.

The *correlation coefficient* $\kappa_{\gamma, y}$ between two random variables γ and y defined by

$$\kappa_{\gamma, y} = \frac{\mathrm{cov}(\gamma, y)}{(\mathrm{var}(\gamma)\,\mathrm{var}(y))^{\frac{1}{2}}} \tag{10}$$

is a normalized (unit-free) measure of the degree to which the two random variables covary. Since $\mathrm{cov}(\gamma, y) = \mathrm{cov}(\widetilde{\gamma}, \widetilde{y})$, the coefficient of correlation satisfies

$$\kappa_{\gamma, y} = \frac{\mathrm{cov}(\widetilde{\gamma}, \widetilde{y})}{\|\widetilde{\gamma}\|_{\rho}\|\widetilde{y}\|_{\rho}} = \frac{[\![\widetilde{\gamma}, \widetilde{y}]\!]_{\rho}}{\|\widetilde{\gamma}\|_{\rho}\|\widetilde{y}\|_{\rho}} = \cos\theta^{\rho}_{\widetilde{\gamma}, \widetilde{y}} \tag{11}$$

The coefficient of correlation between two random variables (γ, y) is the cosine of the angle $\theta^{\rho}_{\widetilde{\gamma}, \widetilde{y}}$ between their purely random components. Thus in the probability induced metric, the statistical measure of correlation becomes a geometric measure of the extent to which the purely random components of the random variables point in the same direction.

In the section that follows, valuations of income streams will be obtained from the differentials of agents' utility functions. It will be important to understand how the gradient representation of a differential under the probability inner product is related to the (more familiar) gradient representation in the standard inner product.

The partial derivative $\frac{\partial f(\bar{x})}{\partial x_s}$ of a function $f : \mathcal{U} \subset \mathbb{R}^S \longrightarrow \mathbb{R}$ at $\bar{x} \in \mathcal{U}$ gives the value of the differential $df_{\bar{x}}(h)$ when the vector h is the vector $h = e_s =$

---

[4] $E(y) = \arg\min \left\{ \sum_{s=1}^{S} \rho_s (y_s - \eta)^2 \mid \eta \in \mathbb{R} \right\}.$

$(0, \ldots, 1, \ldots, 0)$, $s = 1, \ldots, S$, of the standard basis of $\mathbb{R}^S$. It follows that the differential of f at $\bar{x}$ in the standard inner product of $\mathbb{R}^S$ is given by

$$df_{\bar{x}}(h) = \sum_{s=1}^{S} \left[\nabla f(\bar{x}), e_s \right] h_s = \sum_{s=1}^{S} \frac{\partial f(\bar{x})}{\partial x_s} h_s = \left[\nabla f(\bar{x}), h \right] \qquad (12)$$

$\nabla f(\bar{x})$ is the gradient which was defined in Section 7. Since (12) can be written as

$$df_{\bar{x}}(h) = \sum_{s=1}^{S} \rho_s \left(\frac{1}{\rho_s} \frac{\partial f(\bar{x})}{\partial x_s} \right) h_s = \left[\!\left[\nabla^\rho f(\bar{x}), h \right]\!\right]_\rho$$

it follows that

$$\nabla^\rho f(\bar{x}) = \left(\frac{1}{\rho_1} \frac{\partial f(\bar{x})}{\partial x_1}, \ldots, \frac{1}{\rho_S} \frac{\partial f(\bar{x})}{\partial x_S} \right) \qquad (13)$$

is the ρ-gradient which represents the differential of f at $\bar{x}$ in the probability inner product (4) of $\mathbb{R}^S$. If the increments h are restricted to lie in a linear subspace $M \subset \mathbb{R}^S$, then by Proposition 14.12, the ρ-projection of $\nabla^\rho f(\bar{x})$ onto M, denoted by $\nabla^\rho_M f(\bar{x})$, is characterized by

$$df_{\bar{x}}(h) = \left[\!\left[\nabla^\rho f(\bar{x}), h \right]\!\right]_\rho = \left[\!\left[\nabla^\rho_M f(\bar{x}), h \right]\!\right]_\rho, \quad \forall h \in M \qquad (14)$$

so that $\nabla^\rho_M f(\bar{x})$ represents $df_{\bar{x}}$ on M with the probability inner product.

15. VALUATION OF INCOME STREAMS

Let $\mathscr{E}(u, \omega, V)$ be a two-period finance economy. To add more structure to the equilibrium pricing of securities, we make the additional assumption that all agents agree on the probability of occurrence of the states at date 1. The probabilities thus become objective data of the economy.

Assumption $\mathscr{P}$ (Objective Probabilities):   There are objective probabilities of occurrence $\rho = (\rho_1, \ldots, \rho_S)$ of each of the states at date 1, the probability of each state being positive.

Since valuation formulae are simplified if the marketed subspace $\langle V \rangle$ permits the riskless transfer of income between date 0 and date 1, we also make the following assumption.

Assumption $\mathscr{R}$ (Riskless Income Transfer):   The marketed subspace $\langle V \rangle$ permits the riskless transfer of income between date 0 and date 1, that is

$$\mathbb{1} = (1, \ldots, 1) \in \langle V \rangle$$

Valuation of Agent i

Consider first the valuation of date 1 income streams by a typical agent. Standard economic analysis suggests that if $x^i = (x_0^i, x_1^i, \ldots, x_S^i)$ is agent i's consumption stream, then the value he assigns to a date 1 income stream will depend on his present-value vector $\pi^i(x^i)$ defined by equation (4) of Section 7. This valuation vector of agent i defines not only the marginal rate of substitution between date 0 and date 1 (consumption), but also the marginal rates of substitution between each of the states at date 1. It measures, in short, not only the impatience of the agent to consume at date 0 relative to date 1, but also the risk benefits that can be derived from transferring income across the different states at date 1.

The value that agent i assigns to a marginal date 1 income stream $h_1 \in \mathbb{R}^S$ is measured by the maximum amount of date 0 income h_0 that he is prepared to forego, so that he is at least as well off with the new consumption stream $(x_0^i - h_0, x_1^i + h_1)$ as he was with his original consumption stream (x_0^i, x_1^i). If the agent has a differentiable utility function u^i, this value may be obtained by solving the linear equation

$$du_{x^i}^i(-h_0, h_1) = 0 \tag{1}$$

When the standard inner product $[\ ,\ ]$ is used on $\mathbb{R}^{S+1}$, then (1) becomes

$$du_{x^i}^i(-h_0, h_1) = \left[\lambda_0^i(x^i), -h_0\right] + \left[\nabla_1 u^i(x^i), h_1\right] = 0, \quad \forall\, h_1 \in \mathbb{R}^S$$

where

$$\lambda_0^i(x^i) = \frac{\partial u^i(x^i)}{\partial x_0^i} \quad \text{and} \quad \nabla_1 u^i(x^i) = \left(\frac{\partial u^i(x^i)}{\partial x_1^i}, \ldots, \frac{\partial u^i(x^i)}{\partial x_S^i}\right)$$

$\nabla_1 u^i(x^i)$ denoting the date 1 gradient of u^i. Thus the value $c^i(h_1; x^i)$ that agent i assigns to the income stream h_1 is given by

$$c^i(h_1; x^i) = \left[\pi_1^i(x^i), h_1\right], \quad \forall\, h_1 \in \mathbb{R}^S \tag{2}$$

where

$$\pi_1^i(x^i) = \frac{\nabla_1 u^i(x^i)}{\lambda_0^i(x^i)} = (\pi_1^i, \ldots, \pi_S^i)$$

is agent i's date 1 present-value vector. (2) asserts that the *value of* (or *cost that agent i is prepared to pay for*) *the (marginal) date 1 income stream h_1 is its present discounted value to agent i*. This value will be called the *fundamental value to agent i* of the income stream h_1. The date 1 present-value vector $\pi_1^i(x^i)$ at x^i is thus the vector which represents agent i's valuation c^i of income streams in $\mathbb{R}^S$, when the standard inner product is used on $\mathbb{R}^S$.

If agent i's valuation is restricted to income streams lying in the marketed subspace $\langle V \rangle$, then (1) becomes

$$du^i_{x^i}(-h_0, h_1) = \left[\lambda^i_0(x^i), -h_0 \right] + \left[\nabla_V u^i(x^i), h_1 \right] = 0, \quad \forall h_1 \in \langle V \rangle$$

where $\nabla_V u^i(x^i)$ is the orthogonal projection of the date 1 gradient $\nabla_1 u^i(x^i)$ onto $\langle V \rangle$. The value that agent i assigns to an income stream h_1 in the marketed subspace is thus given by

$$c^i(h_1; x^i) = \left[\pi^i_V(x^i), h_1 \right], \quad \forall h_1 \in \langle V \rangle \tag{3}$$

where $\pi^i_V(x^i) = \nabla_V u^i(x^i)/\lambda^i_0(x^i)$ is the orthogonal projection of the agent's date 1 present-value vector $\pi^i_1(x^i)$ onto $\langle V \rangle$. $\pi^i_V(x^i)$ is the unique vector in $\langle V \rangle$ which represents agent i's valuation c^i of income streams in the marketed subspace, under the standard inner product of $\mathbb{R}^S$.

A richer economic interpretation of the risk pricing of income streams implicit in agent i's valuation c^i—in which the means, variances and covariances of the agent's present-value vector and the income stream appear in a natural way—can be obtained if the probability inner product rather than the standard inner product is used for the date 1 income streams. The alternative expression for c^i is obtained if, instead of using the standard inner product $[\, , \,]$ on $\mathbb{R}^{S+1}$ for representing the differential of agent i's utility function in (1), we use the inner product $[\, , \,] \times [\![\, , \,]\!]_\rho$ on $\mathbb{R} \times \mathbb{R}^S$, where $[\![\, , \,]\!]_\rho$ is the probability inner product for $\mathbb{R}^S$ defined by (4) in Section 14. Equation (1) then becomes

$$du^i_{x^i}(-h_0, h_1) = \left[\lambda^i_0(x^i), -h_0 \right] + [\![\nabla^\rho_1 u^i(x^i), h_1]\!]_\rho = 0, \quad \forall h_1 \in \mathbb{R}^S$$

where

$$\nabla^\rho_1 u^i(x^i) = \left(\frac{1}{\rho_1} \frac{\partial u^i(x^i)}{\partial x^i_1}, \ldots, \frac{1}{\rho_s} \frac{\partial u^i(x^i)}{\partial x^i_S} \right)$$

is agent i's date 1 ρ-gradient. The valuation c^i is thus given by

$$c^i(h_1; x^i) = [\![\pi^{\rho,i}_1(x^i), h_1]\!]_\rho, \quad \forall h_1 \in \mathbb{R}^S \tag{4}$$

where $\pi^{\rho,i}_1 = (\pi^i_1/\rho_1, \ldots, \pi^i_S/\rho_S)$ is agent i's date 1 ρ-present-value vector. If agent i's valuation is restricted to income streams lying in the marketed subspace $\langle V \rangle$, then (1) becomes

$$du^i_{x^i}(-h_0, h_1) = \left[\lambda^i_0(x^i), -h_0 \right] + [\![\nabla^\rho_V u^i(x^i), h_1]\!]_\rho = 0, \quad \forall h_1 \in \langle V \rangle$$

where $\nabla^\rho_V u^i(x^i)$ is the ρ-orthogonal projection of $\nabla^\rho_1 u^i(x^i)$ onto $\langle V \rangle$. Thus c^i is given by

$$c^i(h_1; x^i) = [\![\pi^{\rho,i}_V(x^i), h_1]\!]_\rho, \quad \forall h_1 \in \langle V \rangle \tag{5}$$

where

$$\pi_V^{\rho,i}(x^i) = \frac{\nabla_V^\rho u^i(x^i)}{\lambda_0^i(x^i)}$$

is the ρ-orthogonal projection of $\pi_1^{\rho,i}(x^i)$ onto $\langle V \rangle$. $\pi_V^{\rho,i}(x^i)$ is thus the unique vector in $\langle V \rangle$ which represents agent i's valuation c^i of income streams in the marketed subspace, under the probability inner product on $\mathbb{R}^S$. Since $\pi_V^{\rho,i}(x^i)$ lies in $\langle V \rangle$, it can be viewed as a security and will be called the *pricing security of agent i* at x^i.

Ideal Security of Agent i

This security has a special economic significance for agent i. To see this, suppose that agent i were permitted to increase his consumption stream

$$x^i \rightarrow x^i + h$$

subject to the condition that the increment $h = (h_0, h_1)$ satisfies

$$h_1 \in \langle V \rangle, \quad |h_0|^2 + \|h_1\|_\rho^2 = k^2 \tag{6}$$

for some (small) value of k. Since k is small $(u^i(x^i + h) \cong u^i(x^i) + du_{x^i}^i(h))$ agent i would choose h to maximize the differential

$$du_{x^i}^i(h) = \left[\lambda_0^i(x^i), h_0\right] + \left[\!\left[\nabla_V^\rho u^i(x^i), h_1\right]\!\right]_\rho \tag{7}$$

By Proposition 14.18, the vector h^* which maximizes (7) subject to (6) is given by

$$h^* = \alpha \left(\lambda_0^i(x^i), \nabla_V^\rho u^i(x^i)\right) \tag{8}$$

where α is such that the norm of $h^* = (h_0^*, h_1^*)$ is k.

The second constraint in (6) forces agent i to make a trade-off between an increase in date 0 consumption $(|h_0|)$ and a change in date 1 consumption $(\|h_1\|_\rho)$. A change h_1 in the agent's date 1 consumption stream can create a more desirable date 1 income stream $x_1^i + h_1$ by performing two functions: it can increase the resulting income stream by increasing its *mean* and/or it can reduce the *risk* of the resulting income stream by shifting income across the states. Since

$$\|h_1\|_\rho^2 = (E(h_1))^2 + \text{var}(h_1)$$

the ρ-norm on the date 1 income streams makes both functions costly: increasing the mean and reducing risk. The income stream (8) gives the optimal trade-off between these different functions for agent i when his consumption stream is x^i.

Since the problem of maximizing (7) subject to (6) is a homogeneous problem in k, the choice of k is irrelevant to the composition of an optimal income stream which resolves the trade-offs between date 0 and date 1 changes in income. The security $\gamma = h_1^*/h_0^*$, which is independent of k, summarizes all the relevant economic aspects of the agent's local maximum problem.

15.1 Definition: The security $\gamma^i(x^i) = h_1^*/h_0^*$, where (h_0^*, h_1^*) is the income stream which maximizes the increase in utility $du_{x^i}^i(h)$ subject to $h_1 \in \langle V \rangle$ and $|h_0|^2 + \|h_1\|_\rho^2 = k^2$ for any non-zero value of k, is called the *ideal security of agent i* at $x^i \in \mathbb{R}_{++}^{S+1}$ in the marketed subspace.

Note that $\gamma^i(x^i)$ is agent i's locally most preferred security in the *marketed subspace*: it is not the agent's ideal security in $\mathbb{R}^S$, namely the security which maximizes (7) subject to (6), without the restriction $h_1 \in \langle V \rangle$.

15.2 Proposition (Equality of Pricing and Ideal Security):   *For any* $x^i \in \mathbb{R}_{++}^{S+1}$, *the pricing security and the ideal security of agent i coincide*

$$\gamma^i(x^i) = \pi_V^{\rho, i}(x^i)$$

PROOF: Follows from (5) and (8). □

The value to agent i of an income stream h_1 in the marketed subspace can thus be expressed as an inner product with the agent's ideal security

$$c^i(h_1; x^i) = [\![\gamma^i(x^i), h_1]\!]_\rho, \quad \forall h_1 \in \langle V \rangle$$

Since the inner product $[\![\,,\,]\!]_\rho$ can be expressed in terms of the means and covariance of $\gamma^i(x^i)$ and h_1 ((6) in Section 14)

$$c^i(h_1; x^i) = E\left(\gamma^i(x^i)\right) E(h_1) + \text{cov}\left(\gamma^i(x^i), h_1\right), \quad \forall h_1 \in \langle V \rangle \qquad (9)$$

To interpret this valuation, decompose the income stream h_1 into its *certain* and *purely random* parts, $h_1 = \widehat{h}_1 + \widetilde{h}_1$ (equation (8) in Section 14). By the linearity of c^i, the value of h_1 is the sum of the values of these two components

$$c^i(h_1) = c^i(\widehat{h}_1) + c^i(\widetilde{h}_1) \qquad (10)$$

Since

$$c^i(\widehat{h}_1) = [\![\gamma^i, \widehat{h}_1]\!]_\rho = [\![\widehat{\gamma}^i, \widehat{h}_1]\!]_\rho = E(\gamma^i)E(h_1) \qquad (11)$$

$$c^i(\widetilde{h}_1) = [\![\gamma^i, \widetilde{h}_1]\!]_\rho = [\![\widetilde{\gamma}^i, \widetilde{h}_1]\!]_\rho = \text{cov}(\widetilde{\gamma}^i, \widetilde{h}_1) = \text{cov}(\gamma^i, h_1) \qquad (12)$$

(9) expresses the value of h_1 as the sum of the values of its certain and purely random components.

The term $E\left(\gamma^i(x^i)\right)$ in (11) expresses the degree to which agent i is impatient to consume at date 0 rather than at date 1. More precisely, it is the value to agent i at date 0 of one more unit of consumption in each state at date 1— namely the value of the income stream $\mathbb{1} = (1, \ldots, 1)$.

15.3 Definition: If the preference ordering of agent i is represented by a differentiable utility function $u^i : \mathbb{R}^{S+1}_{++} \longrightarrow \mathbb{R}$, then the *rate of impatience* $r^i(x^i)$ of agent i at $x^i \in \mathbb{R}^{S+1}_{++}$ (and the associated *impatience factor* $1/(1 + r^i(x^i))$) is defined by

$$\frac{1}{1 + r^i(x^i)} = \sum_{s=1}^{S} \left(\frac{\partial u^i(x^i)}{\partial x^i_s}\right) \Big/ \left(\frac{\partial u^i(x^i)}{\partial x^i_0}\right) = \sum_{s=1}^{S} \pi^i_s(x^i) \tag{13}$$

Since $\mathbb{1} \in \langle V \rangle$

$$\frac{1}{1 + r^i(x^i)} = \left[\pi^i_1(x^i), \mathbb{1}\right] = c^i(\mathbb{1}; x^i) = \left[\!\left[\gamma^i(x^i), \mathbb{1}\right]\!\right]_\rho = E\left(\gamma^i(x^i)\right) \tag{14}$$

Using (10)–(12), the valuation formula (9) of agent i can be explained as follows. The value the agent assigns to an income stream depends on two sets of factors: his personal needs and on what the income stream offers. The agent's personal needs are summarized by the certain and random parts of his ideal security. The certain component $\widehat{\gamma}^i = E(\gamma^i)\mathbb{1} = 1/(1 + r^i)\mathbb{1}$ expresses the agent's *time preference*; the random component $\widetilde{\gamma}^i = \gamma^i - E(\gamma^i)\mathbb{1}$ expresses the agent's *risk preference* (namely the purely random income stream which most reduces risk for the agent). The characteristics of the income stream are summarized by its certain and risky parts. The certain component $\widehat{h}_1 = E(h_1)\mathbb{1}$ offers a uniform increment to consumption at date 1 relative to date 0; the random component $\widetilde{h}_1 = h_1 - E(h_1)\mathbb{1}$ provides potential risk reduction services. The *first term* of the valuation formula (9) is the product of the certain components of the ideal security and the income stream and gives the *discounted expected value* of the income stream. The smaller the agent's rate of impatience and the greater the uniform increase in income at date 1 offered by the income stream, the greater its value. The *second term* of (9) combines the purely random components of the ideal security and the income stream to give the *risk (covariance) value* of the income stream. The more closely the risk services offered by $\widetilde{h}_1$ conform to the risk needs expressed by $\widetilde{\gamma}^i$ (i.e. if the security offers relatively more (less) income in those states where it is more (less) needed) the greater its value to the agent. In short, the ideal security expresses the agent's needs, and the income stream offers certain services: the more closely the services conform to the needs, the greater the value of the security.

If we consider another agent $j \neq i$ at a consumption stream $x^j \in \mathbb{R}_{++}^{S+1}$, then his valuation of an income stream h_1 is given by

$$c^j(h_1; x^j) = \left[\gamma^j(x^j), h_1 \right]_\rho, \quad \forall h_1 \in \langle V \rangle$$

where $\gamma^j(x^j)$ is the ideal security of agent j at x^j. For arbitrary consumption streams x^i, x^j there is no reason why the two agents will agree on the valuation of the same income stream $h_1, c^j(h_1; x^j) \neq c^i(h_1; x^i)$. However if the income streams x^i and x^j have been obtained by trading on the financial markets, then the two agents will agree on the value of $h_1 \in \langle V \rangle$, since their valuations will coincide with the market value of the income stream.

Equilibrium Valuation

Let $((x, z), q)$ be an equilibrium of the two-period finance economy $\mathscr{E}(u, \omega, V)$. In the equilibrium, the J basic securities, whose date 1 payoffs are the J columns $[V^1 \ldots V^J]$ of the matrix V, are traded on competitive markets at the prices $q = (q_1, \ldots, q_J)$. Any income stream in the marketed subspace $\langle V \rangle$ can be obtained through a portfolio of these J basic securities. The *equilibrium market value* of an income stream $y \in \langle V \rangle$, denoted by $c_q(y)$, is the cost of the portfolio which generates the income stream y

$$c_q(y) = qz, \quad \text{for any } z \in \mathbb{R}^J \text{ such that } y = Vz \tag{15}$$

The function $c_q : \langle V \rangle \longrightarrow \mathbb{R}$ is called the *equilibrium market valuation function*. Since all agents trade the J basic securities at the common vector of prices q, the personal valuation of every agent for each income stream in the marketed subspace will coincide with the equilibrium market valuation of this income stream. From the first-order conditions at the equilibrium (equation (16) in Section 9), for each agent $i = 1, \ldots, I$

$$c_q(y) = qz = \sum_{s=1}^{S} \pi_s^i(x^i) V_s z = \left[\pi_1^i(x^i), y \right] = c^i(y; x^i), \quad \forall y \in \langle V \rangle \tag{16}$$

The equilibrium market value of the riskless income stream $\mathbb{1} = (1, \ldots, 1)$ defines the equilibrium *interest rate* r

$$c_q(\mathbb{1}) = \frac{1}{1+r}$$

Since for a given choice of inner product on $\mathbb{R}^S$, the vector in $\langle V \rangle$ which represents a linear functional on $\langle V \rangle$ is unique, it follows that the ideal securities of all agents coincide.

15.4 Theorem (Equilibrium Valuation of Securities):   *Let* $\mathscr{E}(u, \omega, V)$ *be a finance economy satisfying Assumptions* $\mathscr{U}$, $\mathscr{P}$, $\mathscr{R}$. *If* $((x, z), q)$ *is a financial market equilibrium, then the ideal securities of all agents at their equilibrium consumption streams coincide*

$$\gamma^1(x^1) = \cdots = \gamma^I(x^I) = \gamma \tag{17}$$

and the common vector γ *is called the ideal security at the equilibrium. The equilibrium market value of any income stream* y *in the marketed subspace* $\langle V \rangle$ *is given by*

$$c_q(y) = \frac{E(y)}{1+r} + \mathrm{cov}(\gamma, y) \tag{18}$$

where r *is the equilibrium interest rate.*

PROOF: By Proposition 15.2, $c^i(y; x^i) = \llbracket \gamma^i(x^i), y \rrbracket_\rho$, $\forall y \in \langle V \rangle$, $i = 1, \ldots, I$ and by (16), $c^i(y; x^i) = c_q(y)$, $\forall y \in \langle V \rangle$, $i = 1, \ldots, I$. The Representation Theorem 14.15 implies that there exists a unique vector $\gamma \in \langle V \rangle$ such that

$$c_q(y) = \llbracket \gamma, y \rrbracket_\rho, \quad \forall y \in \langle V \rangle$$

Thus $\gamma^1(x^1) = \cdots = \gamma^I(x^I) = \gamma$: the equilibrium valuation formula (18) then follows from the personal valuation formulae (9) and (14), since $E\left(\gamma^i(x^i)\right) = E(\gamma) = c_q(\mathbb{1}) = 1/(1+r)$, $i = 1, \ldots, I$. $\square$

Economic Interpretation

When markets are incomplete, agents' present-value vectors are generically distinct (Theorem 11.6). Agents may thus assign different values to arbitrary income streams at date 1. Trading on the financial markets under a common vector of security prices leads however to a consensus among agents on the value of income streams which lie in the marketed subspace. This is reflected in the equalization of the ideal securities of the agents (17). *Thus the ideal security at an equilibrium is a social vector which (like the invisible hand) points in the common most preferred direction of agents in the marketed subspace* $\langle V \rangle$.

Applying the decomposition of a random variable into its certain and risky components (equation (8) in Section 14) to the ideal security γ and each individual agent's ideal security γ^i at the equilibrium gives

$$\gamma = \widehat{\gamma} + \widetilde{\gamma}, \quad \gamma^i = \widehat{\gamma}^i + \widetilde{\gamma}^i, \quad i = 1, \ldots, I$$

From the uniqueness of the decomposition and from (17), it follows that the certain (*time preference*) components of these vectors coincide

$$\left(\frac{1}{1+r^i(x^i)}\right) \mathbb{1} = \widehat{\gamma}^i = \widehat{\gamma} = \left(\frac{1}{1+r}\right) \mathbb{1}, \quad i = 1, \dots, I$$

thus $r^i(x^i) = r$, $i = 1, \dots, I$, so that *all agents have the same rate of impatience and this common rate of impatience equals the equilibrium rate of interest.*
  Similarily for the risky components

$$\widetilde{\gamma}^i = \widetilde{\gamma}, \quad i = 1, \dots, I$$

so that $\widetilde{\gamma}$ measures the *equilibrium risk preference* (the purely random income stream which most reduces risk for all agents at the equilibrium).
  Decomposing any income stream y in the marketed subspace $\langle V \rangle$ into its certain and risky components $y = \widehat{y} + \widetilde{y}$, (18) can be written as

$$\begin{aligned} c_q(y) = c_q(\widehat{y}) + c_q(\widetilde{y}) &= [\![\widehat{\gamma}, \widehat{y}]\!]_\rho + [\![\widetilde{\gamma}, \widetilde{y}]\!]_\rho \\ &= \frac{E(y)}{1+r} + \text{cov}(\gamma, y) \end{aligned} \tag{19}$$

Two cases can now be distinguished according as the agents do ($\widetilde{\gamma} \neq 0$) or do not ($\widetilde{\gamma} = 0$) seek risk reduction services at the equilibrium. In the latter case ($\text{var}(\widetilde{\gamma}) = 0$) agents are essentially fully insured at the equilibrium: thus even a risky income stream $y \in \langle V \rangle$, $\text{var}(y) \neq 0$ has no covariance value or cost ($\text{cov}(\gamma, y) = 0$). In this case the value of an income stream coincides with the value of the certain component $\widehat{y}$—namely it is *the discounted value under the equilibrium interest rate of the expected income stream* $E(y)\mathbb{1}$. There are two well-known cases where agents do not seek risk reduction services at the equilibrium. The first arises in an equilibrium of an economy in which some agent i is *risk-neutral* (his utility function is of the form $u^i(x^i) = v_0(x_0^i) + E(x_1^i)$) and has an interior equilibrium consumption $x^i \in \mathbb{R}_{++}^{S+1}$: in this case $\nabla_1^\rho u^i = \mathbb{1}$ so that $\gamma = \alpha\mathbb{1}$, $\alpha > 0$. The second arises in an equilibrium of an economy in which markets are complete, agents have state-independent additively separable utility functions (Definition 16.5), and there is no aggregate risk ($\text{var}(\sum_{i=1}^I \omega_1^i) = 0$). In this case all agents have non-random date 1 equilibrium consumption streams, and $\nabla_1^\rho u^i = \alpha^i\mathbb{1}$, $i = 1, \dots, I$ so that $\gamma = \alpha\mathbb{1}$, $\alpha > 0$ (see Theorem 16.7).
  In the more realistic case where agents have non-trivial risk preferences ($\widetilde{\gamma} \neq 0$) at the equilibrium, the covariance term in (19) is non-zero ($\text{cov}(\gamma, y) \neq 0$) for most income streams in the marketed subspace with a non-trivial risky component ($\widetilde{y} \neq 0$). We call the second term $c_q(\widetilde{y}) = \text{cov}(\gamma, y)$, in the valuation equation (19), the *covariance value* (if $c_q(\widetilde{y}) > 0$) or *cost* (if $c_q(\widetilde{y}) < 0$) of the

income stream y. This term values the risky component $\widetilde{y}$ of the income stream by comparing its behavior as a random variable with the risky component $\widetilde{\gamma}$ of the ideal security. By (10) in Section 14

$$c_q(\widetilde{y}) = \operatorname{cov}(\widetilde{\gamma}, \widetilde{y}) = \kappa_{\widetilde{\gamma}, \widetilde{y}} \left(\operatorname{var}(\widetilde{\gamma}) \operatorname{var}(\widetilde{y}) \right)^{\frac{1}{2}} \tag{20}$$

where $\kappa_{\widetilde{\gamma}, \widetilde{y}}$ is the *correlation coefficient* between $\widetilde{y}$ and $\widetilde{\gamma}$. Three cases can arise according as the risky component $\widetilde{y}$ of the income stream has positive, zero or negative correlation with $\widetilde{\gamma}$.

(i) *If the risky component of the income stream is positively correlated with the risky component of the ideal security, then the security offers risk reducing services whose value at the equilibrium is given by the covariance value $c_q(\widetilde{y}) >$* 0. The risky component of the ideal security indicates those states in which income is relatively more (less) valuable and a positively correlated security provides on average more (less) income in those states where income is more (less) valuable.

In considering different types of securities it is useful to decompose the risks in an economy into two categories: *individual risks* which affect the endowments and preferences of individuals, and *aggregate risks* which affect the behavior of aggregate output across the states. Insurance contracts are securities whose payoffs are contingent on individual states: their income stream is typically positively correlated with the ideal security. Agents are prepared to pay more than the expected value of the income stream to reduce their risks. For such a security the greater the variance of its risky component $(\operatorname{var}(\widetilde{y}))$ and the greater the variance of the ideal security $(\operatorname{var}(\widetilde{\gamma}))$, the greater the risk services that it provides. In the limiting case where there are no aggregate risks and the insurance markets are perfect $(\widetilde{\gamma} = 0)$ agents pay no risk premium at the equilibrium (this case was mentioned above).

(ii) If an income stream is uncorrelated with the return on the ideal security $(\kappa_{\widetilde{\gamma}, \widetilde{y}} = 0)$ then it offers no risk services (incurs no risk costs) and has a zero covariance value. This case arises when y is independent of γ.

(iii) *If the income stream is negatively correlated with the ideal security, then there is a risk cost involved in the purchase of the security whose value at the equilibrium is given by the covariance cost $c_q(\widetilde{y}) < 0$.* The income offered by such a security is on average greater (less) in those states in which income is less (more) valuable. For such securities, an increase in their variance or an increase in the variance of the ideal security leads to a greater covariance cost. Equity contracts fall into this category. These are securities which typically increase the risks incurred by agents, but permit the society as a whole to share the aggregate risks. The profits of firms (and hence the dividends on their equity contracts) are typically high (low) when aggregate output is high (low), but these are typically the states in which the risky component of the ideal security is negative (positive).

Geometric Interpretation

The equilibrium valuation of an income stream can be summarized using the geometry on $\mathbb{R}^S$ induced by the ρ-inner product. An income stream is decomposed into its component on the diagonal $\langle \mathbb{1} \rangle$, and its risky component on the ρ-orthogonal complement $\langle \mathbb{1} \rangle^{\perp}$. The value of the component along the diagonal $\langle \mathbb{1} \rangle$ is obtained by discounting (shrinking) by the factor induced by the rate of interest $E(y)/(1+r)$. By equation (11) in Section 14, the value of the second component (20) can be written as

$$c_q(\widetilde{y}) = \mathrm{cov}(\widetilde{\gamma}, \widetilde{y}) = \cos \theta^{\rho}_{\widetilde{\gamma}, \widetilde{y}} \, \|\widetilde{\gamma}\|_{\rho} \, \|\widetilde{y}\|_{\rho}$$

where $\theta^{\rho}_{\widetilde{\gamma}, \widetilde{y}}$ is the *angle* (in the ρ-inner product) between $\widetilde{y}$ and $\widetilde{\gamma}$. Thus the value of the risky component $\widetilde{y}$ depends on the angle $\theta^{\rho}_{\widetilde{\gamma}, \widetilde{y}}$ between $\widetilde{y}$ and the risky component $\widetilde{\gamma}$ of the ideal security: the smaller the angle the greater the value of the income stream. *The (covariance) value of a security is greater the more closely its risky component points in the direction of the risky component of the ideal security.* When a security points in a *similar direction* $(0 \leq \theta < \pi/2)$ to that of the ideal security, it has a positive covariance value: when it points in an *opposing direction* $(\pi/2 < \theta \leq \pi)$ it has a negative covariance value. The magnitude of the covariance value depends on the lengths $\|\widetilde{\gamma}\|_{\rho}$ and $\|\widetilde{y}\|_{\rho}$ of the risky components of the ideal asset and the income stream.

16. REPRESENTATIVE AGENT ANALYSIS

Theorem 15.4 showed that the equilibrium market value of a security can be explained by the nature of the stochastic dependence between its income stream and the income stream on the ideal security. The security γ depends on the marginal utilities of income of the agents across the states and hence on their equilibrium consumption streams. In general, the equilibrium allocation $x = (x^1, \ldots, x^I)$, and consequently γ, depend in a complicated way on the data (u, ω, V) of the economy. There are however some cases where the ideal security can be expressed directly as a function of the aggregate endowment, this function in turn depending on the preferences and endowments of the individual agents. *In such cases the qualitative properties of security prices can be deduced from the nature of the stochastic dependence between the income stream of the security and aggregate output, without needing to solve for the equilibrium.* We will present three such cases.

(i) The financial markets are *complete* and agents have *additively separable* preferences.

(ii) Agents' endowments lie in the marketed subspace $\langle V \rangle$ and their preferences exhibit *linear risk tolerance* and are sufficiently similar.

(iii) Agents' endowments lie in the marketed subspace $\langle V \rangle$ and their preferences are *mean-variance* (CAPM model).

Economies which satisfy (i) or (ii) have Pareto optimal equilibria. Since a social welfare function is maximized at such an equilibrium allocation, the qualitative properties of the equilibria are the same as those of an economy with a single representative agent. These two cases are studied in this section. By contrast, the equilibria of economies which satisfy (iii) may not be Pareto optimal: the derivation of the properties of the equilibria in this case is based on arguments specific to economies with mean-variance preferences, and these are studied in Section 17.

The intuition behind case (i) can be explained as follows. With (state independent) additively separable preferences, agents seek to equalize their consumption in each state at date 1: since the markets are complete, the extent to which such equalization can be achieved depends on the magnitude of the fluctuations in aggregate output across the states. If there are no differences in the risk aversion of the agents, then the equilibrium consumption of each agent is proportional to aggregate output. With differences in the risk aversion of the agents, equilibrium consumption streams are only positively dependent on the aggregate output. In each case there is an inverse relation between the aggregate output in each state and the associated state price.

This inverse relation can be established by exploiting the property of Pareto optimality of an equilibrium with complete markets. This property permits the construction of a function (which depends on the equilibrium) called the utility function of the representative agent. The surrogate single-agent economy consisting of this utility function, and the aggregate endowment has a unique equilibrium in which the consumption stream is the aggregate output and the vector of state prices is the gradient of the representative agent's utility function at this consumption stream. Furthermore these state prices coincide with the equilibrium state prices of the original economy.

Representative Agent

The first step is to construct the utility function of the representative agent. To this end we introduce the idea of the sup-convolution of a family of utility functions.

16.1 Definition: Let $u^1, \ldots, u^I : \mathbb{R}^n_{++} \longrightarrow \mathbb{R}$ be a family of utility functions. The *sup-convolution* u^* of $u^1, \ldots, u^I$ (denoted by $u^* = u^1 \diamond u^2 \diamond \cdots \diamond u^I$), $u^* : \mathbb{R}^n_{++} \longrightarrow \mathbb{R}$ is defined by

$$u^*(\xi) = \sup \left\{ \sum_{i=1}^{I} u^i(\xi^i) \;\middle|\; \sum_{i=1}^{I} \xi^i = \xi, \quad (\xi^1, \ldots, \xi^I) \in \mathbb{R}^{nI}_{++} \right\} \tag{1}$$

When the functions u^i $(i = 1, \ldots, I)$ are concave, monotonic utility functions, the sup-convolution u^* of these functions is also concave and monotonic and can thus be considered as a (social) utility function. Furthermore if the functions u^i $(i = 1, \ldots, I)$ are differentiable, then u^* is differentiable and the solution of the (social) maximum problem in (1) is obtained when the gradients of all the utility functions u^i are equal; this common vector is the gradient of u^*.

16.2 Proposition (Properties of Sup-convolution): *If* $u^1, \ldots, u^I : \mathbb{R}^n_{++} \longrightarrow \mathbb{R}$ *are concave differentiable functions and if* $u^* = u^1 \diamond \cdots \diamond u^I$ *is the sup-convolution, then*

(i) u^* *is concave;*

(ii) $(\bar{\xi}^1, \ldots, \bar{\xi}^I) \in \mathbb{R}^{nI}_{++}$ *is a solution of the maximum problem (1) at*

$$\bar{\xi} = \bar{\xi}^1 + \cdots + \bar{\xi}^I$$

if and only if there exists $\bar{\pi} \in \mathbb{R}^n$ *such that*

$$\nabla u^1(\bar{\xi}^1) = \cdots = \nabla u^I(\bar{\xi}^I) = \bar{\pi} \tag{2}$$

Furthermore u^* *is differentiable at* $\bar{\xi}$ *and*

$$\nabla u^*(\bar{\xi}) = \bar{\pi} \tag{3}$$

PROOF: The proof is given in the appendix to this chapter (Lemma A3.3 and Proposition A3.5) and is based on the property that the subgraph of u^* is the sum of the subgraphs of the functions u^i $(i = 1, \ldots, I)$. Differentiability is not needed for (i), only for (ii). (2) is simply the first-order condition for the maximum problem (1). A short-cut way of obtaining (3) is to apply the Envelope Theorem to u^* at $\bar{\xi}$. □

Consider an economy in which the financial market equilibria are Pareto optimal: this is always the case if markets are complete (rank $V = S$) and if markets are incomplete (rank $V < S$) can occur for a subclass of economies (studied at the end of this section) with specific restrictions on preferences and endowments. Let $((\bar{x}, \bar{z}), \bar{q})$ be a financial market equilibrium of such an economy. Since the allocation $\bar{x} = (\bar{x}^1, \ldots, \bar{x}^I)$ is Pareto optimal, the present-value vectors $\bar{\pi}^i$ of the agents are equalized

$$\bar{\pi}^i = \pi^i(\bar{x}^i) = \frac{1}{\bar{\lambda}^i_0} \nabla u^i(\bar{x}^i) = \bar{\pi}, \quad i = 1, \ldots, I \tag{4}$$

where $\bar{\lambda}^i_0 = \partial u^i(\bar{x}^i)/\partial x^i_0$. Thus if we define new utility functions $(\bar{u}^i)$ for the agents, obtained by dividing their utility functions by the date 0 marginal utilities of income at their equilibrium consumption streams

$$\bar{u}^i(x^i) = \left(\frac{1}{\bar{\lambda}^i_0}\right) u^i(x^i), \quad i = 1, \ldots, I$$

then (4) can be written as

$$\nabla \bar{u}^1(\bar{x}^1) = \cdots = \nabla \bar{u}^I(\bar{x}^I) = \bar{\pi} \tag{5}$$

If the functions $u^1, \ldots, u^I$ are concave and differentiable, then Proposition 16.2 can be applied to the function $u^* = \bar{u}^1 \diamond \cdots \diamond \bar{u}^I$ and leads to the following definition.

16.3 Definition: Let $((\bar{x}, \bar{z}), \bar{q})$ be a Pareto optimal financial market equilibrium and let $\bar{\lambda}_0^i = \partial u^i(\bar{x}^i)/\partial x_0^i$, $i = 1, \ldots, I$. The function $u^* : \mathbb{R}_{++}^{S+1} \longrightarrow \mathbb{R}$ defined by

$$u^* = \bar{u}^1 \diamond \cdots \diamond \bar{u}^I = \left(\frac{1}{\bar{\lambda}_0^1}\right) u^1 \diamond \cdots \diamond \left(\frac{1}{\bar{\lambda}_0^I}\right) u^I$$

is called the *utility function of the representative agent* at the equilibrium $((\bar{x}, \bar{z}), \bar{q})$.

The utility function u^* is obtained by maximizing a weighted average of the utility functions of the agents, where the weights are chosen so that giving one additional unit of income to any agent at date 0 has the same social value. The function u^* reduces the analysis of the FM equilibrium $((\bar{x}, \bar{z}), \bar{q})$ of the economy $\mathscr{E}(u, \omega, V)$ to the analysis of a single-agent economy $\mathscr{E}(u^*, w, V)$, where $w = \sum_{i=1}^{I} \omega^i$ is the *aggregate endowment*. Since the financial market budget set $\mathbb{B}(\bar{q}, \omega^i)$ is included in the contingent market budget set $B(\bar{\pi}, \omega^i)$ (see Section 10), equation (5) implies that $(\bar{x}, \bar{\pi})$ is a contingent market (CM) equilibrium. The function u^* also reduces the analysis of the CM equilibrium $(\bar{x}, \bar{\pi})$ of the economy $\mathscr{E}(u, \omega)$ to the analysis of the equilibrium of the economy $\mathscr{E}(u^*, w)$ with a representative agent.

16.4 Proposition (Representative Agent Equilibrium):   *Let $\mathscr{E}(u, \omega, V)$ be an economy satisfying Assumption $\mathscr{U}$ in which agents' utility functions are concave and the aggregate endowment $w = \sum_{i=1}^{I} \omega^i$ is strictly positive. If $((\bar{x}, \bar{z}), \bar{q})$ is a Pareto optimal financial market (FM) equilibrium and if $\bar{\pi} \in \mathbb{R}_{++}^{S+1}$ is the common present-value vector of the agents, then*

(i) *the representative-agent economy $\mathscr{E}(u^*, w)$ has a unique CM equilibrium $(w, \bar{\pi})$ and the equilibrium vector of state prices is given by*

$$\bar{\pi} = \nabla u^*(w) \tag{6}$$

(ii) *the representative-agent economy $\mathscr{E}(u^*, w, V)$ has a unique FM equilibrium $((w, 0), \bar{q})$.*

PROOF:　Maximizing u^* over the budget set $\mathbb{B}(\bar{q}, w, V)$ or $B(\bar{\pi}, w)$ requires u^* to be defined on $\mathbb{R}_+^{S+1}$. Since u^* is concave, setting $u^*(\xi) = -\infty$ if $\xi \in \partial\mathbb{R}_+^{S+1}$ extends u^* in an appropriate way. To prove (i) note that since $\bar{x}^1 + \cdots + \bar{x}^I = w$ and (5) is satisfied, $\nabla u^*(w) = \bar{\pi}$. By the concavity of u^* this implies that

$$u^*(w) = \max\left\{u^*(\xi) \mid \xi \in \mathbb{R}_+^{S+1}, \bar{\pi}(\xi - w) = 0\right\} = \max\left\{u^*(\xi) \mid \xi \in B(\bar{\pi}, w)\right\}$$

so that $(w, \bar{\pi})$ is a CM equilibrium of $\mathscr{E}(u^*, w)$.

To prove (ii) note that by the first-order conditions of each agent at equilibrium, $\bar{q} = \bar{\pi}_1 V$ which can be written as $\bar{\pi} W = 0$. For any $x \in \mathbb{B}(\bar{q}, w, V)$ there exists z such that $x - w = Wz$: but then $\bar{\pi}(x - w) = \bar{\pi}Wz = 0$ so that $x \in B(\bar{\pi}, w)$. Thus $\mathbb{B}(\bar{q}, w, V) \subset B(\bar{\pi}, w)$. Thus w also solves the representative agent's FM maximum problem $\max\left\{u^*(\xi) \mid \xi \in \mathbb{B}(\bar{q}, w, V)\right\}$. w is financed by the portfolio $0 = (0, \dots, 0) \in \mathbb{R}^J$ so that $((w, 0), \bar{q})$ is an FM equilibrium. Uniqueness follows from the differentiability of u^* at w. $\square$

The advantage of constructing the function $u^* = \bar{u}^1 \diamond \cdots \diamond \bar{u}^I$ is that properties of the equilibrium vector of state prices can be deduced from properties of u^* without having to explicitly solve the equilibrium problem. If u^* is an expected utility with probabilities given by Assumption $\mathscr{P}$ (a property which holds if each agent's utility function u^i has this form) then equation (6) reduces to $\pi_s = \rho_s \varphi(w_s)$ where φ is a decreasing function: the date 1 ρ-gradient of u^* can then be written as

$$\pi^\rho = \left(\frac{\pi_1}{\rho_1}, \dots, \frac{\pi_S}{\rho_s}\right) = (\varphi(w_1), \dots, \varphi(w_S))$$

each component π_s/ρ_s being a common function $\varphi(w_s)$ of the aggregate endowment in state s. This equation permits the risk price of an income stream y in the marketed subspace to be expressed as a function of its stochastic dependence on the date 1 aggregate endowment.

Before pursuing the analysis further, let us state precisely the additional assumptions on agents' utility functions needed to obtain this formula. It is assumed that for each agent $i = 1, \dots, I$ the utility function u^i has two properties:

　(i) it is additively separable between date 0 and date 1
　(ii) the utility of the date 1 component of a consumption stream is an expected utility with common objective probabilities given by Assumption $\mathscr{P}$.

Property (ii) is commonly referred to as the *von-Neumann-Morgenstern* (VNM) property.

16.5 Definition: The utility function $u^i : \mathbb{R}_+^{S+1} \longrightarrow \mathbb{R}$ of agent i is VNM-*additively separable* if there exist functions $v_0^i, v_1^i : \mathbb{R}_+ \longrightarrow \mathbb{R}$ which are smooth on $\mathbb{R}_{++}$ and satisfy $(t = 0, 1)$

$$v_t^{i\prime}(c) > 0, \; v_t^{i\prime\prime}(c) < 0, \; \forall c \in \mathbb{R}_{++} \quad \text{and} \quad v_t^{i\prime}(c) \to \infty \text{ as } c \to 0 \qquad (7)$$

$$u^i(x^i) = v_0^i(x_0^i) + \sum_{s=1}^{S} \rho_s v_1^i(x_s^i)$$

and we write $u^i \longleftrightarrow (v_0^i, v_1^i)$. u^i is said to exhibit *pure time preference* if

$$\frac{v_1^{i\prime}(c)}{v_0^{i\prime}(c)} < 1 \quad \text{for all} \quad c > 0 \qquad (8)$$

(7) ensures that the utility function u^i satisfies Assumption $\mathscr{U}$. If the rate of impatience $r^i(x^i)$ (Definition 15.3) of agent i is positive for every positive constant consumption stream $x^i = (c, \dots, c)$ then agent i is said to exhibit *pure time preference*. When u^i is VNM additively separable this reduces to (8)

$$\frac{1}{1 + r^i(c, \dots, c)} = \frac{\sum_{s=1}^{S} \rho_s v_1^{i\prime}(c)}{v_0^{i\prime}(c)} = \frac{v_1^{i\prime}(c)}{v_0^{i\prime}(c)} < 1$$

Thus agent i exhibits pure time preference if whenever the consumption he expects in each state at date 1 is the same as his consumption at date 0, then he prefers an additional unit of consumption at date 0 to the promise of an additional unit of consumption in each state at date 1.

VNM additive separability and pure time preference are two further properties (in addition to concavity, monotonicity and differentiability) which are inherited by the sup-convolution (representative agent utility) function u^* from the primitive utility functions u^i $(i = 1, \dots, I)$.

16.6 Proposition (Additive Separability and Pure Time Preference of u*):

Let $\bar{\lambda}_0^i, \; i = 1, \dots, I$ be any positive numbers.

(a) If u^i is VNM-additively separable $\left(u^i \longleftrightarrow (v_0^i, v_1^i)\right)$, and if $\bar{u}^i = u^i / \bar{\lambda}_0^i$, $i = 1, \dots, I$, then $u^* = \bar{u}^1 \diamond \cdots \diamond \bar{u}^I$ is VNM-additively separable $(u^* \longleftrightarrow (v_0^*, v_1^*))$ with

$$v_0^* = \bar{v}_0^1 \diamond \cdots \diamond \bar{v}_0^I, \quad v_1^* = \bar{v}_1^1 \diamond \cdots \diamond \bar{v}_1^I$$

and $\bar{v}_0^i = v_0^i / \bar{\lambda}_0^i, \; \bar{v}_1^i = v_1^i / \bar{\lambda}_0^i, \; i = 1, \dots, I$.

(b) If (v_0^i, v_1^i) satisfies (8) for $i = 1, \dots, I$, then (v_0^*, v_1^*) satisfies (8).

PROOF: (See Appendix A3.6). □

Complete Markets

In an economy with complete markets, a rather thorough description of the properties of a financial market equilibrium can be obtained if agents' utility functions are additively separable. With complete markets, every financial market equilibrium $((\bar{x}, \bar{z}), \bar{q})$ is Pareto optimal: the representative agent analysis can thus be applied. As shown in Theorem 15.4, the equilibrium value of any income stream in the marketed subspace can be deduced from the ideal security $\bar{\gamma}$, which in this case coincides with the common date 1 ρ-present-value vector $\bar{\pi}^\rho$ of all the agents

$$\bar{\gamma} = \bar{\pi}^{\rho,1} = \cdots = \bar{\pi}^{\rho,I} = \bar{\pi}^\rho$$

so that $\bar{\gamma}_s = \bar{\pi}_s/\rho_s$, $s = 1, \ldots, S$ where $\bar{\pi}_s$ is the state price ($s = 1, \ldots, S$) associated with the equilibrium. When markets are complete there is no need to project the agents ρ-present-value vectors $\bar{\pi}^{\rho,i}$ onto the market subspace since $\langle V \rangle = \mathbb{R}^S$. By Proposition 16.4 the ideal security $\bar{\gamma}$ is the date 1 ρ-gradient $\nabla_1^\rho u^*(w)$ of the representative agent at the aggregate endowment w. Using the VNM separability of u^* it is easy to show that $\bar{\gamma}_s$ is inversely related to the aggregate endowment w_s in state s, while the consumption $\bar{x}_s^i$ of each individual agent follows the fluctuations in aggregate output w_s. Since the equilibrium rate of interest $\bar{r}$ is equal to the rate of impatience $r^*(w)$ of the representative agent at the aggregate output, if all agents have pure time preference and aggregate output increases over time then the rate of interest is positive.

16.7 Theorem (Complete Markets Equilibrium): *Let $\mathscr{E}(u, \omega, V)$ be an economy in which the utility functions are VNM-additively separable and $\langle V \rangle = \mathbb{R}^S$. If $((\bar{x}, \bar{z}), \bar{q})$ is a financial market equilibrium with ideal security $\bar{\gamma}$, then*

  (a) *there exists a strictly decreasing function $\varphi : \mathbb{R}_+ \longrightarrow \mathbb{R}_+$, such that*

$$\bar{\gamma}_s = \varphi(w_s), \quad s = 1, \ldots, S \tag{9}$$

      where $\varphi = v_1^{*\prime}$ and $(v_0^*, v_1^*) \longleftrightarrow u^*$ is the utility function of the representative agent at the equilibrium;

  (b) *if all agents have pure time preference and $w_s \geq w_0$, $s = 1, \ldots, S$, then the equilibrium interest rate $\bar{r}$ is positive;*

  (c) *there exist strictly increasing functions $\psi^i : \mathbb{R}_+ \longrightarrow \mathbb{R}_+$, $i = 1, \ldots, I$ such that*

$$\bar{x}_s^i = \psi^i(w_s), \quad s = 1, \ldots, S, \quad i = 1, \ldots, I$$

PROOF: (a) By Proposition 15.2, Theorem 15.4, and $\langle V \rangle = \mathbb{R}^S$

$$\bar{\gamma}_s = \frac{\bar{\pi}_s}{\rho_s}, \quad s = 1, \ldots, S$$

By Proposition 16.4(i), $\bar{\pi}_s = \partial u^*(w)/\partial \xi_s$, $s = 1, \ldots, S$ and by Proposition 16.6, u^* is VNM-additively separable ($u^* \longleftrightarrow (v_0^*, v_1^*)$). Thus the function $\varphi : \mathbb{R}_+ \longrightarrow \mathbb{R}_+$ defined by

$$\bar{\gamma}_s = v_1^{*\prime}(w_s) = \varphi(w_s), \quad s = 1, \ldots, S$$

is strictly decreasing, since $v_1^{*\prime\prime} < 0$.

(c) The first-order conditions for agent i at the equilibrium

$$\bar{\pi}_s^i = \rho_s \frac{v_1^{i\prime}(\bar{x}_s^i)}{\bar{\lambda}_0^i} = \bar{\pi}_s = \rho_s \varphi(w_s), \quad s = 1, \ldots, S$$

imply $v_1^{i\prime}(\bar{x}_s^i) = \bar{\lambda}_0^i \varphi(w_s)$. The function $\psi^i : \mathbb{R}_+ \longrightarrow \mathbb{R}_+ (i = 1, \ldots, I)$ defined by

$$\bar{x}_s^i = (v_1^{i\prime})^{-1} \left(\bar{\lambda}_0^i \varphi(w_s) \right) = \psi^i(w_s), \quad s = 1, \ldots, S$$

is strictly increasing since $v_1^{i\prime\prime} < 0$ and $\varphi' < 0$.

(b) Since the equilibrium rate of interest $\bar{r}$ is equal to the rate of impatience $r^*(w)$ of the representative agent at the aggregate output w

$$\frac{1}{1+\bar{r}} = \frac{1}{1+r^*(w)} = \frac{\sum\limits_{s=1}^{S} \partial u^*(w)/\partial \xi_s}{\partial u^*(w)/\partial \xi_0} = \sum_{s=1}^{S} \rho_s v_1^{*\prime}(w_s)$$

where we have used the fact that $\partial u^*(w)/\partial \xi_0 = v_0^{*\prime}(w_0) = 1$. Since (v_0^*, v_1^*) satisfy (8), if $w_s \geq w_0$, for $s = 1, \ldots, S$ then

$$v_1^{*\prime}(w_s) \leq v_1^{*\prime}(w_0) < v_0^{*\prime}(w_0) = 1, \quad s = 1, \ldots, S$$

so that $\bar{r} > 0$. $\square$

By Theorem 16.7, with complete markets and additively separable preferences the stochastic behavior of the key variables in a financial market equilibrium can be expressed via a simple functional dependence on aggregate output. This theorem has the following consequences.

(1) *If there is no aggregate risk* (var(w_1) = 0) *then the equilibrium consumption stream of each agent is riskless* (var($\bar{x}_1^i$) = 0, $i = 1, \ldots, I$). In such an economy there are only individual risks. The complete set of financial markets acts like a system of insurance markets which enables agents to obtain complete insurance against their individual risks. If all the agents have pure time preference and if aggregate output at date 1 exceeds the output at date 0 then the rate of interest is positive. If the output at date 1 is sufficiently small relative to the output at date 0 then the rate of interest can be negative. *Since*

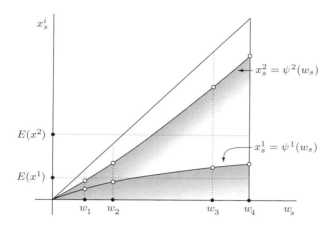

Figure 16.1   Agent 2 is wealthier and less risk averse than agent 1: his average consumption is higher but the variance is also greater.

the ideal security $\bar{\gamma}$ is non-random (var($\bar{\gamma}$) = 0), the covariance value (cost) of every income stream is zero, even if the income stream is risky (var(y) > 0).

(2) If there is aggregate risk (var(w_1) > 0) then the equilibrium consumption stream of each agent is risky (var($\bar{x}_1^i$) > 0, $i = 1, \ldots, I$). Fluctuations in aggregate output lead to fluctuations in the consumption of the agents in the economy, high (low) aggregate output corresponding to high (low) individual consumption. An example (with four states of nature) is shown in Figure 16.1.

When there is aggregate risk the ideal security is risky (var($\bar{\gamma}$) > 0). In this case all income streams which are correlated with $\bar{\gamma}$ have a non-zero covariance value.

Stochastic Dependence

Our objective is to show that the sign of the covariance value depends on the nature of the stochastic dependence between the income stream y and the aggregate output w_1. If the property cov(y, w_1) > 0 (< 0) implied cov($y, \varphi(w_1)$) < 0 (> 0) for every decreasing function $\varphi : \mathbb{R}_+ \longrightarrow \mathbb{R}_+$ then the result would be immediate. While this property is true for joint normally distributed random variables, it is not true for random variables in general (see Exercise 3). To draw the required conclusion, a stronger form of stochastic dependence between the income stream y and the aggregate output w_1 is needed than that implied by cov(y, w_1) > 0 (< 0).

The following concept of stochastic dependence, which is the natural generalization of the concept of *independence* for a pair of random variables, gives the desired result. If $(\mathbf{S}, \mathscr{S}, \mathbb{P})$ is a probability space we use the standard notation of probability theory: for $\alpha \in \mathbb{R}$ and $(\alpha, \beta) \in \mathbb{R}^2$

$$\mathbb{P}[x \leq \alpha] = \mathbb{P}\{s \in \mathbf{S} \mid x(s) \leq \alpha\}$$

and

$$\mathbb{P}[x \leq \alpha, y \leq \beta] = \mathbb{P}\{s \in \mathbf{S} \mid x(s) \leq \alpha, y(s) \leq \beta\}$$

16.8 Definition: A pair of real-valued random variables x, y defined on a probability space $(\mathbf{S}, \mathscr{S}, \mathbb{P})$ is said to be *positively (negatively) dependent* if for all $(\alpha, \beta) \in \mathbb{R}^2$

$$\mathbb{P}[x \leq \alpha, y \leq \beta] \geq (\leq) \ \mathbb{P}[x \leq \alpha]\,\mathbb{P}[y \leq \beta] \tag{10}$$

with strict inequality for some $(\alpha, \beta) \in \mathbb{R}^2$. If there is equality of the two sides in (10), for all $(\alpha, \beta) \in \mathbb{R}^2$, then (x, y) are said to be *independent*.

(10) can be written in a less symmetric but more intuitive form as follows. Recall that the *conditional probability* of event A given that event B has occurred is given by

$$\mathbb{P}[A \mid B] = \frac{\mathbb{P}(A \cap B)}{\mathbb{P}(B)}$$

for $\mathbb{P}(B) > 0$. For positively dependent random variables (10) can be expressed in the equivalent form

$$\mathbb{P}[x \leq \alpha \mid y \leq \beta] \geq \mathbb{P}[x \leq \alpha]$$

Thus the conditional probability that x is small, when it is known that y is small, is greater than the unconditional probability that x is small i.e. when there is no information on y. In short, knowing that y is small makes it more likely that x is small. If the random variables are negatively dependent then the inequality is reversed and knowing that y is small makes it less likely that x is small.

The following proposition makes it clear that the concept of positive (negative) dependence has many natural applications in economics.[1]

16.9 Proposition (Properties of Stochastically Dependent Random Variables):

(i) *If (x, y) are positively (negatively) dependent [independent] random variables and if $f(\cdot)$ is a strictly decreasing function, then $(x, f(y))$ are negatively (positively) dependent [independent] random variables.*

---

[1]To our knowledge, this concept which was introduced by Lehmann (1966) in the statistics literature, has not previously been used in the economics literature except in Magill-Cheng (1985) and Magill-Nermuth (1986).

(ii) *If (x, y) are positively (negatively) dependent [independent] random variables, then $\mathrm{cov}(x, y) > 0$, (< 0), $[= 0]$.*

PROOF: (See Appendix A3.7) □

REMARK. It can be shown that if (x, y) are joint normally distributed then Proposition 16.9 (ii) is an equivalence: (x, y) are positively (negatively) dependent [independent] if and only if $\mathrm{cov}(x, y) > 0$, (< 0), $[= 0]$.

Given the ideal security $\bar{\gamma}$ and the rate of interest $\bar{r}$, the equilibrium market value $c_{\bar{q}}(y)$ of an income stream y is given by (15.18), namely

$$c_{\bar{q}}(y) = \frac{E(y)}{1 + \bar{r}} + \mathrm{cov}(\bar{\gamma}, y)$$

Under the assumptions of Theorem 16.7, $\bar{\gamma}_s = \varphi(w_s)$ (which we write as $\bar{\gamma} = \varphi(w_1)$), where φ is a decreasing function. Thus

$$c_{\bar{q}}(y) = \frac{E(y)}{1 + \bar{r}} + \mathrm{cov}\left(\varphi(w_1), y\right) \tag{11}$$

By Proposition 16.9, the covariance value is positive (negative) if y is negatively (positively) dependent on the aggregate output.

16.10 Proposition (Equilibrium Risk Pricing with Complete Markets): *Let $\mathscr{E}(u, \omega, V)$ be an economy in which the utility functions are VNM-additively separable and $\langle V \rangle = \mathbb{R}^S$, and let $((\bar{x}, \bar{z}), \bar{q})$ be a financial market equilibrium.*

(a) *If the economy has no aggregate risk ($\mathrm{var}(w_1) = 0$), then the equilibrium covariance value of any income stream $y \in \mathbb{R}^S$ is zero.*

(b) *If the economy has aggregate risk ($\mathrm{var}(w_1) > 0$) and if $y \in \mathbb{R}^S$ is an income stream which is independent of aggregate output w_1, then its covariance value is zero; if the income stream is positively (negatively) dependent on aggregate output w_1, then its equilibrium covariance value is negative (positive).*

PROOF: Follows by applying Proposition 16.9 to the formula (11) for the covariance value. □

The advantage of this proposition over Theorem 15.4 is that it provides information about the *sign* of the covariance value of a security without needing to solve for the equilibrium. With complete markets and additively separable preferences, the state prices $\bar{\pi}_s$ and hence the components $\bar{\gamma}_s = \bar{\pi}_s / \rho_s$ of the ideal security are inversely related to aggregate output w_s. With complete markets, agents can insure their individual risks, so that fluctuations in aggregate output are the basic source of risks in the economy. With additively separable preferences, the equilibrium consumption of each agent moves up and down with aggregate output. Since a unit of income has a higher (lower) value in states where aggregate output is low (high), an income stream which is *negatively* dependent on aggregate output has a *positive* covariance value. Within the framework of this model, the observed fact that many contracts such as the equity of firms typically have a *negative* covariance value is explainable by the fact that their income streams (profits) are *positively* dependent on aggregate output.

Linear Risk Tolerance

Representative agent analysis is possible whenever equilibrium allocations are Pareto optimal. In general this property holds for financial market equilibria only when markets are complete. There are however special cases where FM equilibria are Pareto optimal even when markets are incomplete. The intuition behind such cases can be explained as follows. If the attitude towards risk of agents is sufficiently similar and is independent of their levels of consumption (more precisely if they have identical and constant relative risk aversion) then the Pareto optimal allocations are such that the date 1 consumption of each agent is proportional to aggregate output. Thus the risk profile of each agent's date 1 consumption stream is identical to that of aggregate output and is hence independent of the level of consumption. This is clearly a special case, since in general when agents' attitudes toward risk are different, equalization of rates of substitution requires that agents with different levels of consumption have different profiles of consumption (as in Figure 16.1). In order for allocations proportional to the aggregate endowment to be achievable via trading on financial markets, a suitable restriction must be placed on agent's initial endowments relative to the marketed subspace. A sufficient condition is that the date 1 component of each agent's initial endowment lie in the marketed subspace ($\omega_\mathbf{1}^i \in \langle V \rangle$, $i = 1, \ldots, I$). In this case $w_\mathbf{1} = \sum_{i=1}^{I} \omega_\mathbf{1}^i \in \langle V \rangle$ and net trades of the form $b_i w_\mathbf{1} - \omega_\mathbf{1}^i$, can be achieved through trading on the financial markets.

A slight generalization of the above case can be obtained by looking for the restrictions on agents date 1 VNM-utility functions v_1^i which lead to Pareto optimal allocations such that each agent's date 1 consumption is an affine function of aggregate output

$$x_\mathbf{1}^i = a_i \mathbb{1} + b_i w_\mathbf{1}, \quad i = 1, \ldots, I.$$

These conditions have been known in the finance literature for a long time; to express them each function v_1^i needs to be defined on an *appropriate subset*

$\mathcal{V}^i$ of the real line, which in certain cases may include negative consumption. To allow for these cases we modify the definition of additive separability as follows.

16.11 Definition: The utility function $u^i : \mathbb{R}_+ \times (\mathcal{V}^i)^S \longrightarrow \mathbb{R}$ is VNM′-*additively separable* if there exist functions $v_0^i : \mathbb{R}_+ \longrightarrow \mathbb{R}$, $v_1^i : \mathcal{V}^i \longrightarrow \mathbb{R}$ which are smooth on their domains and satisfy

$$v_0^{i\prime}(c) > 0, \quad v_0^{i\prime\prime}(c) < 0, \quad \forall c \in \mathbb{R}_+, \quad v_1^{i\prime}(c) > 0, \quad v_1^{i\prime\prime}(c) < 0, \quad \forall c \in \mathcal{V}^i$$

$$u^i(x^i) = v_0^i(x_0^i) + \sum_{s=1}^{S} \rho_s v_1^i(x_s^i)$$

Just as the rate of impatience expresses an agent's preference for consumption at date 0 relative to date 1, so the following concept expresses an agent's tolerance for risky consumption streams at date 1.

16.12 Definition: For an agent with VNM′-additively separable utility function $\left(u^i \longleftrightarrow (v_0^i, v_1^i)\right)$, the *risk tolerance* $T^i(\xi)$ is defined by

$$T^i(\xi) = -\frac{v_1^{i\prime}(\xi)}{v_1^{i\prime\prime}(\xi)}, \quad \xi \in \mathcal{V}^i$$

Agent i is said to have *linear risk tolerance* (LRT) if there exist $(\alpha_i, \beta_i) \in \mathbb{R}_+ \times \mathbb{R}$ such that

$$T^i(\xi) = \alpha_i + \beta_i \xi \tag{12}$$

for all $\xi \in \mathcal{V}^i = \{\xi \in \mathbb{R} \mid \alpha_i + \beta_i \xi > 0\}$. The coefficient β_i is called agent i's *marginal risk tolerance*.

A date 1 utility function v_1^i which has the property (12) is said to belong to the family of *linear risk tolerance utility functions* (LRT). Since risk tolerance is the inverse of *absolute risk aversion*, linear risk tolerance is equivalent to hyperbolic absolute risk aversion (HARA). For this reason the family of utility functions v_1^i satisfying (12) is also referred to in the finance literature as the HARA family.

16.13 Proposition (Linear Sharing Rule): *Let u^i be VNM′-additively separable utility functions, $i = 1, \ldots, I$. There exist smooth functions $a, b : \mathbb{R}_+^I \longrightarrow \mathbb{R}^I$ satisfying $\sum_{i=1}^{I} a_i(\mu) = 0$, $\sum_{i=1}^{I} b_i(\mu) = 1$ such that the solution of the maximum problem*

$$\max \left\{ \sum_{i=1}^{I} \mu_i u^i(x^i) \ \Bigg| \ \sum_{i=1}^{I} x^i = w, \quad x \in \mathbb{R}^{(S+1)I} \right\} \tag{13}$$

satisfies

$$x_{\mathbf{1}}^i(\mu, w) = a_i(\mu)\mathbb{1} + b_i(\mu)w_{\mathbf{1}}, \quad i = 1, \ldots, I \tag{14}$$

for all $(\mu, w) \in \mathbb{R}_+^I \times \mathbb{R}_{++}^{S+1}$, $\mu \neq 0$ if and only if for all $i = 1, \ldots, I$ there exist $(\alpha_i, \beta) \in \mathbb{R}_+ \times \mathbb{R}$ such that

$$T^i(\xi) = \alpha_i + \beta\xi, \quad i = 1, \ldots, I \tag{15}$$

PROOF: (See Appendix A3.8) □

Since VNM′-additively separable utility functions are concave, the family of solutions to the maximum problem (13) obtained by varying the vector of weights $\mu = (\mu_1, \ldots, \mu_I) \in \mathbb{R}_+^I$ is the set of Pareto optimal allocations of the economy. Proposition 16.13 thus characterizes the class of utility functions for which Pareto optimal allocations are of the form (14). When aggregate output is allocated among agents according to (14), the allocation is said to be obtained by a *linear sharing rule*: the coefficients (a_i, b_i), which depend on agent i's relative weight in the vector μ, determine the agent's consumption as a share (b_i) of aggregate output plus a non-random component (a_i). Such allocations arise in an economy in which each agent has a right to a share of the output of society's productive resources (all firms) and agents can borrow and lend among themselves. Such an outcome will arise as an equilibrium of a bond-equity economy (which will be described shortly) under the assumption that agents have linear risk tolerance with the same coefficient of marginal risk tolerance.

Proposition 16.13 asserts that Pareto optimal allocations satisfy a linear sharing rule if and only if agents' date 1 utility functions v_1^i exhibit linear risk tolerance *with the same marginal risk tolerance*. The utility functions thus satisfy the differential equation

$$-\frac{v_1^{i''}(\xi)}{v_1^{i'}(\xi)} = \frac{1}{\alpha_i + \beta\xi} \tag{16}$$

which when integrated gives the HARA family of utility functions

$$v_1^i(\xi) = \begin{cases} \dfrac{(\alpha_i + \beta\xi)^{1-1/\beta}}{\frac{1}{\beta}(1 - \frac{1}{\beta})} & \text{if } \beta \neq 0,\ \beta \neq 1 \\ -\alpha_i e^{-\xi/\alpha_i} & \text{if } \beta = 0 \\ \log(\alpha_i + \xi) & \text{if } \beta = 1 \end{cases} \tag{17}$$

which is defined on the domain $\alpha_i + \beta\xi > 0$. The sign of β determines whether risk tolerance is increasing $(\beta > 0)$ or decreasing $(\beta < 0)$. The most natural case is $\beta \geq 0$: this includes the power functions with power less than 1, the log and the negative exponential. When $\beta > 0$ and $\alpha_i = 0$ the risk tolerance is proportional to income or alternatively the utility function exhibits constant relative risk aversion. For $\beta = 0$ risk tolerance and absolute risk aversion are constant i.e. independent of income. The frequently used quadratic utility functions correspond to the case $\beta = -1$: they thus have the counterintuitive property of decreasing risk tolerance.

For a given security structure V, allocations satisfying a linear sharing rule are V-feasible (Definition 12.1) if and only if income transfers of the form $a_i \mathbb{1} + b_i w_\mathbf{1} - \omega_\mathbf{1}^i$ lie in the marketed subspace $\langle V \rangle$. A sufficient condition for this is $\mathbb{1} \in \langle V \rangle$, $\omega_\mathbf{1}^i \in \langle V \rangle$, $i = 1, \ldots, I$. When this condition and the common linear risk tolerance condition (15) are satisfied, then the constrained Pareto optimal allocations coincide with the Pareto optimal allocations. Thus under these two conditions, a financial market equilibrium, being constrained Pareto optimal, will result in a Pareto optimal allocation satisfying a linear sharing rule.

16.14 Proposition (Equilibrium with Linear Risk Tolerance):   *Let $\mathscr{E}(u, \omega, V)$ be an economy in which agents' utility functions are VNM'-additively separable and LRT with the same coefficient of marginal risk tolerance. Let agents' endowments satisfy $\omega_\mathbf{1}^i \in \langle V \rangle$, $i = 1, \ldots, I$ and let $\mathbb{1} \in \langle V \rangle$. If $((\bar{x}, \bar{z}), \bar{q})$ is a financial market equilibrium, then $\bar{x}$ is Pareto optimal and the date 1 consumption vectors satisfy a linear sharing rule.*

PROOF: By Theorem 12.3, $\bar{x}$ is constrained Pareto optimal relative to V. $\omega_\mathbf{1}^i \in \langle V \rangle$, $i = 1, \ldots, I$ and $\mathbb{1} \in \langle V \rangle$ imply that the Pareto optimal allocations satisfying (14) lie in the constrained feasible set F_V. Thus $\bar{x}$ is Pareto optimal and satisfies (14). □

Since the equilibrium in Proposition 16.14 is Pareto optimal, the representative agent analysis can be applied. By Proposition 16.4, the common present-value vector $\bar{\pi}$ of all the agents is the gradient vector of the representative agent with utility function $u^* = u^1/\bar{\lambda}_0^1 \diamond \cdots \diamond u^I/\bar{\lambda}_0^I$ at the aggregate endowment, $\bar{\pi} = \nabla u^*(w)$ and the common ρ-present-value vector satisfies $\bar{\pi}^\rho = \nabla^\rho u^*(w)$. The date 1 component $\bar{\pi}_\mathbf{1}^\rho$ is not necessarily the ideal security at the equilibrium since it may not belong to the marketed subspace. It is not however necessary to project onto $\langle V \rangle$ to obtain a common pricing vector since the ρ-present-value vectors $\pi_\mathbf{1}^{\rho, i}$ coincide by Pareto optimality. Thus

$$c_{\bar{q}}(y) = [\![\bar{\pi}_\mathbf{1}^\rho, y]\!]_\rho = [\![\nabla_\mathbf{1}^\rho u^*(w), y]\!]_\rho, \quad \forall y \in \langle V \rangle$$

Since u^* inherits the property of VNM'-additive separability from the utility functions u^i $(i = 1, \ldots, I)$

$$\nabla^\rho u^*(w) = (1, v_1^{*\prime}(w_1), \ldots, v_1^{*\prime}(w_S)) \quad \text{and} \quad \nabla_\mathbf{1}^\rho u^*(w) = \phi(w_\mathbf{1})$$

where $\phi = v_1^{*\prime}$ is strictly decreasing. Thus

$$c_{\bar{q}}(y) = \frac{E(y)}{1+\bar{r}} + \mathrm{cov}\,(\phi(w_1), y)$$

so that the same results (Proposition 16.10) regarding the covariance value of a security can be obtained as in the case of complete markets: *if y is positively (negatively) dependent on aggregate output, then the covariance value of y is negative (positive).*

The Pareto optimality of Proposition 16.14 does not contradict our earlier result (Corollary 11.8) on the generic inefficiency of financial market equilibria when markets are incomplete. Corollary 11.8 applied to an economy with LRT preferences asserts that the FM equilibria of this economy are inefficient for almost all endowment vectors $\omega \in \mathbb{R}_{++}^{(S+1)I}$. The subset of endowment vectors ω satisfying

$$\omega_1^i \in \langle V \rangle, \quad i = 1, \ldots, I \tag{18}$$

which lead to Pareto optimal equilibria is of measure zero in $\mathbb{R}_{++}^{(S+1)I}$ (when $J < S$) and hence is not a generic set. A small perturbation of the endowment vector ω will typically drive each individual agent's date 1 endowment ω_1^i out of the marketed subspace and thus destroy the Pareto optimality of the equilibrium. Thus when financial markets are incomplete, for almost all initial income streams for individuals in the economy (i.e. except for those in the set of measure zero $w_1^i \in \langle V \rangle$, $i = 1, \ldots, I$), the securities will not be well-adapted to sharing risks among the individuals, so that trading on the financial markets will not lead to an efficient risk sharing outcome.

The hypothesis (18) requires that *every individual's risk* (namely the fluctuations in the date 1 endowment ω_1^i) *can be fully traded and hence eliminated on the financial markets.* An agent can thus hedge his initial risks by short selling (at date 0) his future initial endowment ω_1^i, using this income to purchase a sure consumption stream (provided $\mathbb{1} \in \langle V \rangle$), a consumption stream proportional to aggregate output or a combination of the two. (18) is thus a restrictive assumption which cannot be expected to hold in general, for it implies that even if the financial markets are incomplete (in that they do not cover all contingencies), the risk sharing opportunities that they offer are sufficient to permit agents to share all their risks.

Bond-Equity Economy

There is a variant of the general finance model, which satisfies assumption (18), which has been extensively studied in the finance literature. The assumptions made to simplify the equilibrium problem seem well-suited to describe the sector of the economy consisting of *institutional investors* (mutual funds, pension funds and so on) trading on the bond and equity markets—the traditional focus of the finance literature.

The general model of a bond-equity economy can be described as follows. There are two types of securities: those in *zero* net supply (*bonds*) and those in *positive* net supply (*equity*). There are J_1 bonds, where the date 1 payoff of the jth bond is $R^j = (R^j_1, \ldots, R^j_S)$, and J_2 equities, where the date 1 payoff of the jth equity is $y^j = (y^j_1, \ldots, y^j_S)$, the vector of outputs of firm j at date 1. The production plans of the firms are fixed, and for simplicity the date 0 components (the inputs) are omitted. Since an equity contract is taken to represent an ownership share of a firm, the net supply of the equity of each firm is 1. The security payoff matrix V can thus be written as

$$V = \begin{bmatrix} 1 & R^2_1 & \cdots & R^{J_1}_1 & y^1_1 & \cdots & y^{J_2}_1 \\ \vdots & \vdots & \ddots & \vdots & \vdots & \ddots & \vdots \\ 1 & R^2_S & \cdots & R^{J_1}_S & y^1_S & \cdots & y^{J_2}_S \end{bmatrix} = [R \mid Y]$$

where the first bond is assumed to be the riskless bond. Each agent has an initial endowment of income $\omega^i \in \mathbb{R}^{S+1}$ and an initial equity ownership $\delta^i = (\delta^i_1, \ldots, \delta^i_{J_2})$, where δ^i_j is agent i's ownership share of the jth firm. It is assumed that

$$0 \le \delta^i_j \le 1, \quad \sum_{i=1}^{I} \delta^i_j = 1, \quad i = 1, \ldots, I, \quad j = 1, \ldots, J_2$$

Let $\omega = (\omega^1, \ldots, \omega^I)$ denote the vector of agents' initial endowments of income, and let $\delta = [\delta^1 \ldots \delta^I]$ denote the $J_2 \times I$ matrix of their initial ownership shares of equity, then $\mathscr{E}(u, \omega, \delta, V)$ will denote the associated *bond-equity economy*.

Let $q = (q', q'') = (q'_1, \ldots, q'_{J_1}, q''_1, \ldots, q''_{J_2}) \in \mathbb{R}^J$ (where $J = J_1 + J_2$) denote the vector of bond and equity prices, and let $(z^{i\prime}, \theta^i) = (z^{i\prime}_1, \ldots, z^{i\prime}_{J_1}, \theta^i_1, \ldots, \theta^i_{J_2})$ denote the portfolio of bonds and equity purchased by agent i. The budget equations of agent i are given by

$$\begin{aligned} x^i_0 - \omega^i_0 - q''\delta^i &= -q'z^{i\prime} - q''\theta^i \\ x^i_s - \omega^i_s &= R_s z^{i\prime} + Y_s \theta^i, \quad s = 1, \ldots, S \end{aligned} \tag{19}$$

where R_s is row s of R, and Y_s is row s of Y. A pair $((\bar{x}, \bar{z}', \bar{\theta}), \bar{q})$ is a *bond-equity market equilibrium* if each agent chooses an action $(\bar{x}^i, \bar{z}^{i\prime}, \bar{\theta}^i)$ which maximizes his utility over the budget set defined by (19) with $q = \bar{q}$, and the bond and equity markets clear i.e. $\sum_{i=1}^{I} \bar{z}^{i\prime} = 0$ and $\sum_{i=1}^{I} \bar{\theta}^i_j = 1$, $j = 1, \ldots, J_2$.

Since (19) can be written as

$$\begin{aligned} x^i_0 - \omega^i_0 &= -q'z^{i\prime} - q''(\theta^i - \delta^i) \\ x^i_s - \omega^i_s - Y_s\delta^i &= R_s z^{i\prime} + Y_s(\theta^i - \delta^i), \quad s = 1, \ldots, S \end{aligned} \tag{19$'$}$$

if we define $z^i = (z^{i\prime}, z^{i\prime\prime\prime})$ where $z^{i\prime\prime\prime} = (\theta^i - \delta^i)$, then $((\bar{x}, \bar{z}^\prime, \bar{\theta}), \bar{q})$ is a bond-equity market equilibrium if and only if $((\bar{x}, \bar{z}), \bar{q})$ is a financial market equilibrium of the economy $\mathscr{E}(u, \omega, V)$ where $\omega = (\omega^1, \ldots, \omega^I)$ with

$$\omega_0^i = \underline{\omega}_0^i, \quad \omega_s^i = \underline{\omega}_s^i + Y_s \delta^i, \quad s = 1, \ldots, S, \quad i = 1, \ldots, I$$

The subclass of bond-equity economies studied in the finance literature consists of those economies $\mathscr{E}(u, \underline{\omega}, \delta, V)$ for which

$$\underline{\omega}_{\mathbf{1}}^i = 0, \quad i = 1, \ldots, I \quad \text{and} \quad V = \begin{bmatrix} 1 & y_1^1 & \cdots & y_1^K \\ \vdots & \vdots & \ddots & \vdots \\ 1 & y_S^1 & \cdots & y_S^K \end{bmatrix} \tag{20}$$

where for simplicity of notation $K = J_2$ denotes the number of firms.

The problem of each investor is to choose an optimal portfolio of the riskless bond and the K equity contracts. If the investors on these markets have sufficiently *similar risk preferences*—modelled by assuming that their utility functions are LRT with the same marginal risk tolerance—then an interesting characterization of their equilibrium portfolios can be obtained. Since the assumptions of Proposition 16.14 are satisfied, in an equilibrium the investors' after trade date 1 income streams are given by

$$\bar{x}_{\mathbf{1}}^i = a_i \mathbb{1} + b_i w_{\mathbf{1}}, \quad i = 1, \ldots, I \tag{21}$$

The ith agent's income stream is obtained by investing a_i in the riskless bond and purchasing the share b_i of the equity of each firm, since aggregate output at date 1 is the sum of the outputs of the K firms $(w_{\mathbf{1}} = \sum_{k=1}^K y_{\mathbf{1}}^k)$. Each investor thus holds a fully diversified portfolio—investing something in every security in the market

$$(\bar{z}^{i\prime}, \bar{\theta}^i) = (a_i, b_i, \ldots, b_i), \quad i = 1, \ldots, I \tag{22}$$

The special structure of the portfolios (22), suggests another way for the agents to achieve their equilibrium income streams (21). Suppose there are two funds. The first fund markets the riskless bond. The second fund purchases all the equity of the K firms, so that its portfolio $\theta_m = (1, \ldots, 1)$ is the *market portfolio* of all equity contracts. Agent i then invests a_i in the first fund and b_i in the second fund. This property, that agents' equilibrium portfolios (22) can be achieved by investing in two funds rather than purchasing $K + 1$ securities directly on the financial markets, is called the *Two-Fund Separation Property*. This property is just the linear sharing rule (21) expressed in terms of portfolios. Intuitively, if there were fixed transactions costs in the purchase and sale of securities, then investment in the two funds would be less costly than directly purchasing the $K + 1$ securities on the financial markets.

16.15 Proposition (Two-Fund Separation with LRT): *Let $\mathscr{E}(u, \omega, \delta, V)$ be a bond-equity economy satisfying (20), in which investors have VNM'-additively separable LRT utility functions with the same marginal risk tolerance. If $((\bar{x}, \bar{z}', \bar{\theta}), \bar{q})$ is a bond-equity market equilibrium, then there exist constants $(a_1, \ldots, a_I, b_1, \ldots, b_I) \in \mathbb{R}^{2I}$ with $\sum_{i=1}^{I} a_i = 0$, $\sum_{i=1}^{I} b_i = 1$ such that each investor holds a portfolio which consists of investing a_i in the riskless bond and b_i in the market portfolio $\theta_m = (1, \ldots, 1)$ of risky securities*

$$(\bar{z}^{i\prime}, \bar{\theta}^i) = (a_i, b_i \, \theta_m), \quad i = 1, \ldots, I$$

17. CAPITAL ASSET PRICING MODEL (CAPM)

The capital asset pricing model is close in spirit to the model of a bond-equity economy with linear risk tolerance utility functions studied in the last section, the similarity in investors attitudes towards risk being modelled by the alternative assumption of mean-variance preferences. Investors with mean-variance preferences are not concerned with the exact profile of a random consumption stream at date 1—*the income stream is judged solely by the average properties summarized in its mean and variance.* Such an assumption seems unreasonable for a typical consumer for whom the prospect of no consumption (let alone negative consumption) in certain states would be a matter of real concern. This suggests that (as in the previous section) the model should be interpreted as one in which the agents are institutional investors, and it is their *earnings* as opposed to their *consumption* streams that they are ranking.

Mean-variance preferences, combined with the assumptions $\mathbb{1} \in \langle V \rangle$ and $\omega_1^i \in \langle V \rangle$, $i = 1, \ldots, I$, imply that in an equilibrium the ideal security (Theorem 15.4) is of the form

$$\bar{\gamma} = c'\mathbb{1} - cw_1$$

with c' and c positive. The pricing formula (18) in Section 15 then implies that the covariance value of a security is a decreasing linear function of the covariance of its income stream with aggregate output. This result is more precise than that obtained in the previous section where the sign of the covariance value could only be determined for income streams which are positively or negatively dependent on aggregate output.

Since in this model investors rank earnings (as opposed to consumption streams), we follow the practice in finance of allowing the utility functions to be defined on all of $\mathbb{R}^{S+1}$, the utility of negative values reflecting the disutility assigned to losses.

17.1 Definition: $u : \mathbb{R}^{S+1} \longrightarrow \mathbb{R}$ will be called a *mean-variance* utility function if whenever $x = (x_0, x_1)$, $x' = (x_0', x_1') \in \mathbb{R} \times \mathbb{R}^S$ satisfy the semipositive vector inequality[1]

$$(x_0, E(x_1), - \text{var}(x_1)) > (x_0', E(x_1'), - \text{var}(x_1')) \tag{1}$$

then $u(x) > u(x')$.

This definition implies that x is preferred to x' if either of the following conditions is satisfied

$$(x_0, E(x_1)) = (x_0', E(x_1')) \quad \text{and} \quad \text{var}(x_1) < \text{var}(x_1') \tag{1'}$$
$$(x_0, E(x_1)) > (x_0', E(x_1')) \quad \text{and} \quad \text{var}(x_1) = \text{var}(x_1') \tag{1''}$$

Thus if x has the same date 0 component and mean at date 1 as x', but has less variance (1'), then it is preferred (investors dislike *variance*). If the two streams have the same variance, but x has a date 0 component or a mean at date 1 that dominates (1''), then it is preferred (investors like *mean*). In particular this implies that if x is obtained from x' by adding any date 1 income stream of the form $\alpha \mathbb{1}$ with $\alpha > 0$, then x is preferred to x'.

A typical mean-variance utility function is of the form

$$u(x) = h\left(x_0, E(x_1), \text{var}(x_1)\right)$$

where h is an increasing function of $(x_0, E(x_1))$ and a decreasing function of $\text{var}(x_1)$. A well-known example is a quadratic utility function—more precisely a VNM'-additively separable utility function ($u \longleftrightarrow (v_0, v_1)$) with v_1 a quadratic function

$$u(x) = v_0(x_0) - \frac{1}{2} \sum_{s=1}^{S} \rho_s (x_s - \alpha)^2, \quad \alpha > 0$$
$$= v_0(x_0) + \alpha E(x_1) - \frac{1}{2}\left(E(x_1)^2 + \text{var}(x_1)\right) - \frac{\alpha^2}{2}$$

To ensure that u is monotone on the relevant domain of income streams, α must be sufficiently large (for example α greater than the aggregate output in every state).

Since the family of quadratic utility functions (for all $\alpha > 0$ sufficiently large) constitutes a class of LRT utility functions with the same marginal risk tolerance, the properties of an equilibrium of an economy in which all agents have this type of utility function can be derived from Proposition 16.14. Quadratic utility functions are however only very special cases of mean-variance utility functions.

---

[1] $y \in \mathbb{R}^n$ is *semipositive* (written $y > 0$) if it is non-negative ($y \in \mathbb{R}_+^n$), but is not zero ($y \neq 0$).

17.2 Definition: An economy $\mathscr{E}(u, \omega, V)$ satisfies the assumptions of the *capital asset pricing model* (CAPM) if

  (i) there are objective probabilities for the states of nature $(\mathscr{P})$
 (ii) there is a riskless security: $\mathbb{1} \in \langle V \rangle$ $(\mathscr{R})$
(iii) $\omega_1^i \in \langle V \rangle$, $i = 1, \dots, I$
 (iv) $u^i : \mathbb{R}^{S+1} \longrightarrow \mathbb{R}$ is mean-variance, $i = 1, \dots, I$.

To simplify notation the model is analyzed in the standard form $\mathscr{E}(u, \omega, V)$ in which securities are in *zero* net supply. In interpreting the properties of an equilibrium, the model should be viewed as being obtained by a change of variable from a bond-equity economy in which equities are in *positive* net supply—the assumption $\omega_1^i \in \langle V \rangle$ being automatically satisfied if agent i's sole source of initial income at date 1 comes from the ownership of equity of firms $(\omega_1^i = \sum_{k=1}^{K} \delta_k^i y_1^k)$.

17.3 Theorem (CAPM Equilibrium):   If $((\bar{x}, \bar{z}), \bar{q})$ is a financial market equilibrium of an economy $\mathscr{E}(u, \omega, V)$ satisfying the CAPM assumptions with $\mathrm{var}(w_1) > 0$, then

  (i) *there exist strictly positive constants c' and c, such that the ideal security $\bar{\gamma}$ is given by*

$$\bar{\gamma} = c'\mathbb{1} - cw_1$$

 (ii) *the equilibrium market value of any income stream y in the marketed subspace $\langle V \rangle$ is given by*

$$c_{\bar{q}}(y) = \frac{E(y)}{1 + \bar{r}} - c\,\mathrm{cov}(w_1, y) \tag{2}$$

(iii) *there exist $(a, b) = (a_1, \dots, a_I, b_1, \dots, b_I) \in \mathbb{R}^I \times \mathbb{R}_+^I$ with $\sum_{i=1}^{I} a_i = 0$, $\sum_{i=1}^{I} b_i = 1$ such that*

$$\bar{x}_1^i = a_i\mathbb{1} + b_i w_1, \quad i = 1, \dots, I$$

 (iv) *if the utility functions u^i are quasi-concave and satisfy*

$$u^i(x^i) = h^i\left(x_0^i, E(x_1^i), \mathrm{var}(x_1^i)\right), \quad i = 1, \dots, I$$

with h^i differentiable, increasing in the first two variables and decreasing in the third, then the equilibrium allocation $\bar{x}$ is Pareto optimal.

PROOF: We first prove properties (i)–(iii). Since $\omega_1^i \in \langle V \rangle$, the budget constraints of agent i can be written in the equivalent forms

$$\begin{cases} x_0^i - \omega_0^i = -\bar{q}z^i \\ x_1^i - \omega_1^i = Vz^i, z^i \in \mathbb{R}^J \end{cases} \iff \begin{cases} x_0^i - \omega_0^i = c_{\bar{q}}(\omega_1^i) - c_{\bar{q}}(x_1^i) \\ x_1^i \in \langle V \rangle \end{cases} \tag{3}$$

Let $\bar{\gamma}$ be the security in $\langle V \rangle$ (which exists by Theorem 14.15) such that

$$c_{\bar{q}}(y) = [\![\bar{\gamma}, y]\!]_{\rho} = \frac{E(y)}{1 + \bar{r}} + \text{cov}(\bar{\gamma}, y), \quad \forall\, y \in \langle V \rangle \tag{4}$$

since $E(\bar{\gamma}) = c_{\bar{q}}(\mathbb{1}) = 1/(1 + \bar{r})$. For each agent $i = 1, \ldots, I$, let $\hat{x}_1^i$ denote the ρ-projection of $\bar{x}_1^i$ onto the subspace $\langle \mathbb{1}, \bar{\gamma} \rangle$. The following orthogonality relations follow at once from Proposition 14.12:

$$[\![\bar{\gamma}, \bar{x}_1^i - \hat{x}_1^i]\!]_{\rho} = 0 \quad \Longleftrightarrow \quad c_{\bar{q}}(\bar{x}_1^i) = c_{\bar{q}}(\hat{x}_1^i) \tag{5}$$

$$[\![\mathbb{1}, \bar{x}_1^i - \hat{x}_1^i]\!]_{\rho} = 0 \quad \Longleftrightarrow \quad E(\bar{x}_1^i) = E(\hat{x}_1^i) \tag{6}$$

$$[\![\hat{x}_1^i, \bar{x}_1^i - \hat{x}_1^i]\!]_{\rho} = 0 \quad \text{and} \quad (6) \quad \Longrightarrow \quad \text{cov}(\hat{x}_1^i, \bar{x}_1^i - \hat{x}_1^i) = 0 \tag{7}$$

(7) implies that

$$\text{var}(\bar{x}_1^i) = \text{var}(\hat{x}_1^i) + \text{var}(\bar{x}_1^i - \hat{x}_1^i)$$

so that $\text{var}(\bar{x}_1^i) > \text{var}(\hat{x}_1^i)$ if $\text{var}(\bar{x}_1^i - \hat{x}_1^i) > 0$. Since

$$\| \bar{x}_1^i - \hat{x}_1^i \|_{\rho} = \left(\left(E(\bar{x}_1^i - \hat{x}_1^i) \right)^2 + \text{var}(\bar{x}_1^i - \hat{x}_1^i) \right)^{\frac{1}{2}}$$

(6) implies $\bar{x}_1^i - \hat{x}_1^i = 0$ if and only if $\text{var}(\bar{x}_1^i - \hat{x}_1^i) = 0$. Since $\hat{x}_1^i$ and w_1^i both lie in $\langle V \rangle$, by (5), $\hat{x}^i = (\bar{x}_0^i, \hat{x}_1^i)$ satisfies the agent's budget constraints. Since u^i is mean-variance, if $\bar{x}_1^i \neq \hat{x}_1^i$ then $u^i(\bar{x}^i) < u^i(\hat{x}^i)$ since $E(\bar{x}_1^i) = E(\hat{x}_1^i)$ and $\text{var}(\bar{x}_1^i) > \text{var}(\hat{x}_1^i)$, which would contradict the optimality of $\bar{x}^i$. Thus $\bar{x}^i = \hat{x}^i$ and $\bar{x}_1^i = \hat{x}_1^i \in \langle \mathbb{1}, \bar{\gamma} \rangle$, $i = 1, \ldots, I$. It follows that $\sum_{i=1}^{i} \bar{x}_1^i = w_1 \in \langle \mathbb{1}, \bar{\gamma} \rangle$. Since $\text{var}(w_1) > 0$, w_1 is not proportional to $\mathbb{1}$, so we must have $\dim < \mathbb{1}, \bar{\gamma} >= 2$. Thus $\langle \mathbb{1}, \bar{\gamma} \rangle = \langle \mathbb{1}, w_1 \rangle$.

$\bar{\gamma} \in \langle \mathbb{1}, w_1 \rangle$ implies that there exist constants c', c such that $\bar{\gamma} = c'\mathbb{1} - cw_1$. To prove that $c > 0$, observe that

$$c_{\bar{q}}\left(\sum_{i=1}^{I} \bar{x}_1^i \right) = \frac{E\left(\sum_{i=1}^{I} \bar{x}_1^i \right)}{1 + \bar{r}} + \text{cov}\left(\bar{\gamma}, \sum_{i=1}^{I} \bar{x}_1^i \right)$$

$$= \frac{E\left(\sum_{i=1}^{I} \bar{x}_1^i \right)}{1 + \bar{r}} - c\,\text{var}(w_1)$$

since $\sum_{i=1}^{I} \bar{x}_1^i = w_1$ and $\text{cov}(\bar{\gamma}, w_1) = -c\,\text{var}(w_1)$. Since $\text{var}(w_1) > 0$, if $c < 0$ then there must be some agent i for whom $\text{var}(\bar{x}_1^i) > 0$ and $c_{\bar{q}}(\bar{x}_1^i) \geq E(\bar{x}_1^i)/(1 + \bar{r})$. If this were true, then the consumption stream $\tilde{x}^i = \left(\bar{x}_0^i, E(\bar{x}_1^i)\mathbb{1} \right)$, since it is less expensive than $\bar{x}^i$ and lies in $\langle V \rangle$, would satisfy the budget constraints (3) and would be strictly preferred to $\bar{x}^i$, contradicting the optimality of $\bar{x}^i$. Thus $c > 0$. Mean-variance preferences imply that if an agent's maximum problem is to have a solution then $c_{\bar{q}}(\mathbb{1}) > 0$ must be satisfied (adding $\mathbb{1}$ always makes an income stream preferred and thus must have a positive price). Since $c_{\bar{q}}(\mathbb{1}) = E(\bar{\gamma}) = c' - cE(w_1) > 0$ and $E(w_1) \geq 0$, it follows that $c' > 0$, so that (i) is satisfied.

$\bar{x}_1^i \in \langle \mathbb{1}, w_1 \rangle$, $i = 1, \ldots, I$ implies that there exist constants a_i, b_i such that $\bar{x}_1^i = a_i \mathbb{1} + b_i w_1$, $i = 1, \ldots, I$. Since $\sum_{i=1}^{I} \bar{x}_1^i = w_1$ and $(\mathbb{1}, w_1)$ are linearly independent, $\sum_{i=1}^{I} a_i = 0$ and $\sum_{i=1}^{I} b_i = 1$. To prove that $b_i \geq 0$, observe that

$$c_{\bar{q}}(\bar{x}_1^i) = \frac{E(\bar{x}_1^i)}{1+\bar{r}} + \text{cov}(\bar{\gamma}, \bar{x}_1^i) = \frac{E(\bar{x}_1^i)}{1+\bar{r}} - c\, b_i \,\text{var}(w_1)$$

Suppose $b_i < 0$, then $\text{var}(\bar{x}_1^i) > 0$ and $c_{\bar{q}}(\bar{x}_1^i) > E(\bar{x}_1^i)/(1+\bar{r})$. By an argument similar to the one given above this would contradict the optimality of $\bar{x}^i$. Thus $b_i \geq 0$, $i = 1, \ldots, I$ and (iii) is satisfied. Since $c_{\bar{q}}(y) = E(y)/(1+\bar{r}) + \text{cov}(\bar{\gamma}, y)$ and $\bar{\gamma} = c'\mathbb{1} - cw_1$ the valuation formula in (ii) is satisfied for all $y \in \langle V \rangle$.

(iv) To prove that the equilibrium allocation is Pareto optimal it suffices to prove that the equilibrium ρ-present-value vectors of the agents lie in the marketed subspace: $\bar{\pi}_1^{\rho,i} \in \langle V \rangle$, $i = 1, \ldots, I$. Let $h_0^{i\prime}, h_1^{i\prime}, h_2^{i\prime}$ denote the partial derivatives of the function h^i with respect to its three arguments, where $h_0^{i\prime} > 0, h_1^{i\prime} > 0, h_2^{i\prime} < 0$. Since

$$\pi_s^i(\bar{x}^i) = \rho_s \frac{(h_1^{i\prime} + 2h_2^{i\prime}(\bar{x}_s^i - E(\bar{x}_1^i)))}{h_0^{i\prime}}, \quad s = 1, \ldots, S$$

where the partial derivatives $h_0^{i\prime}, h_1^{i\prime}, h_2^{i\prime}$ are evaluated at $(\bar{x}_0^i, E(\bar{x}_1^i), \text{var}(\bar{x}^i))$, and since by (iii), $\bar{x}_1^i = a_i \mathbb{1} + b_i w_1$ it follows that

$$\pi_1^{\rho,i}(\bar{x}^i) = c_i'\mathbb{1} - c_i w_1 \in \langle V \rangle$$

where $c_i' = (h_1^{i\prime} - 2h_2^{i\prime}(a_i - E(w_1)))/h_0^{i\prime}$, $c_i = -2h_2^{i\prime}b_i/h_0^{i\prime}$. By Theorem 15.4, the ρ-projections on $\langle V \rangle$ of the agents' present-value vectors $\pi_1^{\rho,i}(\bar{x}^i)$ are equalized. Since $\pi_1^{\rho,i}(\bar{x}^i)$ lies in $\langle V \rangle$, it coincides with its ρ-projection and $\pi_1^{\rho,i}(\bar{x}^i) = \bar{\gamma}$, $i = 1, \ldots, I$. Since the agents' preferences are convex, the equilibrium is Pareto optimal. □

The CAPM model is normally presented in the framework of a bond-equity economy satisfying the assumption of equation (20) in Section 16: in such an economy the investors have an initial wealth and inherited portfolios of equity at date 0. After laying aside an amount for consumption at date 0, the remainder of their wealth is invested in equity and the riskless bond, which yield a profile of income across the states at date 1. In this model the date 1 aggregate output $w_1 = \sum_{k=1}^{K} y^k$ is the income stream generated by the *market portfolio* $\theta_m = (1, \ldots, 1)$.

(iii) in Theorem 17.3 implies that in a CAPM equilibrium investors' date 1 earnings streams are obtained from aggregate output by a linear sharing rule. It follows therefore (as in Proposition 16.15) that in a CAPM equilibrium investors hold fully diversified portfolios: each investor's portfolio of risky securities is a proportion of the market portfolio. The intuition behind this property of a CAPM equilibrium is best understood by recognizing that it follows directly from the way agents with mean-variance preferences choose their portfolios.

An agent with such preferences always restricts his choice of portfolio to a special subset of diversified portfolios. *Among all portfolios which incur a given initial cost ($\bar{q}z = \bar{c}$) at date 0 and yield a given expected return ($E(Vz) = \bar{v}$) at date 1, an investor with mean-variance preferences selects the portfolio which has minimum variance.* In the finance literature, the family of portfolios obtained by varying the date 1 expected return $\bar{v}$ and the cost $\bar{c}$ is called the *set of efficient portfolios.* It is straightforward to show, by studying the associated minimum variance problem, that since $\mathbb{1} \in \langle V \rangle$ every efficient portfolio is a combination of the riskless bond $\mathbb{1}$ and one portfolio θ^* of the risky securities (see Exercise 6). Since all investors demand only these two securities, the equilibrium prices must be such that the risky portfolio θ^* is the market portfolio $\theta_m = (1, \ldots, 1)$. *Thus in a CAPM equilibrium, diversification is a consequence of the fact that every investor holds an efficient portfolio.* Since all investors consider only date 1 income streams lying in the subspace spanned by $\mathbb{1}$ and w_1 (namely $\langle \mathbb{1}, w_1 \rangle \subset \langle V \rangle$), their date 1 ρ-gradients when projected onto $\langle V \rangle$ must lie in the subspace $\langle \mathbb{1}, w_1 \rangle$. This explains the linear relation $\bar{\gamma} = c' \mathbb{1} - c w_1$ in (ii). Since $\bar{\gamma}$ represents the most preferred direction in the marketed subspace, c' and c are positive; every investor, if permitted to make a costless infinitesimal change in his income stream, would seek to increase his holdings of the riskless bond and reduce his share of aggregate output (equity).

The pricing formula (2) shows that the covariance value of a security is a decreasing linear function of the covariance of its income stream with aggregate output: if a security is positively (negatively) correlated with aggregate output, its covariance value is negative (positive). The interpretation of (2) is thus similar in spirit to the interpretation of the pricing formula (11) in Section 16.

Equilibrium Excess Returns

Since the price of a typical equity contract is less than the discounted expected value of its income stream

$$c_{\bar{q}}(y) < \frac{E(y)}{1 + \bar{r}} \iff \frac{E(y)}{c_{\bar{q}}(y)} > 1 + \bar{r}$$

the expected return on each unit of income invested in this security exceeds the return $\bar{R} = 1 + \bar{r}$ on the riskless bond, the higher return being justified by the risk involved in the investment. Using the return per unit of income (dollar) invested in a security provides a convenient way of comparing the costs and benefits of investing in different securities. This approach is extensively used in the finance literature for analyzing investments in the equity and bond markets.

17.4 Definition: If $c_{\bar{q}}(y) \neq 0$ then the random date 1 *return per unit of income* invested (at date 0) in security y is defined by

$$R_y = \frac{y}{c_{\bar{q}}(y)}, \quad \forall\, y \in \langle V \rangle$$

The (per unit) return on the riskless security is $R_{\mathbb{1}} = (1 + \bar{r})\mathbb{1}$, and the scalar $\bar{R} = 1 + \bar{r}$ is called the *riskless return*. The *excess* return on security y is the random variable $\mathcal{R}_y : \mathbf{S} \longrightarrow \mathbb{R}$ defined by

$$\mathcal{R}_y = R_y - R_{\mathbb{1}}, \quad \forall\, y \in \langle V \rangle$$

and its expected value

$$E(\mathcal{R}_y) = E(R_y) - \bar{R}$$

is called the *risk premium* on security y. In the finance version of a bond-equity economy (i.e. satisfying (20) in Section 16) $w_{\mathbf{1}} = \sum_{k=1}^{K} y_1^k$ is the dividend stream of the market portfolio $\theta_m = (1, \dots, 1)$ consisting of full ownership of all K firms in the economy and

$$R_m = \frac{w_{\mathbf{1}}}{c_{\bar{q}}(w_{\mathbf{1}})} = \frac{\sum_{k=1}^{K} y_1^k}{\sum_{k=1}^{K} \bar{q}_k}$$

is the return on the market portfolio. The risk premium

$$E(\mathcal{R}_m) = E(R_m) - \bar{R}$$

is called the *standard equity premium* of the economy.

The risk premium on an individual security is the additional expected return in excess of the riskless return earned for incurring the risks of investing in this security rather than investing without risk in the sure bond. The equity premium on the economy-wide portfolio θ_m is the reward over and above the riskless return for holding the nondiversifiable aggregate risks in the economy. The equilibrium market valuation formula (2) leads to the following well-known expression for risk premia in a CAPM equilibrium.

17.5 Proposition (CAPM Formula for Equilibrium Risk Premium): *Under the assumptions of Theorem 17.3, the equilibrium risk premium on a security y in the marketed subspace $\langle V \rangle$ is given by*

$$E(R_y) - \bar{R} = \frac{\mathrm{cov}(R_m, R_y)}{\mathrm{var}(R_m)} \left(E(R_m) - \bar{R} \right) \tag{8}$$

PROOF: (2) is equivalent to

$$\frac{E(y)}{c_{\bar{q}}(y)} - \bar{R} = c\,\bar{R}\frac{\mathrm{cov}(w_1, y)}{c_{\bar{q}}(y)} = c\,\bar{R}\,c_{\bar{q}}(w_1)\,\mathrm{cov}(R_m, R_y)$$

so that

$$E(R_y) - \bar{R} = c\,\bar{R}\,c_{\bar{q}}(w_1)\,\mathrm{cov}(R_m, R_y) \tag{9}$$

$$E(R_m) - \bar{R} = c\bar{R}c_{\bar{q}}(w_1)\,\mathrm{var}(R_m) \tag{10}$$

dividing (9) by (10) gives (8). □

Linear Regression

(8) asserts that in equilibrium the risk premium on a security is proportional to the standard equity premium

$$E(\mathcal{R}_y) = \beta_{my}E(\mathcal{R}_m), \quad \beta_{my} = \frac{\mathrm{cov}(\mathcal{R}_m, \mathcal{R}_y)}{\mathrm{var}(\mathcal{R}_m)} \tag{11}$$

since $\mathrm{cov}(R_m, R_y)/\mathrm{var}(R_m) = \mathrm{cov}(\mathcal{R}_m, \mathcal{R}_y)/\mathrm{var}(\mathcal{R}_m)$. The coefficient β_{my}, which is called the *beta coefficient* of the income stream (security) y, will be recognized as the coefficient of regression in a linear regression of $\mathcal{R}_y$ on $\mathcal{R}_m$. Let us recall the following property.

17.6 Proposition (Linear Regression): *If* $(\mathbf{S}, \mathscr{S}, \rho)$ *is a finite probability space and if* $z, x \in \mathbb{R}^S$ *is a pair of random variables with* $var(x) \neq 0$, *then there exists a unique decomposition*

$$z = \alpha\mathbb{1} + \beta x + \epsilon_{xz} \tag{12}$$

with $(\alpha, \beta) \in \mathbb{R}^2, E(\epsilon_{xz}) = 0$, $\mathrm{cov}(\epsilon_{xz}, x) = 0$ *and the coefficients* $(\alpha, \beta) \in \mathbb{R}^2$ *are given by*

$$\alpha = E(z) - \beta E(x), \quad \beta = \frac{\mathrm{cov}(x, z)}{\mathrm{var}(x)} \tag{13}$$

PROOF: Let $\langle \mathbb{1}, x \rangle$ denote the subspace of $\mathbb{R}^S$ spanned by $\mathbb{1}$ and x, then

$$\langle \mathbb{1}, x \rangle^{\perp} = \left\{ \epsilon \in \mathbb{R}^S \mid E(\epsilon) = 0, \quad \mathrm{cov}(x, \epsilon) = 0 \right\}$$

Since $\mathbb{R}^S = \langle \mathbb{1}, x \rangle \oplus \langle \mathbb{1}, x \rangle^{\perp}$ there exist unique vectors z^* and ϵ_{xz} such that

$$z = z^* + \epsilon_{xz}, \quad z^* \in \langle \mathbb{1}, x \rangle, \quad \epsilon_{xz} \in \langle \mathbb{1}, x \rangle^{\perp}$$

Since $\mathrm{var}(x) \neq 0$ implies that $\mathbb{1}$ and x are linearly independent and since $z^* \in \langle \mathbb{1}, x \rangle$, there exist unique coefficients $(\alpha, \beta) \in \mathbb{R}^2$ such that (12) holds. Taking the expectation of (12) gives $E(z) = \alpha + \beta E(x)$ which, with (12) implies

$$z - E(z)\mathbb{1} = \beta \left(x - E(x)\mathbb{1} \right) + \epsilon_{xz}$$

Since $\mathrm{cov}(x, \epsilon_{xz}) = 0$ it follows that $\mathrm{cov}(x, z) = \beta \, \mathrm{var}(x)$. $\square$

REMARK. Since $z^* = \alpha\mathbb{1} + \beta x$ is the ρ-projection of z onto the subspace $\langle \mathbb{1}, x \rangle$, by Proposition 14.14, z^* is the random variable in $\langle \mathbb{1}, x \rangle$ which best approximates z in the sense of the $\| \ \|_\rho$ norm

$$z^* = \underset{\xi \in \langle \mathbb{1}, x \rangle}{\arg \min} \, \| \xi - z \|_\rho$$

z^* is called the *linear (least squares) regression* of z on x.

Let $z = \mathcal{R}_y$ and $x = \mathcal{R}_m$. Consider the linear regression of $\mathcal{R}_y$ on $\mathcal{R}_m$. (8) implies that $\alpha = 0$ in Proposition 17.6, so that

$$\mathcal{R}_y = \beta_{my} \mathcal{R}_m + \epsilon_{my}, \quad E(\epsilon_{my}) = 0, \quad \mathrm{cov}(\mathcal{R}_m, \epsilon_{my}) = 0 \qquad (14)$$

The projection $\mathcal{R}_y^* = \beta_{my}\mathcal{R}_m$ is called the *systematic component* of the excess return $\mathcal{R}_y$, since it measures the systematic variation of $\mathcal{R}_y$ with $\mathcal{R}_m$. The beta coefficient β_{my} (also called the *volatility* of the security) measures the magnitude by which fluctuations in the market excess return $\mathcal{R}_m$ (and hence aggregate output) are translated on average into fluctuations in the excess return $\mathcal{R}_y$. The second component ϵ_{my} in (14) is called the *idiosyncratic component* of security y: it measures the fluctuations in the return $\mathcal{R}_y$ which are not correlated with the market return $\mathcal{R}_m$. Proposition 17.5 asserts that the equilibrium risk premium $E(\mathcal{R}_y)$ on a security is fully explained by the risk premium $\beta_{my}E(\mathcal{R}_m)$ on the systematic component of its excess return $\mathcal{R}_y$: *if a security's excess return is more (less) volatile than aggregate output, then its risk premium is greater (less) than the standard equity premium.* Since in equilibrium the only risks that remain are those arising from fluctuations in aggregate output, the risks induced by fluctuations in the idiosyncratic component of a security's return are diversified away by the portfolio holdings of the agents.

Weaker Assumptions

The assumptions which define a CAPM economy (Definition 17.2) can be weakened in two ways without affecting the basic nature of results (i)–(iii) of Theorem 17.3, namely the properties of equilibrium prices and the linear risk sharing rule.

Consider first assumption (iv) of Definition 17.2. We have seen that an agent with a mean-variance utility function dislikes *variance*, and likes *mean*. This was expressed precisely by asserting that if x and x' are income streams satisfying either equation (1') or equation (1''), then $u(x) > u(x')$. The property of disliking variance can be expressed in a weaker form as follows. A utility function $u : \mathbb{R}^{S+1} \longrightarrow \mathbb{R}$ is said to be *variance-averse* if for any pair of income streams $x = (x_0, x_1)$, $x' = (x'_0, x'_1)$ with $x'_0 = x_0$ and $x'_1 = x_1 + y_1$ where y_1 satisfies

$$y_1 \neq 0, \quad E(y_1) = 0, \quad \text{cov}(y_1, x_1) = 0$$

then $u(x) > u(x')$. This condition is weaker than the ranking implied by (1'), since it does not require that all streams with the same mean can be ranked on the basis of their variance. It only requires that any stream obtained from an initial stream by adding a vector which is ρ-orthogonal to the initial risk and does not increase its expected value, is less preferred.

The property of liking mean (including date 0 consumption) can be expressed in a weaker form as follows. A utility function $u : \mathbb{R}^{S+1} \longrightarrow \mathbb{R}$ is *mean-preferring* if for any pair of income streams $x = (x_0, x_1), x' = (x'_0, x'_1)$ with $x'_0 \geq x_0$ and $x'_1 = x_1 + \alpha \mathbb{1}$, $\alpha \geq 0$, then $u(x) \leq u(x')$ with strict inequality if either $x'_0 > x_0$ or $\alpha > 0$.

It is easy to check that all the steps in the proof of properties (i)–(iii) of Theorem 17.3 (except the one that shows $c' > 0$) can be established if assumption (iv) is replaced by the assumption that agents' utility functions are variance-averse. The property $c' > 0$ can be established if we add the requirement that agents' utility functions are mean-preferring (see Exercise 7).

The proof of the Pareto optimality of the equilibrium allocation does not however go through under these assumptions, since it is based on the explicit representation $h^i(x^i_0, E(x^i_1), \text{var}(x^i_1))$ of a mean-variance utility function. In contrast to the LRT model, the proofs of properties (i)–(iii) in Theorem 17.3 do not depend on the Pareto optimality of the equilibrium.

Secondly, the assumption that there is a riskless security ((ii) of Definition 17.2) can be omitted. There are two cases to consider: either $\mathbb{1} \in \langle V \rangle$ i.e. the riskless transfer of income can be achieved by a suitable portfolio of the securities, in which case the analysis proceeds as before, or $\mathbb{1} \notin \langle V \rangle$ in which case the analysis is less intuitive, but proceeds as follows. By Theorem 14.15 there exists a security $\eta \in \langle V \rangle$ which represents the expectation functional on

$\langle V \rangle$ so that $E(y) = E(\eta y)$ for all $y \in \langle V \rangle$. If $\hat{x}_1^i$ is the ρ-projection of $\bar{x}_1^i$ onto $\langle \eta, \bar{\gamma} \rangle$ then, by the same argument as above, it can be shown that $\bar{x}_1^i = \hat{x}_1^i$ so that the results of Theorem 17.3 become:

(i)$'$ there exist constants c' and c such that

$$\bar{\gamma} = c'\eta - cw_1$$

(ii)$'$ the equilibrium market value of any income stream $y \in \langle V \rangle$ is given by

$$c_{\bar{q}}(y) = (c' - cE(w_1))E(y) - c\operatorname{cov}(w_1, y)$$

(iii)$'$ there exist $(a_i, b_i)_{i=1,\dots,I}$ with $\sum_{i=1}^I a_i = 0, \sum_{i=1}^I b_i = 1$ such that

$$\bar{x}_1^i = a_i\eta + b_i w_1, \quad i = 1, \dots, I$$

If $\dim \langle V \rangle \geq 2$, then there exists a security $e \in \langle V \rangle$ satisfying $c_{\bar{q}}(e) \neq 0$, $\operatorname{cov}(w_1, e) = 0$. The beta pricing formula (8) in Proposition 17.5 becomes

$$E(R_y) - E(R_e) = \beta_{my}\left(E(R_m) - E(R_e)\right)$$

where the security e is called the *zero-beta* security, since $\beta_{me} = 0$.

So far we have assumed that all securities have payoffs denominated in real terms. As we shall see in Chapter 7, when money is introduced into the model, a distinction will be made between the dollar (nominal) and the purchasing power (real) payoff of a security. When uncertainty about inflation leads to fluctuations in the purchasing power of money, then the default-free bond with nominal payoff $\mathbb{1} = (1, \dots, 1)$ has a real payoff which is not risk free. Thus in the setting of a monetary economy, the hypothesis $\mathbb{1} \notin \langle V \rangle$ arises very naturally and is related to many interesting issues that make the study of a "monetary" economy more complex—and more realistic—than the study of a "real" economy.

APPENDIX

Properties of Sup-convolution

Recall that the *sup-convolution* $u^* : \mathbb{R}_{++}^n \longrightarrow \mathbb{R}$ of the family of utility functions $u^i : \mathbb{R}_{++}^n \longrightarrow \mathbb{R}$ $(i = 1, \dots, I)$ is defined by

$$u^*(\xi) = \sup\left\{ \sum_{i=1}^I u^i(\xi^i) \;\middle|\; \sum_{i=1}^I \xi^i = \xi, \quad (\xi^1, \dots, \xi^I) \in \mathbb{R}_{++}^{nI} \right\} \tag{1}$$

and we write $u^* = u^1 \diamond \cdots \diamond u^I$. When $u^1, \ldots, u^I$ are concave functions, the properties of the sup-convolution u^* are readily derived by exploiting the property that the subgraph of a concave function is a convex set.

A3.1 Definition: The *subgraph (graph)* of $u : \mathbb{R}^n_{++} \longrightarrow \mathbb{R}$ is defined by

$$U = \left\{ (\xi, \eta) \in \mathbb{R}^n_{++} \times \mathbb{R} \mid \eta \leq (=) \, u(\xi) \right\}$$

As is well-known, *a function $u : \mathbb{R}^n_{++} \longrightarrow \mathbb{R}$ is concave if and only if its subgraph U is convex.* For a concave differentiable function u, the tangent hyperplane to the graph of u at a point $(\bar{\xi}, u(\bar{\xi}))$ is the supporting hyperplane to the subgraph at $(\bar{\xi}, u(\bar{\xi}))$. This property, which is illustrated in Figure A3.1, is expressed in the following lemma. Let

$$\nabla u(\xi) = \left(\frac{\partial u(\xi)}{\partial \xi_1}, \ldots, \frac{\partial u(\xi)}{\partial \xi_n} \right)$$

denote the standard gradient of u at $\xi \in \mathbb{R}^n_{++}$.

A3.2 Lemma (Supporting Hyperplane to Subgraph): *If $u : \mathbb{R}^n_{++} \longrightarrow \mathbb{R}$ is a concave differentiable function and if U is the subgraph of u, then*[2]

(i) $(\bar{\xi}, u(\bar{\xi})) = \arg \max \left\{ \left(-\nabla u(\bar{\xi}), 1 \right) \cdot (\xi, \eta) \mid (\xi, \eta) \in U \right\}$
(ii) *If $(\bar{\xi}, \bar{\eta}) \in U$ is such that there exists $\bar{\lambda} \in \mathbb{R}^n$ with*

$$(\bar{\xi}, \bar{\eta}) = \arg \max \left\{ (-\bar{\lambda}, 1) \cdot (\xi, \eta) \mid (\xi, \eta) \in U \right\}$$

then $\bar{\eta} = u(\bar{\xi})$ and $\bar{\lambda} = \nabla u(\bar{\xi})$.

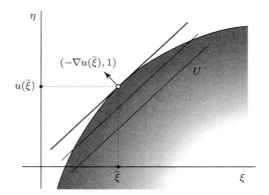

Figure A3.1   Supporting hyperplane to subgraph U

---

[2]For clarity, when vectors are decomposed into two components (e.g. $(\xi, \eta) \in \mathbb{R}^n \times \mathbb{R}$), the inner product is denoted by a dot: in all other cases the usual notation (without dot) is used.

PROOF: (i) A differentiable function u is concave if and only if

$$u(\xi) - u(\bar{\xi}) \leq \nabla u(\bar{\xi})(\xi - \bar{\xi}), \quad \forall \xi \in \mathbb{R}^n_{++}$$

which is equivalent to

$$u(\bar{\xi}) - \nabla u(\bar{\xi})\bar{\xi} \geq u(\xi) - \nabla u(\bar{\xi})\xi \geq \eta - \nabla u(\bar{\xi})\xi, \quad \forall (\xi, \eta) \in U$$

(ii) asserts that $(-\bar{\lambda}, 1)$ generates a supporting hyperplane to the subgraph U at $(\bar{\xi}, \bar{\eta})$. This implies that $(\bar{\xi}, \bar{\eta})$ is a boundary point of U, so that $\bar{\eta} = u(\bar{\xi})$. The differentiability of u implies that the supporting hyperplane is unique and hence coincides with the tangent hyperplane. $\square$

The sup-convolution u^* of a family of utility functions $u^1, \ldots, u^I$ has the important property that its subgraph U^* is the (vector) sum of the subgraphs $U^1, \ldots, U^I$.

A3.3 Lemma (Sum of Subgraphs Property):   Let $u^* = u^1 \diamond \cdots \diamond u^I$ and let $U^*, U^1, \ldots, U^I$ be the associated subgraphs. Then

$$U^* = U^1 + \cdots + U^I \tag{2}$$

Thus if $u^1, \ldots, u^I$ are concave functions, then u^* is concave.

PROOF: (2) follows readily from the definition of u^* and Definition A3.1. If $u^1, \ldots, u^I$ are concave, then $U^1, \ldots, U^I$ are convex subsets of $\mathbb{R}^{n+1}$: thus U^*, as a sum of convex sets, is convex and u^* is concave. $\square$

The following lemma is the familiar property used in proving the second Welfare Theorem: it asserts that a linear function is maximized over a sum of sets if and only if it is maximized over each of the individual sets.

A3.4 Lemma (Maximization Over Sum of Sets):   Let $Z = Z^1 + \cdots + Z^I$, $Z^i \subset \mathbb{R}^n$, $i = 1, \ldots, I$ and let $z \longmapsto az$ for $a \in \mathbb{R}^n$ be a linear functional on $\mathbb{R}^n$. The following properties are equivalent:

(a) $\bar{z} = \arg\max\{az \mid z \in Z\}$
(b) There exists a decomposition $\bar{z} = \bar{z}^1 + \cdots + \bar{z}^I$ with $\bar{z}^i \in Z^i$, $i = 1, \ldots, I$ such that
$$\bar{z}^i = \arg\max\{az^i \mid z^i \in Z^i\}, \quad i = 1 \ldots, I \tag{3}$$

(c) For all decompositions $\bar{z} = \bar{z}^1 + \cdots + \bar{z}^I$ with $\bar{z}^i \in Z^i$, $i = 1, \ldots, I$, (3) holds.

PROOF: It is easy to check that (b) $\Longrightarrow$ (a) $\Longrightarrow$ (c) $\Longrightarrow$ (b). $\square$

We are now in a position to characterize the solution of the problem (1) which defines the sup-convolution, in the case where each of the functions $u^1, \ldots, u^I$ is concave.

A3.5 Proposition (Gradient Property of Sup-convolution): *Let $u^1, \ldots, u^I :$ $\mathbb{R}^n_{++} \longrightarrow \mathbb{R}$ be concave functions and let $u^* = u^1 \diamond \cdots \diamond u^I$. If $\bar{\xi} = \bar{\xi}^1 + \cdots + \bar{\xi}^I$ with $(\bar{\xi}^1, \ldots, \bar{\xi}^I) \in \mathbb{R}^{nI}_{++}$, then $(\bar{\xi}^1, \ldots, \bar{\xi}^I)$ is solution to the problem (1) at $\bar{\xi}$ if and only if there exists $\bar{\pi} \in \mathbb{R}^n$ such that*

$$\nabla u^1(\bar{\xi}^1) = \cdots = \nabla u^I(\bar{\xi}^I) = \bar{\pi} \tag{4}$$

Furthermore $\bar{\pi}$ satisfies

$$\nabla u^*(\bar{\xi}) = \bar{\pi} \tag{5}$$

PROOF: Since a sum of concave functions is concave, (1) involves the maximization of a concave function subject to the linear constraint $\sum_{i=1}^I \xi^i = \bar{\xi}$. $(\bar{\xi}^1, \ldots, \bar{\xi}^I) \in \mathbb{R}^{nI}_{++}$ is a solution if and only if $\sum_{i=1}^I \bar{\xi}^i = \bar{\xi}$ and the first-order conditions are satisfied. These conditions assert that there exists a vector $\bar{\pi} \in \mathbb{R}^n$ such that (4) holds.

To prove (5), note that by Lemma A3.2 (i), (4) implies

$$\left(\bar{\xi}^i, u^i(\bar{\xi}^i)\right) = \arg \max \left\{ (-\bar{\pi}, 1) \cdot (\xi^i, \eta^i) \mid (\xi^i, \eta^i) \in U^i \right\}, \quad i = 1, \ldots, I$$

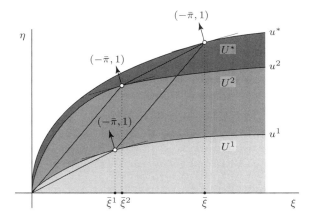

Figure A3.2   The sup-convolution $u^* = u^1 \diamond u^2$ for the case $n = 1$. The figure shows the sum of the subgraphs $(U^* = U^1 + U^2)$ and the gradient property $(\nabla u^*(\bar{\xi}) = \nabla u^1(\bar{\xi}^1) = \nabla u^2(\bar{\xi}^2) = \bar{\pi})$.

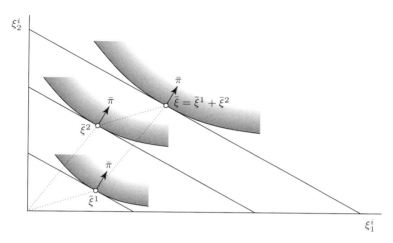

Figure A3.3 The gradient property $\nabla u^*(\bar{\xi}) = \nabla u^1(\bar{\xi}^1) = \nabla u^2(\bar{\xi}^2) = \bar{\pi}$ of the sup-convolution when projected onto ξ plane, for the case $n = 2$.

It follows from (a) $\iff$ (b) in Lemma A3.4 that

$$\sum_{i=1}^{I} \left(\bar{\xi}^i, u^i(\bar{\xi}^i) \right) = \left(\bar{\xi}, u^*(\bar{\xi}) \right) = \arg\max \left\{ (-\bar{\pi}, 1) \cdot (\xi, \eta) \mid (\xi, \eta) \in U^* \right\}$$

Thus $(-\bar{\pi}, 1)$ generates a supporting hyperplane to the subgraph U^* at $\left(\bar{\xi}, u^*(\bar{\xi}) \right)$. The uniqueness of the supporting hyperplane follows from the equivalence (a) $\iff$ (c) in Lemma A3.4 and the differentiability of the functions u^i for $i = 1, \ldots, I$. Thus u^* is differentiable at $\bar{\xi}$ and by Lemma A3.2 (ii), (5) holds. $\square$

Note that if the partial derivatives of $u^1, \ldots, u^I$ are positive, then by (5) the same is true for u^*. Thus u^* inherits the property of monotonicity from $u^1, \ldots, u^I$. The geometric interpretation of Lemma A3.5 is shown in Figure A3.2 for the case of functions of one variable ($n = 1$, $I = 2$) and in Figure A3.3 for the case of functions of two variables ($n = 2$, $I = 2$). In the latter case, only the projection of the three-dimensional figure onto the plane of the variables is shown.

If u^i is additively separable, $u^i(x^i) = \sum_{s=0}^{n} v_s^i(x_s^i)$, $i = 1, \ldots, I$, then the sup-convolution u^* inherits this property. We prove the more precise result stated in Proposition 16.6.

A3.6 (Proof of Proposition 16.6): The first step in proving (a) is immediate:

$$u^*(\xi) = \max_{\sum_{i=1}^I \xi^i = \xi} \left\{ \sum_{i=1}^I \bar{u}^i(\xi^i) \right\}$$

$$= \max_{\sum_{i=1}^I \xi^i = \xi} \left\{ \sum_{i=1}^I \bar{v}_0^i(\xi_0^i) + \sum_{s=1}^S \rho_s \sum_{i=1}^I \bar{v}_1^i(\xi_s^i) \right\}$$

$$= \max_{\sum_{i=1}^I \xi_0^i = \xi_0} \left\{ \sum_{i=1}^I \bar{v}_0^i(\xi_0^i) \right\} + \sum_{s=1}^S \rho_s \max_{\sum_{i=1}^I \xi_s^i = \xi_s} \left\{ \sum_{i=1}^I v_1^i(\xi_s^i) \right\}$$

$$= \left(\bar{v}_0^1 \diamond \cdots \diamond \bar{v}_0^I \right)(\xi_0) + \sum_{s=1}^S \rho_s \left(\bar{v}_1^1 \diamond \cdots \diamond \bar{v}_1^I \right)(\xi_s)$$

It remains to show that the convolution functions v_0^* and v_1^* satisfy (7) in Section 16; we show this for v_0^*. Since

$$v_0^*(\xi) = \max_{\sum_{i=1}^I c^i = \xi} \sum \bar{v}_0^i(c^i) \tag{6}$$

there exists $\bar{\pi}_0 > 0$ such that the solution to (6) is defined by the first-order conditions

$$\bar{v}_0^{1\prime}(\bar{c}^1) = \cdots = \bar{v}_0^{I\prime}(\bar{c}^I) = \bar{\pi}_0, \quad \bar{c}^1 + \cdots + \bar{c}^I = \xi$$

which can be solved as $\bar{c}^i = (\bar{v}_0^{i\prime})^{-1}(\bar{\pi}_0)$, $i = 1, \ldots, I$ and $\sum_{i=1}^I (\bar{v}^{i\prime})^{-1}(\bar{\pi}_0) = \xi$. Since $\bar{v}^{i\prime}$ is differentiable and $v^{i\prime\prime} < 0$, $i = 1, \ldots, I$, $\bar{\pi}_0$ is unique and differentiable and $d\bar{\pi}_0/d\xi < 0$. By Proposition A3.5, $v_0^{*\prime\prime}(\xi) = d\bar{\pi}_0/d\xi < 0$. If $\xi \to 0$ then $\bar{c}^i \to 0$, $i = 1, \ldots, I$ and $v_0^{*\prime}(\xi) = \bar{v}_0^{i\prime}(\bar{c}^i) \to \infty$.

To prove (b), note that by Proposition A3.5

$$\frac{v_1^{*\prime}(\xi)}{v_0^{*\prime}(\xi)} = \frac{\bar{v}_1^{i\prime}(\bar{c}_1^i)}{\bar{v}_0^{i\prime}(\bar{c}_0^i)}, \quad i = 1, \ldots, I \tag{7}$$

where $(\bar{c}_0^1, \ldots, \bar{c}_0^I)$ and $(\bar{c}_1^1, \ldots, \bar{c}_1^I)$ are the solutions to the two maximum problems defining $v_0^*(\xi)$ and $v_1^*(\xi)$ respectively. Since $\bar{c}_0^1 + \cdots + \bar{c}_0^I = \bar{c}_1^1 + \cdots + \bar{c}_1^I = \xi$, for some agent i, $\bar{c}_1^i \geq \bar{c}_0^i$. Since (7) and (8) in Section 16 hold for (v_0^i, v_1^i)

$$\bar{v}_1^{i\prime}(\bar{c}_1^i) \leq \bar{v}_1^{i\prime}(\bar{c}_0^i) < \bar{v}_0^{i\prime}(\bar{c}_0^i)$$

By (7), $v_1^{*\prime}(\xi)/v_0^{*\prime}(\xi) < 1$. $\square$

Stochastically Dependent Random Variables

To prove Proposition 16.9 it suffices to establish (i) and (ii) for the case of positively dependent random variables (x, y). Let us show that if (x, y) are two real-valued random variables on $(\mathbf{S}, \mathscr{S}, \mathbb{P})$ which are positively dependent, then

(i) if $f : \mathbb{R} \longrightarrow \mathbb{R}$ is strictly decreasing, then $(x, f(y))$ are negatively dependent;

(ii) $\operatorname{cov}(x, y) > 0$.

A3.7 (Proof of Proposition 16.9):   To establish (i) above, we first show that the inequality (10) in Section 16, which defines positively dependent random variables, holds if the inequality $x \leq \alpha$ and/or $y \leq \beta$ is replaced by a strict inequality.

$$\mathbb{P}\left[x \leq \alpha, y < \beta\right] \geq \mathbb{P}\left[x \leq \alpha, y \leq \beta - \frac{1}{n}\right] \geq \mathbb{P}\left[x \leq \alpha\right]\mathbb{P}\left[y \leq \beta - \frac{1}{n}\right]$$

If F_y denotes the distribution function of y, then

$$\lim_{n \to \infty} \mathbb{P}\left[y \leq \beta - \frac{1}{n}\right] = \lim_{n \to \infty} F_y\left(\beta - \frac{1}{n}\right) = F_y(\beta^-) = \mathbb{P}\left[y < \beta\right]$$

thus $\mathbb{P}\left[x \leq \alpha, y < \beta\right] \geq \mathbb{P}\left[x \leq \alpha\right]\mathbb{P}\left[y < \beta\right]$.

   Let $f : \mathbb{R} \longrightarrow \mathbb{R}$ be a strictly decreasing function. Suppose first that f is continuous, then

$$\begin{aligned}
\mathbb{P}\left[x \leq \alpha, f(y) \leq \beta\right] &= \mathbb{P}\left[x \leq \alpha, y \geq f^{-1}(\beta)\right] \\
&= \mathbb{P}\left[x \leq \alpha\right] - \mathbb{P}\left[x \leq \alpha, y < f^{-1}(\beta)\right] \\
&\leq \mathbb{P}\left[x \leq \alpha\right] - \mathbb{P}\left[x \leq \alpha\right]\mathbb{P}\left[y < f^{-1}(\beta)\right] \\
&= \mathbb{P}\left[x \leq \alpha\right]\mathbb{P}\left[f(y) \leq \beta\right]
\end{aligned}$$

the inequality being strict for some (α, β). If f is discontinuous and β is such that

$$\lim_{y \to b^+} f(y) \leq \beta \leq \lim_{y \to b^-} f(y)$$

then the inequality $f(y) \leq \beta$ is equivalent to either $y > b$ if $f(b) > \beta$ or $y \geq b$ if $f(b) \leq \beta$. A similar calculation to the one given above completes the proof of (i).

To prove (ii), consider a pair of random variables (x', y') on the probability space $(\mathbf{S}, \mathscr{S}, \mathbb{P})$ having the same joint distribution as (x, y) and such that (x, y) and (x', y') are independent. Then

$$
\begin{aligned}
E\left((x - x')(y - y')\right) &= E(xy) - E(x')E(y) - E(y')E(x) + E(x'y') \\
&= 2\left(E(xy) - E(x)E(y)\right) = 2\operatorname{cov}(x, y) \tag{8}
\end{aligned}
$$

$$
\begin{aligned}
E\left((x - x')(y - y')\right) &= \sum_{s \in \mathbf{S}} \left(x(s) - x'(s)\right)\left(y(s) - y'(s)\right)\mathbb{P}(s) \\
&= \sum_{s \in \mathbf{S}} \left(\int_{x'(s)}^{x(s)} \int_{y'(s)}^{y(s)} du\, dv\right)\mathbb{P}(s) \tag{9}
\end{aligned}
$$

Define the function $I : \mathbb{R}^2 \longrightarrow \mathbb{R}$ by

$$
I(u, \alpha) = \begin{cases} 1 & \text{if} \quad u \geq \alpha \\ 0 & \text{if} \quad u < \alpha \end{cases}
$$

Then (9) can be written as

$$
\begin{aligned}
E&\left((x - x')(y - y')\right) \\
&= E\int_{-\infty}^{\infty}\int_{-\infty}^{\infty} \left(I(u, x') - I(u, x)\right)\left(I(v, y') - I(v, y)\right) du\, dv \\
&= \int_{-\infty}^{\infty}\int_{-\infty}^{\infty} E\left(I(u, x') - I(u, x)\right)\left(I(v, y') - I(v, y)\right) du\, dv \\
&= \int_{-\infty}^{\infty}\int_{-\infty}^{\infty} 2\left(E\left(I(u, x)I(v, y)\right) - EI(u, x)EI(u, y)\right) du\, dv
\end{aligned}
$$

where the last equality follows from the independence of (x, y) and (x', y'). Since

$$
E\left(I(u, x)I(v, y)\right) = \mathbb{P}\left[x \leq u, y \leq v\right] \quad \text{and} \quad EI(u, x) = \mathbb{P}\left[x \leq u\right]
$$

it follows from (8) that

$$
\operatorname{cov}(x, y) = \int_{-\infty}^{\infty}\int_{-\infty}^{\infty} \left(\mathbb{P}\left[x \leq u, y \leq v\right] - \mathbb{P}\left[x \leq u\right]\mathbb{P}\left[y \leq v\right]\right) du\, dv
$$

Since (x, y) are positively dependent the integrand is non-negative and is strictly positive for some pair (u, v). Since the probability space is discrete, the integrand is positive on an open rectangle around (u, v), so that $\operatorname{cov}(x, y) > 0$. $\square$

Pareto Optimal Linear Sharing Rules

Proposition 16.13 characterizes the subclass of economies with additively separable utility functions for which Pareto optimal allocations satisfy a linear sharing rule.

A3.8 (Proof of Proposition 16.13): $(\Longrightarrow)$ u^i VNM$'$-additively separable implies $u^i \longleftrightarrow (v_0^i, v_1^i)$, $i = 1, \dots, I$. In order that

$$x_{\mathbf{1}}^i(\mu, w) = a_i(\mu)\mathbb{1} + b_i(\mu)w_{\mathbf{1}}, \quad i = 1, \dots, I \tag{10}$$

is a solution of the maximum problem

$$\max \left\{ \sum_{i=1}^I \mu_i u^i(x^i) \; \middle| \; \sum_{i=1}^I x^i = w, \quad x \in \mathbb{R}^{(S+1)I} \right\} \tag{11}$$

the first-order conditions

$$\mu_i v_1^{i\prime} \left(a_i(\mu) + b_i(\mu)w_s \right) = \mu_k v_1^{k\prime} \left(a_k(\mu) + b_k(\mu)w_s \right) \tag{12}$$

must be satisfied for all $i, k = 1, \dots, I$, for all $w_s \in \mathbb{R}_{++}$ and for all $\mu \in \mathbb{R}_+^I$. Differentiating (12) with respect to w_s gives

$$\mu_i v_1^{i\prime\prime} \left(x_s^i(\mu, w) \right) b_i(\mu) = \mu_k v_1^{k\prime\prime} \left(x_s^k(\mu, w) \right) b_k(\mu), \tag{13}$$

from which it follows that $b_i(\mu) > 0$ for $\mu_i > 0$. If $\mu_i = 0$ then $a_i(\mu) = b_i(\mu) = 0$ and agent i can be omitted from the maximum problem (11): thus we can assume $\mu_i > 0$, $i = 1, \dots, I$ without loss of generality. Differentiating (12) with respect to μ_i gives

$$\begin{aligned} v_1^{i\prime} \left(x_s^i(\mu, w) \right) + \mu_i v_1^{i\prime\prime} \left(x_s^i(\mu, w) \right) \left(a_{ii}(\mu) + b_{ii}(\mu)w_s \right) \\ = \mu_k v_1^{k\prime\prime} \left(x_s^k(\mu, w) \right) \left(a_{ki}(\mu) + b_{ki}(\mu)w_s \right), \end{aligned} \tag{14}$$

where $a_{ki} = \partial a_k / \partial \mu_i$, $b_{ki} = \partial b_k / \partial \mu_i$. Substituting the value for $v_1^{k\prime\prime}$ given by (13) and $w_s = (x_s^i - a_i)/b_i$ into (14) gives

$$v_1^{i\prime}(x_s^i) + v_1^{i\prime\prime}(x_s^i) \left(\alpha_i(\mu) + \beta_i(\mu)x_s^i \right) = 0, \quad i = 1, \dots, I \tag{15}$$

where

$$\alpha_i = \mu_i \left(\frac{a_{ii}b_i - a_i b_{ii}}{b_i} + \frac{a_i b_{ki} - a_{ki}b_i}{b_k} \right), \quad \beta_i = \mu_i \left(\frac{b_{ii}}{b_i} - \frac{b_{ki}}{b_k} \right)$$

Since (15) must be satisfied for all $w_s > 0$, it must be satisfied for an interval of x_s^i. Thus $\alpha_i(\mu)$ and $\beta_i(\mu)$ are independent of μ so that (15) can be written as

$$\frac{-v_1^{i'}(\xi^i)}{v_1^{i''}(\xi^i)} = \alpha_i + \beta_i \xi^i, \quad i = 1, \ldots, I \tag{16}$$

Integrating (16) gives

$$\log v_1^{i'}(\xi^i) = \begin{cases} -\dfrac{1}{\beta_i} \log(\alpha_i + \beta_i \xi^i) + c_i, & \text{if } \beta_i \neq 0 \\ -\dfrac{1}{\alpha_i} \xi^i + c_i, & \text{if } \beta_i = 0 \end{cases}$$

With this expression for $v_1^{i'}$ it is easy to check that (12) is satisfied for all $w_s > 0$ only if $\beta_i = \beta$, $i = 1, \ldots, I$.

($\Longleftarrow$) Since u^i is additively separable, if $\bar{x}$ is a solution of (11), then

$$\bar{x}_s = (\bar{x}_s^1, \ldots, \bar{x}_s^I) = \arg\max\left\{ \sum_{i=1}^{I} \mu_i v_1^i(x_s^i) \;\middle|\; \sum_{i=1}^{I} x_s^i = w_s, x_s \in \mathbb{R}^I \right\}$$

By strict concavity of v_1^i, the first-order conditions are necessary and sufficient and have a unique solution. The condition

$$T^i(\xi) = \alpha_i + \beta\xi$$

is equivalent to

$$v_1^{i'}(\xi^i) = \begin{cases} \delta_i(\alpha_i + \beta\xi^i)^{1/\beta}, & \text{if } \beta \neq 0 \\ \delta_i e^{-\xi_i/\alpha_i}, & \text{if } \beta = 0 \end{cases}$$

If $\beta \neq 0$ the system of equations

$$\mu_i \delta_i (\alpha_i + \beta x_s^i)^{1/\beta} = \mu_1 \delta_1 (\alpha_1 + \beta x_s^1)^{1/\beta}, \quad i = 2, \ldots, I$$

$$\sum_{i=1}^{I} x_s^i = w_s$$

has a solution of the form $x_s^i = a_i + b_i w_s$, $i = 1, \ldots, I$ with $\sum_{i=1}^{I} a_i = 0$, $\sum_{i=1}^{I} b_i = 1$. A similar calculation holds for $\beta = 0$. $\square$

EXERCISES

1. *Pareto optimal allocations in economies with no aggregate risk and risk-averse agents.*

It follows from Theorem 16.7 that in an economy in which there is no aggregate risk (var $w_1 = 0$), if agents have VNM separable utilities and markets are complete, then at an equilibrium agents have no individual risks (var $\bar{x}_1^i = 0$, $(i = 1, \ldots, I)$. It is easy to show directly that absence of individual risk is a property of Pareto optimal allocations of economies with VNM preferences and no aggregate risk: indeed it is true for a broader class of preferences exhibiting risk aversion, as the reader is asked to show in the following exercise. This property is a well-known and widely used property which generalizes in a straightforward way to economies with many goods at each date.

Consider a two-period, one-good exchange economy $\mathscr{E}(u, \omega)$ with no aggregate risk (var $w_1 = 0$) where $w_1 = \sum_{i=1}^{I} \omega^i$ and $w_1 \in \mathbb{R}_{++}^{S+1}$.

(a) Let u^i be VNM-additively separable, $i = 1, \ldots, I$. Show that if $\bar{x}$ is a Pareto optimal allocation, then var $\bar{x}_1^i = 0$, $i = 1, \ldots, I$. (Hint: proceed by contradiction and use the fact that the concavity of v_1^i implies that agent i is risk averse.)

(b) Find the broadest class of preferences exhibiting risk aversion which imply absence of individual risk at a Pareto optimal allocation.

(c) Give a geometric proof of (a) in the case $I = S = 2$, using an Edgeworth box diagram for the date 1 allocations.

2. *Properties of equilibrium with complete markets: alternative proof.*

The properties of a financial market equilibrium when markets are complete and agents have VNM preferences was studied in Section 16 using *representative agent analysis*. Since this is a powerful tool with many applications the rather lengthy analysis of Section 16 seemed justified. There is however a short and direct way of deriving the properties in Theorem 16.7 as the reader is asked to show in the following exercise.

Consider a two-period finance economy $\mathscr{E}(u, \omega, V)$ in which agents' utility functions are VNM-additively separable (Definition 16.5) and in which the security structure is complete (rank $V = S$). Let $((\bar{x}, \bar{z}), \bar{q})$ be a financial market equilibrium.

(a) Using the first-order conditions of the agents and the assumption of complete markets, deduce that the equilibrium present-value vectors of the agents are the same, $\bar{\pi}^i = \bar{\pi}$, $i = 1, \ldots, I$. Use this to deduce that the date 1 consumption of each agent is a decreasing function of the probability factored state price $\bar{\pi}_s / \rho_s$ i.e. there exists a strictly decreasing function h^i such that $\bar{x}_s^i = h^i(\bar{\pi}_s / \rho_s)$, $s = 1, \ldots, S$, $i = 1, \ldots, I$.

(b) By adding up the date 1 consumption of the agents, deduce that there is a strictly decreasing function ϕ such that $\bar{\pi}_s / \rho_s = \phi(w_s)$, $s = 1, \ldots, S$ (property (a) of Theorem 16.7).

(c) Deduce from (a) and (b) that there exists a strictly increasing function ψ^i such that $\bar{x}^i_s = \psi^i(w_s)$, $s = 1, \dots, S$, $i = 1, \dots, I$ (property (c) of Theorem 16.7).

(d) Using the first-order conditions of the agents and question (b), deduce the pricing formula

$$c_{\bar{q}}(y) = \frac{E(y)}{1+\bar{r}} + \text{cov}(\phi(w_1), y)$$

assuming that one of the securities is the riskless bond.

(e) Suppose the agents' date 1 utility functions are quadratic. Deduce the CAPM formulae

$$c_{\bar{q}}(y) = \frac{E(y)}{1+\bar{r}} - c\,\text{cov}(w_1, y)$$

and

$$E(R_y) - \bar{R} = \beta_{my}(E(R_m) - \bar{R}), \quad \beta_{my} = \frac{\text{cov}(R_m, R_y)}{\text{var}\, R_m}$$

where $R_y = y/c_{\bar{q}}(y)$, $R_m = w_1/c_{\bar{q}}(w_1)$, $\bar{R} = 1 + \bar{r}$ are the returns per unit of income invested in the income stream y, the aggregate output of the economy w_1 and the riskless bond respectively.

(f) The risk premium on the equity of a public utility is typically smaller than that on the equity of corporations in the manufacturing sector. How would you explain this fact using the formulae in (e)?

3. *Covariance and decreasing transformation.*

This exercise shows by a simple example that if two random variables are not positively or negatively dependent, transforming one variable by a decreasing transformation does not always change the sign of the covariance.

Let $S = \{s_1, s_2, s_3\}$ be 3 states of natures, each with probability $1/3$. Let x and y be two random variables on S defined by $x = (3, -6, 9)$, $y = (2, 3, 4)$.

(a) Show that x and y are neither positively nor negatively dependent.

(b) Let $\phi : \mathbb{R}^3 \longrightarrow \mathbb{R}^3$ be a function such that $\phi(2) = 9.5$, $\phi(3) = 1.5$, $\phi(4) = 1$. Show that $\text{cov}(x, y) > 0$ and $\text{cov}(x, \phi(y)) > 0$.

4. *Matrix of ρ-orthogonal projection.* Let $V = [V^1 \cdots V^J]$ be the payoff matrix of J linearly independent securities, where $V^j \in \mathbb{R}^S$, $j = 1, \dots, J$, and let $\rho = (\rho_1, \dots, \rho_S)$ be a probability vector for the states with

$$[\rho] = \begin{bmatrix} \rho_1 & \cdots & 0 \\ \vdots & \ddots & \vdots \\ 0 & \cdots & \rho_S \end{bmatrix}$$

the associated diagonal matrix.

(a) Prove that $V^T [\rho] V$ is positive definite and thus invertible.

(b) Prove that the matrix B associated with the ρ-projection on $\langle V \rangle$ (see Section 14 for the definition) is given by

$$B = V[V^T [\rho] V]^{-1} V^T [\rho]$$

(Hint: use the property that the projection of $x \in \mathbb{R}^S$ on $\langle V \rangle$ is the closest vector to x in $\langle V \rangle$ under the least-squares criterion).

(c) Check that if $x \in \langle V \rangle$ then $Bx = x$.

5. *The case of linear-quadratic preferences.*

This is an example of an economy in which agents have mean-variance utility functions (Definition 17.1) which in addition satisfy the assumption of linear risk tolerance with identical coefficient β for all agents ($\beta^i = -1$ for all $i = 1, \ldots, I$, see Section 16). The exercise shows that with this assumption on preferences, the CAPM pricing formula holds without the assumption $\omega_1^i \in \langle V \rangle$ for all i. The assumption that agents' endowments lie in the marketed subspace is however essential for the property of linear risk sharing and the Pareto optimality of an equilibrium allocation. With linear-quadratic preferences the equilibrium is easy to compute.

Consider a finance economy $\mathscr{E}(u, \omega, V)$ in which agent i's utility function is defined by

$$u^i(x^i) = \lambda_0^i x_0^i + \sum_{s=1}^{S} \rho_s (\alpha^i x_s^i - \frac{1}{2}(x_s^i)^2) = \lambda_0^i x_0^i + E(\alpha^i x_1^i - \frac{1}{2}(x_1^i)^2), \quad i = 1, \ldots, I$$

where $\rho = (\rho_1, \ldots, \rho_S)$ is the vector of probabilities of the states of nature at date 1. Let $\omega^i = (\omega_0^i, \omega_1^i, \ldots, \omega_S^i) = (\omega_0^i, \omega_1^i)$ denote the initial endowment of agent i, and let $w = \sum_{i=1}^{I} \omega^i$ denote the aggregate resources (output) of the economy. It is assumed that $\lambda_0^i > 0$ and $\alpha^i > \max\{w_1, \ldots, w_S\}$. Agents trade the J independent securities with payoff matrix $V = [V^1 \ldots V^J]$.

(a) Compute the risk tolerance $T^i(x^i)$ and the rate of impatience $r^i(x^i)$ of agent i at a consumption stream $x^i = (x_0^i, x_1^i)$. Note that the parameter α^i enters in both the risk and impatience measure for agent i: increasing α^i increases the agent's risk tolerance and reduces his rate of impatience. Show that if x_0^i is fixed and $E(x_1^i)$ increases, $r^i(x^i)$ increases: explain why this property of r^i is intuitive. Show that if the consumption is constant and equal to c for every state $s = 0, 1, \ldots, S$, then r^i decreases with c. Explain why this property is unintuitive. Is it the constant marginal utility of income at date 0 which, while convenient for the computations, induces this undesirable property of the preferences?

(b) In what follows, $(\bar{x}, \bar{z}, \bar{q})$ denotes an equilibrium in which $\bar{x}^i \gg 0$, $i = 1, \ldots, I$. Show that the first-order conditions for the maximum problem of agent i at the equilibrium can be written as

$$\bar{q} = \frac{1}{\lambda_0^i} (\alpha^i \mathbb{1} - \omega_1^i - V\bar{z}^i)^T [\rho] V$$

(c) Let $\lambda_0 = \sum_{i=1}^{I} \lambda_0^i$, $\alpha = \sum_{i=1}^{I} \alpha^i$. Deduce from (b) that the equilibrium price vector for the securities is

$$\bar{q} = \frac{1}{\lambda_0} (\alpha \mathbb{1} - w_1)^T [\rho] V$$

Suppose that security 1 is the riskless bond. Compute the interest rate $\bar{r}$ and show that the security prices satisfy the CAPM formula

$$\bar{q}_j = \frac{E(V^j)}{1 + \bar{r}} - \frac{1}{\lambda_0} \text{cov}(w_1, V^j)$$

Explain the influence of the preference parameters (λ_0, α) and the aggregate endowment w on the equilibrium prices. How does the behavior of the dividend stream V^j affect security j's price? Note that the price of security j is independent of the existence of, or the payoffs on, other securities. This property is convenient for comparing the equilibrium allocations corresponding to different security structures.

(d) Show that the equilibrium allocation satisfies

$$\bar{x}_1^i = w_1^i + \left(\alpha^i - \frac{\lambda_0^i}{\lambda_0} \alpha \right) B \mathbb{1} - B \left(w_1^i - \frac{\lambda_0^i}{\lambda_0} w_1 \right)$$

where B is the projection matrix on $\langle V \rangle$ found in Exercise 4. Deduce the date 1 allocation $\bar{\bar{x}}_1^i$ of agent i in an Arrow-Debreu (contingent market) equilibrium.

(e) Show that if $w_1^i \in \langle V \rangle$ for $i = 1, \ldots, I$, then $\bar{x}_1^i = \bar{\bar{x}}_1^i$. Interpret the coefficients of the linear risk sharing rule.

(f) Show that if $w_1^i \notin \langle V \rangle$ for some i, then the equilibrium allocation is obtained by a net trade vector $\bar{\tau}_1^i = \bar{x}_1^i - w_1^i$ which is the vector in the marketed subspace which lies closest to the first best (Arrow-Debreu) net trade vector $\bar{\bar{\tau}}^i = \bar{\bar{x}}^i - w^i$.

(g) In the case where the equilibrium is Pareto optimal show that the utility function of the representative agent can be written, up to affine transformation, as

$$u^*(\xi) = \lambda_0 \xi_0 + \sum_{s=1}^{S} \rho_s \left(\alpha \xi_s - \frac{1}{2} \xi_s^2 \right)$$

where $\lambda_0 = \sum_{i=1}^{I} \lambda_0^i$, $\alpha = \sum_{i=1}^{I} \alpha_i$. Use this to calculate the ideal security $\bar{\bar{\gamma}}$. Show that this leads immediately to the formula for $\bar{q}$ derived in (c). Show that the equilibrium rate of interest is the representative agent's rate of impatience at the aggregate endowment.

(h) In the case where $w_1^i \notin \langle V \rangle$ for some i, so that the equilibrium is not Pareto optimal, show that the ideal security $\bar{\gamma}$ is the projection of $\bar{\bar{\gamma}}$ onto the marketed subspace $\langle V \rangle$.

6. *Alternative proof of the CAPM properties.*

This exercise presents the most classical proof of the properties of the equilibria of a mean-variance model (Theorem 17.3). It is based on the property that each investor's portfolio must minimize the variance of the date 1 income stream that it generates among the portfolios which have the same cost at date 0 and give the same expected returns.

Consider a two-period bond-equity economy, as described in Section 16, whose security structure consists of the riskless bond which is in zero net supply and K risky securities in positive supply: the returns on these $J = K + 1$ securities are assumed to be linearly independent. Let $y^k = (y_1^k, \ldots, y_S^k)$ denote the dividend stream on risky security k $(k = 1, \ldots, K)$, and let $[y]$ denote the associated $S \times K$ matrix of dividends. There are I investors who have mean-variance preferences (Definition 17.1) and date 0 initial resources (ω_0^i, δ^i), where $\delta^i = (\delta_k^i)_{k=1,\ldots,K}$ is a portfolio of the risky securities (with $\delta^i \geq 0$). Investors do not receive additional resources at date 1. Let $\theta_m = \sum_{i=1}^I \delta^i$ denote the total portfolio of risky securities—the market portfolio— and let $w_1 = [y]\, \theta_m$ denote the date 1 aggregate resources of the economy. Investor i chooses a portfolio (b^i, θ^i) at date 0, where b^i is the investment in the riskless bond and $\theta^i \in \mathbb{R}^K$ is the portfolio of risky securities. Let $(1/(1+r), q)$, with $q \in \mathbb{R}^K$, denote the vector of prices for the bond and the K risky securities.

(a) Write out the budget set of investor i. Define a financial market equilibrium of the bond-equity economy. Show that the change of variable $z_k^i = \theta_k^i - \delta_k^i, k = 1, \ldots, K$, $z_{K+1}^i = b^i$, transforms the model into a model in which all the securities are in zero net supply. Show that the transformed model satisfies the assumptions of a CAPM economy (Definition 17.2). The object of questions (b)–(g) is to show that an alternative proof of Theorem 17.3 can be obtained by calculus, using the model expressed in the original form of a bond-equity economy in which the risky securities are in positive net supply and the portfolios are expressed in terms of the variables $((b^i, \theta^i), (i = 1, \ldots, I)$.

(b) Let $((\bar{b}, \bar{\theta}), (1/(1+\bar{r}), \bar{q}))$ be an FM equilibrium of the economy. Show that the equilibrium portfolio $(\bar{b}^i, \bar{\theta}^i)$ of agent i must be a solution of the problem

$$\min_{(b^i, \theta^i) \in \mathbb{R}^{1+K}} \left\{ \mathrm{var}(\mathbb{1} b^i + [y]\theta^i) \;\middle|\; \begin{array}{l} \dfrac{1}{1+\bar{r}} b^i + \bar{q}\, \theta^i \leq \bar{c}_i \\[2mm] E(\mathbb{1} b^i + [y]\theta^i) \geq \bar{E}_i \end{array} \right\}$$

for appropriate constants $\bar{c}_i$ and $\bar{E}_i$, $i = 1, \ldots, I$.

(c) Let $E(y) = \left(E(y^1), \ldots, E(y^K) \right)^T$ denote the vector of expected payoffs of the risky securities and let

$$\Gamma = \left[\mathrm{cov}\,(y^k, y^{k'}) \right]_{k, k' = 1, \ldots, K}$$

denote their variance-covariance matrix. Show that Γ is positive definite and thus invertible.

(d) Write the problem in (b) in terms of the matrix Γ and show that the solution $(\bar{b}^i, \bar{\theta}^i)$ must satisfy

$$\bar{\theta}^i = \mu_i \Gamma^{-1} \left(\frac{E(y)}{1+\bar{r}} - \bar{q}^T \right)$$

for an appropriate constant $\mu_i \geq 0$, $i = 1, \ldots, I$.

(e) Deduce from (d) that the equilibrium prices must satisfy

$$\frac{E(y)}{1+\bar{r}} - \bar{q}^T = \lambda \Gamma \theta_m$$

for an appropriate constant $\lambda \geq 0$.

(f) Compute $\Gamma \theta_m$ and use the equality $w_1 = [y]\theta_m$ to show that the formula in question (e) is equivalent to

$$\bar{q}_k = \frac{E(y^k)}{1+\bar{r}} - \lambda \operatorname{cov}(w_1, y^k), \quad k = 1, \ldots, K$$

which is the CAPM formula for the security prices. Show that $\operatorname{var}(w_1) > 0$ implies $\lambda > 0$. Give an economic interpretation of λ. Why do we typically expect an equity contract to be worth less than the expected discounted value of its dividend stream?

(g) Deduce from (d) and (e) that the equilibrium portfolios satisfy the two-fund separation property and that the equilibrium allocation satisfies a linear sharing rule.

7. *CAPM equilibrium under weaker assumptions.*

This exercise shows that the properties of a CAPM equilibrium ((i)–(iii) of Theorem 17.3) can be established under the weaker assumption that agents' preferences are variance-averse and mean-preferring. A modification of these properties also holds when $\mathbb{1} \notin \langle V \rangle$, the riskfree bond being replaced by the least risky security in the marketed subspace, in the expression for the ideal security and the linear sharing rule. A zero-beta security replaces the riskfree bond in the beta pricing formula.

Let $\mathscr{E}(u, \omega, V)$ be a CAPM economy with aggregate risk $(\operatorname{var}(w_1) > 0)$.

(a) Let assumption (iv) of Definition 17.2 be replaced by the assumption that agents have variance-averse utility functions.

  (i) Prove that properties (i)–(iii) of Theorem 17.3 (except $c' > 0$) are satisfied.

  (ii) Show that the property $c' > 0$ is satisfied if in addition agents' utility functions are mean-preferring.

(b) Let the assumption in (a) be satisfied, and let assumption (ii) of Definition 17.2 be replaced by $\mathbb{1} \notin \langle V \rangle$. Let η be the security which represents the expectation functional on $\langle V \rangle$.

  (i) Show that η is the least risky security in the marketed subspace. Interpret geometrically the quantity $1 - E(\eta)$. Show that $\operatorname{var}(\eta/E(\eta)) = 1/E(\eta) - 1$ is a statistical measure of the minimum risk on the security markets.

  (ii) Prove that properties (i)′–(iii)′ at the end of Section 17 are satisfied.

  (iii) Show that the beta pricing formula is satisfied with the riskfree bond replaced by a zero-beta security. Give an economic interpretation of the formula.

8. *Dependence of representative agent's utility function on initial income distribution.*

It is shown in Section 16 that when all agents have VNM utility functions with linear risk tolerance $(T^i(\xi) = \alpha_i + \beta_i \xi)$ with the same coefficient β_i $(\beta_i = \beta,$ $i = 1, \ldots, I)$ and have initial endowments satisfying $\omega_1^i \in \langle V \rangle$, (with $1 \in \langle V \rangle$), then the equilibrium prices of the economy are those of a representative-agent economy $\mathscr{E}(u^*, w)$ in which the representative agent owns the aggregate endowment $w = \sum_{i=1}^{I} \omega^i$. The construction of the utility function u^* is explained in Section 16. In general this utility function u^* depends not only of the preferences of the individual agents but also on the *initial distribution of income* among the agents. This simply reflects the fact that the equilibrium prices depend on the income distribution in the economy. This point is illustrated by the following example.

Consider an economy $\mathscr{E}(u, \omega, V)$ such that $1 \in \langle V \rangle$, $\omega_1^i \in \langle V \rangle$ for $i = 1, \ldots, I$ and such that the utility function of agent i is

$$u^i(x^i) = \log x_0^i + \delta_i \left(\sum_{s=1}^{S} \rho_s \log x_s^i \right), \quad i = 1, \ldots, I$$

(a) Show that the utility function u^* of the representative agent at an equilibrium $((\bar{x}, \bar{z}), \bar{q})$ of this economy can be written, up to affine transformation, as

$$u^*(\xi) = \log \xi_0 + \left(\sum_{i=1}^{I} \delta_i \frac{\bar{x}_0^i}{\omega_0} \right) \left(\sum_{s=1}^{S} \rho_s \log \xi_s \right)$$

Interpret the relation between the discount factor of the representative agent and the discount factors of the agents in the economy.

(b) Use (a) to calculate the expression for the equilbrium rate of interest and the prices of the risky securities.

9. *The case of constant risk tolerance.*

This exercise shows that if the agents have VNM utility functions with *constant risk tolerance* $(T^i(\xi) = \alpha_i, i = 1, \ldots, I)$ or equivalently *constant absolute risk aversion* and if the other assumptions of Proposition 16.14 are satisfied, then the utility function u^* of the representative agent does *not* depend on the initial distribution of income among the agents. In such economies, the equilibrium prices depend only on the average risk tolerance, the average discount factor of the agents, and on the profile of the aggregate endowment $w = (w_0, w_1, \ldots, w_S)$.

Consider an economy $\mathscr{E}(u, \omega, V)$ such that $1 \in \langle V \rangle$, $\omega_1^i \in \langle V \rangle$ for $i = 1, \ldots, I$ and agent i has the utility function

$$u^i(x^i) = -\frac{1}{\alpha_i} e^{-x_0^i/\alpha_i} - \delta_i \sum_{s=1}^{S} \rho_s \frac{1}{\alpha_i} e^{-x_s^i/\alpha_i}, \quad i = 1, \ldots, I$$

(a) Interpret the coefficients α_i and δ_i.

(b) Show that the utility function u^* of the representative agent at an equilibrium $((\bar{x}, \bar{z}), \bar{q})$ of this economy can be written, up to affine transformation, as

$$u^*(\xi) = -\frac{1}{\alpha} e^{-\xi_0/\alpha} - \delta \sum_{s=1}^{S} \rho_s \frac{1}{\alpha} e^{-\xi_s/\alpha}$$

with $\alpha = \sum_{i=1}^{I} \alpha_i$, $\delta = \prod_{i=1}^{I} (\delta_i)^{\alpha_i/\alpha}$.

(c) Use (b) to calculate the expression for the equilbrium rate of interest and the prices of the risky securities.

(d) Show that the equilibrium prices of an economy $\mathscr{E}(u, \tilde{\omega}, V)$ with $\sum_{i=1}^{I} \tilde{\omega}^i = \sum_{i=1}^{I} \omega^i$ and $\tilde{\omega}_1^i \in \langle V \rangle$, $\forall i = 1, \dots, I$ are the same as the equilibrium prices of $\mathscr{E}(u, \omega, V)$. Give an economic interpretation of this result.

HISTORICAL REMARKS

In the historical perspective of the emergence of capitalism, few institutions and contracts of a market economy have been the object of so much suspicion and distrust as those connected with money, credit and finance. To the average layperson financial transactions appeared mysterious because, unlike production, they did not involve labor and the creation of some tangible product—they seemed to create something (profit) out of nothing. The widespread suspicion of financial institutions created by the abstract nature of their transactions was well expressed by Hayek (1988):

> Prejudice arising from the distrust of the mysterious reaches an even higher pitch when directed at those most abstract institutions of an advanced civilization on which trade depends, which mediate the most general, indirect, remote and unperceived effects of individual action, and which, though indispensable for the formation of an extended order, tend to veil their guiding mechanisms from probing observation: money and the financial institutions based upon it. The moment that barter is replaced by indirect exchange mediated by money, ready intelligibility ceases and abstract interpersonal processes begin that far transcend even the most enlightened individual perception ... Thus we reach the climax of the progressive replacement of the perceivable and concrete by abstract concepts shaping rules, guiding activity: money and its institutions seem to lie beyond the boundary of laudable and understandable physical efforts of creation, in a realm where the comprehension of the concrete ceases and incomprehensible abstractions rule.[1]

Usury laws were the most obvious manifestation of the suspicion and distrust surrounding the simplest of all financial transactions—the loan contract.[2] The religious prohibition of

---

[1] Hayek (1988, pp. 101–102).

[2] "Accordingly all the saints and all the angels of paradise cry then against [the usurer], saying 'To hell, to hell, to hell.' Also the heavens with their stars cry out, saying, 'To the fire, to the fire, to the fire.' The planets also clamor, 'To the depths, to the depths, to the depths.' " Saint Bernadine, *De Contractibus*, Sermon 45, art. 3; c. 3.

interest was reinforced by civil usury laws of varying severity in all countries of Europe from the beginnings of Christianity and persisted in many until late into the nineteenth century.[3] Usury laws, which were common to all ancient civilizations, can be attributed in part to a misunderstanding of the different functions of money—"money was intended as a means of exchange, whereas interest represents an increase in the money itself . . . and so of all types of business is the most contrary to nature"[4]—and in part to the extreme paucity of financial contracts, particularly insurance contracts. Since for all practical purposes, loans were the only form of financial contract available to most individuals, they were frequently resorted to by those who had suffered substantial and unexpected losses, circumstances that in more modern times would be covered by appropriate private or public insurance: such loans were risky and carried with them a high risk premium. The pawn broker of the Middle Ages extracting weekly interest of 25 percent was overt proof of the extreme incompleteness of the markets in these times.

In Europe the prohibition on lending at interest was never completely or consistently enforced and restrictions on financial dealings progressively gave way under the pressure of the growing needs to finance commercial and productive activities. From the Middle Ages on, commercial banks, insurance contracts, commodity futures and equity contracts emerged progressively with the extended national and international development of trade and industry.[5] At first, access to these markets (contracts) was the exclusive privilege of princes, wealthy merchants and bankers in the large cities and states, but with the course of time the doors were opened to a progressively broader base of the population.

As is true in the development of most economic institutions, practice preceded theory in the evolution of financial institutions—indeed, a proper understanding of the role and functioning of financial markets is essentially a modern phenomenon. An early and remarkable contribution to developing a theory of the rate of interest founded on the theory of capital may be found in the innovative work of John Rae entitled *New Principles on the Subject of Political Economy* (1834). His theory of interest was based on the mutual interplay of impatience (preferences) and the productivity of capital (technology). The intuitive theory of John Rae was developed into a systematic mathematical theory by Irving Fisher in his classic *Theory of Interest* (1930). It is thus to Irving Fisher (1906, 1907, 1930) that we should look for the foundations of the modern theory: he achieved for financial markets what Walras had achieved for goods markets, by introducing a rigorous concept of equilibrium for financial markets based on perfect foresight and maximizing behavior of agents.

Fisher began by introducing the idea of preference orderings for consumption streams over time in an environment without uncertainty. He defined a financial market equilibrium

---

[3] "Thou shalt not lend upon usury to thy brother; usury of money; usury of victuals, usury of anything . . . Unto a stranger thou mayest lend upon usury; but unto thy brother thou shalt not lend upon usury . . ." *Deuteronomy* 23: 19–20.

[4] Aristotle, *The Politics* (Book 1, x).

[5] Banks date from the 13th century in Genoa, Florence and Venice. In the 14th century Exchanges were active in Pisa, Venice, Florence, Genoa, Valencia and Barcelona: the most famous Stock Exchanges were Amsterdam (1530), London (1554), Paris (1563), Berlin (1716), Vienna (1771), and New York (1772). The earliest form of insurance was marine insurance which was active among Lombard and Venetian traders in the Mediterranean in the 15th century. For a historian's vision of the emergence of markets, the reader is referred to Braudel (1979).

in an economy with a finite number of agents over T periods, in which a short-term bond permits the transfer of income between each adjoining period, under the assumption that agents correctly anticipate (foresee) the future interest rates. He showed that in such an equilibrium the rate of interest (between any two periods) is equal to the common rate of impatience of the agents, this in turn being equal to the (marginal) rate of return on capital for each productive venture (between these two periods). In addition he showed that the equilibrium price of any productive asset is equal to the present discounted value of its future stream of income. In Chapter XVI of the earlier book (1906) Fisher developed a formula for the value of a risky income stream (which he called its *commercial value*) obtained by multiplying the expected discounted value of the income stream by a risk factor (the *coefficient of caution*), but he did not attempt to apply this approach in an equilibrium setting.

In the years immediately following Fisher's contributions, there was little significant progress in the theory of the valuation of securities: the typical approach was that of Graham and Dodd's *Security Analysis* (1934) and William's *The Theory of Investment Value* (1938), which are not based on an equilibrium analysis of the security market. An individual investor (with the help of a security analyst) formed his opinion on the likely dividend streams of securities, placing his funds in the security which in his opinion was most undervalued, the value of a security being the expected discounted value of its dividend stream with an allowance for risk which depended on the estimated variability of the dividends.

To make significant progress beyond Irving Fisher's deterministic *Theory of Interest* to a genuine theory of financial markets under uncertainty, what was needed was an appropriate mathematical model in which the income streams of a finite collection of securities could be modelled explicitly as *random variables*. There are two ways in which this can be done and both were discovered almost simultaneously. The first approach is to consider income streams as functions defined on (a finite set of) states of nature: this approach (which is the approach of *probability theory*) was introduced by Arrow (1953) and was discussed in the previous chapter. The second is to characterize the income streams by their joint probability distribution or by the moments of this distribution (the approach of *statistical theory*): the simplest variant of this approach is to describe the income streams by their mean and covariance matrix, and this was the approach introduced by Markowitz (1952). The papers of Arrow and Markowitz are the two pioneering contributions to the modern theory of financial markets. The first led to the general equilibrium model with financial markets,[6] the second led to the *capital asset pricing model* (CAPM) which became the basis for the modern theory of finance.

The key motivation of Markowitz analysis was to explain diversification.[7] He argued that the earlier security analysis mentioned above (Graham and Dodd (1934)) concentrated on finding portfolios which essentially maximized expected return and led to portfolios in which all wealth is invested in the security with the highest expected return. But such a portfolio ignores the principle of risk reduction well-known from insurance: if a collection of risks is independent, then diversification over a sufficiently large number of risks makes the

---

[6] See *Historical Remarks* on Chapter 2.
[7] For a systematic presentation of his ideas, see Markowitz (1959).

variability of the return on a portfolio arbitrarily small. Of course if the risks have positive covariance (as is typically the case for securities) diversification cannot make the variability of the return arbitrarily small, but it will greatly reduce variability—and risk reduction should be the concern of any rational risk-averse investor.

With this in mind Markowitz set up a canonical two-period portfolio choice problem for an investor who has an initial wealth which is to be invested in a finite collection of securities. He characterized the second period returns of the securities by the vector of means and the covariance matrix and formulated the investor's choice problem as the problem of finding the portfolio (defined as the proportion of his initial wealth invested in each of the securities) which minimizes variance for a given expected return. He analyzed the structure of the set of efficient portfolios in the portfolio space (obtained by varying the expected return) and showed that these portfolios generate an increasing curve in the mean-variance space (the so-called *efficient frontier*).

Markowitz analysis was simplified by Tobin (1958) who showed that, when there is a riskless security, the set of efficient portfolios can be characterized by a Two-Fund Separation Theorem: *there is a mutual fund (a portfolio composed of certain proportions of each of the risky securities) with the property that every efficient portfolio consists of holding a certain proportion of wealth in the riskless security (the first fund) and the rest in the mutual fund.* This result was of decisive importance for the development of the first equilibrium model of financial markets under uncertainty—the so-called *capital asset pricing model* (CAPM)—in which the securities are not just *elementary* securities of the kind considered by Arrow (1953) but *composite* securities such as bonds and equity contracts of firms. Under the assumption that all investors have *mean-variance* preferences, Sharpe (1964) and Lintner (1965) showed how the Markowitz-Tobin model could be closed so as to obtain an equilibrium on the financial markets. Since all investors hold the risky securities in the proportions of the mutual fund, the equilibrium prices must be such that this mutual fund is the aggregate portfolio of the economy (the market portfolio). Sharpe and Lintner showed by two different arguments that this property leads to the β-pricing formula (11) in Section 17. Sharpe showed that this formula expresses the fact that in equilibrium, prices and agents' portfolios have adjusted in such a way that the only risk for a security which matters is its systematic risk (the β-coefficient) which measures the volatility of the security's return with respect to the market portfolio—the idiosyncratic risk being diversified away in the equilibrium portfolios of agents.[8] The basic message of the CAPM model—that diversification reduces risk and that the risk which influences the price of a security is the volatility of its return relative to some appropriate index (or family of indices)—has had a lasting impact not only on the finance literature, but also on the thinking that guides the investment policies of professionals in major financial centres, those who manage the portfolios of pension funds, mutual funds, banks and corporations.

Since the influential papers of Sharpe (1964) and Lintner (1965), more abstract techniques have been developed for establishing the properties of a CAPM equilibrium. The proof given in Proposition 17.3 uses the techniques of Hilbert space theory employed by probabilists for studying random variables with finite variance. The idea of exploiting a Hilbert space setting in the study of security pricing seems to have been introduced in

---

[8] The risk pricing formula was extended by Black (1972) to the case where there is no riskless bond.

Chamberlain-Rothschild (1983) and Chamberlain (1983). The argument for deriving the set of efficient portfolios by projecting onto the subspace $\langle \mathbb{1}, \bar{\gamma} \rangle$ is due to Chamberlain-Rothschild (1983, Theorem 1). The use of this argument to prove Theorem 17.3 is given by Duffie (1988). Section 15 is an attempt to extend to the general model with incomplete markets the basic intuitions underlying the risk pricing of securities in CAPM. It is based on the idea that the pricing security has a natural economic interpretation as the ideal security (Theorem 15.4) and provides a unifying principle for analyzing the equilibrium prices of securities.

The LRT (linear risk tolerance) economies studied in Section 16 can be viewed as a confluence of two separate strands of literature; one had its origin in Tobin's Two-Fund Separation Theorem, the other emerged from the study of optimal linear risk-sharing schemes. Since the Two-Fund Separation Theorem exhibited a striking qualitative property of an agent's optimal portfolio, it was natural to enquire into the generality of this result. This question was addressed by Cass and Stiglitz (1970) who studied the following problem: under what conditions on agents' utility functions can optimal portfolios be obtained by investing in a smaller number (k) of appropriately formed mutual funds rather than the J original securities? They showed that if there is a riskless security, there is two fund separation for an agent's optimal portfolio for general security returns if and only if the agent has an LRT (linear risk tolerance) utility function (the sufficiency part had been established by Hakansson (1969)). They also showed that increasing the number of funds $(2 \le k < J)$ does not significantly reduce the restrictive assumptions required on preferences. Ross (1978b) provided restrictions on the distributions of the security returns under which there is k fund separation.

The nature of Pareto optimal risk-sharing rules were studied by Borch (1960, 1962, 1968) and Wilson (1968). Borch was motivated by a problem faced by actuaries—the problem of reinsurance among a collection of insurers. Wilson studied a problem of group decision making, when a collection of individuals must make a common decision under uncertainty that results in a payoff which is shared jointly by rules that are to be determined. In particular he was interested in conditions under which a consensus would be reached by virtue of the existence of a group utility function that could be used as the basis for decision making—essentially a representative agent utility function *independent* of the weights $\bar{\lambda}_0^i$ in Proposition 16.6 (see also Rubinstein (1974)). In looking for *linear* risk-sharing rules these authors were all led to the LRT family of utility functions. Proposition 17.3 is thus essentially due to Borch (1968) and Wilson (1968).

4

STOCHASTIC FINANCE ECONOMY

MOTIVATION AND SUMMARY

Economic activity in the real world is an ongoing process that has no natural terminal horizon. At every date agents trade on markets and make limited commitments regarding their future activities. A realistic model of equilibrium should be able to capture this fact by describing trading on markets as an ongoing sequential process of equilibrium over time: our objective is to construct such a model of equilibrium over an open-ended future. The natural preliminary step is to extend the two-period model of the previous chapters to an equilibrium model over a *finite horizon*: the open-ended model can then be obtained by taking limits of such equilibria for progressively longer horizons.

While the two-period model permits a number of the effects of time and uncertainty to be analyzed in a simple setting, its defect is that it treats the process of information acquisition in too abrupt a way: the transition between *no information* at date 0 and *full information* at date 1 is too sudden, since all the information is acquired in a single moment of time. The advantage of the multiperiod model is that it permits the process of information acquisition to be spread out, so that agents gradually acquire more bits of information over time. This leads to a much richer and more realistic modelling of the observed progressive unfolding of information over time.

The starting point for modelling uncertainty in a multiperiod setting is the same as for a two-period model, and consists of a primitive *set of possible outcomes or states* $\mathbf{S} = \{1, \ldots, S\}$. The fact that there is uncertainty is expressed by saying that an outside party, usually referred to as "nature", draws one of these states at random, $s \in \mathbf{S}$. Agents have no information if they know only that s lies in $\mathbf{S}$, and they have full information if they know exactly the state s which nature has drawn. Progressive acquisition of information over time is modelled by introducing a sequence of partitions of the set of states $\mathbf{S}$ (called *information partitions*) which become progressively finer as time evolves. The information available at time t consists in knowing in which subset of the information partition $\mathbb{F}_t$ at date t the state s lies. Since the partitions become finer as time progresses, the information about s becomes more precise, until at the terminal date T the exact state drawn by nature is revealed. The modelling of the process of information acquisition is thus based on a set of time periods $\mathbf{T} = \{0, 1, \ldots, T\}$, a set of states $\mathbf{S} = \{1, \ldots, S\}$, and a sequence of information partitions $\mathbb{F} = \{\mathbb{F}_t\}_{t \in \mathbf{T}}$, where $\mathbb{F}$ is called the *information structure*.

A multiperiod model of an economy and the associated concept of equilibrium involves an information structure $\mathbb{F}$, exogenously given *data* on characteristics (preferences, endowments and contracts) and *actions* of the agents. The data and actions are functions defined not only on the set of time periods $\mathbf{T}$ but also on the set of states $\mathbf{S}$: in short, they are functions on $\mathbf{T} \times \mathbf{S}$. It is clear that certain restrictions must be imposed on these functions if the information associated with them is to be compatible with the underlying information structure $\mathbb{F}$. Observing the *data* at date t (for example agents' endowments) must not reveal more information than is contained in the information partition $\mathbb{F}_t$ at date t: thus an agent's endowment at date t cannot differ for two states which lie in the same subset of $\mathbb{F}_t$. Furthermore, since at date t, agents do not have enough information to distinguish between two such states, their *actions* at date t—which must be based on the information available to them at date t—cannot differ on two states in the same subset of $\mathbb{F}_t$. A similar property must clearly hold for the prices at date t.

In probability theory, functions of the set of time periods and states $\mathbf{T} \times \mathbf{S}$ which are compatible in this way with the information structure $\mathbb{F}$ are called *stochastic processes adapted to* $\mathbb{F}$. Such stochastic processes can be described in two equivalent ways. The first and simplest approach is called the *event-tree approach*: each subset of the information partition $\mathbb{F}_t$ defines a *node*, and the collection of information partitions $\mathbb{F} = \{\mathbb{F}_t\}_{t \in \mathbf{T}}$ is equivalent to an *event-tree* $\mathbb{D}$. A stochastic process adapted to $\mathbb{F}$ is then equivalent to a function defined on the event-tree $\mathbb{D}$. The advantage of this approach is that the informational restrictions are automatically and straightforwardly incorporated into the event-tree. The second approach, which may be called the *stochastic process approach*, consists in using directly the formalization of probability theory and describing the functions as stochastic processes adapted to $\mathbb{F}$.

Both of these approaches will prove to be useful in the analysis that follows. Certain properties of the equilibrium model such as no-arbitrage, existence and optimality are more conveniently analyzed using the event-tree approach, while other properties such as the informational efficiency of security prices, for which it is convenient to draw on the machinery and concepts of probability theory, are more readily analyzed using the stochastic process approach. In this chapter we show how the event-tree approach can be used to analyze properties of the equilibrium model, while in the chapter that follows we show how the stochastic process approach can be used to analyze the informational efficiency of security prices. Taken together these two chapters are the analogues for the multiperiod model of Chapters 2 and 3 for the two-period model.

In addition to providing a richer modelling of the process of information acquisition, the multiperiod model permits the analysis of a much broader class of financial contracts than the two-period model. A contract is now characterized by its node of issue and the dividend stream that it yields along every path through the event-tree, from its node of issue until a maturity node is reached. An important distinction emerges between *short-lived* contracts (like those in the two-period model) which yield dividends only at the immediate successors of their node of issue and *long-lived* contracts which yield dividends over two or more periods. Short-lived securities are only traded once and are valued exclusively for their dividends. If long-lived securities are liquid (can be retraded at each date), then investors are concerned not only with the securities' dividend streams but also with their resale values in the future. As Keynes emphasized, in such a setting traders may be more concerned with predicting the future capital value of a security (what they think it's worth to other agents) than in assessing the present value to them of its future stream of dividends (its so-called *fundamental value*). Under the idealized conditions of the model we study—a finite horizon model in which all agents are rational and have correct anticipations—the equilibrium price of a long-lived security is always equal to its fundamental value, so that speculative bubbles or more general departures from the fundamental value cannot arise. This important property of security prices is established in Section 21 and is analyzed at greater length in Chapter 5, where it is shown that the capital values change in response to new information in such a way that the price of a security is, at each date, the best estimate of the value of the future stream of dividends, given the current information.

The presence of the capital values of the long-lived securities makes a rigorous mathematical analysis of the multiperiod model somewhat more complicated than the analysis of the earlier two-period model—although many of the techniques developed in Chapter 2 carry over to the multiperiod setting. The difficulty arises from the fact that the dimension of the subspace of income transfers (the market subspace) is no longer determined solely by the exogenously given dividend streams of the securities but depends in addition on the capital values of the long-lived securities. This has two consequences: first, the same security structure can lead to different equilibria in which the market subspace has different dimensions; second, some economies may not have a financial market equilibrium. These difficulties, and an equivalent but more convenient form for analyzing an equilibrium (which we call a *no-arbitrage equilibrium*), are explained in Section 23 and illustrated by an example in Section 24 (see also Example 25.6). These two sections are technical and can be omitted on a first reading—while they do not introduce new conceptual elements as far as the economics is concerned, they do need to be understood by a reader who wants to learn how to work with the multiperiod model. As the example suggests, the presence of several equilibria of different ranks and the nonexistence of equilibrium only arise for exceptional economies: the precise sense in which such economies are exceptional is explained in Section 25.

As far as economic properties of the model are concerned, it is with respect to the *efficiency* of equilibria that the multiperiod model differs most significantly from the two-period model. Not surprisingly, when markets are complete, financial market equilibria are still Pareto optimal. When markets are incomplete, the best that could be hoped for is to show that equilibria are constrained efficient. However finding an appropriate definition of constrained efficiency is much less obvious in a multiperiod than in a two-period economy. The underlying motivation is the same as in Section 12: the idea is to compare what a planner could do relative to what the market mechanism does, without obviously giving the planner access to more instruments for redistributing the income of agents over the event-tree than are available when using the existing financial contracts. With a system of markets, the consumption of an agent at every node ξ after date 0 is given by

$$x^i(\xi) - \omega^i(\xi) = (V(\xi) + q(\xi)) \, z^i(\xi^-) - q(\xi) z^i(\xi) \tag{1}$$

where ξ^- denotes the predecessor of node ξ. In this equation $q(\xi)$ and $z^i(\xi)$ are zero for all nodes at the terminal date T, since the securities yield no dividends after this date. When there are only two periods $(T = 1)$, date 1 is the terminal date and the right side of (1) reduces to $V(\xi)z^i(\xi_0)$, so that agent i's net trade vector at date 1 must lie in the marketed subspace

$$x^i_1 - \omega^i_1 \in \langle V \rangle$$

This condition, combined with the standard feasibility condition $\sum_{i=1}^I (x^i - \omega^i) = 0$, leads at once to the concept of a constrained feasible allocation adopted in Section 12 (Definition 12.1).

However when there are more than two periods it is no longer possible to mimic the right side of (1) for the intermediate dates $t = 1, \ldots, T - 1$ without using prices for the securities.[1] We are thus led to define a notion of constrained feasibility in which the prices of securities after date 0 remain on the right side of (1): the planner intervenes only at date 0, choosing the initial consumption and portfolio (x^i_0, z^i_0) of each agent, the allocation after date 0 being determined as an equilibrium $((x(\xi), z(\xi)), q(\xi), \xi \in \mathbb{D}^+)$ on the markets. In a multiperiod economy with heterogeneous agents in which markets are incomplete, a planner can typically improve on a financial market equilibrium, even when restricted to these limited instruments. When agents have different present-value vectors, such a welfare improvement can be obtained by exploiting the feedback between the initial portfolios (which determine the wealth of the agents at date 1) and the prices of the securities after date 0. Example 25.10 exhibits a simple three-period economy in which a planner can improve on the equilibrium by altering agents' savings decisions at date 0: this leads to a decrease

---

[1] If the price dependent terms $q(\xi) \, (z^i(\xi^-) - z^i(\xi))$ are replaced by transfers which can be chosen by the planner, then the planner is given complete freedom to redistribute income at all nodes in the event-tree except those at date T. But this amounts to ignoring all the subspace constraints imposed by the incompleteness of the markets except those at the terminal date (see equation (12) in Section 23).

in the interest rate in the two possible states at date 1 which, by favoring the agents more when they need to borrow, than it disfavors them when they choose to lend, makes all agents better off.

18. EVENT-TREE COMMODITY SPACE

The object of this section is to introduce a mathematical description of a process of gradual unfolding of information, in which more information is acquired about some underlying random phenomenon as time progresses. The construction is based on the introduction of a finite set $\mathbf{S} = \{1, \ldots, S\}$ of states: the exogenous uncertainty in the economy is expressed by saying that an outside party called "nature" draws one of the states $s \in \mathbf{S}$ at random. All the variables which define the economy are functions of these primitive states, so that knowing the state implies knowing the values of all the variables. Having no information about s amounts to knowing only that s is one of the elements of the set $\mathbf{S}$, while having full information amounts to knowing exactly the state $s \in \mathbf{S}$ which nature has drawn. In the two-period model of Chapter 2 the agents had no information at date $t = 0$ and full information at date $t = 1$.

Information Partition

In the two-period model the revelation of information is very abrupt: agents go from knowing nothing at date 0, to knowing everything at date 1. To formalize the idea of gradual unfolding of information it is necessary

(1) to extend the *set of time periods* to $\mathbf{T} = \{0, 1, \ldots, T\}$ with $T \geq 2$
(2) to formalize the idea of *partial* information.

(2) can be achieved by considering partitions of $\mathbf{S}$. A *partition* of $\mathbf{S}$ is a collection of mutually disjoint subsets of $\mathbf{S}$ whose union is $\mathbf{S}$. The unfolding of information is then described by a sequence of partitions of $\mathbf{S}$,

$$\mathbb{F} = (\mathbb{F}_0, \mathbb{F}_1, \ldots, \mathbb{F}_T) \tag{1}$$

where $\mathbb{F}_0 = \mathbf{S}$, $\mathbb{F}_T = \{\{1\}, \ldots, \{S\}\}$ and $\mathbb{F}_t$ is finer than the partition $\mathbb{F}_{t-1}$ for all $t = 1, \ldots, T$. $\mathbb{F}_t$ is said to be *finer* than $\mathbb{F}_{t-1}$ if

$$\sigma \in \mathbb{F}_t, \quad \sigma' \in \mathbb{F}_{t-1} \Longrightarrow \sigma \subset \sigma' \quad \text{or} \quad \sigma \cap \sigma' = \emptyset \tag{2}$$

The information available at time t is the subset σ of the partition $\mathbb{F}_t$ in which s lies. The fact that the sequence of partitions $\mathbb{F}_t$ becomes finer, expresses the idea that information increases over time.

18.1 Example: Let $\mathbf{T} = \{0, 1, 2, 3\}$, $\mathbf{S} = \{1, 2, 3, 4, 5\}$, and let the sequence of information partitions (1) be given by

$$\mathbb{F}_0 = \{1, 2, 3, 4, 5, \}$$
$$\mathbb{F}_1 = \{\{1, 2, 3\}, \{4, 5\}\}$$
$$\mathbb{F}_2 = \{\{1, 2, \}, \{3\}, \{4, 5\}\}$$
$$\mathbb{F}_3 = \{\{1\}, \{2\}, \{3\}, \{4\}, \{5\}\}$$

(see Figure 18.1(a)). At date 0 no information is available concerning the state s which nature has drawn: it can be any one of the five states. At date 1 it is known if the state s lies in the subset $\{1, 2, 3\}$ or in the subset $\{4, 5\}$. If the state s lies in the subset $\{4, 5\}$, then in moving from date 1 to date 2, no more information is acquired; if the state s lies in the subset $\{1, 2, 3\}$, then at date 2 it is known if the state s is 3 or if it is one of the two states $\{1, 2\}$. At date 3 the state s is revealed: there is complete information (all uncertainty has been resolved). □

The condition $\sigma \subset \sigma'$ in (2) does not require that σ be a strict subset of σ': thus (2) permits no change in information between date $t - 1$ and t. In Example 18.1 this occurs between dates 1 and 2 if the state of nature is either 4 or 5. (2) however excludes the loss of information between dates $t - 1$ and t: there is no "forgetting" what is known at an earlier period.

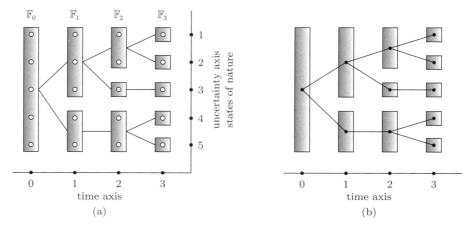

Figure 18.1   A family of partitions (a) and the associated event-tree (b).

Event-tree

The event-tree approach consists in viewing each subset of a partition in the sequence $(\mathbb{F}_0, \mathbb{F}_1, \ldots, \mathbb{F}_T)$ as a node of an event-tree. The event-tree associated with the family of partitions in Example 18.1 is shown in Figure 18.1(b). The formal definition is as follows.

18.2 Definition (Event-tree): Let $\mathbb{F} = (\mathbb{F}_0, \ldots, \mathbb{F}_T)$ be a sequence of partitions of $\mathbf{S}$, with $\mathbb{F}_0 = \mathbf{S}$, $\mathbb{F}_T = \{\{1\}, \ldots, \{S\}\}$ and $\mathbb{F}_t$ finer than $\mathbb{F}_{t-1}$, $t = 1, \ldots, T$. For each date $t \in \mathbf{T}$ and each subset $\sigma \in \mathbb{F}_t$ the pair (t, σ) is called a *date-event* or *node*. The set $\mathbb{D}$ consisting of all date-events (or nodes) is called the *event-tree* induced by $\mathbb{F}$

$$\mathbb{D} = \bigcup_{\substack{t \in \mathbf{T} \\ \sigma \in \mathbb{F}_t}} (t, \sigma)$$

18.3 Definition (Predecessor): Let $\xi = (t, \sigma)$ denote a typical element of the event-tree $\mathbb{D}$. The unique node $\xi_0 = (0, \sigma)$ with $\sigma = \mathbf{S}$ is called the *initial* node. The set of *non-initial* nodes is denoted by $\mathbb{D}^+$ so that

$$\mathbb{D}^+ = \mathbb{D} \setminus \xi_0$$

For each $\xi \in \mathbb{D}^+$, $\xi = (t, \sigma)$, there is a unique subset $\sigma' \in \mathbb{F}_{t-1}$ such that $\sigma' \supset \sigma$; the node $\xi^- = (t - 1, \sigma')$ is called the *predecessor* of ξ.

18.4 Definition (Successor): A node (T, σ) with $\sigma \in \mathbb{F}_T$ is called a *terminal* node. The set of all terminal nodes is denoted by $\mathbb{D}_T$ so that

$$\mathbb{D}_T = \bigcup_{\sigma \in \mathbb{F}_T} (T, \sigma)$$

The set of all *non-terminal* nodes is denoted by $\mathbb{D}^-$ so that

$$\mathbb{D}^- = \mathbb{D} \setminus \mathbb{D}_T$$

For each $\xi \in \mathbb{D}^-$, $\xi = (t, \sigma)$, the set

$$\xi^+ = \{\xi' \in \mathbb{D} \mid \xi' = (t + 1, \sigma'), \quad \sigma' \subset \sigma\}$$

is called the set of *immediate successors* of ξ. The number of elements in the set ξ^+ is called the *branching number* of the node ξ and is denoted by $b(\xi)$. ξ' *succeeds* ξ (strictly) if $\xi' = (t', \sigma')$, $\xi = (t, \sigma)$ satisfy $t' \geq t$ ($t' > t$), $\sigma' \subset \sigma$ and we write $\xi' \geq \xi$ ($\xi' > \xi$).

18.5 Definition (Subtree):   For any node $\bar{\xi} \in \mathbb{D}$, the set of all nodes which succeed $\bar{\xi}$ is called the *subtree* $\mathbb{D}(\bar{\xi})$ starting at $\bar{\xi}$

$$\mathbb{D}(\bar{\xi}) = \left\{ \xi \in \mathbb{D} \mid \xi \geq \bar{\xi} \right\}$$

The set of all *strict successors* of $\bar{\xi}$ is denoted by

$$\mathbb{D}^+(\bar{\xi}) = \left\{ \xi \in \mathbb{D}(\bar{\xi}) \mid \xi > \bar{\xi} \right\}$$

and the set of all *non-terminal successors* of $\bar{\xi}$ is denoted by

$$\mathbb{D}^-(\bar{\xi}) = \left\{ \xi \in \mathbb{D}(\bar{\xi}) \mid \xi \in \mathbb{D}^- \right\}$$

These definitions are illustrated in Figure 18.2 for the event-tree of Example 18.1.

Commodity Space

Our objective is to show how the concept of an information partition and its formulation as an event-tree leads to the basic commodity space for a multi-period economy under uncertainty. The ideas are conveniently introduced by showing how the endowment process of an agent is represented in such an economy.

When there is no uncertainty, an agent's endowment is extended to the multiperiod case by indexing the amount of the good by the date when it becomes available

$$\omega^i = \left(\omega^i(t),\, t \in \mathbf{T} \right)$$

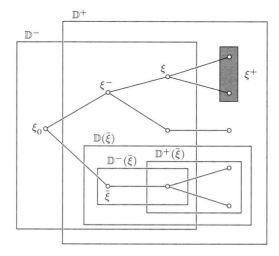

Figure 18.2   Event-tree notation.

The endowment ω^i thus defines a path over time. The introduction of uncertainty means that there is no longer a unique path over time: an agent's endowment can follow one of several paths depending on the state of nature. This is formalized by indexing the path $(\omega^i(t), t \in \mathbf{T})$ by the states of nature

$$\omega^i = \big(\omega^i(t,s), (t,s) \in \mathbf{T} \times \mathbf{S}\big) \tag{3}$$

If nature draws the state $s \in \mathbf{S}$ then the endowment path is $(\omega^i(t,s), t \in \mathbf{T})$.

An additional restriction is however needed if the alternative paths described by (3) are to be consistent with the information structure $\mathbb{F}$. For the information about the state s which nature has drawn is only learned gradually over time—the exact way in which an agent learns about the state s being described by the sequence of information partitions $\mathbb{F} = (\mathbb{F}_t)_{t=0}^T$. At any date $\tau \in \mathbf{T}$, the agent only knows the subset σ of the partition $\mathbb{F}_\tau$ in which s lies. Since agent i is assumed to know the alternative paths (3) that his endowment can trace out over time he knows the function

$$\omega^i : \mathbf{T} \times \mathbf{S} \longrightarrow \mathbb{R} \tag{4}$$

The information revealed by ω^i and $(\mathbb{F}_t)_{t=0}^T$ must be consistent: the agent must not be able to deduce more information about the actual state s that has been drawn by nature by observing the path

$$\big(\omega^i(t,s), t \in [0,\tau]\big) \tag{5}$$

traced out over the interval $[0,\tau]$, than is contained in his knowledge of the subset

$$\sigma \in \mathbb{F}_\tau$$

to which s belongs. This means that for each subset $\sigma \in \mathbb{F}_\tau$, the paths must be the same up to time τ for all states $s \in \sigma$. Thus agent i's endowment process (3) must satisfy

$$\omega^i(t,s) = \omega^i(t,s'), \quad \forall s, s' \in \sigma \in \mathbb{F}_t, \quad \forall t \in [0,\tau], \quad \forall \tau \in \mathbf{T} \tag{6}$$

The commodity space that it is natural to consider thus consists of all functions (processes) (4) satisfying the *information restrictions* (6) induced by the sequence of information partitions $\mathbb{F} = (\mathbb{F}_t)_{t \in \mathbf{T}}$. It should now be clear why the equivalent formulation of $\mathbb{F}$ as the event-tree $\mathbb{D}$ is so convenient. For each subset $\sigma \in \mathbb{F}_\tau$, let $\xi = (\tau, \sigma)$ denote the associated node of the event-tree $\mathbb{D}$, then

$$\omega^i(\xi) = \omega^i(\tau,\sigma) = \omega^i(\tau,s), \quad \forall s \in \sigma$$

defines the common value of agent i's endowment at time τ for all states $s \in \sigma$. A description of the endowment process (3) which includes the informational restrictions (6) is thus given by its *event-tree (node)* representation

$$\omega^i = \left(\omega^i(\xi),\ \xi \in \mathbb{D}\right)$$

18.6 Definition (Commodity Space): Let $\mathbf{S} = \{1,\ldots,S\}$ be a set of states, $\mathbf{T} = \{0,1,\ldots,T\}$ a set of time periods and $\mathbb{F} = (\mathbb{F}_t)_{t \in \mathbf{T}}$ a sequence of partitions satisfying $\mathbb{F}_0 = \mathbf{S}$, $\mathbb{F}_T = \{\{1\},\ldots,\{S\}\}$ and $\mathbb{F}_t$ finer than $\mathbb{F}_{t-1}$, $t = 1,\ldots,T$. Let $\mathbb{D}$ denote the event-tree induced by $\mathbb{F}$. The *commodity space* of a (one-good) economy with $T+1$ time periods and S states of nature, for which the unfolding of information is given by $\mathbb{F}$, is the vector space

$$\mathbb{R}^n = \{x = (x(\xi),\ \xi \in \mathbb{D}) \mid x(\xi) \in \mathbb{R},\ \forall \xi \in \mathbb{D}\}, \quad n = \#\mathbb{D} \qquad (7)$$

where $\#\mathbb{D}$ denotes the number of nodes in the event-tree $\mathbb{D}$.

Implicit in the above analysis is the assumption that all agents have access to the same information at each date. When there are many agents in the economy, it is possible that different agents have access to new information at different rates. In such a setting one would need to associate with each agent i ($i = 1,\ldots,I$) an information structure $\mathbb{F}^i = (\mathbb{F}^i_t)_{t \in \mathbf{T}}$ which describes the information to which agent i has access at each date. Allowing for differential information among agents in the economy creates conceptual problems which we will not attempt to address in this book. The analysis will be based throughout on the following simplifying assumption:

Assumption $\mathcal{I}$ (Information): All agents in the economy have access to the same (common) information structure $\mathbb{F} = (\mathbb{F}_t)_{t \in \mathbf{T}}$.

Under this assumption, the information structure of the economy can be represented by an event-tree $\mathbb{D}$, and all contracts and their prices, as well as the characteristics and actions of all agents are defined on $\mathbb{D}$.

19.   STOCHASTIC EXCHANGE ECONOMY

Given the time-uncertainty setting described by the event-tree $\mathbb{D}$, and the associated commodity space $\mathbb{R}^n$ defined by (7) in the previous section, the description of the economy parallels that of the two-period economy given in Section 6. There are I agents ($i = 1,\ldots,I$) and there is a single (perishable) good at each node of the event-tree. The consumption set of each agent is the non-negative orthant of the commodity space, $X^i = \mathbb{R}^n_+$. Agent i has a preference ordering defined on the consumption set which is represented by a *utility function*

$$u^i : \mathbb{R}^n_+ \longrightarrow \mathbb{R}, \quad i = 1, \ldots, I$$

The Assumptions $\mathscr{U}''$, $\mathscr{U}'$, and $\mathscr{U}$ are the same as those given in Section 6 with $n = \#\mathbb{D}$.

Agent i has an *endowment process*

$$\omega^i = \left(\omega^i(\xi), \, \xi \in \mathbb{D}\right) \in \mathbb{R}^n_+, \quad i = 1, \ldots, I$$

The characteristics of the economy are the event-tree $\mathbb{D}$, the preferences of the agents $u = (u^1, \ldots, u^I)$ and their endowments $\omega = (\omega^1, \ldots, \omega^I)$; let $\mathscr{E}(\mathbb{D}, u, \omega)$ denote the associated *stochastic exchange economy*. For this economy the definitions of a *feasible allocation* and a *Pareto optimum* are given by Definitions 6.1 and 6.2 with $n = \#\mathbb{D}$.

Contingent Markets

As in the two-period economy, two different market structures can be adjoined to the exchange economy $\mathscr{E}(\mathbb{D}, u, \omega)$: a system of *contingent markets* and a system of *financial markets*. Consider the first.

19.1 Definition: A *contingent contract* for node $\xi \in \mathbb{D}$ is a promise to deliver one unit of the single good at node ξ and nothing otherwise. Its price $\pi(\xi)$, payable at date 0, is measured in units of account at date 0.

As a thought experiment, imagine a complete set of such contingent contracts (one for each node in the event-tree) being traded at the initial node ξ_0. Given a system of prices $\pi = (\pi(\xi), \, \xi \in \mathbb{D}) \in \mathbb{R}^n_{++}$ for these contracts, agent i can sell his initial endowment $\omega^i(\xi_0)$ and can also sell forward his entire future endowment stream $(\omega^i(\xi), \, \xi \in \mathbb{D}^+)$ to obtain the *income*

$$\pi \omega^i = \sum_{\xi \in \mathbb{D}} \pi(\xi) \omega^i(\xi)$$

with the standard convention that prices (π) are written as row vectors and quantities (ω^i) as column vectors. The system of contingent markets allows the agent to turn round, the very same instant, to buy the initial consumption $x^i(\xi_0)$ and also to buy forward his future consumption stream $(x^i(\xi), \, \xi \in \mathbb{D}^+)$, provided that the bundle $x^i \in \mathbb{R}^n_+$ lies in his budget set

$$B(\pi, \omega^i) = \left\{ x^i \in \mathbb{R}^n_+ \mid \pi x^i = \pi \omega^i \right\}$$

A *contingent market equilibrium* for the stochastic economy $\mathscr{E}(\mathbb{D}, u, \omega)$ is then given as before by Definition 7.2 with $n = \#\mathbb{D}$. Existence (Theorem 7.4) and Pareto optimality (Theorem 7.6) extend immediately to the economy $\mathscr{E}(\mathbb{D}, u, \omega)$.

19.2 Theorem (Existence and Optimality of CM Equilibrium):

  (i) *If Assumption $\mathscr{U}'$ holds and if $\sum_{i=1}^{I} \omega^i \in \mathbb{R}_{++}^n$, then the stochastic exchange economy $\mathscr{E}(\mathbb{D}, u, \omega)$ has a contingent market equilibrium.*

  (ii) *If Assumption $\mathscr{U}''$ holds, then a contingent market equilibrium allocation is a Pareto optimum.*

Thus with a system of contingent markets, a stochastic exchange economy behaves precisely like a two-period exchange economy. In each case the system of contingent contracts and the associated price system $\pi \in \mathbb{R}_{++}^n$ available at the initial node ξ_0, enable the whole future $(\mathbb{D}^+)$ to be translated back to ξ_0, so that all future commodities are conveniently traded out at ξ_0. This ability to collapse the whole future back to the present and to trade everything out at date 0 is precisely the feature that is unrealistic about the system of contingent markets. However, from a theoretical point of view, this remains an idealized system of markets of great interest.

20.   STOCHASTIC FINANCIAL MARKETS

As in the two-period model, contingent contracts can be viewed as a special case of a more general class of financial contracts which give agents only a limited ability to redistribute income (the single good) across the nodes of the event-tree. It is through this class of financial contracts that the concept of incomplete markets is formalized.

The set of financial contracts that can be modelled in a stochastic economy with T periods is richer than the set of contracts introduced in the two-period economy. In the two-period model all contracts are issued at date zero and expire at date 1. In the multiperiod model contracts can be issued at any date prior to the terminal date or more generally at any non-terminal node $\xi \in \mathbb{D}^-$; they yield payments over a sequence of periods and have an expiration date which can be any date up to time T. When a contract only yields payments at the immediate successors of its node of issue, it is called a *short-lived* contract; when it yields payments after the immediate successors it is called a *long-lived* contract. We assume that a long-lived contract can be retraded at all nodes subsequent to its node of issue and prior to any node at which it expires. For such a contract, a distinction needs to be made between the current payment promised at node ξ, and the total payment that accrues at this node, when in addition the contract is sold for its capital value. We call the former the *dividend* and the latter, the sum of the dividend and the capital value, the *payoff* of the contract at node ξ.

20.1 Definition: *Financial contract* j $(j = 1, \ldots, J)$, which is issued at node $\xi(j) \in \mathbb{D}^-$, is a promise to deliver a dividend process

$$\left\{ V^j(\xi) \in \mathbb{R} \mid \xi \in \mathbb{D}^+(\xi(j)) \right\}$$

at all nodes strictly succeeding its node of issue $\xi(j)$, the dividend at node ξ being measured in units of the good at node ξ.

The expiration nodes of a financial contract can be deduced from its dividend process: if $\xi \in \mathbb{D}\left(\xi(j)\right)$ is such that $V^j(\xi) \neq 0$ and $V^j(\xi') = 0$ for all $\xi' > \xi$, then ξ is an *expiration node* of contract j. The contract is first traded at its node of issue and is then retraded at all succeeding nodes prior to an expiration node. For every node ξ in the subtree $\mathbb{D}\left(\xi(j)\right)$ of its node of issue, let $q_j(\xi)$ denote the price of one unit of the jth contract at node ξ, after its dividend $V^j(\xi)$ at that node has been paid: this is also called the *after-dividend price*. $q_j(\xi)$ is measured in the unit of account at node ξ, which for simplicity is taken to be the unit of the good. The reader can readily verify that when dividends are measured in units of the good, the choice of the unit of account does not influence the budget set of an agent.

The set of financial contracts which are actively traded at node ξ consists of those which have been issued prior to or at node ξ and whose expiration node strictly follows node ξ, since there is no point in trading a security which never yields a dividend.[1] Let $J(\xi)$ denote the set of *actively* traded financial contracts at node ξ

$$J(\xi) = \left\{ j \in \{1, \ldots, J\} \;\middle|\; \begin{array}{l} \xi \in \mathbb{D}\left(\xi(j)\right) \text{ and} \\ V^j(\xi') \neq 0 \text{ for some } \xi' \in \mathbb{D}^+(\xi) \end{array} \right\} \qquad (1)$$

The dividend process of a contract is initially defined only on the subtree $\mathbb{D}^+(\xi(j))$ subsequent to its node of issue, and its price is relevant only on the portion of the subtree $\mathbb{D}\left(\xi(j)\right)$ which precedes the nodes of expiration. Notation is greatly simplified, however, if the definition of the dividends and prices of the contracts is extended to the whole event-tree: this can be done by setting the dividends (prices) equal to zero on the portion of the event-tree on which they are not initially defined.

---

[1] In a finite horizon model when a security ceases to yield a dividend, its price is zero: the value of a security is exclusively attributable to its dividend stream. In Volume 2 we will see that when the horizon is infinite a security can have a positive price, even if it yields no dividend, the value in this case arising from a speculative bubble on the security.

20.2 Definition: The *dividend process* of financial contract j is the vector

$$V^j = \left(V^j(\xi),\ \xi \in \mathbb{D} \right) \in \mathbb{R}^n$$

satisfying $V^j(\xi) = 0$ for all $\xi \notin \mathbb{D}^+(\xi(j))$; its *price process* is the vector

$$q_j = \left(q_j(\xi),\ \xi \in \mathbb{D} \right) \in \mathbb{R}^n$$

satisfying $q_j(\xi) = 0$ for all ξ such that $j \notin J(\xi)$.

20.3 Definition: A *financial structure* (ζ, V) for an economy $\mathcal{E}(\mathbb{D}, u, \omega)$ with J financial contracts is defined by the pair (ζ, V), where ζ is the vector of nodes of issue of the contracts

$$\zeta = (\xi(j),\ j = 1, \ldots, J)$$

and V is the $n \times J$ matrix of dividend processes

$$V = \left[V^1 \ldots V^J \right]$$

Consider some of the standard examples of contracts for the stochastic finance model.

20.4 Example (Contingent Contract):   Contract j is a contingent contract for node $\bar{\xi}$ if it is issued at date 0 ($\xi(j) = \xi_0$) and if its dividend process is

$$V^j(\xi) = \begin{cases} 1 & \text{if } \xi = \bar{\xi} \\ 0 & \text{if } \xi \neq \bar{\xi} \end{cases}$$

20.5 Example (Zero Coupon Bond):   The jth financial contract is a zero coupon bond issued at date 0 with maturity date τ if its dividend process is

$$V^j(\xi) = \begin{cases} 1 & \text{if } \xi = (\tau, \sigma),\ \sigma \in \mathbb{F}_\tau \\ 0 & \text{if } \xi = (t, \sigma),\ t \neq \tau,\ \sigma \in \mathbb{F}_t \end{cases}$$

In calling the contract with this payoff a zero coupon bond, we are using the income interpretation of the finance model. If we use the one-good interpretation, then the contract becomes a futures contract for the good with maturity date τ.

20.6 Example (Short-lived Bond):   Contract j is a short-lived bond issued at node $\bar{\xi}$ if $\xi(j) = \bar{\xi}$ and its dividend process is

$$V^j(\xi) = \begin{cases} 1 & \text{if } \xi \in \bar{\xi}^+ \\ 0 & \text{if } \xi \notin \bar{\xi}^+ \end{cases}$$

20.7 Example (Equity Contract):   Contract j is the equity of firm j if $\xi(j) = \xi_0$ and

$$V^j(\xi) = D^j(\xi), \quad \xi \in \mathbb{D}^+$$

where $D^j(\xi)$ is the firm's dividend at node ξ. □

Let $z^i(\xi) = \left(z_1^i(\xi), \dots, z_J^i(\xi)\right) \in \mathbb{R}^J$ denote the ith agent's *portfolio at node ξ*, giving the number of units of each of the J financial contracts purchased (if $z_j^i(\xi) > 0$) or sold (if $z_j^i(\xi) < 0$) by agent i at node ξ. If the jth contract is not one of the actively traded contracts at node ξ ($j \notin J(\xi)$), then by convention $z_j^i(\xi) = 0$. Since contracts are bought at node ξ after they have yielded their current dividends, there is no point in purchasing a contract at a terminal node, since there is no subsequent period at which it can yield a dividend. Thus the definition of the portfolios can be restricted to the set of non-terminal nodes $\mathbb{D}^-$. The *space of portfolios* is therefore given by

$$\mathbb{Z} = \left\{ z \in \mathbb{R}^{(\#\mathbb{D}^-)J} \;\middle|\; \begin{array}{l} z = (z_1(\xi), \dots, z_J(\xi), \xi \in \mathbb{D}^-) \\ z_j(\xi) = 0 \text{ if } j \notin J(\xi), j = 1, \dots, J \end{array} \right\}$$

Given $\omega^i \in \mathbb{R}_+^n$, the choice of a portfolio $z^i \in \mathbb{Z}$ induces a consumption vector $x^i \in \mathbb{R}^n$ for agent i satisfying

$$x^i(\xi_0) - \omega^i(\xi_0) = -q(\xi_0)z^i(\xi_0) \tag{2}$$
$$x^i(\xi) - \omega^i(\xi) = (V(\xi) + q(\xi))\, z^i(\xi^-) - q(\xi)z^i(\xi), \quad \forall \xi \in \mathbb{D}^+ \cap \mathbb{D}^- \tag{3}$$
$$x^i(\xi) - \omega^i(\xi) = V(\xi)z^i(\xi^-), \quad \forall \xi \in \mathbb{D}_T \tag{4}$$

where $V(\xi) = \left[V^1(\xi) \dots V^J(\xi)\right]$ and $q(\xi) = (q_1(\xi), \dots, q_J(\xi))$ denote the $1 \times J$ matrix of dividends and the (row) vector of prices for the J contracts at node ξ respectively.

In writing (2)–(4), it is assumed that the portfolio $z^i(\xi)$ purchased at any node ξ is sold at each immediate successor of ξ i.e. at each $\xi' \in \xi^+$, and that a new portfolio is then purchased. With no transactions costs in the purchase and sale of securities, there is no loss of generality in writing the budget equations in this form. The typical payoff obtained on the investment $z_j^i(\xi^-)$ in security j at the predecessor ξ^- of node ξ consists of two parts

- the dividend $V^j(\xi)z_j^i(\xi^-)$
- the capital value $q_j(\xi)z_j^i(\xi^-)$

where the latter accrues from the sale of the portfolio at node ξ. The capital value is the new term introduced by extending the model to the multiperiod case: it is absent at both the initial and the terminal dates which are the only dates that appear in the two-period model. The capital value terms account for many of the important differences between the behavior of the multiperiod model and the two-period model.

The W Matrix

The budget equations (2)–(4) can be written in a condensed form similar to that used in Chapter 2 (equation (8.3)) by collecting the payoffs on the J contracts over the nodes of the event-tree $\mathbb{D}$ into a single matrix. Each column of the matrix represents the payoff across all of the $\#\mathbb{D}$ nodes of the event-tree accruing from a one-unit investment in one of the contracts at a non-terminal node $\xi \in \mathbb{D}^-$ of the event-tree, with subsequent sale at each of the immediate successors $\xi \in \xi^+$: the matrix thus has $\#\mathbb{D}$ rows and $(\#\mathbb{D}^-)J$ columns. In the two-period economy of Chapter 2, $\#\mathbb{D} = S + 1$ and $\#\mathbb{D}^- = 1$ so that the payoff matrix was $(S + 1) \times J$. The introduction of this matrix greatly simplifies the analysis of the multiperiod model since it permits many of the arguments developed in the two-period model to be transferred without change to the multiperiod case.

For each node $\xi \in \mathbb{D}$ define the vector of security prices

$$q(\xi) = (q_1(\xi), \ldots, q_J(\xi))$$

(using the convention $q_j(\xi) = 0$ if $j \notin J(\xi)$ in Definition 20.2) and let

$$q = (q(\xi), \xi \in \mathbb{D})$$

denote the vector of security price processes. For each non-terminal node $\xi \in \mathbb{D}^-$ and each $j = 1, \ldots, J$, let

$$V^j(\xi^+) = (V^j(\xi'))_{\xi' \in \xi^+}, \quad q_j(\xi^+) = (q_j(\xi'))_{\xi' \in \xi^+}$$

denote the $b(\xi)$-dimensional column vectors of dividends and capital values arising from a one-unit investment in security j at node ξ, where $b(\xi)$ is the branching number at node ξ. Finally, for $\xi \in \mathbb{D}^-$ define the $b(\xi) \times J$ matrices of dividends and capital values for the J securities at each of the immediate successors of ξ

$$V(\xi^+) = \left[V^1(\xi^+) \cdots V^J(\xi^+) \right], \quad q(\xi^+) = \left[q_1(\xi^+) \cdots q_J(\xi^+) \right]$$

Then the $(\#\mathbb{D}) \times (\#\mathbb{D}^-)J$ *payoff matrix* $W(q,V)$ is given by

$$
W(q,V) =
\begin{array}{c}
\overbrace{\hspace{3cm}}^{\text{J columns for } \xi_0} \quad \overbrace{\hspace{2cm}}^{\text{J columns for } \xi^-} \quad \overbrace{\hspace{2cm}}^{\text{J columns for } \xi} \\
\left[
\begin{array}{ccccc}
-q(\xi_0) & 0 & 0 & 0 & 0 \\
V(\xi_0^+) + q(\xi_0^+) & \cdots & \cdots & 0 & 0 \\
0 & \cdots & \cdots & 0 & 0 \\
0 & 0 & V(\xi) + q(\xi) & -q(\xi) & 0 \\
0 & \cdots & \cdots & 0 & \cdots \\
0 & 0 & 0 & V(\xi^+) + q(\xi^+) & \cdots \\
0 & 0 & 0 & 0 & \cdots
\end{array}
\right]
\begin{array}{l}
\xi_0 \\
\xi_0^+ \\
\\
\xi \\
\\
\xi^+ \\
\end{array}
\end{array}
\quad (5)
$$

Row ξ shows the J returns $V(\xi) + q(\xi)$ corresponding to a one-unit investment in each contract at the predecessor ξ^- and the cost $-q(\xi)$ for a one-unit investment in each contract at node ξ. The columns for node ξ give the returns across all the nodes of the event-tree from a one-unit investment in each contract at node ξ: the cost of the investment $-q(\xi)$ is in row ξ and its returns at the successors ξ^+ of ξ appear as the $b(\xi) \times J$ matrix $V(\xi^+) + q(\xi^+)$, all the remaining entries in the column being zero. (For an example of a payoff matrix W, see Example 22.5).

Using the matrix $W(q,V)$ the budget equations (2)–(4) can be written as

$$
x^i - \omega^i = W(q,V)z^i
$$

Agent i's budget set on the system of financial markets is thus given by

$$
\mathbb{B}(q, \omega^i, V) = \left\{ x^i \in \mathbb{R}_+^n \mid x^i - \omega^i = W(q,V)z^i, \quad z^i \in \mathscr{Z} \right\} \quad (6)
$$

As in the two-period case agent i decides on a pair consisting of a vector of consumption x^i and a portfolio strategy z^i, and the pair (x^i, z^i) defines the *action* of agent i. When agent i chooses a portfolio z^i such that $x^i - \omega^i = Wz^i$, z^i is said to *finance* x^i. The notation

$$
(x^i; z^i) \in \mathbb{B}(q, \omega^i, V) \quad (7)
$$

is used to denote a consumption-portfolio pair $(x^i, z^i) \in \mathbb{B}(q, \omega^i, V) \times \mathscr{Z}$ such that z^i finances x^i. Thus (7) is equivalent to

$$
x^i \in \mathbb{B}(q, \omega^i, V), \quad x^i - \omega^i = Wz^i
$$

If $\bar{x}^i$ is a consumption vector which maximizes agent i's utility $u^i(x^i)$ over the budget set $\mathbb{B}(q, \omega^i, V)$ and if $\bar{z}^i$ is a portfolio which finances $\bar{x}^i$, then we write

$$(\bar{x}^i; \bar{z}^i) \in \arg\max \left\{ u^i(x^i) \mid (x^i; z^i) \in \mathbb{B}(q, \omega^i, V) \right\}$$

Let $\mathscr{E}(\mathbb{D}, u, \omega, \zeta, V)$ denote the stochastic economy over the event-tree $\mathbb{D}$ in which the I agents have the characteristics (u, ω), and the J securities have the nodes of issue $\zeta = (\xi(j), j = 1, \ldots, J)$ and the dividend matrix V.

20.8 Definition: A *financial market (FM) equilibrium* for the stochastic finance economy $\mathscr{E}(\mathbb{D}, u, \omega, \zeta, V)$ is a pair consisting of actions and prices $((\bar{x}, \bar{z}), \bar{q}) \in \mathbb{R}_+^{nI} \times \mathscr{Z}^I \times \mathbb{R}^{nJ}$ such that

(i) $(\bar{x}^i; \bar{z}^i) \in \arg\max \left\{ u^i(x^i) \mid (x^i; z^i) \in \mathbb{B}(\bar{q}, \omega^i, V) \right\}$, $i = 1, \ldots, I$
(ii) $\sum_{i=1}^{I} \bar{z}^i = 0$

21.   ABSENCE OF ARBITRAGE

The idea is the same as in Section 9: there are no arbitrage opportunities on the financial markets if there does not exist a portfolio strategy which generates a positive payoff for at least one date-event and non-negative payoffs at all other date-events. More formally, given (q, V) there are no arbitrage opportunities if there does not exist $z \in \mathscr{Z}$ such that $\tau = W(q, V)z > 0$ (where $\tau > 0$ means $\tau(\xi) \geq 0$, $\forall \xi \in \mathbb{D}$ and $\tau(\xi') > 0$ for some $\xi' \in \mathbb{D}$). In this case q is a *no-arbitrage price process*.

Trading on the financial markets enables agents to redistribute their income across the $\#\mathbb{D}$ date-events (nodes) of the event-tree. The choice of a portfolio strategy

$$z^i \in \mathscr{Z}$$

leads to a vector of income transfers across the nodes of the event-tree

$$\tau^i \in \mathbb{R}^n, \quad \tau^i = W z^i$$

where W is the shorthand notation for $W(q, V)$ and $n = \#\mathbb{D}$. The set of all possible income transfers that can be obtained in this way is the subspace of $\mathbb{R}^n$ spanned by the $(\#\mathbb{D}^-)J$ columns of the matrix W, which is denoted by $\langle W \rangle$. This subspace summarizes the opportunities available on the financial markets.

21.1 Definition: The subspace $\langle W \rangle$ of $\mathbb{R}^n$ spanned by the columns of the matrix W,

$$\langle W \rangle = \{ \tau \in \mathbb{R}^n \mid \tau = W z, \quad z \in \mathscr{Z} \}$$

is called the *market subspace* or the *subspace of income transfers*.

Absence of arbitrage opportunities on the financial markets can then be expressed as the geometric property that the market subspace $\langle W \rangle$ has only one point in common with the non-negative orthant $\mathbb{R}^n_+$, namely the origin

$$\langle W \rangle \cap \mathbb{R}^n_+ = \{0\}$$

Theorem 9.3, which characterizes absence of arbitrage on the financial markets, carries over to the stochastic economy without change, if we set $n = \#\mathbb{D}$ and let $W(q, V)$ and $\mathbb{B}(q, \omega^i, V)$ be defined by equations (5) and (6) in the previous section. Thus absence of arbitrage is equivalent to the existence of a solution to the maximum problem of any agent i $(i = 1, \ldots, I)$

$$\max \left\{ u^i(x^i) \mid x^i \in \mathbb{B}(q, \omega^i, V) \right\}$$

This in turn is equivalent to the existence of a positive vector of node prices $\pi \in \mathbb{R}^n_{++}$ which supports the market subspace

$$\pi W = 0 \iff \pi \in \langle W \rangle^\perp \tag{1}$$

where $\langle W \rangle^\perp$ is the *space of node prices*. When $\pi \in \langle W \rangle^\perp$ is normalized so that $\pi(\xi_0) = 1$, it is called a vector of *present-value prices* since (as we shall see in a moment) $\pi(\xi)$ coincides with the price of the contingent contract for node ξ when such a contract exists (Example 20.4). Since in (1) each of the J columns of W associated with node ξ is premultiplied by the row vector π, (1) is equivalent to

$$\pi(\xi)q_j(\xi) = \sum_{\xi' \in \xi^+} \pi(\xi') \left(V^j(\xi') + q_j(\xi') \right), \quad j \in J(\xi) \tag{2}$$

(2) asserts that the cost of a one-unit investment in security j at node ξ, discounted to date 0, is equal to the present value of the payoff (dividend plus capital value) over the immediate successors ξ^+ of ξ, all discounted to date 0. Multiplying both sides of (2) by $1/\pi(\xi)$ translates the focal date-event for the valuations on both sides of (2) from date 0 to node ξ. (Since $\pi(\xi)$ translates one unit of income from node ξ to date 0, $1/\pi(\xi)$ translates one unit of income from date 0 to node ξ). Thus if node ξ is used as the focal (or reference) date-event for the valuations then (2) becomes

$$q_j(\xi) = \frac{1}{\pi(\xi)} \sum_{\xi' \in \xi^+} \pi(\xi') \left(V^j(\xi') + q_j(\xi') \right), \quad j \in J(\xi) \tag{2'}$$

$\pi(\xi')/\pi(\xi)$ is the present value at node ξ of one unit of income at node ξ'. Thus (2$'$) asserts that the price of security j at node ξ is the present value at node ξ of its payoff (dividend plus capital value) over the immediate successors ξ^+ of ξ.

Solving the system of equations (2) recursively, using the fact that $q(\xi) = 0$ for all terminal nodes, leads to the equivalent formula for the security prices

$$q_j(\xi) = \frac{1}{\pi(\xi)} \sum_{\xi' \in \mathbb{D}^+(\xi)} \pi(\xi') V^j(\xi'), \quad j \in J(\xi) \tag{2$''$}$$

Equation (2$''$) is the fundamental integral formula for the pricing of financial securities. It asserts that the price of security j at node ξ is the present value (at node ξ) of its future stream of dividends over all subsequent nodes of the event-tree (i.e. over all nodes in the subtree $\mathbb{D}^+(\xi)$). Note that if security j is the contingent contract for node ξ, then the date 0 valuation given by (2$''$) is

$$q_j(\xi_0) = \pi(\xi)$$

which justifies the interpretation of $\pi(\xi)$ as the present value at date 0 of one unit of income at node ξ.

First-Order Conditions

When $\bar{q}$ is a no-arbitrage security price process then agent i's maximum problem in a financial market equilibrium ((i) in Definition 20.8) has a solution. The maximum problem is given by

$$\max \left\{ u^i(x^i) \mid x^i - \omega^i = W(q, V)z^i, \quad (x^i, z^i) \in \mathbb{R}^n_+ \times \mathcal{Z} \right\} \tag{3}$$

Let us examine the first-order conditions when the utility function u^i satisfies Assumption $\mathcal{U}$ (in which case no positivity constraint on x^i is binding). The budget constraint at each node $\xi \in \mathbb{D}$ induces a Lagrange multiplier $\lambda^i(\xi)$ and hence a vector of Lagrange multipliers

$$\lambda^i = \left(\lambda^i(\xi), \, \xi \in \mathbb{D} \right)$$

The Lagrangean function is given by

$$L^i \left(x^i, z^i, \lambda^i \right) = u^i(x^i) - \lambda^i \left(x^i - \omega^i - W(\bar{q}, V)z^i \right)$$

The first-order conditions which are necessary and sufficient for $(\bar{x}^i, \bar{z}^i)$ to be a solution of (3) are that there exist $\bar{\lambda}^i \in \mathbb{R}^n_{++}$ such that

$$\nabla L^i(\bar{x}^i, \bar{z}^i, \bar{\lambda}^i) = 0$$

which is equivalent to

$$
\begin{aligned}
\nabla_{x^i} L^i(\bar{x}^i, \bar{z}^i, \bar{\lambda}^i) = 0 &\iff \bar{\lambda}^i = \nabla u^i(\bar{x}^i) \\
\nabla_{z^i} L^i(\bar{x}^i, \bar{z}^i, \bar{\lambda}^i) = 0 &\iff \bar{\lambda}^i W(\bar{q}, V) = 0 \\
\nabla_{\lambda^i} L^i(\bar{x}^i, \bar{z}^i, \bar{\lambda}^i) = 0 &\iff \bar{x}^i - \omega^i = W(\bar{q}, V)\bar{z}^i
\end{aligned}
\tag{4}
$$

Thus $\bar{\lambda}^i$ is the vector of marginal utilities of income at each node in the event-tree. If the *present-value vector* of agent i at $\bar{x}^i$ is defined by

$$
\bar{\pi}^i = \left(\bar{\pi}^i(\xi), \, \xi \in \mathbb{D} \right) = \left(\frac{\bar{\lambda}^i(\xi)}{\bar{\lambda}^i(\xi_0)}, \, \xi \in \mathbb{D} \right)
$$

and if $\bar{\tau}^i = \bar{x}^i - \omega^i$ denotes the *net trade vector*, then the first-order conditions (4) can be written as

$$
\bar{\tau}^i \in \langle W \rangle, \quad \bar{\pi}^i \in \langle W \rangle^\perp
\tag{5}
$$

Agent i is at a maximum at a net trade vector $\bar{\tau}^i \in \langle W \rangle$ when his indifference surface through $\bar{\tau}^i$ is tangent to the market subspace: at such a point his gradient $\bar{\pi}^i$ lies in the orthogonal subspace $\langle W \rangle^\perp$. The orthogonality condition in (5) implies that the pricing formulae (2)–(2″) are satisfied with the present-value vector $\bar{\pi}^i$ of agent i.

22. COMPLETE AND INCOMPLETE MARKETS

The commodity space $\mathbb{R}^n$ can be written as a direct sum of the market subspace and its orthogonal complement

$$
\mathbb{R}^n = \langle W \rangle \oplus \langle W \rangle^\perp
\tag{1}
$$

Since the market subspace must not offer arbitrage opportunities, there exists at least one vector of state prices $\pi \in \langle W \rangle^\perp$. Thus $\dim \langle W \rangle^\perp \geq 1$. Since (1) implies

$$
\dim \langle W \rangle + \dim \langle W \rangle^\perp = n = \#\mathbb{D}
$$

it follows that whenever the market subspace offers no arbitrage opportunities

$$
\dim \langle W \rangle \leq \#\mathbb{D} - 1
$$

Thus $\#\mathbb{D} - 1$ is the maximal dimension of the market subspace. This leads to the following definition of complete (incomplete) markets.

22.1 Definition: Let the market subspace $\langle W(q, V) \rangle$ be arbitrage free. If

$$\dim \langle W(q, V) \rangle = \#\mathbb{D} - 1$$

then the (financial) markets are said to be *complete*: if

$$\dim \langle W(q, V) \rangle < \#\mathbb{D} - 1$$

then the markets are *incomplete*.

Calculating dim $\langle \mathbf{W} \rangle$

In the two-period case the problem of determining the rank of the matrix $W(q, V)$ reduces to the problem of determining the rank of the exogenously given dividend matrix V since rank $W(q, V) = \operatorname{rank} V$ (by Proposition 9.8). In the multiperiod case the rank of $W(q, V)$ in general depends on both the security price q and the dividend matrix V: thus rank $W(q, V)$ can no longer be deduced from properties of the dividend matrix V alone.

The problem of determining the rank of W can be decomposed into the problem of determining the ranks of some simpler submatrices of W.

22.2 Proposition (Rank of W):   *Let q be a no-arbitrage security price, then*

$$\operatorname{rank} W(q, V) = \sum_{\xi \in \mathbb{D}^-} \operatorname{rank} \left(V(\xi^+) + q(\xi^+) \right)$$

PROOF: Let $\pi \in \mathbb{R}^n_{++}$ be a vector of no-arbitrage state prices and let $[\pi]$ denote the $n \times n$ diagonal matrix with diagonal entries $\pi(\xi), \xi \in \mathbb{D}$. The matrix $\widetilde{W} = [\pi]W$ has the same rank as W and is obtained by multiplying row ξ of W by $\pi(\xi)$, $\xi \in \mathbb{D}$. For each node ξ at date $T - 1$, consider the nodes $\xi' \in \xi^+$: there is no column corresponding to ξ' in the matrix $\widetilde{W}$ and the only non-zero entries in row ξ' are given by the J-vector $\pi(\xi')V(\xi')$ which appears in the J columns associated with node ξ. Adding the rows of ξ^+ to row ξ eliminates the J-vector $-\pi(\xi)q(\xi)$ in row ξ of the J-columns of node ξ by virtue of the no-arbitrage relation

$$-\pi(\xi)q(\xi) + \sum_{\xi' \in \xi^+} \pi(\xi')V(\xi') = 0$$

When the terms $-\pi(\xi)q(\xi)$ for each of the nodes ξ at date $T - 1$ have been eliminated, we can proceed to eliminate the terms $-\pi(\xi)q(\xi)$ for the nodes ξ at date $T - 2$ by adding the rows of ξ^+ to row ξ and applying the no-arbitrage relation. Proceeding in this way we obtain a matrix $[\pi]W'$, where W' is obtained from the matrix W in (5) of Section 20 by replacing the terms $-q(\xi)$ by the $J \times 1$ vector 0. Then rank $W = \operatorname{rank} W'$ and rank $W' = \sum_{\xi \in \mathbb{D}^-} \operatorname{rank} \left(V(\xi^+) + q(\xi^+) \right)$. $\square$

Proposition 22.2 reduces the problem of calculating the rank of $W(q, V)$ to calculating the rank of each of the *successor payoff matrices* $V(\xi^+) + q(\xi^+)$ for each non-terminal node ξ. The rank of each of these matrices determines the degree of spanning offered by the financial markets at each non-terminal node.

22.3 Definition: The *spanning numbers* $\rho = (\rho(\xi), \xi \in \mathbb{D}^-)$ for the payoff matrix $W(q, V)$ at the non-terminal nodes of the event-tree are defined by

$$\rho(\xi) = \text{rank}\left(V(\xi^+) + q(\xi^+)\right), \quad \forall \xi \in \mathbb{D}^-$$

The branching number $b(\xi) = \#\xi^+$ is the number of immediate successors of node ξ, so that the total number of nodes in the event-tree is given by

$$\mathbb{D} = 1 + \sum_{\xi \in \mathbb{D}^-} b(\xi)$$

The condition for complete markets can now be stated as a local spanning condition at each non-terminal node of the event-tree.

22.4 Proposition (Complete Markets):   *The market subspace is of maximal dimension* $(\dim \langle W(q, V) \rangle = \#\mathbb{D} - 1)$ *if and only if* $\rho(\xi) = b(\xi)$, *for all* $\xi \in \mathbb{D}^-$.

PROOF: Since $V(\xi^+) + q(\xi^+)$ is a $b(\xi) \times J$ matrix, $\rho(\xi) \leq b(\xi)$, $\forall \xi \in \mathbb{D}^-$. The result follows at once from Proposition 22.2 and the equality $\#\mathbb{D} - 1 = \sum_{\xi \in \mathbb{D}^-} b(\xi)$. □

In the stochastic finance economy $\mathscr{E}(\mathbb{D}, u, \omega, V)$ agents can be viewed as solving a sequence of $(\#\mathbb{D} - 1)$ two-period portfolio decision problems—one at each non-terminal node of the event-tree $\mathbb{D}$. At a typical non-terminal node ξ, $b(\xi) = \#\xi^+$ measures the amount of uncertainty that the agent faces at that node: more precisely, $b(\xi)$ is the number of immediately succeeding contingencies that can arise. The agent's ability to cope with uncertainty by choosing a suitable portfolio $z^i(\xi)$ at node ξ is measured by the spanning number $\rho(\xi)$ of the payoff matrix $W(q, V)$ at node ξ: more precisely, $\rho(\xi)$ measures the dimension of the subspace $\mathbb{R}^{b(\xi)}$ of income transfers at the immediate successors ξ^+ of ξ that can be spanned by trading in the financial securities. For markets to be complete the whole of this successor subspace $\mathbb{R}^{b(\xi)}$ must be spanned and this must hold at each non-terminal node: thus we must have $\rho(\xi) = b(\xi)$ for all $\xi \in \mathbb{D}^-$.

The successor payoff matrix $V(\xi^+) + q(\xi^+)$ at any non-terminal node ξ is a $b(\xi) \times J$ matrix where J is that total number of contracts issued over the event-tree. For spanning purposes however, what matters at node $\xi \in \mathbb{D}^-$ is the number of actively traded securities at this node, since these are the only securities which have non-trivial payoffs at the immediate successors ξ^+. Let

$$j(\xi) = \#J(\xi), \quad \xi \in \mathbb{D}^-$$

denote the number of actively traded securities at each non-terminal node ξ (where $J(\xi)$ is defined by (1) in Section 20). Since all non-active securities (i.e. those not in $J(\xi)$) contribute a column of zeros in the matrix $V(\xi^+) + q(\xi^+)$, the rank $\rho(\xi)$ of this matrix satisfies $\rho(\xi) \leq \min(j(\xi), b(\xi))$. Thus a necessary condition for the financial markets to be complete is that the number of active securities at node $\xi \in \mathbb{D}^-$ be at least as large as the number of immediately succeeding contingencies

$$j(\xi) \geq b(\xi), \quad \forall \xi \in \mathbb{D}^- \tag{2}$$

Condition (2) can be checked directly from the exogenous data on the financial securities—the issue nodes $(\xi(j), \ j = 1, \ldots, J)$ and the dividend matrix V. However it is only in special cases that this exogenous data suffices to determine whether the rank condition

$$\rho(\xi) = b(\xi), \quad \forall \xi \in \mathbb{D}^- \tag{3}$$

is satisfied. Whether or not (3) holds depends in addition on endogenous data of the model—namely the security price process q.

A special case where the spanning numbers $\rho(\xi)$ can be deduced directly from the exogenous dividend data V occurs when all securities are *short-lived*. In this case the only securities that are active at node ξ are those issued at ξ which expire at the immediate successors ξ^+. As a result no capital value terms appear in the successor payoff matrices so that

$$\rho(\xi) = \text{rank}\, V(\xi^+), \quad \forall \xi \in \mathbb{D}^- \tag{4}$$

(4) has an interesting consequence: the theorem on the existence of a FM equilibrium for a two-period economy obtained in Chapter 2 carries over in a straightforward way to a stochastic economy with short-lived securities.

In an economy with long-lived contracts the spanning numbers depend not only on the dividends but also on the capital values of the contracts: the dimension of the market subspace

$$\dim \langle W(q, V) \rangle = \sum_{\xi \in \mathbb{D}^-} \rho(\xi)$$

can thus vary over the set of no-arbitrage security prices. The analysis that follows will show that the changes in the rank of the payoff matrix $W(q, V)$ that can occur in the presence of long-lived securities lead to significant differences in the qualitative behavior of the stochastic finance economy relative to the two-period economy studied in Chapter 2.

If the time periods represent moments of time when relevant new information on the economy is revealed (harvest conditions, new inventions, strikes, political conditions and so on) and if this information is non-trivial (several contingencies can occur at each node i.e. $b(\xi) > 1$) then the number of states of nature grows exponentially with time. For example, if there are b contingencies that can occur at each node, then the number of states of nature in a T-period model is b^T. If all securities were short-lived, then in order to have complete markets a sufficient number (b) of new securities would have to be introduced at each node and the total number of potential securities would have to grow exponentially with time. When some of the securities are long-lived (long-term bonds, equity of firms) the number of newly issued securities does not need to be as large, since retrading the same securities at each node generates spanning opportunities, provided relevant new information is revealed at each node. In terms of the example just considered, to have complete markets it may be sufficient to retrade at each node b securities issued at the initial date which provide dividends up to time T. In a setting where the securities are long-lived, this is often expressed by saying that *frequent trading increases spanning*. For the reasons indicated in Section 3, it may either not be feasible or it may be too costly to constantly introduce new contracts whose returns are appropriately taylored to the contingencies that can occur: the presence of long-lived securities and the possibility for the agents to change their portfolios in response to new information can provide a less costly way of creating spanning opportunities.

Although long-lived securities are convenient for spanning, their presence in the model creates technical difficulties which arise from the fact that the dimension of the subspace $\langle V(\xi^+) + q(\xi^+) \rangle$ may depend on the security prices. This dependence is most easily illustrated by using the simple class of long-lived securities which are issued at date 0 and pay dividends only at the terminal date T. Then, for all nodes prior to date $T - 1$ the successor payoff matrix reduces to the matrix of capital values $q(\xi^+)$: the variation in the security prices as the information unfolds thus determines the spanning opportunities at each of these nodes. Even if there are many securities, if the security prices do not change or if they change in the same manner as new information is revealed, then long-lived securities will not achieve much spanning.

22.5 Example: Suppose there are three periods and four states of nature

$$\mathbf{T} = \{0, 1, 2\}, \quad \mathbf{S} = \{1, 2, 3, 4\}$$

and that the information partitions are given by

$$\mathbb{F}_0 = \{1,2,3,4\}\,, \quad \mathbb{F}_1 = \{\{1,2\},\{3,4\}\}\,, \quad \mathbb{F}_2 = \{\{1\},\{2\},\{3\},\{4\}\}$$

The nodes (date-events) of the associated event-tree are given by

$$\xi_0 = (0,\{1,2,3,4\})\,, \quad \xi_1 = (1,\{1,2\})\,, \quad \xi_2 = (1,\{3,4\})$$
$$\xi_{11} = (2,\{1\})\,, \quad \xi_{12} = (2,\{2\})\,, \quad \xi_{21} = (2,\{3\})\,, \quad \xi_{22} = (2,\{4\})$$

Clearly $\xi_0^+ = \{\xi_1,\xi_2\}$, $\xi_1^+ = \{\xi_{11},\xi_{12}\}$, $\xi_2^+ = \{\xi_{21},\xi_{22}\}$ so that the branching number at each non-terminal node is $b(\xi) = 2$. The event-tree is shown in Figure 22.1.

Suppose that there are two securities which are issued at date 0 and yield dividends only at date $T = 2$. The dividends are given by the matrices (with $a \geq 0$)

$$V(\xi_0^+) = \begin{bmatrix} 0 & 0 \\ 0 & 0 \end{bmatrix}, \quad V(\xi_1^+) = \begin{bmatrix} 1 & 0 \\ 0 & 1 \end{bmatrix}, \quad V(\xi_2^+) = \begin{bmatrix} 1 & 0 \\ 0 & a \end{bmatrix}$$

where the first (second) column gives the dividends on the first (second) security at the immediate successors. The payoff matrix $W(q,V)$ is thus given by

$$
W(q,V) = \left[
\begin{array}{cc:cc:cc}
-q_1(\xi_0) & -q_2(\xi_0) & 0 & 0 & 0 & 0 \\ \hdashline
q_1(\xi_1) & q_2(\xi_1) & -q_1(\xi_1) & -q_2(\xi_1) & 0 & 0 \\
q_1(\xi_2) & q_2(\xi_2) & 0 & 0 & -q_1(\xi_2) & -q_2(\xi_2) \\ \hdashline
0 & 0 & 1 & 0 & 0 & 0 \\
0 & 0 & 0 & 1 & 0 & 0 \\ \hdashline
0 & 0 & 0 & 0 & 1 & 0 \\
0 & 0 & 0 & 0 & 0 & a
\end{array}
\right]
\begin{array}{l}
\xi_0 \\
\xi_1 \\
\xi_2 \\
\xi_{11} \\
\xi_{12} \\
\xi_{21} \\
\xi_{22}
\end{array}
\quad (5)
$$

with column groups: Columns for ξ_0, Columns for ξ_1, Columns for ξ_2.

$$\operatorname{rank} W(q,V) = \rho(\xi_0) + \rho(\xi_1) + \rho(\xi_2)$$

where the spanning numbers are given by

$$\rho(\xi_0) = \operatorname{rank} \begin{bmatrix} q_1(\xi_1) & q_2(\xi_1) \\ q_1(\xi_2) & q_2(\xi_2) \end{bmatrix}, \quad \rho(\xi_1) = \operatorname{rank} \begin{bmatrix} 1 & 0 \\ 0 & 1 \end{bmatrix}, \quad \rho(\xi_2) = \operatorname{rank} \begin{bmatrix} 1 & 0 \\ 0 & a \end{bmatrix}$$

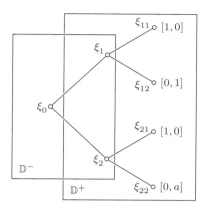

Figure 22.1   Event-tree and security dividends for Example 22.5.

The set of no-arbitrage security prices is given by

$$q_j(\xi_0) = \pi_1 q_j(\xi_1) + \pi_2 q_j(\xi_2), \quad j = 1, 2, \quad \pi_1 > 0, \quad \pi_2 > 0$$
$$q_1(\xi_1) > 0, \quad q_2(\xi_1) > 0, \quad q_1(\xi_2) > 0, \quad q_2(\xi_2) =(>) 0 \text{ if } a =(>) 0$$

If $a = 0$ then $\rho(\xi_0) = \rho(\xi_1) = 2$, $\rho(\xi_2) = 1$. The markets are incomplete since $\rho(\xi_2) < b(\xi_2) = 2$: but the rank of $W(q, V)$ does not vary with q.

If $a > 0$ then $\rho(\xi_0) = 2$ or 1, $\rho(\xi_1) = \rho(\xi_2) = 2$. If there are no variations in the security prices across the nodes at date 1 or if the prices vary proportionally then $\rho(\xi_0) = 1 < b(\xi_0)$ so that the markets are incomplete. If the prices vary across the nodes at date 1 (in a non-proportional way) then $\rho(\xi_0) = 2$ and the markets are complete. Thus for the same dividend structure V, the matrix $W(q, V)$ given by (5) can generate complete or incomplete markets depending on the no-arbitrage security price q. □

Link between Complete Financial Markets and Contingent Markets

When markets are complete, $\langle W \rangle$ is a subspace of dimension $n - 1$ in $\mathbb{R}^n$ where $n = \#\mathbb{D}$. $\langle W \rangle$ is thus a hyperplane in $\mathbb{R}^n$ and there is a unique normalized vector $\pi \in R_{++}^n$ orthogonal to $\langle W \rangle$: this property permits $\langle W \rangle$ to be defined by π

$$\langle W \rangle = \{\tau \in \mathbb{R}^n \mid \pi\tau = 0\}$$

where $\pi\tau = 0$ is the equation of the hyperplane $\langle W \rangle$.

Suppose $((\bar{x}, \bar{z}), \bar{q})$ is a financial market equilibrium in which markets are complete. The observation just made allows us to establish immediately the equality of the budget sets $\mathbb{B}(\bar{q}, \omega^i, V)$ and $B(\bar{\pi}, \omega^i)$, where $\bar{\pi}$ is the unique (normalized) vector satisfying $\bar{\pi} W(\bar{q}, V) = 0$, since

$$\begin{aligned} \mathbb{B}(\bar{q}, \omega^i, V) &= \left\{ x^i \in \mathbb{R}^n_+ \mid x^i - \omega^i \in \langle W(\bar{q}, V) \rangle \right\} \\ &= \left\{ x^i \in \mathbb{R}^n_+ \mid \bar{\pi}(x^i - \omega^i) = 0 \right\} = B(\bar{\pi}, \omega^i) \end{aligned} \tag{6}$$

This observation leads the following proposition.

22.6 Proposition (Complete Markets Equilibrium):

(i) Let $((\bar{x}, \bar{z}), \bar{q})$ be a financial market equilibrium of a stochastic economy $\mathscr{E}(\mathbb{D}, u, \omega, \zeta, V)$. If rank $W(\bar{q}, V) = n - 1$ and if $\bar{\pi} \in \mathbb{R}^n_{++}$ is the unique normalized price vector satisfying $\bar{\pi} W(\bar{q}, V) = 0$, then $(\bar{x}, \bar{\pi})$ is a contingent market equilibrium.

(ii) Let $(\bar{x}, \bar{\pi})$ be a contingent market equilibrium for the economy $\mathscr{E}(\mathbb{D}, u, \omega)$ and let (ζ, V) be a financial structure. If the vector of discounted values of future dividends $\bar{q}$ defined by $(2'')$ in Section 21 with $\pi = \bar{\pi}$ satisfies rank $W(\bar{q}, V) = n - 1$, then there exist portfolios $\bar{z} = (\bar{z}^1, \ldots, \bar{z}^I)$ such that $((\bar{x}, \bar{z}), \bar{q})$ is a financial market equilibrium for $\mathscr{E}(\mathbb{D}, u, \omega, \zeta, V)$.

PROOF: (i) This follows from the equality of the budget sets in (6) and the fact that $\sum_{i=1}^I \bar{z}^i = 0$ implies $\sum_{i=1}^I (\bar{x}^i - \omega^i) = 0$.

(ii) If $\bar{q}$ is defined by $(2'')$ in Section 21 with $\pi = \bar{\pi}$ (and $\bar{q}(\xi) = 0$ if $j \notin J(\xi)$), then $\bar{q}$ satisfies $\bar{\pi} W(\bar{q}, V) = 0$. If rank $W(\bar{q}, V) = n - 1$, then $B(\bar{\pi}, \omega^i) = \mathbb{B}(\bar{q}, \omega^i, V)$ by (6). Thus $\bar{x}$ is agent i's most preferred element in the budget set $\mathbb{B}(\bar{q}, \omega^i, V)$, $i = 1, \ldots, I$. Let $\bar{z}^i \in \mathscr{Z}$ be a portfolio such that $\bar{x}^i - \omega^i = W(\bar{q}, V) \bar{z}^i$, $i = 2, \ldots, I$ and let $\bar{z}^1 = -\sum_{i=2}^I \bar{z}^i \in \mathscr{Z}$. Since $\bar{x}^1 - \omega^1 = -\sum_{i=2}^I (\bar{x}^i - \omega^i)$ implies $\bar{x}^1 - \omega^1 = W(\bar{q}, V) \bar{z}^1$, $((\bar{x}, \bar{z}), \bar{q})$ is an FM equilibrium. $\square$

Proposition 22.6 asserts that whenever a financial market equilibrium generates a market subspace $\langle W(\bar{q}, V) \rangle$ which is an $(n-1)$-dimensional hyperplane in $\mathbb{R}^n$, then agents face a budget set which is identical to that with a system of contingent markets with a price system $\bar{\pi}$, so that the financial markets mimic the ideal behavior of the system of contingent markets. In particular, the equilibrium allocation $\bar{x}$ is Pareto optimal. This proposition explains why we say that markets are complete when rank $W(\bar{q}, V) = n - 1$ (Definition 22.1) for then the financial markets offer each agent the same opportunity set as a complete system of contingent markets.

What does a security structure (ζ, V) have to look like if it is to cope fully with the uncertainties presented by a given event-tree $\mathbb{D}$? Ideally such a condition would be independent of the characteristics (u, ω) of the agents and would describe security structures which are well matched to the information structure. Such a condition can be given when all securities are short-lived: in this case

$$\operatorname{rank} W(\bar{q}, V) = \#\mathbb{D} - 1 \quad \Longleftrightarrow \quad \operatorname{rank} V(\xi^+) = b(\xi), \quad \forall\, \xi \in \mathbb{D}^- \quad (7)$$

For such security structures, the equilibrium allocations on a system of financial markets coincide with the equilibrium allocations with contingent markets: this is the multiperiod version of Theorem 10.6. Thus if $\mathscr{E}(\mathbb{D}, u, \omega, \xi, V)$ is a stochastic economy in which agents' preferences satisfy Assumption $\mathscr{U}''$ and $\sum_{i=1}^{I} \omega^i \in \mathbb{R}_{++}^n$, if the security structure consists solely of short-lived securities which satisfy (7), then a financial market equilibrium exists and every equilibrium allocation is Pareto optimal.

As soon as the security structure includes long-lived securities, a rank condition for complete markets can not be given which is independent of the characteristics of the agents. We saw in Example 22.5 with two long-lived securities that the same dividend structure V can lead to complete or incomplete markets depending on the security price q. If the characteristics (u, ω) are such that the rank condition of Proposition 22.6(ii) is satisfied at a contingent market equilibrium, then for this economy there exists an equilibrium with the two long-lived securities as financial instruments which is Pareto optimal. If the characteristics (u, ω) are such that the rank condition is not satisfied at any contingent market equilibrium, then the proposition does not allow us to infer whether or not a financial market equilibrium exists: if an FM equilibrium exists, it must be an equilibrium with incomplete markets.

23. NO-ARBITRAGE EQUILIBRIUM

Section 10 introduced an alternative way of representing a financial market equilibrium of a two-period economy, called a no-arbitrage equilibrium. This is essentially a constrained contingent market equilibrium based on using present-value prices rather than security prices as the market clearing variables. When the financial markets are complete, such an equilibrium reduces to a contingent market equilibrium. This section shows how the concept of a no-arbitrage equilibrium is derived for a multiperiod economy: as in the two-period case, the construction is based on a change of variable; at each node the price of each security is replaced by the discounted value of the future dividends of the security under a vector of present-value prices. The value of this concept of equilibrium comes from its utility as an analytical tool—it says nothing new in economic terms, but it expresses a financial market equilibrium in a mathematical form which proves to be analytically more tractable.

A positive vector of present-value prices $\pi \in \mathbb{R}^n_{++}$ supports the market subspace $\langle W(q, V) \rangle$ if it satisfies $\pi W(q, V) = 0$. As shown in Section 21 this is equivalent to

$$q_j(\xi) = \frac{1}{\pi(\xi)} \sum_{\xi' \in \mathbb{D}^+(\xi)} \pi(\xi') V^j(\xi'), \quad j \in J(\xi) \tag{1}$$

for all $\xi \in \mathbb{D}$. By the convention which extends the price of the jth security to the whole event tree

$$q_j(\xi) = 0 \quad \text{if} \quad j \notin J(\xi) \tag{2}$$

It is convenient to introduce a notation which permits (1) and (2) to be written simultaneously and in condensed form.

23.1 Definition (Subtree Inner Product):   For a vector of node prices $\pi = (\pi(\xi), \xi \in \mathbb{D})$ and a vector of income $y = (y(\xi), \xi \in \mathbb{D})$ define

$$\pi \underset{\xi}{\bullet} y = \sum_{\xi' \in \mathbb{D}(\xi)} \pi(\xi') y(\xi'), \quad \forall \xi \in \mathbb{D}$$

$\pi \bullet_\xi y$ is the discounted value of the portion of the income stream y restricted to the subtree $\mathbb{D}(\xi)$: this restricted inner product will be called the $\mathbb{D}(\xi)$-*subtree inner product* of π and y.

23.2 Definition (Subtree Inner Product for Security):   For security j ($j = 1, \ldots, J$) with issue node $\xi(j)$ and dividend stream V^j and for a vector of node prices $\pi = (\pi(\xi), \xi \in \mathbb{D})$ define

$$\pi \underset{\xi}{\bullet} V^j = \begin{cases} \displaystyle\sum_{\xi' \in \mathbb{D}(\xi)} \pi(\xi') V^j(\xi') & \text{if } \xi \in \mathbb{D}\left(\xi(j)\right) \\ 0 & \text{if } \xi \notin \mathbb{D}\left(\xi(j)\right) \end{cases}, \quad \forall \xi \in \mathbb{D}$$

Thus for security j, the subtree inner product takes into account its date of issue $\xi(j)$: $\pi \bullet_\xi V^j$ is the discounted value of the dividends of security j on the subtree $\mathbb{D}(\xi)$ if security j exists at node ξ, and is zero otherwise.

With this notation, (1) and (2) can be written as

$$q_j(\xi) = \frac{1}{\pi(\xi)} \sum_{\xi' \in \xi^+} \pi \underset{\xi}{\bullet} V^j, \quad j \in J(\xi) \tag{3}$$

which is equivalent to

$$q_j(\xi) = \frac{1}{\pi(\xi)} \left(\pi \underset{\xi}{\bullet} V^j - \pi(\xi) V^j(\xi) \right) \tag{4}$$

The advantage of this latter expression is that it covers both the case where

$j \in J(\xi)$ and where $j \notin J(\xi)$. If $j \notin J(\xi)$ then either $\xi \notin \mathbb{D}\,(\xi(j))$ and both $\pi \bullet_\xi V^j$ and $\pi(\xi)V^j(\xi)$ are zero or the security has expired in which case $V^j(\xi') = 0$ for all $\xi' > \xi$ and $\pi \bullet_\xi V^j = \pi(\xi)V^j(\xi)$.

To use a more condensed matrix notation define

$$\pi \underset{\xi}{\bullet} V = \left(\pi \underset{\xi}{\bullet} V^1, \ldots, \pi \underset{\xi}{\bullet} V^J \right)$$

Then (4) leads to the formula

$$q(\xi) = \frac{1}{\pi(\xi)} \left(\pi \underset{\xi}{\bullet} V - \pi(\xi)V(\xi) \right), \qquad \forall \xi \in \mathbb{D} \tag{5}$$

(5) *can be used to change variables from the security price vector q to the node price π in the budget equations ((2)–(4) in Section 20).* Performing this change of variable, the budget equations of agent i become (with $z^i \in \mathscr{Z}$)

$$\pi(\xi_0)\left(x^i(\xi_0) - \omega^i(\xi_0)\right) = -\left(\pi \underset{\xi_0}{\bullet} V - \pi(\xi_0)V(\xi_0) \right) z^i(\xi_0)$$

$$\pi(\xi)\left(x^i(\xi) - \omega^i(\xi)\right) = \left(\pi \underset{\xi}{\bullet} V \right) z^i(\xi^-) - \left(\pi \underset{\xi}{\bullet} V - \pi(\xi)V(\xi) \right) z^i(\xi) \tag{6}$$

$$\pi(\xi)\left(x^i(\xi) - \omega^i(\xi)\right) = \left(\pi \underset{\xi}{\bullet} V \right) z^i(\xi^-), \qquad \forall \xi \in \mathbb{D}_T$$

where the second equation must be satisfied for all $\xi \in \mathbb{D}^- \cap \mathbb{D}^+$.

The next step is to rewrite equations (6) in an equivalent form which does not make explicit reference to the portfolio $z^i \in \mathscr{Z}$. To this end let $\mathbb{D}_t$ denote the *set of nodes at date t*

$$\mathbb{D}_t = \bigcup_{\sigma \in \mathbb{F}_t} (t, \sigma)$$

Consider a node ξ at date $T - 1$ ($\xi \in \mathbb{D}_{T-1}$). All the immediate successors of ξ at date T have dividends generated by the same portfolio $z^i(\xi)$, namely

$$z^i(\xi'^-) = z^i(\xi), \qquad \forall \xi' \in \xi^+$$

so that

$$\left(\pi \underset{\xi}{\bullet} V - \pi(\xi)V(\xi) \right) z^i(\xi) = \left(\sum_{\xi' \in \xi^+} \pi \underset{\xi'}{\bullet} V \right) z^i(\xi)$$

$$= \sum_{\xi' \in \xi^+} \pi(\xi')\left(x^i(\xi') - \omega^i(\xi')\right)$$

The budget equation at node $\xi \in \mathbb{D}_{T-1}$ can thus be written as

$$\pi \underset{\xi}{\bullet} (x^i - \omega^i) = \left(\pi \underset{\xi}{\bullet} V\right) z^i(\xi^-) \tag{7}$$

In this expression the cost of the new portfolio $z^i(\xi)$ at node ξ has been taken into account by adding the discounted value of the future net trades to the discounted value of the net trade at node ξ. The portfolio $z^i(\xi)$ only ensures that the vector

$$\left(\pi(\xi') \left(x^i(\xi') - \omega^i(\xi')\right)\right)_{\xi' \in \xi+}$$

lies in the subspace of $\mathbb{R}^{b(\xi)}$ spanned by the J $b(\xi)$-vectors

$$\left(\left(\pi \underset{\xi'}{\bullet} V^1\right)_{\xi' \in \xi+}, \ldots, \left(\pi \underset{\xi'}{\bullet} V^J\right)_{\xi' \in \xi+}\right)$$

This property can be expressed more simply by introducing the following notation.

23.3 Definition (Successor Box-Product):   For a vector of node prices $\pi = (\pi(\xi), \xi \in \mathbb{D})$ and a vector of income $y = (y(\xi), \xi \in \mathbb{D})$, define the *successor box-product* of π and y

$$\pi \underset{\xi+}{\square} y = \left(\pi \underset{\xi'}{\bullet} y\right)_{\xi' \in \xi+} \in \mathbb{R}^{b(\xi)}$$

$\pi \underset{\xi+}{\square} y$ is the vector of discounted values $\pi \underset{\xi'}{\bullet} y$ of the income stream y at each of the successors ξ' of ξ.

23.4 Definition (Successor Box-Product for Security):   For security j with dividend stream V^j and for a vector of node prices $\pi = (\pi(\xi), \xi \in \mathbb{D})$ define

$$\pi \underset{\xi+}{\square} V^j = \begin{cases} \left(\pi \underset{\xi'}{\bullet} V^j\right)_{\xi' \in \xi+} & \text{if } j \in J(\xi) \\ 0 & \text{if } j \notin J(\xi) \end{cases}, \quad \forall \xi \in \mathbb{D}^-$$

and define the $b(\xi) \times J$ matrix $\pi \underset{\xi+}{\square} V$ by

$$\pi \underset{\xi+}{\square} V = \left[\pi \underset{\xi+}{\square} V^1 \cdots \pi \underset{\xi+}{\square} V^J\right]$$

With this notation the budget equations at date T can be written as

$$\pi \underset{\xi+}{\square} (x^i - \omega^i) \in \left\langle \pi \underset{\xi+}{\square} V \right\rangle, \quad \forall \xi \in \mathbb{D}_{T-1} \tag{8}$$

The same transformation can now be applied to a node ξ at date $T - 2$ $(\xi \in \mathbb{D}_{T-2})$. First note that

$$\left(\pi \underset{\xi}{\bullet} V - \pi(\xi)V(\xi) \right) z^i(\xi) = \left(\sum_{\xi' \in \xi^+} \pi \underset{\xi'}{\bullet} V \right) z^i(\xi) \tag{9}$$

Even though $\pi \underset{\bullet\xi}{} V - \pi(\xi)V(\xi)$ is not equal to $\sum_{\xi' \in \xi^+} \pi \underset{\bullet\xi}{} V$ if there is a security j introduced at an immediate successor of ξ $(\xi(j) \in \xi^+)$, formula (9) is valid since $z^i \in \mathscr{Z}$ implies $z^i_j(\xi) = 0$ if $\xi \notin \mathbb{D}\left(\xi(j) \right)$. For the immediate successors ξ' of ξ, equation (7) holds with the portfolio $z^i(\xi'^-) = z^i(\xi)$ so that

$$\left(\pi \underset{\xi}{\bullet} V - \pi(\xi)V(\xi) \right) z^i(\xi) = \sum_{\xi' \in \xi^+} \pi \underset{\xi'}{\bullet} (x^i - \omega^i)$$

and the budget equation for node ξ reduces to

$$\pi \underset{\xi}{\bullet} (x^i - \omega^i) = \left(\pi \underset{\xi}{\bullet} V \right) z^i(\xi^-) \tag{10}$$

Bringing together the nodes of $\mathbb{D}_{T-1}$ which have the same predecessor ξ at date $T - 2$, the budget equation (7) can be written as

$$\pi \underset{\xi^+}{\square} (x^i - \omega^i) \in \left\langle \pi \underset{\xi^+}{\square} V \right\rangle \tag{11}$$

Proceeding recursively in this way leads to an equivalent form for the budget equations in which the financial variables (q, z^i) no longer appear explicitly. Since at date 0 there is no dividend accruing from a previously chosen portfolio, the equation equivalent to (7) or (10) for the only node at date 0 is

$$\pi \underset{\xi_0}{\bullet} (x^i - \omega^i) = \pi(x^i - \omega^i) = 0$$

The budget equations at all other dates $t = 1, \dots, T - 1$ can be written in the form (8) or (11). We are thus led to define the budget set (called the *no-arbitrage budget set*)

$$\mathscr{B}(\pi, \omega^i, V) = \left\{ x^i \in \mathbb{R}^n_+ \; \middle| \; \begin{array}{c} \pi(x^i - \omega^i) = 0 \\ \pi \underset{\xi^+}{\square} (x^i - \omega^i) \in \left\langle \pi \underset{\xi^+}{\square} V \right\rangle, \quad \forall \xi \in \mathbb{D}^- \end{array} \right\} \tag{12}$$

which coincides with the financial market budget set whenever $\pi W(q, V) = 0$.

23.5 Lemma (No-Arbitrage Budget Set): *Let $\mathscr{E}(\mathbb{D}, u, \omega, \zeta, V)$ be a stochastic finance economy. If $q \in \mathbb{R}^{nJ}$ is a no-arbitrage security price process and if $\pi \in \mathbb{R}^n_{++}$ is a vector of node prices satisfying $\pi W(q, V) = 0$, then*

$$\mathscr{B}(\pi, \omega^i, V) = \mathbb{B}(q, \omega^i, V), \quad i = 1, \dots, I$$

where $\mathscr{B}(\pi, \omega^i, V)$ is defined by (12) and $\mathbb{B}(q, \omega^i, V)$ by (6) in Section 20.

PROOF: The above transformations have shown that, if $\pi W(q, V) = 0$, then $\mathbb{B}(q, \omega^i, V) \subset \mathscr{B}(\pi, \omega^i, V)$. To show the reverse inclusion, for any $x \in \mathscr{B}(\pi, \omega^i, V)$ consider a portfolio $z^i \in \mathscr{Z}$ satisfying

$$\pi \underset{\xi+}{_\square} (x^i - \omega^i) = \left[\pi \underset{\xi+}{_\square} V \right] z^i(\xi), \quad \forall \xi \in \mathbb{D}^-$$

which can be written as

$$\pi \underset{\xi}{_\bullet} (x^i - \omega^i) = \left(\pi \underset{\xi}{_\bullet} V \right) z^i(\xi^-), \quad \forall \xi \in \mathbb{D}^+$$

For $\xi \in \mathbb{D}_T$ this gives the last equation in (6) above. Substituting recursively and using (9) gives the middle equation in (6). The equation $\pi(x^i - \omega^i) = 0$ leads to the first equation in (6). The no-arbitrage equations (5) then imply that $(x^i; z^i) \in \mathbb{B}(q, \omega^i, V)$. $\square$

23.6 Example (No-Arbitrage Budget Set):   Let us derive the no-arbitrage budget set of agent i for the financial structure of Example 22.5. It is convenient to write the endowment ω^i as

$$\omega^i = \left(\omega^i(\xi), \xi \in \mathbb{D} \right) = \left(\omega^i_0, (\omega^i_1, \omega^i_2), (\omega^i_{11}, \omega^i_{12}, \omega^i_{21}, \omega^i_{22}) \right)$$

where the subscript of ω^i is the subscript of the appropriate node ($\omega^i_{11} = \omega^i(\xi_{11})$, etc.) and to adopt a similar notation for the consumption vector x^i. The budget equations, written in extensive form, are given by: for ξ_0

$$x^i_0 - \omega^i_0 = -q_1(\xi_0) z^i_1(\xi_0) - q_2(\xi_0) z^i_2(\xi_0) \tag{13}$$

for ξ_0^+ (i.e. for ξ_1 and ξ_2)

$$
\begin{aligned}
x^i_1 - \omega^i_1 &= q_1(\xi_1) z^i_1(\xi_0) + q_2(\xi_1) z^i_2(\xi_0) - q_1(\xi_1) z^i_1(\xi_1) - q_2(\xi_1) z^i_2(\xi_1) \\
x^i_2 - \omega^i_2 &= q_1(\xi_2) z^i_1(\xi_0) + q_2(\xi_2) z^i_2(\xi_0) - q_1(\xi_2) z^i_1(\xi_2) - q_2(\xi_2) z^i_2(\xi_2)
\end{aligned}
\tag{14}
$$

for ξ_1^+ and ξ_2^+

$$
\begin{cases}
x^i_{11} - \omega^i_{11} = z^i_1(\xi_1) \\
x^i_{12} - \omega^i_{12} = z^i_2(\xi_1)
\end{cases}
\qquad
\begin{cases}
x^i_{21} - \omega^i_{21} = z^i_1(\xi_2) \\
x^i_{22} - \omega^i_{22} = a z^i_2(\xi_2)
\end{cases}
\tag{15}
$$

for a portfolio of the two securities

$$z^i = \left(\left(z_1^i(\xi_0), z_2^i(\xi_0) \right), \left(z_1^i(\xi_1), z_2^i(\xi_1) \right), \left(z_1^i(\xi_2), z_2^i(\xi_2) \right) \right) \in \mathcal{Z} = \mathbb{R}^6$$

The no-arbitrage condition implies that there exists a vector of node prices $\pi \in \mathbb{R}^7_{++}$ which can be written as

$$\pi = (1, (\pi_1, \pi_2), (\pi_{11}, \pi_{12}, \pi_{21}, \pi_{22}))$$

such that equation (1) holds. This gives

$$
\begin{aligned}
q_1(\xi_0) &= \pi_{11} + \pi_{21}, & q_2(\xi_0) &= \pi_{12} + a\pi_{22} \\
q_1(\xi_1) &= \frac{\pi_{11}}{\pi_1}, & q_2(\xi_1) &= \frac{\pi_{12}}{\pi_1} \\
q_1(\xi_2) &= \frac{\pi_{21}}{\pi_2}, & q_2(\xi_2) &= \frac{a\pi_{22}}{\pi_2}
\end{aligned}
\tag{16}
$$

The construction leading to equation (7) involves inserting in (14) the security prices and portfolios at date 1 given by (15) and (16): this gives the pair of equations for date 1

$$
\begin{aligned}
\pi_1(x_1^i - \omega_1^i) + \pi_{11}(x_{11}^i - \omega_{11}^i) + \pi_{12}(x_{12}^i - \omega_{12}^i) &= \pi_{11}z_1^i(\xi_0) + \pi_{12}z_2^i(\xi_0) \\
\pi_2(x_2^i - \omega_2^i) + \pi_{21}(x_{21}^i - \omega_{21}^i) + \pi_{22}(x_{22}^i - \omega_{22}^i) &= \pi_{21}z_1^i(\xi_0) + a\pi_{22}z_2^i(\xi_0)
\end{aligned}
\tag{17}
$$

which can be written as

$$
\begin{aligned}
\pi \underset{\xi_1}{\bullet} (x^i - \omega^i) &= \left(\pi \underset{\xi_1}{\bullet} V \right) z^i(\xi_0) \\
\pi \underset{\xi_2}{\bullet} (x^i - \omega^i) &= \left(\pi \underset{\xi_2}{\bullet} V \right) z^i(\xi_0)
\end{aligned}
\tag{18}
$$

where $V = [V^1 \; V^2]$ is the matrix of dividends of securities 1 and 2, with

$$V^1 = (0, (0,0), (1,0,1,0))^T, \quad V^2 = (0, (0,0), (0,1,0,a))^T$$

Using the box product, the two equations in (18) can be written in the more condensed form

$$\pi \underset{\xi_0^+}{\square} (x^i - \omega^i) = \left[\pi \underset{\xi_0^+}{\square} V \right] z^i(\xi_0) \tag{19}$$

with

$$\pi \underset{\xi_0^+}{\square} V = \begin{bmatrix} \pi_{11} & \pi_{12} \\ \pi_{21} & a\pi_{22} \end{bmatrix} \tag{20}$$

The result of the above transformation is to have eliminated the portfolios at date 1 (which appear in (14)) from the date 1 budget equations written in any of the equivalent forms (17), (18) or (19). Since the cost of the portfolio at date 1 has been taken into account, all that remains in (15) is the "spanning" that it offers for date 2. If $a \neq 0$ then (15) imposes no constraint, and if $a = 0$ then the constraint implied by (15) reduces to

$$x_{22}^i - \omega_{22}^i = 0 \tag{21}$$

This conclusion, which is immediate from (15), can also be obtained by using the general procedure to rewrite the date 2 budget equations as follows

$$\begin{bmatrix} \pi_{11}(x_{11}^i - \omega_{11}^i) \\ \pi_{12}(x_{12}^i - \omega_{12}^i) \end{bmatrix} = \begin{bmatrix} \pi_{11} & 0 \\ 0 & \pi_{12} \end{bmatrix} \begin{bmatrix} z_1^i(\xi_1) \\ z_2^i(\xi_1) \end{bmatrix}$$

$$\begin{bmatrix} \pi_{21}(x_{21}^i - \omega_{21}^i) \\ \pi_{22}(x_{22}^i - \omega_{22}^i) \end{bmatrix} = \begin{bmatrix} \pi_{21} & 0 \\ 0 & a\pi_{22} \end{bmatrix} \begin{bmatrix} z_1^i(\xi_2) \\ z_2^i(\xi_2) \end{bmatrix}$$

which, since the date 1 portfolios are unconstrained, is equivalent to

$$\pi \underset{\xi_1^+}{\circ} (x^i - \omega^i) \in \left\langle \pi \underset{\xi_1^+}{\circ} V \right\rangle, \quad \pi \underset{\xi_2^+}{\circ} (x^i - \omega^i) \in \left\langle \pi \underset{\xi_2^+}{\circ} V \right\rangle$$

The constraints for the successors ξ_1^+ are automatically satisfied since the rank of the matrix $\pi \underset{\xi_1^+}{\circ} V$ is 2; they are similarly automatically satisfied for ξ_2^+ if $a \neq 0$. If $a = 0$ the constraints reduce to (21).

The last step involves inserting the expressions for $(q_1(\xi_0), q_2(\xi_0))$ given by (16) into the date 0 budget equation (13) and using (17). The date 0 budget equation then reduces to

$$\pi(x^i - \omega^i) = 0$$

and since $z^i(\xi_0)$ disappears (and hence is not constrained), (19) can be written as

$$\pi \underset{\xi_0^+}{\circ} (x^i - \omega^i) \in \left\langle \pi \underset{\xi_0^+}{\circ} V \right\rangle$$

Thus if $a \neq 0$ the no-arbitrage budget set is

$$\mathscr{B}(\pi, \omega^i, V) = \left\{ x^i \in \mathbb{R}_+^7 \;\middle|\; \begin{array}{l} \pi(x^i - \omega^i) = 0 \\ \pi \underset{\xi_0^+}{\circ} (x^i - \omega^i) \in \left\langle \pi \underset{\xi_0^+}{\circ} V \right\rangle \end{array} \right\}$$

where $\pi \underset{\xi_0^+}{\circ} V$ is given by (20); if $a = 0$, since rank $\pi \underset{\xi_0^+}{\circ} V = 2$

$$\mathscr{B}(\pi, \omega^i, V) = \left\{ x^i \in \mathbb{R}_+^7 \;\middle|\; \begin{array}{l} \pi(x^i - \omega^i) = 0 \\ x_{22}^i - \omega_{22}^i = 0 \end{array} \right\}$$

which completes the derivation of the no-arbitrage budget set for the two possible cases. □

The transformation for each agent from the budget set $\mathbb{B}(q, \omega^i, V)$, which is a function of the security prices, to the budget set $\mathscr{B}(\pi, \omega^i, V)$, which is a function of the node prices, leads to the following concept of equilibrium.

23.7 Definition: A pair $(\bar{x}, \bar{\pi}) \in \mathbb{R}^{nI} \times \mathbb{R}^n_{++}$ is a *no-arbitrage equilibrium* of the economy $\mathscr{E}(\mathbb{D}, u, \omega, \zeta, V)$ if

(i) $\bar{x}^i = \arg\max \left\{ u^i(x^i) \mid x^i \in \mathscr{B}(\bar{\pi}, \omega^i, V) \right\}, i = 1, \ldots, I$

(ii) $\sum_{i=1}^I (\bar{x}^i - \omega^i) = 0$

If $(\bar{x}, \bar{\pi})$ is a no-arbitrage equilibrium and if $\bar{q}$ is defined by (1) and (2) with $\pi = \bar{\pi}$, then there exist portfolios $\bar{z} = (\bar{z}^1, \ldots, \bar{z}^I)$ such that $((\bar{x}, \bar{z}), \bar{q})$ is a financial market equilibrium. This follows from the property $\bar{\pi} W(\bar{q}, V) = 0$, implied by (1) and (2), and the equality of the budget sets $\mathscr{B}(\bar{\pi}, \omega^i, V)$ and $\mathbb{B}(\bar{q}, \omega^i, V)$ asserted by Lemma 23.5. If the financial markets are incomplete, $\dim \langle W(\bar{q}, V) \rangle^\perp > 1$ and there are many node prices $\pi \in \mathbb{R}^n_{++}$ such that $\pi W(\bar{q}, V) = 0$. By Lemma 23.5 all these node prices give rise to the same budget set as that generated by $\bar{\pi}$

$$\mathscr{B}(\pi, \omega^i, V) = \mathscr{B}(\bar{\pi}, \omega^i, V), \quad \forall \pi \in \langle W(\bar{q}, V) \rangle^\perp \cap \mathbb{R}^n_{++}, \quad i = 1, \ldots, I$$

so that for any such node-price vector π, $(\bar{x}, \pi)$ is a no-arbitrage equilibrium corresponding to the same financial market equilibrium $((\bar{x}, \bar{z}), \bar{q})$. This freedom in the choice of node prices for characterizing the agents' budget sets can be exploited to advantage in the same way as in Section 10: thus we choose the present-value vector of a particular agent (agent 1) to represent the node prices associated with the vector of security prices $\bar{q}$. As a result, the budget set $\mathscr{B}(\bar{\pi}^1, \omega^1, V)$ of agent 1 reduces to the contingent market budget set $B(\bar{\pi}^1, \omega^1)$.

23.8 Definition: A pair $(\bar{x}, \bar{\pi}) \in \mathbb{R}^{nI} \times \mathbb{R}^n_{++}$ is *normalized no-arbitrage* (NA) equilibrium of the economy $\mathscr{E}(\mathbb{D}, u, \omega, \xi, V)$ if

(i) $\bar{x}^1 = \arg\max \left\{ u^1(x^1) \mid x^1 \in B(\bar{\pi}, \omega^1) \right\}$
    $\bar{x}^i = \arg\max \left\{ u^i(x^i) \mid x^i \in \mathscr{B}(\bar{\pi}, \omega^i, V) \right\}, i = 2, \ldots, I$

(ii) $\sum_{i=1}^I (\bar{x}^i - \omega^i) = 0$

The following proposition asserts that an NA equilibrium provides an alternative way of analyzing an FM equilibrium.

23.9 Proposition (Equivalence of FM and NA Equilibria): *Let* $\mathscr{E}(\mathbb{D}, u, \omega, \zeta, V)$ *be a stochastic finance economy satisfying Assumption $\mathscr{U}$.*

(i) *If $((\bar{x}, \bar{z}), \bar{q})$ is an FM equilibrium and if $\bar{\pi}^1$ is agent 1's present-value vector, then $(\bar{x}, \bar{\pi}^1)$ is an NA equilibrium.*

(ii) *If $(\bar{x}, \bar{\pi})$ is an NA equilibrium and if $\bar{q} \in \mathbb{R}^n$ is the security price vector defined by (1) and (2) with $\pi = \bar{\pi}$, then there exists a vector of portfolios $\bar{z} = (\bar{z}^1, \dots, \bar{z}^I)$ such that $((\bar{x}, \bar{z}), \bar{q})$ is an FM equilibrium.*

PROOF: The proof is the same as in the two-period case (Proposition 10.3). □

In Chapter 2 the concept of an NA equilibrium was used to prove the existence of an FM equilibrium for a two-period economy. The proof was based on the fact that the aggregate excess demand function for an NA equilibrium has the same properties as the aggregate excess demand function for a CM equilibrium. The proof was thus in all essentials identical to the proof of existence of a CM equilibrium.

In a multiperiod economy with long-lived securities the same argument no longer applies. The subspaces $\langle \pi \,_{\square\,\xi^+} V \rangle$ which constrain the agents' demands in their NA budget sets can change dimension as π varies—as can be readily seen in Example 23.6. When a change of dimension occurs, there is a discontinuity in the agents' demands. With a *discontinuous* aggregate excess demand function Theorem 7.5, or any of the fixed point theorems, no longer applies.

The following example shows that the presence of these discontinuities, induced by changes in the dimension of the market subspace, can lead to non-existence of an FM equilibrium.

24.   EXAMPLE OF NON-EXISTENCE

Let us draw on Example 22.5 to construct a simple three-period economy $\mathscr{E}(\mathbb{D}, u, \omega, \zeta, V)$ for which there is no financial market equilibrium. The event-tree $\mathbb{D}$ with

$$\mathbb{D} = \{\xi_0, (\xi_1, \xi_2), (\xi_{11}, \xi_{12}, \xi_{21}, \xi_{22})\} \tag{1}$$

and the two long-lived securities issued at date 0 with dividend processes

$$\begin{aligned}
V^1 &= (0, (0,0), (1,0,1,0)) \\
V^2 &= (0, (0,0), (0,1,0,a)), \quad a > 0
\end{aligned} \tag{2}$$

are those introduced in Example 22.5 and further studied in Example 23.6. The one-good economy consists of two agents with preferences and endowments defined as follows:

$$u^1(x) = x_1^\alpha + x_2^\alpha + x_1^\beta x_{11}^\alpha + x_{12}^\alpha + x_2^\beta x_{21}^\alpha + x_{22}^\alpha$$
$$u^2(x) = x_1^{\alpha+\beta} + x_2^{\alpha+\beta} + x_{11}^\alpha + x_{12}^\alpha + x_{21}^\alpha + x_{22}^\alpha$$

(3)

$$\omega^1 = (0, (1+\epsilon, 1-\epsilon), (1, 1, 1, 1))$$
$$\omega^2 = (0, (1-\epsilon, 1+\epsilon), (1, 1, 1, 1))$$

(4)

with

$$\alpha > 0, \quad \beta \geq 0, \quad \alpha + \beta < 1, \quad -1 \leq \epsilon \leq 1$$

Thus the agents face risks only at date 1, and then only if $\epsilon \neq 0$. To simplify the computation of equilibrium, we make the special assumption that agents have no endowments at date 0 and that their preferences do not depend on date 0 consumption. At date 0 there is only trading in the securities, and the date 0 budget equation reduces to

$$q_1(\xi_0)z_1^i(\xi_0) + q_2(\xi_0)z_2^i(\xi_0) = 0, \quad i = 1, 2$$

Even though the marginal utility of consumption at date 0 is zero, the multiplier λ_0^i associated with this constraint in the maximum problem of agent i is positive since the securities yield positive income at date 2. The multiplier λ_0^i is the marginal utility of income at date 0 and serves to define the present-value vectors π^i of the agents. An example of an economy with date 0 consumption and properties similar to those of the present example could be constructed at the cost of substantial additional calculations.

For a vector of security prices $q = (q(\xi), \xi \in \mathbb{D})$, the budget equations $x^i - \omega^i = W(q, V)z^i$ are given in extensive form by equations (13)–(15) in Section 23 with $x_0^i = \omega_0^i = 0$, $i = 1, 2$. In Example 23.6 it was shown how the budget set $\mathbb{B}(q, \omega^i, V)$ can be transformed into the no-arbitrage budget set $\mathscr{B}(\pi, \omega^i, V)$. Restricting attention to the case $a > 0$, the no-arbitrage budget set is

$$\mathscr{B}(\pi, \omega^i, V) = \left\{ x^i \in \mathbb{R}_+^7 \;\middle|\; \begin{array}{l} \pi(x^i - \omega^i) = 0 \\ \pi_{\underset{\xi_0^+}{\square}}(x^i - \omega^i) \in \left\langle \pi_{\underset{\xi_0^+}{\square}} V \right\rangle \end{array} \right\}$$

(5)

where

$$\pi_{\underset{\xi_0^+}{\square}} V = \begin{bmatrix} \pi_{11} & \pi_{12} \\ \pi_{21} & a\pi_{22} \end{bmatrix}$$

(6)

The matrix $\pi \underset{\xi_0^+}{\circ} V$ corresponds to the date 1 payoff matrix

$$
\begin{bmatrix}
q_1(\xi_1) & q_2(\xi_1) \\
q_1(\xi_2) & q_2(\xi_2)
\end{bmatrix}
$$

in (5) of Section 22, in which the price of each security is replaced by the present value of the security's dividends.

By Proposition 23.9, a financial market equilibrium exists for the above economy if and only if an NA equilibrium exists. This result is used to show the following:

24.1 Proposition: *For the stochastic economy defined by (1)–(4)*

(i) *there exists $\epsilon^* > 0$ such that if $a = 1$, $\beta > 0$, $0 < |\epsilon| < \epsilon^*$, then the economy has no NA (and hence no FM) equilibrium*

(ii) *if $a \neq 1$, then there exists an NA (and hence an FM) equilibrium.*

PROOF: (i) *Nonexistence with $a = 1$.* If an NA equilibrium (x, π) exists then

$$
\rho(\xi_0) = \text{rank} \left[\pi \underset{\xi_0^+}{\circ} V \right] = 2 \quad \text{or} \quad 1
$$

We shall show that neither case can arise so that no NA equilibrium exists.

Case 1 ($\rho(\xi_0) = 2$): By (5) the NA budget set $\mathscr{B}(\pi, \omega^i, V)$ reduces to the contingent market (CM) budget set $B(\pi, \omega^i)$. The equilibrium (x, π) is thus a CM equilibrium. For $\epsilon = 0$ the initial endowment is Pareto optimal since

$$
\nabla u^1(\omega^1) = \nabla u^2(\omega^2) = ((\alpha + \beta, \alpha + \beta), (\alpha, \alpha, \alpha, \alpha))
$$

(where the date 0 component of the gradients has been omitted). Thus there is a unique CM equilibrium (the no-trade equilibrium) given by

$$
\begin{aligned}
\pi &= (1, (\alpha + \beta, \alpha + \beta), (\alpha, \alpha, \alpha, \alpha)) \\
x^1 &= x^2 = (0, (1, 1), (1, 1, 1, 1))
\end{aligned}
\tag{7}
$$

It follows from the analysis of the CM equilibria of an economy parametrized by endowments (which will be studied in Volume 2) that if the endowments stay close to Pareto optimal endowments then the equilibrium remains unique. Thus there exists $\epsilon^* > 0$ such that there is a unique CM equilibrium for all ϵ such that $|\epsilon| < \epsilon^*$. It is easy to check that for all such ϵ the CM equilibrium is given by (7), since the budget constraints of both agents are still satisfied.

Substituting the price vector π given in (7) into the matrix in (6) gives (for $a = 1$)

$$\text{rank} \begin{bmatrix} \pi \underset{\xi_0^+}{\Box} V \end{bmatrix} = \text{rank} \begin{bmatrix} \alpha & \alpha \\ \alpha & \alpha \end{bmatrix} = 1$$

contradicting the assumption $\rho(\xi_0) = 2$. Thus for $a = 1, |\epsilon| < \epsilon^*$ there is no NA equilibrium with $\rho(\xi_0) = 2$.

Case 2 $(\rho(\xi_0) = 1)$: Note that (with $a = 1$)

$$\text{rank} \begin{bmatrix} \pi \underset{\xi_0^+}{\Box} V \end{bmatrix} = \text{rank} \begin{bmatrix} \pi_{11} & \pi_{12} \\ \pi_{21} & \pi_{22} \end{bmatrix} = 1 \iff \frac{\pi_{11}}{\pi_{21}} = \frac{\pi_{12}}{\pi_{22}} \tag{8}$$

In this case, the budget constraint (5) of agent 2 implies that

$$\pi \underset{\xi_0^+}{\Box} (x^2 - \omega^2) \in \langle (\pi_{11}, \pi_{21})^T \rangle$$

Since π_{11} and π_{21} are both positive, this implies that $\pi \underset{\xi_1}{\bullet} (x^2 - \omega^2)$ and $\pi \underset{\xi_2}{\bullet} (x^2 - \omega^2)$ have the same sign. Since there is no consumption at date 0, the date 0 budget constraint

$$0 = \pi(x^2 - \omega^2) = \pi \underset{\xi_1}{\bullet} (x^2 - \omega^2) + \pi \underset{\xi_2}{\bullet} (x^2 - \omega^2)$$

implies that

$$\pi \underset{\xi_1}{\bullet} (x^2 - \omega^2) = 0, \quad \pi \underset{\xi_2}{\bullet} (x^2 - \omega^2) = 0 \tag{9}$$

If π is an NA equilibrium price, by market clearing, (9) also holds for consumer 1, so that

$$\pi \underset{\xi_1}{\bullet} (x^i - \omega^i) = 0, \quad \pi \underset{\xi_2}{\bullet} (x^i - \omega^i) = 0, \quad i = 1, 2 \tag{10}$$

Intuitively, if there is only one security at date 0 which gives a positive payoff in both nodes at date 1, then if there is trade in this security, one agent must be receiving income at date 0 by sacrificing it at date 1: but neither agent is willing to do this, since the utility of consumption at date 0 is zero.

Thus in an NA equilibrium with $\rho(\xi_0) = 1$ there is no income transfer between nodes ξ_1 and ξ_2 and each agent's consumption must be optimal given the budget constraints (10). Since the utility functions are separable between consumption in the subtrees $\mathbb{D}(\xi_1)$ and $\mathbb{D}(\xi_2)$, an NA equilibrium (x, π) must be such that

$$\left(\left(x_j^1, \left(x_{j1}^1, x_{j2}^1 \right) \right), \left(x_j^2, \left(x_{j1}^2, x_{j2}^2 \right) \right), \left(\pi_j, \left(\pi_{j1}, \pi_{j2} \right) \right) \right)$$

is a CM equilibrium for the economy on the subtree $\mathbb{D}(\xi_j)$ beginning at node ξ_j, for $j = 1, 2$. For the $\mathbb{D}(\xi_1)$ economy, the utility functions and endowments are given by

$$v^1\left(x_1, (x_{11}, x_{12})\right) = x_1^\alpha + x_1^\beta x_{11}^\alpha + x_{12}^\alpha \quad (\omega_1^1, (\omega_{11}^1, \omega_{12}^1)) = (1 + \epsilon, (1, 1))$$
$$v^2\left(x_1, (x_{11}, x_{12})\right) = x_1^{\alpha+\beta} + x_{11}^\alpha + x_{12}^\alpha \quad (\omega_1^2, (\omega_{11}^2, \omega_{12}^2)) = (1 - \epsilon, (1, 1))$$

For the $\mathbb{D}(\xi_2)$ economy the utility functions are the same (the index of node 1 being replaced by the index of node 2) and the endowments are given by

$$(\omega_2^1, (\omega_{21}^1, \omega_{22}^1)) = (1 - \epsilon, (1, 1))$$
$$(\omega_2^2, (\omega_{21}^2, \omega_{22}^2)) = (1 + \epsilon, (1, 1))$$

The only difference between these two economies is that in the $\mathbb{D}(\xi_1)$ economy agent 1 is richer than agent 2 (in terms of initial resources); conversely in the $\mathbb{D}(\xi_2)$ economy.

In the $\mathbb{D}(\xi_j)$ economy agent i maximizes the utility function v^i subject to the CM budget constraint given by (10), namely

$$\pi_j(x_j^i - \omega_j^i) + \pi_{j1}(x_{j1}^i - \omega_{j1}^i) + \pi_{j2}(x_{j2}^i - \omega_{j2}^i) = 0, \quad i = 1, 2, \quad j = 1, 2 \quad (11)$$

Let μ_j^1, μ_j^2 denote the marginal utilities of income of agents 1 and 2 in the $\mathbb{D}(\xi_j)$ economy. Then equilibrium consumption bundles (x_j^1, x_j^2) must satisfy the first-order conditions:

(i) $\alpha(x_j^1)^{\alpha-1} + \beta(x_j^1)^{\beta-1}(x_{j1}^1)^\alpha = \mu_j^1\pi_j, \quad (\alpha+\beta)(x_j^2)^{\alpha+\beta-1} = \mu_j^2\pi_j$

(ii) $\alpha(x_j^1)^\beta(x_{j1}^1)^{\alpha-1} = \mu_j^1\pi_{j1}, \quad \alpha(x_{j1}^2)^{\alpha-1} = \mu_j^2\pi_{j1}$

(iii) $\alpha(x_{j2}^1)^{\alpha-1} = \mu_j^1\pi_{j2}, \quad \alpha(x_{j2}^2)^{\alpha-1} = \mu_j^2\pi_{j2}$

(iv) $x_j^1 + x_j^2 = 2, \ x_{j1}^1 + x_{j1}^2 = 2, \ x_{j2}^1 + x_{j2}^2 = 2$

We will show that these equations imply the following inequalities:

(i)' $\mu_j^1 < \mu_j^2 \implies x_j^1 > 1, \ x_{j1}^1 > 1, \ x_{j2}^1 > 1 \implies \pi_{j1}/\pi_{j2} > 1$

(ii)' $\mu_j^1 = \mu_j^2 \implies x_j^1 = 1, \ x_{j1}^1 = 1, \ x_{j2}^1 = 1 \implies \pi_{j1}/\pi_{j2} = 1 \qquad (12)$

(iii)' $\mu_j^1 > \mu_j^2 \implies x_j^1 < 1, \ x_{j1}^1 < 1, \ x_{j2}^1 < 1 \implies \pi_{j1}/\pi_{j2} < 1$

If $\epsilon > 0$, then in the $\mathbb{D}(\xi_1)$ equilibrium agent 1 is richer than agent 2 so that (i)' must occur; in the $\mathbb{D}(\xi_2)$ equilibrium agent 2 is richer than agent 1 so that (iii)' must occur. When $\epsilon < 0$ these two cases are reversed. Thus when $\epsilon > 0$, $\pi_{11}/\pi_{12} > 1$ and $\pi_{21}/\pi_{22} < 1$; when $\epsilon < 0$, $\pi_{11}/\pi_{12} < 1$ and $\pi_{21}/\pi_{22} > 1$. It follows from (8) that these inequalities contradict the hypothesis $\rho(\xi_0) = 1$. Thus for $a = 1, \ \epsilon \neq 0$ there is no NA equilibrium with $\rho(\xi_0) = 1$.

It remains to prove the inequalities (12). It suffices to prove (i)′, for (ii)′ and (iii)′ then follow by a similar argument. Suppose therefore $\mu_j^1 < \mu_j^2$. Then by (ii) and (iv), $(x_j^1)^\beta (x_{j1}^1)^{\alpha-1} < (2 - x_{j1}^1)^{\alpha-1}$ which implies

$$x_{j1}^1 > \frac{2}{1 + (x_j^1)^{\beta/(\alpha-1)}} \iff x_{j1}^1 > \frac{2(x_j^1)^{\beta/(1-\alpha)}}{1 + (x_j^1)^{\beta/(1-\alpha)}} \tag{13}$$

Thus by (i),

$$\mu_j^1 \pi_j = \alpha(x_j^1)^{\alpha-1} + \beta(x_j^1)^{\beta-1}(x_{j1}^1)^\alpha > \alpha(x_j^1)^{\alpha-1} + \frac{\beta 2^\alpha (x_j^1)^{(\alpha+\beta-1)/(1-\alpha)}}{\left(1 + (x_j^1)^{\beta/(1-\alpha)}\right)^\alpha}$$

Suppose $x_j^1 > 1$ is false, so that $x_j^1 \le 1$. Then the above inequality implies $\mu_j^1 \pi_j > \alpha + \beta$. By (iv), $x_j^1 \le 1 \implies x_j^2 \ge 1 \implies \mu_j^2 \pi_j = (\alpha + \beta)(x_j^2)^{\alpha+\beta-1} \le \alpha + \beta$. Thus $\mu_j^2 < \mu_j^1$ contradicting $\mu_j^1 < \mu_j^2$. Thus we must have $x_j^1 > 1$. By (13), $x_{j1}^1 > 1$. By (iii) and $\mu_j^1 < \mu_j^2$, $x_{j2}^1 > x_{j2}^2$ which implies $x_{j2}^1 > 1$. By (ii) and (iii)

$$(x_j^1)^\beta \left(\frac{x_{j1}^1}{x_{j2}^1}\right)^{\alpha-1} = \left(\frac{x_{j1}^2}{x_{j2}^2}\right)^{\alpha-1} = \frac{\pi_{j1}}{\pi_{j2}} \tag{14}$$

Since $x_j^1 > 1$,

$$\frac{x_{j1}^1}{x_{j2}^1} > \frac{x_{j1}^2}{x_{j2}^2} \implies \frac{x_{j1}^2}{x_{j2}^2} < 1 < \frac{x_{j1}^1}{x_{j2}^2}$$

by (iv). By (14), $\pi_{j1}/\pi_{j2} > 1$ so that (i)′ holds.

Thus we have shown that there exists $\epsilon^* > 0$ such that if $a = 1$, $\beta > 0$, $0 < |\epsilon| < \epsilon^*$, then the economy has no NA equilibrium. By Proposition 23.9 the economy has no FM equilibrium.

REMARK. An intuition for the failure of existence can be given in economic terms as follows. Suppose there are no markets available for trading the two securities at date 0, namely that trading in the securities is only permitted from date 1 on. The prices are such that, viewed from date 0, rank $q(\xi_0^+) = 2$ so that the agents would have an incentive to open markets for the securities at date 0. If markets are opened at date 0 then trading alters the security prices so that rank $q(\xi_0^+) = 1$. Thus the spanning opportunities envisioned with the old prices break down.

(ii) *Existence with $a \ne 1$.* When $a \ne 1$ the CM equilibrium price vector defined by (7) is such that

$$\rho(\xi_0) = \text{rank} \begin{bmatrix} \alpha & \alpha \\ \alpha & a\alpha \end{bmatrix} = 2$$

Thus the CM equilibrium (x, π) defined by (7) is an NA equilibrium with $\rho(\xi_0) = 2$. By Proposition 23.9(ii), it corresponds to an FM equilibrium with security price vector q given by

$$q_1(\xi_0) = 2\alpha, \quad q_2(\xi_0) = \alpha(1 + a)$$

$$q(\xi_0^+) = \begin{bmatrix} q_1(\xi_1) & q_2(\xi_1) \\ q_1(\xi_2) & q_2(\xi_2) \end{bmatrix} = \begin{bmatrix} \dfrac{\alpha}{\alpha + \beta} & \dfrac{\alpha}{\alpha + \beta} \\ \dfrac{\alpha}{\alpha + \beta} & \dfrac{a\alpha}{\alpha + \beta} \end{bmatrix}$$

Since $x_{11}^i - \omega_{11}^i = x_{12}^i - \omega_{12}^i = 0$ and $x_{21}^i - \omega_{21}^i = x_{22}^i - \omega_{22}^i = 0$, the portfolios at date 1 satisfy $z^i(\xi_1) = z^i(\xi_2) = 0$, $i = 1, 2$. The portfolios at date 0 can be deduced from the equation

$$\pi \underset{\xi_0^+}{\square} (x^i - \omega^i) = \left[\pi \underset{\xi_0^+}{\square} V \right] z^i(\xi_0), \quad i = 1, 2$$

which gives

$$z^1(\xi_0) = \begin{bmatrix} z_1^1(\xi_0) \\ z_2^1(\xi_0) \end{bmatrix} = \begin{bmatrix} \alpha & \alpha \\ \alpha & a\alpha \end{bmatrix}^{-1} \begin{bmatrix} -(\alpha + \beta)\epsilon \\ (\alpha + \beta)\epsilon \end{bmatrix}$$

so that

$$z_1^1(\xi_0) = \frac{-(\alpha + \beta)\epsilon(a + 1)}{\alpha(a - 1)} = -z_1^2(\xi_0)$$

$$z_2^1(\xi_0) = \frac{(\alpha + \beta)\epsilon(a + 1)}{\alpha(a - 1)} = -z_2^2(\xi_0)$$

As $a \to 1$, the security prices at date 1 (the columns of the matrix $q(\xi_0^+)$) become close to being collinear and each agent is forced to trade more to achieve the same transfer of income. If $\epsilon > 0$ then $z_1^1(\xi_0) \to -\infty, z_2^1(\xi_0) \to +\infty$ when $a \to 1 (a > 1)$, and the Arrow-Debreu equilibrium with $\rho(\xi_0) = 2$ disappears. $\square$

25. EXISTENCE AND OPTIMALITY

In the first chapter we argued that a market structure consisting of a sequence of spot markets for trading in real goods and a system of financial markets for trading income across time and uncertainty provides a more realistic description of observed markets than the system of contingent markets. We explained that for two reasons—first to study the properties of financial markets and second to serve as a simplified version of the general model—it is of interest to study the financial submodel obtained by freezing out the spot markets.

The equilibria of this model represent the candidate predicted outcomes of trading on a system of financial markets. If the model has no equilibrium then it has no explanatory power. The model cannot therefore provide a useful tool for the analysis of financial markets, if it is a common occurrence that it has no equilibrium.

The example of the previous section has shown that for certain parameter values the economy has no financial market equilibrium: these parameter values are however exceptional. For example, if the economy is parametrized by the dividend parameter a (keeping the utility functions and endowments fixed) then the value $a = 1$ for which an equilibrium fails to exist is exceptional in the space $(0, \infty)$. We shall find that this is a general phenomenon and that a financial market equilibrium exists for most economies. The model thus has at least some explanatory power in that it provides a set of predicted outcomes for trading on financial markets for most—if not all—economies.

Existence

If all securities are short-lived, the problem of nonexistence does not arise since at each non-terminal node the rank of the payoff matrix is independent of the prices. More precisely, for any no-arbitrage price process q and any associated node prices π

$$\text{rank}\left(V(\xi^+) + q(\xi^+)\right) = \text{rank}\left(\pi \underset{\xi^+}{\square} V\right) = \text{rank}\left(V(\xi^+)\right), \quad \forall \xi \in \mathbb{D}^-$$

Thus the following analogue of Theorem 10.5 holds.

25.1 Proposition (Existence of FM Equilbrium with Short-Lived Securities):
Let $\mathscr{E}(\mathbb{D}, u, \omega, \zeta, V)$ be a stochastic finance economy satisfying Assumption $\mathscr{U}$. If $\omega^i \in \mathbb{R}^n_{++}, i = 1, \ldots I$ and if the security structure (ζ, V) is composed solely of short-lived securities, then there exists a financial market equilibrium $((\bar{x}, \bar{z}), \bar{q})$.

PROOF: The proof is the same as for Theorem 10.5. The aggregate excess demand function for a normalized no-arbitrage equilibrium satisfies properties (i)′–(v)′ in the proof of Theorem 7.4 (bounded below, continuity, homogeneity, Walras and boundary behavior, the last property being obtained from the demand function f^1 of agent 1). The existence of an NA equilibrium, which then follows from the Inward-Pointing Vector Field Theorem 7.5, implies the existence of an FM equilibrium by Proposition 23.9. □

When there are long-lived securities a precise meaning needs to be assigned to the statement that an FM equilibrium exists "for most economies". This can be done by using the mathematical technique explained in Section 11 based on the introduction of a parametrized family of economies. The idea is to consider a stochastic economy $\mathscr{E}(\mathbb{D}, u, \omega, \zeta, V)$ as an element of a family of economies, all of which have the same basic structural properties. One way in which this can be done is to leave the basic event-tree $\mathbb{D}$, the preferences (u) and the subsets of actively traded securities at each node $(J(\xi), \xi \in \mathbb{D})$ unchanged, parametrizing the economy by the agent's endowments (ω) and the dividends (V) of the actively traded securities.

To define the admissible dividend streams which respect the subsets of actively traded securities at each node, these subsets must be taken as primitive data of the economy. This leads to the following definition.

25.2 Definition: Let $\mathbf{J} = \{1, \ldots, J\}$ denote a fixed set of securities with nodes of issue $\zeta = (\xi(j), j \in \mathbf{J})$. A collection of subsets $(J(\xi), \xi \in \mathbb{D}^-)$ with $J(\xi) \subset \mathbf{J}$, $\forall \xi \in \mathbb{D}^-$ is a *collection of actively traded securities* at the non-terminal nodes of $\mathbb{D}$ if it satisfies

(i) $j \in J(\xi) \Longrightarrow \xi \in \mathbb{D}(\xi(j))$
(ii) $\xi \in \mathbb{D}(\xi(j))$ and $j \notin J(\xi) \Longrightarrow j \notin J(\xi'), \ \forall \xi' > \xi.$

Condition (i) requires that the collection $(J(\xi), \xi \in \mathbb{D})$ be compatible with the nodes of issue ζ: a security can only be traded if it has already been issued. (ii) requires that a security be traded until its maturity nodes: if a security issued before node ξ is not traded at ξ then it must have expired and is not traded thereafter.

The subsets of actively traded securities $(J_V(\xi), \xi \in \mathbb{D}^-)$ corresponding to a given financial structure (ζ, V) can be deduced from (ζ, V) by formula (1) in Section 20. Clearly $(J_V(\xi), \xi \in \mathbb{D}^-)$ satisfies (i) and (ii) in Definition 25.2. In order to obtain a family of economies in which the dividend streams of the securities can be parametrized without affecting the basic structure of the financial markets, it is natural to require that all admissible dividend streams be compatible with a given collection $(J(\xi), \xi \in \mathbb{D}^-)$ of subsets of actively traded securities. This leads to the following definition.

25.3 Definition: Let $(\mathbf{J}, \zeta, (J(\xi), \xi \in \mathbb{D}^-))$ be a set of securities with nodes of issue ζ and subsets of actively traded securities $(J(\xi), \xi \in \mathbb{D}^-)$. The *set of dividend streams* $\mathscr{V} \subset \mathbb{R}^{nJ}$ compatible with $(\mathbf{J}, \zeta, (J(\xi), \xi \in \mathbb{D}^-))$ is defined by

$$\mathscr{V} = \left\{ V = (V^j(\xi), \xi \in \mathbb{D})_{j \in \mathbf{J}} \ \middle| \ \begin{array}{l} V^j(\xi) = 0 \quad \text{if} \quad \xi \notin \mathbb{D}^+(\xi(j)) \\ J_V(\xi) \subset J(\xi), \quad \forall \xi \in \mathbb{D}^- \end{array} \right\} \tag{1}$$

When the class of securities which is being studied has more specific properties than those described by $(\mathbf{J}, \zeta, J(\xi), \xi \in \mathbb{D}^-)$, further restrictions may need to be imposed on $\mathscr{V}$. An example frequently studied in the multiperiod setting consists of an economy with J long-lived securities issued at the initial node which pay dividends only at the terminal date T. In this case the natural family of dividend streams to consider is given by

$$\mathscr{V} = \left\{ V = \left(V^j(\xi), \xi \in \mathbb{D} \right)_{j \in \mathbf{J}} \ \middle| \ V^j(\xi) = 0, \quad \forall \xi \notin \mathbb{D}_T \right\} \tag{2}$$

For fixed $(\mathbb{D}, u, \mathbf{J}, \zeta, (J(\xi), \xi \in \mathbb{D}^-))$ we are thus led to consider the family of economies

$$\left\{ \mathscr{E}_{\omega, V} \ \middle| \ (\omega, V) \in \Omega \times \mathscr{V} \right\} \tag{3}$$

parametrized by the endowment and dividend streams (ω, V) lying in the *parameter space* $\Omega \times \mathscr{V}$, where $\Omega = \mathbb{R}_{++}^{nI}$ and $\mathscr{V}$ is defined by (1), and $\mathscr{E}_{\omega, V}$ is a simplified notation for the economy $\mathscr{E}(\mathbb{D}, u, \omega, \zeta, V)$.

In the parametrized family of economies (3), the spanning opportunities offered by the financial markets are limited by the number of actively traded securities at each non-terminal node $j(\xi) = \#J(\xi)$. If for some node $\xi \in \mathbb{D}^-$, $j(\xi) < b(\xi)$, then, for all $(\omega, V) \in \Omega \times \mathscr{V}$, every equilibrium of the economy $\mathscr{E}_{\omega, V}$ has incomplete markets. If $j(\xi) \geq b(\xi)$ for all $\xi \in \mathbb{D}^-$, then whether an equilibrium $((\bar{x}, \bar{z}), \bar{q})$ of an economy $\mathscr{E}_{\omega, V}$ has complete markets depends on the rank of the payoff matrix $W(\bar{q}, V)$. This in turn depends on the equilibrium price $\bar{q}$ and the dividend process $\mathscr{V}$. A condition can be given on V which ensures that for almost all endowments ω, in every equilibrium $((\bar{x}, \bar{z}), \bar{q})$ of $\mathscr{E}_{\omega, V}$, the matrix $W(\bar{q}, V)$ has maximal rank. This condition can be stated in two equivalent ways: the simplest is the following.[1]

25.4 Definition: A dividend stream $V \in \mathscr{V}$ is *potentially complete* if there exists a vector of node prices $\pi = (\pi(\xi), \xi \in \mathbb{D}) \in \mathbb{R}^n$ such that

$$\operatorname{rank}\left(\pi \underset{\xi+}{\square} V \right) = b(\xi), \quad \forall \xi \in \mathbb{D}^-$$

It can be shown that if the payoffs (dividends plus capital values) of a given collection of securities give complete markets for *one* vector of node prices (which determine the capital values) then this collection of securities gives complete markets for *almost all* vectors of node prices. It is now possible to assign a precise meaning to the statement that an FM equilibrium exists for most economies.

---

[1] The alternative definition which can be expressed directly in terms of properties of the dividend matrix V is given in Volume 2.

25.5 Theorem (Existence of FM Equilibrium with Long-lived Securities): *Let* $\mathbb{D}$ *be an event-tree,* $u = (u^1, \ldots, u^I)$ *a family of utility functions satisfying Assumption* $\mathscr{U}$ *and* $(\mathbf{J}, \zeta, (J(\xi), \xi \in \mathbb{D}^-))$ *a set of securities with nodes of issue* ζ *and subsets of actively traded securities* $(J(\xi), \xi \in \mathbb{D}^-)$ *at each non-terminal node.*

(i) *Let* $j(\xi) \geq b(\xi)$, $\forall \xi \in \mathbb{D}^-$. *For fixed* $\omega \in \mathbb{R}_{++}^{nI}$ *there exists a set of dividend streams* $\mathscr{V}^* \subset \mathscr{V}$ *of full measure such that, for each* $V \in \mathscr{V}^*$, *the economy* $\mathscr{E}_{\omega,V}$ *has a financial market equilibrium in which markets are complete.*

(ii) *Let* $j(\xi) \geq b(\xi)$, $\forall \xi \in \mathbb{D}^-$. *For a fixed potentially complete dividend stream* $V \in \mathscr{V}$ *there exists a set of endowments* $\Omega^* \subset \Omega$ *of full measure such that, for each* $\omega \in \Omega^*$, *the economy* $\mathscr{E}_{\omega,V}$ *has a financial market equilibrium in which markets are complete.*

(iii) *Let* $j(\xi) < b(\xi)$ *for some* $\xi \in \mathbb{D}^-$. *There exists a set of endowments and dividend streams* $\triangle^* \subset \Omega \times \mathscr{V}$ *of full measure such that, for each* $(\omega, V) \in \triangle^*$, *the economy* $\mathscr{E}_{\omega,V}$ *has a financial market equilibrium.*

PROOF: (i) By Theorem 19.2 the economy $\mathscr{E}(\mathbb{D}, u, \omega)$ has a contingent market equilibrium $(\bar{x}, \bar{\pi})$ in which $\bar{\pi}$ is a vector of present-value prices. We show that this equilibrium can be used to construct a financial market equilibrium for almost all dividend streams $V \in \mathscr{V}$. For $V \in \mathscr{V}$, define the prices $\bar{q}$ of the securities as the present value (at each node) of their future stream of dividends

$$\bar{q}(\xi) = \sum_{\xi'' \in \mathbb{D}^+(\xi)} \frac{\bar{\pi}(\xi'')}{\bar{\pi}(\xi)} V^j(\xi''), \quad \forall j \in J(\xi), \quad \forall \xi \in \mathbb{D}^-$$

If V is such that the rank condition

$$\text{rank}\left(V(\xi^+) + \bar{q}(\xi^+)\right) = b(\xi), \quad \forall \xi \in \mathbb{D}^- \tag{4}$$

is satisfied, then by Proposition 22.4 and Proposition 22.6 (ii), there exist portfolios $\bar{z} = (\bar{z}^1, \ldots, \bar{z}^I)$ such that $((\bar{x}, \bar{z}), \bar{q})$ is a financial market equilibrium with complete markets for the economy $\mathscr{E}(\mathbb{D}, u, \omega, \zeta, V)$. It thus remains to prove that there exists a set of dividend streams $\mathscr{V}^* \subset \mathscr{V}$ of full measure such that the rank condition (4) is satisfied.

Since $\mathbb{D}^-$ has a finite number of nodes and since a finite union of sets of measure zero is a set of measure zero, it suffices to prove that, for each node ξ in $\mathbb{D}^-$, the subset of dividend streams in $\mathscr{V}$ such that

$$\text{rank}\left(V(\xi^+) + q(\xi^+)\right) < b(\xi) \tag{5}$$

is of measure zero. Since

$$\text{rank}\left(V(\xi^+) + q(\xi^+)\right) = \text{rank}\left[\pi(\xi')\left(V^j(\xi') + q_j(\xi')\right)\right]_{\substack{\xi' \in \xi^+ \\ j \in J(\xi)}}$$

$$= \text{rank}\left[\pi \underset{\xi'}{\cdot} V^j\right]_{\substack{\xi' \in \xi^+ \\ j \in J(\xi)}}$$

(5) is equivalent to the existence, for each subset $\tilde{J} \subset J(\xi)$ consisting of $b(\xi)$ securities, of coefficients $(\lambda_j, j \in \tilde{J})$ such that

$$\sum_{j \in \tilde{J}} \lambda_j \bar{\pi} \underset{\xi'}{\cdot} V^j = 0, \quad \forall \xi' \in \xi^+$$

$$\sum_{j \in \tilde{J}} \lambda_j^2 = 1 \tag{6}$$

where the last equation ensures that the linear combination is nontrivial. Since there are only a finite number of subsets of $J(\xi)$ with $b(\xi)$ elements, it suffices to show that for a given subset $\tilde{J} \subset J(\xi)$, the set of $V \in \mathscr{V}$ such that (6) has a solution in λ is of measure zero.

Note that the set of dividend streams $\mathscr{V}$ is isomorphic to $\mathbb{R}^K$ where K is the number of components of a dividend stream $V \in \mathscr{V}$ which are not required to be zero in the definition of $\mathscr{V}$ in (1). Consider $h : \mathbb{R}^{b(\xi)} \times \mathscr{V} \longrightarrow \mathbb{R}^{b(\xi)+1}$ defined by

$$h_{\xi'}(\lambda, V) = \sum_{j \in \tilde{J}} \lambda_j \bar{\pi} \underset{\xi'}{\cdot} V^j, \quad \forall \xi' \in \xi^+$$

$$h_{b(\xi)+1} = \sum_{j \in \tilde{J}} \lambda_j^2 - 1$$

Then (6) can be written as

$$h(\lambda, V) = 0 \tag{7}$$

which is a system of $b(\xi) + 1$ equations in the $b(\xi)$ unknowns $(\lambda_j, j \in \tilde{J})$ parametrized by the dividends $V \in \mathscr{V}$. We are now in a position to apply the technique explained in Section 11. If we show that for every $(\bar{\lambda}, \bar{V})$ satisfying (7)

$$\text{rank}\left[D_{\lambda, V} h(\bar{\lambda}, \bar{V})\right] = b(\xi) + 1 \tag{8}$$

then by Theorem 11.3, there exists a set $\mathscr{V}' \subset \mathscr{V}$ of full measure such that if $V \in \mathscr{V}'$, then (7) has no solution in λ. To prove (8) it suffices to show that for each vector e of the canonical basis for $\mathbb{R}^{b(\xi)+1}$, there exists $(d\lambda, dV)$ such that

$$\left[D_{\lambda, V} h(\bar{\lambda}, \bar{V})\right](d\lambda, dV) = e$$

namely that each of the $b(\xi) + 1$ equations in (7) can be locally controlled independently of the others. To control the equation corresponding to node ξ' choose j' such that $\bar{\lambda}_{j'} \neq 0$ (where j' exists since the last equation of (6) is satisfied by $\bar{\lambda}$). Then

$$d\lambda = 0, \quad dV^{j'}(\xi') = 1/\bar{\lambda}_{j'}, \quad dV^{j}(\xi'') = 0 \text{ if } j \neq j' \text{ or } \xi'' \neq \xi'$$

gives the required increment. To control the last equation, let $d\lambda_{j'} = 1/(2\bar{\lambda}_{j'})$, $d\lambda_j = 0$ if $j \neq j'$, choosing $dV^{j'}(\xi')$ such that $d\lambda_{j'}V^{j'}(\xi') + \bar{\lambda}_{j'}dV^{j'}(\xi') = 0$, $\forall \xi' \in \xi^+$, and $dV^{j}(\xi'') = 0$ if $j \neq j'$ or $\xi'' \notin \xi^+$.

By taking all $b(\xi)$-element subsets $\tilde{J} \subset J(\xi)$ and applying the above argument over all nodes $\xi \in \mathbb{D}^-$ and forming the intersection of all the sets $\mathscr{V}'$ obtained in this way leads to the set $\mathscr{V}'^*$ with the desired property.

Since the proof of (i) depends only on the existence of a contingent market equilibrium for the economy $\mathscr{E}(\mathbb{D}, u, \omega)$ and not on the differentiability of agents' demand functions, Assumption $\mathscr{U}$ (which is needed in the proof of (ii) and (iii)) can be weakened to Assumption $\mathscr{U}'$. Furthermore the proof applies even if additional restrictions are placed on the set $\mathscr{V}$ (for example as in (2)) provided that each actively traded security at node ξ has one component of its dividend stream which can be perturbed in each subtree $\mathbb{D}(\xi')$ for each successor ξ' in ξ^+.

(ii) The proof of (i) is particularly simple because the characteristics $(\mathbb{D}, u, \omega)$ are fixed and a contingent market equilibrium $(\bar{x}, \bar{\pi})$ of the economy $\mathscr{E}(\mathbb{D}, u, \omega)$ provides appropriate state prices $\bar{\pi}$ for constructing an FM equilibrium with complete markets for almost all $V \in \mathscr{V}$. In (ii) the characteristics $(\mathbb{D}, u, \zeta, V)$ are fixed with V potentially complete. Some equilibrium analysis is required to show that for almost all vectors of endowments ω, an FM equilibrium with complete markets of $\mathscr{E}(\mathbb{D}, u, \omega, \zeta, V)$ can be constructed from a CM equilibrium of $\mathscr{E}(\mathbb{D}, u, \omega)$. The first step is to show that if V is potentially complete then the vectors $(\pi \;_{\square\xi^+} V^j)_{j \in J(\xi)}$ have rank $b(\xi)$ for almost all state prices $\pi \in \mathbb{R}^n_{++}$. This part of the proof is similar to the proof in (i). The second step is to show that the set of endowment vectors which yield CM equilibria $(\bar{x}, \bar{\pi})$ such that $\bar{\pi}$ lies in the set of exceptional prices for which the rank condition is not satisfied, is of measure zero. This part of the proof draws on properties of what is known as the *equilibrium manifold* (of CM equilibria), whose analysis requires techniques of differential topology which will be studied in Volume 2. The proof of (ii) is thus postponed to Volume 2.

(iii) The proof of (iii) requires more powerful techniques than the proofs of (i) and (ii), since it can no longer be based on the existence and properties of a CM equilibrium. The mathematical approach, based on degree theory, which has been developed for proving generic existence of equilibrium with incomplete markets will be explained in Volume 2. □

The results of Theorem 25.5 can be explained as follows. When markets are potentially complete ((i) or (ii)), if for some combination of the parameters $(\mathbb{D}, u, \omega, \zeta, V)$, the economy has no FM equilibrium, as in the example of Section 24, then it is sufficient to perturb slightly either the dividend streams or the endowments of the agents to re-establish existence of an equilibrium. When markets are incomplete ((iii)), existence of an equilibrium can be re-established by perturbing slightly both the agents' endowments and the dividend streams.

Since the endowments of the agents are a proxy for their income accruing from the productive services that they own (such as their labor) the economic model does not in general impose any precise conditions on the endowments. A result such as (ii), which holds for almost all endowments, is thus relatively satisfactory. For certain types of securities, such as equity, where the profile of income accruing from a security has no particular structure, it does not seem too restrictive to perturb the dividend stream to obtain existence of an equilibrium. However for other types of securities, such as bonds or futures contracts which have a specific profile of income across the nodes, a perturbation of the dividend stream (of the type required by (i) and (iii)) pushes the security out of the class under consideration and is thus not a satisfactory way of establishing existence.

A more refined version of the existence result (iii) has been developed (the analogue of (ii) for incomplete markets). It can be shown that even if markets are incomplete, there exists a class of dividend streams $\tilde{\mathscr{V}} \subset \mathscr{V}$ such that, for a fixed $V \in \tilde{\mathscr{V}}$, the economy $\mathscr{E}_{\omega,V}$ has an FM equilibrium for almost all $\omega \in \Omega$. Since the definition of the subset $\tilde{\mathscr{V}}$ is somewhat involved, the precise statement of this proposition is postponed to Volume 2.

Optimality

Some of the unintuitive properties of the model of equilibrium on financial markets arise from the fact that the dimension of the market subspace can change when the security prices change. This can either lead to nonexistence of equilibrium, as we saw in Section 24, or to the existence of several equilibria for the same economy, in which the payoff matrix W has a different rank. The following example exhibits an economy with a potentially complete dividend stream which has two equilibria. The first has complete markets and is hence Pareto optimal; in the second, markets are incomplete and the allocation is inefficient.

25.6 Example: Consider the example of Section 24. It was shown that when $a \neq 1$ the contingent market equilibrium defined by (7) in Section 24 corresponds to a financial market equilibrium. It was also shown that an equilibrium in which the prices of the two securities are proportional at nodes ξ_1 and ξ_2, so that $\rho(\xi_0) = 1$, is such that there is no trade in the securities at date 0. The state prices and consumption vectors must then satisfy equations (11) and (i)–(iv) of Section 24, which express the equilibrium conditions for the $\mathbb{D}(\xi_1)$ and $\mathbb{D}(\xi_2)$ subtree economies. Let $(\pi_1^*, \pi_{11}^*, \pi_{12}^*)$ be an equilibrium price for the $\mathbb{D}(\xi_1)$ economy, and let $(\pi_2^*, \pi_{21}^*, \pi_{22}^*)$ be an equilibrium price for the $\mathbb{D}(\xi_2)$ economy. If the payoff a on the second security is chosen so that

$$a = \frac{\pi_{12}^*}{\pi_{11}^*} \frac{\pi_{21}^*}{\pi_{22}^*} \tag{9}$$

then the matrix $\pi \circ_{\xi_0^+} A$, given by (6) in Section 24, has rank 1. Thus for the value of the parameter a given by (9), in addition to the equilibrium with complete markets, there is an equilibrium with incomplete markets ($\rho(\xi_0) = 1$). The latter equilibrium is Pareto inefficient, since the inequalities (12) in Section 24 imply that the two agents' marginal utility vectors (μ_1^1, μ_2^1) and (μ_1^2, μ_2^2) are not proportional. $\square$

In this example the low rank equilibrium occurs only for an exceptional parameter value. This is a general phenomenon: when markets are potentially complete, almost all economies have only Pareto optimal equilibria. Just as existence can be re-established either by perturbing the dividend streams or by perturbing the endowments, so low-rank equilibria can be eliminated by similar perturbations.

25.7 Theorem (Pareto Optimality with Potentially Complete Securities): *Let $\mathbb{D}$ be an event-tree, $u = (u^1, \ldots, u^I)$ a family of utility functions satisfying Assumption $\mathscr{U}$, and $(\mathbf{J}, \zeta, (J(\xi), \xi \in \mathbb{D}^-))$ a set of securities with nodes of issue ζ and subsets of actively traded securities $(J(\xi), \xi \in \mathbb{D}^-)$ at each non-terminal node.*

(i) *Let $j(\xi) \geq b(\xi)$, $\forall \xi \in \mathbb{D}^-$. For fixed $\omega \in \mathbb{R}_{++}^{nI}$, there exists a set of dividend streams $\mathscr{V}^{**} \subset \mathscr{V}$ of full measure such that, for each $V \in \mathscr{V}^{**}$, every financial market equilibrium of the economy $\mathscr{E}_{\omega,V}$ is Pareto optimal.*

(ii) *Let $V \in \mathscr{V}$ be potentially complete. Then there exists a set of endowments $\Omega^{**} \subset \Omega$ of full measure such that, for each $\omega \in \Omega^{**}$, every financial market equilibrium of the economy $\mathscr{E}_{\omega,V}$ is Pareto optimal.*

PROOF: The proof of this theorem is relatively difficult: it must be shown that the set of dividend streams (for (i)) or endowments (for (ii)), for which there exist FM equilibria with rank $(V(\xi^+) + q(\xi^+)) < b(\xi)$ for some node ξ, is of measure zero. Even though the dividend stream is potentially complete, the CM equilibria do not help in studying the FM equilibria for which markets are incomplete, so that the approach used in proving Theorem 25.5 (i) and (ii) is no longer applicable. A direct analysis of the properties of FM equilibria with incomplete markets has to be made, and this is postponed to Volume 2. □

When the dividend stream is not potentially complete, then markets are incomplete, since for all node prices π there exists a node ξ where the rank of $\pi \mathbin{\square}_{\xi+} V$ is less than $b(\xi)$. Since there are not enough markets to equalize the present-value vectors of the agents, for most economies the financial market equilibria are not Pareto optimal. For an FM equilibrium $((\bar{x}, \bar{z}), \bar{q})$, let $\bar{\pi}^i = \pi^i(\bar{x}^i)$ denote the present-value vector of agent i at $\bar{x}^i$: $\bar{\pi}^i = \bar{\lambda}^i / \bar{\lambda}^i_0$ with $\bar{\lambda}^i = \nabla u^i(\bar{x}^i)$, $i = 1, \ldots, I$. The following result is the analogue of Theorem 11.6 for multiperiod economies.

25.8 Theorem (Pareto Inefficiency with Incomplete Markets):

Let $(\mathbb{D}, u, (\mathbf{J}, \zeta, (J(\xi), \ \xi \in \mathbb{D}^-)))$ *be as in Theorem 25.7. If* $j(\xi) < b(\xi)$ *for some* $\xi \in \mathbb{D}^-$ *and* $I \geq 2$, *then there exists a set of endowments and dividend streams* $\Delta^{**} \subset \Omega \times \mathscr{V}$ *such that, if* $(\omega, V) \in \Delta^{**}$, *then in each financial market equilibrium of the economy* $\mathscr{E}_{\omega, V}$ *the present-value vectors of all agents are distinct*

$$\bar{\pi}^i \neq \bar{\pi}^j, \quad \forall i \neq j$$

and the equilibrium allocation is Pareto inefficient.

PROOF: Although the proof is similar in spirit to the proof of Theorem 11.6, there is a problem with the differentiability (even with the continuity) of the agents' demand functions for securities at prices q for which there is a change in the rank of the matrix $W(q, V)$. The methods for coping with this type of difficulty will be explained in Volume 2. □

Constrained Inefficiency

Theorem 25.8 is hardly surprising: with missing markets we do not expect agents' present-value vectors to be equalized. If, for reasons that are exogenous to the model,[2] it is not possible to introduce enough financial instruments to complete the markets, then the most relevant question is whether the trading of securities on the competitive markets that do exist leads to the best allocation that can be expected from such a set of financial instruments.

To formalize the idea of efficiency of a system of markets, it is convenient to introduce a fictional planner who has access to a set of "feasible allocations":

---

[2]The reasons for the incompleteness of markets were discussed at some length in Chapter 1.

if by choosing one of these he can make agents better off than in a equilibrium, then we say that the equilibrium allocation is inefficient. If the planner has access to the standard feasible allocations, then this procedure leads to the test of *Pareto optimality* of an equilibrium allocation. As we have just seen, when markets are incomplete, a financial market equilibrium will typically not pass this test: the planner has more freedom to allocate income across date-events than is provided by the system of financial markets. To obtain a more relevant test of efficiency, when markets are incomplete, the "feasible alloca-tions" available to the planner must be constrained in a way that reflects the restricted ability of the available financial instruments to redistribute income across date-events.

Suppose therefore that the planner is constrained to influencing the alloca-tion exclusively at date 0. He can choose the consumption and portfolio (x_0^i, z_0^i) of each agent at date 0, and thereafter the economy operates free of all inter-vention: all exchanges after date 0 take place in the standard way through the available financial markets. This certainly guarantees that the allocation after date 0 is obtained by using the existing financial markets. An allocation obtained in this way, with the planner choosing the date 0 plans (x_0^i, z_0^i) and the agents choosing optimal plans $\left(x^i(\xi), z^i(\xi), \xi \in \mathbb{D}^+ \right)$ thereafter and facing equilibrium prices $(q(\xi), \xi \in \mathbb{D}^+)$, will be called a *constrained feasible alloca-tion*. To make this definition precise, define the budget set of agent i once the planner has chosen (x_0^i, z_0^i) and the agent is faced with the (after date 0) prices $\hat{q} = (q(\xi), \xi \in \mathbb{D}^+)$

$$\widehat{\mathbb{B}}(x_0^i, z_0^i, \hat{q}) = \left\{ x^i \in \mathbb{R}_+^n \ \middle| \ \begin{array}{l} x^i(\xi_0) = x_0^i \text{ and, for all } \xi \in \mathbb{D}^+, \\ x^i(\xi) - \omega^i(\xi) = (V(\xi) + q(\xi)) \, z^i(\xi^-) - q(\xi) z^i(\xi) \\ \text{for some } z^i \in \mathscr{Z} \text{ with } z^i(\xi_0) = z_0^i \end{array} \right\}$$

To simplify the expression for the budget set $\widehat{\mathbb{B}}$, the budget equations at the terminal nodes $(t(\xi) = T)$ are not written out explicitly. However since $q(\xi) = 0$ at any terminal node, the budget equation at such a node reduces to $x^i(\xi) - \omega^i(\xi) = V(\xi) z^i(\xi^-)$. Note also that the vector of prices $\hat{q}$ does not have any date 0 component since the date 0 allocation is decided by the planner.

25.9 Definition: An allocation $x = (x^1, \ldots, x^I) \in \mathbb{R}_+^{nI}$ is *constrained feasible* if there exist

  (a) a date 0 plan $(x_0, z_0) = (x_0^1, \ldots, x_0^I, z_0^1, \ldots, z_0^I)$ with $\sum_{i=1}^{I}(x_0^i - \omega_0^i) = 0$ and $\sum_{i=1}^{I} z_0^i = 0$
  (b) after date 0 prices $\hat{q} = (q(\xi), \xi \in \mathbb{D}^+)$

such that x satisfies

  (i) $x^i = \arg \max \left\{ u^i(\tilde{x}^i) \ \middle| \ \tilde{x}^i \in \widehat{\mathbb{B}}(x_0^i, z_0^i, \hat{q}) \right\}$, $i = 1, \ldots, I$

(ii) $\sum_{i=1}^{I} \left(x^i(\xi) - \omega^i(\xi) \right) = 0, \; \xi \in \mathbb{D}^+$

An allocation $\bar{x}$ is *constrained Pareto optimal (CPO)* or *constrained efficient* if

(i) $\bar{x}$ is constrained feasible
(ii) there does not exist a constrained feasible allocation x such that, for all $i = 1, \ldots, I$, $u^i(x^i) \geq u^i(\bar{x}^i)$, with strict inequality for at least one i.

In the case of a two-period economy $(T = 1)$, this definition of a constrained feasible and a constrained Pareto optimal allocation coincides with that given in Definitions 12.1 and 12.2. When $T = 1$, since securities are not traded after date 0, their prices are zero, $\hat{q} = (q(\xi), \xi \in \mathbb{D}^+) = 0$: the consumption vector of agent i is thus completely determined once (x_0^i, z_0^i) has been chosen. The budget set $\widehat{\mathbb{B}}$ of agent i is simply a function of (x_0^i, z_0^i)

$$\widehat{\mathbb{B}}(x_0^i, z_0^i) = \left\{ x^i \in \mathbb{R}_+^n \; \middle| \; \begin{array}{c} x^i(\xi_0) = x_0^i \\ x^i(\xi) - \omega^i(\xi) = V(\xi) z_0^i, \quad \forall \xi \in \xi_0^+ \end{array} \right\} \tag{10}$$

With two periods, constraining the planner to the choice of (x_0^i, z_0^i) ensures that the planner has no more ability to redistribute income at date 1 than is permitted by the financial markets. However, when there are more than two periods, the income transfers achievable through the financial markets are not well-defined without equilibrium prices for the securities. To cope with this difficulty, the definition of a constrained Pareto optimum restricts the planner's interference to a minimum—the choice of consumption and portfolio plans at date 0—leaving the remainder of the allocation to be determined by equilibrium on the financial markets. Thus unlike the definition of a Pareto optimum, the definition of a constrained Pareto optimum for a multiperiod economy is not independent of market prices.

It is easy to see that if $((\bar{x}, \bar{z}), \bar{q})$ is a financial market equilibrium, then the allocation $\bar{x}$ is constrained feasible (with respect to the choice $(\bar{x}_0, \bar{z}_0)$ at date 0 and the equilibrium prices $(\bar{q}(\xi), \xi \in \mathbb{D}^+)$ after date 0). If the allocation $\bar{x}$ is to be constrained efficient, then in particular there must not be any *local* changes that are feasible for a "constrained planner" which can improve the welfare of all agents in the economy. More precisely, it must not be possible to find marginal changes at date 0

$$(dx_0, dz_0) \in \mathbb{R}^{2I} \quad \text{with} \quad \sum_{i=1}^{I} dx_0^i = 0, \quad \sum_{i=1}^{I} dz_0^i = 0 \tag{11}$$

which, after adjustments of the subsequent equilibrium plans and prices

$$\left(dx(\xi), dz(\xi); dq(\xi), \xi \in \mathbb{D}^+ \right) \tag{12}$$

around the equilibrium $((\bar{x}, \bar{z}), \bar{q})$, lead to an increase in the welfare of all agents.

To check if an equilibrium allocation has this property, let us compute the effect of marginal changes (11) at date 0 on the welfare of the agents. The date 0 changes (dx_0, dz_0) induce the agents to revise their subsequent portfolio holdings, and this in turn leads to changes $(dq(\xi), \xi \in \mathbb{D}^+)$ in the equilibrium prices. If $\left(dx^i(\xi), \xi \in \mathbb{D}^+\right)$ is the optimal response of agent i to

$$\left(dx_0^i, dz_0^i, \left(dq(\xi), \xi \in \mathbb{D}^+\right)\right)$$

then the change in agent i's utility is given by

$$du^i = \bar{\lambda}_0^i dx_0^i + \sum_{\xi \in \mathbb{D}^+} \bar{\lambda}^i(\xi) dx^i(\xi) \tag{13}$$

where $\bar{\lambda}_0^i = \partial u^i(\bar{x}^i)/\partial x_0^i$, $\bar{\lambda}^i(\xi) = \partial u^i(\bar{x}^i)/\partial x^i(\xi)$, $\xi \in \mathbb{D}^+$. If we let $\bar{\pi}^i = \bar{\lambda}^i/\bar{\lambda}_0^i = \left(1, \bar{\pi}^i(\xi), \xi \in \mathbb{D}^+\right)$ denote the present-value vector of agent i at the equilibrium, then (13) can be written as

$$\frac{du^i}{\bar{\lambda}_0^i} = dx_0^i + \sum_{\xi \in \mathbb{D}^+} \bar{\pi}^i(\xi) dx^i(\xi) \tag{14}$$

To simplify the analysis let us assume that *the utility function u^i of each agent is separable between node ξ_0 and the remaining nodes*, that is u^i is of the form

$$u^i(x^i) = u_0^i(x_0^i) + u_1^i\left(\left(x^i(\xi), \xi \in \mathbb{D}^+\right)\right)$$

Then the change dx_0^i in agent i's date 0 consumption affects the utility of agent i, but not the optimal response $\left(dx^i(\xi), \xi \in \mathbb{D}^+\right)$ after date 0, which is influenced only by dz_0^i: the change dz_0^i affects the wealth of agent i at the immediate successors of ξ_0

$$\omega^i(\xi) + (V(\xi) + q(\xi))\, z^i(\xi_0), \quad \xi \in \xi_0^+$$

and hence influences the consumption-portfolio choice $\left(dx^i(\xi), dz^i(\xi), \xi \in \mathbb{D}^+\right)$ after date 0.

Let us assume that the planner's marginal change (dx_0, dz_0) induces a marginal change

$$\left((dx(\xi), dz(\xi)), dq(\xi), \xi \in \mathbb{D}^+\right)$$

in the equilibrium[3] after date 0. Differentiating the budget constraints of each agent from date 1 on gives, for all $i = 1, \ldots, I$ and all $\xi \in \mathbb{D}^+$

$$dx^i(\xi) = \left(V(\xi) + \bar{q}(\xi)\right) dz^i(\xi^-) + dq(\xi) \left(\bar{z}^i(\xi^-) - \bar{z}^i(\xi)\right) - \bar{q}(\xi)dz^i(\xi) \quad (15)$$

where

$$dz^i(\xi^-) = dz_0^i \quad \text{if} \quad t(\xi) = 1, \quad dz^i(\xi) = \bar{z}^i(\xi) = 0 \quad \text{if} \quad t(\xi) = T \quad (16)$$

and $\bar{q}(\xi) = dq(\xi) = 0$ if $t(\xi) = T$. Using (14)–(16) and the first-order conditions of the agents at the equilibrium

$$\bar{\pi}^i(\xi)\bar{q}(\xi) = \sum_{\xi' \in \xi^+} \bar{\pi}^i(\xi') \left(V(\xi') + q(\xi')\right), \quad \forall \xi \in \mathbb{D}^+ \quad (17)$$

gives for $i = 1, \ldots, I$

$$
\begin{aligned}
\frac{du^i}{\bar{\lambda}_0^i} = {} & dx_0^i + \sum_{\xi \in \xi_0^+} \bar{\pi}^i(\xi) \left(V(\xi) + \bar{q}(\xi)\right) dz_0^i \\
& + \sum_{\xi \in \mathbb{D}^+} \bar{\pi}^i(\xi) dq(\xi) \left(\bar{z}^i(\xi^-) - \bar{z}^i(\xi)\right)
\end{aligned}
\quad (18)
$$

(18) expresses the change in an agent's utility as a sum of three terms:[4] the first two terms are the *direct effect* on agent i's utility arising from the change (dx_0^i, dz_0^i) in the agent's date 0 consumption and portfolio, the last term is the *indirect effect* arising from the change in the market clearing prices $(dq(\xi), \xi \in \mathbb{D}^+)$. By changing the agent's initial portfolio (dz_0^i), the planner changes the initial wealth of the agent at the immediate successors ξ of ξ_0 by $\left(V(\xi) + q(\xi)\right) dz_0^i$ and the second term in (18) is the present value to agent i of this changed profile of date 1 income. Since $\bar{q}(\xi_0) = \sum_{\xi \in \xi_0^+} \bar{\pi}^i(\xi) \left(V(\xi) + q(\xi)\right)$, if the planner chooses (dx_0^i, dz_0^i) so that $dx_0^i = -\bar{q}(\xi_0)dz_0^i$, then the date 0 change in consumption dx_0^i exactly compensates the date 1 wealth effect so that there is no direct effect. For arbitrary changes (dx_0^i, dz_0^i) it is convenient to express dx_0^i as a sum of two components by defining dt^i by the equation

$$dx_0^i = -\bar{q}(\xi_0)dz_0^i + dt^i \quad (19)$$

---

[3]Using techniques of equilibrium theory, it can be shown that for most economies, plans and prices are differentiable around any equilibrium (see Volume 2).

[4]Since the first-order conditions (17) are satisfied at the equilibrium, the local response $(dz^i(\xi), \xi \in \mathbb{D}^+)$ of agent i after date 0 does not directly contribute (to terms of first order) to the local change in utility du^i. This could have been deduced from the Envelope Theorem: because of the maximum property of the equilibrium portfolios, local changes in these portfolios do not lead to a change in utility.

dt^i is the present value to agent i of the direct effect and may be called the *pure transfer* to agent i. Using the variables (dz_0^i, dt^i) agent i's change in utility can be expressed as the sum of the direct and indirect effects

$$\frac{du^i}{\bar{\lambda}_0^i} = dt^i + \sum_{\xi \in \mathbb{D}^+} \bar{\pi}^i(\xi) dq(\xi) \left(\bar{z}^i(\xi^-) - \bar{z}^i(\xi) \right) \tag{20}$$

If we let $dt = (dt^1, \ldots, dt^I)$ denote the vector of pure transfers, then the planner's marginal changes (dx_0, dz_0) satisfying (11) can be expressed equivalently as marginal changes (dz_0, dt) satisfying

$$(dz_0, dt) \in \mathbb{R}^{2I} \quad \text{with} \quad \sum_{i=1}^{I} dz_0^i = 0, \quad \sum_{i=1}^{I} dt^i = 0 \tag{21}$$

the associated vector of date 0 increments dx_0 being given by (19).

If the social welfare is measured by the weighted sum[5] $\sum_{i=1}^{I} \left(\frac{1}{\bar{\lambda}_0^i} \right) u^i(x^i)$, then for any feasible change (dz_0, dt) satisfying (21), the marginal change in social welfare is

$$\sum_{i=1}^{I} \left(\frac{1}{\bar{\lambda}_0^i} \right) du^i = \sum_{i=1}^{I} \sum_{\xi \in \mathbb{D}^+} \bar{\pi}^i(\xi) dq(\xi) \left(\bar{z}^i(\xi^-) - \bar{z}^i(\xi) \right) \tag{22}$$

Under the assumption of node ξ_0 separability of the agents' utility functions, the change in social welfare (22) depends only on dz_0: dt does not influence the response of agents after date 0 and thus does not affect the change $(dq(\xi), \xi \in \mathbb{D}^+)$ in market clearing prices. Let us show that if a feasible change in the initial portfolios dz_0 induces a non-zero change in the social welfare (22), then a vector of pure transfers $dt = (dt^1, \ldots, dt^I)$ of income among the agents can always be found such that the utility of each agent is increased. For suppose $dz_0 \in \mathbb{R}^I$ satisfying $\sum_{i=1}^{I} dz_0^i = 0$ induces changes such that

$$\sum_{i=1}^{I} \sum_{\xi \in \mathbb{D}^+} \bar{\pi}^i(\xi) dq(\xi) \left(\bar{z}^i(\xi^-) - \bar{z}^i(\xi) \right) = \epsilon > 0 \tag{23}$$

---

[5]This welfare function assigns the same value to one additional unit of income for each agent in the economy. In the public economics literature a marginal change in the economic environment which increases the value of this function is said to satisfy the *Hicks-Kaldor criterion* for an improvement in social welfare. As shown in the specific context that we are studying, such a change can always induce, with appropriate transfers, an increase in the utility of each agent in the economy.

If the transfers are defined by

$$dt^i = - \sum_{\xi \in \mathbb{D}^+} \bar{\pi}^i(\xi) dq(\xi) \left(\bar{z}^i(\xi^-) - \bar{z}^i(\xi) \right) + \frac{\epsilon}{I}$$

then by (23), $\sum_{i=1}^I dt^i = 0$ and by (20)

$$\frac{du^i}{\bar{\lambda}_0^i} = \frac{\epsilon}{I} > 0, \quad i = 1, \dots, I$$

so that (dz_0, dt) leads to a Pareto improvement relative to the equilibrium allocation. If dz_0 induces a change such that the sum in (23) is negative and equal to $-\epsilon$, then, by linearity of the differential, $-dz_0$ induces a positive change in social welfare, so that the utility of all agents can be increased by choosing appropriate pure transfers dt associated with the change in initial portfolios $-dz_0$. Thus, under the assumption of node ξ_0 separability of the agents' utility functions, *a necessary condition for a financial market equilibrium to be constrained Pareto optimal is that*

$$\sum_{i=1}^I \sum_{\xi \in \mathbb{D}^+} \bar{\pi}^i(\xi) dq(\xi) \left(\bar{z}^i(\xi^-) - \bar{z}^i(\xi) \right) = 0,$$

$$\text{for all } dz_0 \in \mathbb{R}^I, \text{ with } \sum_{i=1}^I dz_0^i = 0 \tag{24}$$

namely, that the marginal change in social welfare induced by any locally constrained feasible reallocation around the equilibrium be zero.

(24) suggests that it may be possible to find a feasible reallocation (dz_0, dt) which *improves the welfare of all agents* at an equilibrium $((\bar{x}, \bar{z}), \bar{q})$ if, for some node ξ after date 0 ($\xi \in \mathbb{D}^+$), the following three conditions are satisfied:

(i) there are two (or more) agents whose equilibrium valuations of income at this node differ ($\bar{\pi}^i(\xi) \neq \bar{\pi}^k(\xi)$ for some $i \neq k$): for if $\bar{\pi}^i(\xi) = \bar{\pi}(\xi)$, $\forall \xi \in \mathbb{D}^+$, $i = 1, \dots, I$, then the market-clearing equations $\sum_{i=1}^I \bar{z}^i(\xi) = 0$, $\forall \xi \in \mathbb{D}$ imply that (24) is automatically satisfied;

(ii) there is a reallocation (dz_0) of the initial portfolios which changes the price of some actively traded security at this node ($dq_j(\xi) \neq 0$ for some j);

(iii) agents i and k in (i) trade security j in (ii) at the equilibrium ($\bar{z}_j^i(\xi^-) \neq \bar{z}_j^i(\xi)$, $\bar{z}_j^k(\xi^-) \neq \bar{z}_j^k(\xi)$).

If (i)–(iii) hold, then the gains to some agents arising from a reallocation of the initial portfolios may be sufficient to outweigh the losses incurred by other agents, so that after appropriate transfers from gainers to loosers, all agents are better off than at the equilibrium.

Note however that there are subclasses of economies for which one of the conditions (i)–(iii) cannot be satisfied so that an FM equilibrium is *always constrained Pareto optimal*.

(a) *complete markets:* If $((\bar{x}, \bar{z}), \bar{q})$ is an FM equilibrium with complete markets ($\text{rank}[V(\xi^+) + q(\xi^+)] = b(\xi)$ for all $\xi \in \mathbb{D}^-$), then $\bar{\pi}^i(\xi) = \bar{\pi}(\xi)$, $\forall \xi \in \mathbb{D}$, $i = 1, \ldots, I$, so that (i) is not satisfied. In this case not only is the equilibrium allocation constrained Pareto optimal, it is in addition Pareto optimal. This situation is typical if there are enough actively traded securities at each node to cover immediately succeeding contingencies ($j(\xi) \geq b(\xi)$, $\forall \xi \in \mathbb{D}^-$).

(b) *two-periods:* if $T = 1$, then $dq(\xi) = \bar{q}(\xi) = 0$ for all $\xi \in \mathbb{D}^+$, since $\mathbb{D}^+$ consists of the terminal nodes at date 1. In this case, (ii) is not satisfied. Since the securities are not traded after date 0, there is no way for a reallocation of initial portfolios to affect subsequent security prices. This explains why an equilibrium of a two-period economy is always constrained efficient (Theorem 12.3). It also suggests that some caution must be exercised in drawing general conclusions from the two-period model.

(c) *identical homothetic preferences:* if all agents have identical homothetic preferences, then the equilibrium prices of securities do not depend on the distribution of income among the agents. In this case, it is again (ii) which is not satisfied. This is definitely a hairline case if heterogeneity among agents is viewed as typical.

(d) *no-trade:* if the initial endowment is Pareto optimal, then agents will not trade on the financial markets. In this case, (iii) is not satisfied. The circumstances in which there is no trade at an equilibrium are also exceptional.

(e) *single agent:* if there is only one (type) of agent in the economy, then there cannot be any difference in agents' present-value vectors, so that (i) is not satisfied. In this case, even if markets are incomplete, (24) is automat-

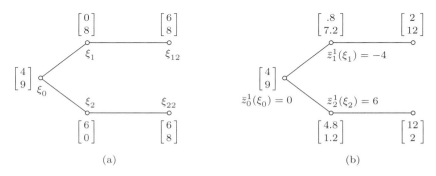

Figure 25.1 (a) Event-tree and initial endowments; (b) equilibrium consumption and portfolios for Example 25.10.

ically satisfied. This is also a special case of (d) since there is no trade at an equilibrium. The assumption that there is only one (type) of agent in an economy with financial contracts is not natural, since financial markets only emerge when there are two or more distinct types of agents for whom trade is mutually advantageous. The single agent assumption is not restrictive however in economies with complete markets if this single agent is understood to be a stand-in *representative agent* (as studied in Section 16). But in this case the property of constrained Pareto optimality of an equilibrium can be deduced from (a).

It can be shown that *condition (24) is typically not satisfied at an FM equilibrium of a multiperiod economy ($T \geq 2$) with heterogeneous agents and incomplete markets: in such economies equilibria are thus typically constrained inefficient.* A formal proof requires techniques of differential topology similar to those explained in Section 11; these techniques are developed in more detail in Volume 2. An understanding of the way in which a reallocation of initial portfolios can improve on an equilibrium allocation can however be explained by a simple example.

25.10 Example: Consider an economy $\mathscr{E}(\mathbb{D}, u, \omega, \zeta, V)$ over three time periods, with the event-tree $\mathbb{D}$ shown in Figure 25.1(a). There are two (types of) agents whose endowments are also shown in Figure 25.1(a)

$$\omega^1 = \left(\omega^1(\xi_0), \omega^1(\xi_1), \omega^1(\xi_2), \omega^1(\xi_{12}), \omega^1(\xi_{22})\right) = (4, 0, 6, 6, 6)$$
$$\omega^2 = \left(\omega^2(\xi_0), \omega^2(\xi_1), \omega^2(\xi_2), \omega^2(\xi_{12}), \omega^2(\xi_{22})\right) = (9, 8, 0, 8, 8)$$

The only uncertainty faced by the agents occurs at date 1: agent 1 (2) has a disastrous harvest if ξ_1 (ξ_2) occurs. The agents' preferences are given by the utility functions ($i = 1, 2$)

$$u^i(x^i) = \log x^i(\xi_0)$$
$$+ \alpha_i \left(\tfrac{1}{2}\left(\log x^i(\xi_1) + \alpha_i \log x^i(\xi_{12})\right) + \tfrac{1}{2}\left(\log x^i(\xi_2) + \alpha_i \log x^i(\xi_{22})\right)\right)$$

with $\alpha_1 = \tfrac{1}{2}$, $\alpha_2 = \tfrac{1}{3}$. Thus both agents have additively separable preferences, and agent 2 discounts future consumption more strongly than agent 1 ($\alpha_2 < \alpha_1$).

The financial structure consists of a short-lived bond at each non-terminal node, which permits the agents to borrow and lend. The securities are indexed by 0, 1, 2 indicating their nodes of issue: security 0 is the short-lived bond issued at date 0 with dividends $V^0(\xi_1) = V^0(\xi_2) = 1$, and security 1 (2) is the short-lived bond issued at node ξ_1 (ξ_2) with dividend $V^1(\xi_{12}) = 1$ ($V^2(\xi_{22}) = 1$).

The equilibrium $((\bar{x}, \bar{z}), \bar{q})$ of this economy is easy to compute (the derivation is left as an exercise):

$$\bar{x}^1 = \left(\bar{x}^1(\xi_0), \bar{x}^1(\xi_1), \bar{x}^1(\xi_2), \bar{x}^1(\xi_{12}), \bar{x}^1(\xi_{22})\right) = (4, 4/5, 24/5, 2, 12)$$

$$\bar{x}^2 = \left(\bar{x}^2(\xi_0), \bar{x}^2(\xi_1), \bar{x}^2(\xi_2), \bar{x}^2(\xi_{12}), \bar{x}^2(\xi_{22})\right) = (9, 36/5, 6/5, 12, 2)$$

$$\bar{z}_0^1(\xi_0) = -\bar{z}_0^2(\xi_0) = 0, \quad \bar{z}_1^1(\xi_1) = -\bar{z}_1^2(\xi_1) = -4, \quad \bar{z}_2^1(\xi_2) = -\bar{z}_2^2(\xi_2) = 6$$

$$\bar{q}_0(\xi_0) = 35/24, \quad \bar{q}_1(\xi_1) = 1/5, \quad \bar{q}_2(\xi_2) = 1/5$$

and the agents' present-value vectors at the equilibrium are

$$\bar{\pi}^1 = \left(\bar{\pi}^1(\xi_0), \bar{\pi}^1(\xi_1), \bar{\pi}^1(\xi_2), \bar{\pi}^1(\xi_{12}), \bar{\pi}^1(\xi_{22})\right) = (1, 5/4, 5/24, 1/4, 1/24)$$

$$\bar{\pi}^2 = \left(\bar{\pi}^2(\xi_0), \bar{\pi}^2(\xi_1), \bar{\pi}^2(\xi_2), \bar{\pi}^2(\xi_{12}), \bar{\pi}^2(\xi_{22})\right) = (1, 5/24, 5/4, 1/24, 1/4)$$

The equilibrium consumption-portfolio plans are shown in Figure 25.1(b). The endowments have been chosen (for convenience) so that the agents do not trade the bond at date 0. The agent with a bad harvest at date 1, borrows against his future income to obtain positive consumption. Since the agent with a good harvest at date 1 has the same endowment at date 2 and is impatient ($\alpha_i < 1$), the rate of interest must be sufficiently high to induce him to save at date 1. On the subtree $\mathbb{D}(\xi_1)$, agent 1 must give up 4 units of consumption at date 2 to be able to consume .8 units at date 1; on $\mathbb{D}(\xi_2)$, agent 2 has to sacrifice 6 units at date 2 to obtain 1.2 units at date 1. The present-value vectors of the two agents are distinct, each agent having a higher present value for income on the subtree with the unfavorable harvest at date 1.

Let us show that any change in the date 0 portfolios $dz_0 = (dz_0^1, -dz_0^1)$ with $dz_0^1 > 0$ accompanied by the change in date 0 consumption $dx_0 = (-\bar{q}_0(\xi_0)dz_0^1, \bar{q}_0(\xi_0)dz_0^1)$ (so that the pure transfers dt^i defined in equation (19) are zero) improves the welfare of both agents. To calculate the effect of the change dz_0 on the date 1 market clearing prices, note that if agent i arrives at date 1 with the wealth

$$\tilde{\omega}^i(\xi_s) = \omega^i(\xi_s) + z_0^i, \quad s = 1, 2, \quad i = 1, 2$$

then his intertemporal budget constraint in the subtree economy $\mathbb{D}(\xi_s)$ is

$$x^i(\xi_s) + q_s(\xi_s)x^i(\xi_{s2}) = \tilde{\omega}^i(\xi_s) + q_s(\xi_s)\omega^i(\xi_{s2}), \quad s = 1, 2$$

since in the $\mathbb{D}(\xi_s)$ economy markets are complete, so that the discounted value of consumption must equal the discounted value of income. Given the form of the utility functions, agent i's demand function is (for $s = 1, 2$)

$$x^i(\xi_s) = \frac{1}{1 + \alpha_i} \left(\tilde{\omega}^i(\xi_s) + q_s(\xi_s)\omega^i(\xi_{s2})\right)$$

$$x^i(\xi_{s2}) = \frac{\alpha_i}{1+\alpha_i}\left(\frac{\tilde{\omega}^i(\xi_s) + q_s(\xi_s)\omega^i(\xi_{s2})}{q_s(\xi_s)}\right)$$

so that the date 1 equilibrium prices are

$$q_s(\xi_s) = \frac{\dfrac{\alpha_1}{1+\alpha_1}\,\tilde{\omega}^1(\xi_s) + \dfrac{\alpha_2}{1+\alpha_2}\,\tilde{\omega}^2(\xi_s)}{\dfrac{1}{1+\alpha_1}\,\omega^1(\xi_{s2}) + \dfrac{1}{1+\alpha_2}\,\omega^2(\xi_{s2})}, \quad s = 1,2$$

A feasible change dz_0 in the date 0 portfolios induces the change $d\tilde{\omega}^1(\xi_s) = dz_0^1$ and $d\tilde{\omega}^2(\xi_s) = -dz_0^1$ in the initial wealth of each agent at date 1. The change in the date 1 equilibrium prices is thus

$$dq_s(\xi_s) = \frac{\left(\dfrac{\alpha_1}{1+\alpha_1} - \dfrac{\alpha_2}{1+\alpha_2}\right) dz_0^1}{\dfrac{1}{1+\alpha_1}\,\omega^1(\xi_{s2}) + \dfrac{1}{1+\alpha_2}\,\omega^2(\xi_{s2})}, \quad s = 1,2 \qquad (25)$$

If α_1 were chosen equal to α_2, then the equilibrium prices would not change, since the agents would have the same homothetic preferences (case (c) above). For the economy considered in this example

$$dq_1(\xi_1) = dq_2(\xi_2) = \frac{1}{120}dz_0^1$$

Recalling that $dt = 0$, the change in utility (20) induced by the change dz_0 is given by

$$\frac{du^i}{\bar{\lambda}_0^i} = \bar{\pi}^i(\xi_1)dq_1(\xi_1)\left(-z_1^i(\xi_1)\right) + \bar{\pi}^i(\xi_2)dq_2(\xi_2)\left(-\bar{z}_2^i(\xi_2)\right)$$

which for agent 1 gives $du^1/\bar{\lambda}_0^1 = \frac{1}{32}dz_0^1$ and for agent 2, $du^2/\bar{\lambda}_0^2 = \frac{1}{18}dz_0^1$. Thus if $dz_0^1 > 0$, then the welfare of each agent increases.

The explanation for this improvement can be found in expression (25) for the change in the bond prices at date 1. When agent 1 is forced to save more at date 0 (and agent 2 to save less) and thus to start with a larger income at date 1, since agent 1 discounts the future less strongly than agent 2 ($\alpha_1 > \alpha_2$), each bond price increases at date 1 or equivalently the rate of interest decreases. The reduction in the rate of interest is the only change which affects the utility of the two agents, since the direct wealth effects at date 1 of the changes dz_0^i in the portfolios are compensated for at date 0 ($dx_0^i = -\bar{q}(\xi_0)dz_0^i$ i.e., no pure transfers). Since for each agent the marginal utility of income is greater in the state in which he has an unfavorable harvest and since this is the state in which he has to borrow, the decrease in the rate of interest helps each agent more in the state where he is a borrower than it hurts him in the state where he is a lender. $\square$

This example shows that a planner with complete information on the characteristics of the agents can, by intervening in the appropriate way, induce a better allocation than that obtained solely by the use of the market mechanism. Results on the constrained suboptimality of equilibrium with incomplete markets which, at first sight, suggest the desirability of government intervention need however to be interpreted with some caution. The government may be able to identify and exploit the presence of *pecuniary externalities* which are not apparent to individual agents operating in the system of competitive markets, or which it is not in the private interest of agents to take into account. In the above example, the pecuniary externalities arise from the way savings decisions at date 0 affect the interest rates at date 1, which in turn affect the welfare of the agents; in the general model, pecuniary externalities arise from the effect of initial portfolio decisions on subsequent equilibrium prices and the way these in turn affect the welfare of agents—in short the way dz_0 affects dq and hence the social welfare (24). However in order to correctly identify and exploit these general equilibrium effects, the government would need extensive information on the characteristics of the agents. To the extent that the government is unlikely to have access to detailed information on the characteristics of all agents in the economy, the externality must be sufficiently important and robust if government intervention, based on only approximate information, is to lead to an improved allocation.

Exploiting pecuniary externalities pre-supposes restricting government intervention within the framework of the existing profile of contracts available in the private sector. However, once the issue of government intervention for an economy with incomplete markets is raised, it is probably more important to ask how the government can attempt to fill in missing markets (i.e. add to the contracts in the private sector) rather than to study the effect of interventions which only make use of the existing structure of markets. In modern economies, governments play an important role in supplementing the private sector provision of insurance and loans, for example through unemployment insurance, social security, health insurance, college loans and so on. The problem here is to understand why certain types of insurance or loans are not readily provided by the private sector, and why the government, in its role as an administrative agency, may have a relative advantage over the private sector in providing such contractual services. The model with incomplete markets studied in this book, in which the structure of contracts is taken as given, is not well adapted to analyzing questions of this kind—it is better adapted to studying the consequences rather than the causes of the incompleteness of markets. A more precise modelling of the imperfections which prevent certain types of contracts from emerging in the private sector would be necessary in order to study the extent to which governments can be expected to fill in markets that are missing in the private sector.

EXERCISES

1. *Generalization of representative agent analysis to multiperiod economy.*

   This exercise asks the reader to show that the representative agent analysis introduced in Section 16 for a two-period economy extends to a multiperiod economy.

Let $\mathscr{E}(\mathbb{D}, u, \omega, \zeta, V)$ be a stochastic exchange economy in which the utility functions of the agents are concave and satisfy Assumption $\mathscr{U}$.
(a) Consider the function $u^* : \mathbb{R}_{++}^n \longrightarrow \mathbb{R}$, with $n = \#\mathbb{D}$, defined by

$$u^*(y) = \max \left\{ \sum_{i=1}^{I} \frac{1}{\bar{\lambda}_0^i} u^i(x^i) \;\middle|\; \sum_{i=1}^{I} x^i = y, \quad x \in \mathbb{R}_+^{nI} \right\} \tag{1}$$

   where $\bar{\lambda}_0^i$, $i = 1, \ldots, I$, are strictly positive parameters.
   (i) Show that u^* is concave.
   (ii) Use the first-order conditions to show that $\bar{x} = (\bar{x}^1, \ldots, \bar{x}^I)$ is a solution of the maximum problem in (1) if and only if

$$\frac{1}{\bar{\lambda}_0^1} \nabla u^1(\bar{x}^1) = \cdots = \frac{1}{\bar{\lambda}_0^I} \nabla u^I(\bar{x}^I).$$

   (iii) Use the Envelope Theorem to show that

$$\nabla u^*(y) = \frac{1}{\bar{\lambda}_0^i} \nabla u^i(\bar{x}^i), \quad i = 1, \ldots, I$$

   at the optimal solution $\bar{x} = (\bar{x}^1, \ldots, \bar{x}^I)$.
(b) Let $((\bar{x}, \bar{z}), \bar{q})$ be an equilibrium of the economy for which the financial markets are complete, and let $\bar{\lambda}_0^i = \partial u^i(\bar{x}^i)/\partial x_0^i$, $i = 1, \ldots, I$. Show that for the representative agent with utility function u^* (defined in (a)) and endowment $w = \sum_{i=1}^{I} \omega^i$, it is optimal not to trade at the equilibrium price vector $\bar{q}$.
(c) Suppose the utility functions of the agents have the form which generalizes the assumption of VNM-additive separability introduced for the two-period case

$$u^i(x^i) = \sum_{\xi \in \mathbb{D}} \rho(\xi) v_{t(\xi)}^i(x^i(\xi)) = \sum_{t=0}^{T} \sum_{\xi \in \mathbb{D}_t} \rho(\xi) v_t^i(x^i(\xi))$$

   where $v_t^i : \mathbb{R}_+ \longrightarrow \mathbb{R}$ are smooth, concave, increasing functions. ρ is a probability on the states of nature, $\rho = (\rho_s)_{s \in \mathbf{S}}$, $\rho_s > 0$, $\sum_{s \in \mathbf{S}} \rho_s = 1$, and for $\xi = (t, \sigma)$, $\rho(\xi) = \sum_{s \in \sigma} \rho_s$ is the probability of node ξ. Prove that the utility function u^* of the representative agent has the same form, namely that there exist functions $v_t^* : \mathbb{R}_+ \longrightarrow \mathbb{R}$, $t = 0, 1, \ldots, T$ which are smooth, concave and increasing such that

$$u^*(y) = \sum_{t=0}^{T} \sum_{\xi \in \mathbb{D}_t} \rho(\xi) v_t^*(y(\xi))$$

(d) Prove that, if the utility functions are VNM-additively separable (as defined in (c)), then the equilibrium consumption $\bar{x}^i$ of agent i at date t is an increasing function of the aggregate endowment w at this date; more precisely that there exist increasing functions $\psi_t^i : \mathbb{R}_+ \longrightarrow \mathbb{R}$, $t = 0, 1, \ldots, T$, $i = 1, \ldots, I$ such that

$$x^i(\xi) = \psi_t^i(w(\xi)), \quad \forall \xi = (t, \sigma), \sigma \in \mathbb{F}_t$$

(e) Suppose that the utility functions v_t^i of the agents are discounted expected utilities with the same discount factor

$$v_t^i(x^i(\xi)) = \delta^t v^i(x^i(\xi)), \quad t = 0, 1, \ldots, T$$

Prove that the equilibrium consumption $\bar{x}^i(\xi)$ of agent i at each date-event ξ is an increasing function of the aggregate endowment $w(\xi)$ i.e. that there exist increasing functions $\psi^i : \mathbb{R}_+ \longrightarrow \mathbb{R}$, $i = 1, \ldots, I$ such that

$$x^i(\xi) = \psi^i(w(\xi)), \quad \forall \xi \in \mathbb{D}$$

Give an economic interpretation for the difference between this case and the case in (d) where the discount factors of the agents can differ.

2. *Multiperiod economy with short-lived securities and complete markets.*

The object of this exercise is to prove directly that an economy with only short-lived securities which span the subsequent contingencies at each node has Pareto optimal equilibria.

Consider a stochastic exchange economy $\mathcal{E}(\mathbb{D}, u, \omega, \zeta, V)$ with three periods ($t = 0, 1, 2$) in which agents' utility functions satisfy Assumption $\mathcal{U}$. Suppose that the financial structure (ζ, V) consists solely of short-lived securities, that at each non-terminal node ξ there are $j(\xi)$ securities with linearly independent payoffs, and that $j(\xi) = b(\xi)$, where $b(\xi)$ is the branching number at node ξ.
(a) Derive the first-order conditions which are necessary and sufficient for an allocation $\bar{x}$ to be Pareto optimal.
(b) Using the first-order conditions at a financial market equilibrium $((\bar{x}, \bar{z}), \bar{q})$, show that the allocation $\bar{x}$ is Pareto optimal.

3. *Discontinuity in demand associated with change in rank.*

This exercise studies the discontinuity in an agent's (no-arbitrage) demand function when there is a change in the rank of the payoff matrix.

Consider a stochastic exchange economy $\mathcal{E}(\mathbb{D}, u, \omega, \zeta, V)$ with three periods ($t = 0, 1, 2$). Let $\mathbb{D}$ be the event-tree induced by the information structure in Example 22.5: each non-terminal node has a branching number equal to two. The financial structure (ζ, V) consists of two securities issued at date 0. One is the short-lived riskless bond which pays 1 unit of the good in each event at date 1; the other is the long-lived riskless bond which pays nothing at date 1 and 1 unit of the good in each state of nature at date 2. Let $(q_S(\xi_0), q_L(\xi_0))$ denote the prices of the short-lived and long-lived bond at date 0 and let $(q_L(\xi_1), q_L(\xi_2))$ denote the price of the long-lived bond when it is retraded at date 1. Use the same notation as in Examples 22.5, 23.6 and in Section 24.

(a) If q is a no-arbitrage price associated with a vector of node prices π, find the no-arbitrage budget set $\mathscr{B}(\pi, \omega^i, V)$ of an agent with endowment ω^i. Show that if

$$\frac{\pi_{11} + \pi_{12}}{\pi_1} \neq \frac{\pi_{21} + \pi_{22}}{\pi_2} \tag{1}$$

then this budget set is described by three constraints, while if

$$\frac{\pi_{11} + \pi_{12}}{\pi_1} = \frac{\pi_{21} + \pi_{22}}{\pi_2} \tag{2}$$

then the budget set involves one additional constraint. Interpret this condition in terms of a property of the matrix W in equation (5) of Section 22.

(b) Suppose each agent has a quadratic utility function of the form

$$u^i(x^i) = \sum_{\xi \in \mathbb{D}} c^i(\xi)(\alpha^i - x^i(\xi))^2$$

where $c^i(\xi_1) = c^i(\xi_2)$ and $c^i(\xi_{s\sigma})$ has the same value for $s = 1, 2$, $\sigma = 1, 2$. Suppose in addition that $\omega_{11}^i + \omega_{12}^i = \omega_{21}^i + \omega_{22}^i$, $i = 1, \dots, I$. Compute the demand function $x^i(\pi, \omega^i)$ of agent i where

$$x^i(\pi, \omega^i) = \arg\max \left\{ u^i(x^i) \mid x^i \in \mathscr{B}(\pi, \omega^i, V) \right\}$$

for all π such that (1) is satisfied.

(c) Let π^ν be a sequence of node prices such that $(\pi_{11}^\nu + \pi_{12}^\nu)/\pi_1^\nu \neq (\pi_{21}^\nu + \pi_{22}^\nu)/\pi_2^\nu$ which converges to $\bar{\pi}$ satisfying (2) and $\bar{\pi}_1 \neq \bar{\pi}_2$. Show that $\lim_{\pi^\nu \to \bar{\pi}} x^i(\pi^\nu, \omega^i)$ does not satisfy the additional constraint which enters the budget set $\mathscr{B}(\bar{\pi}, \omega^i, V)$. Deduce that the demand function of agent i is discontinuous at $\bar{\pi}$.

HISTORICAL REMARKS

The first genuine multiperiod model of equilibrium under uncertainty was due to Debreu (1959, Chapter 7). He introduced the convenient formulation of progressive unfolding of information via an event-tree, the concept of a contingent contract and a contingent market equilibrium. He noted that this formulation of market equilibrium permitted the results of static theory (existence and the two welfare theorems) to be carried over to a multiperiod setting with uncertainty. For a long time much of equilibrium analysis over time was restricted to this concept of equilibrium.[1]

We mentioned in the *Historical Remarks* to Chapter 2 that subsequently two alternative

---

[1] Much of postwar growth theory which formed the basis for the recent real business cycle theory is essentially representative agent analysis of a contingent market equilibrium.

approaches emerged for describing equilibrium for a sequence economy in which agents have limited ability to transfer income across adjoining date-events: the first was the approach of *temporary equilibrium*, the second that of *rational expectations* (or more generally, *correct expectations*) *equilibrium*. The latter approach was formalized in the important paper of Radner (1972) in the setting of a finite-horizon multigood economy. The financial contracts studied by Radner were close to the contingent contracts of Arrow-Debreu: in the terminology of this chapter, each contract was issued at some node ξ of the event-tree and promised to deliver one unit of a given commodity in specified contingencies at a fixed subsequent date (i.e. at certain nodes $\xi' \in \mathbb{D}(\xi)$ such that $t(\xi') = \tau \geq t(\xi)$) and was not retradable after its node of issue. Hart (1975) introduced a more convenient way of describing financial contracts in terms of their dividend streams which subsequently became the standard way of representing financial contracts. Although Hart introduced notation for a three-period model, he exhibited problems of nonexistence and Pareto ranking of equilibria in examples of two-period multigood economies, and this two-period setting was adopted in much of the recent literature, with a few notable exceptions.

One of these was Kreps' paper (1982) which sought conditions under which spanning results similar to those underlying the Black-Scholes (1973) option pricing model might be found in an equilibrium model of financial markets. Kreps studied a finite horizon model with J long-lived securities which pay dividends at the terminal date. He showed that frequent retrading of these securities would lead to complete markets if, for each non-terminal node of the event tree, the rank of the matrix of security prices $q(\xi^+)$ at the successors ξ^+ of ξ is equal to the branching number $b(\xi)$ (Proposition 22.4). Since the security prices $q(\xi^+)$ are equilibrium prices which are endogenously determined, it was clear that such a condition could not be expected to hold for equilibria of all economies. Kreps noted that a similar problem had arisen in an earlier paper of Radner (1979) which studied a closely related model of security markets, in which the emphasis was on differential information among the agents. Following the method introduced by Radner of using differential topology arguments to show that distinct exogenous parameters typically lead to distinct equilibrium prices, Kreps introduced the perturbation argument which underlies the proof of Theorem 25.6 (i): if for an Arrow-Debreu equilibrium the associated security prices in the financial market model do not satisfy the rank condition, then a small perturbation in the dividend streams of the securities restores the rank condition.

As the Radner and Kreps' papers were the first to demonstrate, the methods of differential topology developed in the 1970s for analyzing the standard Arrow-Debreu model have proved to be essential for analyzing the subsequent equilibrium models of financial markets. It is indeed striking how canonical the Arrow-Debreu model has proved to be—that is, how much the understanding of these second-generation equilibrium models has depended on the earlier analytical framework developed for the Arrow-Debreu model.

The analysis of the multiperiod model was further extended by Magill-Shafer (1985/1990) in the context of a multigood economy. They introduced the concept of a potentially complete security structure and showed that this concept permits a precise description of economies whose financial market equilibria typically coincide with the contingent market equilibria. In particular they showed that a given potentially complete security structure generates in almost all economies at least one financial market equilibrium with complete markets and none with incomplete markets (Theorem 25.7 (ii)). In contrast to the proofs of the above mentioned results of Radner and Kreps, the proof of this last property could not rely on mapping the FM equilibria into CM equilibria and exploiting known properties of Arrow-Debreu equilibria. Equilibria with incomplete markets (i.e. those with less than maximum rank) had to be studied directly in order to show that they were exceptional. The methods developed for proving Theorem 25.7 (ii) led directly to the natural way of posing the problem of existence of equilibrium with incomplete markets in a tractable form: the proof of Theorem 25.5 (iii) was given by Duffie-Shafer (1986a) and an alternative proof is given in Magill-Shafer (1991).

We explained earlier the reasons for focusing this volume on the one-commodity (finance) model. First, it permits the economics of the financial markets to be explored in the simplest setting. Second, at least for a two-period economy, it avoids the use of more advanced techniques of equilibrium theory which are needed for the analysis of the multicommodity model. This chapter has shown however that these techniques cannot really be avoided as soon as the finance model is extended to a genuine intertemporal setting: the difficulties of change of rank induced in the multiperiod model by the presence of capital-value terms are essentially the same as those induced in the multicommodity model by the presence of securities whose payoffs depend on the spot prices.

If the problem posed by the change of rank of the market subspace is essentially technical and can be solved by calling on the appropriate mathematical machinery, the problem of the constrained inefficiency of financial market equilibria raises more fundamental economic questions regarding the functioning of a price system in the presence of imperfections. Briefly, there are two traditions for exploring the efficiency properties of a system of incomplete markets. The first seeks to carry over the two Welfare Theorems for an economy with complete markets to a setting where markets are incomplete: Grossman (1977) introduced a concept of weak constrained efficiency with respect to which FM equilibria satisfy the two Welfare Theorems. As we shall show later this result, while of mathematical interest, does not have a natural economic interpretation. The second approach stems from the tax-externality literature of public economics: the idea that taxes—and more general government interventions—can improve social welfare when marginal rates of substitution are not equalized in an economy, can be considered as a folk theorem of public economics, which may be traced back to Pigou (1920). Whether such a result holds in an economy with incomplete markets, when the instruments for intervention respect the inherent restrictions imposed by the incompleteness of markets, was studied in examples by Diamond (1980) and Newberry-Stiglitz (1982), and proposed as a natural test of constrained efficiency of financial market equilibria by Stiglitz (1982). All these papers (which studied models of two-period economies) suggested that constrained efficiency of equilibria was the exception rather than the rule when there are two or more commodities. The first formal proof that, for most two-period exchange economies with more than two agents and more than two goods, all financial market equilibria are constrained inefficient if markets are incomplete, was given by Geanakoplos-Polemarchakis (1986). The proof of generic inefficiency of FM equilibria was extended to production economies by Geanakoplos-Magill-Quinzii-Drèze (1990) who adopted a definition of constrained feasibility that permits more redistribution at date 0, thereby simplifying the proofs. The problem of constrained efficiency has not previously been analyzed for multiperiod economies: the concept of constrained efficiency adopted in this chapter is the natural extension of the concept studied in Geanakoplos-Magill-Quinzii-Drèze.

5

INFORMATIONAL EFFICIENCY
OF SECURITY PRICES

MOTIVATION AND SUMMARY

Some fifty years ago, analysis of the time series of speculative prices revealed a striking property: to a first approximation price changes behave like independent random variables so that the time path of prices is similar to a random walk. At first this revelation came as quite a shock to economists: how could prices determined by demand and supply on organized markets and so central to the functioning of an economy behave in such an apparently erratic way? As Kendall (1953) wrote after an extensive statistical analysis:

> The series looks like a "wandering" one, almost as if once a week the Demon of Chance drew a random number from a symmetrical population of fixed dispersion and added it to the current price to determine the next week's price. And this, we may recall, is not the behavior in some small back water market. The data derive from the Chicago wheat market over a period of fifty years during which at least two attempts were made to corner wheat, and one might have expected the wildest irregularities in the figures.

In retrospect it is not surprising that economists were puzzled: the traditional analysis of markets was concerned with a static demand-supply analysis of price, in which time and uncertainty played no role. Analysis of speculative prices forced economists to come to terms with both time and uncertainty. Soon it was realized that the price changes, far from being erratic, might well reflect timely and accurate responses to new information—if new information emerges randomly then this should translate into random price changes. Thus the random behavior of security prices was bringing to light a new and striking phenomenon in economics—the response of prices to the emergence of new information.

The idea that security prices correctly reflect or exploit all available information has come to be known as the *efficient markets hypothesis*. This hypothesis is not usually

281

expressed as a primitive property of a price process; rather it is expressed indirectly by asserting that a security price process efficiently exploits available information if an investor cannot find trading strategies based on publicly available information which "beat the market", that is, which make an abnormal profit.[1]

It is instructive to begin with the simplest or what we may call the *naive version* of the efficient markets hypothesis: this is the version that holds in an equilibrium of an economy in which agents are *risk neutral*. In an equilibrium there must not be any profitable trades left to exploit: since risk-neutral agents rank income streams by their expected value, if the expected profit on every trading strategy, based on currently available information, is to be zero, then the price of each security must be matched in a precise way to its future dividend stream—intuitively, it must equal the expected value of its future dividends *based on currently available information*.

To make this idea precise requires two mathematical concepts: first, the description of a *process of arrival of new information* over time and second, the idea of a *conditional expectation*. The first was introduced in the previous chapter: the (public) information revealed to agents over time was modelled by a sequence of progressively finer partitions $(\mathbb{F}_t)_{t \in \mathbf{T}}$ of a basic set of states of nature $\mathbf{S}$. The notion of the best estimate of a future random variable based on current information is defined in Section 26 and leads to the concept of a conditional expectation. As we shall see, this is simply a more refined way of taking the average of a random variable using the knowledge (information) that the only relevant states that need to be considered are those associated with a known event σ.

Thus when agents are risk neutral the efficient markets hypothesis can be expressed directly as a property of the security price process: *at each date, the price of each security must equal the conditional expectation (given the event which has occurred at this date) of the sum of its (discounted) future dividends*. The efficiency of prices with respect to the use of information is captured by the best estimate (or optimal predictor) property of the conditional expectation, taken with respect to the objectively given probability measure which characterizes the risk-neutral preferences.

If the assumption that agents are risk neutral is convenient as a preliminary step for analyzing the efficient markets hypothesis, it is hardly a realistic assumption: agents can only be expected to be risk neutral if they are infinitely (extremely) rich, and such

---

[1] The finance literature distinguishes three progressively stronger versions of the efficient markets hypothesis (EMH) according to the "size" of the information set on the basis of which an investor cannot make an abnormal profit. In the *weak* form of EMH, the information consists purely of a knowledge of past prices; if prices satisfy the weak form of EMH then *technical analysis* of (i.e. looking for trading schemes based on patterns in) past prices cannot yield abnormal profit. In the *semi-strong* form of EMH, the information consists of all publicly available information; if the prices satisfy this hypothesis then (the traditionally popular) *fundamental analysis* (i.e. attempting to find undervalued securities by predicting future dividends better than the market) cannot yield abnormal profit. It is this version of EMH which is studied in this chapter. In the *strong* form of EMH, the information consists of all public as well as private (inside) information. This form is more controversial and is difficult to formalize in a satisfactory way.

agents would need no insurance or risk sharing—they could simply self-insure. The presence of security markets on which there is extensive trading can really only be explained by assuming that agents are risk averse and have limited wealth. However in such a world, just as observing the price of a security in excess of (or below) the conditional expectation of its future dividends is no longer proof of inefficient use of information, so a trading strategy which offers a positive expected gain may no longer be perceived as offering the opportunity of an abnormal profit. For when agents are risk averse, the prices of securities involve risk premia, and a strategy which yields a positive expected gain may involve losses in some contingencies which make it unattractive for risk-averse agents with limited wealth.

To judge if at some date-event the discrepancy between the price of a security and the conditional expectation of its future dividends represents inefficient use of available information or is indeed justified as an appropriate risk premium, the risk characteristics of the agents need to be known. However even if no precise specification is made regarding the agents' risk characteristics, there is a minimal condition that security prices must satisfy to meet the requirement of the efficient markets hypothesis: *no investor must be able to find a trading strategy based on publicly available information which yields a sure gain*, that is a positive gain at some date-event and no loss at any other date-event. In short, agents must not be able to make arbitrage profits on the basis of public information. We call a price process satisfying this property *weakly information efficient*. Although the requirement of no sure gains is weak, it yields a rather striking property: *a security price process is weakly information efficient if and only if there exists a probability measure μ on the states of nature such that, at each date-event, the price of each security is the best estimate based on current information (the conditional expectation) of the sum of its discounted future dividends under the probability measure μ*. This result, which is established in Section 28, is often loosely referred to as the *martingale property* of security prices, for reasons that will become clear later.

If a precise specification of agents' characteristics is made, then a more demanding notion of informational efficiency can be introduced. When agents are risk averse, not only do security prices reflect agents' evaluations of the expected future earnings of securities based on current information, they also incorporate the risk premia that agents require as compensation for carrying the risks on the securities' returns, or the risk premia that agents are prepared to pay when the securities offer risk-reduction services. Since information and risk can no longer be separated, the notion of informational efficiency can only be defined relative to the risk characteristics of the agents.

The way agents evaluate risk depends not only on their preference orderings, but also on the profile of their consumption streams. An agent who finds himself with a substantial consumption stream which does not exhibit much variability either across time or across contingencies will typically not be very sensitive to risk. Conversely an agent with a relatively small consumption stream which varies substantially across contingencies will need a high premium to be induced to hold a risky security whose

dividends add to the variability of his consumption stream. Given a utility function and a consumption stream $(u^i; x^i)$ for each agent, a security price process will be called *information efficient* relative to the agents' characteristics $((u^i; x^i),\ i = 1, \ldots, I)$ if no agent can find a profitable trading strategy based on currently available information, that is, a trade which leads to a new consumption stream preferred to the former consumption stream x^i. In particular, if $((\bar{x}, \bar{z}), \bar{q})$ is a financial market equilibrium, then $\bar{q}$ is information efficient relative to the agents' characteristics at the equilibrium allocation $\bar{x}$. In Section 28 we will show that a price process is information efficient if and only if, for each agent, the price of each security is at each date the conditional expectation of the sum of its (discounted) future dividends with respect to a personal probability measure, which weights each state according to the value that the agent assigns to income along the path associated with that state. The optimal use of information is captured by the best estimate or optimal predictor property of the conditional expectation, while the risk characteristics of each agent are incorporated into his personal probability measure on the state space.

The property of informational efficiency of a price process analyzed in this chapter should be distinguished from the property of efficiency of an allocation discussed in the previous chapter. Only when markets are complete are the two properties simultaneously satisfied at an equilibrium, so that security prices both reflect the optimal use of information and lead to an optimal allocation of risk bearing.

26. CONDITIONAL EXPECTATION AND MARTINGALE

This section introduces the mathematical concepts required to formalize the idea of efficient use of information. The formalization is achieved by the concept of the conditional expectation of a random variable, which can be shown to be the best estimate of the random variable conditional on available information. Since the economic model that is studied involves only a finite number of states of nature, the presentation that follows introduces the concepts of probability theory in the simplest setting of a finite probability space.

26.1 Definition: Let $\mathbf{S} = \{1, \ldots, S\}$ be a finite set of states and let $\mathscr{S}$ denote the collection of all subsets of $\mathbf{S}$. A map

$$\mathscr{P} : \mathscr{S} \longrightarrow [0, 1]$$

is called a *probability measure* if $\mathscr{P}(\emptyset) = 0$, $\mathscr{P}(\mathbf{S}) = 1$, and $\mathscr{P}(\sigma \cup \sigma') = \mathscr{P}(\sigma) + \mathscr{P}(\sigma')$ whenever $\sigma, \sigma' \in \mathscr{S}$ and $\sigma \cap \sigma' = \emptyset$. The triple $(\mathbf{S}, \mathscr{S}, \mathscr{P})$ is called a *probability space*.

An element σ of $\mathscr{S}$ is an event: $\mathscr{P}(\sigma)$ measures the likelihood or probability of its occurrence. Information will be expressed by saying that only certain subsets can be observed. If σ and σ' are two observable events, then the events "σ or σ'", "σ and σ'", as well as "not σ" are all observable. This leads to the following definition.

26.2 Definition: A collection $\mathscr{F}$ of subsets of $\mathbf{S}$ is called *a field* if

(i) $\mathbf{S} \in \mathscr{F}$
(ii) for all $\sigma, \sigma' \in \mathscr{F}$, $\mathbf{S} \setminus \sigma$ and $\sigma \cup \sigma' \in \mathscr{F}$.

If $\mathscr{F}$ and $\mathscr{F}'$ are fields and $\mathscr{F}' \subset \mathscr{F}$, then $\mathscr{F}'$ is called a *subfield* of $\mathscr{F}$.

If $\mathbb{F}$ is a family of subsets of $\mathbf{S}$, the *field* $\mathscr{F}(\mathbb{F})$ *generated by* $\mathbb{F}$ is the smallest field containing $\mathbb{F}$ (i.e. the intersection of all fields containing $\mathbb{F}$).

A field is closed under the natural operations on events: union, intersection and complement. The field $\mathscr{F}(\mathbb{F})$ generated by a partition $\mathbb{F}$ thus consists of all finite unions and intersections of elements of $\mathbb{F}$ as well as their complements in $\mathbf{S}$.

In the previous chapter, the information available at a given date $t \in \mathbf{T}$ was defined by a partition $\mathbb{F}_t$ of $\mathbf{S}$. By Definition 26.2 this leads to a field $\mathscr{F}_t = \mathscr{F}(\mathbb{F}_t)$. If $\mathbb{F}_{t+1}$ is finer than $\mathbb{F}_t$ then the field $\mathscr{F}_{t+1}$ is larger than $\mathscr{F}_t$ (contains more subsets): thus the larger the field, the greater the available information. The collection $\mathscr{S}$ of all possible events is the largest field and contains the largest amount of information: it is generated by the finest partition $(\{1\}, \ldots, \{S\})$.

The following definition of an $\mathscr{F}$-measurable random variable formalizes the idea that it is not possible to deduce more information by observing the value taken by the random variable than is contained in the field $\mathscr{F}$.

26.3 Definition: Let $\mathscr{F}$ be a field on $\mathbf{S}$ and let $x : \mathbf{S} \longrightarrow \mathbb{R}$ be a function. x is said to be an $\mathscr{F}$-*measurable random variable* if the inverse image $x^{-1}(I)$ of every open interval $I \subset \mathbb{R}$ is an element of $\mathscr{F}$.

If x is $\mathscr{S}$-measurable, then there is no restriction on x, since $\mathscr{S}$ contains all subsets of $\mathbf{S}$: in this case x is simply called a *random variable*.

26.4 Proposition: *If $\mathscr{F}$ is a field on $\mathbf{S}$ generated by a partition $\mathbb{F}$ then $x : \mathbf{S} \longrightarrow \mathbb{R}$ is $\mathscr{F}$-measurable if and only if x is constant on each subset σ of the partition $\mathbb{F}$*

$$x(s) = x(s'), \quad \forall s, s' \in \sigma, \quad \forall \sigma \in \mathbb{F}$$

PROOF: ($\Longrightarrow$) $\mathscr{F}(\mathbb{F})$ consists of all finite unions and intersections of elements of $\mathbb{F}$ and their complements in $\mathbf{S}$. Thus

$$\sigma \in \mathbb{F}, \ \sigma' \in \mathscr{F}(\mathbb{F}) \Longrightarrow \sigma \subset \sigma' \text{ or } \sigma \cap \sigma' = \emptyset \tag{1}$$

Suppose x is not constant on a subset $\sigma \in \mathbb{F}$, that is, there exist $s, s' \in \sigma$ such that $x(s) \neq x(s')$. If $I \subset \mathbb{R}$ is an open interval such that $x(s) \in I$, $x(s') \notin I$, then $x^{-1}(I) \cap \sigma \neq \emptyset$ and $\sigma \not\subset x^{-1}(I)$ which contradicts (1).

($\Longleftarrow$) If x is constant on each subset of $\mathbb{F}$, then for all open intervals $I \subset \mathbb{R}$, $x^{-1}(I)$ is a union of subsets of $\mathbb{F}$ and thus belongs to $\mathscr{F}$. $\square$

When a probability space $(\mathbf{S}, \mathscr{S}, \mathscr{P})$ is given as exogenous data, $\mathscr{S}$ should not be interpreted as an information set but rather as the domain of definition of the map $\mathscr{P}$ which attributes to each event a number expressing its likelihood. If subsequently it is revealed that a particular event σ has occurred, then it is natural to correct the probabilities to reflect this information. Revising the probabilities in a way that retains the relative likelihood of the states of nature which constitute the event σ, and attributing zero likelihood to all other states, leads to the concept of conditional probability.

26.5 Definition: Let $(\mathbf{S}, \mathscr{S}, \mathscr{P})$ be a probability space. For any $\sigma \in \mathscr{S}$ with $\mathscr{P}(\sigma) > 0$, the *conditional probability given* σ is the function $\mathscr{P}_\sigma : \mathscr{S} \longrightarrow [0, 1]$ defined by

$$\mathscr{P}_\sigma(\sigma') = \frac{\mathscr{P}(\sigma' \cap \sigma)}{\mathscr{P}(\sigma)}, \quad \sigma' \in \mathscr{S}$$

For a random variable $x : \mathbf{S} \longrightarrow \mathbb{R}$, the *conditional expectation $E(x \,|\, \sigma)$ of x given σ* is defined by

$$E(x \,|\, \sigma) = \sum_{s \in \mathbf{S}} x(s) \mathscr{P}_\sigma(s) = \sum_{s \in \sigma} x(s) \frac{\mathscr{P}(s)}{\mathscr{P}(\sigma)}$$

If $\sigma = \mathbf{S}$, $E(x \,|\, \mathbf{S}) = E(x)$ is the *expectation* of x.

In the above definition, $\mathscr{P}(s)$ is a simplified notation for $\mathscr{P}(\{s\})$. The conditional expectation of x given σ is simply the average of x obtained by using the conditional probability induced by σ.

If the events which can occur (for example at a given date) are given by a field $\mathscr{F}$ generated by an information partition $\mathbb{F}$, then the conditional expectation of x given σ can be defined for each possible event σ of the partition $\mathbb{F}$; the collection of numbers $(E(x \,|\, \sigma), \ \sigma \in \mathbb{F})$ can then be used in the natural way to define an $\mathscr{F}$-measurable random variable: for each state $s \in \sigma$ it takes the value $E(x \,|\, \sigma)$. This random variable is called the conditional expectation of x given $\mathscr{F}$.

26.6 Definition: Let $(\mathbf{S}, \mathscr{S}, \mathscr{P})$ be a probability space, and let $\mathscr{F}$ be a subfield of $\mathscr{S}$ generated by a partition $\mathbb{F}$. For a random variable $x : \mathbf{S} \longrightarrow \mathbb{R}$, the *conditional expectation* $E(x \,|\, \mathscr{F})$ *of* x *given* $\mathscr{F}$ is the $\mathscr{F}$-measurable random variable defined by

$$E(x \,|\, \mathscr{F})(s) = E(x \,|\, \sigma) \text{ for } \sigma \in \mathbb{F} \text{ such that } s \in \sigma.$$

REMARK. A more condensed way of writing $E(x \,|\, \mathscr{F})$ can be obtained by using the *indicator function*. For any subset $\sigma \subset \mathbf{S}$, let $\chi_\sigma : \mathbf{S} \longrightarrow \{0, 1\}$ be defined by

$$\chi_\sigma(s) = \begin{cases} 1, & \text{if } s \in \sigma \\ 0, & \text{if } s \notin \sigma \end{cases}$$

Then the function $E(x \,|\, \mathscr{F}) : \mathbf{S} \longrightarrow \mathbb{R}$ can be written as

$$E(x \,|\, \mathscr{F}) = \sum_{\sigma \in \mathbb{F}} E(x \,|\, \sigma) \, \chi_\sigma$$

We have given a simple definition of the conditional expectation $E(x \,|\, \mathscr{F})$ by restricting attention to fields $\mathscr{F}$ generated by partitions. Such fields suffice for the analysis that follows. At the cost of a more abstract definition, $E(x \,|\, \mathscr{F})$ can be defined for an arbitrary subfield $\mathscr{F}$ of $\mathscr{S}$. The properties that follow hold for the general definition.

26.7 Proposition (Properties of Conditional Expectation):   *Let* $(\mathbf{S}, \mathscr{S}, \mathscr{P})$ *be a probability space, and let* $\mathscr{F}$ *be a subfield of* $\mathscr{S}$.

 (i) *If* $x, y : \mathbf{S} \longrightarrow \mathbb{R}$ *are random variables, then*

   (a) $E(ax + by \,|\, \mathscr{F}) = aE(x \,|\, \mathscr{F}) + bE(y \,|\, \mathscr{F})$, $\forall \, a, b \in \mathbb{R}$
   (b) *If* x *is* $\mathscr{F}$-*measurable, then* $E(xy \,|\, \mathscr{F}) = xE(y \,|\, \mathscr{F})$

 (ii)   (a) *Let* $\mathscr{F} = \mathscr{F}_0$ *be the field generated by the trivial partition* $\mathbb{F}_0 = \mathbf{S}$, *then* $E(x \,|\, \mathscr{F}) = E(x)$.
   (b) *Let* $\mathscr{F} = \mathscr{S}$, *then* $E(x \,|\, \mathscr{F}) = x$
(iii) *Let* $\mathscr{H}$ *be a subfield of* $\mathscr{F}$, *then*

$$E(E(x \,|\, \mathscr{F}) \,|\, \mathscr{H}) = E(x \,|\, \mathscr{H})$$

PROOF: We restrict the proof to fields generated by partitions. Properties (i) and (ii) follow at once from Definition 26.6. To show (iii), note that since $\mathscr{H}$ is generated by a partition $\mathbb{H}$, for any $s \in \mathbf{S}$ there is a unique $\sigma \in \mathbb{H}$ such that $s \in \sigma$. Since $\mathscr{F}$ is generated by the partition $\mathbb{F}$ and $\mathscr{H} \subset \mathscr{F}$, there exist $\sigma_1, \ldots, \sigma_k \in \mathbb{F}$ such that $\sigma = \bigcup_{j=1}^{k} \sigma_j$ with $\sigma_j \cap \sigma_{j'} = \emptyset$. Thus

$$
\begin{aligned}
E(x \mid \mathscr{H})(s) &= \frac{1}{\mathscr{P}(\sigma)} \sum_{s' \in \sigma} x(s') \mathscr{P}(s') \\
&= \frac{1}{\mathscr{P}(\sigma)} \sum_{j=1}^{k} \sum_{s' \in \sigma_j} x(s') \frac{\mathscr{P}(s')}{\mathscr{P}(\sigma_j)} \sum_{s'' \in \sigma_j} \mathscr{P}(s'') \\
&= \frac{1}{\mathscr{P}(\sigma)} \sum_{j=1}^{k} \sum_{s'' \in \sigma_j} E(x \mid \mathscr{F})(s'') \mathscr{P}(s'') \\
&= \frac{1}{\mathscr{P}(\sigma)} \sum_{s'' \in \sigma} E(x \mid \mathscr{F})(s'') \mathscr{P}(s'') \\
&= E(E(x \mid \mathscr{F}) \mid \mathscr{H})(s)
\end{aligned}
$$

The property which drives the proof is that, to obtain the average value of x over σ, one can first take averages over the disjoint subsets σ_j of σ and then average these values. □

Conditional Expectation as Best Approximation

Let x be a random variable defined on a probability space $(\mathbf{S}, \mathscr{S}, \mathscr{P})$, and let $\mathscr{F}$ be a field generated by an information partition $\mathbb{F}$. To understand the precise sense in which the conditional expectation $E(x \mid \sigma)$ and $E(x \mid \mathscr{F})$ provide best estimates of x given the information defined by σ or $\mathscr{F}$, it is convenient to introduce three dates $0 < t < T$. At date 0, only the function x and the information partition $\mathbb{F}$ are known: knowing $\mathbb{F}$ means knowing that at the intermediate date t, it will be possible to tell in which event σ of the partition $\mathbb{F}$ the state lies. At date T the state is revealed.

   If the criterion of least squares is used at date 0, then, since there is no information, the best estimate of x is the mean

$$
E(x) = \arg\min_{\alpha \in \mathbb{R}} \sum_{s \in \mathbf{S}} (x_s - \alpha)^2 \mathscr{P}(s) \tag{2}
$$

Since at date 0 it is known that more information will be available at date t, a prediction can be made at date 0 of the way in which the estimate will be revised at date t depending on the event σ which will have occurred. This amounts to associating with each possible event $\sigma \in \mathbb{F}$, a number α_σ which is the predicted estimate of x if σ occurs. What is the optimal way of choosing the coefficients $(\alpha_\sigma, \ \sigma \in \mathbb{F})$? If the error from the perspective of date 0 is measured by the least squares criterion, then the optimal choice of coefficients $(\alpha_\sigma, \sigma \in \mathbb{F})$ is the solution of the problem

$$\min_{(\alpha_\sigma, \, \sigma \in \mathbb{F}) \in \mathbb{R}^k} \sum_{\sigma \in \mathbb{F}} \sum_{s \in \sigma} (x_s - \alpha_\sigma)^2 \mathscr{P}(s) \tag{3}$$

where $k = \#\mathbb{F}$ is the number of elements of the partition $\mathbb{F}$. The solution of (3) is given by

$$\alpha_\sigma^* = \sum_{s \in \sigma} \frac{x_s \mathscr{P}(s)}{\mathscr{P}(\sigma)} = E(x \mid \sigma), \quad \sigma \in \mathbb{F} \tag{4}$$

Suppose that date t arrives and a particular event σ is known to have occurred. Is the date 0 predicted estimate α_σ^* still the best estimate at date-event (σ, t)? Given that it is now known that the state s must lie in σ, it is natural to reduce the probability space to $(\sigma, \widetilde{\mathscr{S}}, \widetilde{\mathscr{P}_\sigma})$, where $\widetilde{\mathscr{S}}$ is the collection of all subsets of σ, and $\widetilde{\mathscr{P}_\sigma}$ is the restriction to $\widetilde{\mathscr{S}}$ of the conditional probability $\mathscr{P}_\sigma$ (i.e. $\widetilde{\mathscr{P}_\sigma}(s) = \mathscr{P}(s)/\mathscr{P}(\sigma), s \in \sigma$). On this probability space, the expectation of x is $E(x \mid \sigma) = \alpha_\sigma^*$, which by (2) is the best estimate of x on the revised probability space. Thus the date 0 predicted estimate is confirmed as the best estimate at date-event (σ, t) under the revised probabilities.

The fact that the conditional expectation coefficients $(E(x \mid \sigma), \sigma \in \mathbb{F})$ solve the minimum problem (3) can be expressed in a more abstract (geometric) form. Let $\mathscr{F}$ denote the field generated by $\mathbb{F}$ and let $Y_{\mathscr{F}}$ denote the linear subspace of $\mathbb{R}^S$ consisting of $\mathscr{F}$-measurable random variables. By Proposition 26.4 this space is given by

$$Y_{\mathscr{F}} = \left\{ y \in \mathbb{R}^S \; \middle| \; y = \sum_{\sigma \in \mathbb{F}} \alpha_\sigma \chi_\sigma, \quad \alpha_\sigma \in \mathbb{R} \right\}$$

Thus the choice of the coefficients $(\alpha_\sigma, \sigma \in \mathbb{F})$ is equivalent to the choice of a vector in $Y_{\mathscr{F}}$.

In Section 14 it was shown that when $\mathbb{R}^S$ is considered as a space of random variables on a probability space $(\mathbf{S}, \mathscr{S}, \mathscr{P})$, the natural inner product is given by

$$[\![x, y]\!]_{\mathscr{P}} = E(xy) = \sum_{s \in \mathbf{S}} x_s y_s \mathscr{P}(s)$$

The associated norm

$$\| x \|_{\mathscr{P}} = \left(E(x^2) \right)^{1/2} = \left(\sum_{s \in \mathbf{S}} x_s^2 \mathscr{P}(s) \right)^{1/2}$$

is precisely adapted to the least squares criterion, since if $y = \sum_{\sigma \in \mathbb{F}} \alpha_\sigma \chi_\sigma$ then

$$\sum_{\sigma \in \mathbb{F}} \sum_{s \in \sigma} (x_s - \alpha_\sigma)^2 \mathscr{P}(s) = \|x - y\|_{\mathscr{P}}^2$$

Thus the minimum problem (3) can be expressed as the problem of finding the $\mathscr{F}$-measurable random variable y which is closest to x in the $\| \ \|_{\mathscr{P}}$ norm

$$\min_{y \in Y_{\mathscr{F}}} \|x - y\|_{\mathscr{P}}$$

The solution of this problem is given by

$$y^* = \sum_{\sigma \in \mathbb{F}} \alpha_\sigma^* \chi_\sigma = \sum_{\sigma \in \mathbb{F}} E(x \,|\, \sigma) \, \chi_\sigma = E(x \,|\, \mathscr{F})$$

The conditional expectation $E(x \,|\, \mathscr{F})$ is the vector in the subspace of $\mathscr{F}$-measurable random variables $Y_{\mathscr{F}}$ which lies closest to x in the probability norm. As we showed in Proposition 14.14, this means that *the conditional expectation $E(x \,|\, \mathscr{F})$ is the projection of x onto the subspace of $\mathscr{F}$-measurable random variables $Y_{\mathscr{F}}$.* In more abstract settings where the state space is not finite and/or the field $\mathscr{F}$ is not generated by a partition, this projection property is often used as a convenient way of defining the conditional expectation $E(x \,|\, \mathscr{F})$.

26.8 Proposition (Conditional Expectation as Best Approximation): *If $x \in \mathbb{R}^S$ is a random variable on the probability space $(\mathbf{S}, \mathscr{S}, \mathscr{P})$ and if $\mathscr{F}$ is a subfield of $\mathscr{S}$ generated by a partition $\mathbb{F}$, then*

$$E(x \,|\, \mathscr{F}) = \arg \min_{y \in Y_{\mathscr{F}}} \|x - y\|_{\mathscr{P}}$$

The conditional expectation $E(x \,|\, \mathscr{F})$ is thus the best $\mathscr{F}$-measurable approximation of x.

PROOF: Since $\mathbb{F}$ is a partition of $\mathbf{S}$, $\sum_{\sigma \in \mathbb{F}} \chi_\sigma = \mathbb{1}$ and $x = \sum_{\sigma \in \mathbb{F}} x\chi_\sigma$. Note that

$$\min_{y \in Y_{\mathscr{F}}} \|x - y\|_{\mathscr{P}}^2 = \min_{(\alpha_\sigma, \ \sigma \in \mathbb{F})} \left\| \sum_{\sigma \in \mathbb{F}} (x - \alpha_\sigma)\chi_\sigma \right\|_{\mathscr{P}}^2 \qquad (5)$$
$$= \min_{(\alpha_\sigma, \ \sigma \in \mathbb{F})} \sum_{\sigma \in \mathbb{F}} \|(x - \alpha_\sigma)\chi_\sigma\|_{\mathscr{P}}^2$$

since $[\![(x - \alpha_\sigma)\chi_\sigma, (x - \alpha_{\sigma'})\chi_{\sigma'}]\!]_{\mathscr{P}} = 0$ for $\sigma \neq \sigma'$. It is easy to see that the solution of

$$\min_{\alpha_\sigma} \sum_{s \in \sigma} (x(s) - \alpha_\sigma)^2 \mathscr{P}(s)$$

is given by $\alpha_\sigma^* = \sum_{s\in\sigma} x(s)\mathscr{P}(s)/\sum_{s\in\sigma}\mathscr{P}(s) = E(x\,|\,\sigma)$, so that the solution of (5) is $y^* = \sum_{\sigma\in\mathbb{F}} E(x\,|\,\sigma)\,\chi_\sigma = E(x\,|\,\mathscr{F})$. $\square$

Process Representation

In the previous chapter the concept of a stochastic economy was constructed from

- a set of time periods $\mathbf{T} = \{0, 1, \ldots, T\}$
- a set of states of nature $\mathbf{S} = \{1, \ldots, S\}$
- a family of partitions $\mathbb{F} = (\mathbb{F}_0, \ldots, \mathbb{F}_T)$ of $\mathbf{S}$

with the interpretation that $s \in \mathbf{S}$ indexes the possible paths that the economy can follow over the $T + 1$ periods, and $\mathbb{F}_t$ defines the information available at time $t \in \mathbf{T}$. The elements $\sigma_t \in \mathbb{F}_t$ are the basic observable events at time t, and the information revealed by observing the characteristics of the economy must be consistent with the unfolding of information expressed by the sequence of partitions $(\mathbb{F}_t)_{t\in\mathbf{T}}$. In Chapter 4, this consistency condition was ensured by defining the characteristics of the economy on the *event-tree* $\mathbb{D}$ associated with $\mathbb{F}$. In this chapter, the concept of *measurability*, introduced in Definition 26.3, is used as an alternative (and equivalent) way of ensuring that the consistency condition holds.

Each partition $\mathbb{F}_t$ generates a field of subsets $\mathscr{F}_t$ of $\mathbf{S}$. Thus a family of information partitions

$$\mathbb{F} = (\mathbb{F}_0, \mathbb{F}_1, \ldots, \mathbb{F}_T)$$

generates a family of fields

$$\mathscr{F} = (\mathscr{F}_0, \mathscr{F}_1, \ldots, \mathscr{F}_T)$$

Reflecting the fact that information increases over time, the family $\mathbb{F}$ satisfies

$$\mathbb{F}_0 = \mathbf{S}, \quad \mathbb{F}_T = \{\{1\}, \ldots, \{S\}\}, \quad \mathbb{F}_t \text{ is finer than } \mathbb{F}_{t-1}, \quad t = 1, \ldots, T$$

Since the partition $\mathbb{F}_t$ is finer than $\mathbb{F}_{t-1}$, the field $\mathscr{F}_t$ has more subsets than $\mathscr{F}_{t-1}$ or equivalently $\mathscr{F}_{t-1} \subset \mathscr{F}_t$. Thus $\mathscr{F}$ is a sequence of subfields of $\mathscr{S}$ such that

$$\mathscr{F}_0 = \{\mathbf{S}, \emptyset\}, \quad \mathscr{F}_T = \mathscr{S}, \quad \mathscr{F}_{t-1} \subset \mathscr{F}_t, \quad t = 1, \ldots, T \tag{6}$$

26.9 Definition: A sequence $\mathscr{F} = (\mathscr{F}_t)_{t\in\mathbf{T}}$ of subfields of $\mathscr{S}$ satisfying (6) is called a *filtration*.

Although the above definition permits more general filtrations, in the analysis that follows filtrations will always be assumed to be generated by a sequence of progressively finer partitions, even when this is not explicitly mentioned.

26.10 Definition: A (vector-valued) process $x : \mathbf{T} \times \mathbf{S} \longrightarrow \mathbb{R}^k$ is said to be *adapted to the filtration* $\mathscr{F} = (\mathscr{F}_t)_{t \in \mathbf{T}}$ if, for all $t \in \mathbf{T}$, each component of the function $x_t : \mathbf{S} \longrightarrow \mathbb{R}$ defined by $x_t(s) = x(t,s)$, $\forall\, s \in \mathbf{S}$, is $\mathscr{F}_t$-measurable.

In Proposition 26.4 it was shown that if $\mathscr{F}_t$ is generated by a partition $\mathbb{F}_t$, then $x_t : \mathbf{S} \longrightarrow \mathbb{R}^k$ is $\mathscr{F}_t$-measurable if and only if x_t is constant on each subset σ_t of $\mathbb{F}_t$. When the filtration $\mathscr{F}$ is generated by a sequence of information partitions $\mathbb{F}$, the requirement that a process x is adapted to $\mathscr{F}$ is equivalent to the condition expressed in equation (6) of Section 18

$$x_t(s) = x_t(s') \quad \forall\, s, s' \in \sigma \in \mathbb{F}_t, \quad \forall\, t \in [0, \tau], \quad \forall\, \tau \in \mathbf{T}$$

This ensures that an agent's observation (or choice) of the process x up to time τ does not reveal (or use) more information than that contained in the partitions $\mathbb{F}_t$ up to time τ. Thus a function $x : \mathbb{D} \longrightarrow \mathbb{R}^k$ defined on the event-tree $\mathbb{D}$ associated with a family of partitions $\mathbb{F}$, which we have written as $x = (x(\xi), \xi \in \mathbb{D})$, is equivalent to a process $x : \mathbf{T} \times \mathbf{S} \longrightarrow \mathbb{R}^k$ adapted to the filtration $\mathscr{F}$ generated by $\mathbb{F}$. The passage from one representation to the other is given by:

- if $\xi \in \mathbb{D}$, $\xi = (t, \sigma)$, $\sigma \in \mathbb{F}_t$, then $x(\xi) = x_t(s)$, $\forall\, s \in \sigma$
- if $(t, s) \in \mathbf{T} \times \mathbf{S}$, then there is a unique $\sigma \in \mathbb{F}_t$, such that $s \in \sigma$ and $x_t(s) = x(\xi)$ for $\xi = (t, \sigma)$.

It is sometimes convenient to use the following notation, which is intermediate between the node notation and the process notation:

$$\text{for } \sigma \in \mathbb{F}_t, \quad x_t(\sigma) = x(\xi) \quad \text{if } \xi = (t, \sigma)$$

or equivalently

$$\text{for } \sigma \in \mathbb{F}_t, \quad x_t(\sigma) = x_t(s), \quad \forall\, s \in \sigma$$

Thus when the unfolding of information in a stochastic economy is described by a family of progressively finer partitions $\mathbb{F} = (\mathbb{F}_0, \dots, \mathbb{F}_T)$, there are two mathematical objects can be associated with $\mathbb{F}$:

- the event-tree $\mathbb{D}$
- the filtration $\mathscr{F}$

The characteristics of the economy and the equilibrium variables (the agents' actions and the prices) can then be expressed in one of two ways as:

- *functions defined on the event-tree* $\mathbb{D}$ (or equivalently as vectors with components indexed by the nodes of $\mathbb{D}$)
- *random processes adapted to the filtration* $\mathscr{F}$.

These two representations are equivalent, and one may adopt whichever is more convenient for the study of the problem at hand. In the previous chapter, the first representation was used to study the properties of equilibrium allocations; in this chapter, the second approach is used (most of the time) to study the properties of equilibrium prices.

Martingale

The idea of a conditional expectation, applied to a random process adapted to a filtration $\mathscr{F} = (\mathscr{F}_t)_{t \in \mathbf{T}}$, leads to the concept of a martingale. This is a process for which the current value is the best estimate, given current information, of its value at any future date.

26.11 Definition: A pair $(x, \mathscr{F})$, where $\mathscr{F}$ is a filtration and x is adapted to $\mathscr{F}$, is called a *martingale* if, for $t, \tau \in \mathbf{T}$,

$$E(x_\tau \,|\, \mathscr{F}_t) = x_t \quad \text{for} \quad \tau \geq t$$

When the filtration $\mathscr{F}$ is generated by a family of information partitions $\mathbb{F} = (\mathbb{F}_t)_{t \in \mathbf{T}}$, then at any node $\xi = (t, \sigma)$, $\sigma \in \mathbb{F}_t$, the best estimate of the value of the random variable x on the successors of ξ at a subsequent date τ is given by the conditional expectation $E(x_\tau \,|\, \sigma)$. For a martingale this value is equal to its current value $x(\xi) = x_t(s)$. The three examples of martingales that follow were the first prototype models that were used to describe the random behavior of security prices.

26.12 Example (Random Walk):   Let $\{\epsilon_t, t \in \mathbf{T}\}$ be a sequence of mutually independent random variables defined on $\mathbf{S}$ with $E(\epsilon_t) = 0$, $t \in \mathbf{T}$. The process x_t defined by the sum

$$x_t = \epsilon_0 + \cdots + \epsilon_t, \quad t \in \mathbf{T}$$

or equivalently by the stochastic difference equation

$$x_{t+1} = x_t + \epsilon_{t+1}, \quad t = 0, \ldots, T-1, \quad x_0 = \epsilon_0 \tag{7}$$

is called a *random walk*. This process has the characteristic that the increment $x_{t+1} - x_t$ is independent of the previous values $x_0, \ldots, x_t$ of the process. It was this property which was observed in the time series of security prices and led to the adoption of the random walk as the first stochastic model of speculative prices.

Let $\sigma(x_0, \ldots, x_t)$ denote the smallest field with respect to which $x_0, \ldots, x_t$ are measurable. If $x_\tau(\mathbf{S})$ denotes the possible values of the random variable x_τ for $\tau = 0, \ldots, t$, then the field $\sigma(x_0, \ldots, x_t)$ is generated by the partition

$$\{\sigma_{k_0, \ldots, k_t}, \; k_\tau \in x_\tau(\mathbf{S}), \; \tau = 0, \ldots, t\} \tag{8}$$

where

$$\sigma_{k_0, \ldots, k_t} = \{s \in \mathbf{S} \mid x_0(s) = k_0, \ldots, x_t(s) = k_t\}$$

If $\mathscr{F}_t = \sigma(x_0, \ldots, x_t)$, then $\mathscr{F} = (\mathscr{F}_t)_{t \in \mathbf{T}}$ is a filtration, and the process $x = (x_t)_{t \in \mathbf{T}}$ is adapted to $\mathscr{F}$. Taking the conditional expectation of (7) gives (by linearity of the conditional expectation)

$$E\left(x_{t+1} \mid \mathscr{F}_t\right) = E(x_t \mid \mathscr{F}_t) + E\left(\epsilon_{t+1} \mid \mathscr{F}_t\right) = x_t + E\left(\epsilon_{t+1} \mid \mathscr{F}_t\right) \tag{9}$$

We want to show that

$$E\left(\epsilon_{t+1} \mid \mathscr{F}_t\right) = E(\epsilon_{t+1}) \tag{10}$$

since $\mathscr{F}_t$ conveys no information about ϵ_{t+1}. Since $\mathscr{F}_t$ is generated by the partition described by (8), showing (10) is equivalent to showing

$$E\left(\epsilon_{t+1} \mid \sigma_{k_0, \ldots, k_t}\right) = E(\epsilon_{t+1}), \quad \forall \, (k_0, \ldots, k_t) \in x_0(\mathbf{S}) \times \cdots \times x_t(\mathbf{S})$$

By definition

$$E\left(\epsilon_{t+1} \mid \sigma_{k_0, \ldots, k_t}\right) = \sum_{s \in \sigma_{k_0, \ldots, k_t}} \epsilon_{t+1}(s) \frac{\mathscr{P}(s)}{\mathscr{P}(s \mid x_0(s) = k_0, \ldots, x_t(s) = k_t)}$$

$$= \sum_{\alpha \in \epsilon_{t+1}(\mathbf{S})} \alpha \frac{\mathscr{P}\left(s \mid \epsilon_{t+1}(s) = \alpha, x_0(s) = k_0, \ldots, x_t(s) = k_t\right)}{\mathscr{P}(s \mid x_0(s) = k_0, \ldots, x_t(s) = k_t)}$$

$$= \sum_{\alpha \in \epsilon_{t+1}(\mathbf{S})} \alpha \mathscr{P}\left(s \mid \epsilon_{t+1}(s) = \alpha\right) = E(\epsilon_{t+1})$$

so that (10) holds. Since $E(\epsilon_{t+1}) = 0$, (9) implies

$$E\left(x_{t+1} \mid \mathscr{F}_t\right) = x_t$$

By induction, using Proposition 26.7(iii), $E\left(x_{t+\tau} \mid \mathscr{F}_t\right) = x_t$ for $\tau \geq 1$, so that $(x, \mathscr{F})$ is a martingale. $\square$

26.13 Example (Multiplicative Random Walk): The fact that security prices must always remain non-negative, and that distributional assumptions on percentage rather than absolute price changes are more natural, leads to modelling the stochastic behavior of a speculative price by the *multiplicative random walk* defined by the product

$$x_t = \epsilon_t \epsilon_{t-1} \cdots \epsilon_0, \quad t \in \mathbf{T}$$

or equivalently by the stochastic difference equation

$$x_{t+1} = \epsilon_{t+1} x_t, \quad t = 0, \dots, T-1, \quad x_0 = \epsilon_0 \tag{11}$$

where $\{\epsilon_t, \ t \in \mathbf{T}\}$ is a sequence of positive, mutually independent random variables defined on $\mathbf{S}$ with $E(\epsilon_t) = 1$, $t \in \mathbf{T}$. In this case, the percentage gains

$$\frac{x_{t+1} - x_t}{x_t} = \frac{x_{t+1}}{x_t} - 1$$

are independent of the previous values $x_0, \dots, x_t$ and are zero on average, $E\left((x_{t+1}/x_t) - 1\right) = 0$.

Let $\mathscr{F}_t = \sigma(x_0, \dots, x_t)$, where $\sigma(x_0, \dots, x_t)$ is defined as in Example 26.12. Taking the conditional expectation of (11) and using Proposition 26.7(i)(b) gives

$$E\left(x_{t+1} \,\middle|\, \mathscr{F}_t\right) = x_t E\left(\epsilon_{t+1} \,\middle|\, \mathscr{F}_t\right) = x_t E(\epsilon_{t+1})$$

since ϵ_{t+1} is independent of $x_0, \dots, x_t$. Since $E(\epsilon_{t+1}) = 1$, $E\left(x_{t+1} \,\middle|\, \mathscr{F}_t\right) = x_t$; by induction, using Proposition 26.7(iii),

$$E\left(x_{t+\tau} \,\middle|\, \mathscr{F}_t\right) = x_t, \quad \tau \geq 1$$

so that $(x, \mathscr{F})$ is a martingale. $\square$

26.14 Example (Conditional Expectation): Let $y : \mathbf{S} \longrightarrow \mathbb{R}$ be a random variable and let $\mathscr{F} = (\mathscr{F}_t)_{t \in \mathbf{T}}$ be a filtration. If x_t is the *conditional expectation* of y given the information $\mathscr{F}_t$ at time t

$$x_t = E(y \,|\, \mathscr{F}_t), \quad t \in \mathbf{T}$$

then by Proposition 26.7(iii)

$$E\left(x_{t+\tau} \,\middle|\, \mathscr{F}_t\right) = E\left(E\left(y \,\middle|\, \mathscr{F}_{t+\tau}\right) \,\middle|\, \mathscr{F}_t\right) = E(y \,|\, \mathscr{F}_t) = x_t, \quad \tau \geq 1$$

so that $(x, \mathscr{F})$ is a martingale. In the next section, we will show that a process of this form provides a useful first approximation to the price process of a security, such as a futures contract, whose sole dividend consists of a random payment y at the terminal date T, x_t denoting its price at any date t prior to the maturity date T. $\square$

Martingales are a remarkable class of stochastic processes which have deep and surprising connections with many parts of modern mathematics. They are of special interest in studying security markets, since they characterize the class of processes against which no trading or gambling strategy based on currently available information can yield an expected profit (can beat the system).

Let $X : \mathbf{T} \times \mathbf{S} \longrightarrow \mathbb{R}^J$ be a vector-valued process in (against) which an investment (a gambling) strategy can be made. X_{jt} is taken to be the gain from holding a one-unit position (gamble) in component j from date 0 to date $t-1$: the difference $X_{jt+1} - X_{jt}$ is thus the gain from a one-unit position in component j during period t. The information is modelled by a filtration $\mathscr{F} = (\mathscr{F}_t)_{t \in \mathbf{T}}$, and X is adapted to $\mathscr{F}$. An investment (gambling) strategy, which only uses information available at each date, is a process $z : \mathbf{T} \times \mathbf{S} \longrightarrow \mathbb{R}^J$ adapted to $\mathscr{F}$ where $z_t(s) = (z_{1t}(s), \ldots, z_{Jt}(s))$ is a J-vector of $\mathscr{F}_t$-measurable random variables describing the amount invested in each component of the process X at date t, conditional on the event which occurs at date t. The *gain* at date t associated with such a strategy is defined by

$$Y_t^z = \sum_{\theta=1}^{t} (X_\theta - X_{\theta-1}) z_{\theta-1}, \quad t = 1, \ldots, T \tag{12}$$

with $Y_0^z = 0$, since at date 0 no gain or loss is inherited from the past. Let $Y^z = (Y_t^z)_{t \in \mathbf{T}}$ denote the associated gain process.

Let $\mathscr{Z}$ denote the set of all $\mathscr{F}$-adapted trading strategies with $z_T = 0$, since trades at the terminal date do not influence the associated gain process

$$\mathscr{Z} = \left\{ z : \mathbf{T} \times \mathbf{S} \longrightarrow \mathbb{R}^J \mid z \text{ is } \mathscr{F}\text{-measurable and } z_T = 0 \right\}$$

The next theorem asserts that the process X is a martingale if and only if for every trading strategy $z \in \mathscr{Z}$, from the perspective of date 0, the expected gain at each date is zero, $E(Y_t^z) = 0$, $t \in \mathbf{T}$. Note that it suffices to impose the zero expected value condition for the gain at the terminal date, since a positive expected gain at date t can be converted into a positive expected gain at date T by stopping the trade at date t and carrying the gain forward to date T. Thus

$$E(Y_t^z) = 0, \quad t \in \mathbf{T}, \quad \forall z \in \mathscr{Z} \Longleftrightarrow E(Y_T^z) = 0, \quad \forall z \in \mathscr{Z}$$

As is shown in Theorem 26.15, the condition of zero expected gain at the terminal date (for every trading strategy) is stronger than it might at first appear, since it implies that from the perspective of any date t the additional expected gain from continuing any trading strategy z until a subsequent date $t + \tau$ (rather than cashing in Y_t) is zero. In fact

$$E(Y_T^z) = 0, \ \forall z \in \mathcal{Z} \Longleftrightarrow E\left(Y_{t+\tau}^z \,\middle|\, \mathcal{F}_t\right) = Y_t^z, \ 0 \leq \tau \leq T - t, \ t \in \mathbf{T}, \ \forall z \in \mathcal{Z}$$

As is shown in the proof below, this follows from the fact that a positive additional expected gain at a particular date-event (t, σ) can be converted into an expected gain from date 0, by employing the the trading strategy z only from node (t, σ) onwards, eliminating trading before date t, and, if the event σ does not occur, after date t as well. Furthermore, since z is not constrained to be non-negative, a negative additional expected gain can always be converted into a positive additional expected gain by reversing the sign of the trading strategy (replacing z by $-z$).

26.15 Theorem (Martingale is Equivalent to Zero Expected Gain): *Let $X : \mathbf{T} \times \mathbf{S} \longrightarrow \mathbb{R}^J$ be a process adapted to a filtration $\mathcal{F} = (\mathcal{F}_t)_{t \in \mathbf{T}}$ and, for any strategy $z \in \mathcal{Z}$, let Y^z be the associated gain process given by*

$$Y_0^z = 0, \quad Y_t^z = \sum_{\theta=1}^{t}(X_\theta - X_{\theta-1})z_{\theta-1}, \quad t = 1, \ldots, T$$

The following conditions are equivalent:

(i) X *is a martingale*
(ii) Y^z *is a martingale,* $\forall z \in \mathcal{Z}$
(iii) $E(Y_T^z) = 0, \ \forall z \in \mathcal{Z}$

PROOF: (i) $\Longleftrightarrow$ (ii) For $0 \leq t \leq T - 1$

$$E\left(Y_{t+1}^z - Y_t^z \,\middle|\, \mathcal{F}_t\right) = E\left((X_{t+1} - X_t)z_t \,\middle|\, \mathcal{F}_t\right) = \left(E\left(X_{t+1} \,\middle|\, \mathcal{F}_t\right) - X_t\right)z_t$$

since X_t and z_t are $\mathcal{F}_t$-measurable (see Proposition 26.7). Thus the property $E\left(Y_{t+1}^z \,\middle|\, \mathcal{F}_t\right) = Y_t^z$, for all $\mathcal{F}$-adapted z and all t satisfying $0 \leq t \leq T - 1$, is equivalent to the property $E\left(X_{t+1} \,\middle|\, \mathcal{F}_t\right) = X_t$, $0 \leq t \leq T - 1$. Using Proposition 26.7(iii) completes the proof.

(ii) $\Longrightarrow$ (iii) If Y^z is a martingale with $Y_0^z = 0$, then by Proposition 26.7(ii)(a)

$$E(Y_T^z) = E(Y_T^z \,|\, \mathcal{F}_0) = Y_0^z = 0$$

(iii) $\Longrightarrow$ (ii) Suppose that for some $\bar{z} \in \mathcal{Z}$, $Y^{\bar{z}}$ is not a martingale, then there exist $\bar{t}, \bar{\tau}$ and $\bar{\sigma} \in \mathbb{F}_{\bar{t}}$ such that $E\left(Y_{\bar{t}+\bar{\tau}}^{\bar{z}} \,\middle|\, \bar{\sigma}\right) \neq Y_{\bar{t}}^{\bar{z}}(\bar{\sigma})$. Consider the trading strategy z defined by

$$z_t(s) = \begin{cases} 0 & \text{if } t < \bar{t} \text{ or } t \geq \bar{t} + \bar{\tau} \text{ or } s \notin \bar{\sigma} \\ \bar{z}_t(s) & \text{otherwise} \end{cases}$$

the associated gain process is

$$
Y_t^z(s) = \begin{cases} 0, & \text{if } t < \bar{t} \text{ or } s \notin \bar{\sigma} \\ Y_t^{\bar{z}}(s) - Y_{\bar{t}}^{\bar{z}}(s), & \text{if } \bar{t} \leq t \leq \bar{t} + \bar{\tau} \text{ and } s \in \bar{\sigma} \\ Y_{\bar{t}+\bar{\tau}}^{\bar{z}}(s) - Y_{\bar{t}}^{\bar{z}}(s), & \text{if } t \geq \bar{t} + \bar{\tau} \text{ and } s \in \bar{\sigma} \end{cases}
$$

and the expected profit at the terminal date is

$$
\begin{aligned}
E(Y_T^z) &= \sum_{s \in \bar{\sigma}} \left(Y_{\bar{t}+\bar{\tau}}^{\bar{z}}(s) - Y_{\bar{t}}^{\bar{z}}(s) \right) \mathscr{P}(s) \\
&= E\left(Y_{\bar{t}+\bar{\tau}}^{\bar{z}} - Y_{\bar{t}}^{\bar{z}} \,\middle|\, \bar{\sigma} \right) \mathscr{P}(\bar{\sigma}) \neq 0
\end{aligned}
$$

which contradicts (iii). $\square$

Note that the informational requirement on the trading strategies $z \in \mathscr{Z}$, namely that at each date $t \in \mathbf{T}$, z_t is $\mathscr{F}_t$-measurable, does not impose any limits on the sophistication employed in constructing z_t from the information available at date t: since the past values of X, z and Y are known, z_t can use all this information i.e. it can be any function of $(X_0, \ldots, X_t, z_0, \ldots, z_{t-1}, Y_0, \ldots, Y_t)$. In particular it can involve any rule for going in and out of the market, based on properties of the time series of X up to date t or on the realized gain Y up to date t. None of these strategies can beat the market if X is a martingale—they all make zero profit on average.

27. EFFICIENT MARKETS UNDER RISK NEUTRALITY

Ownership of a financial security gives the right to a stream of dividends in the future, and the chief characteristic of such streams is that they are random, that is, they cannot be predicted with certainty. A firm may make substantial profits and hence offer substantial dividends if a new product that it has recently launched proves to be timely and well-adapted to the needs of consumers; if the product is not well received, then the firm will be left with little or no return on its investment with which to reward its equity owners. As time evolves, it becomes progressively clearer if the product is of just the kind to catch the whims of consumers or if it will simply sit unsold on the shelves of supermarkets. The story is familiar, but the point is important: as time evolves, investors are constantly discovering more about the likely prospects of future dividends. On modern security markets there is a huge array of such financial contracts, and information is constantly pouring onto the market regarding their future earnings prospects. How do the prices of securities respond to this flow of new information?

Experience suggests what the efficient markets hypothesis affirms: since securities traded on public exchanges are readily bought and sold at small cost, prices of securities respond promptly to new information, rising when signals indicate more favorable future dividends and falling when unfavorable news arrives regarding their future earnings prospects. The process of price formation and market making is a complex phenomenon, but loosely speaking it is the buying and selling activity of the professional investors (those who trade on these markets all day and every day) in response to the latest news that accounts for the rapid revision of prices to reflect new information.[1] For professional traders the name of the game is to be constantly on the lookout for securities whose prices are mismatched to their most recently revised earnings prospects: in the presence of such active trading, unexploited profit opportunities do not sit around for long. The efficient markets hypothesis postulates that the adjustment of prices to information is so fast that, to all intents and purposes, prices adjust "immediately" to reflect new information. Thus the typical investor, who is not involved in such market making activity, can not expect to earn abnormal profit by exploiting new information better than the market.

The objective of this chapter is to show how the appealing (albeit vague) intuition behind the efficient markets hypothesis can be made precise in the framework of a formal model. This requires two steps: the first consists in formalizing the idea that prices leave no opportunities for abnormal profit based on current information; the second, in characterizing the properties of price processes which satisfy this condition.

It is instructive to begin the analysis in the idealized setting of an economy with risk-neutral agents. The rarefied atmosphere in which risk-neutral agents with zero time preference conduct their affairs is, strictly speaking, far removed from the real world—after all, agents can only be assumed to be risk neutral if they are so rich that they can face the possibility of incurring substantial losses without their consumption being reduced to the point where a marginal unit is very valuable. Few agents in the real world reach this blissful state. Furthermore the existence of an elaborate system of financial markets could not possibly be justified in an economy in which all agents are risk neutral and have no time preference; such agents would find no gains from trading on financial markets.

---

[1] In asserting that the prices of securities on the whole adjust in a timely and accurate way to the arrival of new information, we do not take into account the phenomenon of *speculative phases* created by fads, fashions and other market moods which can lead prices of securities far out of line with any reasonable estimate of their future dividends. The circumstances in which such speculative phenomena arise are as yet not well understood but seem to be—at least in their most extreme forms—somewhat exceptional. The theory presented in this chapter does not attempt to account for such speculative phenomena.

However, as we shall see, the thought process involved in analyzing the pricing of securities in such an idealized setting provides a valuable short-cut or guide to the analysis of pricing in the real world where agents are risk averse. Furthermore, the properties of equilibrium prices in an economy with risk-neutral agents may be *approximately* verified in an economy with risk-averse agents, if some of the agents or institutions trading on the financial markets are extremely wealthy. Such agents (institutions), who can be considered as approximately risk neutral, will be willing to exploit strategies which yield positive expected profit even if they involve substantial losses in some contingencies, and will drive the prices of securities close to the value predicted by the assumption of risk neutrality.

In an economy in which agents are risk neutral, any trade with a positive expected value is viewed as a profitable trade. Since in an equilibrium there are by definition no unexploited profit opportunities left, equilibrium prices must be such that every trade based on currently available information yields zero expected profit. A good intuition for the implications of this condition for the pricing of securities may be obtained by considering a strikingly simple example—the pricing of a futures contract on a commodity. Such a contract has a dividend process which is zero at every date prior to its maturity date T, at which date its dividend is the current spot market value of (one unit of) the commodity. Its date T dividend is thus a random variable which we denote by

$$p_T = (p(T, s), s \in \mathbf{S})$$

The contract is traded at every date between 0 and $T - 1$, and its price process is

$$q = (q_t(s), (t, s) \in \mathbf{T} \times \mathbf{S})$$

The process of information acquisition is described by a sequence $\mathbb{F} = (\mathbb{F}_t)_{t \in \mathbf{T}}$ of progressively finer partitions, and there is an objective probability $\rho_s > 0$, $s \in \mathbf{S}$ for the occurrence of each state.

Suppose that at date $t \in \mathbf{T}$ the economy has reached node $\xi = (t, \sigma)$. Given the information $\sigma \in \mathbb{F}_t$, the best estimate of the future spot price p_T is, by Proposition 26.8

$$E(p_T \mid \sigma) = \frac{\sum\limits_{s \in \sigma} \rho_s p(T, s)}{\sum\limits_{s \in \sigma} \rho_s}$$

If, as a first approximation, not only the risk aversion but also the time preference of agents can be ignored, then the price $q_t(s)$ of the futures contract must coincide with this best estimate of the future spot price

$$q_t(\sigma) = E(p_T \mid \sigma) \tag{1}$$

For suppose $q_t(\sigma) < E(p_T \,|\, \sigma)$, then an investor can make a positive expected profit by using the following strategy: at node $\xi = (t, \sigma)$ the investor buys one unit of the futures contract for the price $q_t(\sigma)$ and earns the dividend $p(T, s)$ at date T if state s occurs. The expected gain is thus

$$-q_t(\sigma) + E(p_T \,|\, \sigma) > 0$$

If $q_t(\sigma) > E(p_T \,|\, \sigma)$ then selling one unit of the futures contract at node ξ yields a positive expected profit. Since this reasoning can be made at each node, in the absence of impatience and risk aversion, the price process q_t of the futures contract must satisfy

$$q_t = E(p_T \,|\, \mathscr{F}_t), \quad t = 0, \ldots, T - 1 \tag{2}$$

(2) is a prototype formula for a security price—the price is a conditional expectation of some future variable (in this case the future spot price).

To be more concrete, and to illustrate the way such a conditional expectation changes with the arrival of new information, consider in more detail the factors which influence the future spot price of a commodity like wheat. Suppose date T is the harvest time. In practice (to exaggerate a little), the principal source of randomness in the spot price at harvest time comes from the supply side, the demand for wheat being relatively stable and inelastic: a poor (bumper) crop thus translates into a high (low) spot price.[2] The weather conditions during the course of the growing season are the principal factors influencing the size of the harvest, and there is a critical period during the growing season when the exact profile of weather conditions (temperature, humidity) plays a particularly important role in determining the size of the subsequent harvest. Prior to this period the conditional expectation (futures price) fluctuates around the spot price corresponding to the average harvest, and the fluctuations are relatively small since only a small amount of information about the size of the final crop is being revealed. When the weather conditions during the critical period are revealed, there is typically a substantial change in the futures price, reflecting the fact that the future harvest is then largely determined. If during the critical period weather conditions were favorable (unfavorable) then the subsequent futures price typically exhibits

---

[2]This description of the wheat market is purposefully stylized. By assuming that demand is a relatively stable function of the spot price the usual general equilibrium dependence on prices of other goods is factored out. Furthermore wheat is a storable good, so the spot price (at the harvest time) depends both on the size of the new crop and the size of the carryover into the next year. The latter in turn is influenced by the size of the carryover from the previous period and the expected future spot price. Finally in a world economy where wheat is produced in different climactic zones in both hemispheres, the "harvest time" is more evenly spread over the calendar year.

small fluctuations around the low (high) spot price associated with a bumper (poor) harvest, unless some unlikely event (such as a severe drought or flood) occurs which significantly changes the estimates for the future crop.

Since the futures price process $(q_t, t = 0, 1, \ldots, T-1)$ is the conditional expectation of a random variable, it is a martingale (see Example 26.14). Equation (2) suggests that the price of the futures contract at date T should be taken to be the spot price

$$q_T = E(p_T \,|\, \mathscr{F}_T) = p_T \tag{3}$$

Adopting this convention amounts to defining the price of the futures contract as the "before-dividend" price i.e. as the price at date T before the one unit of commodity has been delivered.[3] With q_T defined by (3), the process $(q_t)_{t \in \mathbf{T}}$ is a martingale

$$q_t = E(q_\tau \,|\, \mathscr{F}_t), \quad t \le \tau, \quad t, \tau \in \mathbf{T} \tag{4}$$

(2) and (4) express remarkable properties of a futures price: not only is the price of the futures contract at date t the best estimate of the spot price at the terminal date, it is also the best estimate at date t of what the best predictor $q_{t+\tau}$ will be at any later date when more information will have been revealed. This implies that a trading strategy which consists of buying one unit of the futures contract at date t in order to sell it at a later date, can not yield an expected profit. The rule for choosing the right moment to sell—the optimal stopping time—can be as sophisticated as imaginable, based on the presence of head and shoulders, neckline, or bear-trap formations in the series of past prices,[4] or any related devices for extrapolating from current information, and still on average the profit will be zero.

The argument which led to the pricing formula (2) was simply an application of the "zero expected profit" condition at each node in the event-tree: this led at once to formula (4), asserting that the futures price is a martingale. This result is a particular application of Theorem 26.15 which asserts, in a much more general setting, that a payoff process X against which no trading strategy based on current information can ever make an expected profit over any time intervals, no matter how they are chosen, must be a martingale. Let us show how this result can be used to obtain pricing formulae, which are the

---

[3]This involves a temporary change in the convention normally adopted in this book, by which the price of a financial contract is the "after-dividend" price, so that the price of a security at date T is zero. This change of convention, convenient in the case of a futures contract, is exceptional and limited to this paragraph.

[4]These terms are taken from so-called *technical analysis* which seeks methods for determining the appropriate moments to "enter" and "exit" the market, based on patterns in the behavior of past prices (see Gould (1973)).

analogues of (2) and (4), for an arbitrary family of securities traded on the financial markets on the time interval $\mathbf{T}$.

Let $(\mathbf{S},\mathscr{S},\mathscr{P})$ denote a probability space, and let $\mathscr{F} = (\mathscr{F}_t)_{t\in\mathbf{T}}$ be a filtration describing the common information available to all agents in the economy at each date t on the time interval $\mathbf{T} = \{0, 1, \ldots, T\}$, $\mathscr{F}$ being derived from a family of partitions $\mathbb{F} = (\mathbb{F}_t)_{t\in\mathbf{T}}$ with associated event-tree $\mathbb{D}$. Consider a financial structure (ζ, V) consisting of J securities issued on the time interval $\mathbf{T}$ (see Definition 20.3), with the usual convention that $V_t^j(s) = 0$ if j has not been issued at date t in state s. Let t_j denote the date at which security j is issued: $\xi(j) = (t_j, \sigma_j)$, $\sigma_j \in \mathbb{F}_{t_j}$. Investors are assumed to be risk neutral: to simplify the analysis further, we assume that agents have no time preference, so that they rank income streams $y : \mathbf{T} \times \mathbf{S} \longrightarrow \mathbb{R}$ by the expected value of their total income $E(\sum_{t\in\mathbf{T}} y_t)$. The effect of time preference will be studied shortly.

To connect the framework of security markets with the language of Theorem 26.15, let X_{jt} denote the total earnings from holding one unit of security j from date 0 to date $t - 1$ (and selling it at date t)

$$X_{j0} = q_{j0}, \quad X_{jt} = \sum_{\theta=1}^{t} V_\theta^j + q_{jt}, \quad t \geq 1 \tag{5}$$

where q_{jt} is the price of the security at date t. Let $X_t = (X_{1t}, \ldots, X_{Jt})$ denote the associated vector of earnings for the J securities up to date t, $X = (X_t)_{t\in\mathbf{T}}$ denoting the associated earnings process. If $z = (z_t)_{t\in\mathbf{T}} \in \mathscr{Z}$ is a trading strategy for the J securities, then the *gain* from following the strategy z from date 0 to date $t - 1$ is given by (for $t \geq 1$)

$$\begin{aligned} Y_t^z = &\left(V_t + q_t - q_{t-1}\right) z_{t-1} + \left(V_{t-1} + q_{t-1} - q_{t-2}\right) z_{t-2} \\ &+ \cdots + \left(V_1 + q_1 - q_0\right) z_0 \end{aligned} \tag{6}$$

In view of (5), this can be written as

$$Y_t^z = \left(X_t - X_{t-1}\right) z_{t-1} + \left(X_{t-1} - X_{t-2}\right) z_{t-2} + \cdots + \left(X_1 - X_0\right) z_0 \tag{7}$$

Since $\mathbb{F} = (\mathbb{F}_t)_{t\in\mathbf{T}}$ represents the flow of information accruing to agents over time, the dividend, price, and trading processes (V, q, z) must be $\mathscr{F}$-adapted. By Theorem 26.15—if we make the efficient markets hypothesis that there is no trading strategy (based on current information) which yields an expected profit over any time interval—then the process X must be a martingale. Since the vector of dividend processes $V = (V^1, \ldots, V^J)$ is taken as exogenously given, this means that *an equilibrium price process for the J securities in an economy with risk-neutral investors with no time preference must satisfy the martingale condition*

$$q_{jt} + \sum_{\theta=1}^{t} V_\theta^j = E\left(\sum_{\theta=1}^{\tau} V_\theta^j + q_{j\tau} \,\middle|\, \mathcal{F}_t\right), \quad t_j \le t < \tau \le T \tag{8}$$

for $j = 1, \ldots, J$, which implies

$$q_{jt} = E\left(\sum_{\theta=t+1}^{\tau} V_\theta^j + q_{j\tau} \,\middle|\, \mathcal{F}_t\right), \quad t_j \le t < \tau \le T \tag{9}$$

and since $q_{jT} = 0$ (with the convention that prices are after dividends)

$$q_{jt} = E\left(\sum_{\theta=t+1}^{T} V_\theta^j \,\middle|\, \mathcal{F}_t\right), \quad t_j \le t < T \tag{10}$$

(10) and (9) are the analogues—for a security which pays a stream of dividends up to the terminal date—of formulae (2) and (4) for a futures contract. (10) asserts that the price of a security at date t is the best estimate which can be made on the basis of available information of the sum of its future dividends. By (9), the price is also the best estimate at date t of what the future price q_τ will be at any later date τ, after allowance is made for the intervening dividends $\left(\sum_{\theta=t+1}^{\tau} V_\theta^j\right)$. If new information arrives more frequently than the periods at which dividends are distributed (for example, information arrives daily and dividends are paid quarterly) then for any $t < \tau$ for which there are no intervening dividends, (9) reduces to (4), so that the security price q_{jt} is the best estimate (at date t) of what the price will be at time τ when more information will have been revealed. Thus with the assumption of risk neutrality and zero time preference, the efficient markets hypothesis leads to striking consistency properties for the prices of securities.

The simplest way of showing the effect of introducing time preference is to consider an economy in which all agents have the same utility function

$$u^i(x^i) = E\left(\sum_{t=0}^{T} \delta^t x_t^i\right), \quad 0 < \delta \le 1 \tag{11}$$

the economy just studied corresponding to the case $\delta = 1$. Suppose there is a riskless bond which permits short term borrowing and lending at each date-event. Then the short-term interest rate is constant, $r_t(s) = r$, with

$$\frac{1}{1+r} = \delta$$

With preferences given by (11), an equilibrium price process must have the property that for all trading strategies $z \in \mathscr{Z}$, the expectation of

$$Y_t^z = \sum_{\theta=1}^{t} \frac{1}{(1+r)^\theta} \left(V_\theta + q_\theta - q_{\theta-1} \right) z_{\theta-1} \tag{12}$$

is zero for each $t \geq 1$, that is, the expectation of the discounted gain on every trading strategy must be zero. Let Δ_t^τ denote the discount factor between date τ and date t (with $\tau \geq t$)

$$\Delta_t^\tau = \frac{1}{(1+r)^{\tau-t}}$$

then the discounted earnings process of the securities (analogous to (5)) is given by

$$X_{j0} = q_{j0}, \quad X_{jt} = \sum_{\theta=1}^{t} \Delta_0^\theta V_\theta^j + \Delta_0^t q_{jt}, \quad t \geq 1 \tag{13}$$

In view of (12) and (13), Y^z can once again be written as in equation (7). It follows from Theorem 26.15 that X is a martingale. Thus the equilibrium price of each security ($j = 1, \ldots, J$) satisfies

$$q_{jt} = E\left(\sum_{\theta=t+1}^{\tau} \Delta_t^\theta V_\theta^j + \Delta_t^\tau q_{j\tau} \,\middle|\, \mathscr{F}_t \right), \quad t_j \leq t < \tau \leq T \tag{14}$$

and by the terminal condition $q_T = 0$

$$q_{jt} = E\left(\sum_{\theta=t+1}^{T} \Delta_t^\theta V_\theta^j \,\middle|\, \mathscr{F}_t \right), \quad t_j \leq t < T \tag{15}$$

(14) and (15) have exactly the same interpretation as (9) and (10), after taking into account the effect of discounting.

28.   EFFICIENT MARKETS WITH RISK AVERSION

In the previous section we studied the efficient markets hypothesis in an economy in which agents are risk neutral: we saw that the hypothesis implies that the price of a security at any date can be expressed as the best estimate of the sum of its (discounted) future dividends, given current information. When agents are risk averse the conditional expectation of the sum of the future dividends is only one element in determining the value of a security, the other being the perceived risk attached to its future dividend stream. This can also be expressed by saying that a trading strategy which yields a positive expected profit is not always attractive to a risk-averse agent, since it may involve losses in precisely those contingencies where income is really at a premium, and gains when the marginal value of income is small. The property which characterizes equilibrium prices—namely *that there are no advantageous trades left to exploit*—cannot be expressed without reference to the preferences (risk aversion) and consumption streams of the agents. Analyzing the efficient markets hypothesis in an economy in which agents are risk averse is thus necessarily more complicated than in the risk-neutral case, since the presence of risk will distort prices away from the conditional expectation of their future dividends.

Weak Informational Efficiency

There is however a *minimal consistency property* linking the arrival of new information to the changes in security prices which must be satisfied, no matter what the characteristics of the agents happen to be: in any economy, equilibrium prices must not permit agents to cleverly use available information to obtain a *sure* gain. In the previous chapter this property of equilibrium prices—the property of no-arbitrage—was expressed, and explored, in the language appropriate to an event-tree description of an economy. When the variables which describe an equilibrium, the prices and agents' actions (strategies), are expressed as functions of the nodes of an event-tree, all informational restrictions are automatically incorporated into these variables. The merit of the event-tree description—to bring out the similarity between a two-period and a multiperiod economy, thus facilitating the use of standard techniques of equilibrium theory—is also its main drawback: it has the somewhat deceptive effect of making the economy appear "static", flattened as it were onto the event-tree, thereby hiding the sequential, informational side of the story. When expressed in process language, the property of no-arbitrage describes an efficiency property of security prices with respect to information, since it requires that no strategy based on currently available information yields a sure gain. This property combines the consistency of the prices of the different securities at each date-event (the *cross-sectional consistency* analyzed in the two-period model) with the consistency of prices with respect to the arrival of new information (*intertemporal consistency*). To focus attention more directly on the way prices and decisions are related as new information unfolds, and to reinforce the change of perspective from the event-tree to the process description, it will be helpful to adopt a different terminology to express the idea of no-arbitrage.

28.1 Definition: Let (ζ, V) be a financial structure adapted to an information filtration $\mathscr{F} = (\mathscr{F}_t)_{t \in \mathbf{T}}$. An $\mathscr{F}$-adapted price process q is *weakly information* *efficient* if there does not exist an $\mathscr{F}$-adapted trading strategy which yields a sure gain i.e. there does not exist $z \in \mathscr{Z}$ such that

$$(V_t(s) + q_t(s)) \, z_{t-1}(s) - q_t(s) z_t(s) \geq 0, \quad \forall \, (t, s) \in \mathbf{T} \times \mathbf{S}$$

with at least one strict inequality.

This definition provides one possible (albeit crude) formalization of the efficient markets hypothesis. While it prevents investors from finding riskless trading strategies that beat the market, it does not prevent an agent with a given preference ordering and consumption stream from finding a risky trading strategy that he views as profitable (leading to a preferred consumption stream). The next proposition shows however that the property of weak informational efficiency is sufficient to ensure that a price process behaves like a conditional expectation with respect to some probability measure, that is, under this probability measure the price of each security is at each date the best estimate of the sum of its (discounted) future dividends conditional on current information.

To obtain such a valuation formula, the security structure must contain securities which permit a minimum transfer of income over time, the prices of these securities permitting income in the future to be translated (discounted) to an earlier date. The simplest instruments for transferring income over time are the riskless bonds,[1] and these can be distinguished by their maturity date. The valuation formula obtained depends upon the basic set of riskless bonds chosen as the reference point for defining discount factors. For a variety of reasons, the choice of short-term interest rates for discounting income seems most natural: short-term bonds are the simplest, and permit the analysis to be extended to an open-ended future.

Assumption $\mathscr{R}$ (Short-term Riskless Bonds): At each date-event $\xi = (t, \sigma)$, $0 \leq t \leq T - 1$, $\sigma \in \mathbb{F}_t$, there is a short-term riskless bond j_ξ paying one unit of account at each immediate successor of ξ, and nothing otherwise.

The price of the short-term bond at each date-event defines the short-term interest rate: if $\xi = (t, \sigma)$, $0 \leq t \leq T - 1$, $\sigma \in \mathbb{F}_t$ then

$$q_{j_\xi}(\xi) = \frac{1}{1 + r(\xi)} = \frac{1}{1 + r_t(s)}, \quad \forall \, s \in \sigma$$

---

[1]The analysis of this chapter is based on a "real" model which does not take into account the risks of inflation. We retain the assumption made in Chapter 4 that the unit of account at each date-event is one unit of the (composite) consumption good and that the dividends on all securities are denominated in this unit of account.

The *discount factor* Δ_t^τ between a future date τ and the current date t is the random variable defined by

$$\Delta_t^\tau(s) = \frac{1}{(1 + r_t(s)) \cdots (1 + r_{\tau-1}(s))}, \quad 0 \le t < \tau \le T$$

The inverse of the discount factor (i.e. the product of the short-term interest rates between date t and date $\tau - 1$) is called the *accumulation factor* Γ_t^τ between date t and date τ

$$\Gamma_t^\tau(s) = \frac{1}{\Delta_t^\tau(s)} = (1 + r_t(s)) \cdots (1 + r_{\tau-1}(s)), \quad 0 \le t < \tau \le T$$

The accumulation factor is the return on a composite security obtained by investing one unit of income in the riskless bond at date t and rolling over the returns in subsequent short-term bonds until date τ. The discount and accumulation factors have the multiplicative property

$$\Delta_t^\theta \Delta_\theta^\tau = \Delta_t^\tau, \quad \Gamma_\theta^\tau \Gamma_t^\theta = \Gamma_t^\tau, \quad \Gamma_0^T \Delta_0^t = \Gamma_t^T, \quad 0 \le t < \theta < \tau \le T$$

We can now state formally the property which characterizes weakly information-efficient price processes.

28.2 Theorem (Characterization of Weak Informational Efficiency): *Let (ζ, V) be financial structure, satisfying Assumption $\mathscr{R}$, which is adapted to a filtration $\mathscr{F}$ on $(\mathbf{S}, \mathscr{S})$. A security price process q is weakly information efficient if and only if there exists a probability measure μ on $(\mathbf{S}, \mathscr{S})$, with $\mu_s > 0$ for all $s \in \mathbf{S}$, such that the following equivalent properties hold:*

(i) *The (discounted) earnings process $X : \mathbf{T} \times \mathbf{S} \longrightarrow \mathbb{R}^J$ defined by*

$$X_{j0} = q_{j0}, \quad X_{jt} = \sum_{\theta=1}^{t} \Delta_0^\theta V_\theta^j + \Delta_0^t q_{jt}, \quad j = 1, \ldots, J$$

is a martingale on $(\mathbf{S}, \mathscr{S}, \mu)$, i.e.

$$X_{jt} = E_\mu(X_{j\tau} \,|\, \mathscr{F}_t), \quad t_j \le t \le \tau \le T$$

(ii) $q_{jt} = E_\mu\left(\sum_{\theta=t+1}^{\tau} \Delta_t^\theta V_\theta^j + \Delta_t^\tau q_{j\tau} \,\Big|\, \mathscr{F}_t\right), \quad t_j \le t < \tau \le T$

(iii) $q_{jt} = E_\mu\left(\sum_{\theta=t+1}^{T} \Delta_t^\theta V_\theta^j \,\Big|\, \mathscr{F}_t\right), \quad t_j \le t < T$

where t_j is the date associated with the node of issue $\xi(j) = (t_j, \sigma_j)$ of security j.

PROOF: In Section 21 it was shown that a price process q offers no arbitrage opportunities if and only if there exists a strictly positive vector of node prices $\pi = (\pi(\xi), \xi \in \mathbb{D})$ such that

$$q_j(\xi) = \frac{1}{\pi(\xi)} \sum_{\xi' \in \mathbb{D}^+(\xi)} \pi(\xi') V^j(\xi'), \quad j \in J(\xi), \quad \xi \in \mathbb{D}^- \tag{1}$$

It thus suffices to show that under Assumption $\mathscr{R}$, the existence of a vector of node prices π such that (1) holds is equivalent to the existence of a probability measure μ satisfying (i), (ii), (iii).

($\Longrightarrow$) Suppose there exists a strictly positive vector of node prices π satisfying equation (1), where π is normalized so that $\pi(\xi_0) = 1$. Consider the composite security obtained by investing one unit of income in the riskless bond at node $\xi = (t, \sigma)$ and rolling over the returns in short-term bonds until date T. (1) implies

$$\pi(\xi) = \sum_{\xi' \in \mathbb{D}_T(\xi)} \Gamma_t^T(\xi') \pi(\xi') = \sum_{s \in \sigma} \Gamma_t^T(s) \pi_T(s) \tag{2}$$

When $t = 0$, since $\pi(\xi_0) = 1$, (2) implies

$$1 = \sum_{s \in \mathbf{S}} \Gamma_0^T(s) \pi_T(s)$$

where $\Gamma_0^T(s) > 0$, since no-arbitrage implies $1 + r_t(s) > 0$, $s \in \mathbf{S}$, $0 \le t < T$. Thus

$$\mu = (\mu_s)_{s \in \mathbf{S}} = \left(\Gamma_0^T(s) \pi_T(s) \right)_{s \in \mathbf{S}} \tag{3}$$

defines a probability measure on $(\mathbf{S}, \mathscr{S})$ with $\mu_s > 0$, $s \in \mathbf{S}$. Since Γ_0^t is $\mathscr{F}_t$-measurable (i.e. $\Gamma_0^t(s)$ is known at date t), if $\xi = (t, \sigma)$ then (2) can be written as

$$\pi(\xi) = \pi_t(s) = \frac{1}{\Gamma_0^t(\sigma)} \sum_{s \in \sigma} \Gamma_0^T(s) \pi_T(s) = \frac{1}{\Gamma_0^t(\sigma)} \mu(\sigma)$$

so that

$$\pi(\xi) = \Delta_0^t(\sigma) \mu(\sigma), \quad \xi = (t, \sigma), \quad \sigma \in \mathbb{F}_t \tag{4}$$

Thus for $\sigma \in \mathbb{F}_t$, $t_j \leq t < T$, (1) can be written as

$$
\begin{aligned}
q_{jt}(\sigma) &= \sum_{\substack{\sigma' \subset \sigma \\ \sigma' \in \mathbb{F}_\theta \\ t < \theta \leq T}} \frac{\Delta_0^\theta(\sigma')\mu(\sigma')V_\theta^j(\sigma')}{\Delta_0^t(\sigma)\mu(\sigma)} \\
&= \sum_{s \in \sigma} \sum_{\theta=t+1}^T \Delta_t^\theta(s)V_\theta^j(s)\frac{\mu_s}{\mu(\sigma)} \\
&= E_\mu\left(\sum_{\theta=t+1}^T \Delta_t^\theta V_\theta^j \,\bigg|\, \sigma\right)
\end{aligned}
\tag{5}
$$

which is equivalent to

$$
q_{jt} = E_\mu\left(\sum_{\theta=t+1}^T \Delta_t^\theta V_\theta^j \,\bigg|\, \mathscr{F}_t\right), \quad t_j \leq t < T
\tag{6}
$$

namely formula (iii) in Theorem 28.2. It is straightforward to show (iii) $\Longleftrightarrow$ (ii) $\Longleftrightarrow$ (i).

($\Longleftarrow$) Suppose there exists μ such that (6) holds. If π is defined by (4), then the computation in (5) leads back to formula (1). $\square$

The theorem asserts that a weakly information-efficient price process exhibits remarkable consistency properties, akin to those obtained under the assumption of risk neutrality. In both cases security prices react to the arrival of new information by Bayesian updating of the best estimate of the future dividends on the securities. Given a security structure (ζ, V), the fact that a weakly information-efficient price process q is "supported" by a pair (Δ_0, μ) consisting of a date 0 discount process $(\Delta_0 = (\Delta_0^t)_{t \in \mathbf{T}})$ and a probability measure μ—in the sense that any one of the equivalent valuation formulae (i), (ii), or (iii) is satisfied—is equivalent to q being supported by a present-value vector π, in the sense that the fundamental-value formula (1) holds. The advantage of the valuation formulae (i), (ii), or (iii) is that they bring out more clearly otherwise hidden consistency conditions linking the intertemporal behavior of prices to the arrival of new information.

If the price process q is assumed to be not only weakly information efficient, but to be the equilibrium price process of a fully specified stochastic economy $\mathscr{E}(\mathbb{D}, u, \omega, \zeta, V)$, then the valuation formulae (ii) or (iii) can be given a richer economic interpretation.

Equilibrium Price Process

Consider an equilibrium $((\bar{x}, \bar{z}), \bar{q})$ of a stochastic economy $\mathcal{E}(\mathbb{D}, u, \omega, \zeta, V)$ satisfying Assumption $\mathcal{R}$. From the analysis of Chapter 4 it follows that if $\bar{\pi}^i = \pi^i(\bar{x}^i)$ denotes the present-value process of agent i at his equilibrium consumption $\bar{x}^i$ ($\bar{\pi}^i(\xi) = \frac{\partial u^i(\bar{x}^i)}{\partial x^i(\xi)} / \frac{\partial u^i(\bar{x}^i)}{\partial x^i(\xi_0)}$, $\xi \in \mathbb{D}$), then the price process $\bar{q}$ must satisfy the agent's first-order conditions

$$\bar{q}_j(\xi) = \sum_{\xi' \in \mathbb{D}^+(\xi)} \frac{\bar{\pi}^i(\xi') V^j(\xi')}{\bar{\pi}^i(\xi)}, \quad j \in J(\xi), \quad \xi \in \mathbb{D}^- \tag{7}$$

Let $\bar{\Delta}_0 = (\bar{\Delta}_0^t)_{t \in \mathbf{T}}$ and $\bar{\Gamma}^T = (\bar{\Gamma}_t^T)_{t \in \mathbf{T}}$ denote the equilibrium discount and accumulation processes defined by the equilibrium short-term interest rate process $\bar{r} = (\bar{r}_t)_{t \in \mathbf{T}}$. The proof of Theorem 28.2 shows that if $\bar{\mu}^i$ is the probability measure for agent i defined by

$$\bar{\mu}^i = (\bar{\mu}_s^i)_{s \in \mathbf{S}} = \left(\bar{\Gamma}_0^T(s) \bar{\pi}_T^i(s) \right)_{s \in \mathbf{S}} \tag{8}$$

then (given $\bar{\Delta}_0$) (7) is equivalent to

$$\bar{q}_{jt} = E_{\bar{\mu}^i} \left(\sum_{\theta=t+1}^T \bar{\Delta}_t^\theta V_\theta^j \,\middle|\, \mathscr{F}_t \right), \quad t_j \le t < T, \quad j = 1, \ldots, J \tag{9}$$

Thus under the measure $\bar{\mu}^i$, the price of each active security is, at each date, the best estimate that agent i can make of the sum of its discounted future dividends given currently available information. The measure $\bar{\mu}^i$ weights the state s by the value for agent i of one unit of income accumulated along the path associated with s ($\bar{\Gamma}_0^T(s) \bar{\pi}_T^i(s)$).

The valuation of agent i in (9) is, just like the earlier valuation (7), a marginal valuation by the agent from the standpoint of his equilibrium consumption $\bar{x}^i$. The logic which underlies this formula can be understood as follows. Suppose that to purchase a marginal unit dz_j of security j at date t in event σ, agent i borrows $\bar{q}_j(\sigma) dz_j$ using the short-term bond at date-event (t, σ), and plans to roll over the debt $(\bar{q}_j(\sigma) dz_j)$ in subsequent short-term loans until date T. Whenever dividends accrue from the security, the agent invests them in the short-term bond, rolling over the earnings obtained until date T. Since the purchase of the security at date-event (t, σ) was financed by a loan, the only change in consumption occurs at date T. If the state $s \in \sigma$ occurs, agent i will have to pay back the accumulated principal and interest

$$\bar{\Gamma}_t^T(s) \bar{q}_{jt}(\sigma) dz_j = \bar{\Delta}_0^t(\sigma) \bar{\Gamma}_0^T(s) \bar{q}_{jt}(\sigma) dz_j$$

and will have earned on the accumulated dividends

$$\sum_{\theta=t+1}^{T} \bar{\Gamma}_{\theta}^{T}(s)V_{\theta}^{j}(s)dz_{j} = \sum_{\theta=t+1}^{T} \bar{\Delta}_{0}^{\theta}(\sigma)\bar{\Gamma}_{0}^{T}(s)V_{\theta}^{j}(s)dz_{j}$$

The difference between these two terms gives the change in consumption in state s at date T, and the value to agent i (from the perspective of date 0) of this change in consumption is

$$\left(\sum_{\theta=t+1}^{T} \bar{\Delta}_{0}^{\theta}(s)V_{\theta}^{j}(s) - \bar{\Delta}_{0}^{t}(\sigma)\bar{q}_{jt}(\sigma)\right)\bar{\Gamma}_{0}^{T}(s)\bar{\pi}_{T}^{i}(s)dz_{j}$$

Since at the equilibrium the agent has maximized utility it must be the case that

$$\frac{du^{i}}{\bar{\lambda}_{0}^{i}} = \left(\sum_{s\in\sigma}\left(\sum_{\theta=t+1}^{T} \bar{\Delta}_{0}^{\theta}(s)V_{\theta}^{j}(s) - \bar{\Delta}_{0}^{t}(\sigma)\bar{q}_{jt}(\sigma)\right)\Gamma_{0}^{T}(s)\bar{\pi}_{T}^{i}(s)\right)dz_{j} = 0 \quad (10)$$

(10) is equivalent to (9) when both sides of (9) are multiplied by the $\mathscr{F}_{t}$-measurable discount factor $\bar{\Delta}_{0}^{t}$. Each component of the sum in the inner bracket in (10) is first discounted to date 0 and then upcounted to date T by the factor $\Gamma_{0}^{T}(s)$, multiplication by $\bar{\pi}_{T}^{i}(s)$ giving the value at date 0 of this date T income (consumption).

The valuation formula (9) combines into a single expression both the way agent i uses information (to update a best estimate) and the way he evaluates risk (through the measure μ^{i}). If the stronger assumption of rational expectations is invoked—namely that there are objective probabilities of occurrence for the states on which agents agree—then it is possible (at least to some extent) to separate out informational and risk components of the valuation.

Assumption $\mathscr{P}$ (Objective Probabilities): There is an objective probability measure ρ on $(\mathbf{S},\mathscr{S})$ with $\rho_{s} > 0$ for every $s \in \mathbf{S}$.

As in Chapter 3, define the present-value process obtained by factoring out the probabilities of events

$$\bar{\pi}^{\rho,i} = \left(\frac{\bar{\pi}^{i}(\xi)}{\rho(\sigma)}, \xi \in \mathbb{D}\right) \quad \text{with} \quad \xi = (t,\sigma)$$

as the ρ-present-value process of agent i. For example, if the utility function of agent i is a sum of discounted expected utility

$$u^{i}(x^{i}) = E\sum_{t=0}^{T}\delta_{i}^{t}v^{i}(x_{t}^{i})$$

then

$$\bar{\pi}_t^{\rho,i}(s) = \frac{\delta_i^t v^{i\prime}\left(\bar{x}_t^i(s)\right)}{v^{i\prime}(\bar{x}_0^i)}$$

Under Assumption $\mathscr{P}$, the probability measure $\bar{\mu}^i$ of agent i can be viewed as a rescaling of the objective probability measure ρ

$$\bar{\mu}_s^i = m^i(s)\rho_s, \quad m^i(s) = \Gamma_0^T(s)\bar{\pi}_T^{\rho,i}(s), \quad s \in \mathbf{S} \tag{11}$$

It follows from (11) that if $y : \mathbf{S} \longrightarrow \mathbb{R}$ is a random variable, then for any $\sigma \in \mathscr{S}$

$$E_{\bar{\mu}^i}(y\,|\,\sigma) = \frac{\displaystyle\sum_{s\in\sigma} y_s m^i(s)\rho_s}{\displaystyle\sum_{s\in\sigma} m^i(s)\rho_s} = \frac{E\left(m^i y\,|\,\sigma\right)}{E\left(m^i\,|\,\sigma\right)} = E(y\,|\,\sigma) + \frac{\mathrm{cov}\left(m^i, y\,|\,\sigma\right)}{E\left(m^i\,|\,\sigma\right)} \tag{12}$$

Equation (4) above defines the following relation between $\bar{\pi}^i$ and $\bar{\mu}^i$

$$\bar{\pi}^i(\xi) = \bar{\pi}_t^i(\sigma) = \bar{\Delta}_0^t(\sigma)\bar{\mu}^i(\sigma), \quad \xi = (t,\sigma), \quad \sigma \in \mathbb{F}_t$$

which can also be written as

$$\bar{\Gamma}_0^t(\sigma)\bar{\pi}_t^{\rho,i}(\sigma) = E\left(m^i\,|\,\sigma\right) \tag{13}$$

(12) and (13) imply

$$\bar{q}_{jt} = E\left(\sum_{\theta=t+1}^T \bar{\Delta}_t^\theta V_\theta^j \,\middle|\, \mathscr{F}_t\right) + \mathrm{cov}\left(\frac{\bar{\Gamma}_t^T \bar{\pi}_T^{\rho,i}}{\bar{\pi}_t^{\rho,i}}, \sum_{\theta=t+1}^T \bar{\Delta}_t^\theta V_\theta^j \,\middle|\, \mathscr{F}_t\right) \tag{14}$$

where the conditional covariance $\mathrm{cov}(\cdot,\cdot\,|\,\mathscr{F}_t)$ means that for each $\sigma \in \mathbb{F}_t$ the covariance is taken with respect to the conditional probability $(\rho_s/\rho(\sigma), s \in \sigma)$. The first component in (14) is the best estimate of the (discounted) future earnings based on current information under the objective probability measure ρ, and may be called the *purely informational component* of the valuation. The second component is the conditional covariance value of the future earnings for agent i: this part depends not only on current information but also on the attitude toward risk of the agent and on the risk profile of future earnings, and may be called the *risk component* of the valuation.

To understand the expression for the risk component in (14), suppose that at date t in event σ, agent i buys an additional marginal amount dz_j of the security and borrows—not the full amount $\bar{q}_{jt}(s)dz_j$—but the expected value $E(\sum_{\theta=t+1}^T \bar{\Delta}_t^\theta V_\theta^j\,|\,\sigma)$ using the short-term bond at date-event (t,σ), subsequently rolling over the debt in short-term bonds until date T. At date-event (t, σ) the change in consumption is

$$dx_t^i(\sigma) = \left(-\bar{q}_{jt}(\sigma) + E\left(\sum_{\theta=t+1}^T \bar{\Delta}_t^\theta V_\theta^j \,\bigg|\, \sigma \right) \right) dz_j \tag{15}$$

which when multiplied by $\bar{\pi}_t^i(\sigma) = \pi_t^{\rho,i}(\sigma)\rho(\sigma)$ gives the marginal change in utility. Suppose (as in the earlier argument) that the agent reinvests all dividends accruing from the security until date T, by rolling them over in the short-term bonds. At date T, if state $s \in \sigma$ occurs, the change in consumption is

$$dx_T^i(s) = \left(\sum_{\theta=t+1}^T \bar{\Delta}_t^\theta(s) V_\theta^j(s) - E\left(\sum_{\theta=t+1}^T \bar{\Delta}_t^\theta V_\theta^j \,\bigg|\, \sigma \right) \right) \bar{\Gamma}_t^T(s) dz_j \tag{16}$$

being the difference between the accumulated value of the dividends and the amount repayable on the debt. Since at equilibrium the agent has maximized utility, (15) and (16) imply

$$\frac{du^i}{\bar{\lambda}_0^i} = \left(-\bar{q}_{jt}(\sigma) + E\left(\sum_{\theta=t+1}^T \bar{\Delta}_t^\theta V_\theta^j \,\bigg|\, \sigma \right) \right) \pi_t^{\rho,i}(\sigma)\rho(\sigma)$$

$$+ \sum_{s\in\sigma} \left(\sum_{\theta=t+1}^T \bar{\Delta}_t^\theta(s) V_\theta^j(s) - E\left(\sum_{\theta=t+1}^T \bar{\Delta}_t^\theta V_\theta^j \,\bigg|\, \sigma \right) \right) \bar{\Gamma}_t^T(s) \bar{\pi}_T^{\rho,i}(s) \rho_s = 0$$

which reduces to formula (14), after exploiting the identity for any pair of random variables (x, y)

$$E\left((x - E(x))\, y \right) = \mathrm{cov}(x, y)$$

When the agent cashes in the expected value of the future earnings

$$E\left(\sum_{\theta=t+1}^T \bar{\Delta}_t^\theta V_\theta^j \,\bigg|\, \sigma \right)$$

at date-event (t, σ), he is left with the *purely random component* of future earnings

$$\sum_{\theta=t+1}^T \bar{\Delta}_t^\theta(s) V_\theta^j(s) - E\left(\sum_{\theta=t+1}^T \bar{\Delta}_t^\theta V_\theta^j \,\bigg|\, \sigma \right), \quad s \in \sigma$$

and it is *the value of this random income stream which gives the risk component in the valuation* (14). Whenever realized earnings $\sum_{\theta=t+1}^T \bar{\Delta}_t^\theta(s) V_\theta^j(s)$

exceed (fall short of) expected earnings $E(\sum_{\theta=t+1}^{T} \bar{\Delta}_t^\theta V_\theta^j \,|\, \sigma)$, the gain (loss) is translated along the path leading to state s by the factor $\bar{\Gamma}_t^T(s)\bar{\pi}_T^{\rho,i}(s)\rho_s$ which values the gain (loss) along the path from t to s. The number $1/\bar{\pi}_t^{\rho,i}$ simply translates the above valuation from a focal date at 0 to a focal date at t.

Informational Efficiency

The original motivation for the efficient markets hypothesis (EMH) came from the analysis of time series of speculative prices: prices were observed to change frequently and in an apparently random manner. EMH expressed the idea that these price changes are a timely and accurate response to the arrival of new (random) information. In the previous section we analyzed the naive version of the efficient markets hypothesis—namely the version obtained in an economy where risk is unimportant since all agents are risk neutral. We found that if a price process offers no further profitable trades for the agents based on current information, then the price of each security is the best estimate of its future earnings under the objective probability measure ρ. Thus in an economy in which risk can be ignored, price changes represent optimal responses to the arrival of new information.

But analyzing security markets without risk is like Hamlet without the Prince. *If valuation formulae in an economy with risk-averse agents incorporate both information and risk elements in an essential way, is it still possible to formalize the efficient markets hypothesis?*

It seems natural to retain the idea that a price process responds in an efficient way to new information if it offers no further profitable trades for the agents based on current information. The only difference relative to the risk-neutral case is that profitable trades for an agent cannot be defined without reference to his consumption stream and preference ordering, since these are needed to evaluate whether or not a risky trade, which alters the profile of his consumption across time and contingencies, leads to a preferred consumption stream. A pair $(u^i; x^i)$, which induces a preference ordering on net trades from x^i, will be called the *risk-impatience characteristics* of agent i. A trade is said to be *profitable* for agent i if it leads to a consumption stream preferred to x^i.

28.3 Definition: Let (ζ, V) be a financial structure adapted to an information filtration $\mathscr{F} = (\mathscr{F}_t)_{t \in \mathbf{T}}$. An $\mathscr{F}$-adapted price process q is *information efficient* relative to the risk-impatience characteristics $((u^i; x^i),\ i = 1, \ldots, I)$ of the agents in the economy, if no agent can find a profitable $\mathscr{F}$-adapted trading strategy.

To analyze the conditions for no profitable trades, assume that agents' preferences are represented by utility functions satisfying Assumption $\mathscr{U}$. The present-value vector $\pi^i(x^i)$ of agent i at x^i is collinear to the gradient $\nabla u^i(x^i)$

$$\pi^i(x^i) = \frac{1}{\lambda_0^i(x^i)} \nabla u^i(x^i), \quad \lambda_0^i(x^i) = \frac{\partial u^i(x^i)}{\partial x^i(\xi_0)}$$

and, given the quasi-concavity of u^i,

$$u^i(x^i + h) > u^i(x^i) \implies \nabla u^i(x^i)h > 0 \iff \pi^i(x^i)h > 0$$

A consumption stream $x^i + h$ which is preferred to x^i costs more under the agent's supporting price $\pi^i(x^i)$. Conversely if there exists a net trade h from x^i such that $\pi^i(x^i)h > 0$, then it can be scaled down to αh, $0 < \alpha \leq 1$, so that $u^i(x^i + \alpha h) > u^i(x^i)$, since $du_{x^i}^i(h) = \nabla u^i(x^i)h > 0$. (For a formal statement and proof of these properties see Proposition 31.2 in Chapter 6.)

If agent i can only change his consumption by trading on a system of financial markets with payoff matrix $W(q, V)$ (see equation (5) in Section 20) then any trading strategy $z^i \in \mathscr{Z}$ which leads to a preferred consumption stream must satisfy

$$\pi^i(x^i)W(q, V)z^i > 0$$

and there exists no profitable trade for agent i if and only if

$$\pi^i(x^i)W(q, V)z^i = 0, \quad \forall z^i \in \mathscr{Z} \tag{17}$$

(17) is equivalent to

$$\pi^i(x^i)W(q, V) = 0$$

which in turn is equivalent to

$$q_j(\xi) = \frac{1}{\pi^i(\xi)} \sum_{\xi' \in \mathbb{D}^+(\xi)} \pi^i(\xi')V^j(\xi'), \quad j \in J(\xi), \quad \xi \in \mathbb{D}^- \tag{18}$$

with $\pi^i = \pi^i(x^i)$.

A number of composite rates of substitution can be derived from the agent's present-value vector $\pi^i(x^i)$. The rate of impatience (introduced in the two-period setting in Definition 15.3) can be defined at every node ξ, and expresses the preference of agent i for consumption at node ξ rather than at its immediate successors $\xi' \in \xi^+$. These rates of impatience (or personalized interest rates) in turn induce discount and accumulation factors for agent i when combined over a sequence of periods.

28.4 Definition: Let (u^i, x^i) be the risk-impatience characteristics of agent i, and let $\pi^i = \pi^i(x^i)$ be the associated present-value vector. Agent i's *rate of impatience at node* ξ, $r^i(\xi)$, is defined by

$$\frac{1}{1 + r^i(\xi)} = \frac{\displaystyle\sum_{\xi' \in \xi^+} \pi^i(\xi')}{\pi(\xi)}, \quad \forall \xi \in \mathbb{D}^-$$

The process of rates of impatience $r^i = (r^i_t)_{t \in \mathbf{T}}$ is given by

$$r^i_t(s) = r^i(\xi), \quad \xi = (t, \sigma), \quad \sigma \in \mathbb{F}_t, \quad s \in \sigma, \quad 0 \le t < T$$

(with the convention $r^i_T(s) = \infty$). The *discount* and *accumulation factors of agent* i between a future date τ and the current date t are the random variables defined by

$$\Delta^{\tau,i}_t(s) = \frac{1}{(1 + r^i_t(s)) \cdots (1 + r^i_{\tau-1}(s))}, \quad \Gamma^{\tau,i}_t(s) = \frac{1}{\Delta^{\tau,i}_t(s)}, \quad 0 \le t < \tau \le T$$

As we saw earlier, agent i's present-value vector $\pi^i(x^i)$ also defines a probability measure μ^i on $(\mathbf{S}, \mathscr{S})$, which permits the agent's valuation formula (18) to be expressed as a conditional expectation.

28.5 Definition: Let $(u^i; x^i)$ be the risk-impatience characteristics of agent i, and let $\pi^i = \pi^i(x^i)$ be the associated present-value vector. The *probability measure* of agent i on $(\mathbf{S}, \mathscr{S})$ is defined by

$$\mu^i = (\mu^i_s)_{s \in \mathbf{S}} = \left(\Gamma^{T,i}_0(s) \pi^i_T(s)\right)_{s \in \mathbf{S}}$$

The argument used in the proof of Theorem 28.2 shows that agent i's valuation formula (18) is equivalent to

$$q_{jt} = E_{\mu^i}\left(\sum_{\theta=t+1}^{T} \Delta^{\theta,i}_t V^j_\theta \,\middle|\, \mathscr{F}_t\right), \quad t_j \le t < T \tag{19}$$

If $X^i : \mathbf{T} \times \mathbf{S} \longrightarrow \mathbb{R}^J$ is the i-discounted earnings process for the securities obtained by using the discount process Δ^i_0 of agent i

$$X^i_{j0} = q_{j0}, \quad X^i_{jt} = \sum_{\theta=1}^{t} \Delta^{\theta,i}_0 V^j_\theta + \Delta^{t,i}_0 q_{jt}, \quad j = 1, \ldots, J \tag{20}$$

then (19) is equivalent to

$$E_{\mu^i}\left(\sum_{t=1}^{T} \left(X^i_t - X^i_{t-1}\right) z^i_{t-1}\right) = 0, \quad \forall z^i \in \mathscr{Z}$$

which is the process equivalent of (17). Thus the condition that the financial markets do not offer any profitable trades for agent i from the consumption stream x^i is equivalent to the condition that *all trading strategies based on current information yield a zero expected profit under the discount factor and probability measure of agent i.*

In an economy in which agents have the risk-impatience characteristics $((u^i; x^i), i = 1, \ldots, I)$, an information-efficient price process can thus be characterized as follows.

28.6 Proposition (Characterization of Informational Efficiency): *Let (ζ, V) be a financial structure adapted to a filtration $\mathscr{F}$ on $(\mathbf{S}, \mathscr{S})$. A security price process q is information efficient relative to the risk-impatience characteristics $((u^i; x^i), i = 1, \ldots, I)$ of the agents in the economy if and only if the following equivalent conditions hold for every agent $i = 1, \ldots, I$:*

(i) $E_{\mu^i}\left(\sum_{t=1}^{T}\left(X_t^i - X_{t-1}^i\right) z_{t-1}^i\right) = 0, \quad \forall z^i \in \mathscr{Z}$

(ii) X^i *is a martingale on* $(\mathbf{S}, \mathscr{S}, \mu^i)$ *i.e.*

$$X_{jt}^i = E_{\mu^i}\left(X_{j\tau}^i \,\middle|\, \mathscr{F}_t\right), \quad t_j \le t < \tau \le T$$

(iii) $q_{jt} = E_{\mu^i}\left(\sum_{\theta=t+1}^{\tau} \Delta_t^{\theta,i} V_\theta^j + \Delta_t^{\tau,i} q_{j\tau} \,\middle|\, \mathscr{F}_t\right), \quad t_j \le t < \tau \le T$

(iv) $q_{jt} = E_{\mu^i}\left(\sum_{\theta=t+1}^{T} \Delta_t^{\theta,i} V_\theta^j \,\middle|\, \mathscr{F}_t\right), \quad t_j \le t < T$

where (Δ_0^i, μ^i) is the discount process and probability measure of agent i at x^i, X^i is given by (20), and t_j is the date associated with the node of issue $\xi(j) = (t_j, \sigma_j)$ of security j.

PROOF: It was shown above that (18) characterizes a price process which does not offer profitable trades to agent i. The equivalence of (18) and (19) can be established as in the proof of Theorem 28.2. Assumption $\mathscr{R}$ is not needed since the personalized interest rates r^i, discount factors Δ^i, and accumulation factors Γ^i replace their market-based equivalents (r, Δ, Γ) taken as given in Theorem 28.2: in particular (π^i, Γ^i) satisfy equation (2), which was the basis for establishing the equivalence between (1) and (6). The equivalence of (ii), (iii), (iv) is immediate, and the equivalence with (i) follows from Theorem 26.15. □

We can now state precisely the sense in which the efficient markets hypothesis holds in the equilibrium model of an economy with risk-averse agents.

28.7 Proposition (Efficient Markets Hypothesis): *If $((\bar{x}, \bar{z}), \bar{q})$ is an equilibrium of a stochastic economy $\mathscr{E}(\mathbb{D}, u, \omega, \zeta, V)$ satisfying Assumption $\mathscr{U}$, then the security price process $\bar{q}$ is information efficient relative to the risk-impatience characteristics $((u^i; \bar{x}^i), i = 1, \ldots, I)$ of the agents at the equilibrium.*

PROOF: The result is an immediate consequence of Proposition 28.6 and the definition of an equilibrium. □

The property that in an equilibrium security prices are information efficient relative to the risk-impatience characteristics of the agents is another way of stating that the price of each security is equal to its fundamental value for each agent. The advantage of expressing agents' equilibrium valuations in the form (iii) or (iv) of Proposition 28.6 is that it formalizes the idea that security prices are best estimators of their future dividend streams, that is, they make best possible use of current information. This property holds under the sole assumption that agents have correct anticipations of future dividends and security prices: they need not agree on the probabilities of the states (u^i may involve a subjective probability measure ρ^i), markets may be incomplete (the measures μ^i can differ), and there need not be an objective market discount factor (the agents' discount factors Δ^i can differ).

However, to make a direct comparison between the efficient markets hypothesis for an economy with risk-averse agents and the naive version based on risk neutrality, Assumptions $\mathscr{P}$ (objective probabilities of the states) and $\mathscr{R}$ (riskless short-term bond at each date-event) must be invoked. Under these assumptions, the naive version of the efficient markets hypothesis states that the price of a security is always an unbiased estimate (the conditional expectation with respect to the objective probabilities) of its future discounted stream of dividends, given current information. As explained in Section 27, this is equivalent to asserting that no investor trading on the basis of publicly available information can make systematic profits on financial markets, i.e. positive profit on average.

When agents are risk averse, the price of a security will typically be a *biased estimate* of its future dividend stream, the bias

$$E\left(\sum_{\theta=t+1}^{T} \bar{\Delta}_t^\theta V_\theta^j \,\middle|\, \mathscr{F}_t \right) - \bar{q}_{jt} \tag{21}$$

corresponding to the *risk premium* that is implicitly paid as compensation for holding the risky security (the premium being given by equation (14)). This implies that *investors who take risks on financial markets can expect to make systematic profits i.e. to receive a positive profit on average for their risk taking, without having access to more information or making better use of it than the market*. This consequence of the efficient markets hypothesis under risk aversion, namely that investors on financial markets are rewarded not for knowing better than the market what the future has in store, but rather for risk bearing, was clearly stated by Keynes[2] (1923b). He argued that the conventional theory of his day

> presumes that the speculator is better informed on average than the producers and consumers themselves, which, speaking generally, is a rather dubious proposition. The most important function of the speculator in the great organised 'futures' markets is, I think, somewhat different. He is not so much a prophet...as a *risk-bearer*.... Without paying the slightest attention to the prospects of the commodity he deals in or giving a thought to it, he may, one decade with another, earn substantial remuneration *merely* by running risks and allowing the results of one season to average with those of others; just as an insurance company makes profits without pretending to know more about an individual's prospects of life or the chances of his house taking fire than he knows himself.[3]

However Keynes' estimates of the bias[4] given by (21) for commodity futures, of the order of 10% per annum has proved somewhat of an overestimate relative to subsequent empirical work (see Gray and Rutledge (1971)).

In this chapter we have studied the informational efficiency of security prices: this must be distinguished from the study of the allocational efficiency induced by trading on the financial markets. In Section 25 we showed that in a multiperiod economy when markets are incomplete, not only is an equilibrium allocation generically inefficient, it is also constrained inefficient. Thus prices of securities can be efficient in the sense of making best use of available information, without co-ordinating efficiently risk sharing among the agents. Only in the ideal case where financial markets are complete does an equilibrium simultaneously exhibit the properties of informational and risk-sharing efficiency, prices correctly anticipating future events and correctly co-ordinating risk sharing among agents.

---

[2] For another statement of his ideas on futures markets see Keynes' *Treatise on Money* (1930, ch. 29).

[3] Keynes (1923b, Section 2).

[4] "What abatement below the probable future price, as he estimates it, must the producer accept in order to induce the speculative market to relieve him of risk? ... the price is very high—much higher than is charged for any other form of insurance, though perhaps it is inevitable that a risk which only averages out over units spread *through time* should be less easy to insure than one which averages out over units which are nearly simultaneous—for we have to wait too long for the actuarial result. I should doubt whether in the largest and most organised market the cost of a hedge-sale works out at less than 10 per cent per annum (e.g., 5 per cent for a sale six months forward) and often rises to 20 per cent per annum (e.g., 5 per cent for a sale three months forward) and even much higher figures." (Keynes (1923b, Section 3)).

EXERCISES

1. *Multiperiod equilibrium risk premium on securities.*

This exercise shows that an agent's first-order conditions for the choice of an optimal trading strategy can be expressed equivalently as a risk pricing formula for each security at each date, conditional on current information.

Consider a stochastic exchange economy $\mathcal{E}(\mathbb{D}, u, \omega, \zeta, V)$ on an event-tree $\mathbb{D}$ and let $\mathcal{F} = (\mathcal{F}_t)_{t \in \mathbf{T}}$ denote the associated filtration describing the unfolding of information. The economy satisfies Assumption $\mathcal{P}$ (there is an objective probability ρ on the states of nature), $\mathcal{R}$ (at each date the short-term riskless bond is traded), and the utility functions u of the agents satisfy Assumption $\mathcal{U}$. Let $((\bar{x}, \bar{z}), \bar{q})$ be a financial market equilibrium of this economy (Definition 20.8). For each agent i, let $\bar{\pi}^i$ and $\bar{\pi}^{\rho,i}$ denote the present-value and probability factored present-value vector of agent i at the equilibrium $(\bar{\pi}^{\rho,i}(\xi) = \bar{\pi}^i(\xi)/\rho(\xi), \xi \in \mathbb{D})$.

(a) Show that the first-order conditions for the choice of an optimal trading strategy by agent i (written in event-tree notation in Chapter 4) can be expressed in stochastic process notation as

$$\bar{\pi}_t^{\rho,i} \bar{q}_{jt} = E\left(\bar{\pi}_{t+1}^{\rho,i}(\bar{q}_{jt+1} + V_{t+1}^j) \,\middle|\, \mathcal{F}_t\right), \quad t = 0, \ldots, T, \quad j = 1, \ldots, J$$

Give an economic interpretation of this condition.

(b) The *rate of return* on the jth security during period t is defined as the sum of its dividend yield and its capital gain yield

$$r_{jt} = \frac{V_{t+1}^j + q_{jt+1} - q_{jt}}{q_{jt}}$$

Let r_t denote the riskless rate of interest between date t and date $t+1$ (i.e. the rate of return on the short-term riskless bond). Show that the formula in (a) is equivalent to

$$E(\bar{r}_{jt} \,|\, \mathcal{F}_t) - \bar{r}_t = -\operatorname{cov}\left(\bar{r}_{jt}, \frac{\bar{\pi}_t^{\rho,i}}{E(\bar{\pi}_t^{\rho,i})} \,\middle|\, \mathcal{F}_t\right), \quad t = 0, \ldots, T, \quad j = 1, \ldots, J$$

Give an economic interpretation of the risk premium.

(c) Show that if agents have additively separable utility functions of the form

$$u^i(x^i) = E \sum_{t=0}^T v_t^i(x_t^i), \quad i = 1, \ldots, I$$

and if the financial markets are complete at the equilibrium, then the risk premium formula in (b) can be expressed as

$$E(\bar{r}_{jt} \,|\, \mathcal{F}_t) - \bar{r}_t = -\operatorname{cov}\left(\bar{r}_{jt}, \frac{v_t^{*\prime}(w_t)}{E(v_t^{*\prime}(w_t))} \,\middle|\, \mathcal{F}_t\right), \quad t = 0, \ldots, T, \quad j = 1, \ldots, J$$

where $u^*(y) = E \sum_{t=0}^{T} v_t^*(y_t)$ is the utility function of the representative agent at the equilibrium (see Exercise 1, Chapter 4) and $w_t = \sum_{i=1}^{I} \omega_t^i$ is the aggregate output at date t. Give an economic interpretation of this formula.

2. *Multiperiod CAPM equilibrium risk premium.*

This exercise derives the analogue for a multiperiod economy of the two-period CAPM formula (8) in Proposition 17.5, under the assumption of complete markets and additively separable quadratic utility functions.

Consider a stochastic economy $\mathscr{E}(\mathbb{D}, u, \omega, \zeta, V)$ which is the multiperiod analogue of a bond-equity economy defined in Section 16. In addition to an array of long and short-term bonds, there are equity contracts for K corporations which are traded at each date. The production plan $\bar{y}^k = (\bar{y}^k(\xi), \xi \in \mathbb{D})$ of the kth corporation is taken as fixed and exogenously given for $k = 1, \ldots, K$. Each agent i has an initial portfolio $\delta^i = (\delta_1^i, \ldots, \delta_K^i) \in \mathbb{R}_+^K$ of ownership shares of the K corporations and $\sum_{i=1}^{I} \delta_k^i = 1$. Agents inherit no initial credit or debt at date 0 with respect to the securities in zero net supply, and have no initial resources after date 0 ($\omega^i(\xi) = 0$, $\xi > \xi_0$, $i = 1, \ldots, I$)—the agents are thus thought of as institutional investors whose sole source of income (after date 0) comes from trading on the financial markets. Suppose the agents have additively separable utility functions as in Exercise 1(c), the VNM utility functions $v_t^i, t = 0, \ldots, T$, being quadratic

$$v_t^i(x_t^i) = -\frac{1}{2}\delta_i^t(\alpha_t^i - x_t^i)^2, \quad i = 1, \ldots, I$$

where $\alpha_0^i > w_0 = \sum_{i=1}^{I} \omega_0^i + \sum_{k=1}^{K} \bar{y}_0^k$ and $\alpha_t^i > w_t + \sum_{k=1}^{K} \bar{y}_t^k$, $t \geq 1$. Consider an equilibrium of this economy in which the financial markets are complete.

(a) Show that there exist coefficients α_t, a_t such that the representative agent's utility functions $v_t^*(y_t)$, $t = 0, \ldots, T$, can be written as

$$v_t^*(y_t) = -\frac{1}{2}a_t(\alpha_t - y_t)^2$$

(b) For all non-terminal nodes $\xi \in \mathbb{D}^-$, let $\theta_m(\xi)$ be the portfolio whose total return (dividend plus capital value) is the aggregate output $w(\xi)$, and let $\bar{q}_m(\xi)$ denote the price of this portfolio. Let $\bar{q}_{mt}$ denote the stochastic process notation for this price, and let $\bar{r}_{mt}$ denote the rate of return on the portfolio θ_m during period t. Applying the formula derived in Exercise 1(c) to $\bar{r}_{jt}$ and $\bar{r}_{mt}$, show that the equilibrium risk premium on each security satisfies the "CAPM-like" formula

$$E(\bar{r}_{jt} \,|\, \mathscr{F}_t) - \bar{r}_t = \beta_{mj}^t(E(\bar{r}_{mt} \,|\, \mathscr{F}_t) - \bar{r}_t), \quad t = 0, \ldots, T, \quad j = 1, \ldots, J$$

with

$$\beta_{mj}^t = \frac{\text{cov}(\bar{r}_{mt}, \bar{r}_{jt} \,|\, \mathscr{F}_t)}{\text{var}(\bar{r}_{mt} \,|\, \mathscr{F}_t)}$$

(c) Show that if $t(\xi) = T - 1$, then $\theta_m(\xi)$ is the market portfolio $(\theta_m(\xi) = (1, \ldots, 1) \in \mathbb{R})$, and if $t(\xi) < T - 1$, then $\theta_m(\xi)$ is not the market portfolio. Use this to explain why the formula in (b) differs from the standard CAPM expression for the risk premium in Proposition 17.5.

3. *Term structure of interest rates.*

This exercise explores the conditions under which the expectations hypothesis and the liquidity preference hypothesis on the term structure of interest rates are satisfied.

Consider a stochastic exchange economy $\mathscr{E}(\mathbb{D}, u, \omega, \zeta, V)$ as in Exercise 1 in which agents (investors) have additively separable utility functions $E \sum_{t=0}^{T} v_t^i(x_t^i)$, where the expectation is taken with respect to the objective probability ρ of the states of nature. Suppose the security structure has zero coupon bonds of all maturities issued at each node, which are retraded until the date prior to their maturity. Let r_t (resp. q_t) denote the interest rate on (resp. price of) the one-period bond at date t, and let $r_{t\tau}$ (resp. $q_{t\tau}$) denote the *yield to maturity* on (resp. price of) the bond with maturity date $\tau > t$ where

$$q_{t\tau} = \frac{1}{(1 + r_{t\tau})^{\tau - t}}, \quad 0 \le t < \tau \le T$$

The prices at date 0 of the bonds with different maturity dates also define the sequence of *forward interest rates* r_t^f for $0 \le t \le T$ by

$$q_{0t} = \frac{q_{0,t-1}}{1 + r_t^f}$$

To keep the analysis simple, consider the case $T = 2$ (we let the reader generalize the results for $T \ge 3$). The *expectations hypothesis* on the term structure of interest rates states that the forward rate r_1^f is the expected value of the short-term interest rate r_1 at date 1. The *liquidity preference hypothesis* asserts that the forward rate r_1^f exceeds the expected short-term interest rate r_1 by a risk premium which compensates investors holding the long-term bond for the risks incurred (by changes in capital value) when selling the bond at date 1.

Consider a financial market equilibrium $((\bar{x}, \bar{z}), \bar{q})$ of the economy.

(a) Let $\bar{\mu}^i$ denote the equilibrium probability measure of agent i (Definition 28.5). Show that for $i = 1, \ldots, I$

$$\frac{1}{1 + \bar{r}_1^f} = E_{\bar{\mu}^i} \left(\frac{1}{1 + \bar{r}_1} \right)$$

(b) Use this to show that if agents are risk-neutral and if the date 1 interest rate r_1 takes sufficiently small values, then the expectations hypothesis is approximately verified, although strictly speaking $\bar{r}_1^f < E(\bar{r}_1)$.

(c) Show that for $i = 1, \ldots, I$ the formula in (a) can also be written as

$$\frac{1}{1 + \bar{r}_1^f} = E \left(\frac{1}{1 + \bar{r}_1} \right) + \text{cov} \left(\frac{1}{1 + \bar{r}_1}, \frac{\bar{\pi}_1^{\rho, i}}{E(\bar{\pi}_1^{\rho, i})} \right)$$

Under what conditions does this formula support the liquidity preference hypothesis?

(d) Suppose that the financial markets are complete so that there is a representative agent and suppose that at each date there is uncertainty about the aggregate endowment which can take on one of two values $w^L < w^H$ with equal probability. Show that the liquidity preference hypothesis is likely to hold in this case. Illustrate your reasoning with a simple example with specific utility functions and endowment process. How would you expect the results to be modified if there is serial correlation in the aggregate endowment process or if agents' marginal utilities of income are influenced by consumption in other periods?

HISTORICAL REMARKS

The emergence of the dynamic theory of security pricing is a remarkable instance of the mutual interplay between observation of data and attempts to formulate a theory that "fits". There are few prices on which such an extraordinary wealth of data has been available over such long periods of time and to such a fine gradation of the time axis (daily, weekly, ...) as for the prices of securities, bonds, options, and futures contracts.

The observation that price changes seem to behave like independent random variables with zero expectation led to the adoption of the *random walk model* (Example 26.12) as the first stochastic model of a speculative price. Thus q_t was taken to satisfy

$$q_{t+1} = q_t + \epsilon_{t+1}, \quad t = 0, 1, \ldots \tag{1}$$

where $(\epsilon_t, \epsilon_{t+1}, \ldots)$ is a sequence of mutually independent, identically distributed random variables satisfying the zero expected gains condition

$$E(\epsilon_{t+1} \mid \mathscr{F}_t) = 0, \quad t = 0, 1, \ldots \tag{2}$$

The first formal use of this process (or more accurately its continuous time analogue *Brownian motion*) appeared in the seminal thesis of Bachelier (1900) on the valuation of options. He developed a theory of the valuation of options when the price of the underlying security follows what would now be called a Brownian motion process. Bachelier's strikingly original work was far ahead of its time both as a contribution to the theory of stochastic processes and as an innovative contribution to the theory of security pricing. The importance of his ideas[1] for the theory of derivative pricing remained entirely unknown to economists until the 1960s.

A separate but ultimately related branch of the literature can be traced to the work of Slutsky (1937) and Working (1934) who were interested in the irregular cyclical fluctuations characteristic of economic time series more generally. They noted that series generated by forming weighted sums of independent random variables look strikingly like many economic

---

[1] The book of readings edited by Cootner (1967) brings together many early papers on security pricing and contains an English translation of Bachelier's thesis.

time series—in particular indices of economic activity (business cycles) and the time series of security prices. They put forward the provocative and far reaching hypothesis that the fluctuations characteristic of both business cycles and security prices result from the cumulative effects of many independent disturbances, some favorable and some unfavorable. This approach contrasted with most contemporary models of business cycles and price fluctuations which generated strictly periodic fluctuations—such models having the defect of generating time series which do not exhibit the irregular fluctuations characteristic of actual time series and also of not being arbitrage-proof (rational). The idea that independent random shocks might provide a foundation for models of the business cycle was subsequently explored by Frisch (1933), Magill[2] (1977) and, in a systematic way, in the *real business cycle theory* of the 1980s (Kydland-Prescott (1982), Long-Plosser (1983), and Lucas (1987)).

Kendall (1953) was one of the first to attempt a systematic and extensive statistical analysis of security prices. He showed that time series analysis of security prices indicates that knowledge of past price changes yields no information about future price changes: namely if (1) is used as a model, then the $(\epsilon_t, \epsilon_{t+1}, \dots)$ sequence appears to be a sequence of mutually independent random variables. Subsequent statistical tests served to further confirm the serial independence of price changes (Osborne (1959), Granger-Morgenstern (1963, 1970)).

The random walk behavior of security prices came as quite a shock to economists: it seemed difficult to reconcile the standard demand and supply analysis of price formation with such erratic behavior for prices. How could one possibly account for such frequent and unsystematic price changes? Working (1949), who spent his career analyzing speculative prices, seems to have been the first to explain clearly why it might be theoretically reasonable to assume that security prices satisfy (1)–(2): he argued that the random walk of a futures price is the price behavior that would result from the perfect functioning of a futures market—a perfect futures market being defined as one in which the current market price constitutes at each date the best estimate that can be made, from currently available information, of what the price of the futures contract will be at its delivery date (namely the future spot price). Working called this a *theory of anticipatory prices* (see Working (1958)). He seems to have been the first to recognize the fundamental role of expectations and the unfolding of new information in explaining the behavior of speculative prices. This remarkable work essentially contained all the ingredients of the *rational expectations hypothesis* first formally introduced by Muth (1961).

The random walk model was the prototype model of speculative prices: it emerged as

---

[2] In Magill (1977) it was shown that the long-run analysis of optimal capital accumulation under random shocks to technology leads, as a byproduct, to a short-run analysis of the business cycle. The response of investment to technological shocks leads to paths of output by the different sectors of the economy that correspond closely with the observed irregular short-run fluctuations characteristic of the business cycle: even if the shocks are uncorrelated, the resulting time paths of the economic variables exhibit serial correlation. In particular it was shown explicitly how the spectral distribution of output—namely the relative importance of the different frequencies in a Fourier series expansion with random coefficients—depends on the underlying preferences and technology of the economy. It is most natural that the two literatures on fluctuations in security prices and fluctuations in economic activity should come together: they are dual aspects of the same underlying economic phenomenon.

the simplest model to capture the main characteristic of observed speculative price series—
that price changes behave like independent random variables with zero expectation. While
useful as a preliminary statistical model it was clear that it could not survive as a plausible
economic model: after all, in a random walk there is no room for maximizing and equilibrium
behavior, and most economists would probably argue that this is the most natural point
of departure for any economic theory of speculative markets. Samuelson (1965) was the
first to suggest a more general model of speculative prices which could at the same time
accommodate the "zero expected profit on random price changes" and maximizing behavior
on the part of agents. His analysis was essentially a formalization of the ideas of Working
(1949, 1958) and was first laid out in the context of a futures market—namely as a rational
model of the price of a futures contract on some underlying commodity. He argued that
the price of a futures contract is the *conditional expectation* of the commodity's future
spot price given current information, so that the price process of the futures contract is a
martingale (Example 26.14). As was shown in Example 26.12, a random walk is just another
example of a martingale. Samuelson's paper, by formalizing the intuition of Working, had the
effect of shifting attention to the economic forces (expectations and new information) that
underlie the pricing of speculative securities, rather than focusing attention on the purely
statistical properties of these prices. If, under ideal conditions, a futures price is indeed the
conditional expectation of the future spot price, then at each instant the futures price is the
best predictor (given current information) of the future spot price. Later Samuelson (1973)
showed how the analysis could be generalized to cover securities which generate not just
a random income stream at the maturity date (as with a futures contract) but a random
income stream at each date until maturity (as with an equity contract). The formula he
obtained however was not quite appropriate, since he assumed that discounting and risk
aversion could be embodied into the pricing formula as the product of an exogenously given
sequence of factors.

The representative-agent model of Lucas (1978) provided a strikingly simple and yet
fruitful framework for analyzing the intertemporal pricing of securities, in a way that could
explicitly take into account both discounting and risk aversion. In the setting of an (infinite horizon) economy consisting of identical agents with additively separable preferences
and with endowments following a Markov process, Lucas showed that the first-order conditions of the representative agent's maximum problem imply that the security prices and
their dividends satisfy equation (2) of Section 21, with state prices equal to the discounted
marginal utilities of the representative agent consuming the total endowment of the economy. Lucas' single-agent exchange model was further studied by Prescott-Mehra (1980)
and extended to include production by Brock (1979, 1982). This latter model provides a
setting in which properties of the business cycle and properties of security prices can be
studied simultaneously.

The hypothesis that prices on financial markets adjust in such a way that there are no
systematic unexploited profit opportunities—so that speculative prices fluctuate in a way
that accurately reflects the arrival of new information—became the accepted framework of
analysis in finance in the 1970s. In his influential article, Fama (1970) referred to this perfect
informational functioning of the security markets, under symmetric information for the
participants, as the *efficient markets hypothesis* (EMH). Most statistical tests have focused
on what we have called the *naive version* of EMH, namely that obtained in an economy with

risk-neutral investors in which the price of a security is equal to the conditional expectation of its discounted future dividends (equation (15) in Section 27). The well-known fact that a best predictor should be more sluggish than the process it predicts was made the basis for a new approach to testing the risk-neutral version of EMH by LeRoy-Porter (1981) and Shiller (1979). Since the variance of a conditional expectation is smaller than the variance of the process it predicts, the variance of a security price should be smaller than the variance of the sum of its discounted future dividends. Both papers conclude that the hypothesis that the variance of the security price is less than the variance of its dividends is strongly rejected by econometric tests.[3] These results created quite a stir, since they seriously questioned the validity of at least the risk-neutral version of EMH. However they did not take into account either the effect of substantial fluctuations in interest (discount) rates, or the fact that fluctuations in economic activity can lead to substantial fluctuations in agents' income and hence in their marginal valuation of income (the effect of risk aversion).

The fact that including risk aversion increases the variability of the predicted value of future dividends—but not sufficiently to justify the observed volatility of security prices—was exploited by Grossman-Shiller (1981), who used aggregate consumption data to evaluate the discounted marginal utility of dividends for a representative agent with constant relative risk aversion. Subsequent attempts to refine the use of Lucas' (1978) asset pricing model have shown that there are serious limitations on the ability of representative-agent models to generate time series for security prices that conform satisfactorily with the data (Hansen-Singleton (1982, 1983), Singleton (1987)). Related difficulties in the use of the representative agent model were encountered by Mehra-Prescott (1985) in an attempt to explain the long-observed undervaluation of stocks relative to bonds:[4] in a model with additively separable utility, no reasonable specification of time preference and risk aversion permits the return on bonds to be as low as that observed, while simultaneously generating returns on equity as high as those observed. The relative stability in the observed historical time path of aggregate consumption prevents the representative-agent model from generating sufficient variability in the marginal utility of consumption to explain the observed variability of security prices or the high risk premium on equity. The ability of rational expectations models to fit the data could probably be substantially improved by taking into account the fact that insurance (security) markets are incomplete and that the personal consumption of agents varies much more than aggregate consumption.

The study of martingales had its origin in the study of gambling strategies and became the precise mathematical way of expressing the fact that no gambling scheme can beat the house in a fair game (Theorem 26.15, see Doob (1953)). Samuelson (1965, 1973) was the first to recognize the relation between the fair game property and the valuation of securities on competitive markets. When the valuation model was extended to the non-risk-neutral case (LeRoy (1973), Lucas (1978)) it was thought that the martingale property was no longer satisfied. Harrison-Kreps (1979) were the first to establish that any no-arbitrage

---

[3]Serious objections have been raised to the econometric procedures used in the variance-bounds tests of LeRoy-Porter (1981) and Shiller (1979). Even when more sophisticated procedures are employed, the phenomenon of excess volatility does not seem to disappear (see LeRoy (1989)).

[4]An interesting discussion of the issues may be found in Keynes' (1925) book review assessing a study of the long-term returns on equity relative to bonds in the U.S. over the period 1866–1922.

price process has the property that, under an appropriate change of measure on the state space, each security price can be expressed as the conditional expectation of its dividends (Theorem 28.2). Subsequently the martingale measure proved to be a powerful tool in the theory of pricing of derivative securities—an excellent exposition of the results is given by Duffie (1992). In this chapter, we have chosen to emphasize the fact that the martingale property provides a natural way of formalizing the informational efficiency of security prices in a financial market equilibrium, both in the case where investors are risk averse and in the case where they are risk neutral.

6

PRODUCTION IN A FINANCE ECONOMY

MOTIVATION AND SUMMARY

The analysis of the functioning of an economy is typically broken down into two steps. The first consists in modelling economic activity by an *exchange economy*: the key simplification consists in assuming that the goods available to the agents are exogenously given and attention is focused on how the available financial markets enable agents to share the risks involved in their initial holdings. In short, with supply fixed, the focus is on exchange.

The second step consists of grafting onto this model a description of how the supply of goods is created by productive activity. Since in a modern economy, such productive activity is a long and complex process which involves initiative, organization and co-operation, it is a much greater challenge to model satisfactorily the activity of agents in a *production economy*. There is now potentially far more to be explained: why agents come together to form firms, why firms specialize in the production of certain types of goods and services and are organized in certain ways, and how the activities of the different firms are co-ordinated through markets. A single theory cannot explain everything, so it has to take certain elements as given. The model of a production economy studied in this chapter is based on some traditional simplifications. The economy is taken to be composed of an exogenously given collection of firms (no explanation of how they come about); the outcomes arising from alternative modes of specialization and organization open to each firm are expressed in reduced form as a menu of productive options (a technology set); the focus of attention is on the interface between firms' activities and markets—how a firm's choice among productive options is influenced by the opportunities available on the financial markets.

The interplay between productive activity of firms and financial markets arises from a simple fact: *most production takes time*. The cost of an investment must be incurred before the revenue is obtained from the sale of its output. This mismatching of disbursements and receipts implies that every production plan must be accompanied by an appropriate method of financing. There is also a close connection between the ownership structure of a firm and the method used to finance its investment.

Three principal types of ownership structure can be distinguished: the *sole proprietorship* (*individually owned firm*), the *partnership* and the *corporation*. From a historical perspective these three types correspond to successive stages in the development of capitalism, although all three types still coexist in a modern economy. The firms in these three categories differ in their size, their organizational structure and the way in which they are financed. The category into which a particular firm falls depends essentially on the scale of its operation. This in turn depends on the extent of the potential economies of scale and indivisibilities associated with its technology and on the size of the market that it faces. Since the problem of integrating economies of scale and indivisibilities presents many difficulties for a general equilibrium analysis we shall not attempt to explicitly incorporate them into the analysis that follows. In all cases production sets are assumed to be convex: this amounts to assuming that firms operate at a scale where decreasing returns are prevalent and that the number of firms in each market is sufficient to allow us as a first approximation to abstract from non-competitive behavior.

The distinction that is made between the three types of firms is based on differences in the financial sources to which they have access and the ownership and control structure that this implies. The individually owned firm and the partnership do not have access to the stock market, and the ownership and control are vested in the individual or partners who subscribe the initial capital. A corporation sells ownership shares on the stock market. It is thus owned by shareholders, but is typically run by a separate group of agents specialized in the job of management.

In the case of an individually owned firm, it is natural to assume that the owner (entrepreneur) manages the firm in his own interests, so that there is no problem in assigning an objective function to the firm. In a partnership, the owners do not change during the lifetime of the firm, unless the firm goes public, in which case it becomes a corporation. However in an environment where the outcome of production is uncertain and where markets are incomplete, there may be disagreement among the partners on the objective to be assigned to the firm even if the partnership shares are endogenously chosen.

The potential disagreement among the partners has its origin in the basic property of an economy with incomplete markets which was studied in the previous chapters:[1] when financial markets are incomplete, agents differ in the way they value future (risky) income streams. To resolve such differences of opinion, some method needs to be introduced to decide how strongly the opinions of the different partners should be weighted to obtain a collective objective function, on the basis of which decisions can be made for the partnership. A way of resolving the problem has been proposed

---

[1] In particular in Section 11.

by Drèze (1974): it consists in assuming that transfer payments can be used among partners to reach unanimity. In Section 32 it is shown how this approach leads to a well-defined objective function for a partnership in which each partner's present-value vector is weighted by his share in the initial investment of the partnership. This is a natural and intuitively reasonable way of resolving potential disagreements.

Historically the partnership came to be widely adopted when the initial capital required to set up a business became too large to be provided by individual entrepreneurs. While the presence of bond markets (and other more informal sources of loanable funds) enabled the partners to further augment their access to capital, the risky returns involved in their investment limited their access to such funds, for the group of partners had to remain solvent even in the face of unfavorable returns on their investment. The introduction of the legal status of *limited liability*, which limited the debts of the company for which individual partners were liable to their share of the initial capital, made it more attractive for potential investors to undertake risky capital projects. However, limiting the liability of partners increases the risk to which bond holders are exposed, and hence limits the access of a partnership to loanable funds.

As the size of the market expanded and as technical change increased the potential payoffs from large scale production, firms needed to have access to larger amounts of capital. What was needed to finance such firms was a way of spreading the risks associated with the investment among a much larger number of individuals. A solution was found by introducing the *equity contract* which made it possible to sell ownership shares of a firm on a stock market. Thus emerged the third form of business enterprise called a *corporation*. A corporation may be defined as a firm with three properties:

(i) its capital (ownership) is divided into shares (equity contracts);
(ii) each shareholder is liable for the company's debts up to an amount limited to the current value of his equity share;
(iii) the company's equity contracts are traded on a stock market.

Property (iii) is the new feature which distinguishes a corporation from a (limited liability) partnership and makes it possible to collect the required capital from a large number of shareholders. It increases the willingness of potential investors to contribute funds to the firm by making the investment liquid. An investor who purchases an equity contract has the flexibility to revise his commitment at any later date if the need should arise, by selling his ownership share on the market. An investment in a corporation thus stands in sharp contrast to an investment in a partnership which essentially involves a permanent commitment.

The corporation brought with it a new phenomenon: *the separation of ownership and control*. The greatly increased number of owners and the often temporary nature of the commitment of many of the shareholders made it unpractical, and in fact undesirable, for the owners to be responsible for the (routine) management of the firm. Corporations became run by salaried managers who were not necessarily significant shareholders in the firm. Whether managers in fact act in the best interests of shareholders (if this can be defined) has been the subject of extensive debate. The systematic formal study of the corporation as an organization is too recent to have brought a definite conclusion on the subject. It is clear however that if the compensation of managers is closely correlated to the market value of the firms' shares, then the interests of the managers will probably not significantly differ from the interests of the shareholders.

In the analysis of this chapter, shareholders are taken to be well-informed about the options open to the corporation, and to take an active part in influencing its (long-run) investment decision. As with a partnership, the problem is to determine how the opinions and objectives of a diverse collection of shareholders can be aggregated into a workable (well-defined) criterion for making decisions on behalf of the collective entity called "the corporation". The new complicating element is the possibly transient nature of the owners of a corporation: given the liquidity of the equity contract, a shareholder has the option of selling his shares between the time when the investment decision is made and the future period when its payoff (dividend) is earned. A shareholder is thus concerned with the effect of an investment decision on the market value of his shares.

When the financial markets are complete, present-value prices are well-defined and competitive markets value an investment by the present value of its future dividend stream. In such a setting all shareholders are unanimous and agree that the investment decision should be taken which maximizes the market value of the firm. When the financial markets are incomplete, present-value prices are not unique: the market thus no longer provides a well-defined signal for the value of an investment. In such a setting how does a shareholder estimate the value that "the market" will attribute to the dividend stream generated by an investment, when the dividend stream does not lie in the marketed subspace? What is needed is a way of extending the pricing of income streams—which is well-defined on the marketed subspace—to the space of all possible income streams. A natural approach, introduced by Grossman-Hart (1979), is to assume that each agent bases his estimate of the market value of a future income stream on the value obtained by using his own present-value vector. Forming expectations in this way does not assume more knowledge on the part of agents than is contained in the equilibrium prices: furthermore such expectations are rational in the sense that they are confirmed in equilibrium, since the market value of each corporation's dividend stream coincides with its fundamental value for each agent. Under this method of assessing market value (called *competitive price perceptions*), the problem of finding an objective function for the corporation which aggregates the divergent opinions of the shareholders is equivalent to the problem of finding an objective function for a partnership.

29. CHARACTERISTICS OF PRODUCTION ECONOMY

An income or finance model of an economy when taken literally may appear as something of a fiction. Actually, there is a perfectly legitimate way of interpreting a finance-exchange economy as the income part of a general multigood exchange economy if the vector of spot prices for the goods is fixed at an equilibrium value. In the same way, a finance-production economy can be interpreted as the income part of a general multigood production economy.

In a two-period multigood economy there are L goods at date 0 and in each of the states at date 1. A production economy with I consumers and K firms is characterized by the preferences and initial endowments (u^i, ω^i), $i = 1, \ldots, I$, of the consumers and by the production (opportunity) sets $Y^k \subset \mathbb{R}^{L(S+1)}$, $k = 1, \ldots, K$, of the firms. If $\bar{p} = (\bar{p}_0, \bar{p}_1, \ldots, \bar{p}_S)$ is an equilibrium vector of spot prices for the multigood model, then the *profit opportunity* set of firm k in the finance model is given by

$$\widetilde{Y}_k = \left\{ \widetilde{y}^k \in \mathbb{R}^{S+1} \mid (\widetilde{y}_0^k, \ldots, \widetilde{y}_S^k) = (\bar{p}_0 y_0^k, \ldots, \bar{p}_S y_S^k), \quad y^k \in Y^k \right\} \qquad (1)$$

Thus a production plan $(y_0^k, \ldots, y_S^k)$ involving the L goods is replaced by an *income stream* $(\bar{p}_0 y_0^k, \ldots, \bar{p}_S y_S^k)$ in the finance model. In a two-period model it is natural to interpret the vector y_0^k as a vector of inputs at date 0 which generates the vector of outputs y_s^k in state s at date 1: $\bar{p}_0 y_0^k$ is thus the *investment cost* incurred at date 0, while $\bar{p}_s y_s^k$ is the *revenue* which it generates in state s at date 1.

The characteristics of consumer i in the finance model consist of the agent's *indirect utility function* $\widetilde{u}^i$ (defined by (6) in Section 5) and his *initial income* $\widetilde{\omega}^i$, which is the value of his initial endowment ω^i under the vector of spot prices $\bar{p}$ (see (12) in Section 5). Thus the characteristics of a finance-production economy are given by

$$(\widetilde{u}, \widetilde{\omega}, \widetilde{Y}) = (\widetilde{u}^1, \ldots, \widetilde{u}^I, \widetilde{\omega}^1, \ldots, \widetilde{\omega}^I, \widetilde{Y}^1, \ldots, \widetilde{Y}^K)$$

With the vector of spot prices fixed at $\bar{p}$, this model is a one-good version of the general model. As in the case of an exchange economy, it is convenient to omit explicit reference to the vector $\bar{p}$, analyzing the model directly as a one-good model. As before, depending on the context, we take the liberty of switching between the one-good and the income interpretation of the model.

With this convention, a two-period one-good production economy can be characterized as follows. There are I consumers, where consumer i is described by a utility function $u^i : \mathbb{R}_+^{S+1} \longrightarrow \mathbb{R}$ and an initial endowment $\omega^i \in \mathbb{R}_+^{S+1}$ for $i = 1, \ldots, I$. There are K exogenously given *technology sets*:[1] $Y^k \subset \mathbb{R}^{S+1}$ describes the income streams $y^k = (y_0^k, y_1^k, \ldots, y_S^k)$ generated by investment projects available to "firm" k, for $k = 1, \ldots, K$. At this point a "firm" is an abstract concept assimilated with its production set: later, when an ownership

---

[1] The usual sign convention is adopted: $y_s^k < 0$ indicates an *input* (investment), while $y_s^k > 0$ implies *output* (revenue) in state s: typically $y_0^k < 0$ and $y_s^k > 0$, $s = 1, \ldots, S$.

structure is introduced, the firm will become a more precise entity, consisting of either an individually owned firm (proprietorship), a partnership or a corporation. In each case an appropriate concept of equilibrium is introduced. To keep the necessary techniques to a minimum the problem of existence will not be discussed in this chapter:[2] however to ensure the existence of an equilibrium, in addition to the earlier assumptions on preferences, the following conditions are imposed on the technology sets.

Assumption $\mathscr{T}$ (Technology Sets):   The technology sets Y^k $(k = 1, \ldots, K)$ have the following properties:

(1) $Y^k \subset \mathbb{R}^{S+1}$ is closed
(2) Y^k is convex
(3) $Y^k \supset \mathbb{R}^{S+1}_-$
(4) $Y^k \cap \mathbb{R}^{S+1}_+ = \{0\}$
(5) $(w + \sum_{k=1}^{K} Y^k) \cap \mathbb{R}^{S+1}_+$ is compact for all $w \in \mathbb{R}^{S+1}_+$.

These are standard assumptions of general equilibrium theory (see Debreu (1959, Chapter 3)). (1) is a mild technical assumption. (2) implies that the technology sets exhibit *constant* or *decreasing returns*. (3) is the assumption of *free disposal* and implies $0 \in Y^k$ (the possibility of inaction). (4) is the assumption of *no free goods in production*: a production plan cannot create something (positive output) out of nothing (zero input). (5) asserts that the production possibilities of the economy as a whole are bounded: only a limited amount of output can be produced from limited initial resources, when the productive capacities of all firms are combined.

To analyze the first-order conditions at an equilibrium and more generally to illustrate the theory in the sections that follow, it will often be instructive to consider technology sets which have the additional property that their boundaries are defined by differentiable functions.

Assumption $\mathscr{T}'$ (Transformation Functions):   Each production set Y^k can be represented by a transformation function $T^k : \mathbb{R}^{S+1} \longrightarrow \mathbb{R}$

$$Y^k = \{y \in \mathbb{R}^{S+1} \mid T^k(y) \leq 0\}$$

where $T^k(\cdot)$ is non-decreasing, quasi-convex, and differentiable, and satisfies $T^k(0) = 0$.

Let $(u, \omega, Y) = (u^1, \ldots, u^I, \omega^1, \ldots, \omega^I, Y^1, \ldots, Y^K)$ denote the characteristics of the I consumers and K firms, and let $\mathscr{E}(u, \omega, Y)$ denote the associated

---

[2]The proofs are either standard or presented in Volume 2.

finance-production economy. For such an economy the definitions of feasible and Pareto optimal allocations are straightforward.

29.1 Definition: An *allocation* $(x, y) = (x^1, \ldots, x^I, y^1, \ldots, y^K)$ for the economy $\mathscr{E}(u, \omega, Y)$ consists of a consumption stream $x^i \in \mathbb{R}^{S+1}$ for each consumer $(i = 1, \ldots, I)$ and a production plan $y^k \in \mathbb{R}^{S+1}$ for each firm $(k = 1, \ldots, K)$. An allocation (x, y) is *feasible* if

(i) $x^i \in \mathbb{R}_+^{S+1}$, $i = 1, \ldots, I$

(ii) $y^k \in Y^k$, $k = 1, \ldots, K$

(iii) $\sum_{i=1}^{I} (x^i - \omega^i) \le \sum_{k=1}^{K} y^k$

We let F denote the *set of feasible allocations* so that

$$F = \left\{ (x, y) \in \mathbb{R}_+^{(S+1)I} \times \prod_{k=1}^{K} Y^k \;\middle|\; \sum_{i=1}^{I} (x^i - \omega^i) \le \sum_{k=1}^{K} y^k \right\}$$

29.2 Definition: An allocation $(\bar{x}, \bar{y})$ is a *Pareto optimum* if (i) $(\bar{x}, \bar{y}) \in F$ (ii) there does not exist $(x, y) \in F$ such that $u^i(x^i) \ge u^i(\bar{x}^i)$, $i = 1, \ldots, I$ with strict inequality for at least one i.

Contingent Market Equilibrium

The concept of a contingent contract was made precise in Definition 7.1. Classical general equilibrium theory assumes that at date 0 there is a complete set of contingent contracts for the good in each state $s = 0, 1, \ldots, S$. Let $\pi = (\pi_0, \pi_1, \ldots, \pi_S)$ denote the associated *contingent prices.* Consumer i has income which comes from two sources: the sale of his initial endowment ω^i and the firms' profits derived from his ownership shares in the firms. At date 0 consumer i can sell not only his date 0 endowment ω_0^i at the price π_0 but also each component ω_s^i of the (correctly anticipated) date 1 endowment $\omega_1^i = (\omega_1^i, \ldots, \omega_S^i)$ at the price $\pi_s (s = 1, \ldots, S)$. Agent i thus obtains the income $\pi \omega^i = \sum_{s=0}^{S} \pi_s \omega_s^i$ from the sale of his lifetime endowment. The ownership of the firms is assumed to be distributed among the consumers and is taken as initial data given exogenously. Let $\delta^i = (\delta_1^i, \ldots, \delta_K^i)$ denote the vector of initial ownership shares of agent i, δ_k^i denoting agent i's share of firm k, and let $\delta = (\delta^1, \ldots, \delta^I)$. It is assumed that δ satisfies

$$\delta^i \in \mathbb{R}_+^K, \quad i = 1, \ldots, I \quad \text{and} \quad \sum_{i=1}^{I} \delta_k^i = 1, \quad k = 1, \ldots, K$$

We let $\mathscr{E}(u, \omega, \delta, Y)$ denote the associated private ownership production economy.

If $y = (y^1, \ldots, y^K)$ are the production plans chosen by the firms, then agent i receives the *dividend income*

$$\sum_{k=1}^{K} \delta_k^i \pi y^k = \sum_{k=1}^{K} \delta_k^i \left(\sum_{s=0}^{S} \pi_s y_s^k \right)$$

from his ownership shares in the J firms. The *contingent market budget set* of agent i is thus given by

$$B(\pi, y, \omega^i, \delta^i) = \left\{ x^i \in \mathbb{R}_+^{S+1} \;\middle|\; \pi x^i = \pi \left(\omega^i + \sum_{k=1}^{K} \delta_k^i y^k \right) \right\}$$

Each firm is owned by its shareholders and is assumed to be run by a manager. Although the managerial function is not explicitly modelled, the cost of management can be included in the opportunity set Y^k. Since there is no asymmetry of information, there is no problem of moral hazard involved in inducing the manager to act in the best interest of the shareholders: provided the manager is a shareholder of the firm, his best interest coincides with the best interest of all other shareholders of the firm. Under the price-taking assumption of the competitive model, these interests are best served if the profit of the firm is maximized. Assuming that the manager of each firm acts in this way leads to the following classical concept of equilibrium.

29.3 Definition: A *contingent market (CM) equilibrium* for the economy $\mathscr{E}(u, \omega, \delta, Y)$ with one good is a pair consisting of an allocation and a vector of prices $((\bar{x}, \bar{y}), \bar{\pi}) \in \mathbb{R}_+^{(S+1)I} \times \mathbb{R}^{(S+1)K} \times \mathbb{R}_+^{S+1}$ such that

(i) $\bar{x}^i \in \arg \max \left\{ u^i(x^i) \;\middle|\; x^i \in B(\bar{\pi}, \bar{y}, \omega^i, \delta^i) \right\}$, $i = 1, \ldots, I$

(ii) $\bar{y}^k \in \arg \max \left\{ \bar{\pi} y^k \;\middle|\; y^k \in Y^k \right\}$, $k = 1, \ldots, K$

(iii) $\sum_{i=1}^{I} (\bar{x}^i - \omega^i) = \sum_{k=1}^{K} \bar{y}^k$

It is a standard result of general equilibrium theory that under Assumptions $(\mathscr{U}', \mathscr{T})$, if $\left(\sum_{i=1}^{I} \omega^i + \sum_{k=1}^{K} Y^k \right) \cap \mathbb{R}_{++}^{S+1} \neq \emptyset$, then the production economy $\mathscr{E}(u, \omega, \delta, Y)$ has a contingent market equilibrium.

The striking property of the competitive model with complete contingent markets is that profit maximization by firms, which from a positive point of view can be justified by the self-interest of the shareholders, is also optimal for the economy as a whole. A system of contingent markets is thus an ideal system of markets which perfectly co-ordinates the activities of all agents in the economy.

29.4 Theorem (Pareto Optimality of CM Equilibrium):   Let $\mathscr{E}(u, \omega, Y, \delta)$ be an economy satisfying Assumption $\mathscr{U}''$. If $((\bar{x}, \bar{y}), \bar{\pi})$ is a contingent market equilibrium, then the allocation $(\bar{x}, \bar{y})$ is a Pareto optimum.

PROOF: The proof is a simple adaptation of that for Theorem 7.6. □

Assuming that there is a complete set of contingent markets simplifies (or perhaps more accurately trivializes) the theory of the firm.[3] The fact that there is a complete set of markets on which all goods are traded and paid for at date 0 has the following consequences.

(1) Since firms can sell their contingent plans in advance and all payments are made at date 0, the cost of inputs is immediately covered by the revenue obtained from the forward sale of output: there is thus no need to consider a *financial policy* for matching date 0 payments with date 1 receipts.

(2) Since there is a date 0 market price π_s for the good in each state, the *profit* $\pi y^k = \sum_{s=0}^{S} \pi_s y_s^k$ associated with a production plan y^k is well-defined.

(3) Since each shareholder is given his share of the date 0 profit, all shareholders agree with the objective of *maximizing profit*. Thus the production plan which is chosen does not depend on who the manager is nor who the shareholders are.

In Section 3 it was argued that there are many reasons why in practice it is either unfeasible or unpractical to have a complete set of contingent markets which would permit firms to sell contingent plans in advance, all payments being made at some initial date. In the simplest two-period setting, a model which conforms more closely with what is observed in the real world is a model of a *sequence economy* in which there are limited financial markets for the transfer of income between the initial date and the states at date 1. In such an economy, since firms cannot obtain payment at date 0 for their date 1 outputs, a production plan needs to be accompanied by a *financial policy* describing how the investment at the initial date is financed. The next section analyses the investment and financial policies in the simplest case where firms are individually owned.

30. SOLE PROPRIETORSHIPS

Consider a two-period finance economy with I agents and $K \leq I$ firms, in which each firm has a sole proprietor. Thus for each firm k ($k = 1, \ldots, K$) there is an agent $i(k) \in \{1, \ldots, I\}$ who is the founder, owner, and manager of firm k: such an agent will be called an *entrepreneur*. The ownership structure of the firms

---

[3] "The firm fits into general equilibrium theory as a balloon fits into an envelope: flattened out! Try with a blown-up balloon: the envelope may tear, or fly away: at best, it will be hard to seal and impossible to mail … Instead, burst the balloon flat, and everything becomes easy. Similarly with the firm and general equilibrium". (Drèze (1985)).

is taken as exogenously given: there is no attempt to explain entrepreneurship endogenously. It will often be convenient to invert the ownership map $k \mapsto i(k)$: thus $i \mapsto k(i)$ indicates the firm which belongs to agent i, with the convention that $k(i) = \emptyset$ if agent i does not own a firm.

The entrepreneur of firm k is assumed to have at his disposal a variety of alternative investment projects which are summarized in a production set Y^k satisfying Assumption $\mathcal{T}$. A typical element of Y^k is denoted by $y^k = (y_0^k, y_1^k, \ldots, y_S^k)$. There are financial markets on which J bonds are traded: R_s^j denotes the exogenously given payoff of the jth bond in state s ($s = 1, \ldots, S$) and

$$R_s = (R_s^1, \ldots, R_s^J), \quad s = 1, \ldots, S$$

denotes the vector of payoffs of the J bonds in state s. Let $q = (q_1, \ldots, q_J)$ denote the vector of prices for the J bonds.

The entrepreneur of firm k chooses a production plan $y^k = (y_0^k, y_1^k, \ldots, y_S^k)$ and pays for the initial investment y_0^k. He can however use the financial markets to borrow, but is personally responsible for the payment of debts at date 1: thus an entrepreneur is assumed to have *unlimited liability* for any debts incurred by his firm. In addition there is no possibility of default for individuals as consumers: implicitly, the legal penalties for default are so high that no consumer ever chooses a financial strategy which would lead to default.

Each agent i chooses a consumption plan $x^i = (x_0^i, x_1^i, \ldots, x_S^i)$, a portfolio $\xi^i = (\xi_1^i, \ldots, \xi_J^i)$ of the J bonds and if agent i owns a firm, a production plan $y^{k(i)}$. With the convention[1]

$$Y^{k(i)} = \{0\} \quad \text{if} \quad k(i) = \emptyset$$

the same notation can be used for all agents, so that $y^{k(i)} = 0$ if agent i does not own a firm. The *budget set* of agent i is defined by

$$\mathbb{B}(q, \omega^i, R, Y^{k(i)}) = \left\{ x^i \in \mathbb{R}_+^{S+1} \;\middle|\; \begin{array}{l} x_0^i = \omega_0^i - q\xi^i + y_0^{k(i)} \\ x_s^i = \omega_s^i + R_s\xi^i + y_s^{k(i)}, \ s = 1, \ldots, S \\ (\xi^i, y^{k(i)}) \in \mathbb{R}^J \times Y^{k(i)} \end{array} \right\} \quad (1)$$

---

[1]Strictly speaking, the production set of an agent who does not own a firm should be written as $Y^{k(i)} = \mathbb{R}_-^{S+1}$ in order that Assumption $\mathcal{T}(3)$ be satisfied. When an analysis is made of the existence of equilibrium, this is the convention which should be adopted. However there is no loss of generality in adopting the more intuitive convention $Y^{k(i)} = \{0\}$ when analyzing the properties of equilibria, since at an equilibrium in which agents maximize utility, the choice is obviously $y^{k(i)} = 0$. Since the analysis that follows is restricted to properties of equilibria, we adopt the simpler convention.

If W denotes the matrix of financial market payoffs

$$W = W(q, R) = \begin{bmatrix} -q \\ R \end{bmatrix} = \begin{bmatrix} -q_1 & \cdots & -q_J \\ R_1^1 & \cdots & R_1^J \\ \vdots & \ddots & \vdots \\ R_S^1 & \cdots & R_S^J \end{bmatrix} \tag{2}$$

then the budget set can be written as

$$\mathbb{B}(q, \omega^i, R, Y^{k(i)}) = \left\{ x^i \in \mathbb{R}_+^{S+1} \;\middle|\; \begin{array}{l} x^i - \omega^i = W\xi^i + y^{k(i)} \\ (\xi^i, y^{k(i)}) \in \mathbb{R}^J \times Y^{k(i)} \end{array} \right\} \tag{3}$$

Each agent chooses a triple $(x^i, \xi^i, y^{k(i)})$ consistent with his budget set so as to maximize his utility. A financial policy ξ^i such that $x^i - \omega^i = W\xi^i + y^{k(i)}$ is said to *finance* $(x^i, y^{k(i)})$; the notation

$$(x^i; \xi^i, y^{k(i)}) \in \mathbb{B}(q, \omega^i, R, Y^{k(i)})$$

is used to denote a consumption-finance-production plan $(x^i, \xi^i, y^{k(i)}) \in \mathbb{B}(\cdot) \times \mathbb{R}^J \times Y^{k(i)}$ such that ξ^i finances $(x^i, y^{k(i)})$. A vector denoting the actions of the I agents in the economy is given by

$$(x, \xi, y) = (x^1, \ldots, x^I, \xi^1, \ldots, \xi^I, y^1, \ldots, y^I)$$

The concept of a competitive equilibrium for an entrepreneurial economy in which agents correctly anticipate their future consumption and production plans is then defined as follows. The qualification "reduced-form" introduced in Definition 30.1 will be explained shortly: in essence it means that no distinction is made between the role of an agent as a consumer and his role as an entrepreneur.

30.1 Definition: A (reduced-form) *entrepreneurial equilibrium* is a pair consisting of actions and prices $((\bar{x}, \bar{\xi}, \bar{y}), \bar{q}) \in \mathbb{R}_+^{(S+1)I} \times \mathbb{R}^{JI} \times \mathbb{R}^{(S+1)I} \times \mathbb{R}^J$ such that

(i) Each agent i $(i = 1, \ldots, I)$ chooses a triple $(\bar{x}^i, \bar{\xi}^i, \bar{y}^{k(i)})$ consistent with his budget set $\mathbb{B}(\bar{q}, \omega^i, R, Y^{k(i)})$ and

$$(\bar{x}^i; \bar{\xi}^i, \bar{y}^{k(i)}) \in \arg\max \left\{ u^i(x^i) \;\middle|\; (x^i; \xi^i, y^{k(i)}) \in \mathbb{B}(\bar{q}, \omega^i, R, Y^{k(i)}) \right\}$$

(ii) $\sum_{i=1}^I \bar{\xi}^i = 0$

Note that (ii) implies that the implicit "spot market" for the good clears in each state

$$\sum_{i=1}^{I}(\bar{x}_s^i - \omega_s^i) = \sum_{k=1}^{K} \bar{y}_s^k, \quad s = 0, 1, \ldots, S$$

The concept of equilibrium just defined is the natural concept to consider in a model where agents are proprietors of their own firms and can borrow and lend on the bond market. However it does not respect the classical dichotomy between the activities of agents in the production and consumption (distribution) sectors of the economy. As an entrepreneur (producer), an agent looks for profit opportunities; as a consumer he looks for the most preferred consumption stream compatible with his income. Let us show how the above concept of equilibrium can be *transformed* so as to respect this distinction between the role of an agent as an entrepreneur and his role as a consumer.

First-Order Conditions

The simplest way of finding this transformation is to consider the first-order conditions for the maximum problem of an agent in an equilibrium

$$\max \left\{ u^i(x^i) \mid (x^i; \xi^i, y^{k(i)}) \in \mathbb{B}(\bar{q}, \omega^i, R, Y^{k(i)}) \right\} \tag{4}$$

For an agent without a firm ($Y^{k(i)} = \{0\}$) this problem is the consumption-portfolio problem of an agent in a financial market equilibrium studied in Section 9. In this case the first-order conditions can be written (using the net trade vector $\tau^i = x^i - \omega^i$) as

$$\bar{\tau}^i \in \langle W \rangle, \quad \bar{\pi}^i \in \langle W \rangle^{\perp}$$

where $\bar{\pi}^i$ is agent i's present-value vector at the optimal consumption plan $\bar{x}^i$.

An agent who is an entrepreneur chooses in addition a production plan $y^{k(i)}$ from the collection of projects $Y^{k(i)}$ to which he has access. If the utility function u^i satisfies Assumption $\mathscr{U}$ and if his technology set $Y^{k(i)}$ can be represented by a differentiable transformation function T^k (Assumption $\mathscr{T}'$), then the first-order conditions can be derived by standard techniques of calculus. The maximum problem of entrepreneur i, who owns firm $k = k(i)$, can be written as

$$\max \left\{ u^i(x^i) \left| \begin{array}{l} x_0^i - \omega_0^i = -q\xi^i + y_0^k \\ x_s^i - \omega_s^i = R_s\xi^i + y_s^k, \quad s = 1, \ldots, S \\ T^k(y^k) \leq 0 \\ (x^i, \xi^i, y^k) \in \mathbb{R}_+^{S+1} \times \mathbb{R}^J \times \mathbb{R}^{S+1} \end{array} \right. \right\} \tag{5}$$

In view of Assumption $\mathscr{U}$, the non-negativity constraint $x^i \in \mathbb{R}^S_+$ will not be binding. Let $\lambda^i = (\lambda^i_0, \lambda^i_1, \ldots, \lambda^i_S)$ denote the vector of Lagrange multipliers induced by the $S+1$ budget constraints and let μ^k be the multiplier induced by the technology constraint. Forming the Lagrangean

$$L^i(x^i, \xi^i, y^k, \lambda^i, \mu^k) = u^i(x^i) - \lambda^i_0(x^i_0 - \omega^i_0 + q\xi^i - y^k_0)$$
$$- \sum_{s=1}^{S} \lambda^i_s(x^i_s - \omega^i_s - R_s\xi^i - y^k_s) - \mu^k T^k(y^k)$$

the first-order conditions, which are necessary and sufficient for $(\bar{x}^i, \bar{\xi}^i, \bar{y}^k)$ to be a solution of (5), are that there exist $(\bar{\lambda}^i, \bar{\mu}^k) \in \mathbb{R}^{S+1}_{++} \times \mathbb{R}_{++}$ such that

$$\nabla L^i(\bar{x}^i, \bar{\xi}^i, \bar{y}^k, \bar{\lambda}^i, \bar{\mu}^k) = 0$$

which is equivalent to

$$\nabla u^i(\bar{x}^i) = \bar{\lambda}^i \tag{6}$$

$$-\bar{\lambda}^i_0\bar{q} + \sum_{s=1}^{S} \bar{\lambda}^i_s R_s = 0 \tag{7}$$

$$\bar{\mu}^k \nabla T^k(\bar{y}^k) = \bar{\lambda}^i \tag{8}$$

$$\bar{x}^i - \omega^i = W\bar{\xi}^i + \bar{y}^k, \quad T^k(\bar{y}^k) = 0 \tag{9}$$

(6) and (7) are identical to the first-order conditions for the agent's consumption-portfolio choice derived in Section 9 (equations (13) and (14)). $\bar{\lambda}^i$ is the vector of marginal utilities of income, which, in the finance model, coincides with the vector of marginal utilities of the good across the states. Let $\bar{\pi}^i = \bar{\lambda}^i/\bar{\lambda}^i_0$ denote the present-value vector (the normalized gradient) of agent i, then (7) expresses the fact that the price $\bar{q}_j$ of each security coincides with the present value to agent i of its future stream of dividends $\sum_{s=1}^{S} \bar{\pi}^i_s R^j_s$. As explained in Section 9, this condition can also be written as

$$\bar{\pi}^i \in \langle W \rangle^\perp$$

Condition (8) on the choice of production plan can be written as

$$\bar{\pi}^i_s = \frac{\dfrac{\partial u^i(\bar{x}^i)}{\partial x^i_s}}{\dfrac{\partial u^i(\bar{x}^i)}{\partial x^i_0}} = \frac{\dfrac{\partial T^k(\bar{y}^k)}{\partial y^k_s}}{\dfrac{\partial T^k(\bar{y}^k)}{\partial y^k_0}}, \quad s = 1, \ldots, S \tag{10}$$

which is equivalent to

$$\bar{\pi}^i = \left(\frac{1}{\bar{\lambda}_0^i}\right)\nabla u^i(\bar{x}^i) = \left(\frac{\bar{\mu}^k}{\bar{\lambda}_0^i}\right)\nabla T^k(\bar{y}^k) \tag{11}$$

(10) expresses the requirement that *the marginal rates of transformation between each pair of goods on the production surface at $\bar{y}^k$ must equal the corresponding marginal rates of substitution on the indifference surface through $\bar{x}^i$.*
If this condition were not satisfied, then by a small reallocation (dx^i, dy^k) in his consumption-production plan,[2] the entrepreneur could move to an alternative plan $(\bar{x}^i + dx^i, \bar{y}^k + dy^k)$, which is technologically feasible $(T^k(\bar{y}^k + dy^k) = 0)$, satisfies the budget equations $(dx^i = dy^k)$, and leads to a higher level of utility $\left(u^i(\bar{x}^i + dx^i) > u^i(\bar{x}^i)\right)$.

Condition (11) has an important consequence: it permits the optimal plan $\bar{y}^k$ to be viewed as a production plan which is chosen as a result of profit maximization by the entrepreneur under his present-value vector $\bar{\pi}^i$. This can be seen as follows. Suppose entrepreneur i, taking $\bar{\pi}^i$ as given, looks for a production plan which maximizes profit; that is, he solves the maximum problem

$$\max\left\{\bar{\pi}^i y^k \mid T^k(y^k) \leq 0\right\} \tag{12}$$

The first-order conditions for this problem are that there exist $\nu_k > 0$ such that

$$\bar{\pi}^i = \nu_k \nabla T^k(\bar{y}^k) \tag{13}$$

(13) is equivalent to (11), and by quasi-convexity of $T^k(\cdot)$ (or equivalently by the convexity of Y^k) the condition (13) is necessary and sufficient for $\bar{y}^k$ to solve the maximum problem (12). *Thus the entrepreneur's decision $(\bar{x}^i, \bar{\xi}^i, \bar{y}^k)$ can be thought of as being decomposed into two decisions: taking production $\bar{y}^k$ as given, agent i solves a standard consumption-portfolio problem to find $(\bar{x}^i, \bar{\xi}^i)$; taking $(\bar{x}^i, \bar{\xi}^i)$ as given, and hence the vector $\bar{\pi}^i = \pi^i(\bar{x}^i)$, agent i chooses the production plan y^k which maximizes profit $\bar{\pi}^i y^k$ over the production set Y^k.*

This decomposition of the maximum problem in (5), induced by the agent's present-value vector $\bar{\pi}^i$ at the optimum, has been derived under the assumption that the technology set Y^k can be represented by a differentiable function T^k. Using this assumption, the first-order conditions (11) and (13) were derived using calculus and the standard Lagrange multiplier technique. Assumption $\mathscr{T}'$ is however a rather restrictive condition to impose on technology sets: among other properties, it implies that the output (income) y_s^k in state s can be

---

[2]A reallocation which leads to a preferred plan can be found as follows. Since (10) (or equivalently (11)) is not satisfied, $\nabla u^i(\bar{x}^i)$ is not collinear to $\nabla T^k(\bar{y}^k)$. Thus there exists $\eta \in \mathbb{R}^{S+1}$ satisfying $\nabla T^k(\bar{y}^k)\eta = 0$ such that $\nabla u^i(\bar{x}^i)\eta \neq 0$. If $\nabla u^i(\bar{x}^i)\eta > 0$, let $dx^i = dy^k = \eta$, if $\nabla u^i(\bar{x}^i)\eta < 0$, let $dx^i = dy^k = -\eta$.

marginally altered by adjusting the initial investment y_0^k without affecting the output y_σ^k in any other state $\sigma \neq s$ at date 1. Even in an income model, realistic opportunity sets available to an entrepreneur are unlikely to permit such flexible adjustments among alternative production plans. Fortunately a natural generalization of the first-order conditions (11) and (13) can readily be obtained, without invoking Assumption $\mathscr{T}'$, and using only the property that the technology set Y^k is convex, provided a few elementary concepts of *convex analysis* are introduced.

In (11), the gradient $\nabla T^k(\bar{y}^k)$ to the production surface at $\bar{y}^k$ is used to express the first-order conditions. Since the gradient $\nabla T^k(\bar{y}^k)$ is orthogonal to the tangent hyperplane to the surface $T(y^k) = 0$ at $\bar{y}^k$, (11) can be expressed geometrically as the condition that the vector $\bar{\pi}^i$ is orthogonal to the production set at $\bar{y}^k$. When Y^k is convex, this geometric condition, which is expressed in terms of the gradient $\nabla T^k(\bar{y}^k)$ under $\mathscr{T}'$, can be expressed (without Assumption $\mathscr{T}'$) by using the concept of a normal cone to a convex set.

30.2 Definition: Let $C \subset \mathbb{R}^n$ be a convex set. If $\bar{x} \in C$, then the *normal cone* to C at $\bar{x}$ is defined by $N_C(\bar{x}) = \{ \pi \in \mathbb{R}^n \mid \pi\bar{x} \geq \pi x, \ \forall x \in C \}$.

If $\bar{x}$ is a boundary point of the convex set C, then it follows[3] from the Separation Theorem A2.6 that there is a hyperplane $H_\pi = \{ x \in \mathbb{R}^n \mid \pi x = \pi\bar{x} \}$ with the property that C lies (entirely) in the *half-space* $H_\pi^- = \{ x \in \mathbb{R}^n \mid \pi x \leq \pi\bar{x} \}$: when this condition is satisfied, the hyperplane H_π is said to *support* C at $\bar{x}$. *The normal cone to C at $\bar{x}$ thus consists of all those vectors π which generate*

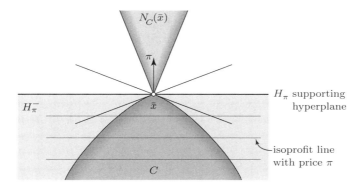

Figure 30.1   A supporting hyperplane H_π to C at $\bar{x}$: C is contained in the half-space H_π^-; this corresponds to profit maximization under π at $\bar{x}$. The normal cone $N_C(\bar{x})$ is the set of all price vectors π under which $\bar{x}$ is profit maximizing.

---

[3] Apply the standard separation Theorem A2.6(i) with $K = \{\bar{x}\}$ and $M = \mathrm{int}\, C$. Extend the inequality (7) in A2.6 to $C \subset \overline{\mathrm{int}\, C}$ by continuity of the inner product.

hyperplanes which support C at $\bar{x}$. When $\bar{x}$ is a boundary point, there is always at least one supporting hyperplane, so that the normal cone $N_C(\bar{x})$ contains at least one half-line. In economic terms, the normal cone to a set C at $\bar{x}$ consists of all those price systems π under which profit is maximized at $\bar{x}$. A boundary point of a convex set thus has the property of being profit maximizing for at least one price vector, a property frequently used in microeconomics. As the following proposition shows, the normal cone is precisely the concept required to express the first-order conditions when a utility function is maximized over a convex set.

30.3 Proposition (First-Order Conditions for Convex Maximum Problem): *Let $u : \mathbb{R}^n \longrightarrow \mathbb{R}$ be differentiable and quasi-concave, and let $\nabla u(x) \neq 0$, $\forall\, x \in C$ where $C \subset \mathbb{R}^n$ is a non-empty convex set. Then $\bar{x}$ is a solution of the problem*

$$\max\{u(x) \mid x \in C\} \tag{14}$$

if and only if $\bar{x} \in C$ and

$$\nabla u(\bar{x}) \in N_C(\bar{x}) \tag{15}$$

PROOF: The proof, which is based on the Separation Theorem for convex sets, is given in Appendix A6.2. □

A geometric interpretation of the proposition is shown in Figure 30.2: (15) requires that the gradient $\nabla u(\bar{x})$ lie in the normal cone to C at $\bar{x}$. The supporting hyperplane H induced by the gradient $\nabla u(\bar{x})$ at $\bar{x}$ separates C from the preferred set, since C lies in the half-space H^- and the preferred set lies in the half-space H^+: this property ensures that u attains a global maximum over C at $\bar{x}$.

Entrepreneur i in solving the maximum problem (4) chooses two variables, his portfolio and the production plan of his firm. This leads to a problem in which two variables enter additively in the utility function, for which the first-order conditions are given by the following corollary to Proposition 30.3.

30.4 Corollary: *Let $u : \mathbb{R}^n \longrightarrow \mathbb{R}$ be differentiable and quasi-concave, and let $Y \subset \mathbb{R}^n$, $Z \subset \mathbb{R}^n$ be non-empty convex sets. Then $(\bar{y}, \bar{z})$ is a solution of the problem*

$$\max\{u(y + z) \mid y \in Y, z \in Z\} \tag{16}$$

if and only if

$$\nabla u(\bar{y} + \bar{z}) \in N_Y(\bar{y}) \cap N_Z(\bar{z}) \tag{17}$$

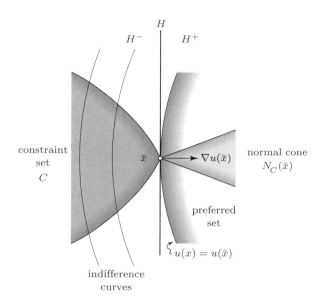

Figure 30.2   First-order conditions for $\max\{u(x) \mid x \in C\}$: the gradient $\nabla u(\bar{x})$ must lie in the normal cone to C at $\bar{x}$.

PROOF: Let $v : \mathbb{R}^n \times \mathbb{R}^n \longrightarrow \mathbb{R}$ be defined by $v(y, z) = u(y + z)$. Then the maximum problem (16) is equivalent to

$$\max\{v(y, z) \mid (y, z) \in Y \times Z\} \tag{18}$$

By Proposition 30.3, $(\bar{y}, \bar{z})$ is a solution of (18) if and only if

$$\left(\nabla_y v(\bar{y}, \bar{z}), \, \nabla_z v(\bar{y}, \bar{z})\right) \in N_{Y \times Z}(\bar{y}, \bar{z}) \tag{19}$$

where $\nabla_y v$ (resp. $\nabla_z v$) denotes the gradient of v with respect to y (resp. z). It is easy to check from Definition 30.2 of a normal cone that

$$N_{Y \times Z}(\bar{y}, \bar{z}) = N_Y(\bar{y}) \times N_Z(\bar{z})$$

and from the definition of the function v that

$$\nabla_y v(\bar{y}, \bar{z}) = \nabla_z v(\bar{y}, \bar{z}) = \nabla u(\bar{y} + \bar{z})$$

so that (19) reduces to (17). □

Consider the maximum problem (4) of entrepreneur i. As in the earlier analysis, suppose that the utility function u^i satisfies Assumption $\mathscr{U}$ so that the non-negativity condition $x^i \in \mathbb{R}_+^{S+1}$ can be omitted. To simplify the notation let $k = k(i)$ denote the ith entrepreneur's firm; then problem (4) can be written as

$$\max \left\{ u^i(x^i) \mid x^i - \omega^i = W\xi^i + y^k, \quad (\xi^i, y^k) \in \mathbb{R}^J \times Y^k \right\} \qquad (20)$$

Since the choice of a portfolio $\xi^i \in \mathbb{R}^J$ is equivalent to the choice of a vector of income transfers $\tau^i = W\xi^i$ lying in the market subspace $\langle W \rangle$, (20) can be written as

$$\max \left\{ u^i(\omega^i + \tau^i + y^k) \mid (\tau^i, y^k) \in \langle W \rangle \times Y^k \right\} \qquad (21)$$

By Corollary 30.4, $(\bar{\tau}^i, \bar{y}^k)$ is a solution of (21) if and only if

$$(\bar{\tau}^i, \bar{y}^k) \in \langle W \rangle \times Y^k, \quad \nabla u^i(\bar{x}^i) \in \langle W \rangle^\perp \cap N_{Y^k}(\bar{y}^k) \qquad (22)$$

where $\bar{x}^i = \omega^i + \bar{\tau}^i + \bar{y}^k$ is the optimal consumption stream of entrepreneur i. Using the normalized gradient $\bar{\pi}^i = \pi^i(\bar{x}^i)$, the first-order conditions (22) can be decomposed into the pair of conditions

$$\bar{\tau}^i \in \langle W \rangle, \quad \bar{\pi}^i \in \langle W \rangle^\perp \qquad (23)$$

$$\bar{y}^k \in Y^k, \quad \bar{\pi}^i \in N_{Y^k}(\bar{y}^k) \qquad (24)$$

(23) is just the first-order condition for the choice of an optimal trade vector $\bar{\tau}^i$ lying in the market subspace $\langle W \rangle$. (24) is the first-order condition for the choice of an optimal production vector $\bar{y}^k$ lying in the production set Y^k. The condition $\bar{\pi}^i \in \langle W \rangle^\perp$ requires that the entrepreneur's (normalized) gradient be orthogonal to the market subspace. This is simply a geometric way of saying that the price of each security is equal to the present value to entrepreneur i of its future dividend stream. The condition $\bar{\pi}^i \in N_{Y^k}(\bar{y}^k)$ requires that his (normalized) gradient lie in the normal cone to his production set at $\bar{y}^k$. From the definition of the normal cone, this condition is equivalent to

$$\bar{y}^k \in \arg \max \left\{ \bar{\pi}^i y^k \mid y^k \in Y^k \right\} \qquad (25)$$

If the entrepreneur uses his present-value vector $\bar{\pi}^i$ to evaluate the present value of any income stream y^k lying in his opportunity set Y^k, then the production plan $\bar{y}^k$ maximizes the present value of his profit. *Thus an entrepreneur is at his most preferred trade and production vector when the present value of his profit is maximized under his present-value vector and his indifference surface is tangent to the market subspace.* When the production set Y^k can be represented by a differentiable transformation function T^k, the normal cone $N_{Y^k}(\bar{y}^k)$ to Y^k at $\bar{y}^k$ reduces to the half-line generated by the gradient $\nabla T^k(\bar{y}^k)$, so that the condition $\bar{\pi}^i \in N_{Y^k}(\bar{y}^k)$ reduces to condition (11) or (13).

A geometric interpretation of (23) and (24) is shown in Figure 30.3 for the

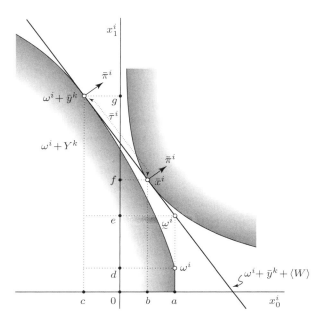

Figure 30.3   Maximizing behavior of an entrepreneur in the case $S = J = 1$ (complete markets). An entrepreneur first seeks the production plan $\bar{y}^k$ which maximizes profit $\bar{\pi}^i y^k$ and then looks for the most preferred consumption stream $\bar{x}^i$ in the opportunity set $\omega^i + \bar{y}^k + \langle W \rangle$. (Since this opportunity set is unaffected by the firm's choice of financial policy, which merely alters the agent's starting point $\underline{\omega}^i$ on the line $\omega^i + \bar{y}^k + \langle W \rangle$, this figure also provides a geometric interpretation of Theorem 30.7 on the irrelevance of a firm's financial policy.)

simplest case $S = J = 1$. Agent i starts with the initial endowment ω^i. As a producer he maximizes the present value of profit over his production set using the present-value vector $\bar{\pi}^i = (1, \bar{\pi}^i_1)$. Since in this case the market is complete this vector is the unique normalized vector orthogonal to the market subspace $\langle W \rangle$. This production activity leads him to the income vector $\omega^i + \bar{y}^k$: this is his initial vector of income as a consumer. He then chooses a net trade vector $\bar{\tau}^i$ in the market subspace $\langle W \rangle$ which takes him to his most preferred consumption vector $\bar{x}^i$: he borrows cb at date 0 and pays back gf at date 1.

We can now transform the concept of an entrepreneurial equilibrium (Definition 30.1) into an equivalent profit-maximizing concept of equilibrium, where the role of each agent as an entrepreneur is separated from his activity as a consumer. To separate out the agent's activity as a consumer, we take the production activity $y^{k(i)}$ as given and define the budget set

$$\mathbb{B}(q, \omega^i, R, y^{k(i)}) = \left\{ x^i \in \mathbb{R}^{S+1}_+ \ \middle| \ x^i - \omega^i - y^{k(i)} = W\xi^i, \quad \xi^i \in \mathbb{R}^J \right\}$$

30.5 Proposition (Profit-Maximizing Entrepreneurial Equilibrium): *Consider an entrepreneurial economy satisfying Assumptions $(\mathscr{U}, \mathscr{T})$. $\left((\bar{x}, \bar{\xi}, \bar{y}), \bar{q}\right)$ is a reduced-form entrepreneurial equilibrium (Definition 30.1) if and only if*

(i) $(\bar{x}^i; \bar{\xi}^i) = \arg\max\left\{u^i(x^i) \mid (x^i; \xi^i) \in \mathbb{B}(\bar{q}, \omega^i, R, \bar{y}^{k(i)})\right\}$, $i = 1, \ldots, I$

(ii) $\bar{y}^{k(i)} \in \arg\max\left\{\pi^i(\bar{x}^i)y^k \mid y^k \in Y^{k(i)}\right\}$, $i = 1, \ldots, I$

(iii) $\sum_{i=1}^{I} \bar{\xi}^i = 0$

A pair $\left((\bar{x}, \bar{\xi}, \bar{y}), \bar{q}\right)$ satisfying (i)–(iii) is called a profit-maximizing entrepreneurial equilibrium.

PROOF: In view of Assumption $\mathscr{U}$, $(\bar{x}^i, \bar{\xi}^i)$ satisfies (i) if and only if (23) holds. By convexity of $Y^{k(i)}$, (ii) is satisfied if and only if (24) holds. Since $(\bar{x}^i, \bar{\xi}^i, \bar{y}^{k(i)})$ satisfies (i) in Definition 30.1 (the maximum problem (4)) if and only if (23) and (24) hold, $\left((\bar{x}, \bar{\xi}, \bar{y}), \bar{q}\right)$ is an entrepreneurial equilibrium if and only if it is a profit-maximizing entrepreneurial equilibrium. □

Proposition 30.5 defines a concept of equilibrium for an economy with entrepreneurial firms, in which there is a separation between the activity of each agent as a consumer and his activity as an entrepreneur: for (i) implies that agent i, in choosing his consumption-portfolio plan (x^i, ξ^i), takes the dividend income $\bar{y}^{k(i)}$ from his firm as given, while (ii) implies that, in selecting the production plan $y^{k(i)}$ for his firm, entrepreneur i takes his consumption-portfolio plan $(\bar{x}^i, \bar{\xi}^i)$—and hence the present-value vector $\bar{\pi}^i = \pi^i(\bar{x}^i)$—as given.

Evaluation of Risks by Entrepreneurs

An interesting consequence of this alternative characterization of an entrepreneurial equilibrium is that it leads to a better understanding of how entrepreneurs evaluate alternative risky projects at an equilibrium. By converting the choice of a production plan into the solution of a profit-maximizing problem using the entrepreneur's present-value vector at the equilibrium, the risk-return considerations involved in the choice of the optimal plan $\bar{y}^k$ can be made explicit. A mean-covariance form for the profit-maximizing criterion (ii) can be obtained by invoking the assumption of rational expectations, namely that agents agree on the probabilities $\rho = (\rho_1, \ldots, \rho_S)$ of occurrence of the states at date 1. The present value of an income stream $y^k = (y_0^k, y_1^k, \ldots, y_S^k)$ for entrepreneur i can then be written as

$$\bar{\pi}^i y^k = y_0^k + \sum_{s=1}^{S} \rho_s \bar{\pi}_s^{\rho,i} y_s^k = y_0^k + E\left(\bar{\pi}_1^{\rho,i} y_1^k\right)$$
$$= y_0^k + E\left(\bar{\pi}_1^{\rho,i}\right) E\left(y_1^k\right) + \mathrm{cov}\left(\bar{\pi}_1^{\rho,i}, y_1^k\right) \tag{26}$$

where $\bar{\pi}_{\mathbf{1}}^{\rho,i} = \left(\bar{\pi}_1^i/\rho_1, \ldots, \bar{\pi}_S^i/\rho_S\right)$ is agent i's date 1 present-value vector with the probabilities factored out. If, in addition, one of the securities is the riskless bond (say $R^1 = (1, \ldots, 1)^T = \mathbb{1}$) whose price $\bar{q}_1$ defines the equilibrium interest rate $\bar{r}$ $(\bar{q}_1 = 1/(1 + \bar{r}))$ then $E(\bar{\pi}_{\mathbf{1}}^{\rho,i}) = 1/(1 + \bar{r})$ so that (26) reduces to

$$\bar{\pi}^i y^k = y_0^k + \frac{E(y_1^k)}{1 + \bar{r}} + \mathrm{cov}\left(\bar{\pi}_{\mathbf{1}}^{\rho,i}, y_1^k\right) \tag{27}$$

The first two terms correspond to the *expected present value* of the project y^k. This can be thought of as an entrepreneur's first approximation to the true present value of the project, and, when there is no uncertainty about the outcome of the project, it gives the precise present value. When the outcome of a project is uncertain $(\mathrm{var}(y_1^k) \neq 0)$, the additional element that enters into the entrepreneur's calculation is the risk of the project: this is measured by the covariance term $\mathrm{cov}(\bar{\pi}_{\mathbf{1}}^{\rho,i}, y_1^k)$. Since this term is typically negative, the present value of a project is (normally) less than its expected present value, and the term $\mathrm{cov}(\bar{\pi}_{\mathbf{1}}^{\rho,i}, y_1^k)$ may be called the *covariance risk* of the project for entrepreneur i. Unlike the expected present value, which is a market-based valuation, the covariance risk may depend on the personal perceptions and attitude toward risk of the entrepreneur. Indeed, if markets are incomplete, then the way two different entrepreneurs evaluate the risk of the same project may differ substantially, so that the project chosen for firm $k = k(i)$ may be strongly influenced by the personal characteristics (u^i, ω^i) of its owner.

The extent of the possible differences in entrepreneurs' evaluations of the risks of projects can be evaluated by decomposing the covariance risk into two components: the first is the component that can be evaluated by the market, the second is the residual idiosyncratic component which is evaluated by the entrepreneur. Such a decomposition can be obtained as follows.

In Section 14 it was shown that under the probability induced inner product $[\![x, y]\!]_\rho = \sum_{s=1}^S \rho_s x_s y_s$, the marketed subspace[4] $\langle V \rangle$ leads to a ρ-orthogonal decomposition of the space of date 1 random income streams

$$\mathbb{R}^S = \langle V \rangle \oplus \langle V \rangle^{\perp\!\!\!\perp}$$

Entrepreneur i's ρ-present-value vector $\bar{\pi}_1^{\rho,i}$ can thus be decomposed into two components

$$\bar{\pi}_{\mathbf{1}}^{\rho,i} = \bar{\pi}_V^{\rho,i} + \check{\pi}_{\mathbf{1}}^{\rho,i}, \quad \bar{\pi}_V^{\rho,i} \in \langle V \rangle, \quad \check{\pi}_{\mathbf{1}}^{\rho,i} \in \langle V \rangle^{\perp\!\!\!\perp} \tag{28}$$

In Chapter 3 it was shown that trading on the security markets leads to the

---

[4]Although in this section the only marketed securities are bonds (i.e. $\langle V \rangle = \langle R \rangle$), it is convenient to use the notation $\langle V \rangle$ for the marketed subspace since the arguments that follow are applicable for any security structure (for example when equity contracts are also present, as in Section 32).

equalization of the projections $\bar{\pi}_V^{\rho,i}$ of agents (Theorem 15.4) and the common projection was called the ideal security $\bar{\gamma}$ in $\langle V \rangle$. Thus

$$\bar{\pi}_1^{\rho,i} = \bar{\gamma} + \check{\pi}_1^{\rho,i} \tag{29}$$

Since the riskless bond $\mathbb{1} = (1, \ldots, 1)$ is one of the marketed securities, the ideal security can be decomposed as

$$\bar{\gamma} = E(\bar{\gamma})\mathbb{1} + \widetilde{\gamma}, \quad E(\widetilde{\gamma}) = 0 \tag{30}$$

where $E(\bar{\gamma}) = 1/(1 + \bar{r})$ is the market's *intertemporal discount factor* expressed in terms of the equilibrium rate of interest $\bar{r}$, and $\widetilde{\gamma}$ is the market's *equilibrium risk pricing vector* which evaluates marketed risks.

The date 1 component y_1^k of a project $y^k = (y_0^k, y_1^k)$ can also be decomposed into two components (see Figure 30.4)

$$y_1^k = y_V^k + \check{y}_1^k, \quad y_V^k \in \langle V \rangle, \quad \check{y}_1^k \in \langle V \rangle^\perp \tag{31}$$

Since (26) can be expressed as

$$\bar{\pi}^i y^k = y_0^k + \left[\!\left[\bar{\pi}_1^{\rho,i}, y_1^k \right]\!\right]_\rho$$

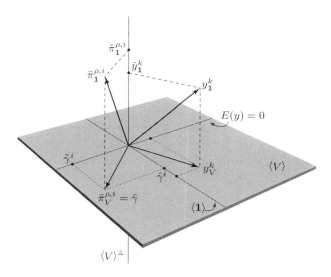

Figure 30.4   The decomposition of entrepreneur i's present-value vector $\bar{\pi}_1^{\rho,i}$ and the date 1 component y_1^k of a project, induced by projecting them onto the market subspace $\langle V \rangle$ and its orthogonal component $\langle V \rangle^\perp$, provides a decomposition of the risk of the project (to agent i) into the market risk cov $\left(\widetilde{\gamma}, y_V^k \right)$ and the entrepreneurial risk cov $\left(\bar{\pi}_1^{\rho,i}, \check{y}_1^k \right)$.

the decompositions (28)–(31) imply that the present value of the project y^k can be written as

$$\bar{\pi}^i y^k = y_0^k + \left[\!\left[\bar{\gamma}, y_V^k \right]\!\right]_\rho + \left[\!\left[\check{\pi}_{\mathbf{1}}^{\rho,i}, \check{y}_{\mathbf{1}}^k \right]\!\right]_\rho$$

so that

$$\bar{\pi}^i y^k = y_0^k + \frac{E(y_{\mathbf{1}}^k)}{1+\bar{r}} + \operatorname{cov}(\widetilde{\gamma}, y_V^k) + \operatorname{cov}(\check{\pi}_{\mathbf{1}}^{\rho,i}, \check{y}_{\mathbf{1}}^k) \qquad (32)$$

The last two terms express the covariance risk of the project y^k as the sum of two terms

$$\operatorname{cov}(\bar{\pi}_{\mathbf{1}}^{\rho,i}, y_{\mathbf{1}}^k) = \operatorname{cov}(\widetilde{\gamma}, y_V^k) + \operatorname{cov}(\check{\pi}_{\mathbf{1}}^{\rho,i}, \check{y}_{\mathbf{1}}^k)$$

The first may be called the *market risk* of the project and the second its *entrepreneurial risk*.

If the projects y^k available to entrepreneur i all lie in the marketed subspace ($Y^k \subset \langle V \rangle$)—a condition which is always satisfied if markets are complete— then the market rate of interest ($\bar{r}$) and the market's equilibrium risk-pricing vector ($\widetilde{\gamma}$) provide an objective market-based assessment for the present value of any project in Y^k. The covariance risk of a project is given by its market risk, and the choice of an optimal plan for firm k does not depend on the characteristics of its owner—the choice of production plan is thus completely determined by the market. If the markets are incomplete and if some of the firms' projects lie outside the marketed subspace then the entrepreneurial risk $\operatorname{cov}(\check{\pi}_{\mathbf{1}}^{\rho,i}, \check{y}_{\mathbf{1}}^k)$ of some projects may be non-zero. In this case, the choice of production plan may be influenced by personal characteristics of the owner. This is the case which seems most likely in an economy with entrepreneurial firms. Indeed, suppose that the financial markets are very incomplete, in the sense that there are no markets for risk sharing, the only security being the riskless bond ($V = \mathbb{1}$). In this case $\bar{\gamma} = 1/(1+\bar{r})\mathbb{1}$ and $\widetilde{\gamma} = 0$ so that the covariance risk consists solely of entrepreneurial risk. To further analyze the evaluation of risks in such an economy, suppose that agents' preferences can be represented by VNM additively separable utility functions

$$u^i(x^i) = v_0^i(x_0^i) + \sum_{s=1}^{S} \rho_s v_1^i(x_s^i), \quad i = 1, \dots I$$

Then

$$\bar{\pi}^{\rho,i} = \frac{v_1^{i\prime}(\bar{x}_{\mathbf{1}}^i)}{v_0^{i\prime}(\bar{x}_0^i)} \quad \text{and} \quad \frac{1}{1+\bar{r}} = \frac{E\left(v_1^{i\prime}(\bar{x}_{\mathbf{1}}^i)\right)}{v_0^{i\prime}(\bar{x}_0^i)}$$

The ρ-projection of $\bar{\pi}_1^{\rho,i}$ onto $\langle \mathbb{1} \rangle$ is

$$\bar{\pi}_V^{\rho,i} = \bar{\gamma} = \frac{E\left(v_1^{i\prime}(\bar{x}_1^i)\right)}{v_0^{i\prime}(\bar{x}_0^i)} \mathbb{1}$$

and the idiosyncratic component $\check{\pi}_1^{\rho,i}$ can be written as

$$\check{\pi}_1^{\rho,i} = \frac{1}{1+\bar{r}} \frac{v_1^{i\prime}(\bar{x}_1^i) - E\left(v_1^{i\prime}(\bar{x}_1^i)\right)\mathbb{1}}{E\left(v_1^{i\prime}(\bar{x}_1^i)\right)}$$

so that the present value of project y^k to entrepreneur i is given by

$$\bar{\pi}^i y^k = y_0^k + \frac{1}{1+\bar{r}}\left(E(y_1^k) + \text{cov}\left(\frac{v_1^{i\prime}(\bar{x}_1^i)}{E(v_1^{i\prime}(\bar{x}_1^i))}, y_1^k \right) \right)$$

The relative importance of the mean and covariance terms in the evaluation of y^k depends on the variability of the agent's marginal utility of income $v_1^{i\prime}(\bar{x}_1^i)$. This in turn depends on the personal circumstances of the entrepreneur at the equilibrium: if he is wealthy or if his preferences exhibit high tolerance to risk, then the ratio $v_1^{i\prime}(\bar{x}_s^i)/E(v_1^{i\prime}(\bar{x}_1^i))$ is close to one for all states, and the project is evaluated principally by its expected present value. The project $\bar{y}^k$ which is optimal for the mean-covariance trade-off of entrepreneur i would not be optimal for a less risk-tolerant or less wealthy entrepreneur.

Separation of Financial Policies

In a profit-maximizing entrepreneurial equilibrium defined by Proposition 30.5, the separation between the activities of an agent as an entrepreneur and his activities as a consumer is not complete. Agent $i(k)$ in his capacity as an entrepreneur chooses the production plan $\bar{y}^k$ which maximizes profit, *but does not worry about financing the project* $\bar{y}^k$: his portfolio activity $\bar{\xi}^i$ on the financial markets simultaneously finances the production plan $\bar{y}^{k(i)}$ of his firm and his personal consumption plan $\bar{x}^i$. The reader will no doubt argue that all this is most unprofessional since the financing of his business is mixed with the financing of his private affairs.

Let us distinguish therefore between the financial accounts of firms and the financial accounts of consumers. The entrepreneur of firm k chooses a production plan $y^k \in Y^k$, a portfolio policy $b^k \in \mathbb{R}^J$, and a dividend policy $D^k = (D_0^k, D_1^k, \ldots, D_S^k)$, where D^k is the stream of payments made by the firm to the entrepreneur. Given the production plan y^k, a portfolio-dividend policy (b^k, D^k) is said to balance the *financial accounts of the firm* if

$$D^k = y^k + W b^k \Longleftrightarrow \begin{cases} D_0^k = y_0^k - q b^k \\ D_s^k = y_s^k + R_s b^k, \quad s = 1, \ldots, S \end{cases}$$

When this equation is satisfied we also say that the firm's portfolio-dividend policy *finances* its production plan. Since, for a given production plan, the dividend payments are determined as soon as the portfolio policy has been chosen, it will be convenient in the analysis that follows to refer more briefly to b^k as the *financial policy* of the firm.

The entrepreneur clearly has considerable flexibility in his choice of financial policy and in particular with the manner in which the initial investment y_0^k is financed. If $D_0^k = y_0^k - qb^k$ is non-negative, then he does not contribute any of his initial wealth but instead finances the inputs by borrowing on the bond market. If $D_0^k = y_0^k - qb^k$ is negative, then he contributes part of his initial wealth to financing the firm. $D_s^k = y_s^k + R_s b^k$ is the residual income in state s at date 1 after all debts have been paid and when positive, constitutes the dividend received by the entrepreneur. If $D_s^k < 0$ then the entrepreneur, being responsible for the debts of his firm, must draw on his personal wealth to pay the portion of the debts not covered by his firm's earnings y_s^k.

As a consumer, agent i receives the dividend stream D^k generated by his firm: his initial income is thus $\varpi^i = \omega^i + D^k$. The agent then chooses a consumption bundle $x^i \in R_+^{S+1}$ and a portfolio $z^i \in \mathbb{R}^J$ which balances his *financial accounts as a consumer*

$$x^i = \omega^i + D^k + W z^i \iff \begin{cases} x_0^i = \omega_0^i + D_0^k - qz^i \\ x_s^i - \omega_s^i + D_s^k + R_s z^i, \quad s = 1, \dots, S \end{cases}$$

The budget set of agent i as a consumer can thus be written as

$$\mathbb{B}(q, \omega^i, R, D^{k(i)}) = \left\{ x^i \in \mathbb{R}_+^{S+1} \ \middle| \ x^i - \omega^i - D^{k(i)} = W z^i, \quad z^i \in \mathbb{R}^J \right\}$$

The dividend stream $D^{k(i)}$ is the income stream received by agent i from his firm. In his capacity as entrepreneur, it is natural that he should choose the production and financing of the firm so that the resulting dividend stream has a maximum present value under his present-value vector π^i. We are thus led to the final concept of an entrepreneurial equilibrium in which, by contrast with the earlier Definition 30.1, the private activities of agents as consumers are separated from their professional activities as entrepreneurs, the private and professional activities of agents being written out in extensive form.

30.6 Definition: An (extensive-form) *entrepreneurial equilibrium* is a pair consisting of actions and prices

$$\left((\bar{x}, \bar{z}), (\bar{y}, \bar{b}), \bar{q} \right) \in \mathbb{R}_+^{(S+1)} \times \mathbb{R}^{JI} \times \mathbb{R}^{(S+1)I} \times \mathbb{R}^{JI} \times \mathbb{R}^J$$

such that

(i) $(\bar{x}^i; \bar{z}^i) \in \arg\max \left\{ u^i(x^i) \mid (x^i; z^i) \in \mathbb{B}(\bar{q}, \omega^i, R, \overline{D}^{k(i)}) \right\}$

     with $\overline{D}^{k(i)} = \bar{y}^{k(i)} + W\bar{b}^{k(i)}$, $i = 1, \ldots, I$

(ii) $\left(\bar{y}^{k(i)}; \bar{b}^{k(i)} \right) \in \arg\max \left\{ \pi^i(\bar{x}^i)D^k \;\middle|\; \begin{array}{l} D^k = y^k + Wb^k \\ (y^k, b^k) \in Y^{k(i)} \times \mathbb{R}^J \end{array} \right\}$, $i = 1, \ldots, I$

(iii) $\sum_{i=1}^{I}(\bar{z}^i + \bar{b}^{k(i)}) = 0$

Interdeterminacy of Financial Policies

Does the financial policy of a firm matter? There are two reasons why a firm's financial policy might be of concern to the entrepreneur: it might affect

(1) the present value of the dividend stream generated by the firm
(2) his budget set.

The following proposition shows that at an equilibrium, neither of these effects is present: the financial policies of firms are indeterminate and have no effect on the real equilibrium allocation.

30.7 Proposition (Invariance of Entrepreneurial Equilibrium w.r.t. Financial Policies): *Consider an economy satisfying Assumptions $(\mathscr{U}, \mathscr{T})$ which has entrepreneurial firms and in which there is no default for consumers and no bankruptcy for firms.*

(i) *If $\big((\bar{x}, \bar{z}), (\bar{y}, \bar{b}), \bar{q}\big)$ is an extensive-form entrepreneurial equilibrium, then $\big((\bar{x}, \bar{\xi}, \bar{y}), \bar{q}\big)$ is a reduced-form entrepreneurial equilibrium where $\bar{\xi}^i = \bar{z}^i + \bar{b}^{k(i)}$, $i = 1, \ldots, I$.*
(ii) *If $\big((\bar{x}, \bar{\xi}, \bar{y}), \bar{q}\big)$ is a reduced-form entrepreneurial equilibrium, then $((\bar{x}, z), (\bar{y}, b), \bar{q})$ is an extensive-form equilibrium for all $(z, b) \in \mathbb{R}^{J(I+K)}$ satisfying $z^i + b^{k(i)} = \bar{\xi}^i$, $i = 1, \ldots, I$.*

PROOF: (i) Let us first show that $(\bar{x}, \bar{\xi}, \bar{y})$ satisfies the first-order conditions (23) and (24) so that condition (i) in Definition 30.1 is satisfied. The first-order conditions for the consumer's problem in 30.6(i)

$$\bar{x}^i = \omega^i + \overline{D}^{k(i)} + W\bar{z}^i, \quad \pi^i(\bar{x}^i)W = 0 \tag{33}$$

can be written as

$$\bar{x}^i = \omega^i + \bar{y}^{k(i)} + W\bar{\xi}^i, \quad \pi^i(\bar{x}^i)W = 0$$

since $\bar{\xi}^i = \bar{z}^i + \bar{b}^{k(i)}$, so that (23) holds. The condition $\pi^i(\bar{x}^i)W = 0$ implies that for all $(y^k, b^k) \in Y^{k(i)} \times \mathbb{R}^J$, the present value to entrepreneur i of the dividend stream of firm $k(i)$ reduces to

$$\pi^i(\bar{x}^i)D^k = \pi^i(\bar{x}^i)y^k + \pi^i(\bar{x}^i)Wb^k = \pi^i(\bar{x}^i)y^k$$

Thus the entrepreneur's problem in 30.6(ii) is equivalent to

$$\bar{y}^{k(i)} \in \arg\max \left\{ \pi^i(\bar{x}^i)y^k \;\middle|\; y^k \in Y^{k(i)} \right\}$$

for which the first-order conditions are given by (24). Finally, since the market clearing condition $\sum_{i=1}^{I} \bar{\xi}^i = \sum_{i=1}^{I}(\bar{z}^i + \bar{b}^{k(i)}) = 0$ holds, the result follows.

(ii) If $(\bar{x}^i, \bar{\xi}^i, \bar{y}^{k(i)})$ is the solution of 30.1(i), then the first-order conditions (23) and (24) are satisfied. This implies that, for any $b^{k(i)} \in \mathbb{R}^J$

$$(\bar{y}^{k(i)}; b^{k(i)}) \in \arg\max \left\{ \pi^i(\bar{x}^i)\left(y^k + Wb^k\right) \;\middle|\; (y^k; b^k) \in Y^{k(i)} \times \mathbb{R}^J \right\}$$

since by (23), $\pi^i(\bar{x}^i)W = 0$. Pick any $b^{k(i)} \in \mathbb{R}^J$, and define

$$z^i = \bar{\xi}^i - b^{k(i)}, \quad \overline{D}^{k(i)} = \bar{y}^{k(i)} + Wb^{k(i)}$$

then (33) is satisfied by $(\bar{x}^i, z^i)$. Thus $(\bar{x}^i, z^i)$ is a solution of 30.6(i). Since $(\bar{y}^{k(i)}; b^{k(i)})$ is a solution of 30.6(ii) and $0 = \sum_{i=1}^{I} \bar{\xi}^i = \sum_{i=1}^{I} z^i + b^{k(i)}$, the result follows. □

The equivalence between the reduced-form equilibrium and extensive-form entrepreneurial equilibrium in which the financial policies of firms are explicitly modelled is the simplest version of the well-known Modigliani-Miller Theorem which asserts that the precise nature of a firm's financial policy does not matter provided that it finances the firm's productive activity. In Sections 31 and 32 we will show that a similar result holds in more general settings.

There are two properties that make the theorem work. The first is that the financial market opportunities available to consumers are the same as those available to firms,[5] and are described by the market subspace $\langle W \rangle$. The second is that the present value of an income stream in the market subspace is always zero for any state price vector lying in the orthogonal subspace $\langle W \rangle^{\perp}$. The first property enables an agent as a consumer to repackage the financial component of the dividend stream offered to him by his firm: in short, *consumers can*

---

[5]This is a natural assumption to make in a model in which the implicit presence of infinite penalties rules out default for individuals and bankruptcy for firms. If the model is extended to permit default and bankruptcy and if agents use collateral to back their debts, then this assumption of equal access to the financial markets by individuals and firms ceases to be appropriate.

always undo whatever firms do on the financial markets. The second property implies that *the present value of the dividends distributed by the firm to its owner depends only on its production plan, and not on its choice of financial policy.*

A geometric interpretation of Proposition 30.7 for the simplest case $S = J = 1$ can be obtained by using Figure 30.3. Different financial policies of the firm, when combined with the production plan $\bar{y}^k$, lead to different initial points for the consumer on the line $\omega^i + \bar{y}^k + \langle W \rangle$. The consumer in each case undertakes the appropriate financial policy which leads him to the consumption plan $\bar{x}^i$. For example, if the firm is self-financing, so that it borrows the entire cost of its inputs $(\bar{y}_0^k)$, then agent i as a consumer has an initial income stream ω^i: he contributes nothing to the financing of the firm at date 0, and the firm borrows the entire cost ac of the initial investment from the market. At date 1 the firm pays back the principal and interest eg on its debt and pays the dividend de to its owner. Agent i who has lent ab to the market at date 0 is reimbursed ef which, when added to the dividend de and his initial resources od, gives the date 1 consumption of.

31.   PARTNERSHIPS

Historically the partnership emerged when the initial capital required to undertake profitable ventures (i.e. to set up efficient production plants) became too large to be provided by individual entrepreneurs. In a partnership, a group of agents (the partners) come together to undertake a venture whose outcome is uncertain: each partner contributes a share of the initial investment and obtains the same share of the subsequent profits. The challenging part in the description of a partnership equilibrium is to explain why agents are better off undertaking business ventures jointly as partners rather than individually as entrepreneur-owners of firms: in short we need to explain why agents would seek to move out of the first stage of capitalist organization described in the previous section.

The realistic element which would need to be introduced to give a satisfactory explanation for the formation of partnerships is an explicit modelling of the relation between size and efficiency—a larger initial investment leads to a more efficient plant—while preserving the essential element that the return on the venture is risky: for if a project were known to have a sure return, then no matter how large the initial investment required (provided it is feasible for the economy as a whole), any individual could borrow to finance the project. A realistic model of partnerships would thus require the assumption of increasing returns to scale in production. But this creates difficulties for a competitive analysis.

On the other hand the assumption of decreasing returns is incompatible with
the model of partnerships that we present in this section. The partners create
a firm by investing in a project: since the firm does not exist before the partnership is formed, there are no rents to the previously invested factors, which
is the natural interpretation of decreasing returns to scale. This can also be
expressed by saying that there are no initial owners of the available production
opportunities and hence no markets for buying and selling partnership shares.
The best compromise that we can make between realism and tractability is to
assume that each production set exhibits constant returns to scale.

Assumption $\mathscr{T}^*$ (Constant Returns to Scale):   The technology sets $Y^k(k =
1,\ldots,K)$ satisfy Assumption $\mathscr{T}$ and exhibit constant returns to scale:

$$y^k \in Y^k \Longrightarrow \lambda y^k \in Y^k, \quad \forall \lambda \in \mathbb{R}_+$$

The production set Y^k can be interpreted as the envelope of a family of
technology sets with progressively larger fixed costs (as shown in Figure 31.1 for
the case without uncertainty). The choice of a production plan in the original
constant-returns technology set Y^k can then be interpreted as the choice of
an initial fixed cost a and an associated plan in the tangential production set
$\widetilde{Y}^k(a)$ induced by this fixed cost.

To describe a partnership equilibrium, consider an economy with I agents
whose preferences and initial endowments are given by $(u^i,\omega^i, i = 1,\ldots,I)$.
As in the previous section each agent in his role as a consumer can trade
on J bond markets with prices $q = (q_1,\ldots,q_J)$ and date 1 payoff matrix R.
There are K business ventures available to the community, summarized by K
technology sets Y^k, $k = 1,\ldots,K$ which satisfy Assumption $\mathscr{T}^*$. Every agent
is free to become a partner in any of these business ventures. Agent i becomes

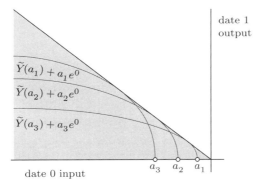

Figure 31.1 Y^k as an envelope of a family of production sets $ae^0 + \widetilde{Y}^k(a)$ where $a < 0$
and $e^0 = (1,0,\ldots,0)$.

a partner in the kth venture by contributing the share $\theta^i_k > 0$ of the initial capital cost $(-y^k_0 > 0)$: this gives him the right to the share θ^i_k of its random income stream $y^k_1 = (y^k_1, \ldots, y^k_S)$ at date 1. Thus there are two sets of decisions that the agents make in addition to their financial decisions $(z^1, \ldots, z^I)$ on the bond markets:

(a) each agent decides on his partnership share in each of the business ventures $(\theta^i = (\theta^i_1, \ldots, \theta^i_K), \ i = 1, \ldots, I)$

(b) the partners of each business venture must decide how the venture is to be operated $(y^k = (y^k_0, y^k_1, \ldots, y^k_S), \ k = 1, \ldots, K)$

At an equilibrium these two sets of decisions must be compatible. The partnership shares θ^i of agent i must be optimal, given the production plan y^k adopted by each venture: if not, agent i would have an incentive to alter his partnership shares. Similarly the production plan chosen by the partners of each venture must be optimal in the sense that there is no other plan which they would all prefer.

If the financial markets are complete, then there are uniquely defined prices for income in each state, and the partners of the kth venture will agree on any production plan which maximizes the present value of profit under these state prices: any such plan maximizes the utility of each partner regardless of his choice of partnership share in the kth venture. Thus with complete markets, the choice of a production plan is independent of the partnership shares chosen by the agents. Given the choice of production plans $y = (y^k, k = 1, \ldots, K)$ for each of the K ventures, each agent decides on his partnership shares $\theta^i = (\theta^i_1, \ldots, \theta^i_K)$ and bond portfolio $z^i = (z^i_1, \ldots, z^i_J)$ as the solution of a combined portfolio problem in which the matrix of payoffs is given by

$$\begin{bmatrix} -q & y_0 \\ R & y_1 \end{bmatrix}$$

When the financial markets are incomplete, the mutual dependence between the decisions in (a) and (b) may create difficulties. By arguments similar to those used in the previous section, if agent i is a partner in the kth venture, then a production plan $\bar{y}^k$ is optimal from his perspective if

$$\bar{y}^k \in \arg \max \left\{ \pi^i(\bar{x}^i) y^k \mid y^k \in Y^k \right\} \tag{1}$$

If there are several partners and if the $\bar{\pi}^i$ vectors of the partners are distinct, then there may not be any production plan which simultaneously satisfies this profit maximizing condition for each of the partners. This will typically be the case if Y^k contains projects which are not in the market subspace. Such risky projects do not have an objective market-based valuation and may be given a different valuation by different partners. Thus a concept of equilibrium which is to be applicable in the case of incomplete markets cannot require that the production plans of each venture always be unanimously agreed upon by all the partners.

Some compromise criterion is required which appropriately reflects the different preferences of the partners. The weakest criterion which respects the idea that partners (as owners) should have some say in the choice of a production plan is the *Pareto criterion* applied to the partners: *a production plan $\bar{y}^k \in Y^k$ should not be chosen if there is a production plan $y^k \in Y^k$ which is preferred by every partner.* As a first step it is useful to study the concept of equilibrium based on this minimal requirement for respecting the preferences of partners. To this end, define the budget set of agent i, for given production plans y for the ventures

$$\mathbb{B}(q, \omega^i, R, y) = \left\{ x^i \in \mathbb{R}_+^{S+1} \mid x^i - \omega^i = W z^i + y\theta^i, \, (z^i, \theta^i) \in \mathbb{R}^J \times \mathbb{R}_+^K \right\}$$

where

$$W = \begin{bmatrix} -q \\ R \end{bmatrix} \quad \text{and} \quad y = [y^1 \ldots y^K]$$

is the $(S+1) \times J$ matrix of payoffs on the J bonds and the $(S+1) \times K$ matrix of payoffs on the K ventures respectively.

31.1 Definition: A *Pareto partnership equilibrium* is a pair consisting of actions and prices

$$\left((\bar{x}, \bar{z}, \bar{\theta}, \bar{y}), \bar{q} \right) \in \mathbb{R}_+^{(S+1)I} \times \mathbb{R}^{JI} \times \mathbb{R}_+^{KI} \times \mathbb{R}^{(S+1)K} \times \mathbb{R}^J$$

such that

(i) $\left(\bar{x}^i; \bar{z}^i, \bar{\theta}^i \right) \in \arg \max \left\{ u^i(x^i) \mid (x^i; z^i, \theta^i) \in \mathbb{B}(\bar{q}, \omega^i, R, \bar{y}) \right\}, i = 1, \ldots, I$

(ii) there does not exist $y^k \in Y^k$ such that $u^i \left(\bar{x}^i + (y^k - \bar{y}^k)\bar{\theta}^i_k \right) \geq u^i(\bar{x}^i)$ with strict inequality for at least one i, for $k = 1, \ldots, K$

(iii) $\sum_{i=1}^I \bar{z}^i = 0$ (iv) $\sum_{i=1}^I \bar{\theta}^i_k = 1, \, k = 1, \ldots, K$

The properties of this concept of equilibrium are more readily understood if the Pareto optimality criterion in (ii) is transformed into an equivalent profit maximizing criterion. This transformation is based on the following proposition which is a familiar result of equilibrium theory.

31.2 Proposition (Preferred Consumption is More Expensive): *If $u : \mathbb{R}^n \longrightarrow \mathbb{R}$ is differentiable and quasi-concave, and if $\bar{x} \in \mathbb{R}^n$ is such that $\nabla u(\bar{x}) \neq 0$, then*

(i) $u(\bar{x} + \xi) > (\geq) \, u(\bar{x})$ *implies* $\nabla u(\bar{x})\xi > (\geq) \, 0$;

(ii) *if u is weakly monotone, $\nabla u(\bar{x})\xi > 0$ implies that for some $\mu \in (0, 1]$, $u(\bar{x} + \mu\xi) > u(\bar{x})$.*

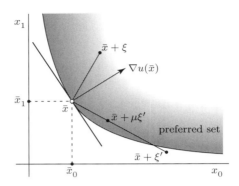

Figure 31.2   The relation between the set of consumption vectors preferred to $\bar{x}$ and those that are more expensive than $\bar{x}$.

PROOF: The proof is given in Appendix A6.1. $\square$

The geometric intuition underlying this proposition is shown in Figure 31.2. The preferred set to $\bar{x}$, being convex, lies entirely on the same side of the tangent hyperplane (in the same half-space) as the gradient $\nabla u(\bar{x})$, so that a change ξ in consumption which leads to a preferred consumption $\bar{x} + \xi$ must satisfy $\nabla u(\bar{x})\xi > 0$: in economic terms, any preferred-consumption vector $\bar{x} + \xi$ is more expensive than $\bar{x}$ under the prices induced by the gradient at $\bar{x}$. Conversely, if ξ' lies in the same half-space as the gradient, $\nabla u(\bar{x})\xi' > 0$, then ξ' can be scaled down to $\mu\xi'$ in such a way that $\bar{x} + \mu\xi'$ lies in the preferred set: a consumption stream $\bar{x} + \xi'$ which is more expensive than $\bar{x}$ can always be made into a stream which is strictly preferred to $\bar{x}$ by suitably scaling down the increment ξ'.

This proposition can be used to transform condition (ii), which is expressed in terms of production plans preferred by the partners, into a condition expressed in terms of production plans making a greater profit under the present-value vectors of the partners. Let $I_k = \left\{ i \mid \bar{\theta}_k^i > 0 \right\}$ denote the set of partners of venture k at equilibrium.

31.3 Proposition (Profit-Maximizing Form of Pareto Criterion):   *Under Assumptions* $(\mathscr{U}, \mathscr{T}^*)$, *the Pareto criterion* (ii) *in Definition 31.1 is equivalent to each of the following conditions:*

(ii)′ *there does not exist* $y^k \in Y^k$ *such that* $\bar{\pi}^i y^k > \bar{\pi}^i \bar{y}^k$ *for all* $i \in I_k$, *for*
     $k = 1, \ldots, K$

(ii)″ *for each* $k = 1, \ldots, K$ *there exists* $\alpha_k = (\alpha_k^1, \ldots, \alpha_k^I) \in \mathbb{R}_+^I$ *with* $\bar{\theta}_k^i \alpha_k^i > 0$
for some $i \in I_k$ *such that*

$$\bar{y}^k \in \arg\max \left\{ \left(\sum_{i \in I_k} \alpha_k^i \bar{\theta}_k^i \bar{\pi}^i \right) y^k \;\middle|\; y^k \in Y^k \right\}$$

where $\bar{\pi}^i = \pi^i(\bar{x}^i)$ *for* $i = 1, \ldots, I$.

PROOF: (ii) $\implies$ (ii)′ Suppose (ii)′ does not hold, then there exists $y^k \in Y^k$
such that for all $i \in I_k$, $\bar{\pi}^i y^k > \pi^i \bar{y}^k$, so that $\bar{\pi}^i(\bar{x}^i + (y^k - \bar{y}^k)\bar{\theta}_k^i) > \bar{\pi}^i \bar{x}^i$, for
all $i \in I_k$. By Proposition 31.2 (ii) there exists $\mu^i \in (0,1]$ such that

$$u^i \left(\bar{x}^i + \mu^i(y^k - \bar{y}^k)\bar{\theta}_k^i \right) > u^i(\bar{x}^i), \quad \forall\, i \in I_k$$

By strict quasi-concavity of u^i, this inequality holds for all $\widetilde{\mu}^i \in (0, \mu^i]$. Thus
if $\mu = \min_{i \in I_k} \mu^i$ then

$$u^i \left(\bar{x}^i + \mu(y^k - \bar{y}^k)\bar{\theta}_k^i \right) > u^i(\bar{x}^i), \quad \forall\, i \in I_k \tag{2}$$

Let $\hat{y}^k = \bar{y}^k + \mu(y^k - \bar{y}^k)$. By convexity of Y^k, $\hat{y}^k \in Y^k$ and (2) can be written
as

$$u^i \left(\bar{x}^i + (\hat{y}^k - \bar{y}^k)\bar{\theta}_k^i \right) > u^i(\bar{x}^i), \quad \forall\, i \in I_k \tag{3}$$

so that (ii) does not hold.

(ii)′ $\implies$ (ii) Suppose (ii) does not hold, then there exists $y^k \in Y^k$, $y^k \neq \bar{y}^k$
such that $u^i \left(\bar{x}^i + (y^k - \bar{y}^k)\bar{\theta}_k^i \right) \geq u^i(\bar{x}^i)$, $\forall\, i \in I_k$. The strict quasi-concavity
of u^i implies that for any $0 < \mu < 1$, (2) is satisfied. Choose any such μ
and let $\hat{y}^k = \bar{y}^k + \mu(y^k - \bar{y}^k)$. As shown above, $\hat{y}^k \in Y^k$ and satisfies (3).
Proposition 31.2(i) then implies that $\bar{\pi}^i \hat{y}^k > \bar{\pi}^i \bar{y}^k$, $\forall\, i \in I_k$, contradicting (ii)′.

(ii)′ $\iff$ (ii)″ It is immediate that (ii)″ implies (ii)′. The proof of the converse
is given in Appendix A6.4. It is based on the Minkowski-Farkas Lemma, a
classical result of convex analysis. □

(ii)′ asserts that an equilbrium plan $\bar{y}^k$ of venture k is such that it is not
possible to find an alternative plan y^k which increases the present value of its
profit from the perspective of all of its partners. By (ii)″ a plan $\bar{y}^k$ has this
property if it maximizes profit under a present-value vector which is a weighted
average of the present-value vectors of the partners of the kth venture.

When the Pareto criterion (ii) is written in the equivalent profit-maximizing
form (ii)″, it becomes apparent why Assumption $\mathscr{T}^*$ of constant returns for the
technology sets of the ventures is essential to obtain a meaningful (consistent)

concept of a partnership equilibrium.[1] If the opportunity sets Y^k were to exhibit (strictly) decreasing returns to scale, then a solution $\bar{y}^k$ of the profit-maximizing problem (ii)″ would yield a positive profit[2] and would thus satisfy $\bar{\pi}^i \bar{y}^k > 0$ for some partner i. But this would not be inconsistent with the first-order conditions for his optimal choice of partnership shares which requires $\bar{\pi}^i \bar{y}^k = 0$ when $\bar{\theta}^i_k > 0$.

Condition (ii)″ reveals a weakness of the concept of a Pareto partnership equilibrium: when the trading opportunities available to the agents are incomplete, the $\bar{\pi}^i$ vectors are typically distinct, so that different vectors of weights $\alpha_k = (\alpha^1_k, \ldots, \alpha^I_k)$ give rise to different average present-value vectors $\sum_{i=1}^I \alpha^i_k \bar{\theta}^i_k \bar{\pi}^i$ and hence different production plans $\bar{y}^k$. Since all non-zero vectors of weights lead to a Pareto partnership equilibrium, there is in general a continuum of such equilibria.

All the models that we have considered so far have the important property that the equilibrium outcomes that they predict are finite in number: this will be proved in Volume 2 where it will also be shown that an equilibrium model cannot in general be expected to predict a unique outcome but rather several possible outcomes. A model which typically predicts a finite number of equilibrium outcomes is said to be *determinate*; when this is not the case, a model typically has a continuum of equilibria, in which case the model is said to be *indeterminate*. This latter property is normally viewed as an undesirable feature in that the predictive (explanatory) power of the model is greatly reduced.

The reason for the indeterminacy of the Pareto partnership equilibrium when markets are incomplete is clear: since the Pareto criterion is compatible with any non-negative vector of weights $\alpha_k = (\alpha^1_k, \ldots, \alpha^I_k)$, it is compatible with any scheme for taking into account the different opinions of the partners. A determinate model of a partnership equilibrium can be obtained by adopting a specific scheme for resolving these differences of opinion, and one natural way of resolving a collective choice problem when agents have differences of opinion is to introduce *transfer payments*. To obtain a unique[3] optimal production plan for a partnership, we will thus require that the chosen production plan be robust to change by unanimous vote of the partners, given that they can make transfer payments among themselves to reach unanimity.

Suppose $\bar{y}^k$ is a production plan which is currently under consideration by the

---

[1] It can be shown that under Assumptions $(\mathscr{U}, \mathscr{T}^*)$ and $\omega^i \in \mathbb{R}_{++}, i = 1, \ldots, I$, a Pareto partnership equilibrium exists for every $\alpha = (\alpha^i_k, i = 1, \ldots, I, k = 1, \ldots, K) \in \mathbb{R}^{KI}_{++}$.

[2] $\bar{y}^k$ maximizes profit with respect to a strictly positive vector of state prices $\bar{\pi} = \sum_{i \in I_k} \alpha^i_k \bar{\theta}^i_k \bar{\pi}^i$. If Y^k exhibits strictly decreasing returns to scale, then $\mu \bar{y}^k \in \text{int } Y^k$ for $0 < \mu < 1$, so that there exists $\widetilde{y}^k \in Y^k$ such that $\bar{\pi}\widetilde{y}^k > \mu\bar{\pi}\bar{y}^k$. If $\bar{\pi}\bar{y}^k = 0$, this contradicts the profit maximizing property of $\bar{y}^k$.

[3] Up to scalar multiplication because of constant returns.

partners of the kth venture, and suppose that an alternative plan y^k is proposed by a subgroup of the partners. Suppose also that the partners favoring the new plan can offer to compensate the other partners for the losses that they would incur if this alternative plan were adopted. When will y^k be adopted in place of $\bar{y}^k$? If the payments that the partners in favor of the change are prepared to make to the partners who are opposed are sufficient to compensate the latter for the losses incurred, then the new plan y^k will be adopted in place of $\bar{y}^k$. More precisely, suppose partner i is in favor of the proposed change then

$$u^i\left(\bar{x}^i + (y^k - \bar{y}^k)\bar{\theta}^i_k\right) > u^i(\bar{x}^i)$$

Let $\tau^i_k > 0$ denote the maximum amount that he is prepared to pay to compensate those against the change. If $e^0 = (1, 0, \ldots, 0) \in \mathbb{R}^{S+1}$, then τ^i_k is defined by

$$u^i\left(\bar{x}^i + (y^k - \bar{y}^k)\bar{\theta}^i_k - \tau^i_k e^0\right) = u^i(\bar{x}^i) \tag{4}$$

Suppose now that i is a partner who is against the change. Then the same formula with $\tau^i_k < 0$ gives the minimum amount $(-\tau^i_k)$ that he has to be paid to compensate him for the loss, and to make him agree to the change. When the payments τ^i_k of all partners have been assessed in this way, y^k will be adopted in place of $\bar{y}^k$ if

$$\sum_{i \in I_k} \tau^i_k > 0 \tag{5}$$

where τ^i_k is defined by (4) for $i \in I_k$. Requiring that the production plan adopted by each venture is stable, in the sense that there is no alternative plan which is unanimously preferred by the partners after side payments, leads to the following concept of equilibrium.

31.4 Definition: *A partnership equilibrium* (derived from the Pareto criterion with side payments) is a pair consisting of actions and prices

$$\left((\bar{x}, \bar{z}, \bar{\theta}, \bar{y}), \bar{q}\right) \in \mathbb{R}_+^{(S+1)I} \times \mathbb{R}^{JI} \times \mathbb{R}_+^{KI} \times \mathbb{R}^{(S+1)K} \times \mathbb{R}^J$$

such that

   (i) $(\bar{x}^i; \bar{z}^i, \bar{\theta}^i) \in \arg\max\left\{u^i(x^i) \mid (x^i; z^i, \theta^i) \in \mathbb{B}(\bar{q}, \omega^i, R, \bar{y})\right\}, i = 1, \ldots, I$
   (ii) there does not exist $(y^k, \tau_k) \in Y^k \times \mathbb{R}^I$ with $\sum_{i \in I_k} \tau^i_k \geq 0$, such that

$$u^i\left(\bar{x}^i + (y^k - \bar{y}^k)\bar{\theta}^i_k - \tau^i_k e^0\right) \geq u^i(\bar{x}^i), \quad i \in I_k$$

   with strict inequality for at least one i, for $k = 1, \ldots, K$
   (iii) $\sum_{i=1}^I \bar{z}^i = 0$ (iv) $\sum_{i=1}^I \bar{\theta}^i_k = 1, k = 1, \ldots, K$.

This concept of equilibrium is close in spirit to the original idea that motivates the formation of partnerships. A collection of agents, any one of whom is individually unable to fund the initial investment, agree to pool their financial resources and to share the risks involved in a business venture. However, the benefits of pooling their funds and sharing the risks can only be put to advantage by the (potential) partners if they can resolve their differences of opinion on the best way to operate the business. It is natural for the partners to begin with a preliminary phase in which they discuss the relative merits of alternative investment plans. An equilibrium plan $\bar{y}^k$ is a plan on which a consensus has been reached by the partners: after much discussion they have not been able to come up with any alternative plan which would be preferred by all partners after suitable persuasion (side payments).

A weakness of this concept of equilibrium is that it does not provide a well-defined bargaining process by which partners could come up with such an agreement. Such a criticism is however applicable to all equilibrium analysis where certain "equilibrium states" of the economy are defined as candidate outcomes, even though no explicit process (dynamics) is described by which such equilibrium states can be attained.

Analyzing the properties of a partnership equilibrium in the form presented in Definition 31.4 is cumbersome since the Pareto criterion with side payments in (ii) yields a complicated objective function for each venture. The next proposition provides a simpler characterization of a partnership equilibrium in which the criterion (ii), based on the nonlinear utility functions of the partners, is replaced by a linear objective of profit maximization. The vector of state prices for venture k under which its profit is maximized is the average of the present-value vectors of its partners, each partner being weighted by his share in the partnership. Replacing the nonlinear vector maximum problem in (ii) for each venture by a scalar maximum problem with a linear objective function leads to a more tractable way of analyzing the properties of a partnership equilibrium.

31.5 Proposition (Profit-Maximizing Characterization of Partnership Equilibrium):   *Consider a partnership economy satisfying Assumptions $(\mathscr{U}, \mathscr{T}^*)$. $\big((\bar{x}, \bar{z}, \bar{\theta}, \bar{y}), \bar{q}\big)$ is a partnership equilibrium if and only if*

(i) $(\bar{x}^i; \bar{z}^i, \bar{\theta}^i) \in \arg\max\big\{ u^i(x^i) \mid (x^i; z^i, \theta^i) \in \mathbb{B}(\bar{q}, \omega^i, R, \bar{y}) \big\}$, $i = 1, \ldots, I$

(ii)′ $\bar{y}^k \in \arg\max\Big\{ \sum_{i \in I_k} \bar{\theta}^i_k \bar{\pi}^i y^k \mid y^k \in Y^k \Big\}$, $k = 1, \ldots, K$ *where* $\bar{\pi}^i = \pi^i(\bar{x}^i)$, $i = 1, \ldots, I$

(iii) $\sum_{i=1}^I \bar{z}^i = 0$ (iv) $\sum_{i=1}^I \bar{\theta}^i_k = 1$, $k = 1, \ldots, K$.

PROOF: It suffices to show that (ii)′ is equivalent to (ii) in Definition 31.4.

(ii) $\Longrightarrow$ (ii)$'$ Suppose that (ii)$'$ does not hold. Then there exists $y^k \in Y^k$ such that $\sum_{i=1}^{I} \theta_k^i \bar{\pi}^i(y^k - \bar{y}^k) > 0$. Let $\tau_k^i = \bar{\theta}_k^i \bar{\pi}^i(y^k - \bar{y}^k) - \epsilon$, with $\epsilon > 0$. Then for ϵ sufficiently small

$$\sum_{i \in I_k} \tau_k^i \geq 0 \tag{6}$$

and $\bar{\pi}^i\left(\bar{\theta}_k^i(y^k - \bar{y}^k) - \tau_k^i e^0\right) = \epsilon > 0$, $i \in I_k$. Let

$$\xi^i = \bar{\theta}_k^i(y^k - \bar{y}^k) - \tau_k^i e^0, \quad i \in I_k$$

then $\bar{\pi}^i \xi^i > 0$, $i \in I_k$. By Proposition 31.2(ii), for each $i \in I_k$ there exists $\mu^i \in (0,1]$ such that $u^i(\bar{x}^i + \mu^i \xi^i) > u^i(\bar{x}^i)$. By strict quasi-concavity of u^i, if $0 < \mu \leq \min_{i \in I_k} \mu^i$ then

$$u^i\left(\bar{x}^i + \mu \xi^i\right) > u^i(\bar{x}^i), \quad i \in I_k \tag{7}$$

$\mu \xi^i$ can be written as $\mu \xi^i = \bar{\theta}_k^i(\hat{y}^k - \bar{y}^k) - \mu \tau_k^i e^0$ where $\hat{y}^k = \bar{y}^k + \mu(y^k - \bar{y}^k)$. By convexity of Y^k, $\hat{y}^k \in Y^k$. By (6) and (7), (ii) does not hold.

(ii) $\Longleftarrow$ (ii)$'$ Suppose (ii) does not hold. Then by redistributing the transfers $(\tau_k^i) \to (\tilde{\tau}_k^i)$ among the partners so as to make each partner strictly better off, there exists $(y^k, \tilde{\tau}_k) \in Y^k \times \mathbb{R}^I$ with $\sum_{i \in I_k} \tilde{\tau}_k^i \geq 0$ such that

$$u^i\left(\bar{x}^i + (y^k - \bar{y}^k)\bar{\theta}_k^i - \tilde{\tau}_k^i e^0\right) > u^i(\bar{x}^i), \quad i \in I_k \tag{8}$$

By Proposition 31.2(i), (8) implies

$$\bar{\pi}^i\left((y^k - \bar{y}^k)\bar{\theta}_k^i - \tilde{\tau}_k^i e^0\right) > 0, \quad i \in I_k \tag{9}$$

Since $\sum_{i \in I_k} \tilde{\tau}_k^i \geq 0$, (9) implies

$$\sum_{i \in I_k} \bar{\theta}_k^i \bar{\pi}^i y^k > \sum_{i \in I_k} \bar{\theta}_k^i \bar{\pi}^i \bar{y}^k$$

which contradicts (ii)$'$. $\square$

It is tempting to interpret the objective of profit maximization in (ii)$'$ as the objective of a manager who runs the firm on behalf of the partners. The manager is informed of their preferences and aggregates them into an overall objective function for the firm, the preference of each partner being weighted by his share in the venture. The equilibrium plan $\bar{y}^k$ is then a plan which maximizes this managerial objective function. This interpretation, however, runs into difficulties. If the partners know the manager's objective function, then they will have an incentive to misrepresent their preferences so as to alter the manager's decision to their advantage. Furthermore it is not clear what incentive system will induce the manager to act as an arbitrator among partners who do not agree among themselves.

It is more appropriate to view the profit-maximizing form of a partnership equilibrium as a description of the way risks are evaluated by each partnership after the bargaining process has brought the partners to an agreement. The mean-covariance form for the profit-maximizing criterion $(ii)'$ can be obtained by invoking the assumption that there are objective probabilities $\rho = (\rho_1, \ldots, \rho_S)$ for the states at date 1 and that one of the securities is the riskless bond. If for simplicity we assume that $\bar{\theta}_k^i > 0$ for all i and k then the present value of a project for the kth partnership can be written as

$$\sum_{i \in I_k} \bar{\theta}_k^i \bar{\pi}^i \bar{y}^k = y_0^k + \frac{E(y_1^k)}{1 + \bar{r}} + \text{cov}(\widetilde{\gamma}, y_V^k) + \text{cov}\left(\sum_{i \in I_k} \bar{\theta}_k^i \check{\pi}_1^{\rho,i}, \check{y}_1^k \right) \qquad (10)$$

where $\widetilde{\gamma}$ is the risk-pricing component of the ideal security $\bar{\gamma}$ in the marketed subspace $\langle V \rangle = \langle [\, R \; \bar{y}_1 \,] \rangle$ and $\check{\pi}_1^{\rho,i}$ is the component of $\pi_1^{\rho,i}$ on the orthogonal complement $\langle V \rangle^{\perp\!\!\!\perp}$. (10) is the analogue for a partnership of the present-value formula (32) derived in Section 30 for an entrepreneurial firm. It is clear from this expression that the only source of disagreement among partners arises from projects $y^k \in Y^k$ which are not fully priced in the market ($\check{y}_1^k \neq 0$). In the equilibrium evaluation of risk, this disagreement is resolved by weighting the idiosyncratic risk components $\check{\pi}_1^{\rho,i}$ of the partners by their shares in the partnership: in the collective criterion of the firm the evaluation of nonmarket risk is thus an average of the individual partners' valuations.

Under criterion (ii) or $(ii)'$, the production decisions of the K firms are made separately, the partners of each venture taking the plans of all other ventures as given when coming to an agreement on their production plan. Since agents in this model will typically diversify their risks by being partners of several ventures, an agent would need to consider simultaneously all the proposed changes of production plans of the ventures of which he is a partner in deciding which changes he favors (or disfavors) and how much he is prepared to pay (or needs to be paid) to have them implemented. The following proposition shows that the equilibrium of Definition 31.4 has the property of being robust to *simultaneous changes* in the production plans of all ventures, when side payments can be used to obtain unanimity, and unanimity is required to implement any proposed change. Just as $I_k = \left\{ i \mid \bar{\theta}_k^i > 0 \right\}$ denotes the agents who are partners of venture k, so it is natural to let $K_i = \left\{ k \mid \bar{\theta}_k^i > 0 \right\}$ denote the ventures of which agent i is a partner (at equilibrium).

31.6 Proposition (Robustness to Simultaneous Changes): *Under Assumptions $(\mathscr{U}, \mathscr{T}^*)$, (ii) in Definition 31.4 is equivalent to* (ii)″ *there does not exist* $(y, \tau) \in \prod_{k=1}^{K} Y^k \times \mathbb{R}^{IK}$ *with* $\sum_{i \in I_k} \tau_k^i \geq 0$ *for* $k = 1, \ldots, K$ *such that*

$$u^i \left(\bar{x}^i + \sum_{k \in K_i} (y^k - \bar{y}^k) \bar{\theta}_k^i - \sum_{k \in K_i} \tau_k^i e^0 \right) \geq u^i(\bar{x}^i), \quad i = 1, \ldots, I \quad (11)$$

with strict inequality for at least one i.

PROOF: It is immediate that (ii)″ implies (ii); let us show that (ii) $\Longrightarrow$ (ii)″. Suppose (ii)″ does not hold. Then there exists $(y, \tau) \in \prod_{k=1}^{K} Y^k \times \mathbb{R}^{IK}$ with $\sum_{i \in I_k} \tau_k^i \geq 0$ for $k = 1, \ldots, K$ such that (11) holds with strict inequality for at least one i. By Proposition 31.2(i)

$$\pi^i \left(\sum_{k \in K_i} (y^k - \bar{y}^k) \bar{\theta}_k^i - \sum_{k \in K_i} \tau_k^i e^0 \right) \geq 0, \quad i = 1, \ldots, I$$

with strict inequality for at least one i. Summing over the agents gives

$$\sum_{k=1}^{K} \left(\sum_{i=1}^{I} \bar{\theta}_k^i \pi^i \right) y^k > \sum_{k=1}^{K} \left(\sum_{i=1}^{I} \bar{\theta}_k^i \pi^i \right) \bar{y}^k$$

so that (ii)′ is contradicted for at least one k. Since (ii)′ $\Longleftrightarrow$ (ii), this contradiction completes the proof. □

Constrained Pareto Optimality

In a partnership equilibrium, agents are assumed to choose their partnership shares, taking the production plans of each venture as given; the plan for each venture is in turn chosen to maximize the present value of its profit, taking the partnership shares as given. Thus portfolios are chosen given production plans, and production plans are chosen given portfolios: as a result there may be incomplete co-ordination between the risk-sharing decisions and the choice of investment plans in the economy.

To examine the efficiency properties of a partnership equilibrium, it is useful to imagine an alternative way of allocating resources in which a planner instead of the agents chooses the allocation (x, z, θ, y). The planner can then choose the portfolios and production plans simultaneously. As in Section 12 the planner is constrained to use the existing financial instruments (partnership shares and bond holdings) to allocate date 1 consumption.

31.7 Definition: In a partnership economy a plan (x, z, θ, y) is *constrained feasible* if

(i) $x^i \in \mathbb{R}_+^{S+1}$, $i = 1, \ldots, I$

(ii) $\sum_{i=1}^{I}(x_0^i - \omega_0^i) = \sum_{k=1}^{K} y_0^k$

(iii) $x_1^i = \omega_1^i + Rz^i + y_1\theta^i$, $(z^i, \theta^i) \in \mathbb{R}^J \times \mathbb{R}_+^K$, $i = 1, \dots, I$

(iv) $\sum_{i=1}^{I} z^i = 0$

(v) $\sum_{i=1}^{I} \theta_k^i = 1$, $k = 1, \dots, K$

(vi) $y^k \in Y^k$, $k = 1, \dots, K$

Let $Y = Y^1 \times \cdots \times Y^K$ denote the cartesian product of the production sets. The *set of constrained feasible plans* $F_{R,Y}$ is given by

$$F_{R,Y} = \left\{ (x, z, \theta, y) \in \mathbb{R}^{(S+1)I} \times \mathbb{R}^{JI} \times \mathbb{R}^{KI} \times \mathbb{R}^{(S+1)K} \ \middle| \ \text{(i)–(vi) hold} \right\}$$

A plan $(\bar{x}, \bar{z}, \bar{\theta}, \bar{y})$ is *constrained Pareto optimal* if $(\bar{x}, \bar{z}, \bar{\theta}, \bar{y}) \in F_{R,Y}$ and there does not exist $(x, z, \theta, y) \in F_{R,Y}$ such that $u^i(x^i) \geq u^i(\bar{x}^i)$, $i = 1, \dots, I$, with strict inequality for at least one i; for brevity we also write: $(\bar{x}, \bar{z}, \bar{\theta}, \bar{y})$ is CPO. A plan which is not constrained Pareto optimal is called *constrained Pareto suboptimal*.

The important point to notice is that the set of constrained feasible plans $F_{R,Y}$ is not convex. The non-convexity comes from the quadratic production-portfolio term $y_1\theta^i$ which gives the agent's date 1 income from his partnership holdings. The functions $(y_s, \theta^i) \longrightarrow \sum_{k=1}^{K} y_s^k \theta_k^i$ (for $s = 1, \dots, S$) from $\mathbb{R}^K \times \mathbb{R}^K \longrightarrow \mathbb{R}$ being homogeneous of degree two, are not concave: thus the constraints in Definition 31.7(iii), which could be written in the inequality form

$$x_1^i \leq \omega_1^i + Rz^i + y_1\theta^i, \quad i = 1, \dots, I$$

without changing the CPO, do not define a convex set.

The next proposition shows that a partnership equilibrium satisfies the first-order conditions for constrained optimality. However, since the set of constrained feasible plans is not convex, the first-order conditions are not sufficient to guarantee optimality. The following notation is useful for expressing (constrained) Pareto optimality in condensed form. Let $u : \mathbb{R}^m \longrightarrow \mathbb{R}^I$ with $u = (u^1, \dots, u^I)$ be a vector-valued function, and let F be a subset of $\mathbb{R}^m$. $\bar{\xi} \in \mathbb{R}^m$ is said to be a solution of the *vector maximum problem*

$$\max \{ u(\xi) \mid \xi \in F \} \tag{12}$$

if there does not exist $\xi \in F$ such that $u(\xi) > u(\bar{\xi})$, where the vector inequality $>$ means that the difference $u(\xi) - u(\bar{\xi})$ is semipositive ($u^i(\xi) \geq u^i(\bar{\xi})$ for $i = 1, \dots, I$ with strict inequality for at least one i). If $u = (u^1, \dots, u^I)$ denotes the vector of utility functions of I agents, and F is the set of (constrained) feasible allocations then a solution of the vector maximum problem (12) is a (constrained) Pareto optimal allocation.

31.8 Proposition (Partnership Equilibrium Satisfies FOC for CPO):   *Let*
$\mathscr{E}(u, \omega, Y)$ *be an economy satisfying Assumptions* $(\mathscr{U}, \mathscr{T}^*)$. *If* $((\bar{x}, \bar{z}, \bar{\theta}, \bar{y}), \bar{q})$
is a partnership equilibrium, then the plan $(\bar{x}, \bar{z}, \bar{\theta}, \bar{y})$ *satisfies the first-order
conditions for the vector maximum problem*

$$\max \left\{ u(x) \mid (x, z, \theta, y) \in F_{R,Y} \right\} \tag{13}$$

where $u(x) = \left(u^1(x^1), \ldots, u^I(x^I) \right)$.

PROOF: It is convenient to incorporate the nonconvexity in problem (13) into
the objective functions rather than in the constraints. This can be done by
substituting for x_1^i from (iii) in Definition 31.7 and defining the function $v =
(v^1, \ldots, v^I)$ with

$$v^i(x_0, z, \theta, y) = u^i(x_0^i, \omega_1^i + y_1 \theta^i + R z^i), \quad i = 1, \ldots, I$$

A constrained feasible plan is defined, as before, with (i) and (iii) replaced by

$$\text{(i)}' \quad (x_0, \omega_1 + y_1 \theta + R z) \in \mathbb{R}_+^{(S+1)I} \qquad \text{(iii)}' \quad (z, \theta) \in \mathbb{R}^{JI} \times \mathbb{R}_+^{KI}$$

In view of Assumption $\mathscr{U}$, the nonnegativity condition (i)$'$ cannot be binding:
thus the constraint (i)$'$ can be omitted. Consider the set

$$C = \left\{ (x_0, z, \theta, y) \in \mathbb{R}_+^I \times \mathbb{R}^{JI} \times \mathbb{R}_+^{KI} \times \prod_{k=1}^{K} Y^k \; \middle| \; \begin{array}{l} \sum_{i=1}^{I} (x_0^i - \omega_0^i) = \sum_{k=1}^{K} y_0^k \\ \sum_{i=1}^{I} z^i = 0, \; \sum_{i=1}^{I} \theta^i = e \end{array} \right\}$$

where $e = (1, \ldots, 1) \in \mathbb{R}^K$. If we let $\xi = (x_0, z, \theta, y)$ then (13) is equivalent to
the vector maximum problem

$$\max \left\{ v(\xi) \mid \xi \in C \right\} \tag{14}$$

where C is a convex set. The normal cone $N_C(\xi)$ to C at ξ is thus well-defined.
Since by Assumption $\mathscr{U}$ each component v^i of the vector-valued function $v =
(v^1, \ldots, v^I)$ is differentiable we can make use of the following result, in which
the functions v^i are not required to be quasi-concave.

31.9 Proposition (FOC for Vector Maximum Problem):   *Let* $v = (v^1, \ldots, v^I) :
\mathbb{R}^m \longrightarrow \mathbb{R}^I$ *be differentiable and let* $C \subset \mathbb{R}^m$ *be a non-empty convex set. If*
$\bar{\xi}$ *is a solution of the vector maximum problem* (14), *then there exists* $\alpha =
(\alpha_1, \ldots, \alpha_I) \in \mathbb{R}_+^I$, $\alpha \neq 0$ *such that*

$$\sum_{i=1}^{I} \alpha_i \nabla v^i(\bar{\xi}) \in N_C(\bar{\xi}) \tag{15}$$

PROOF: See Appendix A6.5. □

C is defined through cartesian products and intersections of convex sets. It is readily verified from the definition of the normal cone that if C_1 and C_2 are convex sets then

$$N_{C_1 \times C_2} = N_{C_1} \times N_{C_2}, \quad N_{C_1 \cap C_2} = N_{C_1} + N_{C_2} \tag{16}$$

Associating the multiplier λ_0 with (ii) in Definition 31.7, $\mu^i = (\mu_1^i, \ldots, \mu_K^i)$, $i = 1, \ldots, I$ with the positivity constraints on θ in (iii)$'$, $q = (q_1, \ldots, q_J)$ with (iv), $\rho = (\rho_1, \ldots, \rho_K)$ with (v), and letting $\nabla_1 u^i = (\partial u^i / \partial x_1^i, \ldots, \partial u^i / \partial x_S^i)$ denote the date 1 gradient of u^i, the first-order conditions (15) can be written using (16) as: there exist non-negative vectors $\alpha = (\alpha_1, \ldots, \alpha_I)$ and $(\lambda_0, \mu^1, \ldots, \mu^I, q, p)$ such that

$$\left.\begin{aligned}
\alpha_i \frac{\partial u^i(\bar{x}^i)}{\partial x_0^i} &= \lambda_0 \\
\alpha_i \nabla_1 u^i(\bar{x}^i) R &= q \\
\alpha_i \nabla_1 u^i(\bar{x}^i) \bar{y}_1 &= \rho - \mu^i, \quad \mu_k^i \bar{\theta}_k^i = 0, \quad k = 1, \ldots, K
\end{aligned}\right\} \quad i = 1, \ldots, I$$

$$\left(\lambda_0, \sum_{i=1}^I \alpha_i \bar{\theta}_k^i \nabla_1 u^i(\bar{x}^i)\right) \in N_{Y^k}(\bar{y}^k), \quad k = 1, \ldots, K$$

where $\bar{x}^i$ is deduced from $\bar{\xi}$ by

$$\bar{x}^i = (\bar{x}_0^i, \omega_1^i + \bar{y}_1 \bar{\theta}^i + R\bar{z}^i), \quad i = 1, \ldots, I$$

$\lambda_0 \neq 0$ since $\alpha = (\alpha_1, \ldots, \alpha_I) \neq 0$. Since the conditions are homogeneous of degree one in the multipliers we can normalize so that $\lambda_0 = 1$. Then $\alpha_i = 1/\frac{\partial u^i}{\partial x_0^i}$, $i = 1, \ldots, I$, and $(\bar{x}_0, \bar{z}, \bar{\theta}, \bar{y}) \in C$ satisfies the first-order conditions for (14) if there exist vectors $(q, \rho) \in \mathbb{R}^J \times \mathbb{R}^K$ such that for $i = 1, \ldots, I$:

$$\pi_1^i(\bar{x}^i) R = q \tag{17}$$
$$\pi_1^i(\bar{x}^i) \bar{y}_1^k \leq \rho_k \quad \text{with equality if} \quad \bar{\theta}_k^i > 0, \quad k = 1, \ldots, K \tag{18}$$

and for $k = 1, \ldots, K$:

$$\sum_{i=1}^I \bar{\theta}_k^i \pi^i(\bar{x}^i) \in N_{Y^k}(\bar{y}^k) \tag{19}$$

Let us show that if (18) and (19) are satisfied, then $\rho_k = -\bar{y}_0^k$, $k = 1, \ldots, K$. Let $\bar{\pi}^k = \sum_{i \in I_k} \bar{\theta}_k^i \pi^i(\bar{x}^i)$. Since by Assumption $\mathcal{T}^*$, Y^k is a convex cone, (19) implies $\bar{\pi}^k \bar{y}^k = 0$. Since $\bar{\pi}_0^k = 1$, and since (18) and $\sum_{i \in I_k} \bar{\theta}_k^i = 1$ imply that

$\bar{\pi}_1^k \bar{y}_1^k = \rho_k$, it follows that $\bar{y}_0^k + \rho_k = 0$. Thus in the statement of the first-order conditions, (18) can be written as

$$\pi_1^i(\bar{x}^i)\,\bar{y}_1^k \le -\bar{y}_0^k \text{ with equality if } \bar{\theta}_k^i > 0, \quad k = 1, \ldots, K \qquad (18')$$

If $\big((\bar{x}, \bar{z}, \bar{\theta}, \bar{y}), \bar{q}\big)$ is a partnership equilibrium then (17) and (18′) are the first-order conditions for the utility maximizing problem ((i) in Definition 31.4) of each agent. (19) is the first-order condition for the problem of maximizing profit ((ii)′ in Proposition 31.5) for each venture. Since $(\bar{x}_0, \bar{z}, \bar{\theta}, \bar{y}) \in C$, the first-order conditions for (13) are satisfied in a partnership equilibrium. □

REMARK. The first-order conditions for a partnership equilibrium can be written in the geometric form analogous to the conditions (23) and (24) for an entrepreneurial equilibrium. Let

$$W = \begin{bmatrix} -\bar{q} \\ R \end{bmatrix} \quad \text{and} \quad \bar{y} = \begin{bmatrix} \bar{y}^1 \cdots \bar{y}^K \end{bmatrix}$$

denote the matrix of payoffs on the bond market and the matrix of partnership payoffs respectively. If $\langle \bar{y} \rangle_+$ denotes the cone generated by taking non-negative linear combinations of the columns of the matrix $\bar{y}$, then the first-order conditions of a consumer can be written as

$$\bar{\tau}^i \in \langle W \rangle + \langle \bar{y} \rangle_+, \quad \bar{\pi}^i \in \langle W \rangle^\perp \cap N_{\langle \bar{y} \rangle_+}(\bar{\theta}^i), \quad i = 1, \ldots, I \qquad (20)$$

and those for the kth partnership as

$$\bar{y}^k \in Y^k, \quad \sum_{i \in I_k} \bar{\theta}_k^i \bar{\pi}^i \in N_{Y^k}(\bar{y}^k), \quad k = 1, \ldots, K \qquad (21)$$

Even though the first-order conditions for constrained Pareto optimality are satisfied in a partnership equilibrium, the following examples of Drèze (1974) show that these equilibria can be constrained Pareto suboptimal—or as we shall say for brevity, *constrained inefficient*. Since the constrained feasible set is nonconvex, the first-order conditions do not guarantee that a global (nor even a local) maximum is reached.

Examples of Constrained Inefficient Equilibria

The first example is simple and very striking, but the agents' utility functions do not satisfy Assumption $\mathscr{U}$(ii) which ensures that equilibrium consumption streams are strictly positive. As a result, agents' consumption streams can (and in the example do) lie on the boundary of their consumption sets. This in no way alters the fact that a partnership equilbrium satisfies the first-order conditions for CPO, since the above analysis can be readily adapted by introducing additional multipliers to cope with the non-negativity constraints on consumption. To show that constrained inefficiency is not an artifact arising from boundary solutions, the second example exhibits a constrained inefficient interior equilibrium for an economy satisfying Assumption $\mathscr{U}$. The third example exhibits a new phenomenon that can arise in a production economy when markets are incomplete: in a partnership economy there can be a trade-off between productive efficiency and spanning. Productive efficiency would require that only the more efficient partnership produce: however also using the less efficient partnership provides greater spanning opportunities for sharing risks.

31.10 Example: Consider a production economy $\mathscr{E}(u, \omega, Y)$ with the following properties. There are two states of nature, two agents, and two ventures $(S = I = K = 2)$. There are no bond markets. The agents' utility functions do not depend upon consumption at date 0: this simplifies the analysis of the equilibria. The agents have initial resources only at date 0 (one unit of the good (income) for each agent). They thus invest the full amount of their initial resources at date 0 in production to obtain consumption at date 1. The production sets (Y^1, Y^2) of the two ventures exhibit constant returns to scale: the outputs (y_1^k, y_2^k) in the two states at date 1, which can be obtained from one unit of input at date 0, are shown in Figure 31.3: ab (AB) is the boundary of $Y^1(Y^2)$ with $y_0^k = -1$. Firm 1(2) is more efficient at producing the good in state 1(2). The utility functions (u^1, u^2) are such that agent 1(2) prefers the good in state 1(2). Since $\omega^i = (\omega_0^i, \omega_1^i, \omega_2^i) = (1, 0, 0)$ and since there is no date 0 consumption, the budget set of each agent, for given production plans $y = (y^1, y^2)$ for the two ventures, is given by

$$\mathbb{B}(\omega^i, y) = \left\{ x^i \in \mathbb{R}_+^2 \;\middle|\; \begin{array}{l} 0 = 1 + \theta_1^i y_0^1 + \theta_2^i y_0^2 \\ x_{\mathbf{1}}^i = \theta_1^i y_{\mathbf{1}}^1 + \theta_2^i y_{\mathbf{1}}^2, \quad \theta^i \in \mathbb{R}_+^2 \end{array} \right\} \tag{22}$$

Two partnership equilibria are shown in Figure 31.3: one at (B, a), the other at (b, A). In the equilibrium (B, a), agent 1(2) is the only partner of firm 2(1): thus $\bar{\theta}^1 = (0, 1)$, $\bar{\theta}^2 = (1, 0)$. The budget set (22) of each agent is the segment aB. The production plan chosen by each venture is optimal for its owner, and given these production plans, the agents do not want to become partners in the other venture. Since the owner of each firm is more interested in the good

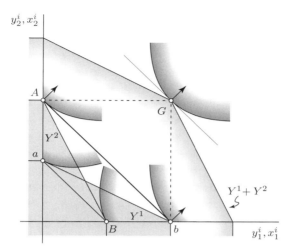

Figure 31.3   Equilibria of Example 31.10.

which his firm produces relatively inefficiently, there is a misallocation of the partnership shares $(\bar{\theta}^1, \bar{\theta}^2)$ which in turn induces a misallocation of production. As a result the equilibrium (B, a) is constrained inefficient. The equilibrium (B, a) is however a *local* maximum of the vector maximum problem (13): a planner restricting himself to small simultaneous changes in the partnership shares and productions plans of the two ventures could not improve the welfare of both agents.

In the equilibrium (b, A) agent 1(2) is the only partner of firm 1(2): $\bar{\theta}^1 = (1, 0)$, $\bar{\theta}^2 = (0, 1)$. The budget set (22) of each agent is the segment Ab. In this case the relative efficiency of each venture in producing the good in each state is appropriately matched to the preferences of its owner. As a result the equilibrium is constrained efficient and hence a global maximum of the problem (13). In fact the equilibrium (b, A) is a Pareto optimum: it can be obtained as a contingent market equilibrium with any initial distribution of ownership shares among the agents (since there are zero profits). A contingent price vector $\bar{\pi}_1$ is shown in Figure 31.3: the contingent market budget line coincides with the budget line Ab for the partnership equilibrium. The segment Ab also gives the profit maximizing line for each firm.[4] □

31.11 Example: This example also gives an economy with one constrained inefficient and one efficient equilibrium: in this case the inefficient equilibrium is not a local maximum for the problem (13). The utility functions satisfy

---

[4]The Pareto optimality of (b, A) is shown geometrically in Figure 31.3 by the separation of the sum of the preferred sets of agent 1 at b and agent 2 at A from the aggregate production set $Y^1 + Y^2$ by the hyperplane (line) defined by $\bar{\pi}_1$ which passes through G.

Assumption $\mathscr{U}$ (with respect to date 1 consumption), so that the equilibrium consumption vectors lie in the interior of the agents' (date 1) consumption sets.

The agents' endowment vectors and the production sets are the same as in Example 31.10. The utility functions (u^1, u^2) are changed so that agent 1(2) predominantly likes the good in state 1(2), but likes the good in state 2(1) more than in Example 31.10.

Two partnership equilibria are shown in Figure 31.4: one with date 1 production and consumption at C, the other with date 1 production at (b, A) and consumption at (D, F). The equilibrium at C corresponds to the equilibrium at (B, a) in the previous example: as a result of the modification of the preferences the two points B and a have come together at point C, and each venture has the same production plan given by the point C. Thus the budget line, which in the previous example was given by the line segment Ab, is now reduced to the point C. Agent 1(2) is the sole owner of venture 2(1). However, since the production plans of each venture coincide, each agent is indifferent between partnership shares in the two firms. As before, there is a misallocation of the partnership shares and production plans so that the equilibrium at C is constrained inefficient. However, in this case a small change in the production plan of venture 1 towards b and of venture 2 towards A, accompanied by small changes in the partnership shares, with agent 1 obtaining a small share of venture 1 and agent 2 a small share of venture 2, improves the welfare of both agents. Thus, unlike the equilibrium (B, a) in the previous example, *the*

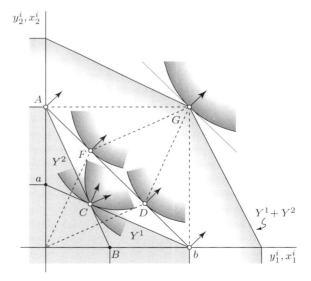

Figure 31.4   Equilibria of Example 31.11.

equilibrium at C is not a local maximum of the planner's maximum problem (13).

In the second equilibrium, production is at (b, A) and consumption at (D, F). The budget set (22) is the line segment Ab, and in the equilibrium the agents are partners in both ventures

$$\bar{\theta}^1 = (2/3, \, 1/3), \quad \bar{\theta}^2 = (1/3, \, 2/3)$$

The (normalized) gradients of the two agents coincide and lie in the normal cones to the two production sets at A and b, so that the equilibrium is not only constrained efficient, but also Pareto optimal.[5] □

Productive Inefficiency

If $(\bar{x}, \bar{y})$ is a Pareto optimal allocation then

(a) $\bar{x}$ is *distribution-efficient*; this means that there does not exist a vector $x = (x^1, \ldots, x^I) \in \mathbb{R}_+^{(S+1)I}$ of consumption streams for the agents which is feasible

$$\sum_{i=1}^{I} (x^i - \omega^i) = \sum_{k=1}^{K} \bar{y}^k$$

such that every agent is at least as well off and at least one agent is strictly better off i.e. $u(x) > u(\bar{x})$;

(b) $\bar{y}$ is *production-efficient*; this means that there does not exist an alternative production plan $y = (y^1, \ldots, y^k) \in \prod_{k=1}^{K} Y^k$ which either uses less total input, or produces more total output in some state, or both, i.e. such that $\sum_{k=1}^{K} y^k > \sum_{k=1}^{K} \bar{y}^k$.

If $(\bar{x}, \bar{y})$ is constrained Pareto optimal, then $\bar{x}$ is distribution-efficient given the constraints on the way agents can obtain their income: in this section the constraints are

$$x_{\mathbf{1}}^i - \omega_{\mathbf{1}}^i \in \langle R \rangle + \langle \bar{y}_{\mathbf{1}} \rangle_+, \quad i = 1, \ldots, I$$

since agents obtain their net income from their bond holdings and their partnership shares. However $\bar{y}$ is not necessarily production-efficient as the following example shows.

---

[5]The same comment as in the previous footnote applies to the Pareto optimality of (b, A): the sum of the preferred sets of the two agents at D and F and the aggregate production set $Y^1 + Y^2$ are separated by the hyperplane (line) passing through G defined by the common normalized gradient of the two agents.

31.12 Example: The preferences and endowments are the same as in Example 31.10. The technologies of the two firms are changed so that for any level of input at date 0, firm 1 produces more output at date 1 than firm 2. In Figure 31.5 the segment ab (AB) is the date 1 frontier of firm 1(2) from one unit of input at date 0. (A, b) is a partnership equilibrium. Since $\bar{y}_1^1 = b$, $\bar{y}_1^2 = A$, the budget line of each agent is the segment Ab. Agent 1 chooses the optimal point b, agent 2 the optimal point A: thus agent 1(2) is the sole owner of venture 1(2). Given this ownership structure, the optimal production plan of venture 1 is at b, and that of venture 2 is at A.

The efficient production plans are obtained by using the two units of input available at date 0 in firm 1: this gives the frontier $a'b'$ in Figure 31.5. When all production is done by venture 1, then the two agents must be partners: their date 1 consumption vectors must thus be collinear. However, there is no date 1 output vector on the segment $a'b'$, which after being shared by the two agents, increases their utilities (relative to the utility at b (A) respectively). Any output on the segment $a'D$ (Fb') makes agent 1(2) worse off, even if he is given all the output. Furthermore, no output on the segment DF can be shared in a way that improves the utility of both agents. For a point like C, agent 1 requires at least OC', leaving the amount $C'C$ which is less than the amount OC'' required to improve the utility of agent 2.

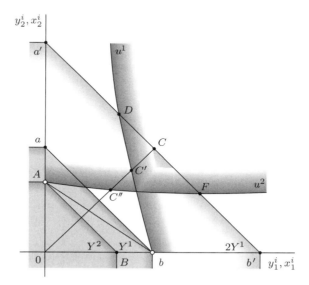

Figure 31.5 (A, b) is a partnership equilibrium which is constrained efficient but is not production-efficient.

In this example, if a planner were to simultaneously choose the partnership shares and production plans, he would face a trade-off between productive efficiency and spanning. If only the productive venture is used, then two agents with quite different needs will have to share the common income stream. On the other hand, if the less efficient firm is also used then there is greater (in fact, complete) spanning. This permits the two agents to undertake distinct projects better suited to their needs. □

Indeterminacy of Financial Policies

So far it has been assumed that the date 0 input of a venture is paid for by its partners. While the partners can borrow and lend on their personal accounts, the venture has not been permitted, as a separate legal entity, to borrow on its own account. If the partners are fully liable for the debts of the venture (so that date 1 dividends may be negative), then permitting the venture access to the bond markets on its own account does not affect the allocation (consumption and production) in a partnership equilibrium. The analysis amounts to distinguishing between the financial accounts of partners in their activity as producers and their private financial accounts as consumers. A similar analysis has already been carried out in the previous section for the case of entrepreneurial firms: this analysis extends in a straightforward way to the case of partnerships. From the point of view of the partners, the present value of the venture's profit is independent of its financial policy. Furthermore if we assume that partners as individuals have access to the same financial opportunities as the ventures in which they participate, then whatever packaging of income streams is achieved by the financial policy of a venture can always be undone by individuals on their private accounts. The proof that the financial policies of ventures are indeterminate and without consequence for the real equilibrium allocation is thus identical to that for Proposition 30.7.

As mentioned earlier, the status of *limited liability* was introduced for partnerships so as to encourage investment in risky capital projects by limiting the risk incurred by partners. Introducing limited liability into the above model of partnerships limits the liability of partners to their date 0 contribution, so that the date 1 dividends that they receive from the venture are non-negative. As a result, if part of the date 0 input has been financed by debt, then the venture may not fully reimburse its debt to the bond holders at date 1. The debt of a venture then becomes a personalized security whose date 1 returns and hence price are influenced by the financial policy chosen by the venture. The formal analysis of the choice of an optimal financial policy then presents some new difficulties: since these difficulties are similar to those encountered in determining the optimal production and financial policy of a corporation, the discussion of limited liability and bankruptcy is postponed to the next section.

32.   CORPORATIONS

Consider an economy in which, with the passage of time, some firms which perhaps began as individually owned firms or as partnerships, have reached the corporate stage where their ownership shares are traded on a stock market. Although in a modern economy, the three types of firms—sole proprietorships, partnerships, and corporations—co-exist, it simplifies the analysis to study a model with only one type of firm at a time. This simplification, adopted in the two previous sections, will be retained here in order to focus attention on the new elements introduced by corporations.[1]

An investment in a corporation differs from that in a partnership in that agents who are shareholders in a firm at one point in time can at a later date sell their equity holdings at the current market price. As a result, the shareholders who at an initial date influence the choice of an investment plan for the firm may not be the agents who at a later date obtain the payoff on the firm's investment in the form of dividends, since they may decide to sell their shares in the intervening period. Their concern is therefore to assess how the market price of the firm's equity depends on its investment and financing decisions. Many of the conceptual difficulties that arise in modelling the corporation come from the problem of finding a satisfactory way of explaining how agents perceive the relation between a firm's market value and its investment and financing decisions.

The story begins with K corporations which have already been formed, each being owned by a group of shareholders. The initial ownership of the corporations is not explained and is taken as exogenously given. On the production side, each corporation is characterized by a set Y^k satisfying Assumption $\mathcal{T}$ in Section 29. In contrast to the previous section, where the initial phase of the formation of partnerships was studied under the assumption of constant returns, in this section it is natural to assume that some capital has already been invested in the firms so that their production sets exhibit decreasing returns to scale. The decision-making process of the firm is modelled in a stylized and perhaps overly simplified way: in particular the agency problem arising from the separation between ownership and control, which is typical of a modern corporation, is ignored. The original shareholders make the production and financing decisions for the firm, and these decisions are implemented by a salaried manager. As an initial step for simplifying the description of the decision-making process, it is assumed that the production plan is financed

---

[1] A corporation is taken to be a firm whose equity contracts are publicly traded on an exchange. The theory of *closely-held* corporations whose shares can only be transferred with the collective consent of all shareholders is closer in spirit to the theory of partnerships and is not studied here.

by the original shareholders; later in the section it is shown how the financial decisions can be incorporated into the analysis.

In addition to the bond market, which was considered in the previous sections, there is a stock market on which the equity contracts for the K corporations are traded. Let $\delta^i = (\delta^i_1, \ldots, \delta^i_K)$ denote the vector of initial ownership shares of agent i in the K firms: the ownership shares $\delta = (\delta^1, \ldots, \delta^I)$ satisfy

$$\delta^i \in \mathbb{R}^K_+, \quad i = 1, \ldots, I \quad \text{and} \quad \sum_{i=1}^I \delta^i_k = 1, \quad k = 1, \ldots, K$$

Since all transactions on the financial markets are taken to be costless, it may be assumed that agent i sells his portfolio $\delta^i = (\delta^i_1, \ldots, \delta^i_K)$ of initial ownership shares and purchases the new portfolio $\theta^i = (\theta^i_1, \ldots, \theta^i_K)$. These new portfolios satisfy

$$\theta^i \in \mathbb{R}^K, \quad i = 1, \ldots, I$$

so that agents can either purchase ($\theta^i_k > 0$) or short sell ($\theta^i_k < 0$) the shares of each corporation ($k = 1, \ldots, K$). As before, $z^i = (z^i_1, \ldots, z^i_J) \in \mathbb{R}^J$ denotes agent i's portfolio of the J bonds. The vector of prices of the J bonds and the K equity contracts is denoted by

$$q = (q', q'') = (q'_1, \ldots, q'_J, q''_1, \ldots, q''_K)$$

As an initial shareholder of firm k, agent i contributes $y^k_0 \delta^i_k$ as his share of the input costs of firm k. The sale of his initial share δ^i_k earns him the income $q''_k \delta^i_k$, while the purchase of the new share θ^i_k involves the cost $q''_k \theta^i_k$. The new share θ^i_k entitles agent i to the income stream $y^k_1 \theta^i_k = (y^k_1 \theta^i_k, \ldots, y^k_S \theta^i_k)$ at date 1. Agent i's transactions on the financial markets thus generate the income

$$-\sum_{j=1}^J q'_j z^i_j + \sum_{k=1}^K (y^k_0 + q''_k)\delta^i_k - \sum_{k=1}^K q''_k \theta^i_k = -q'z^i + (y_0 + q'')\delta^i - q''\theta^i$$

at date 0, and the income stream

$$\sum_{j=1}^J R^j_s z^i_j + \sum_{k=1}^K y^k_s \theta^i_k = R_s z^i + y_s \theta^i, \quad s = 1, \ldots, S$$

at date 1. If the *matrix of financial market payoffs* is defined by

$$W(q, R, y) = \begin{bmatrix} -q' & -q'' \\ R & y_1 \end{bmatrix} = \begin{bmatrix} -q'_1 & \cdots & -q'_J & -q''_1 & \cdots & -q''_K \\ R^1_1 & \cdots & R^J_1 & y^1_1 & \cdots & y^K_1 \\ \vdots & \ddots & \vdots & \vdots & \ddots & \vdots \\ R^1_S & \cdots & R^J_S & y^1_S & \cdots & y^K_S \end{bmatrix} \tag{1}$$

and if $e^0 = (1, 0, \ldots, 0) \in \mathbb{R}^{S+1}$, then the budget set of agent i can be written as

$$
\mathbb{B}(q, \omega^i, \delta^i, R, y) = \left\{ x^i \in \mathbb{R}^{S+1}_+ \; \middle| \; \begin{array}{l} x^i - \omega^i = (y_0 + q'')\delta^i e^0 + W \begin{bmatrix} z^i \\ \theta^i \end{bmatrix} \\ (z^i, \theta^i) \in \mathbb{R}^J \times \mathbb{R}^K \end{array} \right\} \quad (2)
$$

Imagine now that the original shareholders $I_k = \{i \mid \delta^i_k > 0\}$ of firm k meet to decide on its production plan y^k, taking the production plans $y^{-k} = (y^{k'}, k' \neq k)$ of all other firms as given. Each shareholder will be affected by the choice of a production plan y^k in two ways. First, as an original shareholder (δ^i_k) of firm k the agent earns the net income at date 0

$$
(y^k_0 + q''_k)\delta^i_k \quad (3)
$$

Second, as a new shareholder (θ^i_k) the agent has access to the income stream across the $S + 1$ states

$$
\begin{bmatrix} -q''_k \\ y^k_1 \end{bmatrix} \theta^i_k \quad (4)
$$

which is simply the multiple θ^i_k of the $(J + k)^{\text{th}}$ column of the payoff matrix W. In assessing (3), agent i is interested in the way that the choice of the firm's production plan affects its (net) *market value*; in assessing (4), the agent is concerned with the way the firm's production plan influences the terms of the equity contract which he is trading on the stock market—namely the *spanning services* of the firm's equity contract. *The traditional arguments which lead to a well-defined objective function for the firm are based on the idea that the market value term* (3) *dominates the spanning services term* (4). Roughly speaking these arguments are of three types.

 (i) If the terms θ^i_k are very small because there are many firms, and agents hold well-diversified equity portfolios, and if the initial shareholdings δ^i_k (exogenously given) are assumed to be non-negligible, then the market value term (3) dominates. This argument is somewhat ad-hoc since the θ^i_k of to-day will be the δ^i_k of tomorrow: thus if the θ^i_k are negligible then the δ^i_k should also be negligible.

 (ii) If firms are grouped into industries and if firms within each industry have similar production sets, then changes in the production plan of a particular firm, while altering the spanning services offered by its equity contract, will not (significantly) affect the spanning services offered by the industry to which it belongs and hence will not significantly affect the market subspace $\langle W \rangle$. Agents can always adapt their equity portfolio within the industry to accommodate changes in the spanning services offered by a particular firm. The idea that a particular firm cannot create new spanning opportunities by altering its production plan is formalized later in this section using the concept of *partial spanning*.

(iii) The third argument is based on an assumption about the way each agent perceives the relation between the date 1 income stream y_1^k generated by a firm's equity contract and its market price q_k''. If each agent perceives that the benefit accruing from the dividend stream y_1^k (for any choice of y_1^k) is always exactly compensated by the cost q_k'' of the equity contract, then the spanning term (4) does not affect the agent's choice among production plans.

On the basis of any one of these arguments, it can be assumed that the shareholders of firm k have the objective of maximizing the (net) market value $y_0^k + q_k''$ of the firm when deciding on its production plan. The market value of each firm depends however not only on its own production plan (y^k) but also on the production plans $y^{-k} = (y^{k'},\ k' \neq k)$ of all other firms. The relation between the vector of production plans $y = (y^1, \dots, y^K)$ and the vector of market values $q'' = (q_1'', \dots, q_K'')$ is obtained by solving for an equilibrium of the exchange economy $\mathscr{E}(u, \omega, \delta, R, y)$ *with fixed production plans* y and running through all possible plans $y \in \prod_{k=1}^{K} Y^k$. To exhibit clearly the exchange economy induced by each choice $y = (y^1, \dots, y^K)$ of production plans by the firms, let us introduce the *virtual endowments* $\underset{\sim}{\omega} = (\underset{\sim}{\omega}^1, \dots, \underset{\sim}{\omega}^I)$ defined by

$$\underset{\sim}{\omega}^i = \omega^i + \sum_{k=1}^{K} \delta_k^i y^k, \quad i = 1, \dots, I \tag{5}$$

and the net portfolio trades $z^i \in \mathbb{R}^{J+K}$ (for $i = 1, \dots, I$)

$$z_j^i = z_j^i, \quad j = 1, \dots, J, \quad z_{J+k}^i = \theta_k^i - \delta_k^i, \quad k = 1, \dots, K. \tag{6}$$

Then the budget set (2) of agent i can be written in the standard form for an exchange economy (equation (3) in section 8)

$$\mathbb{B}(q, \underset{\sim}{\omega}^i, R, y) = \left\{ x^i \in \mathbb{R}_+^{S+1} \mid x^i - \underset{\sim}{\omega}^i = W z^i, \quad z^i \in \mathbb{R}^{J+K} \right\} \tag{7}$$

where $W = W(q, R, y)$ is defined by (1). This leads naturally to the following concept of a stock market equilibrium with fixed production plans.

32.1 Definition: A *stock market equilibrium* for the economy $\mathscr{E}(u, \omega, \delta, R, y)$ *with fixed production plans* $y \in \prod_{k=1}^{K} Y^k$ is an equilibrium of the induced exchange economy $\mathscr{E}(u, \underset{\sim}{\omega}, R, y)$, namely a pair $((\bar{x}, \bar{z}), \bar{q}) \in \mathbb{R}_+^{(S+1)I} \times \mathbb{R}^{(J+K)I} \times \mathbb{R}^{J+K}$ such that

(i) $(\bar{x}^i; \bar{z}^i) \in \arg \max \left\{ u^i(x^i) \mid (x^i; z^i) \in \mathbb{B}(\bar{q}, \underset{\sim}{\omega}^i, R, y) \right\}, i = 1, \dots, I$

(ii) $\sum_{i=1}^{I} \bar{z}^i = 0$

where $(\underset{\sim}{\omega}, \bar{z}, \mathbb{B})$ are defined by (5)–(7).

Non-competitive approach

While this definition suggests a non-competitive approach to a theory of market-value maximization, such an approach encounters a number of difficulties. For suppose that the agents understand the correspondence

$$\bar{q}''(\ ) : Y^1 \times \cdots \times Y^K \longrightarrow \mathbb{R}^K$$

which assigns to each vector of production plans $y = (y^1, \ldots, y^K)$ the possible equilibrium equity prices $\bar{q}''(y)$. If this correspondence is not single-valued (i.e. if there are multiple equilibria) and if the number of equilibria changes as the production plans y are changed, then any selection of the equilibrium correspondence will be discontinuous. Even if this problem can be overcome (by imposing conditions which guarantee *uniqueness* of the equilibrium—although no such conditions are currently known when markets are incomplete), then the natural approach is to assume that the shareholders of each firm k seek the production plan $\bar{y}^k$ which maximizes the value of the kth firm given the production plans $\bar{y}^{-k}$ of all other firms, namely

$$\bar{y}^k = \arg\max\left\{ y_0^k + \bar{q}_k''(y^k, \bar{y}^{-k}) \mid y^k \in Y^k \right\}$$

This approach leads to a consistent concept of equilibrium. However such an equilibrium may not exist. Since the market value function $y^k \longmapsto \bar{q}_k''(y^k, \bar{y}^{-k})$ has no reason to be quasi-concave, the firm's reaction function may be discontinuous so that standard fixed-point theorems are not applicable: these difficulties are of course common to all non-competitive models of general equilibrium. Since in addition to these technical difficulties, the assumption that agents know the market value correspondence $\bar{q}''(\cdot)$ seems much too demanding, it is natural to begin by formulating a consistent competitive approach to market-value maximization.

Competitive Approach

What do we mean by a competitive approach to the valuation of income streams? An income stream (for example the dividend stream $y_1^k = (y_1^k, \ldots, y_S^k)$ offered by the equity contract of firm k) is a bundle of goods—actually a bundle of the single good (income) across the S states at date 1. Two ideas underlie the competitive pricing of a bundle of goods (an income stream):

  (i) the price of a bundle of goods is the sum of the prices of its components
  (ii) the unit price of each component is independent of the number of units of the good (income) purchased or sold.

We say that agents make valuations of date 1 income streams with *competitive expectations* if they expect the price q_k'' of an income stream $y_1^k = (y_1^k, \ldots, y_S^k)$ (the market value of firm k's equity contract) to be

$$q_k'' = \sum_{s=1}^{S} \pi_s y_s^k \tag{8}$$

where π_s is the price of income in state s. When (8) is satisfied, agents expect the market value of the kth firm to be a linear function of its date 1 dividend stream, so that property (i) is satisfied. In (8) it is assumed that the state price π_s is uninfluenced by the magnitude of y_s^k, so that property (ii) is satisfied. Thus the competitive assumption implies that agents do not take into account the fact that changes in the firm's production plan could have an impact on the state prices π_s.

In a model with financial markets, the equilibrium prices are the prices of the financial contracts: the state prices, whose existence is implied by the absence of arbitrage, are implicit in the security prices, but are not directly observable. When valuing income streams using (8), agents must use a no-arbitrage vector of state prices, so that the valuation of any income stream in the marketed subspace coincides with its observed price.

Complete Markets

If the financial markets are complete (rank $[\, R \; y_1 \,] = S$), then by absence of arbitrage

$$\pi_1 [\, R \; y_1 \,] = q \tag{9}$$

there is a unique (normalized) vector of state prices $\pi = (1, \pi_1, \ldots, \pi_S)$ consistent with an observed vector of security prices q. In this case all agents necessarily use the same vector of state prices to evaluate the present value of a production plan, so that they all agree on the production plan which maximizes the market value of a firm. This leads to the following definition of an equilibrium.

32.2 Definition: A pair $((\bar{x}, \bar{z}, \bar{y}), \bar{q})$ with rank $[\, R \; \bar{y}_1 \,] = S$ is a *stock market equilibrium* for the economy $\mathscr{E}(u, \omega, \delta, R, Y)$ in which markets are complete, if $((\bar{x}, \bar{z}), \bar{q})$ is a stock market equilibrium with fixed production plans $\bar{y}$ and

$$\text{(iii)} \quad \bar{y}^k \in \arg\max \left\{ \bar{\pi} y^k \mid y^k \in Y^k \right\}, \quad k = 1, \ldots, K$$

where $\bar{\pi}$ is the unique (up to normalization) solution of the no-arbitrage equation $\pi W(\bar{q}, R, \bar{y}) = 0$.

The concept of a contingent market equilibrium for the production econ-
omy $\mathscr{E}(u, \omega, \delta, Y)$ was defined in Section 29. Using the transformation to a
no-arbitrage equilibrium, introduced in Section 10, it is easy to check that if
$((\bar{x}, \bar{z}, \bar{y}), \bar{q})$ is a stock market equilibrium for the economy $\mathscr{E}(u, \omega, \delta, R, Y)$,
with rank $[\, R \, \bar{y}_1 \,] = S$, then $((\bar{x}, \bar{y}), \bar{\pi})$ is a contingent market equilibrium for
the production economy $\mathscr{E}(u, \omega, \delta, Y)$. The converse is only true for those contingent market equilibria satisfying the condition rank $[\, R \, \bar{y}_1 \,] = S$.

Partial Spanning

If markets are incomplete the situation is more complicated, for in this case
there is a whole continuum of state price vectors which are solutions of (9)
for a given (no-arbitrage) security price q. As a result when agents use (8) to
value income streams, different agents may choose different state price vectors
and hence may arrive at different estimates of the market value of the firm. In
such circumstances the original shareholders of firm k may not agree on the
production plan which is optimal for the firm.

Such divergences of opinion are however restricted to production plans which
lie outside the span of the marketed securities $\langle [\, R \, \bar{y}_1 \,] \rangle$. For if a date 1 production plan y_1^k is a linear combination of the basic marketed securities, then its
market value under (8) is the corresponding linear combination of the prices
of the basic securities, regardless of the state-price vector π used. In the language of Chapter 3, all (normalized) no-arbitrage state-price vectors project
onto the same vector in the marketed subspace, so that an income stream lying
in the marketed subspace has the same value (using (8)) for all no-arbitrage
state-price vectors. Thus if the kth firm cannot generate any date 1 income
stream which lies outside the span of the marketed securities $\langle [\, R \, \bar{y}_1 \,] \rangle$, then
the original shareholders will (as in the case of complete markets) agree on the
production plan which maximizes the firm's market value.

Implicit in much of the finance literature is the idea that, because firms
within a given industry have similar technologies and are exposed to similar
exogenous shocks, their profit (income) streams are similar. In such a setting
an individual firm cannot offer an income stream that is significantly different
from the array of income streams already offered by the market. A particularly
simple way of formalizing this idea is to assume that the income streams (production sets) available to all firms in the economy lie in a common subspace
Z of $\mathbb{R}^{S+1}$ with dim $Z \leq K \leq S$.

Assumption $\mathscr{P}.\mathscr{S}$ (Partial Spanning): There is a linear subspace $Z \subset \mathbb{R}^{S+1}$
whose dimension is at most K, such that $Y^k \subset Z$, $k = 1, \ldots, K$.

Under this assumption, provided that the production plans $(\bar{y}^1, \ldots, \bar{y}^K)$ of the firms span Z, the original shareholders of each firm k will agree on the production plan which maximizes its market value. This leads to the following concept of equilibrium.

32.3 Definition: Let the production economy $\mathscr{E}(u, \omega, \delta, R, Y)$ satisfy the assumption of partial spanning $(\mathscr{P}\mathscr{S})$. A pair $((\bar{x}, \bar{z}, \bar{y}), \bar{q})$ with rank $[\bar{y}] = \dim Z$ is a *stock market equilibrium* if $((\bar{x}, \bar{z}), \bar{q})$ is a stock market equilibrium with fixed production plans $\bar{y}$, and

(iii) $\bar{y}^k \in \arg\max\left\{\pi y^k \mid y^k \in Y^k\right\}, \quad k = 1, \ldots, K$

where π is any solution of the no-arbitrage equation $\pi W(\bar{q}, R, \bar{y}) = 0$.

REMARK. Recall the pricing function on the marketed subspace

$$c_q : \langle V \rangle \longrightarrow \mathbb{R}$$

defined by equation (15) in Section 15. Here $V = [R\, y_1]$ and $q = (q', q'')$. Thus, at an equilibrium, for any income stream $\tau \in \langle [R\, \bar{y}_1] \rangle$

$$\text{if } \tau = \sum_{j=1}^{J} \alpha_j R^j + \sum_{k=1}^{K} \beta_k \bar{y}_1^k \quad \text{then} \quad c_{\bar{q}}(\tau) = \sum_{j=1}^{J} \alpha_j \bar{q}_j' + \sum_{k=1}^{K} \beta_k \bar{q}_k''.$$

With this notation, the profit-maximizing criterion in (iii) of Definitions 32.2 and 32.3 can be written as

(iii)′ $\bar{y}^k \in \arg\max\left\{y_0^k + c_{\bar{q}}(y_1^k) \mid y^k \in Y^k\right\}, \quad k = 1, \ldots, K$

Thus in the two cases just considered (complete markets and partial spanning) agents do not need to explicitly calculate state prices in order to evaluate the market value of alternative production plans: they simply use the prices of the $J + K$ basic securities, which are directly observable, and price by linearity.

Incomplete Markets

In situations where firms face investment opportunities which are quite different from those currently offered by the market—these opportunities may involve creating new goods or services or some other form of innovation—the prices of existing securities will not provide a useful guide to the shareholders in their attempt to evaluate the best investment opportunity or, more accurately, the investment opportunity which they think the market will value most highly.

If shareholders are to use the competitive formula (8) to value income streams which lie outside the marketed subspace, then they must choose a state-price vector which is compatible with the observed prices of the marketed securities. *Which state-price vector is it most reasonable for agent i to use?* If the agent is purchasing the income stream y_1^k, then it is reasonable for him to use his own present-value vector $\bar{\pi}_1^i$ in assessing its value. But if, as an original shareholder, he is selling the income stream y_1^k, then the information he would really like to have is what this income stream is worth to potential buyers. However it is not in the spirit of a competitive analysis—which limits the information of an agent to the signals (prices) observable in the markets—to assume that an agent knows the present-value vectors of other agents. Thus to retain the competitive nature of the model we assume that an agent does not have access to information on the present-value vectors of other agents and, in his role as a seller, uses his own state price vector in assessing the value of an income stream. This is formalized in the following assumption.

Assumption $\mathscr{C}$ (Competitive Price Perceptions): If $((\bar{x}, \bar{z}), \bar{q})$ is an equilibrium with fixed production plans $\bar{y}$, then agent i $(i = 1, \dots, I)$ expects the price of a date 1 income stream τ to be $c_{\bar{q}}^i(\tau) = \sum_{s=1}^{S} \pi_s^i(\bar{x}^i)\tau_s$.

In contrast to the pricing function $c_{\bar{q}}$ which is defined only for income streams lying in the marketed subspace, the pricing functions $c_{\bar{q}}^i : \mathbb{R}^S \longrightarrow \mathbb{R}$ are defined for all date 1 income streams. The expectations of agents can only differ for income streams lying outside the marketed subspace since

$$c_{\bar{q}}^i(\tau) = c_{\bar{q}}(\tau), \quad \forall \tau \in \langle [\, R\, \bar{y}_1\,] \rangle, \quad i = 1, \dots, I$$

For an agent with competitive price perceptions, the production plan $\bar{y}^k$ of firm k is optimal if and only if

$$\bar{y}^k \in \arg\max \left\{ \sum_{s=0}^{S} \pi_s^i(\bar{x}^i) y_s^k \;\middle|\; y^k \in Y^k \right\}$$

But this is exactly the criterion (1) in Section 31: *under Assumption $\mathscr{C}$, the problem of finding a production plan which is in the best interest of the original shareholders is formally equivalent to the problem of finding a production plan which is in the best interest of a group of partners.* This problem was studied in Section 31. As explained in that section, if shareholders use side payments to reach unanimity, then a determinate concept of equilibrium is obtained. It is convenient to revert to the original form (z^i, θ^i) of writing the agents' trades rather than the net trade form adopted in Definitions 32.2 and 32.3. Let $I_k = \{ i \mid \delta_k^i > 0 \}$ denote the original shareholders of firm k.

32.4 Definition: Let $\mathscr{E}(u,\omega,\delta,R,Y)$ be an economy with K corporations whose initial ownership is divided among the I agents according to the ownership shares δ. A (reduced form) *stock market equilibrium* for $\mathscr{E}(u,\omega,\delta,R,Y)$ (derived from the Pareto criterion with side payments) is a pair consisting of actions and prices $\big((\bar{x},\bar{z},\bar{\theta},\bar{y}),\bar{q}\big) \in \mathbb{R}_{+}^{(S+1)I} \times \mathbb{R}^{JI} \times \mathbb{R}^{KI} \times \mathbb{R}^{(S+1)K} \times \mathbb{R}^{J+K}$ such that

(i) $(\bar{x}^i; \bar{z}^i, \bar{\theta}^i) \in \arg\max \big\{ u^i(x^i) \,\big|\, (x^i; z^i, \theta^i) \in \mathbb{B}(\bar{q}, \omega^i, \delta^i, R, \bar{y}) \big\}$, $i = 1,\dots,I$

(ii) $\sum_{i=1}^{I} \bar{z}^i = 0$ (ii)' $\sum_{i=1}^{I} \bar{\theta}^i_k = 1$, $k = 1,\dots,K$

(iii) $\bar{y}^k \in \arg\max \Big\{ \sum_{i\in I_k} \delta^i_k \pi^i(\bar{x}^i) y^k \,\Big|\, y^k \in Y^k \Big\}$, $k = 1,\dots,K$

In the two cases studied earlier, where the financial markets are complete or the production sets satisfy the condition of partial spanning, the present values $\pi^i(\bar{x}^i) y^k$ of all agents coincide for all production plans $y^k \in Y^k$, and the equilibrium just defined coincides with that in Definitions 32.2 and 32.3. In these two cases there is no need for Assumption $\mathscr{C}$—namely an assumption on the way agents form price expectations for income streams which are *not* in the marketed subspace. Assumption $\mathscr{C}$ is necessary only when corporations need to be able to evaluate the profitability of production plans which are not priced by the market at the equilibrium: it permits each corporation to check that the plan which it has chosen is in fact optimal—that is, it yields a higher profit than any other production plan which it could have chosen ($y^k \in Y^k$) which *differs* from those currently being produced in the economy (i.e. which cannot be expressed as a linear combination of the currently chosen equilibrium production plans of all firms). Assumption $\mathscr{C}$ respects the two ideas that underlie competitive pricing: first, that pricing is a linear functional (as discussed in conjunction with equation (8)); second, that it does not require more information on the part of agents than is contained in the knowledge of the equilibrium prices and their own characteristics. Furthermore it is rational or self-fulfilling, since the equilibrium price of any marketed income stream (in particular the market value of corporation k) coincides with the price expected by each agent (in particular by the initial shareholders of corporation k).

It can be shown that under Assumptions ($\mathscr{U}$, $\mathscr{T}'$), a stock market equilibrium exists for most parameters (u,ω,δ,R,Y) characterizing the economy. Existence is not guaranteed for all parameter values, since the rank of the date 1 payoff matrix $[\,R\,y_1\,]$ is endogenous and depends on the date 1 production plans y_1 chosen by the firms. Since changes in the firms' plans y_1 can change the rank of the payoff matrix, agents' demands for securities can exhibit discontinuities which lead to non-existence of an equilibrium as in the example of Section 24. The techniques for proving the generic existence of an equilibrium when such discontinuities can arise are studied in Volume 2.

In deriving the objective function (iii) for each firm, it was assumed that the original shareholders of a firm do not take into account their interests as new shareholders as reflected in the spanning services term (4): *to terms of first order, Assumption $\mathscr{C}$ justifies neglecting this term.* This can be shown as follows. Let $\big((\bar{x}, \bar{z}, \bar{\theta}, \bar{y}), \bar{q}\big)$ be a stock market equilibrium. Consider agent i's maximum problem. We want to calculate the anticipated change in utility for agent i arising from a small change in the firms' production plans $\bar{y} \longrightarrow \bar{y} + dy$. Such a change will (under Assumption $\mathscr{C}$) induce an anticipated change $\bar{q} \longrightarrow \bar{q} + dq$ in the agent's perception of the security prices (where $dq = (dq', dq'')$)

$$dq' = 0, \quad dq'' = \sum_{s=1}^{S} \pi_s^i(\bar{x}^i) dy_s$$

Under Assumption $\mathscr{U}$, if rank $[\, R \ \bar{y}_1 \,] = J + K$, the agent's optimal portfolio $(\tilde{z}^i(q, y), \tilde{\theta}^i(q, y))$ is a smooth function of (q, y) in a neighborhood of $(\bar{q}, \bar{y})$ (see Lemma 11.5). Let $\tilde{u}^i(y)$ denote the agent's anticipated utility as a function of y (in a neighborhood of $\bar{y}$). Then

$$\tilde{u}^i(y) = u^i(\omega_0^i + (y_0 + q'')\delta^i - q'\tilde{z}^i - q''\tilde{\theta}^i, \omega_1^i + R\tilde{z}^i + y_1\tilde{\theta}^i)$$

so that

$$\begin{aligned} d\tilde{u}^i = \lambda_0^i(\bar{x}^i)\Big(& (dy_0 + dq'')\delta^i - \bar{q}'d\tilde{z}^i - dq''\tilde{\theta}^i - \bar{q}''d\tilde{\theta}^i \\ & + \pi_1^i(\bar{x}^i)(Rd\tilde{z}^i + dy_1\tilde{\theta}^i + \bar{y}_1 d\tilde{\theta}^i)\Big) \end{aligned}$$

By the agent's first-order conditions for a maximum

$$-\bar{q}' + \pi_1^i(\bar{x}^i)R = 0, \quad -\bar{q}'' + \pi_1^i(\bar{x}^i)\bar{y}_1 = 0$$

and by Assumption $\mathscr{C}$,

$$-dq'' + \pi_1^i(\bar{x}^i)dy_1 = 0$$

so that

$$d\tilde{u}^i = \lambda_0^i(\bar{x}^i)\,(dy_0 + dq'')\,\delta^i$$

Thus agent i only perceives the impact of the change in the net market-value term $(y_0 + q'')\delta^i$ when assessing the effect of a marginal change in the firms' production plans dy.

This proof formalizes the third argument that was presented at the beginning of this section for justifying the criterion of market-value maximization: agents who anticipate being future shareholders do not expect to obtain a gain by changing the dividend stream on an equity contract which they have to buy, since the change in its price is expected to precisely match the changed value of its dividend stream.

Evaluation of Risks by Corporations

Equity contracts constitute one of the most important instruments for sharing the risks arising from the unavoidable fluctuations in productive activity in a modern economy. How does the presence of such contracts influence the way corporations evaluate risks and choose production plans in a stock market equilibrium? This question is most conveniently analyzed under the assumption that there is an objective probability $\rho = (\rho_1, \dots, \rho_S)$ for the states and that the riskless bond is one of the traded securities, so that the rate of interest is well-defined. Then an analysis similar to that for entrepreneurial firms (leading to formula (32) in Section 30) implies that the equilibrium production plan $\bar{y}^k$ of corporation k satisfies

$$\bar{y}^k \in \arg\max_{y^k \in Y^k} \left\{ y_0^k + \frac{E(y_1^k)}{1 + \bar{r}} + \mathrm{cov}(\widetilde{\gamma}, y_V^k) + \mathrm{cov}\left(\sum_{i \in I_k} \delta_k^i \check{\pi}_1^{\rho,i}, \check{y}_1^k \right) \right\} \qquad (10)$$

where $\widetilde{\gamma}$ is the risk pricing component of the ideal security in the marketed subspace $\langle V \rangle = \langle [\, R \ \bar{y}_1 \,] \rangle$ and $\check{\pi}_1^{\rho,i}$ are the idiosyncratic components of the present-value vectors of the shareholders ($\check{\pi}_1^{\rho,i} \in \langle V \rangle^{\perp}$, $i \in I_k$). Each project y^k is decomposed into the date 0 investment y_0^k, the component of the date 1 returns which lie in the marketed subspace y_V^k, and the idiosyncratic returns $\check{y}_1^k$ (i.e. $y_1^k = y_V^k + \check{y}_1^k$ where $y_V^k \in \langle V \rangle$ and $\check{y}_1^k \in \langle V \rangle^{\perp}$).

In a production economy, risks are of two kinds: those which come from the production sector, arising from fluctuations in the outputs (y^k) of the K corporations, and those which come from the consumption sector and are modelled here by the fluctuations in the agents' initial endowments (ω^i). When the production plans of the firms are taken to be those at equilibrium, then the *individual risks* born by agents are given by their virtual endowments

$$\underset{\sim}{\omega}^i = \omega^i + \sum_{k=1}^{K} \delta_k^i \bar{y}^k, \quad i = 1, \dots, I$$

and the aggregate or economy-wide risk is the *equilibrium aggregate output*

$$\bar{w} = \sum_{i=1}^{I} \underset{\sim}{\omega}^i = \sum_{i=1}^{I} \omega^i + \sum_{k=1}^{K} \bar{y}^k$$

In an economy in which all production is undertaken by corporations whose equity contracts are traded on financial markets, the risks arising from productive activity can be shared in the markets ($\sum_{k=1}^{K} \delta_k^i \bar{y}_1^k \in \langle \bar{y}_1 \rangle$, $i = 1, \dots, I$). If in addition the remaining financial markets, modelled by the matrix of returns

R, are well-adapted to sharing the consumers' risks[2] ($\omega_\mathbf{1}^i \in \langle R \rangle$, $i = 1, \ldots, I$), then all the risks involved in the agent's virtual endowments can be shared in the markets ($\omega_\mathbf{1}^i \in \langle V \rangle, i = 1, \ldots, I$). If some restrictions are placed on agents' preferences—VNM separability if the markets are complete and LRT or mean-variance if the markets are incomplete—then, as shown in Chapter 3, the equilibrium is Pareto optimal ($\check{\pi}_\mathbf{1}^{\rho,i} = 0$, $i = 1, \ldots I$) and the ideal security $\bar{\gamma}$, which coincides with the (date 1) present-value vector of the representative agent ($\bar{\gamma} = \pi_\mathbf{1}^*$), can be expressed as a decreasing function of equilibrium aggregate output

$$\bar{\gamma}_s = \varphi(\bar{w}_s), \quad s = 1, \ldots, S$$

In the two cases (LRT with common marginal risk tolerance or complete markets and VNM) where the representative agent's utility function is VNM additively separable ($u^* \longleftrightarrow (v_0^*, v_1^*)$), the function φ is given by $\varphi(\bar{w}_s) = v_1^{*\prime}(\bar{w}_s)/v_0^{*\prime}(\bar{w}_0)$. Thus the certain and risky components of $\bar{\gamma}$, which express the discount factor ($1/(1+\bar{r})$) and the risk pricing vector ($\widetilde{\gamma}$), are given by

$$\frac{1}{1+\bar{r}} = \frac{E\left(v_1^{*\prime}(\bar{w}_\mathbf{1})\right)}{v_0^{*\prime}(\bar{w}_0)}, \quad \widetilde{\gamma} = \frac{v^{*\prime}(\bar{w}_\mathbf{1}) - E\left(v_1^{*\prime}(\bar{w}_\mathbf{1})\right) \mathbb{1}}{v_0^{*\prime}(\bar{w}_0)}$$

so that $\widetilde{\gamma}$ can be written as

$$\widetilde{\gamma} = \frac{1}{1+\bar{r}} \left(\frac{v_1^{*\prime}(\bar{w}_\mathbf{1}) - E\left(v_1^{*\prime}(\bar{w}_\mathbf{1})\right) \mathbb{1}}{E\left(v_1^{*\prime}(\bar{w}_\mathbf{1})\right)} \right)$$

(10) thus reduces to

$$\bar{y}^k \in \underset{y^k \in Y^k}{\arg\max} \left\{ y_0^k + \frac{1}{1+\bar{r}} \left(E(y_\mathbf{1}^k) + \mathrm{cov}\left(\frac{v_1^{*\prime}(\bar{w}_\mathbf{1})}{E\left(v_1^{*\prime}(\bar{w}_\mathbf{1})\right)}, y_\mathbf{1}^k \right) \right) \right\}$$

The relative importance of the mean and covariance terms thus depends on aggregate characteristics of the economy. For a typical firm, the available projects $y^k \in Y^k$ are positively dependent on aggregate output (in the sense of Definition 16.8). Since $v_1^{*\prime}$ is a decreasing function, by Proposition 16.9 the covariance term is negative: uncertainty in the date 1 income stream $y_\mathbf{1}^k$ reduces its value below the expected present value. The extent to which the dependence of the project on aggregate output (the degree of procyclicity of the project) decreases its value depends on the variability of $v_1^{*\prime}(\bar{w}_\mathbf{1})$, which measures the extent to which fluctuations in aggregate output affect the welfare of agents. This in turn depends on the average risk aversion of the agents and the variability of aggregate output at the equilibrium.

A similar type of analysis holds when agents have mean-variance prefer-

---

[2] This is not a realistic assumption when the endowment ω^i is a proxy for the income generated by human capital subject to the risk of unemployment.

ences. In a CAPM economy, the function φ is given by $\varphi(w_s) = c' - cw_s$ (Theorem 17.3), so that the equilibrium production plan of corporation k must satisfy

$$\bar{y}^k \in \underset{y^k \in Y^k}{\arg\max} \left\{ y_0^k + \frac{E(y_1^k)}{1 + \bar{r}} - c \operatorname{cov}\left(\bar{w}_1, y_1^k\right) \right\}$$

The market risk of a project is measured directly by its covariance with equilibrium aggregate output, the parameter c being a measure of average risk aversion of agents in the economy at equilibrium. There are thus two market based forces guiding each corporation in the choice of its production plan: the first is to maximize the expected discounted value of output (profit), while the second is to minimize the plan's susceptibility to business cycle fluctuations. *Thus at equilibrium, each corporation is induced by the market to minimize its contribution to business cycle fluctuations*: this is because in an equilibrium with optimal risk sharing all agents have relatively low (high) income and consumption when aggregate output is low (high); agents thus assign a high value to production plans which generate high output when the economy-wide output is low. Furthermore, the importance attached to minimizing a firm's contribution to economy-wide fluctuations depends on the average risk aversion of the agents at equilibrium—the greater the aversion to risk, the greater the importance attached to choosing projects whose payoffs are countercyclical.

When the assumptions mentioned above ($\omega_1^i \in \langle V \rangle$, $i = 1, \ldots, I$ and specific types of preferences) are not satisfied, it is less easy to trace the dependence of the ideal security $\bar{\gamma}$ on the average characteristics of the economy. If the assumption of partial spanning holds then all projects available to the corporations are priced by the market ($\check{y}_1^k = 0$, $\forall y^k \in Y^k$, $k = 1, \ldots, K$), and (10) reduces to

$$\bar{y}^k \in \underset{y^k \in Y^k}{\arg\max} \left\{ y_0^k + \frac{E(y_1^k)}{1 + \bar{r}} + \operatorname{cov}(\widetilde{\gamma}, y_1^k) \right\}$$

But without additional assumptions $\widetilde{\gamma}$ can no longer be related in a simple way to aggregate output. However since at equilibrium firms choose production plans which maximize the same linear functional, it follows that the plans chosen by the K corporations are production efficient.

If partial spanning is not satisfied because some corporations have access to "new" projects not priced by the market, then the idiosyncratic risk prices of the shareholders ($\check{\pi}_1^{\rho,i}$) play a role in the evaluation of risks. Assumption $\mathscr{C}$ leads to an objective function for each corporation in which the idiosyncratic risk prices of initial shareholders are weighted by their shares in the corporation. Since different corporations may have different shareholders or the same shareholders with different weights, the objective functions of corporations will typically differ: as a result,when markets are incomplete, the plans chosen by the K corporations will typically not be production efficient.

Financial Policies of Corporations

So far it has been assumed that the date 0 investment of a corporation is paid directly by the original shareholders. In practice the funds for covering the cost of an initial investment (y_0^k) come from two sources: the first is *internal* (to the firm) and consists of retained earnings; the second is *external* and consists of borrowing on the bond market (debt) or issuing new equity. To model retained earnings as a source of funds, we would need to introduce (as exogenously given parameters) earnings for each firm arising from production activity prior to date 0. The date 0 dividend accruing to the original shareholders would then equal these initial earnings minus the earnings retained to finance the investment y_0^k. Requiring the original shareholders to pay for the date 0 investment costs then amounts to restricting the firm to financing by retained earnings (i.e. the internal source of funds). The next step is to extend the analysis to include the external sources of funds.

Let us assume therefore that the corporations, like the consumers, have access to the bond and equity markets. Let $b^k = (b_1^k, \ldots, b_J^k) \in \mathbb{R}^J$ denote the portfolio of the J bonds purchased (or sold short) by the kth firm, and let $\zeta^k = (\zeta_1^k, \ldots, \zeta_K^k) \in \mathbb{R}^K$ denote its portfolio of the K equity contracts. The purchase (sale) of $\zeta_{k'}^k$ units of the equity contract of firm k' gives firm k the right to receive (the obligation to deliver) the multiple $\zeta_{k'}^k$ of the dividend offered by firm k' in each state s ($s = 1, \ldots, S$) at date 1. This description of the functioning of the equity market does not distinguish between two segments of the market which in practice are kept distinct. There is a *primary* equity market on which the outstanding shares of a firm are traded and on which the positions of all agents are positive. The agents who hold these shares have ownership (and hence control) rights to firm k'. Trade on the primary equity market transfers ownership of firm k' from one group of agents to another. Parallel to this market, there is a *secondary* equity market on which a financial contract is traded which promises to deliver the dividend stream of firm k', on which agents are free to take arbitrarily long or short positions and on which the contracts traded are in zero net supply: the agents who hold these contracts have no ownership (and hence no control) rights to firm k'. Trade on the secondary equity market simply transfers income streams between agents on the long and the short sides of the market.

In the model that we are considering, a firm makes its production decision before its shares are traded on the equity market. The ownership (control) rights attached to the shares traded on the primary market are virtual since they do not influence the firm's production decision. Thus the equity contracts traded on the primary and secondary market are indistinguishable and have the same price. Even if under an alternative modelling we assumed that some part of a firm's production decision were to be taken after its shares have been traded on the equity market, a competitive model would assume that each agent views himself as a sufficiently small proportion of the whole market so as not to perceive the effect of his ownership share on the firm's production decision. Thus once again the prices on the two markets would coincide.

In the model introduced above when $0 < \zeta_k^k < 1$, firm k can either be viewed as buying back the proportion ζ_k^k of its outstanding shares on the primary market or as taking the long position ζ_k^k on the secondary market. Similarly if $\zeta_k^k < 0$, firm k can either be viewed as issuing new shares on the primary market in an amount such that the original shares are reduced to the fraction $1/(1 - \zeta_k^k)$ of the shares outstanding after the issue, or as taking the short position ζ_k^k on the secondary market. It is easy to check that these two interpretations lead to the same dividend stream for the firm.

Unlimited Liability (no Bankruptcy)

Let $D^k = (D_0^k, D_1^k, \ldots, D_S^k)$ denote the stream of dividends paid on the equity of firm k, and let

$$D_s = (D_s^1, \ldots, D_s^K), \quad s = 0, 1, \ldots, S$$

denote the vector of dividends paid by the K firms in state s. The production plans y^k, financial policies (b^k, ζ^k), and dividends D^k of the firms are linked by a system of budget equations $(k = 1, \ldots, K)$

$$D_0^k = y_0^k - q'b^k - q''\zeta^k \tag{11}$$

$$D_s^k = y_s^k + R_s b^k + D_s \zeta^k, \quad s = 1, \ldots, S \tag{12}$$

D_0^k is the dividend received by the original shareholders. As explained above, when $D_0^k < 0$, part of the financing takes place through retained earnings. D_s^k is the dividend received by the new shareholders. Initially the date 1 dividends are not required to be non-negative: *thus the new shareholders assume unlimited liability for the debts of the firm.*

In order that the budget equations (12) lead to well-defined dividends for each firm, the matrix

$$[I_K - \zeta] = \begin{bmatrix} 1 - \zeta_1^1 & -\zeta_1^2 & \cdots & -\zeta_1^K \\ -\zeta_2^1 & 1 - \zeta_2^2 & \cdots & -\zeta_2^K \\ \vdots & \vdots & \ddots & \vdots \\ -\zeta_K^1 & -\zeta_K^2 & \cdots & 1 - \zeta_K^K \end{bmatrix} \tag{13}$$

must be invertible, where ζ is the $K \times K$ matrix of *inter-firm shareholdings.*

When this condition is satisfied, the $S \times K$ matrix of date 1 dividends for the K firms can be written as

$$D_{\mathbf{1}} = [\, y_{\mathbf{1}} + Rb \,]\,[\, I_K - \varsigma \,]^{-1} \quad \text{where } b = \begin{bmatrix} b_1^1 & \cdots & b_1^K \\ \vdots & \ddots & \vdots \\ b_J^1 & \cdots & b_J^K \end{bmatrix} \tag{14}$$

is the $J \times K$ matrix of *firm bond holdings*. If the matrix of *financial market payoffs* is defined by

$$W(q, R, D) = \begin{bmatrix} -q' & -q'' \\ R & D_{\mathbf{1}} \end{bmatrix} = \begin{bmatrix} -q_1' & \cdots & -q_J' & -q_1'' & \cdots & -q_K'' \\ R_1^1 & \cdots & R_1^J & D_1^1 & \cdots & D_1^K \\ \vdots & \ddots & \vdots & \vdots & \ddots & \vdots \\ R_S^1 & \cdots & R_S^J & D_S^1 & \cdots & D_S^K \end{bmatrix} \tag{15}$$

and if $e^0 = (1, 0, \dots, 0) \in \mathbb{R}^{S+1}$, then the budget set of consumer i can be written as $(i = 1, \dots, I)$

$$\mathbb{B}\left(q, \omega^i, \delta^i, R, D\right) = \left\{ x^i \in \mathbb{R}_+^{S+1} \;\middle|\; \begin{array}{l} x^i - \omega^i = (D_0 + q'')\delta^i e^0 + W \begin{bmatrix} z^i \\ \theta^i \end{bmatrix} \\ (z^i, \theta^i) \in \mathbb{R}^J \times \mathbb{R}^K \end{array} \right\}$$

The object of the analysis that follows is to extend the concept of a (reduced-form) stock market equilibrium, in which the actions of corporations consist solely of the choice of their production plans (y^k), to an (extensive-form) stock market equilibrium in which their actions consist of the simultaneous choices of production plans and financial policies (y^k, b^k, ς^k). To make this extension, the objective of a corporation in making its production and financing decisions needs to be made explicit. In principle, the interdependence of the corporate dividend streams (see (11) and (14)) makes the derivation of an individual corporation's objective more complicated than before. It will be shown however that the criterion for a corporation can be reduced to (iii) in Definition 32.4, even in this more general setting where the corporations simultaneously choose production plans and financial policies and are permitted to make investments in other corporations in the economy.

An (extensive-form) stock market equilibrium will describe actions $(\bar{x}, \bar{z}, \bar{\theta})$ for each of the I consumers, actions $(\bar{y}, \bar{b}, \bar{\varsigma})$ for each for the K corporations, and prices $\bar{q} = (\bar{q}', \bar{q}'')$ on the bond and equity markets such that

(a) each consumer chooses an optimal consumption-portfolio plan $(\bar{x}^i, \bar{z}^i, \bar{\theta}^i)$ $(i = 1, \dots, I)$

(b) each corporation chooses a production-portfolio plan $(\bar{y}^k, \bar{b}^k, \bar{\varsigma}^k)$ which is optimal (in a sense to be defined) for its group of original shareholders

(c) the bond and equity markets clear.

In such a concept of equilibrium, (a) and (c) express the fact that $\big((\bar{x}, \bar{z}, \bar{\theta}), \bar{q}\big)$ is a stock market equilibrium given the actions $(\bar{y}, \bar{b}, \bar{\zeta})$ of the firms. This leads to the following generalization of Definition 32.1.

32.5 Definition: For the economy $\mathscr{E}(u, \omega, \delta, R, \bar{y}, \bar{b}, \bar{\zeta})$, a *stock market equilibrium with fixed actions* $(\bar{y}, \bar{b}, \bar{\zeta})$ for the corporations, where $[\, I_K - \bar{\zeta}\,]$ is invertible, is a pair $\big((\bar{x}, \bar{z}, \bar{\theta}), \bar{q}\big)$ such that

(i) $(\bar{x}^i; \bar{z}^i, \bar{\theta}^i) \in \arg\max \big\{ u^i(x^i) \,\big|\, (x^i; z^i, \theta^i) \in \mathbb{B}(\bar{q}, \omega^i, \delta^i, R, \overline{D}) \big\}$, $i = 1, \ldots, I$

(ii) $\sum_{i=1}^{I} \bar{z}^i + \sum_{k=1}^{K} \bar{b}^k = 0$

(ii)′ $\sum_{i=1}^{I} \bar{\theta}^i + \sum_{k=1}^{K} \bar{\zeta}^k = e_K$, $e_K = (1, \ldots, 1) \in \mathbb{R}^K$

where $\overline{D}$ is defined by (11) and (14) with $(y, b, \zeta, q) = (\bar{y}, \bar{b}, \bar{\zeta}, \bar{q})$.

Consider such an equilibrium with actions $(\bar{y}, \bar{b}, \bar{\zeta})$ chosen by the firms. An original shareholder of firm k with (initial) shareholding δ^i_k receives the income $(\overline{D}^k_0 + \bar{q}''_k)\delta^i_k$ from firm k. To decide if the action $(\bar{y}^k, \bar{b}^k, \bar{\zeta}^k)$ of firm k is optimal, agent i must form his estimate $E^i(D^k_0 + q''_k)$ of the net market value $D^k_0 + q''_k$ for alternative actions

$$(y^k, b^k, \zeta^k) \in Y^k \times \mathbb{R}^J \times \mathbb{R}^K \tag{16}$$

taking the actions $(\bar{y}^{-k}, \bar{b}^{-k}, \bar{\zeta}^{-k})$ of the other firms as given. In view of the interdependence of the firms' dividends, a new action (16) of firm k induces a new matrix of date 1 dividends D_1 for all the firms, defined by (14) with

$$(y, b, \zeta) = (y^k, \bar{y}^{-k}, b^k, \bar{b}^{-k}, \zeta^k, \bar{\zeta}^{-k})$$

Let $\widetilde{D}_1(y^k, b^k, \zeta^k)$ denote the function induced in this way. The new date 1 dividends will lead to new security prices $q = (q', q'')$ which the agent must estimate in order to obtain the new estimate of $D^k_0 + q''_k$ (using (11)). If the agent has competitive price perceptions (Assumption $\mathscr{C}$) then his estimate of the new security prices is given by

$$E^i(q') = \bar{q}' = \pi^i_1(\bar{x}^i)R \tag{17}$$

$$E^i(q'') = \pi^i_1(\bar{x}^i)\widetilde{D}_1(y^k, b^k, \zeta^k) \tag{18}$$

so that (by (11))

$$E^i(D^k_0 + q''_k) = y^k_0 - \pi^i_1(\bar{x}^i)Rb^k - \pi^i_1(\bar{x}^i)\widetilde{D}_1\zeta^k + \pi^i_1(\bar{x}^i)\widetilde{D}^k_1$$

Since (14) is equivalent to (12), replacing $\widetilde{D}^k_1$ by its value in (12) gives

$$E^i(D^k_0 + q''_k) = y^k_0 + \pi^i_1(\bar{x}^i)y^k_1 = \pi^i(\bar{x}^i)y^k \tag{19}$$

Thus the action $(\bar{y}^k, \bar{b}^k, \bar{\zeta}^k)$ of firm k is optimal for agent i if it maximizes (19): *the net market value of firm k, as estimated by agent i, is independent of the firm's financial policy (b^k, ζ^k) and depends only on its choice of production plan y^k.* The problem of deriving a criterion for the corporation on the basis of (19) is thus the same as before. If markets are incomplete, agents will typically have distinct present-value vectors $\pi^i(\bar{x}^i)$, and if $y_1^k \notin \langle [\, R \; \bar{y}_1 \,] \rangle$ different shareholders will typically derive different estimates for the market value of the corporation: there will thus be no production plan which simultaneously maximizes (19) for all original shareholders. If side payments among the shareholders can be used to induce unanimity, then the action $(\bar{y}^k, \bar{b}^k, \bar{\zeta}^k)$ of the kth corporation is optimal for the group of original shareholders I_k if and only if

$$\bar{y}^k \in \arg\max \left\{ \sum_{i \in I_k} \delta_k^i \pi^i(\bar{x}^i) y^k \;\middle|\; y^k \in Y^k \right\} \tag{20}$$

This derivation of the corporate objective function can be summarized as follows.

32.6 Proposition (Corporate Objective is Independent of Financial Policy): *Let $\big((\bar{x}, \bar{z}, \bar{\theta}), \bar{q}\big)$ be a stock market equilibrium with fixed actions $(\bar{y}, \bar{b}, \bar{\zeta})$ for the corporations, with $[\, I_K - \bar{\zeta} \,]$ invertible. If shareholders have competitive price perceptions (Assumption $\mathscr{C}$) and if side payments are used to obtain unanimity among the original shareholders, then the action $(\bar{y}^k, \bar{b}^k, \bar{\zeta}^k)$ of the kth corporation is optimal if and only if (20) is satisfied.*

This leads to the following concept of an extensive-form stock market equilibrium.

32.7 Definition: An (extensive form) *stock market equilibrium* for an economy $\mathscr{E}(u, \omega, \delta, R, Y)$ with K corporations (derived from the Pareto criterion with side payments) is a pair consisting of actions and prices

$$\big((\bar{x}, \bar{z}, \bar{\theta}), (\bar{y}, \bar{b}, \bar{\zeta}), \bar{q}\big) \in \mathbb{R}_+^{(S+1)I} \times \mathbb{R}^{JI} \times \mathbb{R}^{KI} \times \mathbb{R}^{(S+1)K} \times \mathbb{R}^{JK} \times \mathbb{R}^{KK} \times \mathbb{R}^{J+K}$$

such that

(0) $[\, I_K - \bar{\zeta} \,]$ is invertible

(i) $(\bar{x}^i; \bar{z}^i, \bar{\theta}^i) \in \arg\max \left\{ u^i(x^i) \;\middle|\; (x^i; z^i, \theta^i) \in \mathbb{B}(\bar{q}, \omega^i, \delta^i, R, \overline{D}) \right\}$, $i = 1, \dots, I$

(ii) $\sum_{i=1}^I \bar{z}^i + \sum_{k=1}^K \bar{b}^k = 0$

(ii)$'$ $\sum_{i=1}^I \bar{\theta}^i + \sum_{k=1}^K \bar{\zeta}^k = e_K$, $e_K = (1, \dots, 1)$

(iii) $\bar{y}^k \in \arg\max \left\{ \sum_{i \in I_k} \delta_k^i \pi^i(\bar{x}^i) y^k \;\middle|\; y^k \in Y^k \right\}$, $k = 1, \dots, K$

where $\overline{D}$ is defined by (11) and (14) with $(y, b, \zeta, q) = (\bar{y}, \bar{b}, \bar{\zeta}, \bar{q})$.

In a reduced-form equilibrium, only consumers have access to the financial markets: corporations are restricted to internal sources of funds for financing investment. In an extensive-form equilibrium, corporations can also trade on the financial markets. *When the corporations are given access to the financial markets, does the equilibrium allocation change?* In the case of entrepreneurial firms it was shown in Proposition 30.7 that giving firms access to the financial markets does not change the equilibrium allocation. The next proposition shows that this result extends to the more complex setting where firms are corporations whose equity is traded on the stock market, if the following four conditions are satisfied.

(a) Consumers and corporations have complete and frictionless access to the financial markets (i.e. no restricted participation, indivisibilities, or transactions costs).

(b) All agents in the economy have competitive price perceptions regarding the valuation of income streams (Assumption $\mathscr{C}$).

(c) Consumers may not default and the shareholders of each corporation have unlimited liability for the repayment of its debts (i.e. no bankruptcy for firms).

(d) The original shareholders of each corporation use side payments to achieve unanimity regarding the production plan that it should adopt.

(a) and (b) characterize competitive frictionless markets. The role of the no-bankruptcy condition in (c) will become clear in the next subsection which analyzes the case where shareholders have limited liability for a firm's debts. (d) closes the model by providing a well-defined corporate objective function.[3] As shown in Proposition 32.6, this objective function (which is defined by (20)) does not depend on the firm's choice of financial variables: thus the financial policy of each corporation is indeterminate. This result is a consequence of Assumption $\mathscr{C}$, for with competitive price perceptions no shareholder perceives the possibility of affecting the present value of the firm's profit stream by altering the firm's financial policy. To show that the equilibrium is unaffected by the firms' choices of financial policies it remains to show that, given their production plans $\bar{y} = (\bar{y}^1, \ldots, \bar{y}^K)$, the market subspace $\langle W \rangle$ does not change when firms change their financial policies. The following proposition is a generalized version of the Modigliani-Miller Theorem asserting the irrelevance (or more accurately the indeterminacy) of corporate financial policies.

---

[3] There is a much broader family of corporate objective functions than that implied by (d) which also leads to Propositions 32.7 and 32.8. As far as the objective function of a corporation is concerned, all that matters for the proof of these results is that it be a linear function of the firm's dividend stream $\beta^k D^k$, where β^k is a present-value vector which is independent of the firm's actions and is compatible with the observed prices of the securities i.e. $\beta^k W = 0$ (see Exercise 9). In particular if β^k is a linear combination of the present-value vectors of any (possibly endogenously determined) group of new or original shareholders, then the financial policies of the firm are indeterminate and do not affect the equilibrium allocation.

32.8 Proposition (Invariance of Stock Market Equilibrium w.r.t. Financial Policies):   *Consider an economy $\mathscr{E}(u, \omega, \delta, R, Y)$ with K corporations satisfying Assumptions $(\mathscr{U}, \mathscr{T})$ in which there is no default for consumers and shareholders have unlimited liability for the debts of the corporations. Let all agents have competitive price perceptions (Assumption $\mathscr{C}$).*

(i) *If $\big((\bar{x}, \bar{z}, \bar{\theta}), (\bar{y}, \bar{b}, \bar{\zeta}), \bar{q}\big)$ is an extensive-form stock market equilibrium and if $(\hat{z}, \hat{\theta}, \hat{q})$ are defined by*

$$\begin{bmatrix} \hat{z} \\ \hat{\theta} \end{bmatrix} = \begin{bmatrix} I_J & -\bar{b} \\ 0 & I_K - \bar{\zeta} \end{bmatrix}^{-1} \begin{bmatrix} \bar{z} \\ \bar{\theta} \end{bmatrix} \tag{21}$$

$$\hat{q} = (\hat{q}', \hat{q}'') = (\bar{q}', \bar{q}'') \begin{bmatrix} I_J & -\bar{b} \\ 0 & I_K - \bar{\zeta} \end{bmatrix} \tag{22}$$

then $\big((\bar{x}, \hat{z}, \hat{\theta}, \bar{y}), \hat{q}\big)$ is a reduced-form stock market equilibrium.

(ii) *If $\big((\bar{x}, \hat{z}, \hat{\theta}, \bar{y}), \hat{q}\big)$ is a reduced-form stock market equilibrium, then for all $(\bar{b}, \bar{\zeta}) \in \mathbb{R}^{JK} \times \mathbb{R}^{KK}$ there exist $(\bar{z}, \bar{\theta}, \bar{q})$ satisfying (21)–(22) such that $\big((\bar{x}, \bar{z}, \bar{\theta}), (\bar{y}, \bar{b}, \bar{\zeta}), \bar{q}\big)$ is an extensive-form stock market equilibrium.*

PROOF: The financial market payoff matrices

$$\overline{W} = W(\bar{q}, R, \overline{D}) \quad \text{and} \quad \widehat{W} = W(\hat{q}, R, \bar{y})$$

in the extensive-form and reduced-form equilibrium are defined by equations (15) and (1), respectively. The associated budget sets of agent i are given by

$$\mathbb{B}\left(\bar{q}, \omega^i, \delta^i, R, \overline{D}\right) = \left\{ x^i \in \mathbb{R}^{S+1}_+ \;\middle|\; \begin{array}{c} x^i - \omega^i = (\overline{D}_0 + \bar{q}'')\delta^i e^0 + \overline{W} \begin{bmatrix} z^i \\ \theta^i \end{bmatrix} \\ (z^i, \theta^i) \in \mathbb{R}^J \times \mathbb{R}^K \end{array} \right\} \tag{23}$$

$$\mathbb{B}\left(\hat{q}, \omega^i, \delta^i, R, \bar{y}\right) = \left\{ x^i \in \mathbb{R}^{S+1}_+ \;\middle|\; \begin{array}{c} x^i - \omega^i = (\bar{y}_0 + \hat{q}'')\delta^i e^0 + \widehat{W} \begin{bmatrix} z^i \\ \theta^i \end{bmatrix} \\ (z^i, \theta^i) \in \mathbb{R}^J \times \mathbb{R}^K \end{array} \right\} \tag{24}$$

Note first that for any fixed vector of financial policies for the firms $(\bar{b}, \bar{\zeta}) \in \mathbb{R}^{JK} \times \mathbb{R}^{KK}$ with $[I_K - \bar{\zeta}]$ invertible, the equations (21)–(22) define a bijection between $(\bar{z}, \bar{\theta}, \bar{q})$ and $(\hat{z}, \hat{\theta}, \hat{q})$. To prove (i) and (ii) we need to show that for $(\bar{b}, \bar{\zeta}) \in \mathbb{R}^{JK} \times \mathbb{R}^{KK}$ with $[I_K - \bar{\zeta}]$ invertible, if $(\bar{z}, \bar{\theta}, \bar{q})$ and $(\hat{z}, \hat{\theta}, \hat{q})$ satisfy equations (21)–(22) then

(α) the budget sets (23) and (24) are the same for each agent $i = 1, \ldots, I$. This in turn implies that

$$\begin{cases} (\bar{x}^i; \bar{z}^i, \bar{\theta}^i) = \arg\max \left\{ u^i(x^i) \mid (x^i; z^i, \theta^i) \in \mathbb{B}(\bar{q}, \omega^i, \delta^i, R, \overline{D}) \right\} \\ \qquad\qquad\qquad\qquad \Updownarrow \\ (\bar{x}^i; \hat{z}^i, \hat{\theta}^i) = \arg\max \left\{ u^i(x^i) \mid (x^i; z^i, \theta^i) \in \mathbb{B}(\hat{q}, \omega^i, \delta^i, R, \bar{y}) \right\} \end{cases}$$

(β) the market-clearing equations for the two equilibria are equivalent

$$\left. \begin{array}{l} \displaystyle\sum_{i=1}^{I} \bar{z}^i + \sum_{k=1}^{K} \bar{b}^k = 0 \\ \displaystyle\sum_{i=1}^{I} \bar{\theta}^i + \sum_{k=1}^{K} \bar{\zeta}^k = e_K \end{array} \right\} \Longleftrightarrow \left\{ \begin{array}{l} \displaystyle\sum_{i=1}^{I} \hat{z}^i = 0 \\ \displaystyle\sum_{i=1}^{I} \hat{\theta}^i = e_K \end{array} \right.$$

which, if we define $e_I = (1, \ldots, 1) \in \mathbb{R}^I$ (considered as a column vector), can be written in more condensed form as

$$\left. \begin{array}{l} \bar{z}e_I + \bar{b}e_K = 0 \\ \bar{\theta}e_I + \bar{\zeta}e_K = e_K \end{array} \right\} \Longleftrightarrow \left\{ \begin{array}{l} \hat{z}e_I = 0 \\ \hat{\theta}e_I = e_K \end{array} \right.$$

Let us begin by showing the equivalence (β). By (21)

$$\hat{z}e_I = 0 \Longleftrightarrow (\bar{z} + \bar{b}\,[\,I_K - \bar{\zeta}\,]^{-1}\,\bar{\theta})e_I = 0$$
$$\Longleftrightarrow \bar{z}e_I + \bar{b}\hat{\theta}e_I = 0 \tag{25}$$

$$\hat{\theta}e_I = e_K \Longleftrightarrow [\,I_K - \bar{\zeta}\,]^{-1}\,\bar{\theta}e_I = e_K$$
$$\Longleftrightarrow \bar{\theta}e_I = [\,I_K - \bar{\zeta}\,]e_K = e_K - \bar{\zeta}e_K$$
$$\Longleftrightarrow \bar{\theta}e_I + \bar{\zeta}e_K = e_K \tag{26}$$

(25) and (26) imply the equivalence (β).

To prove (α), we first note that by (11) and (22)

$$\overline{D}_0 + \bar{q}'' = \bar{y}_0 - \bar{q}'\bar{b} - \bar{q}''\bar{\zeta} + \bar{q}'' = \bar{y}_0 - \bar{q}'b + \bar{q}''\,[\,I_K - \bar{\zeta}\,] = \bar{y}_0 + \hat{q}''$$

To show equality of the budget sets (23) and (24) it remains to show that

$$\langle\,\overline{W}\,\rangle = \langle\,\widehat{W}\,\rangle \tag{27}$$

Since (14) implies

$$\bar{y}_1 = \overline{D}_1\,[\,I_K - \bar{\zeta}\,] - R\bar{b}$$

the date 1 payoff matrices in the reduced- and extensive-form equilibria are related by

$$[\, R\ \bar{y}_1\,] = [\, R\ \overline{D}_1\,] \begin{bmatrix} I_J & -\bar{b} \\ 0 & I_K - \bar{\zeta} \end{bmatrix} \tag{28}$$

(22) and (28) imply

$$\begin{bmatrix} -\hat{q}' & -\hat{q}'' \\ R & \bar{y}_1 \end{bmatrix} = \begin{bmatrix} -\bar{q}' & -\bar{q}'' \\ R & \overline{D}_1 \end{bmatrix} \begin{bmatrix} I_J & -\bar{b} \\ 0 & I_K - \bar{\zeta} \end{bmatrix} \Longleftrightarrow \widehat{W} = \overline{W} \begin{bmatrix} I_J & -\bar{b} \\ 0 & I_K - \bar{\zeta} \end{bmatrix}$$

Since $[\, I_K - \bar{\zeta}\,]$ is invertible, the matrix $\begin{bmatrix} I_J & -\bar{b} \\ 0 & I_K - \bar{\zeta} \end{bmatrix}$ is invertible so that (27) holds. $\square$

The main ideas of Propositions 32.6 and 32.8 can be summarized as follows.

(1) The group of shareholders I_k of corporation k evaluates the action of the firm using the vector of state prices $\bar{\beta}^k = \sum_{i \in I_k} \delta_k^i \pi^i(\bar{x}^i)$. Since the corporation's financial policy $(\bar{b}^k, \bar{\zeta}^k)$ induces transfers of income in the market subspace $\langle \overline{W} \rangle$ and since the net present value of all such transfers is zero ($\bar{\beta}^k \overline{W} = 0$), the firm's objective is not influenced by its financial policy, and depends only on its production plan $\bar{y}^k$.

(2) The basic securities that agents can invest in are the production plans of the firms (with payoff matrix $\bar{y}_1$) and the bonds (with payoff matrix R): investment in these securities generates the market subspace $\langle \widehat{W} \rangle$. The financial policies of the corporations alter their dividends (from $\bar{y}_1$ to $\overline{D}_1$) but only through a repackaging of the basic securities. Since equity prices adjust (linearly) to this repackaging of their income streams, the new market subspace $\langle \overline{W} \rangle$ coincides with the original subspace $\langle \widehat{W} \rangle$. Thus the opportunity sets of the agents are not affected by the corporations' choices of financial policies.

(3) Since neither the *objectives* of the firms nor the *investment opportunities* of the agents are affected by the corporations' financial policies $(\bar{b}, \bar{\zeta})$, these policies are indeterminate and do not affect the equilibrium allocation $(\bar{x}, \bar{y})$.

Formula (28) expresses the relation between the payoffs on the basic securities $[\, R\ \bar{y}_1\,]$ in a reduced-form equilibrium and their payoffs $[\, R\ \overline{D}_1\,]$ in an associated extensive-form equilibrium in which the financial policies of the corporations are $(\bar{b}, \bar{\zeta})$: this formula is the key to understanding the relations (21) and (22) between the portfolios and equity prices in the two types of equilibria. (22) expresses how the equity prices adjust to the change in dividends induced by the corporations' financial policies. (21) describes how each agent adjusts his portfolio $\hat{z}^i \longrightarrow \bar{z}^i$ so as to finance the same consumption stream $\bar{x}^i$

$(i = 1, \ldots, I)$, when corporations alter their financial policies: it shows how each agent "undoes" what corporations "do" on the financial markets.

Limited Liability (Bankruptcy)

The development of large modern corporations whose ownership is divided among numerous shareholders, who, for that reason, cannot all directly intervene in the running of the firm, was made possible by introducing the legal status of limited liability for shareholders. The analysis of this subsection shows that when limited liability is taken into account, the result of Proposition 32.8 on the invariance of the equilibrium allocation with respect to the financial policies of firms no longer holds. It also shows that a more precise modelling of institutional aspects of bankruptcy (liquidation, cost of bankruptcy, etc.) needs to be explicitly introduced to obtain a more insightful analysis of bankruptcy and its consequences for the financial policies of firms.

The equity contract of the kth corporation is said to have *limited liability* if the date 1 dividend stream that it pays is constrained to be non-negative: this means that if in some state the earnings of the firm are not sufficient to cover the payment of its debt, then the (new) shareholders are not called upon to make the payment. In such a state the bondholders are not fully paid, and firm k is said to be *bankrupt*. With the introduction of bankruptcy, it becomes natural to endogenize the payoffs of the risky bonds which, up to now, have been taken as exogenously given. Any corporate bond can be thought of as being derived from the riskless bond with payoff stream $(1, \ldots, 1)$: if a corporation borrows and goes bankrupt in some state, then the payoff on its loan contract is less than that on the riskless bond in that state. Since the amount that a corporation pays on its debt contract is a function of its actions, its debt contract becomes a *named* contract specific to firm k.

Suppose therefore that the financial contracts consist of $J = K + 1$ debt contracts and K equity contracts with limited liability. The kth debt contract (bond) is that of corporation k $(k = 1, \ldots, K)$ and the $(K + 1)^{\text{st}}$ is the riskless bond. If firm k does not go bankrupt in any state, then its debt contract coincides with the riskless bond. As in the earlier analysis, individual agents have unlimited liability for the repayment of their debts i.e. *default* is not permitted for consumers.

Let $(b^k, \zeta^k) \in \mathbb{R}^{K+1} \times \mathbb{R}^K$ denote the financial policy of firm k. To simplify the computation of the payoffs of the firms' bonds, we assume that there is no interfirm bond or share holding: each firm is thus restricted to trading its own debt and equity contracts

$$b^k = (0, \ldots, b^k_k, \ldots, 0) \in \mathbb{R}^{K+1}, \quad b^k_{k'} = 0, \quad \forall \, k' \neq k \tag{29}$$

$$\zeta^k = (0, \ldots, \zeta^k_k, \ldots, 0) \in \mathbb{R}^K, \quad \zeta^k_k \neq 1, \quad \zeta^k_{k'} = 0, \quad \forall \, k' \neq k \tag{30}$$

It is assumed that each firm's technology set satisfies

$$y_0^k \leq 0, \quad y_s^k \geq 0, \quad s = 1, \ldots, S, \quad \forall \, y^k \in Y^k, \quad k = 1, \ldots, K$$

The budget equations (11) and (12) of firm k $(k = 1, \ldots, K)$ reduce to

$$D_0^k = y_0^k - q_k' b_k^k - q_k'' \zeta_k^k \tag{31}$$

$$(1 - \zeta_k^k) D_s^k = y_s^k + R_s^k b_k^k, \quad s = 1, \ldots, S \tag{32}$$

Limited liability of the kth equity contract requires that

$$D_s^k \geq 0, \quad s = 1, \ldots, S$$

The payoff R_s^k on its debt contract adjusts to maintain this inequality

$$R_s^k = \begin{cases} 1 & \text{if} \quad y_s^k + b_k^k \geq 0 \\ \dfrac{-y_s^k}{b_k^k} & \text{if} \quad y_s^k + b_k^k < 0 \end{cases}$$

which can be written more compactly as

$$-b_k^k R_s^k = \min \left\{ -b_k^k, \quad y_s^k \right\} \tag{33}$$

If the firm lends $(b_k^k \geq 0)$ or borrows $(b_k^k < 0)$ in such a way that it never goes bankrupt $(y_s^k + b_k^k \geq 0, \ s = 1, \ldots, S)$ then the payoff of its debt contract is the same as that of the riskless bond. If the firm borrows up to the point where it goes bankrupt in some state $(y_s^k + b_k^k < 0)$ then its debt contract becomes a risky bond. Since we want to permit the firm to finance part of its date 0 investment costs by retained earnings (which implies $D_0^k < 0$) D_0^k is not required to be non-negative.

Given the actions (y, b, ζ) of the firms (where (b, ζ) satisfy (29)–(30)), the consumers have access to financial markets described by the payoff matrix

$$W(q, R, D) = \begin{bmatrix} -q' & -q'' \\ R & D_{\mathbf{1}} \end{bmatrix}$$

$$= \begin{bmatrix} -q_1' & \cdots & -q_K' & -q_{K+1}' & -q_1'' & \cdots & q_K'' \\ R_1^1 & \cdots & R_1^K & 1 & D_1^1 & \cdots & D_1^K \\ \vdots & \ddots & \vdots & \vdots & \vdots & \ddots & \vdots \\ R_S^1 & \cdots & R_S^K & 1 & D_S^1 & \cdots & D_S^K \end{bmatrix} \tag{34}$$

where the matrices R and $D_{\mathbf{1}}$ are defined by (33) and (32). It is straightforward to adapt the concept of a stock market equilibrium with fixed actions $(\bar{y}, \bar{b}, \bar{\zeta})$ for the firms given by Definition 32.5 to the present context. The important point to notice is that, because of bankruptcy, when firms vary their financial policies (b, ζ) the market subspace $\langle W(q, R, D) \rangle$ can change, even if the production plans y of the firms stay fixed.

Consider a stock market equilibrium with fixed actions $(\bar{y}, \bar{b}, \bar{\zeta})$ for the firms. To decide if the action $(\bar{y}^k, \bar{b}^k, \bar{\zeta}^k)$ of firm k is optimal, agent i (as an original shareholder) must form his estimate of $D_0^k + q_k''$ for alternative actions (y^k, b^k, ζ^k). If we wish to express the idea that shareholders take into account the full effect on $D_0^k + q_k''$ of changes in the marketed subspace induced by changes in (y^k, b^k, ζ^k), then we must resort to a non-competitive analysis. Since agents must be able to calculate equilibrium security prices for a marketed subspace $\langle [\, R \; D_{\mathbf{1}} \,] \rangle$ different from the one which they observe, they must understand the correspondence

$$(y, b, \zeta) \longrightarrow q(y, b, \zeta) \tag{35}$$

which associates with each vector of actions of the firms, the possible equilibrium vectors of bond and equity prices. The technical difficulties involved in carrying out such a non-competitive analysis—in particular in proving that an equilibrium exists in which agents understand the correspondence (35)— were explained earlier: these difficulties are now compounded by the fact that bankruptcy induces additional discontinuities in the market subspace (arising from changes in the rank of W) when firms change their financial policies. Moreover, requiring that agents know what the prices would be in a hypothetical and unobserved market structure calls for a considerable degree of understanding on the part of agents.

For these reasons, we are once again led to adopt a competitive approach based on Assumption $\mathscr{C}$. With the assumption of competitive price perceptions, the analysis leading to Proposition 32.6, summarized in formulae (17)–(20), is essentially unchanged. The only change is that the matrix of payoffs $\widetilde{R}(y, b, \zeta)$ of the bonds is now endogenous. Thus (17) must be replaced by

$$E^i(q') = \pi_{\mathbf{1}}^i(\bar{x}^i) \widetilde{R}(y, b, \zeta) \tag{36}$$

while (18)–(20) continue to hold.

Thus even if bankruptcy is permitted, if shareholders have competitive price perceptions, then the shareholders of firm k do not perceive the possibility of affecting the net market value of the firm's equity by the choice of a financial policy. If $\big((\bar{x}, \bar{z}, \bar{\theta}), \bar{q} \big)$ is a stock market equilibrium with fixed actions $(\bar{y}, \bar{b}, \bar{\zeta})$ of the firm (satisfying (29)–(30)), then the action $(\bar{y}^k, \bar{b}^k, \bar{\zeta}^k)$ is optimal for the shareholders of firm k if $\bar{y}^k$ satisfies (20) i.e. if $\bar{y}^k$ maximizes the present value of its profit stream, where the vector of state prices is the average present-value vector of the shareholders. Any combination (b^k, ζ^k, D_0^k) of bond financing, equity financing, and financing by retained earnings satisfying (31)–(32) is equivalent for the shareholders, so that the firm's financial policy is indeterminate even when bankruptcy is permitted.

If firms adopt the criterion (20) in choosing their production plans then, with obvious modifications, Definition 32.7 can be used to define a *stock market equilibrium with bankruptcy*: the firms' financial policies are restricted to satisfy (29)–(30), the date 1 dividends D_1 are defined by (31)–(32), and the bond payoffs $R = (R^1, \ldots, R^K, R^{K+1})$ are given by (33) for $(R^1, \ldots, R^K)$ and by $R^{K+1} = (1, \ldots, 1)$ for the riskless bond.

While the financial policies of firms are a matter of indifference to shareholders they are not a matter of indifference to consumers whenever these policies can affect the market subspace by altering the span $\langle [R\, D_1] \rangle$ of the date 1 payoff matrix. This can be seen by taking a simple example of an economy with one firm $(K = 1)$. Let $\big((\hat{x}, \hat{z}, \hat{\theta}), (\hat{y}, 0, 0), \hat{q} \big)$ be a (reduced form) stock market equilibrium in which the firm finances its investment by retained earnings. The payoff matrix of the financial markets (34) is given by

$$\widehat{W} = \begin{bmatrix} -\hat{q}_1' & -\hat{q}_2' & -\hat{q}_1'' \\ 1 & 1 & \hat{y}_1^1 \\ \vdots & \vdots & \vdots \\ 1 & 1 & \hat{y}_S^1 \end{bmatrix}$$

with $\hat{q}_1' = \hat{q}_2'$, where the first column is the firm's bond (on which there is zero trade), the second column is the riskless bond, and the third column is the firm's equity contract. Let us assume that the income stream $(\hat{y}_1^1, \ldots, \hat{y}_S^1)$ is risky, so that rank $\widehat{W} = 2$. Let $\big((\bar{x}, \bar{z}, \bar{\theta}), (\bar{y}, \bar{b}, 0), \bar{q} \big)$ be an (extensive form) stock market equilibrium in which the firm borrows up to the point where it is bankrupt in the state in which output (profit) is the lowest, which we may call state 1. Then the payoff matrix (34) is given by

$$\overline{W} = \begin{bmatrix} -\bar{q}_1' & -\bar{q}_2' & -\bar{q}_1'' \\ -\dfrac{\bar{y}_1^1}{\bar{b}} & 1 & 0 \\ 1 & 1 & \bar{y}_2^1 + \bar{b} \\ \vdots & \vdots & \vdots \\ 1 & 1 & \bar{y}_S^1 + \bar{b} \end{bmatrix}$$

If $S = 2$, then $\langle [\widehat{R}\, \widehat{D}_1] \rangle = \langle [\overline{R}\, \overline{D}_1] \rangle = \mathbb{R}^2$ so that markets are complete. If $\bar{y} = \hat{y}$, $\bar{q}_2' = \hat{q}_2'$ and $(\bar{q}_1', \bar{q}_1'')$ are deduced by linearity from $(\hat{q}_2', \hat{q}_1'')$, then $\langle \overline{W} \rangle = \langle \widehat{W} \rangle$, the consumption plans of the consumers do not change, $\bar{x} = \hat{x}$, and the proof of Proposition 32.8 goes through. *With complete markets, even if shareholders have limited liability (i.e. bankruptcy is permitted) the real equilibrium allocation is invariant with respect to the choice of financial policies by firms.* Bankruptcy does not matter since it does not affect the span of the date 1 payoff matrix.

If $S > 2$, since dim $\langle [\, \widehat{R} \; \widehat{D}_1 \,] \rangle = 2$ in the reduced-form equilibrium, markets are incomplete. Since dim $\langle [\overline{R} \; \overline{D}_1 \,] \rangle = 3$, provided $\bar{y}_s^1 \neq \bar{y}_2^1$ for some $s > 2$ (which we take to be satisfied), the market subspaces must differ in the two equilibria

$$\langle \overline{W} \rangle \neq \langle \widehat{W} \rangle$$

Thus in general $\bar{x} \neq \hat{x}$ (the argument can be made precise using techniques of differential topology similar to those used in the next chapter (see Section 35). If $(\hat{x}, \hat{y})$ is a reduced-form stock market equilibrium allocation, then there exist financial policies for the firms, which induce bankruptcy, such that the resulting equilibrium allocation $(\bar{x}, \bar{y})$ satisfies $(\bar{x}, \bar{y}) \neq (\hat{x}, \hat{y})$. *With incomplete markets, if bankruptcy is permitted then the financial policies of firms have real effects.*

Without bankruptcy, the profit stream of a firm is divided into a risky stream (the equity contract) and a riskless stream (the riskless bond), where the latter is the same for all firms. Bankruptcy augments the span of the markets by splitting the profit stream of a firm into two risky streams: the equity contract, whose downside risk is reduced by limited liability, and the debt contract, which is firm specific and whose downside risk is increased by the possibility of bankruptcy. Trading equity contracts on a stock market permits the production risks in an economy to be divided among a large number of shareholders: introducing limited liability further increases the instruments available for risk sharing by inducing bondholders to carry part of the production risks.

It should be noted that the independence of a corporation's objective function from its financial policy, when shareholders have limited liability, is valid only if production and financing decisions are made simultaneously: this independence property is no longer true if some of the firm's production decisions are made after long-term debts have been incurred. Suppose that a corporation from its past decisions has inherited certain capital equipment and earnings opportunities summarized in its production set Y^k and in addition has an inherited debt, which was issued at some earlier date to finance part of the existing capital. Suppose that as a result of this past borrowing, the firm must pay $\bar{b}^k$ units of income in each state at date 1 to exogenously specified bondholders. When the firm chooses the production plan y^k, since the shareholders have limited liability, the bondholders will receive $\min\{y_s^k, -\bar{b}^k\}$ in state s. Let $\mathbf{S} = \{1, \ldots, S\}$ denote the set of states of nature and, for a choice of production plan y^k, let $\mathbf{S}(\bar{b}^k, y^k)$ denote the subset of states in which the kth firm is not bankrupt

$$\mathbf{S}(\bar{b}^k, y^k) = \left\{ s \in \mathbf{S} \mid y_s^k + \bar{b}^k \geq 0 \right\}$$

If the concept of a stock market equilibrium is modified to take into account inherited debts, retaining all the other earlier assumptions—in particular Assumption $\mathscr{C}$ and that decisions at date 0 are made by the date 0 shareholders—then the equilibrium production plan of corporation k must satisfy

$$\bar{y}^k \in \arg\max \left\{ \sum_{i \in I_k} \sum_{s \in \mathbf{S}(\bar{b}^k, y^k)} \delta_k^i \bar{\pi}_s^i (y_s^k + \bar{b}^k) + y_0^k \;\middle|\; y^k \in Y^k \right\} \tag{37}$$

If the firm does not go bankrupt in any state at equilibrium, then $\mathbf{S}(\bar{b}^k, \bar{y}^k) = \mathbf{S}$, and the equilibrium production plan $\bar{y}^k$ maximizes the present-value criterion (20). If there are *bankrupt states* ($\mathbf{S}(\bar{b}^k, \bar{y}^k) \neq \mathbf{S}$), then the equilibrium production plan $\bar{y}^k$ maximizes the criterion (37), which differs from (20) in that it places no value on output in bankrupt states. In this case the solution $\bar{y}^k$ of (37) will typically differ from the plan $\hat{y}^k$ which would solve (20). Let $\beta^k = \sum_{i \in I_k} \delta_k^i \bar{\pi}^i$ denote the state price vector of corporation k. Since $\bar{y}^k$ is optimal for the shareholders

$$\bar{y}_0^k + \sum_{s \in \mathbf{S}(\bar{b}^k, \bar{y}^k)} \beta_s^k \bar{y}_s^k \;\geq\; \hat{y}_0^k + \sum_{s \in \mathbf{S}(\bar{b}^k, \bar{y}^k)} \beta_s^k \hat{y}_s^k \tag{38}$$

and since $\hat{y}^k$ is present-value maximizing

$$\beta^k \bar{y}^k = \bar{y}_0^k + \sum_{s \in \mathbf{S}} \beta_s^k \bar{y}_s^k \;\leq\; \hat{y}_0^k + \sum_{s \in \mathbf{S}} \beta_s^k \hat{y}_s^k = \beta^k \hat{y}^k$$

it follows that

$$\sum_{s \in \mathbf{S} \setminus \mathbf{S}(\bar{b}^k, \bar{y}^k)} \beta_s^k \bar{y}_s^k \;\leq\; \sum_{s \in \mathbf{S} \setminus \mathbf{S}(\bar{b}^k, \bar{y}^k)} \beta_s^k \hat{y}_s^k \tag{39}$$

Thus when there is bankruptcy, the compensation of bondholders is less with the plan $\bar{y}^k$ chosen by the shareholders than it would have been with the plan $\hat{y}^k$ which maximizes present value. *Since shareholders make no effort to minimize losses in bankrupt states, focusing instead on maximizing profit in the favorable states, they are led to choose a riskier production plan which generates more profit (for them) when it succeeds, but less return for the bondholders when it fails.*[4] The limited liability status of the equity contract induces a distortion

---

[4]Bondholders often seek to mitigate this problem by requiring that covenants be appended to the long-term bonds issued by corporations. A *covenant* is basically a modification of the debt contract which may set limits to the future financial policy of the firm (for example, by preventing an increase in the debt-equity ratio either directly or indirectly through mergers and acquisitions) or seek to reduce the incentives of shareholders to engage in risky activities at the expense of the bondholders (for example, by making the debt convertible into equity at the discretion of the bondholders). A discussion of the role and form of covenants is given by Smith-Warner (1979). Including covenants in the long-term debt contracts issued by corporations is

in the incentives of shareholders, leading to a loss $\beta^k(\bar{y}^k - \hat{y}^k)$ in the present value of production. This loss is a measure of the agency cost of bankruptcy arising from the conflict of interest between equity holders and bondholders when there are long-term debts.

APPENDIX

Subgradients

Most of the analysis of this book has been made under the assumption that agents' utility functions are differentiable. Many of the results—basically all except those based on the Transversality Theorem (Theorem 11.3 in Chapter 2)—hold without assuming differentiability, provided the utility functions are monotone and quasi-concave (i.e. adopting Assumption $\mathscr{U}'$ instead of $\mathscr{U}$). It suffices to replace the notion of the gradient of the utility function at x by the notion of the subgradient of u at x. For a reader interested in getting a flavor of how *convex analysis* can replace usual calculus-based marginal reasoning, we present here (a brief introduction to) the notion of a subgradient and show that Propositions 30.3 and 31.2 are readily proved without assuming the differentiability of u.

If u is continuous and quasi-concave, the *preferred set at $\bar{x}$*

$$U_{\bar{x}} = \{x \in \mathbb{R}^n \mid u(x) \geq u(\bar{x})\}$$

is closed and convex. The normal cone $N_{U_{\bar{x}}}(\bar{x})$ to $U_{\bar{x}}$ at $\bar{x}$

$$N_{U_{\bar{x}}}(\bar{x}) = \{\pi \in \mathbb{R}^n \mid \pi x \leq \pi\bar{x}, \quad \forall x \in U_{\bar{x}}\}$$

defines the set of supporting hyperplanes to $U_{\bar{x}}$ at $\bar{x}$, and the negative of this cone (which defines the same supporting hyperplanes) is the set of prices $\pi \in \mathbb{R}^n$ at which all elements of the preferred set cost at least as much as $\bar{x}$. This set, which is denoted by $\partial u(\bar{x})$, is called the *subgradient* of u at $\bar{x}$: thus

$$\partial u(\bar{x}) = -N_{U_{\bar{x}}}(\bar{x})$$

---

often in the (ex-ante) interest of shareholders, since covenants typically reduce the cost of issuing debt: the more confident bondholders are that shareholders will not engage in policies which increase the probability of bankruptcy or decrease the payoff in case of bankruptcy, the smaller the return that they require in nonbankrupt states.

The next proposition establishes the exact relation between the set $U_{\bar{x}}$ of consumption streams which are preferred to $\bar{x}$ and the set

$$\{x \in \mathbb{R}^n \mid \pi x \geq \pi \bar{x}, \quad \forall\, x \in \partial u(\bar{x})\}$$

of consumption streams which are more expensive than $\bar{x}$ for all prices in the subgradient. It also shows in (iii) that if u is differentiable, then the subgradient reduces to the half-line generated by the gradient

$$\partial u(\bar{x}) = \{\pi \in \mathbb{R}^n \mid \pi = \lambda \nabla u(\bar{x})\}, \quad \lambda \geq 0$$

A6.1 Proposition (Preferred Consumption is More Expensive): *If $u : \mathbb{R}^n \longrightarrow \mathbb{R}$ is continuous and quasi-concave and if $\bar{x} \in \mathbb{R}^n$, then*

   (i) *$u(\bar{x} + \xi) >(\geq) u(\bar{x})$ implies $\pi \xi >(\geq) 0$, $\forall\, \pi \in \partial u(\bar{x})$, $\pi \neq 0$;*
  (ii) *if u is weakly monotone,[5] $\pi \xi > 0$, $\forall\, \pi \in \partial u(\bar{x})$, $\pi \neq 0$, implies that for some $\mu \in (0, 1]$, $u(\bar{x} + \mu \xi) > u(\bar{x})$;*
 (iii) *if u is differentiable and $\nabla u(\bar{x}) \neq 0$ then (i) and (ii) of Proposition 31.2 are satisfied.*

PROOF: (i) By definition of $\partial u(\bar{x})$, if $\pi \in \partial u(\bar{x})$ then

$$\pi x \geq \pi \bar{x}, \quad \forall\, x \in U_{\bar{x}} \tag{1}$$

We need to show that the inequality is strict if $x \in \text{int } U_{\bar{x}}$. Suppose $x \in \text{int } U_{\bar{x}}$ then there exists a ball $B(x, \epsilon)$ of radius $\epsilon > 0$ around x such that $B(x, \epsilon) \subset \text{int } U_{\bar{x}}$. If $\pi x = \pi \bar{x}$, $\pi \neq 0$, then there exists $x' \in B(x, \epsilon)$ such that $\pi x' < \pi \bar{x}$, which contradicts (1). Letting $x = \bar{x} + \xi$, gives (i).

(ii) Since u is continuous and weakly monotone,

$$\text{int } U_{\bar{x}} = \{x \in \mathbb{R}^n \mid u(x) > u(\bar{x})\}$$

Let $[\bar{x}, \bar{x} + \xi]$ denote the line segment joining $\bar{x}$ and $\bar{x} + \xi$. Then

$$[\bar{x}, \bar{x} + \xi] \cap \text{int } U_{\bar{x}} = \varnothing \tag{2}$$

is equivalent to the condition that there does not exist $\mu \in (0, 1]$ such that $u(\bar{x} + \mu \xi) > u(\bar{x})$. If (ii) is not satisfied, then there exists $\xi \in \mathbb{R}^n$ satisfying (2) and

$$\pi \xi > 0, \quad \forall\, \pi \in \partial u(\bar{x}), \quad \pi \neq 0 \tag{3}$$

_____

[5] u is *weakly monotone* if $x' \gg x$ implies $u(x') > u(x)$.

If (2) is satisfied, by the standard Separation Theorem for convex sets (A2.6(i)), there exists $\widetilde{\pi} \in \mathbb{R}^n, \widetilde{\pi} \neq 0$ such that

$$\widetilde{\pi}a \leq \widetilde{\pi}x, \quad \forall\, a \in [\bar{x}, \bar{x} + \xi], \quad \forall\, x \in \operatorname{int} U_{\bar{x}}$$

Setting $a = \bar{x}$ gives $\widetilde{\pi}\bar{x} \leq \widetilde{\pi}x, \forall\, x \in \operatorname{int} U_{\bar{x}}$. By continuity of u, $\widetilde{\pi}\bar{x} \leq \widetilde{\pi}x$, $\forall\, x \in U_{\bar{x}}$ so that $\widetilde{\pi} \in \partial u(\bar{x})$. Since $\bar{x} \in \overline{\operatorname{int} U_{\bar{x}}} = U_{\bar{x}}$, $\widetilde{\pi}a \leq \widetilde{\pi}\bar{x}$, $\forall\, a \in [\bar{x}, \bar{x} + \xi]$. Setting $a = \bar{x} + \xi$ gives $\widetilde{\pi}\xi \leq 0$, contradicting (3).

(iii) Let us show that, if u is differentiable and $\nabla u(\bar{x}) \neq 0$, then

$$\partial u(\bar{x}) = \{\pi \in \mathbb{R}^n \mid \pi = \lambda \nabla u(\bar{x}), \quad \lambda \geq 0\}$$

(i) and (ii) of Proposition 31.2 then follow from (i) and (ii) above.

First, we show that $\nabla u(\bar{x}) \in \partial u(\bar{x})$. This is equivalent to $\nabla u(\bar{x})(x - \bar{x}) \geq 0$, $\forall\, x \in U_{\bar{x}}$, or to

$$u(\bar{x} + \xi) \geq u(\bar{x}) \Rightarrow \nabla u(\bar{x})\xi \geq 0 \tag{4}$$

Suppose (4) does not hold. Then there exists $\bar{\xi}$ such that $u(\bar{x} + \bar{\xi}) \geq u(\bar{x})$ and $\nabla u(\bar{x})\bar{\xi} < 0$. By the quasi-concavity of u,

$$u(\bar{x} + \mu\bar{\xi}) = u\left((1 - \mu)\bar{x} + \mu(\bar{x} + \bar{\xi})\right) \geq u(\bar{x}), \quad 0 \leq \mu \leq 1 \tag{5}$$

On the other hand, by Taylor's expansion, $u(\bar{x} + \mu\bar{\xi}) - u(\bar{x})$ has the same sign as $\mu\nabla u(\bar{x})\bar{\xi} < 0$ for μ sufficiently small, which contradicts (5).

Secondly, let us show that all vectors in $\partial u(\bar{x})$ are collinear to $\nabla u(\bar{x})$. Suppose not: then there exists $\pi \in \partial u(\bar{x})$, $\pi \neq 0$ such that $\pi \neq \lambda \nabla u(\bar{x})$ for all $\lambda > 0$. But then there exists $\xi \in \mathbb{R}^n$ such that $\pi\xi \leq 0$ and $\nabla u(\bar{x})\xi > 0$. This is obvious geometrically, and formally follows from the Minkowski-Farkas Lemma (Proposition A6.3 below). By Taylor's expansion, if $\mu > 0$ is sufficiently small, then $u(\bar{x} + \mu\xi) > u(\bar{x})$. But $\pi\mu\xi \leq 0$, which contradicts (i). $\square$

Convex Maximum Problem

The theorem in this subsection gives the first-order conditions which characterize a solution of the *convex programming problem* $\max\{u(x) \mid x \in C\}$, when u is quasi-concave and C is convex. This is a result which has been used repeatedly in this book in the case where u is differentiable and C is defined by differentiable functions. When the model involves production, it is simpler, and more convenient, to directly invoke the assumption that the production sets are convex than to define these sets as intersections of subsets defined by differentiable functions: thus it is useful to be able to dispense with the assumption that the constraint set C is defined by differentiable functions. In this chapter, for expositional reasons, we have maintained the assumption that

u is differentiable, but this is not necessary, and the geometry of the problem is best understood without the differentiability restriction.

A6.2 Theorem (First-Order Conditions for Convex Programming Problem):
Let $u : \mathbb{R}^n \longrightarrow \mathbb{R}$ be continuous, monotonic, and quasi-concave, and let $C \subset \mathbb{R}^n$ be a non-empty convex set. Then $\bar{x}$ is a solution of the problem

$$\max \{ u(x) \mid x \in C \} \tag{6}$$

if and only if $\bar{x} \in C$ and

$$\partial u(\bar{x}) \cap N_C(\bar{x}) \neq \{0\} \tag{7}$$

If u is differentiable and $\nabla u(x) \neq 0$, $\forall x \in C$, then $\bar{x}$ is a solution of the problem (6) if and only if $\bar{x} \in C$ and

$$\nabla u(\bar{x}) \in N_C(\bar{x}) \tag{8}$$

PROOF: When u is differentiable, $\partial u(x) = \{ \pi \in \mathbb{R}^n \mid \pi = \lambda \nabla u(x), \ \lambda \geq 0 \}$ when $\nabla u(x) \neq 0$. Since in this case (8) is equivalent to (7), it suffices to prove that (6) is equivalent to (7).

($\Longrightarrow$) $\bar{x}$ is a solution of (6) if and only if $\bar{x} \in C$ and

$$\operatorname{int} U_{\bar{x}} \cap C = \emptyset$$

By the standard Separation Theorem for convex sets (A2.6(i)), there exists $\pi \in \mathbb{R}^n, \pi \neq 0$ such that

$$\pi x \leq \pi x', \quad \forall x \in C, \quad \forall x' \in \operatorname{int} U_{\bar{x}}$$

Since $\bar{x} \in C$,

$$\pi \bar{x} \leq \pi x', \ \forall x' \in \operatorname{int} U_{\bar{x}}$$

By the continuity of u, $\overline{\operatorname{int} U_{\bar{x}}} = U_{\bar{x}}$, and by the continuity of the scalar product,

$$\pi \bar{x} \leq \pi x', \ \forall x' \in U_{\bar{x}} \quad \Longleftrightarrow \quad \pi \in \partial u(\bar{x})$$

Since $\bar{x} \in U_{\bar{x}}$

$$\pi x \leq \pi \bar{x}, \ \forall x \in C \quad \Longleftrightarrow \quad \pi \in N_C(\bar{x})$$

so that (7) is satisfied.

($\Longleftarrow$) Suppose that $\bar{x} \in C$ and there exists $\pi \in \partial u(\bar{x}) \cap N_C(\bar{x})$, $\pi \neq 0$. If $\bar{x}$ is not a solution of (6) then there exists $x' \in \operatorname{int} U_{\bar{x}} \cap C$. Since $\pi \in \partial u(\bar{x})$, by Proposition A6.1(i)

$$\pi x' > \pi \bar{x}$$

But since $\pi \in N_C(\bar{x})$ and $x' \in C$, it follows that $\pi x' \le \pi \bar{x}$ which contradicts the above inequality. $\square$

Minkowski-Farkas Lemma

Proposition 31.3 asserts that the Pareto criterion for a partnership is equivalent to maximizing profit under a present-value vector which is a weighted sum of the present-value vectors of the partners. The existence of the "weights" in the criterion follows from a classical result of convex analysis known as the Minkowski-Farkas Lemma.

A6.3 Proposition (Minkowski-Farkas Lemma):   *Let $\bar{\pi}, \bar{\pi}^i \in \mathbb{R}^n, i = 1, \dots, I$. The inequality $\bar{\pi}y \ge 0$ is a consequence of the system of inequalities*

$$\bar{\pi}^i y \ge 0, \quad i = 1, \dots, I$$

if and only if there exist non-negative real numbers $(\alpha_1, \dots, \alpha_I)$ such that

$$\bar{\pi} = \sum_{i=1}^{I} \alpha_i \bar{\pi}^i \tag{9}$$

PROOF: ($\Longrightarrow$) Let

$$K(\bar{\pi}^1, \dots, \bar{\pi}^I) = \left\{ \pi \in \mathbb{R}^n \,\middle|\, \pi = \sum_{i=1}^{I} \alpha_i \bar{\pi}^i, \, \alpha_i \ge 0, \, i = 1, \dots, I \right\}$$

denote the closed convex cone generated by $\bar{\pi}^1, \dots, \bar{\pi}^I$. If (9) is not satisfied, then $\bar{\pi} \notin K(\bar{\pi}^1, \dots, \bar{\pi}^I)$. By the strict Separation Theorem for convex sets (A2.6 (ii)), there exists $\bar{y} \in \mathbb{R}^n$ such that

$$\bar{\pi}\bar{y} < \pi\bar{y}, \quad \forall \pi \in K(\bar{\pi}^1, \dots, \bar{\pi}^I) \tag{10}$$

Since $0 \in K(\bar{\pi}^1, \dots, \bar{\pi}^I)$, $\bar{\pi}\bar{y} < 0$. On the other hand (10) implies $\bar{\pi}^i\bar{y} \ge 0$, $i = 1, \dots, I$. For suppose there exists i' such that $\bar{\pi}^{i'}\bar{y} < 0$, then $\alpha_{i'}\bar{\pi}^{i'}\bar{y} \to -\infty$ as $\alpha_{i'} \to \infty$, contradicting (10). But $\bar{\pi}^i\bar{y} \ge 0$, $i = 1, \dots, I$ and $\bar{\pi}\bar{y} < 0$ contradicts the assumption that $\bar{\pi}\bar{y} \ge 0$ is a consequence of the inequalities $\bar{\pi}^i\bar{y} \ge 0$, $i = 1, \dots, I$.

($\Longleftarrow$) immediate. $\square$

A6.4 (Proof of Proposition 31.3, (ii)$'$ $\Longrightarrow$ (ii)$''$):   Define the set

$$Z = Z(\bar{y}^k, \bar{\pi}^1, \dots, \bar{\pi}^I) = \left\{ y \in \mathbb{R}^{S+1} \,\middle|\, \bar{\pi}^i y > \bar{\pi}^i \bar{y}^k, \, i \in I_k \right\}$$

(ii)$'$ is equivalent to $Y^k \cap Z = \emptyset$. By the standard Separation Theorem for convex sets (A2.6(i)), there exists $\bar{\pi} \in \mathbb{R}^{S+1}, \bar{\pi} \neq 0$ such that

$$\bar{\pi} y^k \geq \bar{\pi} y, \quad \forall \, y^k \in Y^k, \quad \forall \, y \in Z \tag{11}$$

Since $\bar{y}^k \in Z$, (11) implies

$$\bar{\pi} y^k \geq \bar{\pi} \bar{y}^k, \, \forall \, y^k \in Y^k \quad \Longleftrightarrow \quad \bar{\pi} \in N(\bar{y}^k) \tag{12}$$

Since $\bar{y}^k \in Y^k$, (11) implies

$$\bar{\pi} \bar{y}^k \geq \bar{\pi} y, \quad \forall \, y \in Z \tag{13}$$

Since Z is defined by a system of inequalities, (13) is equivalent to

$$\bar{\pi}^i (y - \bar{y}^k) \geq 0, \, i \in I_k \quad \Longrightarrow \quad \bar{\pi}(y - \bar{y}^k) \geq 0$$

By Proposition A6.3, there exist non-negative coefficients $(\tilde{\alpha}_k^i, \, i \in I_k)$ such that $\bar{\pi} = \sum_{i \in I_k} \tilde{\alpha}_k^i \bar{\pi}^i$. Let $\tilde{\alpha}_k^i = \alpha_k^i \bar{\theta}_k^i, \, i \in I_k$. Then $\bar{\pi}$ can be written as $\bar{\pi} = \sum_{i \in I_k} \alpha_k^i \bar{\theta}_k^i \bar{\pi}^i$ with $\alpha_k^i \geq 0, \, i \in I_k$. Since $\bar{\pi} \neq 0$, $\alpha_k^i \bar{\theta}_k^i > 0$ for at least one $i \in I_k$. By (12), $\sum_{i \in I_k} \alpha_k^i \bar{\theta}_k^i \bar{\pi}^i \in N_{Y^k}(\bar{y}^k)$ which is equivalent to (ii)$''$. $\square$

Vector Maximum Problem

The proposition in this subsection gives the first-order conditions for the *vector maximum problem* $\max \{ v(\xi) \mid \xi \in C \}$ where $v(\xi) = (v^1(\xi), \dots, v^I(\xi))$ is a vector-valued function whose components $v^i(\xi)$ are differentiable but not necessarily quasi-concave, and where C is a convex set. The first-order conditions, which are the same as the first-order conditions for the maximum of a social welfare function which assigns a weight to the utility of each agent, are necessary but not sufficient.

A6.5 Proposition (FOC for Vector Maximum Problem): *Let* $v = (v^1, \dots, v^I)$: $\mathbb{R}^m \longrightarrow \mathbb{R}^I$ *be differentiable, and let* $C \subset \mathbb{R}^m$ *be a non-empty convex set. If* $\bar{\xi}$ *is a solution of the vector maximum problem*

$$\max \{ v(\xi) \mid \xi \in C \} \tag{14}$$

then there exists $\alpha = (\alpha_1, \dots, \alpha_I) \in \mathbb{R}_+^I, \, \alpha \neq 0$, *such that*

$$\sum_{i=1}^{I} \alpha_i \nabla v^i(\bar{\xi}) \in N_C(\bar{\xi}) \tag{15}$$

PROOF: If $h \in \mathbb{R}^m$ satisfies $\nabla v^i(\bar{\xi}) h > 0$, $i = 1, \ldots, I$, then for $a \in \mathbb{R}$ sufficiently small

$$v^i(\bar{\xi} + ah) > v^i(\bar{\xi}), \ i = 1, \ldots, I \quad \Longleftrightarrow \quad v(\bar{\xi} + ah) \gg v(\bar{\xi})$$

Since C is convex and $\bar{\xi} \in C$, if $\bar{\xi} + h \in C$, then $\bar{\xi} + ah \in C$ for $a \in [0, 1]$. Thus if $\bar{\xi}$ is a solution of (14), then there must not exist $h \in \mathbb{R}^m$ such that

$$\bar{\xi} + h \in C \quad \text{and} \quad \nabla v^i(\bar{\xi}) h > 0, \quad i = 1, \ldots, I$$

Let $H = \{ h \in \mathbb{R}^m \mid \nabla v^i(\bar{\xi}) h > 0, \ i = 1, \ldots, I \}$. Since $(\bar{\xi} + H) \cap C = \emptyset$, the standard Separation Theorem for convex sets (A2.6(i)) implies that there exists $\rho \in \mathbb{R}^m$, $\rho \neq 0$ such that

$$\rho(\bar{\xi} + h) \geq \rho \xi, \quad \forall h \in H, \quad \forall \xi \in C$$

Since $0 \in \overline{H}$,

$$\rho \bar{\xi} \geq \rho \xi, \ \forall \xi \in C \quad \Longleftrightarrow \quad \rho \in N_C(\bar{\xi}) \tag{16}$$

Since $\bar{\xi} \in C$, $\rho h \geq 0$, $\forall h \in H$. By continuity of the scalar product, $\rho h \geq 0$ for all $h \in \overline{H}$, which is equivalent to

$$\nabla v^i(\bar{\xi}) h \geq 0, \ i = 1, \ldots, I \quad \Longrightarrow \quad \rho h \geq 0$$

By the Minkowski-Farkas Lemma A6.3, there exists $\alpha = (\alpha_1, \ldots, \alpha_I) \in \mathbb{R}^I_+$, $\alpha \neq 0$ such that $\rho = \sum_{i=1}^I \alpha_i \nabla v^i(\bar{\xi})$. By (16), $\sum_{i=1}^I \alpha_i \nabla v^i(\bar{\xi}) \in N_C(\bar{\xi})$. $\square$

EXERCISES

1. *Interest rate, impatience, and productivity.*

This exercise, which is a continuation of Exercise 1 in Chapter 2, shows how the *productivity* of capital, in conjunction with the *rate of impatience*, determines the equilibrium rate of interest. This constitutes what Irving Fisher, in his *Theory of Interest* (1930), called the second approximation to the rate of interest (see chapters VI and XI of Fisher (1930)).

Consider a simple one-good two-period economy without uncertainty ($S = 1$). There are two (types of) agents ($i = a, b$) with utility functions

$$u^i(x_0^i, x_1^i) = v^i(x_0^i) + \delta_i v^i(x_1^i)$$

where $v^i(\xi) = \log \xi$ and $0 < \delta_i \leq 1$. There is only one firm in the economy $(K = 1)$, with technology set

$$Y = \{(-y_0, y_1) \in \mathbb{R}^2 \mid y_1 \leq c\sqrt{y_0}\}, \quad c > 0$$

and agent a is its sole proprietor. The profits of this firm are the only source of income for agent a (i.e. $\omega^a = (0,0)$). Agent b is a worker with initial endowment $\omega^b = (\eta, 0)$ who offers his services to agent a. The bond which pays one unit of income at date 1 is the only security $(J = 1)$. If q denotes its price, then the rate of interest r is defined by $q = 1/(1+r)$.

(a) Find the equilibrium bond price (rate of interest) and the equilibrium production, consumption, and security trades as a function of the parameters (η, c, δ_i).

(b) Just for this part of the exercise, replace the production inequality $y_1 \leq c\sqrt{y_0}$ by the inequality $f(y_0, y_1) \leq 0$. Give an economic interpretation of the first-order conditions for each agent at an equilibrium and show that they reduce to

$$\frac{\text{rate of return}}{\text{in production}} = \text{rate of interest} = \frac{\text{rate of impatience}}{\text{(of each agent)}}$$

where the rate of return μ in production is defined by

$$\frac{1}{1 + \mu(y)} = \frac{\dfrac{\partial f(y)}{\partial y_1}}{\dfrac{\partial f(y)}{\partial y_0}}$$

(c) Study how the equilibrium values of the rate of interest, production, consumption and bond trades vary as a function of the parameters (η, c, β_i). (For example, how does a technical improvement (increase in c) affect the interest rate and the agents' consumption?)

(d) Suppose $\delta_a = \delta_b = 1$, $\eta = 100{,}000$, $c = 1{,}000$. By combining the ideas in Figures 10.1 and 30.3, draw a (reasonably accurate) figure to illustrate the equilibrium. Note that since a is the owner of the firm and b is the worker, $x^a \in \bar{y} + \langle W \rangle$ and $x^b \in \omega^b + \langle W \rangle$.

2. *First-order conditions for constrained Pareto optimality under Assumption $\mathcal{T}'$.*

When the production sets Y^k can be represented by differentiable transformation functions T^k, then the first-order conditions for constrained Pareto optimality can be derived using the Kuhn-Tucker theorem.

Consider a one-good two-period production economy $\mathcal{E}(u, \omega, Y, R)$. $u = (u^1, \ldots, u^I)$ are the utility functions of the agents (satisfying Assumption $\mathcal{U}$), $\omega = (\omega^1, \ldots, \omega^I) \in \mathbb{R}_{++}^{I(S+1)}$ are the endowments of the agents, $Y = (Y^1, \ldots, Y^K)$ are the technology sets (satisfying Assumption $\mathcal{T}'$) and R is the $S \times J$ matrix of dividends on J securities in zero net supply (bonds).

(a) Let $F_{R,Y}$ denote the set of constrained feasible plans in Definition 31.7, and let $F_{R,Y}^*$ denote the subset of constrained Pareto optimal plans. Note that these definitions apply in both a partnership and a corporate economy. Derive the first-order necessary conditions for any plan $(x, z, \theta, y) \in F^*_{R,Y}$ using the Kuhn-Tucker theorem.

(b) Give a geometric interpretation of these conditions and compare them with the conditions derived in Section 31 for technology sets satisfying Assumption $\mathscr{T}^*$.

(c) Suppose that the technology sets also satisfy Assumption $\mathscr{T}^*$. Let $((\bar{x}, \bar{z}, \bar{\theta}, \bar{y}), \bar{q})$ be a partnership equilibrium of the economy $\mathscr{E}(u, \omega, Y, R)$. Show that the plan $(\bar{x}, \bar{z}, \bar{\theta}, \bar{y})$ satisfies the first-order conditions derived in (a). Give an economic interpretation of the first-order conditions at the equilibrium.

(d) Why are the first-order conditions in (a) not sufficient to ensure that a plan (x, z, θ, y) lies in $F^*_{R,Y}$?

(e) Let $\widetilde{F}_{R,Y}$ denote the set of constrained feasible plans in Definition 31.7 with the no-short sales condition $\theta^i \in \mathbb{R}^K_+$, $i = 1, \ldots, I$ removed, and let $\widetilde{F}^*_{R,Y}$ denote the subset of constrained Pareto optimal plans. Derive the first-order necessary conditions for any plan $(x, z, \theta, y) \in \widetilde{F}^*_{R,Y}$.

(f) Let $((\bar{x}, \bar{z}, \bar{\theta}, \bar{y}), \bar{q})$ be a (reduced form) stock market equilibrium.

   (i) Suppose the financial markets (stocks and bonds) are complete at the equilibrium. Show that the equilibrium is Pareto optimal.

   (ii) Suppose the financial markets are incomplete at the equilibrium. Explain why the first-order conditions in (e) are typically not satisfied at the equilibrium.

3. *Constrained-inefficient partnership equilibrium (first example).*

This exercise provides specific utility functions and technology sets for Example 31.10.

Consider a one-good two-period production economy $\mathscr{E}(u, \omega, Y)$ with two states of nature at date 1 $(S = 2)$ and two (types of) agents $i = 1, 2$. The agents' utility functions, which do not depend on consumption at date 0, are given by

$$u^1(x^1_1, x^1_2) = 5\sqrt{x^1_1} + x^1_2, \quad u^2(x^2_1, x^2_2) = x^2_1 + 5\sqrt{x^2_2}$$

Both agents have 1 unit of the good at date 0 and no resources at date 1: $\omega^i = (1, 0, 0)$, $i = 1, 2$.

Two ventures are available with constant returns technology sets defined by

$$Y^1 = \{(-y^1_0, y^1_1, y^1_2) \in \mathbb{R}^3 \mid y^1_0 \geq 0, \quad y^1_1 \leq 2y^1_0, \quad y^1_2 \leq y^1_0, \quad y^1_1 + 2y^1_2 \leq 2y^1_0\}$$
$$Y^2 = \{(-y^2_0, y^2_1, y^2_2) \in \mathbb{R}^3 \mid y^2_0 \geq 0, \quad y^2_1 \leq y^2_0, \quad y^2_2 \leq 2y^2_0, \quad 2y^2_1 + y^2_2 \leq 2y^2_0\}$$

The date 1 production possibilities that arise when one unit of input is invested in technology 1 is given by the segment ab in Figure 31.3, and when invested in technology 2 is given by the segment AB. In order to obtain consumption at date 1, the agents must invest their date 0 resources in one or both of the productive ventures. Thus each agent is a potential partner in each venture: let $\theta^i = (\theta^i_1, \theta^i_2)$ denote the partnership shares of agent $i = 1, 2$.

(a) This part of the exercise shows that (B, a) in Figure 31.3 is a partnership equilibrium allocation.

(i)   Show that, if firm 1 has the production plan $\bar{y}^1 = (-1, 0, 1)$ and firm 2 the production plan $\bar{y}^2 = (-1, 1, 0)$, then $\bar{\theta}^1 = (0, 1)$ and $\bar{\theta}^2 = (1, 0)$ are the optimal choices of partnership shares for agents 1 and 2.

(ii) Show that, if agent 1 is the owner of firm 2 i.e. $\bar{\theta}^1 = (0, 1)$ and agent 2 is the owner of firm 1 i.e. $\bar{\theta}^2 = (1, 0)$, then the production plans $\bar{y}^1$ and $\bar{y}^2$ in (a) maximize the profits of the firms given their owners. For each firm, exhibit the present-value vector which is used for maximizing its profit.

(iii) Conclude that the plan $(\bar{x}, \bar{\theta}, \bar{y})$, which is defined by (B, a) in Figure 31.3, is a partnership equilibrium for the economy $\mathscr{E}(u, \omega, Y)$.

(b) This part of the exercise shows that (b, A) in Figure 31.3 is a partnership equilibrium allocation. Answer questions (i)–(iii) in (a) with $\hat{y}^1 = (-1, 2, 0)$, $\hat{y}^2 = (-1, 0, 2)$, $\hat{\theta}^1 = (1, 0)$, $\hat{\theta}^2 = (0, 1)$.

(c) Show that the allocation $\hat{x}^1 = (0, 2, 0)$, $\hat{x}^2 = (0, 0, 2)$, $\hat{y}^1 = (-1, 2, 0)$, $\hat{y}^2 = (-1, 0, 2)$, and the vector of prices $\hat{\pi} = (1, \frac{1}{2}, \frac{1}{2})$ is a contingent market equilibrium of the economy $\mathscr{E}(u, \omega, Y)$.

(d) Conclude that the partnership equilibrium in (b) is Pareto optimal (and hence CPO), while the partnership equilibrium in (a) is constrained Pareto suboptimal.

(e) What is it about the concept of a partnership equilibrium which makes possible the mismatching between agents and firms exhibited in (a)?

4. *Constrained-inefficient partnership equilibrium (second example).*

The object of this exercise is to provide utility functions and technology sets for Example 31.11.

Let the agents' endowments and the technology sets be the same as in Exercise 3. Find utility functions for the two (types of) agents $u^1(x_1^1, x_2^1), u^2(x_1^2, x_2^2)$ such that the two allocations, (i) with production and consumption at C and (ii) with production at (b, A) and consumption at (D, F) in Figure 31.4, can be made into partnership equilibria. Show that the first equilibrium is constrained Pareto suboptimal and that the second is Pareto optimal.

5. *Productively inefficient partnership equilibrium.*

This exercise gives utility functions and technology sets for Example 31.12.

Let the utility functions and endowments of the agents be the same as in Exercise 3. Suppose the technology sets of the two ventures are given by

$$Y^1 = \left\{ (-y_0^1, y_1^1, y_2^1) \mid y_0^1 \geq 0, \ y_1^1 \leq y_0^1, \ y_2^1 \leq y_0^1, \ y_1^1 + y_2^1 \leq y_0^1 \right\}$$
$$Y^2 = \left\{ (-y_0^2, y_1^2, y_2^2) \mid y_0^2 \geq 0, \ y_1^2 \leq \alpha y_0^2, \ y_2^2 \leq \alpha y_0^2, \ y_1^2 + y_2^2 \leq \alpha y_0^2 \right\}$$

(a) Show that for all $\alpha \in (0, 1)$ there are four partnership equilibria: the first (x^*, θ^*, y^*) corresponds to (A, b) in Figure 31.5; the second is the symmetric equilibrium $(x^{**}, \theta^{**}, y^{**})$ corresponding to (a, B); the third is $(\bar{x}, \bar{\theta}, \bar{y})$ with $\bar{x}^1 = (0, 1/2, 1/2) = \bar{x}^2$, $\bar{\theta}^1 = (1/2, 0) = \bar{\theta}^2$, $\bar{y}^1 = (-2, 1, 1)$, $\bar{y}^2 = 0$; and the fourth is $(\hat{x}, \hat{\theta}, \hat{y})$ with $\hat{x}^1 = (0, \alpha/2, \alpha/2) = \hat{x}^2$, $\hat{\theta}^1 = (0, 1/2) = \hat{\theta}^2$, $\hat{y}^1 = 0$, $\hat{y}^2 = (-2, \alpha, \alpha)$.

(b) Show that for all $\alpha \in (0,1), (\hat{x}, \hat{\theta}, \hat{y})$ is not CPO

(c) Show that there exist $0 < \alpha_1 < \alpha_2 < 1$ such that

    (i)   if $\alpha \in (\alpha_2, 1)$ then (x^*, θ^*, y^*) (and its symmetric) is CPO, and $(\bar{x}, \bar{\theta}, \bar{y})$ is not CPO

    (ii) if $\alpha \in (\alpha_1, \alpha_2)$ then (x^*, θ^*, y^*) (and its symmetric) and $(\bar{x}, \bar{\theta}, \bar{y})$ are CPO

    (iii) if $\alpha \in (0, \alpha_1)$ then (x^*, θ^*, y^*) (and its symmetric) is not CPO but $(\bar{x}, \bar{\theta}, \bar{y})$ is CPO.

(d) Calculate (α_1, α_2).

6. *Partnership equilibrium with multiplicative uncertainty.*

Diamond (1967) introduced an interesting type of technology set described by a production function with multiplicative uncertainty: for a venture with this type of technology set the problem of disagreement among partners over the production plan to be selected does not arise.

Consider a partnership economy with I agents and K business ventures summarized by technology sets Y^k ($k = 1, \ldots, K$). Suppose these technology sets exhibit *multiplicative uncertainty* and constant returns to scale, that is, for each $k = 1, \ldots, K$ there exists a fixed vector $\eta^k = (\eta_1^k, \ldots, \eta_S^k) \in \mathbb{R}_+^S$ such that

$$Y^k = \left\{ (-y_0^k, y_1^k) \in \mathbb{R}^{S+1} \;\middle|\; y_1^k = \eta^k y_0^k, \quad y_0^k \geq 0 \right\}$$

Thus the relative payoffs across the states are fixed, and the only choice is the scale at which the kth process should be operated. Let $\eta = (\eta^1, \ldots, \eta^K)$ denote the vectors of per-unit payoffs from the K ventures. Each agent i has preferences represented by a utility function $u^i : \mathbb{R}_+^{S+1} \longrightarrow \mathbb{R}$ satisfying Assumption $\mathscr{U}$ and has the initial resources $\omega^i \in \mathbb{R}_+^{S+1}$, $i = 1, \ldots, I$. There is only one financial security, the riskless bond with price q. Each agent i chooses the amount to lend (b^i) and his share (θ_k^i) in venture k ($k = 1, \ldots, K$, $i = 1, \ldots, I$). Let $\tau_k^i = \theta_k^i y_0^k$ denote the amount invested by agent i in venture k with $\theta^i = (\theta_1^i, \ldots, \theta_K^i)$ and $\tau = (\tau^1, \ldots, \tau^I)$.

(a) Show that the budget set $\mathbb{B}(q, \omega^i, y)$ of agent i can be written as a function of the decision variables $(b^i, \tau^i) \in \mathbb{R} \times \mathbb{R}_+^K$ with parameters (q, ω^i, η).

(b) Prove that at equilibrium all partners agree on the optimal plan of each venture. Show that at an equilibrium, the economy functions as if each agent chose the scale at which to operate each venture which is optimal for him, the activity level of each venture simply being the sum of the activity levels chosen by the individual partners, so that no conflict of interest can arise.

(c) Consider the set of constrained feasible allocations for a planner. Show that this set can be written as a function of the variables (x, b, τ, y_0) and prove that it is convex.

(d) Prove that a partnership equilibrium of this economy is constrained Pareto optimal. Relate this result to the property established in (b).

(e) Suppose that there is a venture k such that $\eta_s^k \geq 1$ for $s = 1, \ldots, S$. Prove that the equilibrium interest rate $\bar{r}$ is non-negative. Interpret this result.

7. *Stock market equilibrium with multiplicative uncertainty.*

This example establishes the two classical results of Diamond (1967) for an economy in which all corporations have technology sets with multiplicative uncertainty: shareholders are unanimous about the firm's production decision and a stock market equilibrium is constrained efficient.

Consider an economy $\mathscr{E}(u, \omega, \delta, R, Y)$ with I agents and K corporations. Suppose that the technology sets of the corporations exhibit *multiplicative uncertainty* and decreasing returns to scale, that is, for each $k = 1, \ldots, K$ there exists a fixed vector $\eta^k = (\eta_1^k, \ldots, \eta_S^k) \in \mathbb{R}_+^S$ and a (differentiable) production function $f_k : \mathbb{R}_+ \longrightarrow \mathbb{R}$ with $f_k' > 0, f_k'' \leq 0$ such that

$$Y^k = \left\{ (-y_0^k, y_1^k) \in \mathbb{R}^{S+1} \;\middle|\; y_0^k \geq 0, \quad y_1^k \leq \eta^k f_k(y_0^k) \right\}$$

Each agent i has a utility function u^i satisfying Assumption $\mathscr{U}$, initial resources $\omega^i \in \mathbb{R}_+^{S+1}$, and initial shares in the corporations $\delta^i = (\delta_1^i, \ldots, \delta_K^i) \in \mathbb{R}_+^K$, $\sum_{i=1}^I \delta_k^i = 1$, $k = 1, \ldots, K$. Agents trade shares of the corporations on the stock market with prices $q'' = (q_1'', \ldots, q_K'')$ and trade the riskless bond ($J = 1$) with price q'. The shares are traded after the initial shareholders have financed the date 0 investment of each corporation.

(a) Find the first-order conditions satisfied at a stock market equilibrium with fixed production plans $(\bar{y}^1, \ldots, \bar{y}^K)$.

(b) Prove that the production plan $\bar{y}^k$ is optimal for initial shareholder i if

$$\left(\sum_{s=1}^S \bar{\pi}_s^i \eta_s^k \right) f_k'(\bar{y}_0^k) = 1$$

where $\bar{\pi}^i$ is the present-value vector of agent i at the stock market equilibrium in (a).

(c) Deduce from (a) and (b) that if

$$\frac{\bar{q}_k''}{f_k(\bar{y}_0^k)} = \frac{1}{f_k'(\bar{y}_0^k)}$$

then the shareholders of firm k are unanimous that the production $\bar{y}^k$ is optimal. Interpret this condition, showing that it implies that the firm's scale of production is optimal when the marginal cost equals the price of output, for an appropriate definition of output.

(d) Show that the set of constrained-feasible plans (using the definition $\widetilde{F}_{R,Y}$ in Exercise 2) can be expressed in terms of the variables (x, z, τ, y_0) where $\tau_k^i = \theta_k^i f_k(y_0^k)$ and that in these variables it is convex.

(e) Show that a (reduced-form) stock market equilibrium of $\mathscr{E}(u, \omega, \delta, R, Y)$ is constrained Pareto optimal (with the definition of CPO corresponding to $\widetilde{F}_{R,Y}^*$).

(f) Explain carefully why the result in (e) does not contradict the assertion in (f)(ii) of Exercise 2 that a stock market equilibrium in an economy in which corporations have technology sets satisfying Assumption $\mathcal{T}'$ is typically not CPO. (Hint: a production set with multiplicative uncertainty is 2-dimensional and is thus much thinner than a production set satisfying Assumption $\mathcal{T}'$ which is $(S+1)$-dimensional. Thus if there is genuine uncertainty ($S \geq 2$), then selecting an optimal production plan from a technology set with multiplicative uncertainty involves much less choice (only the scale of operation) than selecting a plan from a technology set satisfying Assumption $\mathcal{T}'$ where both the scale of operation and the composition of output across the states at date 1 (i.e. the risk profile of the plan) must be determined).

8. *Stock market equilibrium with factor structure.*

Diamond's (1967) results on unanimity and constrained Pareto optimality generalize to the case where firms' production sets satisfy the condition of *partial spanning* (Assumption $\mathcal{PS}$ in Section 32). Partial spanning is equivalent to having a factor structure (in the sense of Ross (1976)), and multiplicative uncertainty corresponds to the case where each firm is influenced by only one of the factors.

Consider an economy $\mathcal{E}(u, \omega, \delta, R, Y)$ with I agents and K corporations, as in Exercise 7, the only difference in the characteristics of the economy being that the technology sets Y are more general. The technology sets $Y^1, \ldots, Y^K$ are said to have a *factor structure* if there exist M linearly independent vectors $\eta^m = (\eta_1^m, \ldots, \eta_S^m) \in \mathbb{R}_+^S, m = 1, \ldots, M$ and K functions $f_m^k : \mathbb{R}_+ \longrightarrow \mathbb{R}$ satisfying $f_m^{k\prime} \geq 0$, $f_m^{k\prime\prime} \leq 0$ for $k = 1, \ldots, K$ such that

$$Y^k = \left\{ (-y_0^k, y_1^k) \in \mathbb{R}^{S+1} \;\middle|\; y_0^k \geq 0,\; y_1^k = \eta^1 f_1^k(y_0^k) + \cdots + \eta^M f_M^k(y_0^k) \right\}$$

Moreover there are genuine differences between the firms in the sense that the *factor rank condition*

$$\mathrm{rank} \begin{bmatrix} f_1^1(y_0^1) & \cdots & f_1^K(y_0^K) \\ \vdots & \ddots & \vdots \\ f_M^1(y_0^1) & \cdots & f_M^K(y_0^K) \end{bmatrix} = M$$

is satisfied for all $(y_0^1, \ldots, y_0^K) \in \mathbb{R}_{++}^K$.

(a) Find the first-order conditions satisfied at a stock market equilibrium with fixed production plans $(\bar{y}^1, \ldots, \bar{y}^K)$. Show that for each factor

$$\sum_{s=1}^S \bar{\pi}_s^1 \eta_s^m = \cdots = \sum_{s=1}^S \bar{\pi}_s^I \eta_s^m, \quad m = 1, \ldots, M$$

where $\bar{\pi}^i$ is the present-value vector of agent i at the equilibrium. Let $\bar{\mu}_m$ denote this common value for the mth factor: give an economic interpretation of $\bar{\mu}_m$ and (optional) calculate $\bar{\mu}_m$ (at the equilibrium).

(b) Prove that the production plan $\bar{y}^k$ is optimal for shareholder i if

$$\sum_{m=1}^{M}\sum_{s=1}^{S} \bar{\pi}_s^i \eta_s^m f_m^{k\prime}(\bar{y}_0^k) = 1$$

(c) Show that if the production plan $\bar{y}^k$ satisfies

$$\sum_{m=1}^{M} \bar{\mu}_m f_m^{k\prime}(\bar{y}_0^k) = 1$$

then the shareholders of corporation k are unanimous that the plan $\bar{y}^k$ is optimal. Interpret this condition.

(d) Show that, with an appropriate change of variable, the set of constrained-feasible plans is convex.

(e) Prove that, if the technology sets have a factor structure, then a (reduced-form) stock market equilibrium is constrained Pareto optimal.

9. *Independence of production decisions from financing.*

This exercise shows that Proposition 32.6, namely the assertion that a firm's production decision is independent of its financial policy, holds for any linear objective function consistent with no-arbitrage.

Suppose that an (extensive form) stock market equilibrium is defined as in Definition 32.7, except that the objective (iii) for the kth corporation is replaced by the more general objective

$$\bar{y}^k \in \arg\max\left\{ \bar{\beta}^k D^k(y,b,\zeta,q) \;\middle|\; (y^k,b^k,\zeta^k) \in Y^k \times \mathbb{R}^J \times \mathbb{R}^K \right\} \qquad \text{(iii}^\prime\text{)}$$

for $k = 1, \ldots, K$, the dividends D^k being defined by (11) and (12) in Section 32. $\beta^k = (1, \beta_1^k, \ldots, \beta_S^k) \in \mathbb{R}_{++}^{S+1}$ is a present-value vector whose value $\bar{\beta}^k$ (at the equilibrium) can be influenced by variables determined at equilibrium.

(a) Prove that the maximum problem (iii$^\prime$) of the kth corporation has a solution if and only if $\bar{\beta}^k W(\bar{q}, R, \overline{D}) = 0$. Interpret this result.

(b) Show that when the maximum problem (iii$^\prime$) has a solution, it is equivalent to

$$\bar{y}^k \in \arg\max\left\{ \bar{\beta}^k \bar{y}^k \;\middle|\; y^k \in Y^k \right\} \qquad \text{(iii}^{\prime\prime}\text{)}$$

(c) Show that the financial policy of the firm is indeterminate and does not affect the equilibrium allocation. Interpret this result.

HISTORICAL REMARKS

The first formal theory of finance and production in a one-good economy appeared in Irving Fisher's *Theory of Interest* (1930). He presented a model of a sequence economy without uncertainty, over a finite number of periods, in which there is a short-term bond at each date which enables agents to redistribute their income across time. Each agent is both a consumer and an entrepreneur, and as an entrepreneur, has access to a set of production opportunities defined by a transformation function (Assumption $\mathscr{T}'$). Each agent makes a consumption-portfolio-production decision and Fisher's definition of equilibrium is precisely a (reduced-form) entrepreneurial equilibrium (Definition 30.1). His most striking result, which is often referred to as the *Fisher Separation Theorem*, asserts that an entrepreneurial firm should choose its production plan so as to maximize the present discounted value of its profit. This result has two important consequences: first, *the firm's objective function is independent of the preferences of the owner*; second, *the production decision is independent of the financing decision, in the sense that financing needs do not influence the firm's choice of production plan*. He showed that the sequence of interest rates over time are determined on the one hand by resource availability and investment opportunities, and on the other by the impatience (preference for present over future consumption) of agents.[1] These results have formed the basis for all subsequent results in the theory of production in a finance economy.

The first extension of the Fisher Separation Theorem to a setting with uncertainty was made in the well-known paper of Modigliani-Miller (1958): they showed that the market value of a corporation depends only on its profit stream and not on the way the claims to this income stream are divided between debt and equity holders. While the model used to establish this result was a partial equilibrium model based on somewhat ad hoc assumptions,[2] the most interesting feature of the paper was the arbitrage argument used to establish their result. If a levered firm (part debt, part equity) were to have greater value than an unlevered firm with the same profit stream, then an individual investor could make a profit by short-selling the levered firm and borrowing on his personal account to buy the same number of shares of the unlevered firm. As we have seen in this chapter, since the principle of no-arbitrage carries over to a general setting with incomplete markets, the Modigliani-Miller result holds quite generally provided that investors and firms have the same access to financial markets. The first proof of this result in a general equilibrium model was due to Stiglitz (1969, 1974) who noted that the result can fail to hold, when markets are incomplete, for debt policies which may lead to bankruptcy. A more recent analysis which takes into account firms' production decisions and interfirm security holdings (but not bankruptcy) was given by Duffie-Shafer (1986b) and DeMarzo (1988).

The problem of determining the appropriate objective function for a multi-owner firm in a setting with uncertainty presented much greater difficulties. The finance literature

---

[1] This is well-expressed by the full title of the book which reads: *The Theory of Interest as Determined by Impatience to Spend Income and Opportunity to Invest it.*

[2] In particular the idea that the profit streams of firms can be divided into risk classes in such a way that, within a given risk class, investors rank profit streams by their expected value.

was based on the criterion of maximizing the firm's market value i.e. the value of equity plus debt. An important foundation was thus provided by the Modigliani-Miller Theorem since it showed that, whatever the appropriate expression for a firm's market value as a function of its actions, it would not depend on the manner in which its production plan was financed. While the expression for market value used by Modigliani-Miller was not based on primitive assumptions, this deficiency was subsequently corrected, under the assumptions of the CAPM model, by Sharpe (1964) and Lintner (1965).

A systematic discussion of the problem of optimal choice of production plan for a multi-owner firm—both from the perspective of its shareholders and from the normative perspective of the efficiency of equilibrium—began with the influential paper of Diamond (1967). He showed that under the assumption of multiplicative uncertainty (see Exercise 7), market-value maximization is a well-defined criterion that leads to a constrained optimal allocation. Although this property was not emphasized by Diamond, in his model the shareholders of each firm unanimously agree on the optimality of the firm's production plan at equilibrium.

Subsequent attempts to generalize these two properties of Diamond's model—unanimity of shareholders with respect to choice of production and constrained Pareto optimality of the equilibrium allocation—revealed that neither of these properties holds under conditions of any generality when markets are incomplete. However these attempts at generalizing Diamond's results played an important role in developing much of the subsequent theory during the 1970s. Ekern-Wilson (1974) identified the conditions for shareholder unanimity— that all the production plans available to each firm are priced by the market at equilibrium. A primitive assumption on the technology sets of firms which ensures that this condition is satisfied was given by Radner (1974): we have called this the condition of partial spanning (Assumption $\mathscr{PS}$). Ekern-Wilson showed that their condition is also satisfied under the conditions of the CAPM model (Definition 17.2). The Ekern-Wilson approach amounts to asking for conditions under which the "market" tells a firm what it should do; these conditions are summarized by formula (10) in Section 32: any conditions that lead either to Pareto optimality ($\check{\pi}_1^{\rho,i} = 0$, $i = 1, \ldots, I$) or partial spanning ($\check{y}_1^k = 0$, $k = 1, \ldots, K$) suffice.

Drèze (1974) sought a generalization of Diamond's model by examining the constrained Pareto optimality of a stock market equilibrium. He showed that there is a well-defined criterion for each firm, derived from the first-order conditions for CPO, which is unanimously agreed on by the shareholders, provided two conditions are satisfied: first that side payments among shareholders are permitted to induce unanimity, and second that production decisions are made by the new shareholders (i.e. after shares have been traded on the stock market). The analysis of Drèze was strongly influenced by the work on public economics of the 1960s and early 1970s. He viewed the decision problem of a corporation as a public-good problem for the group of shareholders in which the decision to be taken is the output to be produced. The first-order conditions for constrained Pareto optimality lead to the shareholder-weighted criterion $\sum_{i \in I_k} \bar{\theta}_k^i \bar{\pi}^i y^k$: this is the analogue of the criterion obtained for choosing the optimal amount of a public good in a Lindahl equilibrium, the weighted prices $\bar{\theta}_k^i \bar{\pi}^i$, $i = 1, \ldots, I$ (reflecting the fact that agent i receives only the share $\bar{\theta}_k^i$ of output) playing the role of the personalized prices in the public-good problem.

The important contribution of Drèze's paper was to show a way of resolving the conflict among shareholders which arises when the "market" no longer tells the firm what it should do. However Grossman-Hart (1979) pointed out that the second condition postulated by Drèze, namely that production decisions are made after the firm's shares are traded, prevents the analysis from being extended to a multiperiod setting: while in a two-period model the timing of the production decision postulated by Drèze permits the shareholders to ignore the effects of the production decision on the firm's equity price, this effect can not be ignored when there are more than two periods. In a multiperiod setting, shares will always be traded after a production decision is made, so that shareholders must take into account the influence of production decisions not only on the firm's subsequent dividends but also on the subsequent capital value of its shares.

Grossman-Hart were thus led to re-examine the two-period model under the alternative timing assumption that firms' production decisions are made before their shares are traded. The important contribution of their analysis is to have introduced the assumption of *competitive price perceptions* (Assumption $\mathscr{C}$) which extends the notion of competitive pricing to a setting with incomplete markets: this hypothesis leads to a determinate way of valuing production plans not priced by the market. The analysis of Grossman-Hart forms the basis for the concept of a reduced-form stock market equilibrium presented in Section 32.

Since one of the principal characteristics which distinguishes a partnership from a corporation is that its shares are not traded on a stock market (or stated more generally, are not transferable) we have chosen to use the analysis of Drèze as the basis for a theory of partnerships. Since a partner cannot sell his shares, he does not attempt to estimate what they might be worth to others, so that the Grossman-Hart criticism of Drèze does not apply: all that matters to a partner is what the present value of the dividend stream is to him.

As we have stressed, the theory of incomplete markets is first and foremost a theory of the organization of economic activity in a sequential setting where time and uncertainty play an essential role. In this chapter we have attempted to show how the earlier results of Modigliani-Miller, Diamond, Drèze and Grossman-Hart can be put together to provide a more systematic picture of the organization of productive activity in an economy. Sole proprietorships, partnerships, and corporations are the three principal types of business enterprise through which such productive activity takes place. In much of the finance literature, the focus is principally on large corporations whose equity is traded on the stock market. In practice, sole proprietorships and partnerships are also, by many measures, important types of business enterprise which should be included in a realistic theory. On a purely numerical basis, of the 21.5 million business enterprises in the U.S. in 1989, 16.1 million were sole proprietorships, 1.8 million partnerships, and 3.6 million corporations: by far the largest number of corporations were closely-held, less than 8,000 having publicly traded equity.

The earliest and perhaps still the soundest explanation for the formation of firms was due to Adam Smith (1776, Book 1, Chapters 1–3): his theory focused on the gains from specialization and co-operation in reducing the per-unit costs of production. He stressed that the extent to which such economies of scale could be exploited are limited by the size of the market. At the time of Adam Smith and until the 1850s the size of business was by modern standards very limited—the traditional sole proprietorship and partnership providing both sufficient capital and adequate organization to meet the needs of the time. It was only with the great innovations in transport (railroads, steamships) and communication (telegraph, postal service) after the 1850s that markets became sufficiently large and accessible on a regular basis to permit the exploitation of economies of scale of a wholly new order. This transformation of business enterprise in the middle of the 19th century, first with the great railroad companies and subsequently, with the introduction of mass production and mass distribution, is the story of the *Second Industrial Revolution*, which has been documented with great clarity and vision by Chandler (1962, 1977, 1990). The efficiency in production obtained by exploiting economies of scale could only be realized however if parallel innovations in *financing* and *organization* were achieved. The emergence of the modern corporation with its widely dispersed ownership, limited liability, and ready transferability of shares, was the financial innovation needed to supply business enterprises with the funds needed to finance their massive capital projects. The benefits from large fixed-capital investments could only be reaped if the organizational capabilities of the firm could be adapted to ensure that the volume of production (the *throughput* in Chandler's language) was constantly maintained at the high level needed to keep unit costs low. This required developing a network of suppliers who could ensure a steady flow of inputs, internal hierarchies to co-ordinate and supervise the production process, as well as an organized system of distribution and marketing to assure the regular and efficient distribution of its products. The financing needs which led to widely dispersed ownership and liquidity of equity contracts, combined with the organizational needs of a skilled and specialized management, led inevitably to the separation of ownership and control, one of the important characteristics of the modern corporation.

Although these developments took place between 1850 and 1950, the central core of economic theory that developed during this period did not choose to focus on these phenomena. This period saw the development of neoclassical economics and the formalization of the theory of resource allocation through a price mechanism. The theory was fundamentally static: a firm was assimilated to a set of blueprints for transforming inputs into outputs, the price system (which reflects preferences, technology, and the availability of economy-wide resources) indicating the best combination for the firm to choose. The only notable exception was the Austrian School,[3] who had a dynamic view of the economy, and saw the strength of capitalism in its propensity to innovate and adapt to new techniques of production. Perhaps the most visionary representative of this school was Schumpeter (1912, 1942) who proposed an essentially *evolutionary* theory of competition and capitalism, advancing the idea—which was certainly not fashionable at the time, and is probably not to this day—that the oligopolistic behavior of large corporations is a minor cost compared to the major cost reductions that they typically succeed in achieving by exploiting economies of scale.[4] Schumpeter's theory—or should we say, *vision*—fits remarkably well with Chandler's detailed account of evolutionary capitalism during the Second Industrial Revolution.

---

[3]Menger (1871), von Wieser (1914), von Mises (1912, 1949), Schumpeter (1912, 1942), Hayek (1948).

[4]As Schumpeter (1942) explained at some length, the inspiration for many of his ideas came from Marx (1867) perceptive and original critique of the evolutionary forces inherent in capitalist economies.

   Much of the modern economic literature on the theory of the firm can be traced to the provocative paper of Coase (1937). He pointed out that economic theory did not have a theory of the firm which was capable of explaining why some activities are *internal* to a firm while others are carried out via *markets*. He introduced the notion of a firm as a party that is contracting with various agents—a view which forms the basis for much of the modern theory. In a long series of penetrating papers and books, Simon (1947, 1957) studied the internal structure of organizations and showed that "the principle of bounded rationality lies at the very core of organization theory, and at the core, as well, of any 'theory of action' that purports to treat human behavior in complex situations" (Simon (1957, p. 200)). By combining the notions of contract, transaction cost, and bounded rationality with the idea that agents behave opportunistically (i.e. in their self-interest), Williamson (1975, 1985) developed a powerful qualitative approach to the analysis of organizations, which gave much insight into the structure of firms and went a long way towards answering some of the questions posed by Coase; this theory has come to be known as the *transactions cost* approach to the theory of the firm. The advent of information economics in the 1970s permitted a more formal mathematical theory of contracting between agents with different objectives and different information to be developed—whose connections with the theory of the firm are well explained by Holmstrom and Tirole (1989).

   If the modern economic literature on the firm can be traced to the paper of Coase, much of the modern theory of the firm in the finance literature (which has concentrated almost exclusively on the corporation) can be traced to the well-known book *The Modern Corporation and Private Property* by Berle and Means (1932). Their central message was the inadequacy of traditional theory for throwing light on (what they identified as) the key problem posed by the modern corporation—the resolution of the conflict of interest between the apparent owners (the shareholders) and the actual controllers (the board of directors and managers). This problem, which was ignored (or at least lay dormant) for a long time, became the subject of an active literature after the stimulating paper of Jensen and Meckling (1976). They re-opened discussion of the Modigliani-Miller Theorem by arguing that the optimal financial structure for a corporation should minimize the agency costs caused by the divergence of interest of three claimants on the corporation's income stream—inside equity holders who control the firm (assimilated to the managers), outside equity holders, and bondholders. The conflict of interest between equity holders and bondholders, when shareholders have limited liability, was studied at the end of Section 32: this phenomenon, which seems to have been first noted by Fama-Miller (1972, ch. 4), was argued by Jensen-Meckling (1976) to be an active force limiting the debt held by corporations. Different ways in which either the market (in particular the market for managers), or reputation effects, or explicit control and monitoring procedures, correct distortions in the corporation's decisions induced by the conflicts of interest between managers and equity holders on the one hand, and bondholders and shareholders on the other, have given rise to an extensive formal literature summarized by Harris-Raviv (1992) and to more qualitative analysis such as in Fama (1980), and Fama-Jensen (1983a,b).

7
MONETARY ECONOMY

Which way shall I persuade a Man to serve me, when the Service, I can repay him in, is such as he does not want or care for? . . . Money obviates and takes away all those Difficulties, by being an acceptable Reward for all the Services Men can do to one another.

Fable of the Bees, Part II (1729), B. Mandeville

It is my belief that the far-reaching and in some respects fundamental difference between the conclusions of a monetary economy and those of the more simplified real-exchange economy have been greatly underestimated by the exponents of traditional economics.

A Monetary Theory of Production, (1933), J. M. Keynes

If a serious monetary theory comes to be written, the fact that contracts are indeed made in terms of money will be of considerable importance. . . The Keynesian revolution cannot be understood if proper account is not taken of the powerful influence exerted by the future . . . and by the large modifications that must be introduced into . . . value theory . . . if the requisite futures markets are missing.

General Competitive Analysis, (1971), K. J. Arrow and F. H. Hahn.

MOTIVATION AND SUMMARY

By far the most dramatic and innovative of all the financial contracts that the human being has invented is the contract called money. This was also the earliest economic invention—or should we say convention since it evolved, and continues to evolve, by a process of trial and error.[1] There is no financial contract that is more important and more pervasive in its impact on the functioning of an economy and yet is more complicated and elusive to model than money. Economic theory has as yet no satisfactory abstract model of money that brings out in a clear way the different functions that it performs. Fundamentally, money is an instrument introduced to facilitate the process of making transactions. But once money is introduced, it does much more than facilitate the immediate, short-run process of exchange: it has an important impact on the way agents undertake their contractual commitments over time. Experience proves that in their business affairs agents find it convenient to make contractual commitments in which money is used as the standard for their deferred payments. Such contracts are called *nominal contracts*: they constitute a significant proportion of all contracts signed by Federal, State and Local governments, businesses, and individuals in a modern economy. The object of this chapter is to show that when agents in the

---

[1] Its systematic recorded use (at least in metallic form) dates back over four thousand years.

private sector choose to commit themselves to such contractual agreements, if the overall system of contracts is incomplete, then money inevitably has an important impact on the outcome of economic activity. We show this in the setting of a simple, highly stylized model of a monetary economy. The underlying message is however likely to be quite robust to different specifications of the way money circulates and facilitates the process of exchange.

Broadly speaking there are two important categories of contracts: those with future payments based on the value of real goods, which we call *real* contracts, and those with future payments consisting of a given amount of money, which we call *nominal* contracts. An example of a real contract is an insurance contract which promises to replace a car in case of accident; an example of a nominal contract is a discount bond promising to pay 1000 dollars at the end of next year regardless of what happens.

In the previous chapters we have studied a one-good model, with the convention that the payoffs on contracts were expressed in units of the single good: the model was intended to serve as the simplest version of a model in which all contracts are real. In such a model, price levels do not matter: when the price level doubles, the payoffs on all contracts double as well as the income that accrues to agents from their endowments. Thus the opportunities available to agents from trading on the markets (i.e. their budget sets) are isolated from the effects of inflation and depend only on relative prices.

In an economy with real contracts, the absence of a monetary theory explaining the determination of price levels does not present a conceptual problem for the hypothesis of correct price anticipations: since price levels do not affect budget sets, agents do not need to correctly anticipate future price levels[2]—if the price level turns out to be twice the level that an agent had anticipated, it is of no consequence, since his income from the real contracts and from his endowment adjusts accordingly. Not only is an agent isolated from the effects of inflation, he does not even need to correctly anticipate inflation. The story is completely different in an economy with nominal contracts: now price levels matter since they determine the purchasing power of the money payoffs of contracts. In deciding whether or not to purchase a discount bond at a given price to-day, it is now essential that an agent correctly anticipates future inflation in order to estimate the bundle of commodities that he will be able to purchase with the 1000 dollars payable next year.

Agents can only be expected to form correct anticipations of future inflation if they understand the economic forces that lie behind the determination of price levels. Furthermore these economic forces, which we take to be monetary, must explicitly determine price levels in the model—if not, the assumption that agents correctly anticipate inflation inevitably involves an element of magic.[3] The simplest monetary theory of the

---

[2]Of course agents must correctly anticipate future relative prices.

[3]An element of mystery is a convenient way of closing a model but is liable to lead to a certain amount of confusion (if not among the agents, at least among economists).

determination of price levels is based on the idea that agents use money as a *medium of exchange* in their transactions, and perhaps the simplest modelling of the role of money as a medium of exchange is that introduced by Clower (1967), which separates the moments at which goods are sold (in exchange for money) from the moments at which the acquired money balances are used to purchase goods. In Section 34 an explicit transactions process is introduced by subdividing date 0 and each of the states at date 1 into three subperiods: in the first, agents acquire money balances from the sale of their endowments to a Central Exchange; in the second, agents transact (or at date 1 receive their dividends from transactions) on the financial markets; and in the third subperiod agents use the money balances acquired in the two previous subperiods to purchase commodities. The simplicity of the model comes from the device of the Central Exchange which avoids the need to force agents to carry money balances across periods, thus permitting the analysis to be restricted to a finite horizon model. Suppressing the role of money as a store of value across periods, while certainly undesirable in a general model of money, is a convenient simplification for the purposes of this chapter. The analysis focuses on the effects of fluctuations in the money supply on the income transfers achievable by agents in the private sector through use of nominal contracts, thus abstracting from the inflation tax imposed on agents' money balances arising from an overall increase in the money supply.

Monetary policy is said to be *neutral* if the real outcome (i.e. the equilibrium allocation) is independent of the money supply; if money is *non-neutral*, different monetary policies can lead to different real outcomes. The idea that the non-neutrality of money can be attributed to the presence of nominal contracts is a theme that has a long history in monetary theory.[4] Under the influence of Keynes (1936), and more recently with the discovery of the statistical relation between inflation and unemployment, known as the Phillips Curve,[5] the discussion of the real effects of monetary policy has focused on the presence of nominal wage contracts. Friedman (1968) attributed the short-run non-neutrality of money to errors or lags in the expectations of agents trading nominal contracts: if agents sign contracts based on a lower anticipated inflation rate than the one that is induced by monetary policy, then inflation has the effect of redistributing income from lenders to borrowers, or for labor contracts, from workers to firms. Such effects were straightforward to establish under the hypothesis of adaptive expectations, the standard expectations assumption until the early seventies.

The assumption of adaptive expectations leads to policy recommendations based on systematic errors on the part of agents. Sooner or later, however, agents in the

---

[4] It became the focus of considerable attention by classical economists such as Jevons (1875), Marshall (1923), Pigou (1927), and Fisher (1911) because of the substantial fluctuations in the purchasing power of money experienced during the nineteenth century.

[5] As is well-known, this was in fact a rediscovery of statistical evidence which had been earlier reported by Irving Fisher (1926) and was known to other economists of that period (see Pigou (1927, ch.22)).

private sector come to understand the consequences of monetary policy for inflation and incorporate this into their expectations. This became abundantly clear in the early seventies, and led the economics profession to shift from the assumption of *adaptive expectations* to the assumption of *rational expectations*. As shown by Sargent-Wallace (1975), when agents correctly anticipate the consequences of monetary policy and adjust their behavior accordingly, results of non-neutrality under adaptive expectations can become results of neutrality under rational expectations. Fischer (1977) pointed out that the Sargent-Wallace neutrality result depends crucially on the assumption that contracts are renegotiated at the same moments that monetary policy can be changed: he showed that if contracts are fixed over longer periods, then even under rational expectations, monetary policy is non-neutral.

The main objective of this chapter is to extend these earlier results of Sargent-Wallace and Fischer, by deriving conditions under which monetary policy is neutral or non-neutral under the assumption that agents correctly anticipate monetary policy. For the model that we study, non-neutrality requires four conditions:

(i) *non-indexed nominal contracts*: indexing transforms nominal into real contracts, and, in an economy with real contracts, monetary policy is always neutral (Section 37);

(ii) *a random monetary policy* i.e. a policy which is not known for sure at the time when the contracts are signed. If the money supply is non-random, then the implied inflation is incorporated directly into the prices of the nominal contracts and has no real effects (Proposition 35.3);

(iii) *incomplete markets*: with complete markets, agents can always adjust their portfolios to retain the same consumption stream regardless of the variability or the level of anticipated inflation, so that monetary policy is neutral (Proposition 35.4);

(iv) *heterogeneous agents*: money can have real effects only if agents trade, and agents will trade only if they are heterogeneous in their characteristics.

The analysis of Section 35 shows that if these four conditions are fulfilled, and if there are enough agents that are heterogeneous (at least with respect to their endowments), then typically monetary policy is non-neutral. The model studied by Fischer satisfies these four conditions—hence the non-neutrality result—while the model studied by Sargent-Wallace does not satisfy (ii), so that money is neutral. Many cash-in-advance models assume that there is a representative agent and that markets are complete and thus imply neutrality of money (Sargent (1987)).

In Section 36 the model is used to formalize an idea which underlies much of classical monetary theory and which has more recently been expressed in forceful terms by Friedman (1968): a monetary policy which introduces additional shocks into the economy over and above the unavoidable real shocks that affect technology and resources is never optimal.

33. REAL AND NOMINAL CONTRACTS

Recall the two-period exchange economy introduced in Section 5, in which there are L goods at date 0 and in each state at date 1. Each agent has an initial endowment $\omega^i = (\omega_0^i, \omega_1^i, \ldots, \omega_S^i) \in \mathbb{R}_+^{L(S+1)}$, consisting of the vector $\omega_0^i = (\omega_{01}^i, \ldots, \omega_{0L}^i) \in \mathbb{R}_+^L$ of the L goods at date 0 and the vector $\omega_s^i = (\omega_{s1}^i, \ldots, \omega_{sL}^i)$, which he correctly anticipates, for each state s at date 1. The agent's preference ordering over consumption bundles $x^i = (x_0^i, x_1^i, \ldots, x_S^i) \in \mathbb{R}_+^{L(S+1)}$ is represented by a utility function $u^i : \mathbb{R}_+^{L(S+1)} \longrightarrow \mathbb{R}$.

In each state s there are spot markets on which the L goods can be bought and sold at the current spot prices $p_s = (p_{s1}, \ldots, p_{sL})$. By a mechanism that will be made explicit in Section 34, agents acquire money balances from the sale of their endowments and then, after transacting on the financial markets, purchase their desired vector of consumption. The price $p_{s\ell}$ of good ℓ in state s is thus expressed in units of money. Let $p = (p_0, p_1, \ldots, p_S) \in \mathbb{R}_+^{L(S+1)}$ denote the vector of *spot prices* across the $S + 1$ states.

Since goods are paid for with money, it is natural for the payoffs of the financial securities to be expressed in units of money. This leads naturally to a distinction between two categories of financial contracts: those whose payoff in each state is a function of the current spot prices and those whose payoff in each state is an exogenously specified amount of money which is independent of the current spot price.

33.1 Definition: A financial contract is said to be a *real contract* if its payoff in state s is the value $V_s^j = p_s A_s^j$ of a specified bundle $A_s^j = (A_{s1}^j, \ldots, A_{sL}^j)$ of the L goods under the spot prices p_s for $s = 1, \ldots, S$.

The payoff V_s^j on a real contract is a linear homogeneous function of the spot price vector p_s. A real contract is thus *inflation proof* in the sense that doubling the spot prices in state s doubles its payoff: more precisely, $V_s^j(\alpha p_s) = \alpha V_s^j(p_s)$ for all $\alpha > 0$. This property of real contracts is of central importance in the analysis that follows. By contrast, the payoff on the second type of contract is independent of the current spot prices: thus, doubling the spot prices in state s cuts the purchasing power of its payoff in half.

33.2 Definition: A financial contract is said to be a *nominal contract* if its payoff in state s is a specified amount of money N_s^j which is independent of the spot prices p_s for $s = 1, \ldots, S$.

Two important examples of real contracts are futures contracts and the equity contracts of corporations (provided the corporations are not financed by debt). A *futures contract* for good ℓ is a promise to deliver one unit of good ℓ (or the spot market value of one unit of good ℓ) in each state at date 1. If contract j is a futures contract for good ℓ then $A^j_{s\ell'} = 1$ if $\ell' = \ell$ and zero otherwise, so that $V^j_s = p_{s\ell}$, $s = 1, \ldots, S$. If the production plan $y^j = (y^j_0, y^j_1, \ldots, y^j_S) \in \mathbb{R}^{L(S+1)}$ of corporation j is financed at date 0 by retained earnings then its *equity contract* pays the dividend $V^j_s = p_s y^j_s$, which is the profit from its production plan $A^j_s = y^j_s$ in state s, for $s = 1, \ldots, S$.

The simplest example of a nominal contract is the bond which pays one unit of money in each state s at date 1, namely the dividend stream $\mathbb{1} = (1, \ldots, 1)$. In the previous chapters, where there was only one good ($L = 1$) and this good was taken to be the unit of account in each state, it was appropriate to call this contract the riskless bond. However, when payments in each state are made in money and when the purchasing power of money can vary across the states, it is no longer appropriate to call this security the riskless bond. In this chapter therefore, the bond with dividend stream $\mathbb{1} = (1, \ldots, 1)$ will be called the *default-free bond*: there is no risk of default, but there is risk arising from fluctuations in the purchasing power of money.

There are many contracts whose payoffs have both real and nominal components. If, as in Section 32, a corporation is partly financed by debt and for simplicity there are no interfirm shareholdings, then its equity contract pays the dividend $D^j_s = p_s y^j_s - b^j$ in state s, where b^j is the nominal value of its debt: thus the equity contract of a corporation which is debt financed is not inflation proof. When there is risk of bankruptcy, the corporation's bond is no longer a (purely) nominal contract, since its return R^j_s is one unit of money if $p_s y^j_s \geq b^j$, and $p_s y^j_s$ if $p_s y^j_s < b^j$. Since the analysis of contracts which have both real and nominal components is more complex, attention in this chapter will focus on securities that are either real or nominal.

Real Contracts

We begin by considering the case which leads to the concept of equilibrium which is the most straightforward generalization of the one studied in the earlier chapters: this case arises when the all the contracts are *real*. Let $A_s = [A^1_s \ldots A^J_s]$ denote the $L \times J$ matrix of commodity payoffs from the J real securities in state s, and let $A = (A_s, s = 1, \ldots, S)$ denote the collection of all commodity payoff matrices across the S states at date 1. When all the securities are real, the budget set of agent i can be written as

$$
\mathbb{B}(p, q, \omega^i, A) = \left\{ x^i \in \mathbb{R}^{L(S+1)}_+ \;\middle|\; \begin{array}{l} p_0(x^i_0 - \omega^i_0) = -qz^i, \; z^i \in \mathbb{R}^J \\ p_s(x^i_s - \omega^i_s) = p_s A_s z^i, \; s = 1, \ldots, S \end{array} \right\} \quad (1)
$$

Given the date 0 prices (p_0, q) and the anticipated spot prices $p_1 = (p_1, \ldots, p_S)$

at date 1, agents choose their date 0 consumption and portfolio (x_0^i, z^i), anticipating their date 1 consumption stream $x_1^i = (x_1^i, \ldots, x_S^i)$, so as to maximize their utility over their budget sets (1). An equilibrium is obtained on the system of spot and financial markets when the date 0 markets clear and the anticipated consumption streams of agents are compatible, in the sense that at the date 1 spot price p_s, the L spot markets will clear in state s, for each state $s = 1, \ldots, S$. The date 1 market-clearing equations thus not only imply that the anticipated consumption vector x_s^i of each agent can be realized whichever state s occurs, but also that *the price anticipations of the agents are correct*. This concept, which Radner (1972) aptly called an equilibrium of plans, prices, and price expectations, we have called more briefly a correct expectations equilibrium (Section 5). In this chapter, to place more emphasis on the market structure rather than on agents' expectations and to focus on the fact that goods and income are traded on two distinct types of markets, we will call this a *spot-financial market equilibrium*.

33.3 Definition: A *spot-financial market equilibrium* for the two-period L-good economy $\mathscr{E}(u, \omega, A)$ with real contracts is a pair of actions and prices

$$((\bar{x}, \bar{z}), (\bar{p}, \bar{q})) \in \mathbb{R}_+^{nI} \times \mathbb{R}^{JI} \times \mathbb{R}_+^n \times \mathbb{R}^J, \quad n = L(S + 1)$$

such that

(i) $(\bar{x}^i; \bar{z}^i) \in \arg \max \{ u^i(x^i) \mid (x^i; z^i) \in \mathbb{B}(\bar{p}, \bar{q}, \omega^i, A) \}, \, i = 1, \ldots, I$

(ii) $\sum_{i=1}^I (\bar{x}^i - \omega^i) = 0$ (iii) $\sum_{i=1}^I \bar{z}^i = 0$

Walras Consistency Test

A long time ago Walras (1874) suggested a simple test for determining whether an equilibrium has been appropriately described. He was referring, of course, to a mathematical description of an equilibrium: this involves a collection of variables (unknowns), which are typically the prices, and a collection of equations that must be satisfied by these variables, which express equality between demand and supply for the commodities or contracts in question. He wanted the equilibrium to be *determinate*: for this to hold, *the number of independent equations must equal the number of unknowns*. It is instructive to apply this test to the equations which define a spot-financial market equilibrium.

Let $\tilde{x}^i(p, q) = (\tilde{x}_0^i(p, q), \ldots, \tilde{x}_S^i(p, q))$ denote agent i's demand[1] for the L goods at date 0 and in each of the states at date 1, as a function of the

---

[1] If the agents' utility functions are strictly quasi-concave, then the maximum problem in Definition 33.3(i) yields a demand function for the L goods; if rank $V(p) = J$ for all $p \in \mathbb{R}_+^{L(S+1)}$, then each agent has a well-defined portfolio demand function for the J securities. The way to handle changes in the rank of the matrix $V(p)$ are explained in the second volume.

vector of spot prices $p = (p_0, \ldots, p_S)$ and the security prices q. Similarly, let $\tilde{z}^i(p, q) = (\tilde{z}_1^i(p, q), \ldots, \tilde{z}_J^i(p, q))$ denote the agent's demand for the J securities. The pair $(\tilde{x}^i, \tilde{z}^i) = (\tilde{x}^i(p, q), \tilde{z}^i(p, q))$ is thus a solution of the agent's maximum problem in (i) of Definition 33.3.

Let $F(p, q) = \sum_{i=1}^I (\tilde{x}^i(p, q) - \omega^i)$ denote the aggregate excess demand for the L goods on the $S + 1$ spot markets: thus F is a vector with components $F_{s\ell}$, $s = 0, 1, \ldots, S$, $\ell = 1, \ldots, L$, where $F_{s\ell}$ denote the excess demand for good ℓ on spot market s. Similarly let $G(p, q) = \sum_{i=1}^I \tilde{z}^i(p, q)$ denote the aggregate excess demand for the J securities: thus G is a vector with components G_j, $j = 1, \ldots, J$, where G_j is the excess demand for security j. A vector of equilibrium prices (p, q) is a solution of the system of $L(S + 1) + J$ equations expressing equality between demand and supply for each of the goods and each of the securities ((ii) and (iii) in Definition 33.3)

$$\left.\begin{array}{cc} F_{01}(p, q) = 0 & G_1(p, q) = 0 \\ \vdots & \vdots \\ F_{SL}(p, q) = 0 & G_J(p, q) = 0 \end{array}\right\} \iff \left\{\begin{array}{l} F(p, q) = 0 \\ G(p, q) = 0 \end{array}\right. \tag{2}$$

Are these $L(S + 1) + J$ market-clearing equations independent? Certainly not. Since each agent fully spends his income both at date 0 $(p_0(x_0^i - \omega_0^i) + qz^i = 0)$ and in each state s at date 1 $(p_s(x_s^i - \omega_s^i) - V_s z^i = 0$, with $V_s = p_s A_s)$, it follows by summing over the agents that we have the $S + 1$ Walras' Laws

$$p_0 F_0 + qG = 0, \quad p_s F_s - V_s G = 0, \quad s = 1, \ldots, S \tag{3}$$

(3) expresses $S + 1$ relations of dependence between the components of the aggregate excess demands: there are thus at most $L(S + 1) + J - (S + 1)$ independent equations in the system of equilibrium equations (2). To understand more intuitively what the relations of dependence (3) imply, note that when the security markets clear $(G(p, q) = 0)$, then the value of aggregate excess demand for goods is zero in each state

$$p_s F_s(p, q) = \sum_{\ell=1}^L p_{s\ell} F_{s\ell}(p, q) = 0 \iff F_{sL}(p, q) = -\frac{1}{p_{sL}} \sum_{\ell=1}^{L-1} p_{s\ell} F_{s\ell}(p, q)$$

Thus, market clearing for the securities and for $L - 1$ of the goods in each state, automatically entails market clearing for the Lth good in every state: in other words, the $S + 1$ equations $F_{sL}(p, q) = 0$, $s = 0, 1, \ldots, S$ are redundant and could be dropped from the equilibrium equations (2).

Since there are less independent equations $(L(S + 1) + J - (S + 1))$ than unknowns (the $L(S + 1) + J$ prices (p, q)), *the system of equilibrium equations (2) is indeterminate in the prices: there are $S + 1$ too few equations*. Does this mean that the equilibrium concept in Definition 33.3 has something missing?

In a sense, yes: the equilibrium equations only serve to determine the relative prices of the goods in each state—the $S + 1$ price levels are completely indeterminate. As it happens, however, *when the contracts are real, changing the price levels (while leaving the relative prices unchanged) does not affect the equilibrium allocation*: thus while there is indeterminacy in the price component of an equilibrium, there is no indeterminacy in the quantity component i.e. in the allocation. This can be seen as follows. Suppose the vector of spot prices p_s is multiplied by the factor $\beta_s > 0$ for $s = 1, \ldots, S$. Agent i's budget equations at date 1 become

$$\beta_s p_s (x_s^i - \omega_s^i) = \beta_s p_s A_s z^i, \quad s = 1, \ldots, S$$

which are the same as the date 1 budget equations in (1). Thus while the prices of the goods in state s have been multiplied by the factor β_s, the income that the agent receives from the securities has increased by the same factor: the change in the price level for state s does not affect the agent's opportunity set since real securities are inflation proof. If the prices (p_0, q) at date 0 are changed to $(\beta_0 p_0, \beta_0 q)$ for some $\beta_0 > 0$, then the date 0 equation becomes

$$\beta_0 p_0 (x_0^i - \omega_0^i) = -\beta_0 q z^i$$

so that once again the agent's budget set in unaffected. The change in the $S+1$ price levels can be conveniently expressed as follows: for $\beta = (\beta_0, \ldots, \beta_S) \in \mathbb{R}^{S+1}$ and $p = (p_0, \ldots, p_S) \in \mathbb{R}^{L(S+1)}$ define the *scalar box-product*

$$\beta \square p = (\beta_0 p_0, \ldots, \beta_S p_S)$$

We have shown that for any $\beta \in \mathbb{R}_{++}^{S+1}$

$$\mathbb{B}(\beta \square p, \beta_0 q, \omega^i, A) = \mathbb{B}(p, q, \omega^i, A) \tag{4}$$

It follows that the agent's demand for goods and securities is unchanged, $\tilde{x}^i(\beta \square p, \beta_0 q) = \tilde{x}^i(p, q)$ and $\tilde{z}^i(\beta \square p, \beta_0 q) = \tilde{z}^i(p, q)$, which in turn implies that aggregate demand for goods and securities is unaffected

$$F(\beta \square p, \beta_0 q) = F(p, q), \quad G(\beta \square p, \beta_0 q) = G(p, q) \tag{5}$$

Thus if (p, q) is an equilibrium price then $(\beta \square p, \beta_0 q)$ is also an equilibrium price, and the equilibrium allocation is unchanged, for any $\beta \in \mathbb{R}_{++}^{S+1}$.

From a mathematical point of view, the $S + 1$ homogeneity conditions in (5) express the fact that there are $S + 1$ directions in the price space $\mathbb{R}_+^{L(S+1)} \times \mathbb{R}^J$ in which price changes have no real effects: as far as the equilibrium model is concerned there seems to be redundancy in the prices, since only relative prices matter. If a normalization[2] of the prices in each state is introduced so as to eliminate this redundancy, then the equilibrium equations (2) become a system for which the number of (independent) equations $(L(S+1) + J - (S+1))$ is equal to the number of unknowns and is hence determinate. This property, that $S+1$ normalizations are required to make the system of equilibrium equations (2) determinate, reflects the fact that a deeper monetary phenomenon is missing in the description of an equilibrium given by Definition 33.3. This will become clear in the next section.

Nominal Contracts

We now consider the case where all the contracts are nominal. The payoff of security j in state s is N_s^j units of money. Let

$$N = \begin{bmatrix} N_1^1 & \cdots & N_1^J \\ \vdots & \ddots & \vdots \\ N_S^1 & \cdots & N_S^J \end{bmatrix}$$

denote the $S \times J$ payoff matrix of the nominal contracts. Given the endowment ω^i, the matrix N, and faced with the spot and security prices (p, q), the budget set of agent i is

$$\mathbb{B}(p, q, \omega^i, N) = \left\{ x^i \in \mathbb{R}_+^{L(S+1)} \;\middle|\; \begin{array}{l} p_0(x_0^i - \omega_0^i) = -qz^i, \; z^i \in \mathbb{R}^J \\ p_s(x_s^i - \omega_s^i) = N_s z^i, \; s = 1, \ldots, S \end{array} \right\} \quad (6)$$

Formally, the equilibrium described by Definition 33.3 for real securities can be carried over to the case where the securities are nominal, the only change being that (6) replaces the earlier budget set (1). Let $(\tilde{x}^i(p, q), \tilde{z}^i(p, q))$ denote agent i's optimal consumption and portfolio choice over this new budget set, then an equilibrium price (p, q) is a solution of the system of equations (2). The Walras consistency test can be applied as before. The argument showing that the $L(S+1)$ goods market and the J security market equations are not independent is entirely unchanged: the agents still fully spend their income, and this leads at the aggregate level to the $S+1$ relations of dependence (3). There are thus $S+1$ less independent equations than prices, so that the system of equations (2) will not lead to a determinate solution for the prices. All this is just as before.

   With real securities we found that all was not lost, since $S+1$ homogeneity relations lay behind the scenes, which exactly offset this $S+1$-dimensional deficiency in the number of equations, thereby ensuring that the equilibrium

---

[2]Standard normalizations are $p_{s1} = 1$, $s = 0, 1, \ldots, S$ or $\sum_{\ell=1}^L p_{s\ell}^2 = 1$, $s = 0, 1, \ldots, S$ or $\sum_{\ell=1}^L p_{s\ell} = 1$, $s = 0, 1, \ldots, S$.

allocation (namely the real side) is determinate. With nominal securities no such rescue job is possible: the whole equilibrium concept, both the allocation and the prices become indeterminate. The intuition for this can be explained as follows.

Suppose the spot prices p_s in state s are doubled (or more generally multiplied by some factor $\beta_s > 0$). Since doubling the spot prices doubles the net expenditure $(\beta_s p_s (x_s^i - \omega_s^i))$ needed to purchase the agent's consumption bundle, but leaves the dividend income from the securities completely unchanged $(N_s z^i)$, the agent can no longer afford the same consumption bundle. Doubling the spot prices has halved the purchasing power of the dividend income accruing from the nominal securities. More precisely, with nominal securities there are (in general) only two "directions" in which the prices (p, q) can be changed without affecting the agents' budget sets. First, since multiplying both sides of the date 0 budget equation by a factor $\beta_0 > 0$ leaves the equation unchanged, multiplying the date 0 prices (p_0, q) by the factor β_0 does not affect the agents' budget sets. Second, if all spot prices $p_1 = (p_1, \ldots, p_S)$ at date 1 are doubled (multiplied by a common factor $\beta > 0$, $p_1 \longrightarrow \beta p_1$) and if the security prices are halved $(q \longrightarrow q/\beta)$ to compensate for the decreased purchasing power of the securities' dividends, since agents can afford to double their portfolios $(z^i \longrightarrow \beta z^i)$ they can still afford the same consumption bundles: in short,

$$\left. \begin{array}{l} p_0(x_0^i - \omega_0^i) = -\dfrac{q}{\beta}(\beta z^i) \\ \beta p_s(x_s^i - \omega_s^i) = N_s(\beta z^i) \end{array} \right\} \Longleftrightarrow \left\{ \begin{array}{l} p_0(x_0^i - \omega_0^i) = -q z^i \\ p_s(x_s^i - \omega_s^i) = N_s z^i \end{array} \right.$$

These two directions of price change

$$(p_0, q) \longrightarrow (\beta_0 p_0, \beta_0 q) \quad \text{and} \quad (p_1, q) \longrightarrow (\beta p_1, q/\beta)$$

do not affect the agents' budget sets, and hence do not affect their demands $(\tilde{x}^i, \tilde{z}^i)$ or the aggregate demand (F, G) in a way that fundamentally alters the equilibrium, since

$$\begin{array}{ll} F(\beta_0 p_0, p_1, \beta_0 q) = F(p_0, p_1, q), & G(\beta_0 p_0, p_1, \beta_0 q) = G(p_0, p_1, q) \\ F(p_0, \beta p_1, q/\beta) = F(p_0, p_1, q), & G(p_0, \beta p_1, q/\beta) = \beta G(p_0, p_1, q) \end{array}$$

Thus if (p_0, p_1, q) is an equilibrium, so is $(\beta_0 p_0, p_1, \beta_0 q)$ for any $\beta_0 > 0$, and so is $(p_0, \beta p_1, q/\beta)$ for any $\beta > 0$. In the latter case all agents have scaled up their portfolios $(z^i \longrightarrow \beta z^i)$, but this simply reflects the fact that security prices have fallen $(q \longrightarrow q/\beta)$ and does not alter the equilibrium allocation $x = (x^1, \ldots, x^I)$. Portfolios, after all, are only a means to an end: all that matters is the consumption that they make possible (the equilibrium allocation x), their actual magnitude being in every other respect of no significance.

Indeterminacy

In the next section it will be shown that under appropriate assumptions these are the only directions of price changes which do not affect the aggregate demand for commodities F. If these two homogeneity conditions are factored out by appropriate normalizations,[3] then there are still $S - 1$ less independent equations than unknowns. Thus, when Walras' consistency test is applied to the equilibrium described by Definition 33.3 for an economy with nominal contracts, then the equilibrium is found to be indeterminate since there are $S - 1$ too few equations for determining the unknown prices. The $S - 1$ directions in which price changes affect aggregate demand can be shown, by a more complete analysis, to translate into $S - 1$ dimensions of distinct real equilibrium allocations.[4] Thus, even though the equilibrium described by Definition 33.3 is indeterminate when the contracts are real, the indeterminacy is much more serious when the contracts are nominal.

The economic reason for the indeterminacy is clear. Different profiles of price levels across the states of nature lead to different purchasing power for the nominal securities' payoffs across the states. When the financial markets are *incomplete*, changes in the purchasing power of the nominal payoffs lead to changes in the subspace of income transfers achievable by trading the securities. It is this freedom to vary the price levels and hence to tilt the subspace of income transfers—i.e. to change the basic risk sharing opportunities offered by the securities—that leads to the continuum (or more precisely, $S - 1$-dimensional set) of equilibrium allocations.

The indeterminacy of the equilibrium outcomes reflects two important deficiencies of the model. First, a model with a continuum of outcomes is severely limited in its predictive and explanatory power: looked at another way, indeterminacy suggests that there is perhaps an important element which is missing in the model. Second, indeterminacy creates conceptual difficulties with the assumption that agents correctly anticipate future spot prices—and hence, in particular, future spot price levels. When price levels matter, all agents must anticipate the same price levels to arrive at an equilibrium. But since there is nothing in the concept of equilibrium (Definition 33.3) for determining the price levels, it is difficult to see how the agents' expectations regarding future price levels come to be co-ordinated. Even if agents have a good understanding of how the economy functions, the model does not make any data available to them on the basis of which they could calculate future price levels. Thus when

---

[3]For example $p_{01} = 1$ and $\sum_{s=1}^{S} p_{s1} = 1$.

[4]A more precise statement is that the set of equilibrium allocations contains an $S - 1$-dimensional smooth manifold. This property can be established by making precise the notion of a smooth manifold and by drawing on techniques of differential topology. The appropriate notions and techniques are introduced and studied in Volume 2.

the contracts are nominal, if the assumption of correct price anticipations is to be retained, then some mechanism must be introduced for determining price levels.

Nominal contracts reflect the fact that we live in a monetary economy in which transactions take place through a medium of exchange. Thus when nominal contracts are introduced into the model, a more explicit account needs to be given of the way money circulates in the economy, how transactions take place via the medium of exchange, and how the volume of these transactions in conjunction with the available supply of fiat money determine price levels.

34. MONETARY EQUILIBRIUM

Money is traditionally said to perform three functions: to act as a *medium of exchange*, to provide a *store of value*, and to serve as a *unit of account* for current as well as deferred payments. The primary function of money is to facilitate the process of exchange—a highly complex process in a modern economy with a huge multiplicity of goods and contracts and an immense specialization of tasks—and it does so by serving as an indirect medium of exchange. In an economy without money, that is, in a *barter economy*, goods would have to be exchanged for goods: an agent with $\omega_{s\ell}^i$ units of (say) labor services would have to find some other agent offering the very goods he wants to obtain in exchange for $\omega_{s\ell}^i$. With extensive specialization and a large number of commodities, such a process would be extraordinarily cumbersome and most costly in the time and effort required to search and find a "satisfactory" matching of agents and goods. By a process of trial and error (that, after all, is how most contracts and institutional arrangements are discovered) the individuals in even the earliest societies rapidly hit on the much cleverer idea of selecting one of the goods to serve as a medium of exchange, thereby breaking up the single barter act of exchanging good ℓ for good ℓ' into the double operation of first selling good ℓ in exchange for money and then subsequently using the acquired money balances to purchase good ℓ' (see Figure 34.1). It is traditional to say that the introduction of money solves the problem of *double coincidence of wants* faced in a barter economy.

In the four thousand or so years that money has been used as a medium of exchange, it was normally important that the "object" singled out to serve as a medium of exchange was a commodity which had a substantial value in its own right for the services it performed as a commodity, quite apart from the value it acquired by serving as a medium of exchange. It is a relatively modern phenomenon that individuals in society by a combination of custom, convention, and fiat have come to accept an inconvertible paper currency (which is intrinsically worthless) as the universal medium of exchange for transactions.

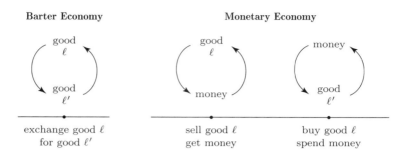

Figure 34.1   Exchange in a barter and a monetary economy.

In performing its function as a medium of exchange, money must also act as a *store of value* between the time it is received (in exchange for good ℓ) and the time when it is spent (on the purchase of good ℓ'). In the model that we outline in the next section, money will always perform this function across the subperiods at which goods are sold and those at which they are bought: in short, money always acts as a "current" or short-period store of value—hence the term "currency". It is more difficult however to model (in a satisfactory way) the role of money as a long-period (across the periods) store of value when there are other securities such as the default-free bond which offer a positive rate of return: for no individual wants to hold money balances across the periods (since doing so means forfeiting the positive default-free return on the bond) and yet the private sector as a whole must do so. As we shall see in the next section some "device" is needed to cope with this problem.

When a particular commodity or fiat money comes to be used as a medium of exchange, experience has shown that it is convenient to use the units of the commodity or money as the *unit of account* for "current" transactions. The price of each good is thus expressed as so many units of money per unit of the good, and all accounts are normally kept in the units of the medium of exchange. During periods of extremely variable inflation, even though money may continue to act as a medium of exchange, individuals in the community may decide to use some other unit for keeping accounts and measuring the prices of goods. Typically in periods of hyperinflation, agents will use the currency of some foreign country to act as the unit of account: thus in the famous German hyperinflation of 1923 the US dollar was used as the unit for keeping accounts. The unit of account function of money is thus sometimes described as a secondary (albeit important) function which can be dispensed with, at the cost of considerable inconvenience.

When the purchasing power of money is relatively stable, it also comes to be used as the *standard for deferred payments* i.e. as the unit of account for "long-period" transactions. In the normal course of business, individuals find it convenient to sign nominal contractual commitments expressed in the units of the established medium of exchange, provided its purchasing power is not too variable, and it is precisely when money comes to be extensively used as the standard for deferred payments in long-period contracts that a monetary economy begins to depart in a substantial way from the essentially real economy that we have studied so far. However when there is too much fluctuation in the purchasing power of money, agents seek to index their contracts:[1] just as money ceases to perform its function of a short-period unit of account, so also it ceases to perform its long-period function of acting as a standard for deferred payments.

Modelling Money

While it is relatively straightforward to describe the functions of money in general and intuitive terms, it is much harder to capture these functions in a coherent model which simultaneously incorporates the real sector, the financial sector, and money. At this stage it is difficult to tell whether a more satisfactory modelling of the basic function of money—its *exchange-facilitating* role—will involve switching from the general equilibrium approach based on "markets" to an approach based on an explicit process of bilateral exchanges with either "random meeting" among agents or a "search process" in which agents, who are imperfectly informed about trading opportunities, spend time searching for trading partners in a possibly complex random environment.[2] For the moment, the models based on explicit bilateral exchanges are too limited in the trading environments that they can describe to provide a workable alternative to the general equilibrium approach.

  If the model does not explain, through an explicit meeting and transaction process, why agents are better off using money as a medium of exchange, it must however, by some device or hypothesis, assign a special role to money which serves to distinguish it from the other commodities and contracts. There are two principal short-cuts for introducing the medium-of-exchange role of money into an equilibrium model. The first and oldest device is to model the *convenience yield* of real money balances: this approach, championed in recent times by Patinkin (1965) in his integration of monetary and value theory, was used long before by Walras (1874, Part VI; 1886) as the basis for a penetrating

---

[1] This is discussed in more detail in Section 37.

[2] For models based on random meetings see Hellwig (1976) and Kiyotaki-Wright (1989): for a more general discussion of this approach see Hellwig (1993). For the search approach see Diamond (1984a). More generally, Diamond (1984b, 1994) has suggested that a search theoretic approach may provide a more satisfactory microfoundation for macroeconomics than an approach based on general equilibrium.

analysis of money.[3] The idea is to model the convenience yield derived in each period from having a stock of money available for carrying out transactions during this period. This approach, which is flexible and convenient, has proved useful for studying certain questions of monetary theory.[4] However, since the approach amounts to making real money balances another argument of each agent's utility function, money becomes essentially just another good whose sole distinguishing feature is to play the role of a numeraire, and such a modelling does not capture the specific attribute of fiat money of being worthless as a commodity for consumption, only acquiring value by serving as an instrument that assures agents that they can carry out their desired commodity transactions. Hahn (1965) expressed this criticism by showing that a model, in which preferences for real money balances satiate at some finite level, always has a non-monetary equilibrium in which the price of money is zero: seeking to avoid this difficulty, by assuming that agents' preferences for real money balances are always strictly monotonic, amounts to assuming that fiat money has intrinsic value.

Our analysis will be based on the alternative device known as the *cash-in-advance constraint*. This approach, which was introduced by Clower (1967), comes closer to capturing the exchange role of money. The idea is to model in a stylized fashion the way money is used in transactions, by separating the moments when agents sell goods in exchange for money from the moments when they use this money to purchase goods. In an equilibrium setting (as in Grandmont-Younes (1972) or Lucas (1980)) this is modelled by assuming that the money balances agents acquire from the sale of their goods (endowments) cannot immediately be used for the purchase of commodities. Agents are thus forced to hold money balances in order to be able to purchase their consumption bundle and are at the same time obliged to carry money balances from one period to the next. The models of Grandmont-Younes and Lucas depend in an essential way on the fact that there is an *infinite horizon*.[5] For if there were a last period, then the money received from the sale of goods in this period would have no subsequent use: thus the value of money balances in the last period would be zero, and by backward induction, it would be zero in all previous periods. No exchange would be possible using money as a medium of exchange, and the only equilibrium would be the zero trade equilibrium. This is a familiar property of any equilibrium model in which money is used as a store of value across periods: if an equilibrium is to exist in which money has

---

[3]Note that Walras, who lived under a gold standard, was modelling *commodity* money, while Patinkin was modelling *fiat* money.

[4]See Sidrauski (1967) and Brock (1975).

[5]As every capital theorist and game theorist knows, an infinite horizon should never be taken literally: it is simply a convenient modelling device for expressing the fact (idea) that the future is open ended i.e. that there is no known date when the world comes to an end.

a positive price, there cannot be a last period unless some artificial device is introduced which serves to give money a positive value at the terminal date.

An infinite horizon model with a cash-in-advance constraint can be approximated by a model on a finite horizon $[0, T]$ in which agents are required to have money balances to make tax payments at the terminal date.[6] If the horizon T is sufficiently distant, such a model can provide a convenient way of deriving qualitative properties which mimic those of the infinite horizon model. Since, for the sake of simplicity we want to work with a two-period model and since such a model would involve exclusively the two periods which are exceptional—the initial and the terminal periods[7]—it seems easier to introduce directly an alternative device, which factors out the role of money as a store of value across periods, but still retains Clower's idea that "money buys goods and goods buy money, but goods do not buy goods". While the model is highly stylized and is tailored to study the effects of variability in the purchasing power of money in an economy with nominal contracts, the effects which are exhibited will be present in more elaborate models of a monetary economy, as long as they involve variable inflation and nominal contracts.

Monetary Equilibrium

To describe the way money circulates through the economy and is used to carry out transactions, each state s $(s = 0, 1, \ldots, S)$ is decomposed into three subperiods (s_1, s_2, s_3): in the first subperiod (s_1), agents sell their endowment of goods in exchange for money, in the second (s_2), agents transact on the financial markets—an activity which leads to a redistribution of the money balances—and in the last subperiod (s_3), agents use their transactions balances to purchase goods.

Let $\omega_s^i \in \mathbb{R}_+^L$ $(s = 0, 1, \ldots, S)$ denote the initial endowment of agent i in subperiod s_1. There is an institution which we call the Central Exchange which performs the basic function of marketing the agents' endowments (ω_s^i): agents' endowments are not directly consumable but need to be *processed* through a constant returns technology before they are suitable for consumption. The processing as well as the marketing of the agents' endowments is performed by

---

[6]This requirement is sometimes justified by invoking Knapp's (1924) state theory of money, which asserts that inconvertible paper currency acquires value because it is needed to pay taxes. However since there is no explanation of what the government is to do with these money balances once the taxes have been paid, it is simply a device which replaces one problem (money has zero value for agents in the private sector) by another (what the government is to do with the tax money). If money has no value to agents in the private sector, why should it have any value to the government? After all, the world *has* come to an end.

[7]In the first period, money balances are inherited and not chosen, and in the second period, agents must pay their taxes: there is no typical period in which money balances are chosen optimally for transactions purposes.

the Central Exchange. Thus we assume that *in the first subperiod s_1 of each state ($s = 0, 1, \ldots, S$) each agent sells the full amount of his endowment ω_s^i to the Central Exchange.* This assumption is present in most models of a monetary economy in one form or another: it can be viewed as the assertion that agents have no direct utility for their own initial endowment, or, in the more graphic language of Diamond (1984a) that there is a "taboo" on consuming one's own initial endowment. Behind it, lies the idea that money permits the high degree of specialization characteristic of a modern (production) economy, in which consumers offer highly specialized labor services to firms which process and transform these into consumption goods. In the simplified framework of the present exchange model, the processing of goods by the Central Exchange can be viewed as a surrogate for this roundabout process of transforming specialized inputs into consumption goods.

In the first subperiod 0_1, each agent i receives the money income $m_0^i = p_0 \omega_0^i$, where $p_0 = (p_{01}, \ldots, p_{0L})$ is the vector of prices for the goods at date 0. In subperiod 0_2, J nominal securities are traded, where the jth contract promises to pay the stream $N^j = (N_1^j, \ldots, N_S^j)$ of dollars at date 1 (written as a column vector) and costs q_j dollars (payable at date 0). These securities are taken to be in zero net supply. Buyers and sellers are assumed to meet directly on the financial markets, so that the exchange of contracts for money is carried out directly without the intervention of the Central Exchange. If, in subperiod 0_2, agent i purchases the portfolio $z^i = (z_1^i, \ldots, z_J^i) \in \mathbb{R}^J$, and if $q = (q_1, \ldots, q_J)$ is the vector of security prices, then the money balances he has available are $\widetilde{m}_0^i = p_0 \omega_0^i - q z^i$. The transactions balances $\widetilde{m}_0^i$ are used in subperiod 0_3 to buy the consumption bundle $x_0^i = (x_{01}^i, \ldots, x_{0L}^i) \in \mathbb{R}_+^L$ from the Central Exchange at the price $p_0 = (p_{01}, \ldots, p_{0L})$. The transactions activities of agent i in the three subperiods of date 0 can thus be summarized by the equation

$$p_0 x_0^i = \widetilde{m}_0^i = p_0 \omega_0^i - q z^i \tag{1}$$

At date 1, one of the states s ($s = 1, \ldots, S$) occurs. In the first subperiod s_1, agent i receives the money income $m_s^i = p_s \omega_s^i$ in exchange for his endowment ω_s^i, which is sold to the Central Exchange at the vector of spot prices $p_s = (p_{s1}, \ldots, p_{sL})$ for state s. In the second subperiod s_2, agent i receives the dividend income $N_s z^i = \sum_{j=1}^{J} N_s^j z_j^i$. Thus in the third subperiod s_3, he has available the transactions balances $\widetilde{m}_s^i = m_s^i + N_s z^i$ for purchasing the consumption bundle $x_s^i = (x_{s1}^i, \ldots, x_{sL}^i) \in \mathbb{R}_+^L$ from the Central Exchange at the spot prices $p_s = (p_{s1}, \ldots, p_{sL})$. The transactions of agent i in state s can thus be summarized by the equation

$$p_s x_s^i = \widetilde{m}_s^i = p_s \omega_s^i + N_s z^i, \quad s = 1, \ldots, S \tag{2}$$

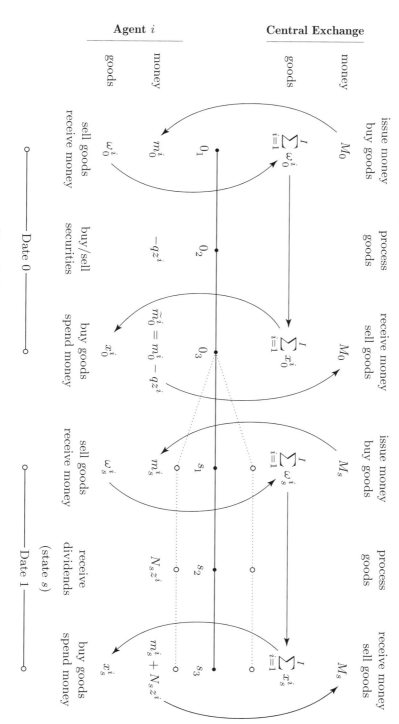

Figure 34.2 Transactions and the circulation of money.

In addition to its role of processing and marketing commodities, the Central Exchange determines the supply of fiat money

$$M_s = \sum_{i=1}^{I} m_s^i, \quad s = 0, 1, \ldots, S$$

that is injected into the economy in each state s. We call the vector $M = (M_0, M_1, \ldots, M_S) \in \mathbb{R}_{++}^{S+1}$ the *monetary policy*. In subperiod 0_1, the Central Exchange injects the money supply $M_0 = \sum_{i=1}^{I} m_0^i$ into the economy: since agents spend the transactions balances $\widetilde{m}_0^i = m_0^i - qz^i$ (acquired after trading on the financial markets) on the purchase of goods in subperiod 0_3, the money M_0 returns to the Central Exchange[8] in subperiod 0_3. In the same way when state s occurs at date 1, in the first subperiod s_1, it injects the money supply $M_s = \sum_{i=1}^{I} m_s^i$ into the economy: since agents spend the transactions balances $\widetilde{m}_s^i = m_s^i + N_s z^i$ (acquired after receiving dividends on their portfolio holdings) on the purchase of goods in subperiod s_3, the money M_s returns to the Central Exchange in subperiod s_3. Figure 34.2 shows in a schematic way how money circulates in the economy and is used to carry out transactions at date 0 and in each state s at date 1.

The monetary policy $M = (M_0, M_1, \ldots, M_S)$, which is determined by the monetary authorities (Central Exchange), is the additional vector of parameters which needs to be added to the preferences, endowments and security characteristics (u, ω, N) to fully specify the *monetary exchange economy* $\mathscr{E}(u, \omega, N, M)$. Note that the trading opportunities of an agent in this economy, described by equations (1) and (2), lead to the same budget set $\mathbb{B}(p, q, \omega^i, N)$ as in equation (6) of the previous section. We are thus led to the following concept of a monetary equilibrium for the economy $\mathscr{E}(u, \omega, N, M)$.

34.1 Definition: A *monetary equilibrium* for the economy $\mathscr{E}(u, \omega, N, M)$ is a pair of actions and prices

$$((\bar{x}, \bar{z}), (\bar{p}, \bar{q})) \in \mathbb{R}_+^{nI} \times \mathbb{R}^{JI} \times \mathbb{R}_+^n \times \mathbb{R}^J, \quad n = L(S+1)$$

such that

(i) $(\bar{x}^i; \bar{z}^i) \in \arg\max \{u^i(x^i) \mid (x^i; z^i) \in \mathbb{B}(\bar{p}, \bar{q}, \omega^i, N)\}$, $i = 1, \ldots, I$
(ii) $\sum_{i=1}^{I}(\bar{x}^i - \omega^i) = 0$ (iii) $\sum_{i=1}^{I} \bar{z}^i = 0$
(iv) $\bar{p}_s \sum_{i=1}^{I} \bar{x}_s^i = M_s$, $s = 0, 1, \ldots, S$

[8]It is assumed that no agent in the private sector holds money balances between the last subperiod 0_3 of date 0 and the first subperiod (state) s_1 at date 1: in short, money is not used as a store of value between date 0 and date 1. As our colleague Andy Neumeyer has suggestively said of our model: money "sleeps" overnight in the Central Exchange. This assumption is discussed after Definition 34.1.

The difference between this concept of equilibrium and that in Definition 33.3 is that money has been explicitly introduced into the transactions process: the endogenously determined transactions demand for money $(\sum_{i=1}^{I} \bar{p}_s \bar{x}_s^i)$ combined with the exogenously given money supply (M_s), serve to determine the equilibrium price level in each state. The monetary equations (iv) are $S+1$ *quantity theory equations* linking the price level in each state to the quantity of money. Since the money injected into the economy in each state is used only once to carry out transactions, the velocity of circulation is one.[9]

Implicit in our description of the way agents acquire and use their money balances is the assumption that agents do not (may not) carry money from date 0 to date 1: the money balances $\widetilde{m}_0^i$ available to each agent after trading on the security markets are spent on consumption at date 0. If there is a default-free bond on which the nominal interest rate is positive, no agent will ever choose to carry money from date 0 to date 1, since money is dominated by the bond as a store of value (see Exercise 1(a)). Thus for parameter values of the money supply M for which the nominal interest rate is positive, there is no need for an assumption preventing agents from carrying money from date 0 to date 1. However, for those monetary policies M which lead to a negative nominal interest rate, the equilibrium described by Definition 34.1 differs from the equilibrium that would be obtained if agents were permitted to carry money from date 0 to date 1: for if the rate of interest is negative, agents— if permitted to do so—will always choose to transfer purchasing power from date 0 to date 1 in the form of money rather than lending at a negative interest rate. The model can be extended to permit agents to carry money balances from date 0 to date 1, but the analysis becomes much more complicated since the velocity of circulation differs from one when agents transfer money to date 1 (see Magill-Quinzii (1992)). To avoid these complications, we can either add the assumption that money issued at date 0 is not accepted as a means of payment at date 1 or, to avoid this rather artificial assumption, restrict attention to monetary policies leading to equilibria in which the nominal rate of interest is positive. (See Exercise 1(b))

The quantity theory equations (iv) provide the $S+1$ equations needed to determine the price levels which are missing in the earlier concept of equilibrium (Definition 33.3). By providing the relations needed to endogenously determine

---

[9]The determination of price levels by quantity theory equations with a velocity of circulation one, is a common feature of most cash-in-advance models. The timing of transactions in Lucas type cash-in-advance models puts 0_1 after 0_3 (agents having positive initial money balances) and s_1 after s_3 (see Sargent (1987, ch. 5)). This avoids recourse to a Central Exchange since money stays in the private sector, being carried over from one period to the next by agents— but requires an infinite horizon. However the fact that price levels are determined by quantity theory equations of the type (iv) is identical. A slightly more general approach which leads to a variable velocity of circulation is the model of Lucas-Stokey (1983, 1987) which distinguishes between goods paid for with money and goods paid by credit.

the purchasing power of money, these equations serve to close the model, so
that a monetary equilibrium—unlike the earlier equilibrium concept—is determinate. This can be seen (heuristically) by applying the Walras Consistency
Test. The equations defining a monetary equilibrium are given by

$$F(p,q) = \sum_{i=1}^{I} (\tilde{x}^i(p,q) - \omega^i) = 0 \tag{3}$$

$$G(p,q) = \sum_{i=1}^{I} \tilde{z}^i(p,q) = 0 \tag{4}$$

$$H_s(p,q) = \sum_{i=1}^{I} p_s \tilde{x}_s^i - M_s = 0, \quad s = 0, 1, \ldots, S \tag{5}$$

There are $L(S+1)+J$ unknown prices (p,q). As before there are $S+1$ Walras'
Laws (equation (3) in Section 33) for the market-clearing equations (3) and
(4). The $S+1$ monetary equations (5) exactly compensate for the equations
missing as a result of the $S+1$ Walras' Laws.

One of the difficult problems of monetary theory is to explain in a satisfactory equilibrium setting how changes in the monetary base, over which the
monetary authority has control, translate into changes in the money supply,
where the latter consists of cash and bank deposits (so-called $M1$) and perhaps
more generally includes money market accounts (so-called $M2$). Since the very
simple model considered here has no banking system, no attempt is made to
model how base money is multiplied up by a whole process of transactions
through the banking system into a money supply.[10] We take the short-cut of
assuming that the monetary authority has direct control over the money supply, the state contingent function $M = (M_s)_{s=0}^S$ being the monetary policy
rule.

The monetary equations (iv) express the simplest (or as a monetary theorist would say, the naive) version of the quantity theory: an increase in the
money supply in any state leads to a proportional increase in the price level
in that state. Modulo the timing problem encountered in practice, namely the
separation between the moment money is injected and the time when prices
increase, empirical data usually suggest that increases in the money supply
lead to more than proportionate increases in the price level: similarly a decrease in the money supply leads to a more than proportionate decrease in the
price level. When prices increase, the rate of interest increases, which in turn
increases the velocity of circulation of money. Mathematically, M_s in equation
(iv) would need to be replaced by $v_s M_s$, where v_s is the velocity of circulation

---

[10]For a discussion of the factors influencing the base money multiplier, see any Money and
Banking textbook, for example Mishkin (1995).

in state s, which would depend on the endogenously derived average money balances held by each agent in state s. The basic message that we want to convey would not, however, be altered by moving to a more refined model that permits the velocity of circulation to be variable and endogenously determined. All that really matters is that, when the money supply in some state changes, then the price level changes.[11]

The monetary equations imply a significant new level of foresight and understanding on the part of agents in the private sector, regarding the functioning of the economy. In a monetary equilibrium each agent is expected to understand the relation between monetary policy and inflation. In a world where many of the contracts made by consumers and businessmen involve commitments to make and receive payments in dollar amounts over intervals that extend to relatively distant times in the future, it is natural that they should apply all the rationality (and experience) at their disposal in forming their expectations regarding future inflation. We are assuming, in essence, that, in a modern economy, agents will make use of this understanding (and experience) combined with the extensive and continuous sources of information on many government activities to form conjectures regarding monetary policy, and that they recognize that increases in the money supply typically lead to inflation. In short, agents are aware of what is going on, what the government is up to, and have learned (perhaps via Chicago) a little monetary theory.

Consider, therefore, an economy in which agents in the private sector understand the monetary policy rule and correctly anticipate future inflation. Does a perfectly anticipated change in monetary policy affect the outcome of economic activity? Namely, is monetary policy neutral or does the presence of nominal contracts in the economy make monetary policy non-neutral? This is the question to which we now turn our attention.

35. NON-NEUTRALITY OF MONETARY POLICY

This section studies the conditions under which monetary policy is neutral and non-neutral respectively. The objective is to establish precise but straightforward results without drawing on more technique than that developed in

---

[11] "There is perhaps no empirical regularity among economic phenomena that is based on so much evidence for so wide a range of circumstances as the connection between substantial changes in the quantity of money and in the level of prices. There are few if any instances in which a substantial change in the quantity of money per unit of output has occurred without a substantial change in the level of prices in the same direction ... And instances in which prices and the quantity of money have moved together are recorded for many centuries of history, for countries in every part of the globe, and for a wide diversity of monetary arrangements." (Friedman (1987)).

Chapter 2: this can be done by restricting the analysis of monetary equilibria to the one-good case.[1]

Consider a monetary economy $\mathscr{E}(u, \omega, N, M)$ with one good $(L = 1)$. A typical agent chooses a consumption plan $x^i = (x_0^i, x_1^i, \ldots, x_S^i) \in \mathbb{R}^{S+1}$, consisting of the amount of the single good to be consumed in each state, and a portfolio $z^i = (z_1^i, \ldots, z_J^i) \in \mathbb{R}^J$ of the J securities whose date 1 payoff matrix is given by N. The vector of prices (p, q) now consists of money (dollar) prices $p = (p_0, p_1, \ldots, p_S)$ for the good (payable) in each state and the dollar prices $q = (q_1, \ldots, q_J)$ for the J securities payable at date 0. The budget set in a one-good monetary economy

$$\mathbb{B}(p, q, \omega^i, N) = \left\{ x^i \in \mathbb{R}_+^{S+1} \ \middle| \ \begin{array}{l} p_0(x_0^i - \omega_0^i) = -qz^i, \ z^i \in \mathbb{R}^J \\ p_s(x_s^i - \omega_s^i) = N_s z^i, \ s = 1, \ldots, S \end{array} \right\} \quad (1)$$

can be written as

$$\mathbb{B}(p, q, \omega^i, N) = \left\{ x^i \in \mathbb{R}_+^{S+1} \ \middle| \ \begin{array}{l} x_0^i - \omega_0^i = -\dfrac{q}{p_0} z^i, \ z^i \in \mathbb{R}^J \\ x_s^i - \omega_s^i = \dfrac{1}{p_s} N_s z^i, \ s = 1, \ldots, S \end{array} \right\} \quad (2)$$

In an equilibrium of $\mathscr{E}(u, \omega, N, M)$ the price of the good in each state (which is also the price level in each state) is determined by the monetary equations

$$p_s w_s = M_s, \quad s = 0, 1, \ldots, S \quad (3)$$

where $w_s = \sum_{i=1}^I \omega_s^i$ is the aggregate output in state s $(s = 0, 1, \ldots, S)$. A one-good monetary economy thus has the special property that, once the aggregate endowment and monetary policy are known, equilibrium spot prices can be written out directly without needing to solve for a monetary equilibrium. If, to a monetary economy $\mathscr{E}(u, \omega, N, M)$, we associate the parameters $(\nu_0, \nu_1, \ldots, \nu_S)$ defined by

$$\nu_s = \frac{w_s}{M_s}, \quad s = 0, 1, \ldots, S \quad (4)$$

then the monetary equations (3) can be written as

$$\frac{1}{p_s} = \nu_s, \quad s = 0, 1, \ldots, S \quad (5)$$

---

[1]More precise comparative statics properties of equilibria, which also cover the case of many goods, can be obtained by drawing on a broader array of techniques and concepts of differential topology which are studied in the second volume. These more general results are similar in spirit if not in (exact) statement to the results given in this chapter.

Thus in a monetary equilibrium, the parameter ν_s represents the *purchasing power* of one unit of money in state s for $s = 0, 1, \ldots, S$.

When the agent's budget set is written in the form (2), it is clear that this opportunity set is the budget set of the agent in a real economy in which the (real) returns on the securities in each state (V_s^j) are obtained by multiplying the nominal returns (N_s^j) by the purchasing power of money $(1/p_s)$. The following notation will be useful for expressing this conversion from a monetary to a real economy. Let $\nu = (\nu_1, \ldots, \nu_S)$ denote the random variable which is the (date 1) *vector of purchasing power of money* and let $[\nu]$ denote the associated *diagonal matrix*

$$[\nu] = \begin{bmatrix} \nu_1 & \cdots & 0 \\ \vdots & \ddots & \vdots \\ 0 & \cdots & \nu_S \end{bmatrix} \tag{6}$$

The payoffs of the securities in the associated real economy when the spot prices satisfy (5) are thus given by

$$V_s = \nu_s N_s, \quad s = 1, \ldots, S \iff V = [\nu] N \tag{7}$$

The following proposition expresses the relation between monetary equilibria of the economy $\mathscr{E}(u, \omega, N, M)$ and the financial market equilibria of the real economy $\mathscr{E}(u, \omega, V)$, which were introduced (Definition 8.2) and studied in Chapter 2.

35.1 Proposition (Equilibria of Monetary and Real Economy): $((x, z), (p, q))$ *is a monetary equilibrium of the (one-good) economy* $\mathscr{E}(u, \omega, N, M)$ *if and only if*

  (i) p *satisfies* (5)
 (ii) $((x, z), \nu_0 q)$ *is an FM equilibrium of the real economy* $\mathscr{E}(u, \omega, V)$ *where* $V = [\nu] N$ *and* ν *is defined by* (4).

PROOF: The proof follows from the equality of the budget set $\mathbb{B}(p, q, \omega^i, N)$ in (1) and the budget set $\mathbb{B}(\widetilde{q}, \omega^i, V)$ defined by equation (3) in Section 8 with $V = [\nu] N$ and $\widetilde{q} = \nu_0 q$. $\square$

Thus, if agents' preferences satisfy Assumption $\mathscr{U}$, if their endowments are strictly positive $(\omega^i \in \mathbb{R}_{++}^{S+1}, i = 1, \ldots, I)$, and if the money supply is strictly positive $(M \in \mathbb{R}_{++}^{S+1})$, then the economy $\mathscr{E}(u, \omega, N, M)$ has a monetary equilibrium, since by Theorem 10.5 the associated real economy $\mathscr{E}(u, \omega, V)$ has an equilibrium.

Our objective is to study whether equilibria of a monetary economy are affected by changes in monetary policy. The first step is to make precise what it means to "affect an equilibrium". We are not concerned with prices or portfolios per se—what matters is the real outcome, the equilibrium consumption achieved by the agents. If, at a monetary equilibrium, changing the money supply only affects the prices and agents' portfolios without affecting their equilibrium consumption, then we say that monetary policy is neutral; if there is some change in the money supply which alters some agent's equilibrium consumption, then monetary policy is said to be non-neutral. It is convenient to express this more formally as follows.

35.2 Definition: Let $((x,z),(p,q))$ be a monetary equilibrium of the economy $\mathscr{E}(u,\omega,N,M)$. Monetary policy is said to be *neutral* if, for any change in monetary policy from M to $M' \in \mathbb{R}_{++}^{S+1}$, there exist portfolios z' for the agents and prices (p',q'), such that $((x,z'),(p',q'))$ is a monetary equilibrium of $\mathscr{E}(u,\omega,N,M')$. If this is not true, then monetary policy is said to be *non-neutral*.

There are two types of changes in monetary policy which are always neutral. Let $((x,z),(p,q))$ be a monetary equilibrium of the economy $\mathscr{E}(u,\omega,N,M)$. Suppose the date 0 money supply is doubled (increased by the factor β_0, $M_0 \longrightarrow \beta_0 M_0$). By the quantity theory equations (3), the date 0 spot price will double ($p_0 \longrightarrow \beta_0 p_0$). If at the same time the security prices double ($q \longrightarrow \beta_0 q$) in response to the increased money supply, then it follows from (1) that agents' budget sets are unaffected, so that their optimal decisions (x,z) remain unchanged. Thus the only effect of a change in the date 0 money supply is to change the date 0 prices $(p_0,q) \longrightarrow (\beta_0 p_0, \beta_0 q)$. The fact that date 0 monetary changes are always neutral also follows at once from Proposition 35.1, since the real economy $\mathscr{E}(u,\omega,V)$ associated with $\mathscr{E}(u,\omega,N,M)$ is independent of M_0.

If the date 1 money supplies are doubled (increased by the factor β, $M_s \longrightarrow \beta M_s$, $s = 1, \ldots, S$), by the quantity theory equations (3), the date 1 spot prices will double ($p_s \longrightarrow \beta p_s$, $s = 1, \ldots, S$). If the security prices are halved ($q \longrightarrow q/\beta$) to reflect the decreased purchasing power of the securities' dividends, then, since agents can afford to double their portfolios ($z^i \longrightarrow \beta z^i$), they can still afford the same consumption bundles. Thus when the money supply is changed from $(M_0, M_1, \ldots, M_S)$ to $(M_0, \beta M_1, \ldots, \beta M_S)$, prices change to $(p_0, \beta p_1, \ldots, \beta p_S, q/\beta)$ and portfolios change to βz, the agents' consumption plans x remaining unchanged. The fact that a uniform change for date 1 money supplies is always neutral also follows directly from Proposition 35.1, since a reader familiar with the analysis of Chapter 2 will recognize[2] that changing the diagonal matrix of purchasing power from $[\nu]$ to $(1/\beta)[\nu]$ does not change the market subspace of the associated real economy ($\langle [\nu] N \rangle = \langle (1/\beta)[\nu] N \rangle$) so

---

[2]The no-arbitrage budget set $\mathscr{B}(\pi, \omega^i, V)$, in equation (7) of Section 10, depends only on $\langle V \rangle$.

that the equilibrium allocation is unchanged. These two neutrality properties of monetary policy can be summarized as follows.

35.3 Proposition (Two Types of Neutrality of Monetary Policy): *In the monetary economy $\mathscr{E}(u, \omega, N, M)$, there are two types of changes in monetary policy which are always neutral: a change in the money supply at date 0 and a uniform proportional change in the money supply in all states at date 1, namely*

(i) $M = (M_0, M_1, \ldots, M_S) \longrightarrow M' = (\beta_0 M_0, M_1, \ldots, M_S),\ \forall \beta_0 > 0$
(ii) $M = (M_0, M_1, \ldots, M_S) \longrightarrow M' = (M_0, \beta M_1, \ldots, \beta M_S),\ \forall \beta > 0$

The *inflation* η in a monetary equilibrium $((x, z), (p, q))$ is the random variable $\eta : \mathbb{R}^S \longrightarrow \mathbb{R}$ defined by

$$\eta = (\eta_1, \ldots, \eta_S) = \left(\frac{p_1}{p_0}, \ldots, \frac{p_S}{p_0} \right) \tag{8}$$

Proposition 35.3 asserts that inflation can be multiplied by a scalar without affecting the equilibrium allocation, the scalar being the resultant of multiplying the denominator in (8) by β_0 and the numerator by β. In short, *in an economy $\mathscr{E}(u, \omega, N, M)$, changing the magnitude of inflation leaves the real equilibrium outcome unchanged*: this property comes from the fact that agents do not carry money balances from date 0 to date 1 and, because they correctly anticipate the consequences of monetary policy, always adjust their portfolios to cancel the effect of anticipated inflation.

It is clear from the way money operates in the economy $\mathscr{E}(u, \omega, N, M)$ that what really matters about a monetary policy M is how it affects the purchasing power of money ν. This is essentially the economic content of Proposition 35.1. In the analysis that follows, the neutrality or non-neutrality properties of monetary policy which are derived—which are less obvious than those described in Proposition 35.3—are often conveniently expressed in terms of the purchasing power ν.

The basic idea is the following: all that matters about the security structure $V = [\nu] N$ as far as the equilibrium allocations of the real economy $\mathscr{E}(u, \omega, V)$ are concerned, is the *subspace* $\langle V \rangle$ of $\mathbb{R}^S$ spanned by V. Thus a change in ν which does not affect the market subspace $\langle [\nu] N \rangle$ is neutral, since agents can adjust their portfolios to compensate for the change in the purchasing power of the securities' dividends. Conversely, any change in the purchasing power ν which "tilts" the market subspace $\langle [\nu] N \rangle$ of the associated real economy, in general affects the equilibrium allocation.

Consider first the idealized case where the monetary economy $\mathscr{E}(u, \omega, N, M)$ has a sufficiently rich structure of financial securities to make the financial markets complete (rank $N = S$). Then, for any positive vector of purchasing power $\nu \in \mathbb{R}^S_{++}$, rank $[\nu]\, N = S$, since the diagonal matrix $[\nu]$ is non-singular. Thus for any $\nu \in \mathbb{R}^S_{++}$, the financial markets are complete in the associated real economy $\mathscr{E}(u, \omega, V)$

$$\langle N \rangle = \mathbb{R}^S \quad \Longleftrightarrow \quad \langle V \rangle = \langle [\nu]\, N \rangle = \mathbb{R}^S \text{ for all } \nu \in \mathbb{R}^S_{++} \tag{9}$$

In Section 10 it was shown that the equilibrium allocations of an economy $\mathscr{E}(u, \omega, V)$, for which the financial markets are complete, coincide with the contingent market (Arrow-Debreu) equilibrium allocations of the economy $\mathscr{E}(u, \omega)$. It follows that *the equilibrium allocations of an economy $\mathscr{E}(u, \omega, V)$ are independent of the exact form of the security structure V whenever the securities span the whole space,* $\langle V \rangle = \mathbb{R}^S$. We are thus led to a class of economies whose equilibria are invariant with respect to monetary policy.

35.4 Proposition (Neutrality of Monetary Policy with Complete Markets): *If the financial markets of the monetary economy $\mathscr{E}(u, \omega, N, M)$ are complete, then monetary policy is neutral. For every choice of monetary policy $M \in \mathbb{R}^{S+1}_{++}$, the equilibrium allocations of the economy $\mathscr{E}(u, \omega, N, M)$ coincide with the contingent market equilibrium allocations of the economy $\mathscr{E}(u, \omega)$.*

PROOF: The proof follows from Proposition 35.1, (9), and Proposition 10.6. □

When markets are complete, it is as if agents could sign contracts contingent on the state of nature and thus, in particular, contingent on the purchasing power of money. Any anticipated change in monetary policy will lead to changes in portfolios and security prices, but will not affect the real economy.

The adjustment of the agents' actions and the prices to a change in monetary policy can be explained as follows. Let $((x, z), (p, q))$ be an equilibrium of the economy $\mathscr{E}(u, \omega, N, M)$. If the change in monetary policy from M to M' changes the purchasing power of money from ν to ν', then the real returns on the securities change $([\nu]\, N \longrightarrow [\nu']\, N)$. Since the financial markets are complete, agents can always find new portfolios $(z^i \longrightarrow z^{i\prime})$ which finance the same date 1 consumption plan $(x^i_s - \omega^i_s = \nu'_s N_s z^{i\prime}, \ s = 1, \ldots, S)$. The prices of the securities adjust $(q \longrightarrow q')$ to reflect the new purchasing power of their dividends, and they do so in such a way that agents can afford the same date 0 consumption $(x^i_0 - \omega^i_0 = -q' z^{i\prime})$.

To analyze the effects of monetary policy when the financial markets are incomplete we make the following assumption.

Assumption $\mathscr{D}$ (Default-Free Bond): $\mathbb{1} \in \langle N \rangle$

When Assumption $\mathscr{D}$ is satisfied, there is no loss of generality in assuming that the default-free bond is one of the securities, $N^1 = \mathbb{1}$. This assumption is most natural: the bond $\mathbb{1}$ is perhaps the most extensively traded nominal financial contract. Its presence as one of the nominal securities provides a simple tool for exhibiting the effects of changes in monetary policy, since its real return is the purchasing power of money ν.

Our objective is to show that for most monetary economies, if financial markets are incomplete, then monetary policy is non-neutral. The idea of the proof is simple and can be broken down into three steps. The first is provided by Proposition 35.1 which asserts that analyzing the equilibria of the monetary economy $\mathscr{E}(u, \omega, N, M)$ can be reduced to the simpler task of analyzing the equilibria of the real economy $\mathscr{E}(u, \omega, V)$ in which the (real) returns on the securities are given by $V = [\nu] N$. The second step is to exhibit the changes in the purchasing power parameters ν which change the span of the financial markets $\langle [\nu] N \rangle$ in the real economy. The third step is to show that if a change in monetary policy from M to M' changes the span of the market in the associated real economy ($\langle [\nu] N \rangle \neq \langle [\nu'] N \rangle$), then the equilibrium allocation must change ($x' \neq x$).

The first step being disposed of by Proposition 35.1, consider the second. Under Assumption $\mathscr{D}$, there is a way of changing the purchasing power of money which is sure to change the market subspace $\langle [\nu] N \rangle$: it consists in tilting the purchasing power vector ν in a direction which is orthogonal to the market subspace

$$\nu \to \nu' = \nu + (\nu' - \nu) \quad \text{with} \quad \nu' - \nu \in \langle [\nu] N \rangle^{\perp}$$

for then the new purchasing power vector ν' cannot lie in the original market subspace $\langle [\nu] N \rangle$. Since $\dim \langle [\nu] N \rangle^{\perp} = S - J$, there is at least a subspace of dimension $S - J$ of changes in the purchasing power of money which change the span of the markets in the associated real economy.

35.5 Proposition (Monetary Policies which Alter the Market Subspace): *Let $\mathscr{E}(u, \omega, N, M)$ be an monetary economy satisfying Assumption $\mathscr{D}$ with random date 1 purchasing power of money ν given by (4). There is a subspace $\Delta \subset \mathbb{R}^S$ with $\dim \Delta \geq S - J$ such that, if monetary policy is changed from M to M' in such a way that the purchasing power changes from ν to ν' with $\nu' - \nu \in \Delta$, then $\langle [\nu'] N \rangle \neq \langle [\nu] N \rangle$.*

PROOF: Since $N^1 = \mathbb{1}$, $\nu = [\nu] \mathbb{1} \in \langle [\nu] N \rangle$. Let $\Delta = \langle [\nu] N \rangle^{\perp}$. Any $\nu' \in \mathbb{R}^S$ can be written as $\nu' = \nu + (\nu' - \nu)$ with $\nu' - \nu$ denoting the change in purchasing power. Pick $\nu' \in \mathbb{R}^S$, $\nu' \neq \nu$ with $\nu' - \nu \in \Delta$. $\nu' \notin \langle [\nu] N \rangle$, since $\nu' \in \langle [\nu] N \rangle$ would imply

$$\nu' - \nu \in \langle [\nu] N \rangle \cap \langle [\nu] N \rangle^{\perp} = \{0\}$$

which contradicts $\nu' \neq \nu$. Since $\nu' \in \langle [\nu'] N \rangle$ it follows that $\langle [\nu] N \rangle \neq \langle [\nu'] N \rangle$ for all $\nu' \neq \nu$ such that $\nu' - \nu \in \Delta$. Since $\dim \langle [\nu] N \rangle = \dim \langle N \rangle = J$, $\dim \Delta = S - J$. □

REMARK. The proof of Proposition 35.5 uses only two properties of N: $N^1 = \mathbb{1}$ and $\dim N = J$. Thus the remaining financial contracts ($j = 2, \ldots, J$) do not need to be nominal: they can be real (like equity contracts) or have real and nominal components (like the bonds of corporations subject to risk of bankruptcy). Provided the markets are incomplete and the default-free (nominal) bond is traded, the result of Proposition 35.5 holds.

Proving that changes in monetary policy can change the market subspace $\langle V \rangle = \langle [\nu] N \rangle$ of the associated real economy $\mathscr{E}(u, \omega, V)$ is not sufficient to prove that it can affect the equilibrium allocation x. For suppose that a different monetary policy leads to a subspace $\langle V' \rangle = \langle [\nu'] N \rangle$ with $\langle V' \rangle \neq \langle V \rangle$. If the agents' (date 1) net trade vectors all lie in the intersection

$$x_1^i - \omega_1^i \in \langle V' \rangle \cap \langle V \rangle, \quad i = 1, \ldots, I$$

then, without further information, it can not be deduced that changing monetary policy will change the equilibrium allocation. One way of being sure that such a conclusion can be drawn is to exhibit a family of economies for which the agents' equilibrium net trade vectors $(x_1^i - \omega_1^i)$, $i = 1, \ldots, I$ span the whole subspace $\langle V \rangle$: in this case they cannot all lie in the smaller subspace $\langle V \rangle \cap \langle V' \rangle$ when monetary policy is changed. To establish such a result, there must be enough agents: the number I of agents must be at least J, the dimension of the subspace $\langle V \rangle$. Actually the analysis that follows requires that there is (at least) one more agent than the dimension of $\langle V \rangle$. It is clear that there are some economies for which agents' net trades $x_1^i - \omega_1^i$, $i = 1, \ldots, I$ will not span the market subspace. For example, if the vector of initial endowments is Pareto optimal, then there is no trade at the equilibrium, $x_1^i - \omega_1^i = 0$, $i = 1, \ldots, I$—no spanning whatsoever is achieved by the agents' net trades. *The spanning property can thus at best be a "typical" property of equilibria of monetary economies.*

The mathematical approach for establishing that a certain property is typical at equilibrium was explained in Section 11. It consists in introducing a parametrized family of economies: a property is then said to be typical if it holds for the equilibria of almost all economies of the family, where "almost all" means for a subset of full measure of the parameter space. The characteristics of a monetary economy $\mathscr{E}(u, \omega, N, M)$ are the preferences (utility functions $u = (u^1, \ldots, u^I)$), the vector of endowments ω, the dividend matrix N, and the monetary policy M. There are a number of ways of parametrizing monetary economies. Since the dividend matrix represents specific types of nominal contracts, such as the default-free bond or bonds that may not pay off under specified contingencies, it is natural to keep the dividend matrix N fixed. The remaining characteristics (u, ω, M) can in general be taken as parameters: for the properties of a monetary economy that are studied in this section, it is natural to choose (ω, M) as parameters, taking $u = (u^1, \ldots, u^I)$ to be a fixed profile of utility functions satisfying Assumption $\mathscr{U}$. Variations in ω model the heterogeneity of the agents, while variations in M reflect the possible choices of monetary policy. The parameter space for the family of monetary economies is thus taken to be

$$\Omega = \mathbb{R}_{++}^{(S+1)I} \times \mathbb{R}_{++}^{S+1}$$

35.6 Definition: $\{\mathscr{E}(u, \omega, N, M) \mid (\omega, M) \in \Omega\}$ is said to be a *standard family* of monetary economies if (i) agents' utility functions $u = (u^1, \ldots, u^I)$ satisfy Assumption $\mathscr{U}$, and (ii) the dividend matrix N has rank J.

The next proposition formalizes the idea that for a typical endowment profile and monetary policy (ω, M), in an equilibrium agents trade heterogeneously i.e. they exploit differently (through their portfolios z^i) the trading opportunities offered by the market subspace.

35.7 Proposition (Spanning Property of Date 1 Net Trade Vectors): *Let* $\{\mathscr{E}(u, \omega, N, M) \mid (\omega, M) \in \Omega\}$ *be a standard family of monetary economies in which there are more agents than securities* $(I > J)$. *There exists a set of full measure* $\Omega^* \subset \Omega$ *such that, if* $(\omega, M) \in \Omega^*$ *and* $((x, z), (p, q))$ *is a monetary equilibrium of* $\mathscr{E}(u, \omega, N, M)$, *then the date 1 net trade vectors of the first* J *agents,* $x_1^i - \omega_1^i$, $i = 1, \ldots, J$, *are linearly independent.*

PROOF: Since rank $N = J$, the linear independence of the net trade vectors $x_1^i - \omega_1^i$, $i = 1, \ldots, J$ is equivalent to the linear independence of the portfolio vectors $z^i, i = 1, \ldots, J$ of the first J agents: if $\mu = (\mu_1, \ldots, \mu_J) \in \mathbb{R}^J$ is a vector of coefficients of linear combination, then

$$\mu_1(x_1^1 - \omega_1^1) + \cdots + \mu_J(x_1^J - \omega_1^J) = 0 \tag{10}$$
$$\Longleftrightarrow \quad [\nu] N(\mu_1 z^1 + \cdots + \mu_J z^J) = 0$$
$$\Longleftrightarrow \quad \mu_1 z^1 + \cdots + \mu_J z^J = 0 \tag{11}$$

Thus $\mu = 0$ is the only solution of (10), if and only if $\mu = 0$ is the only solution of (11).

The method for proving that a property (P)—in this case the linear independence of the portfolio vectors—is typically satisfied at an equilibrium,

has been explained in Section 11. It consists in showing that, if the property
(P′)—that (P) does *not* hold—is expressed by a system of equations (in this
case the equations (P′) express the linear dependence of the portfolio vectors),
and if these equations are added to the equations of equilibrium (E), then the
resulting system of equations has more equations than unknowns. If the rank
condition (ii) in Theorem 11.3 can be shown to hold, then for most parameter
values the combined system of equations (E,P′) does not have a solution.

Using the notation of Section 11, define $\tilde{z}^i(q, \omega^i, V)$ as agent i's portfolio
demand in the real economy $\mathscr{E}(u, \omega, V)$ viewed as a function of the security prices q, the agent's endowment ω^i and the matrix of real dividends V.
By Proposition 35.1, agent i's portfolio demand in the monetary economy
$\mathscr{E}(u, \omega, N, M)$ is given by $\tilde{z}^i(\nu_0 q, \omega^i, [\nu] N)$ where q is the nominal price of the
securities and (ν_0, ν) are the functions of (ω, M) defined by (4). Thus for fixed
N, agent i's portfolio demand in a monetary economy can be expressed as a
function z^i of (q, ω, M) defined by

$$z^i(q, \omega, M) = \tilde{z}^i(\nu_0 q, \omega^i, [\nu] N) \tag{12}$$

Since for all $(\omega, M) \in \Omega$, rank $[\nu] N = $ rank $N = J$, a simple extension of the
argument in Lemma 11.5 shows that z^i *is a smooth function defined on the
open set* $Q \times \Omega$ where $Q = \{q \in \mathbb{R}^J \mid q = \pi_1 N, \pi_1 \in \mathbb{R}^S_{++}\}$ is the set of no-
arbitrage prices for the matrix N—which is the same as for the matrix $[\nu] N$
for all $\nu \in \mathbb{R}^S_{++}$.

If $f : Q \times \Omega \longrightarrow \mathbb{R}^J$ is the aggregate excess demand function for the J
securities in the monetary economy $\mathscr{E}(u, \omega, N, M)$ defined by $f(q, \omega, M) = \sum_{i=1}^I z^i(q, \omega, M)$, then $q \in Q$ is an equilibrium price if and only if it is a
solution of the equilibrium equations

$$f(q, \omega, M) = 0 \tag{E}$$

The portfolios $z^1, \ldots, z^J$ at an equilibrium (where $z^i = z^i(q, \omega, M)$) are linearly
dependent if there exists a vector $\mu = (\mu_1, \ldots, \mu_J) \neq 0$ such that (11) holds,
namely if

$$\sum_{i=1}^J \mu_i z^i(q, \omega, M) = 0 \tag{13}$$

is satisfied. Since the system of J equations (13) is homogeneous in μ, if μ is
non-zero, then it can be chosen to have unit length, that is, it can be taken to
satisfy

$$\sum_{i=1}^J \mu_i^2 = 1 \tag{14}$$

(13) and (14) are $J+1$ equations which express the property (P′) that the first J agents' portfolios are linearly dependent at equilibrium. Thus there exists an equilibrium of the economy $\mathscr{E}(u, \omega, N, M)$ in which the first J agents' portfolios are linearly dependent if and only if there exists a vector of prices and a vector of coefficients of dependence $(q, \mu) \in Q \times \mathbb{R}^J$ such that the system of equations (E,P′) is satisfied. This is a system of $2J+1$ equations (J for (E), $J+1$ for (P′)) in $2J$ unknowns (J for q, J for μ), parametrized by $(\omega, M) \in \Omega$.

Define the function $g : Q \times \mathbb{R}^J \times \Omega \longrightarrow \mathbb{R}^{J+1}$ by

$$
\begin{aligned}
g_j(q, \mu, \omega, M) &= \sum_{i=1}^{J} \mu_i z_j^i(q, \omega, M), \quad j = 1, \ldots, J \\
g_{J+1}(q, \mu, \omega, M) &= \sum_{i=1}^{J} \mu_i^2 - 1
\end{aligned}
\tag{15}
$$

If $h : Q \times \mathbb{R}^J \times \Omega \longrightarrow \mathbb{R}^{2J+1}$ is defined by $h = (f, g)$, then the system of equations (E,P′) can be written as

$$
h(q, \mu, \omega, M) = 0
\tag{16}
$$

By Theorem 11.3, if for every solution $(\bar{q}, \bar{\mu}, \bar{\omega}, \bar{M})$ of (16),

$$
\operatorname{rank}\left[D_{q, \mu, \omega, M} h(\bar{q}, \bar{\mu}, \bar{\omega}, \bar{M})\right] = 2J + 1
\tag{17}
$$

then there exists a set of full measure $\Omega^* \subset \Omega$ such that, if $(\omega, M) \in \Omega^*$, then (16) has no solution in (q, μ). Since the equilibrium equations (E) have a solution in q for all $(\omega, M) \in \Omega$, if $(\omega, M) \in \Omega^*$, then there is no non-zero vector μ expressing a linear dependence between the equilibrium portfolios of the first J agents. Thus for $(\omega, M) \in \Omega^*$ the spanning property asserted in the proposition—namely that the net trade vectors $(x_1^i - \omega_1^i), i = 1, \ldots, J$ span $\langle [\nu] N \rangle$—is satisfied.

In the proof of Theorem 11.6 we showed a useful technique for establishing that a rank condition of the form (17) is satisfied, which amounts to showing that each of the $2J+1$ equations can be *locally controlled* independently of the others. The method of controlling the first J equations (i.e. the equilibrium equations (E)) was shown in the proof of Theorem 11.6. By (12), if the $(J+1)^{\text{th}}$ agent's endowment is changed by $d\omega^{J+1} = (\bar{\nu}_0 \bar{q}_j, -\bar{\nu}_1 N_1^j, \ldots, -\bar{\nu}_S N_S^j)$, while M is changed so that (to terms of first order) $(\bar{\nu}_0, \bar{\nu})$ do not change, then the optimal response of agent $J+1$ will be to purchase one more unit of security j. The change in M must be such that $d\nu_s = 0 \iff dw_s/\bar{M}_s - w_s dM_s/\bar{M}_s^2 = 0 \iff dM_s = \bar{M}_s dw_s/w_s$ for $s = 0, 1, \ldots, S$. If $dq = 0$, $d\mu = 0$ and $d\omega^i = 0$, $i \neq J+1$, then the demands of the other agents are not affected: furthermore, since the portfolio of agent $J+1$ does not appear in the system of equations (P$'$), equations (13) and (14) are unaffected. Thus the jth equation in (E) has been controlled, all other equations remaining unchanged. (Note that this argument has made use of the assumption $I > J$.) To control the jth equation in (13) (for $j = 1, \ldots, J$), choose an agent i such that $\bar{\mu}_i \neq 0$: such an agent exists since (14) holds, and, since the agents can always be relabelled, this may be taken to be agent $i = 1$. If agent 1's endowment is changed by $d\omega^1 = \frac{1}{\bar{\mu}^1}(\bar{\nu}_0 \bar{q}_j, -\bar{\nu}_1 N_1^j, \ldots, -\bar{\nu}_S N_S^j)$ and if $(\bar{\nu}_0, \bar{\nu})$ do not change, then agent 1 responds with $dz_j^1 = 1/\bar{\mu}^1$. If $dq = 0$, $d\mu = 0$, $d\omega^i = 0$, $i \neq 1$ and $i \neq J + 1$, and if $d\omega^{J+1} = -d\omega^1$, then the change in demand of agent $J + 1$ cancels the change in demand of agent 1 so that (E) is satisfied; furthermore agent $(J + 1)$'s changed portfolio demand does not affect the equations (P$'$). Since the aggregate endowment does not change, if $dM = 0$, then $d\nu_s = 0$ for $s = 0, 1, \ldots, S$. Thus the jth equation in (13) has been controlled (increased by one unit), all other equations remaining unchanged.

To control the last equation (14), choose an agent (without loss of generality agent 1) such that $\bar{\mu}_1 \neq 0$. If $d\mu$ is changed so that $2\bar{\mu}_1 d\mu_1 = 1$ and $d\mu_i = 0$, $i \neq 1$ then $d\left(\sum_{i=1}^{J} \mu_i^2\right) = 1$ so that the last equation has (to terms of first order) been increased by one unit. To ensure that the equations (13) are unchanged, the portfolio of agent 1 must change so that

$$\bar{\mu}_1 dz^1 + d\mu_1 z^1(\bar{q}, \omega, M) = 0$$

This change in agent 1's portfolio demand can be induced by changing agent 1's endowment by

$$d\omega^1 = \frac{d\mu^1}{\bar{\mu}^1}\left(-\bar{\nu}_0 \bar{q}z^1, \bar{\nu}_1 N_1 z^1, \ldots, \bar{\nu}_S N_S z^1\right)$$

provided that $(\bar{\nu}_0, \bar{\nu})$ remain unchanged. If $dq = 0$, $d\mu^i = 0$, $i \neq 1$, $d\omega^i = 0$, $i \neq 1$, and $i \neq J + 1$, and if $d\omega^{J+1} = -d\omega^1$, then the change in demand of agent $J + 1$ cancels the change in demand of agent 1 so that (E) is satisfied. Since the aggregate endowment does not change, if $dM = 0$, then $d\nu_s = 0$ for $s = 0, 1, \ldots, S$. Thus the last equation has been controlled, all other equations remaining unchanged, and the rank condition (17) is satisfied. $\square$

REMARK. Proposition 35.7 asserts that, if there are sufficiently many agents, then for most endowment profiles $\omega = (\omega^1, \ldots, \omega^I)$ and for most monetary policies M (purchasing powers of money ν), J of the agents will trade differently i.e. act like distinct (heterogeneous) agents as far as their trade on the financial markets is concerned. This is true for arbitrary (but fixed) preferences for the agents (provided they satisfy Assumption $\mathscr{U}$) and holds in particular if the preferences of the agents are identical, or belong to one of the special families studied in Chapter 3.

Combining Propositions 35.5 and 35.7 gives sufficient conditions for monetary policy to be non-neutral when financial markets are incomplete: if there is at least one nominal security which pays dividends in all states—for example the default-free bond—and if there are sufficiently many heterogeneous agents, then there are at least $S - J$ directions of change for the purchasing power of money ν at date 1 which lead to changes in the equilibrium allocation.

35.8 Proposition (Non-neutrality of Monetary Policy with Incomplete Markets): Let $\{\mathscr{E}(u, \omega, N, M) \mid (\omega, M) \in \Omega\}$ be a standard family of monetary economies with more agents than securities ($I > J$), and let $\Omega^* \subset \Omega$ denote the subset of full measure given by Proposition 35.7. If the dividend matrix N satisfies Assumption $\mathscr{D}$, and if the financial markets are incomplete ($J < S$), then for each economy $\mathscr{E}(u, \omega, N, M)$ with $(\omega, M) \in \Omega^*$ there exists a subspace $\Delta \subset \mathbb{R}^S$ with $\dim \Delta \geq S - J$, such that all changes in monetary policy from M to M', which induce changes in the purchasing power of money $\nu' - \nu \in \Delta$, are non-neutral.

PROOF: Consider an economy $\mathscr{E}(u, \omega, N, M)$ with $(\omega, M) \in \Omega^*$. Let $\langle V \rangle = \langle [\nu] N \rangle$ denote the market subspace of the associated real economy. By Proposition 35.5, if M changes to M' in such a way that $\nu' - \nu \in \Delta = \langle V \rangle^{\perp}$, then $\langle V' \rangle = \langle [\nu'] N \rangle \neq \langle V \rangle$. Thus $\dim \langle V' \rangle \cap \langle V \rangle < J$ since $\dim \langle V \rangle = \dim \langle V' \rangle = \dim \langle N \rangle = J$. Let x and x' denote equilibrium allocations for the economies $\mathscr{E}(u, \omega, N, M)$ and $\mathscr{E}(u, \omega, N, M')$ respectively. By Proposition 35.7, $(x_1^i - \omega_1^i)$, $i = 1, \ldots, J$ span $\langle V \rangle$; thus some of these net trade vectors do not lie in $\langle V \rangle \cap \langle V' \rangle$. Since all the net trade vectors $(x_1^{i'} - \omega_1^i)$, $i = 1, \ldots, I$ lie in $\langle V' \rangle$, $x' \neq x$. □

Technicality aside, the above result is obtained by showing that changes in monetary policy which tilt the real return on the default-free bond out of the current market subspace are of dimension $S - J$. This result is intuitive: the greater the dimension J of the market subspace, the harder it is to find changes which tilt ν out of this subspace.

The above reasoning focuses exclusively on the default-free bond, and if this is the only security, it gives the best result that can be obtained. If there are other nominal securities (i.e. $J \geq 2$) then changing the purchasing power of money changes their returns as well: there are thus (in principle) more possibilities for affecting the market subspace by altering the purchasing power than indicated by the above proposition. Since by Proposition 35.3 there is one dimension of change $\nu' - \nu$—namely when $\nu' - \nu$ is collinear to ν—which is neutral, the maximum dimension for the subspace of non-neutral changes Δ in the purchasing power ν is $S - 1$. To obtain a more refined result, which reflects the possibility of "tilting" not just the default-free bond $\mathbb{1}$ but the other securities as well, an additional hypothesis needs to be made about the returns on the other securities: the maximum dimension $S - 1$ is attained under the following assumption.

35.9 Definition: An $S \times J$ matrix N, with $J \leq S$, is in *general position* if every $J \times J$ submatrix of N has rank J.

This algebraic condition can be expressed geometrically as follows: whenever the columns $N^1, \ldots, N^J$ of N, which are J-vectors in $\mathbb{R}^S$, are projected onto any J-dimensional co-ordinate subspace of $\mathbb{R}^S$, the projections must be linearly independent vectors.[3] This assumption is natural from a mathematical point of view, since general position is a typical property of $S \times J$ matrices (i.e. the matrices that do not have this property are a set of measure zero in $\mathbb{R}^{SJ}$). However it is less natural from an economic point of view: typical nominal contracts, such as the default-free bond, risky bonds, or nominal insurance contracts, offer to reimburse a constant sum in most states—for example, zero for an insurance contract, except when an accident occurs, when it pays one, and one for a risky bond, except when default occurs, when it pays zero: such contracts have payoffs which are easy to describe and are thus easy to enforce. Thus, what is typical from a mathematical point of view may not be typical from an economic point of view.

For example, suppose there are two contracts N^1, N^2 and suppose N^1 is the default-free bond, then the matrix $N = [N^1 N^2]$ is in general position if and only if all components of the second contract N_s^2, $s = 1, \ldots, S$ are different

$$\det \begin{bmatrix} 1 & N_s^2 \\ 1 & N_{s'}^2 \end{bmatrix} \neq 0 \quad \text{for all} \quad s \neq s'$$

Requiring that the payoff on the second contract be completely state contingent in this way is a strong assumption: for example, it would not permit the second contract to be a bond which defaults in a subset $\mathbf{S}'$ of states, since the payment is still constant and equal to 1 in all non-default states $(\mathbf{S} \setminus \mathbf{S}')$. Thus the following result is less broadly applicable than Proposition 35.5 in models of a monetary economy. However it is of theoretical interest, since it shows that as soon as markets are incomplete, there can be market structures for which *all* changes in monetary policy which alter the variability of inflation are non-neutral.

---

[3]Let $e^1 = (1, \ldots, 0), \ldots, e^S = (0, \ldots, 1)$ denote the standard basis for $\mathbb{R}^S$. The jth column of N can be written as $N^j = \sum_{s=1}^{S} N_s^j e^s$. For all collections $(i_1, \ldots, i_J)$ of J indices drawn from $\{1, \ldots, S\}$, consider the J-dimensional co-ordinate subspace $\langle e^{i_1}, \ldots, e^{i_J} \rangle$. Projecting N^j onto this subspace gives the vector $(N_{i_1}^j, \ldots, N_{i_J}^j)$. Asking that $\{(N_{i_1}^j, \ldots, N_{i_J}^j), j = 1, \ldots, J\}$ be linearly independent means that they span the subspace $\langle e^{i_1}, \ldots, e^{i_J} \rangle$.

35.10 Proposition (Maximum Dimension of Non-neutral Monetary Changes):
Let $\mathscr{E}(u, \omega, N, M)$ be a monetary economy with incomplete markets ($J < S$)
for which the dividend matrix N is in general position, and let ν (given by
(4)) be the purchasing power of money in this economy. There is a subspace
$\Delta \subset \mathbb{R}^S$ with $\dim \Delta = S - 1$ such that, if monetary policy is changed from
M to M' in such a way that the purchasing power changes from ν to ν' with
$\nu' - \nu \in \Delta$, then $\langle [\nu'] N \rangle \neq \langle [\nu] N \rangle$.

PROOF: Suppose that $\langle [\nu'] N \rangle = \langle [\nu] N \rangle$. This implies that for $j = 1, \ldots, J$,
$[\nu'] N^j$ is a linear combination of the vectors $[\nu] N^1, \ldots, [\nu] N^J$. The coefficients expressing these linear combinations form a $J \times J$ matrix C such that

$$[\nu'] N = [\nu] N C$$

which can be written as

$$\frac{\nu_1'}{\nu_1} N_1 = N_1 C$$
$$\vdots \tag{19}$$
$$\frac{\nu_S'}{\nu_S} N_S = N_S C$$

Thus for $s = 1, \ldots, S$, ν_s'/ν_s must be an eigenvalue of C^T, and the row $N_s \in \mathbb{R}^J$
must be an associated eigenvector. The eigenspaces associated with distinct
eigenvalues of a linear map have the property that they form a direct sum.[4]
Thus if C^T has two or more distinct eigenvalues, then each eigenspace is
of dimension less than J. Since each of the S vectors $N_1, \ldots, N_S$ must belong to an eigenspace, at least one of these eigenspaces must contain more
vectors $N_1, \ldots, N_S$ than its dimension: this contradicts the general position
assumption that every collection of J row vectors from $\{N_1, \ldots, N_S\}$ is linearly independent. Thus if $\langle [\nu'] N \rangle = \langle [\nu] N \rangle$, then the matrix C expressing
the linear combinations must have the property that there exists $\beta \neq 0$ (the
unique eigenvalue) such that $\nu_s'/\nu_s = \beta$, $s = 1, \ldots, S$. Conversely if $\nu_s' = \beta \nu_s$,
$s = 1, \ldots, S$, then $\langle [\nu'] N \rangle = \langle [\nu] N \rangle$, the matrix of coefficients being $C = \beta I$
(where I is the $J \times J$ identity matrix). Thus the only changes from ν to ν'
which do not affect the market subspace are those lying in the one-dimensional
subspace $\nu' - \nu \in \langle \nu \rangle$. All other changes, in particular all changes such that
$\nu' - \nu \in \langle \nu \rangle^\perp$, are such that $\langle [\nu'] N \rangle \neq \langle [\nu] N \rangle$. $\square$

The role of the general position assumption on N in the proof of Proposition 35.10 can be understood geometrically as follows. Suppose $S = 3$ and

---

[4]If β_1 and β_2 are distinct eigenvalues of C and if E_{β_1} and E_{β_2} denote the associated eigenspaces
in $\mathbb{R}^J$, if $y \in E_{\beta_1} \cap E_{\beta_2}$, then $C^T y = \beta_1 y = \beta_2 y \Longrightarrow (\beta_1 - \beta_2) y = 0 \Longrightarrow y = 0$ since $\beta_1 \neq \beta_2$.
Thus $E_{\beta_1} \cap E_{\beta_2} = \{0\}$.

$J = 2$, and let $\nu = (1, 1, 1)$. If (e^1, e^2, e^3) is the standard basis for $\mathbb{R}^3$, then $[\nu] N^j = \sum_{s=1}^{3} N_s^j e^s$, for $j = 1, 2$. Let $\nu' = (\nu_1', \nu_2', \nu_3') \neq \nu$, then $[\nu'] N^j = \sum_{s=1}^{3} N_s^j \nu_s' e^s$, so that changing from ν to ν' amounts to changing units on each of the co-ordinate axes, a geometric transformation which is called an affine distortion. The mathematical problem reduces to studying the distortions ν' which leave the subspace $\langle N \rangle$ invariant. If the two vectors N^1 and N^2 are not in general position, then their projections n^1 and n^2 onto one of the three co-ordinate planes, say $\langle e^1, e^2 \rangle$, are collinear. If the projections $n^1 = (N_1^1, N_2^1)$ and $n^2 = (N_1^2, N_2^2)$ are collinear, whenever $\nu' = (\nu_1', \nu_2', \nu_3')$ satisfies $\nu_1' = \nu_2'$, then $(\nu_1' N_1^1, \nu_2' N_2^1)$ and $(\nu_1' N_1^2, \nu_2' N_2^2)$ are also collinear to n^1 and n^2. For any ν_3', the vectors $[\nu'] N^1$ and $[\nu'] N^2$ lie in the same plane as (N^1, N^2) (see Figure 35.1). In this case the distortions ν' which leave the subspace $\langle N \rangle$ invariant, i.e. $\langle [\nu'] N \rangle = \langle N \rangle$, are given by $\widetilde{\Delta} = \{\nu' \in \mathbb{R}^3 \mid \nu_1' = \nu_2'\}$ which is two-dimensional. The changes in purchasing power $\nu' - \nu \neq 0$ which lead to a change in the market subspace must be such that $\nu' - \nu \in \widetilde{\Delta}^C$, a set which contains subspaces of dimension one, like $\Delta = \widetilde{\Delta}^\perp$, but no subspace of dimension $2 \ (= S - 1)$ as asserted in Proposition 35.10.

The distinction between Propositions 35.5 and 35.10 should be clear. The first proposition exhibits a *minimal* subspace of changes in purchasing power which change the market subspace. This subspace is given by $\Delta = \langle [\nu] N \rangle^\perp$, so that $\dim \Delta = S - J$. As soon as the new vector of purchasing power ν' moves out of the current market subspace $\langle [\nu] N \rangle$, in particular if $\nu' - \nu \in \langle [\nu] N \rangle^\perp$, then the market subspace is altered. Proposition 35.10 (under the additional hypothesis that N is in general position) exhibits a *maximal* subspace of ν-changes: this subspace is given by $\Delta = \langle \nu \rangle^\perp$ so that $\dim \Delta = S - 1$. As soon as the new vector of purchasing power ν' moves out of the subspace generated by the current vector of purchasing power, in particular if $\nu' - \nu \in \langle \nu \rangle^\perp$, then the market subspace changes.

REMARK. Combining Propositions 35.7 and 35.10 gives a result on the non-neutrality of monetary policy for a typical economy, analogous to Proposition 35.8, for which the subspace of non-neutral changes in purchasing power is of dimension $S - 1$.

Indeterminacy

This result also establishes the indeterminacy properties for economies with nominal securities discussed in Section 33. If in Definition 34.1 the monetary equations (iv) are omitted, then a concept of equilibrium is obtained for an economy $\mathscr{E}(u, \omega, N)$ with nominal securities in which the purchasing power of money is a free variable: it is the one-good version of the concept of equilibrium discussed in Section 33. The indeterminacy of such equilibria suggested

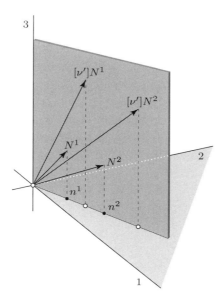

Figure 35.1   The role of the general position assumption in Proposition 35.10 when $S = 3$, $J = 2$: N^1 and N^2 are not in general position since they project onto the collinear vectors n^1 and n^2. For any vector of purchasing power $\nu' = (\nu_1', \nu_2', \nu_3') \in \mathbb{R}_{++}^3$ such that $\nu_1' = \nu_2'$, $\langle [\nu'] N \rangle = \langle N \rangle$.

by the Walras Consistency Test is established by Propositions 35.8 and the analogous result derived from Proposition 35.10 when N is in general position: the equilibrium allocations of $\mathscr{E}(u, \omega, N)$ are the union of the equilibrium allocations for monetary economies $\mathscr{E}(u, \omega, N, M)$ for all $M \in \mathbb{R}_{++}^{S+1}$. When the monetary policy is non-neutral, the monetary equilibria depend on M, so that there is a continuum of equilibria of the economy $\mathscr{E}(u, \omega, N)$. Using the concept of a smooth manifold, it can be shown that the "dimension" of the set of equilibrium allocations of $\mathscr{E}(u, \omega, N)$ is typically at least $S - J$ under the assumptions of Proposition 35.5, and is $S - 1$ under the assumptions of Proposition 35.10.

36.   OPTIMAL MONETARY POLICY

One of the recurrent themes of monetary theory is that an important objective of monetary policy should be to keep the purchasing power of money stable.[1]

---

[1] With slight exaggeration this was the principal theme of classical monetary theory: see Ricardo (1816), Mill (1848), Walras (1886), and Marshall (1923). For a more sophisticated modern version of this theory see Friedman's (1968) well-known Presidential address to the American

Monetary policy should not introduce additional uncertainty (shocks) into the economy over and above the unavoidable real shocks which affect the availability of resources, the technology (in an economy with production), and the preferences of the agents.

In a modern economy a large proportion of business contracts involve deferred payment in the medium of exchange: this is true not only for contracts made between firms, but also for loan contracts, mortgages, and leases as well as for the wages and salaries paid to employees. Nominal contracts are used because they are simple and convenient: but these qualities are greatly impaired by fluctuations in the purchasing power of money which introduce additional uncertainty over and above the standard uncertainties of business. The idea that agents should be able to borrow and lend without excessive risk to either creditors or debtors, that labor contracts, while expressed in nominal terms, should approximately represent the real value of services rendered, not exposing employees to substantial cuts in their standard of living nor employers to substantial increases in their costs—all these are classical arguments extolling the virtues of stability in the purchasing power of money. We shall show that there is a simple setting where the classical argument can be proved to be right: in a two-period exchange economy, introducing monetary shocks is never optimal since it adds a new element of uncertainty into the economy which impairs the functioning of the financial markets in the private sector.

Economy with Monetary Risks

Consider first an economy in which the only source of uncertainty comes from fluctuations in the money supply. To keep the analysis within the framework of this chapter, suppose there are two periods ($t = 0, 1$) and a single good ($L = 1$) and suppose that the government's date 1 monetary policy can be expressed as a function $M_1 : (\mathbf{K}, \rho) \longrightarrow \mathbb{R}_{++}$ on a finite probability space $(\mathbf{K}, \rho)$, where $\mathbf{K} = \{1, \ldots, K\}$ is a set of states, and $\rho = (\rho_1, \ldots, \rho_K)$ denotes the probabilities of the states. The reason for this change of notation from $\mathbf{S}$ to $\mathbf{K}$ will become clear shortly when we distinguish between the state space $\mathbf{S}$ which reflects real sources of uncertainty and the state space $\mathbf{K}$ which reflects monetary sources of uncertainty. In keeping with the assumption of rational expectations, all agents in the private sector are assumed to correctly anticipate the government's monetary policy—that is, they know the policy function M_1—and understand the consequences of this policy for the functioning of markets in the private sector.

The agents in the economy do not like uncertainty: more precisely, they have

---

Economic Association: "The first and most important lesson that history teaches about what monetary policy can do—and it is a lesson of the most profound importance—is that monetary policy can prevent money itself from being a major source of economic disturbance."

preferences which exhibit risk aversion and state independence in the following sense: in addition to Assumption $\mathscr{U}'$, the utility function u^i of agent i satisfies

$$u^i(x_0^i, x_{\mathbf{1}}^i) \le u^i(x_0^i, E(x_{\mathbf{1}}^i)\mathbb{1}) \quad \text{for all} \quad (x_0, x_1) \in \mathbb{R}_{++}^{K+1} \tag{1}$$

with strict inequality if $x_{\mathbf{1}}^i \ne E(x_{\mathbf{1}}^i)\mathbb{1}$, where $x_{\mathbf{1}}^i = (x_1^i, \dots, x_K^i)$ is the agent's random consumption at date 1 and $\mathbb{1} = (1, \dots, 1)$ is the constant random variable. (1) expresses the fact that given any date 0 consumption $x_0^i \in \mathbb{R}_{++}$, the agent always prefers to replace any random date 1 consumption $x_{\mathbf{1}}^i \in \mathbb{R}_{++}^K$ by its expected value under the known probabilities $\rho = (\rho_1, \dots, \rho_K)$

$$E(x_{\mathbf{1}}^i) = \sum_{k \in \mathbf{K}} \rho_k x_k^i$$

for sure. State independence of preferences is implicit in (1), since the expected value of any date 1 random consumption is preferred, regardless of the way it distributes consumption across the states. In particular, (1) is satisfied if agent i has von-Neumann-Morgenstern preferences

$$u^i(x_0^i, x_{\mathbf{1}}^i) = \sum_{k \in \mathbf{K}} \rho_k v^i(x_0^i, x_k^i)$$

where $v^i : \mathbb{R}_{++}^2 \longrightarrow \mathbb{R}$ is strictly concave and increasing.

To express the idea that the only source of uncertainty comes from fluctuations in the money supply, the date 1 endowments of the agents are assumed to be non-random. Thus the endowment of each agent satisfies

$$\omega^i = (\omega_0^i, \omega_1^i \mathbb{1}) \quad \text{where} \quad (\omega_0^i, \omega_1^i) \in \mathbb{R}_{++}^2 \tag{2}$$

We assume that the economy has the simplest possible financial structure; the only security is the default-free nominal bond: thus $J = 1$ and

$$N = \mathbb{1} \tag{3}$$

(3) implies that there are no nominal risks, since the lending contract is default-free; however there are real risks associated with either borrowing or lending, arising from the possible random inflation created by fluctuations in the money supply. It is assumed that when agents make their contractual commitments, they do not write indexing clauses into their contracts to counteract fluctuations in the purchasing power of money.[2] Let $\mathscr{E}(u, \omega, N, M)$ denote the resulting monetary economy satisfying assumptions (1)–(3). Later we will relax

---

[2] The conditions under which agents prefer not to include indexing clauses into their contracts are discussed in Section 37.

assumptions (2) and (3), permitting both real uncertainty in the endowments and a richer structure of financial securities.

As usual, we define the *aggregate output w* of an exchange economy $\mathscr{E}(u, \omega)$ by $w = (w_0, w_1, \ldots, w_K)$ where $w_k = \sum_{i=1}^{I} \omega_k^i$, and say that there is *no aggregate risk* if the date 1 output $w_{\mathbf{1}} = (w_k, \ k \in \mathbf{K})$, is non-random

$$w_{\mathbf{1}} = w_1 \mathbb{1} \tag{4}$$

Agent i is said to have *no individual risk* if his endowment ω^i satisfies (2). In the economy outlined above there is neither aggregate nor individual risk.

Consider the two-period certainty economy $\mathscr{E}(v, \underset{\sim}{\omega})$ in which agent i has preferences defined by the utility function

$$v^i(\underset{\sim}{x}^i) = v^i(x_0^i, x_1^i) = u^i(x_0^i, x_1^i \mathbb{1}) \quad \text{for all} \quad (x_0^i, x_1^i) \in \mathbb{R}_{++}^2 \tag{5}$$

where $\underset{\sim}{x}^i = (x_0^i, x_1^i)$ denotes his consumption at date 0 and date 1, and in which his initial endowment is

$$\underset{\sim}{\omega}^i = (\omega_0^i, \omega_1^i)$$

Let $\underset{\sim}{w} = (w_0, w_1)$ denote the aggregate output in the certainty economy. To emphasize the fact that Pareto optima of an economy depend only on the agents' preferences and the aggregate output, let $\mathscr{E}_w(u)$ denote the economy with utility functions u and aggregate output w, while $\mathscr{E}_{\underset{\sim}{w}}(v)$ denotes the certainty economy with utility functions v and aggregate output $\underset{\sim}{w}$. The assiduous reader will already have established the following result (see Exercise 1 of Chapter 3).

36.1 Proposition (Pareto Optima of an Economy with no Real Risk):

Let $\mathscr{E}_w(u)$ be an economy without aggregate risk in which agents' utility functions satisfy (1). An allocation $x = (x^1, \ldots, x^I) \in \mathbb{R}_+^{(K+1)I}$ is Pareto optimal if and only if for each agent $i = 1, \ldots, I$ there exists a two-period consumption plan $\underset{\sim}{x}^i = (x_0^i, x_1^i) \in \mathbb{R}_+^2$ such that $x^i = (x_0^i, x_1^i \mathbb{1})$ and $\underset{\sim}{x} = (\underset{\sim}{x}^1, \ldots, \underset{\sim}{x}^I)$ is a Pareto optimum of the certainty economy $\mathscr{E}_{\underset{\sim}{w}}(v)$.

PROOF: ($\Longrightarrow$) Let x be a Pareto optimum for $\mathscr{E}_w(u)$. Suppose that for some agent (without loss of generality, agent 1) $x_{\mathbf{1}}^1$ is risky i.e. $x_{\mathbf{1}}^1 \neq E(x_{\mathbf{1}}^1)\mathbb{1}$. Since there is no aggregate risk, the riskless allocation $\hat{x}$ defined by giving each agent the same date 0 consumption and the expected value of his date 1 consumption for sure, namely

$$\hat{x}^i = (\hat{x}_0^i, \hat{x}_{\mathbf{1}}^i) = (x_0^i, E(x_{\mathbf{1}}^i)\mathbb{1}) \tag{6}$$

is feasible, since $x_0 = \hat{x}_0$ and $\sum_{i=1}^{I} \hat{x}_{\mathbf{1}}^i = \sum_{i=1}^{I} E(x_{\mathbf{1}}^i)\mathbb{1} = w_1 \mathbb{1}$. The assumption of risk aversion in (1) implies that every agent prefers the sure consumption stream (6) and it is strictly preferred by agent 1, contradicting the Pareto optimality of x. Thus each agent's date 1 consumption is riskless, so that x^i can be written as $x^i = (x_0^i, x_1^i \mathbb{1})$, $i = 1, \ldots, I$. Let $\underset{\sim}{x}^i = (x_0^i, x_1^i)$ denote agent i's consumption in the associated two-period certainty economy $\mathscr{E}_{\underset{\sim}{w}}(v)$: then by (4) the allocation $\underset{\sim}{x} = (\underset{\sim}{x}^1, \ldots, \underset{\sim}{x}^I)$ is feasible. If there were a Pareto improvement of $\underset{\sim}{x}$ in $\mathscr{E}_{\underset{\sim}{w}}(v)$, then there would be a Pareto improvement of x in $\mathscr{E}_w(u)$.

($\Longleftarrow$) Let $\underset{\sim}{x}$ be a Pareto optimum for $\mathscr{E}_{\underset{\sim}{w}}(v)$. Suppose the allocation $x = (x^1, \ldots, x^I)$ with $x^i = (x_0^i, x_1^i \mathbb{1})$, $i = 1, \ldots, I$ is not Pareto optimal in $\mathscr{E}_w(u)$. Then there exists a feasible allocation $\hat{x}$ such that $u^i(\hat{x}^i) \geq u^i(x^i)$ with strict inequality for some i. By (1) and the absence of aggregate risk, the allocation $(\hat{x}_0^i, E(\hat{x}_1^i)\mathbb{1})$, $i = 1, \ldots, I$ Pareto dominates x in $\mathscr{E}_w(u)$, which in turn implies that $(\hat{x}_0^i, E(\hat{x}_1^i))$, $i = 1, \ldots, I$ Pareto dominates $\underset{\sim}{x}$ in $\mathscr{E}_{\underset{\sim}{w}}(v)$, which is a contradiction. Thus x is Pareto optimal in $\mathscr{E}_w(u)$. $\square$

This proposition asserts that in an economy in which there is no aggregate risk and in which agents' preferences exhibit risk aversion and state independence, any Pareto optimal allocation $x = (x^1, \ldots, x^I)$ has the property that each agent's consumption $x^i = (x_0^i, x_1^i \mathbb{1})$ is free of individual risk: in short, absence of aggregate risk translates into absence of individual risk for Pareto optima. The absence of individual risk in the Pareto optima of the original economy $\mathscr{E}_w(u)$ in turn translates into Pareto optimality of these allocations in the certainty economy $\mathscr{E}_{\underset{\sim}{w}}(v)$.

In the study of markets, only those economies are of interest in which the initial endowments are not Pareto optimal, since these are the only economies in which there is trade. Since the endowments of a monetary economy satisfying (2) can be viewed as the endowments of a two-period certainty economy, these endowments can be parametrized by

$$\Omega = \{\underset{\sim}{w} = (\underset{\sim}{w}^1, \ldots, \underset{\sim}{w}^I) \in \mathbb{R}_{++}^{2I}\}$$

Thus if we define

$$\Omega^* = \{\underset{\sim}{w} \in \Omega \mid \underset{\sim}{w} \text{ is not PO for } \mathscr{E}_{\underset{\sim}{w}}(v)\}$$

and if the monetary economies satisfying (2) are parametrized by endowments, then it follows from Proposition 36.1 that Ω^* is the subset of economies in which there are *gains from trade*.

36.2 Proposition (Optimal Monetary Policy with no Real Risk): *Consider a monetary economy $\mathscr{E}(u, \omega, N, M)$ satisfying (1)–(3) in which there are gains from trade, $\underset{\sim}{w} \in \Omega^*$. The equilibria of $\mathscr{E}(u, \omega, N, M)$ are Pareto optimal if and only if the monetary policy does not introduce monetary shocks i.e. M is non-random, $M = (M_0, M_1 \mathbb{1})$ for some $M_1 > 0$.*

PROOF: ($\Longleftarrow$) Suppose $M = (M_0, M_1\mathbb{1})$ is a non-random monetary policy. Since there is no aggregate risk ($w_1 = w_1\mathbb{1}$ with $w_1 = \sum_{i=1}^{I} \omega_1^i$), the date 1 purchasing power of money is constant $\nu = \nu_1\mathbb{1}$ with $\nu_1 = w_1/M_1$. Let $((\bar{x}, \bar{z}), (\bar{p}, \bar{q}))$ be a monetary equilibrium of $\mathscr{E}(u, \omega, N, M)$. Then $\bar{p}_k = 1/\nu_1$ for $k \in \mathbf{K}$, and $\bar{x}^i$ is optimal in the budget set

$$\left\{ x^i \in \mathbb{R}_{++}^{K+1} \;\middle|\; \begin{array}{l} x_0^i - \omega_0^i = -\nu_0\bar{q}z^i, \; z^i \in \mathbb{R} \\ x_k^i - \omega_1^i = \nu_1 z^i, \; k \in \mathbf{K} \end{array} \right\}$$

$$\Longleftrightarrow \quad \left\{ x^i \in \mathbb{R}_{++}^{K+1} \;\middle|\; \begin{array}{l} x^i = (x_0^i, x_1^i\mathbb{1}) \\ x_0^i - \omega_0^i = -\dfrac{\nu_0}{\nu_1}\bar{q}z^i, \; z^i \in \mathbb{R} \\ x_1^i - \omega_1^i = z^i \end{array} \right\}$$

Thus $\bar{\underline{x}}^i = (\bar{x}_0^i, \bar{x}_1^i)$ is optimal in the budget set $\mathbb{B}(q, \underline{\omega}^i, 1)$ of the certainty economy $\mathscr{E}(v, \underline{\omega}, 1)$ in which the only security is the real bond with price $q = (\nu_0/\nu_1)\bar{q}$ and $\bar{\underline{x}} = (\bar{\underline{x}}^1, \dots, \bar{\underline{x}}^I)$ is an equilibrium allocation of this economy. Since in $\mathscr{E}(v, \underline{\omega}, 1)$ the financial market is complete, the allocation $\bar{\underline{x}}$ is Pareto optimal in $\mathscr{E}_w(v)$ and thus by Proposition 36.1, $\bar{x}$ is Pareto optimal in $\mathscr{E}_w(u)$.

($\Longrightarrow$) Suppose each monetary equilibrium $((\bar{x}, \bar{z}), (\bar{p}, \bar{q}))$ of $\mathscr{E}(u, \omega, N, M)$ is Pareto optimal and suppose that M is random i.e. there are states $k \neq k'$ such that $M_k \neq M_{k'}$. Then

$$\bar{x}_k^i - \omega_1^i = \nu_k\bar{z}^i, \quad \bar{x}_{k'}^i - \omega_1^i = \nu_{k'}\bar{z}^i, \quad i = 1, \dots I$$

and $\nu_k = w_1/M_k \neq w_1/M_{k'} = \nu_{k'}$. If $\bar{z}^i = 0$ for $i = 1, \dots, I$, then $\bar{x} = \omega$: but since $\omega \in \Omega^*$ this contradicts the assumption that $\bar{x}$ is Pareto optimal. If $\bar{z}^i \neq 0$ for some i, then $\bar{x}_k^i \neq \bar{x}_{k'}^i$ and by Proposition 36.1, $\bar{x}$ is not Pareto optimal. Thus M is non-random. $\square$

Real and Monetary Risks

The characterization of an optimal monetary policy in Proposition 36.2 can be extended to economies with real risks, provided these risks are fully covered by the contracts traded in the private sector. To establish such a property, a distinction needs to be made between the real and monetary risks in an economy. A natural way of making this distinction is to decompose the underlying state space—on which the description of uncertainty is based—into a product of two spaces

$$\mathbf{S} \times \mathbf{K} = \{1, \dots, S\} \times \{1, \dots, K\} \tag{7}$$

each state $s \in \mathbf{S}$ representing a *real* shock and each state $k \in \mathbf{K}$ a *monetary* shock: a state of nature is then a pair $(s, k) \in \mathbf{S} \times \mathbf{K}$. The vector of *probabilities*

$$\rho = (\rho_{sk}, (s, k) \in \mathbf{S} \times \mathbf{K}) \tag{8}$$

is assumed to be known (correctly anticipated) by all agents. To express the idea that there is an underlying *real risk economy* in which the initial endowments of the agents are only affected by the real shocks, the initial resources of the agents are assumed to depend only on s i.e.. to be constant for all states $(s, k), k \in \mathbf{K}$ for a fixed $s \in \mathbf{S}$. Thus, for each agent i $(i = 1, \ldots, I)$, there exists a vector $\underset{\sim}{\omega}^i = (\omega_0^i, \omega_1^i, \ldots, \omega_S^i) \in \mathbb{R}_+^{S+1}$ such that

$$\omega_0^i = \underset{\sim}{\omega}_0^i, \quad \omega_{sk}^i = \underset{\sim}{\omega}_s^i \quad \text{for all} \quad (s, k) \in \mathbf{S} \times \mathbf{K} \tag{9}$$

The simplest way of expressing, in this more general setting, the fact that agents do not like uncertainty (the property expressed by equation (1) for an economy with no real risk) is to assume that agents have separable, von-Neumann-Morgenstern utility functions of the form

$$u^i(x_0^i, x_1^i) = \sum_{(s,k) \in \mathbf{S} \times \mathbf{K}} \rho_{sk} v^i(x_0^i, x_{sk}^i) \tag{10}$$

where $v^i : \mathbb{R}_+^2 \longrightarrow \mathbb{R}$ is strictly concave and increasing.

Although the most realistic assumption is that there are both real and nominal securities, the analysis that follows is simpler if all securities are taken to be nominal. This assumption is stronger than necessary: the results that follow depend only on the existence of some nominal securities. In addition, payoffs on the securities are assumed to depend only on the underlying real risks: thus for each real state $s \in \mathbf{S}$ there exists a vector of payoffs on the J securities $\underset{\sim}{N}_s = (\underset{\sim}{N}_s^1, \ldots, \underset{\sim}{N}_s^J)$ such that

$$N_{sk} = \underset{\sim}{N}_s \quad \text{for all} \quad (s, k) \in \mathbf{S} \times \mathbf{K} \tag{11}$$

In this economy, only the monetary policy

$$M = (M_0, M_1) \quad \text{with} \quad M_1 = (M_{sk}, (s, k) \in \mathbf{S} \times \mathbf{K}) \tag{12}$$

can depend on both the real and the monetary sources of uncertainty. Let $\mathscr{E}(u, \omega, N, M)$ denote the resulting monetary economy satisfying assumptions (7)—(12), and let $\mathscr{E}_w(u)$ denote the real economy with preference profile $u = (u^1, \ldots, u^I)$ and aggregate endowment $w = \sum_{i=1}^I \omega^i$.

To such an economy one can associate the economy $\mathscr{E}(\underline{u}, \underline{\omega})$ defined on the real states $\mathbf{S}$ in which the characteristics of each agent are given by $(\underline{u}^i, \underline{\omega}^i)$, where $\underline{u}^i : \mathbb{R}_+^{S+1} \longrightarrow \mathbb{R}$ is defined by

$$\underline{u}^i(\underline{x}_0^i, (\underline{x}_s^i)_{s \in S}) = \sum_{s \in \mathbf{S}} \rho_s v^i(\underline{x}_0^i, \underline{x}_s^i), \quad \rho_s = \sum_{k \in \mathbf{K}} \rho_{sk}$$

and $\underline{\omega}^i$ is the endowment vector in (9). $\mathscr{E}_{\underline{w}}(\underline{u})$ is the economy with preference profile $\underline{u} = (\underline{u}^1, \dots, \underline{u}^I)$ and aggregate endowment $\underline{w} = \sum_{i=1}^I \underline{\omega}^i$. Proposition 36.1 can then be generalized as follows.

36.3 Proposition (Pareto Optima of Economy Satisfying (7)–(10)): *Let $\mathscr{E}_w(u)$ be an economy in which aggregate output depends only on the real risks and in which agents' utility functions satisfy (10). An allocation $x = (x^1, \dots, x^I) \in \mathbb{R}_+^{(SK+1)I}$ is Pareto optimal if and only if for each agent $i = 1, \dots, I$ there is a consumption plan $\underline{x}^i = (\underline{x}_0^i, \underline{x}_1^i, \dots, \underline{x}_S^i)$ which depends only on the real risks, such that $x_0^i = \underline{x}_0^i$, $x_{sk}^i = \underline{x}_s^i$ for all $(s, k) \in \mathbf{S} \times \mathbf{K}$ and $\underline{x} = (\underline{x}^1, \dots, \underline{x}^I)$ is a Pareto optimum of the economy $\mathscr{E}_{\underline{w}}(\underline{u})$.*

PROOF: The proof is a straightforward generalization of the proof of Proposition 36.1 and is based on the feasibility of the allocation $\underline{x}$ defined by $\underline{x}_0^i = x_0^i$, $\underline{x}_s^i = (1/\rho_s) \sum_{k \in \mathbf{K}} \rho_{sk} x_{sk}^i$ and the risk aversion of each agent which implies that $u^i(x^i) \leq \underline{u}^i(\underline{x}^i)$ with strict inequality if $x_{sk}^i \neq x_{sk'}^i$ for some $k \neq k'$. $\square$

Since monetary policy can only influence the outcome of economies in which there is trade, we restrict attention to those economies in which there are *gains from trade*

$$\Omega^* = \left\{ \underline{\omega} \in \mathbb{R}^{(S+1)I} \ \middle| \ \underline{\omega} \text{ is not PO for } \mathscr{E}_{\underline{\omega}}(\underline{u}) \right\}$$

The analogue of Proposition 36.2 can then be stated as follows.

36.4 Proposition (Optimal Monetary Policy with Complete Markets for Real Risks): *Let $\mathscr{E}(u, \omega, N, M)$ be a monetary economy satisfying (7)–(12) in which the markets for real risks are complete (rank $N = S$) and in which there are gains from trade, $\underline{\omega} \in \Omega^*$. The equilibria of $\mathscr{E}(u, \omega, N, M)$ are Pareto optimal if and only if the monetary policy does not introduce additional uncertainty (shocks) into the economy i.e. there exists $\underline{M}_{\mathbf{1}} = (\underline{M}_s, \ s \in \mathbf{S})$ such that M satisfies $M_{sk} = \underline{M}_s$ for all $(s, k) \in \mathbf{S} \times \mathbf{K}$.*

PROOF: The proof is a straightforward generalization of the proof of Proposition 36.2 and is based on Proposition 36.3 and the fact that an agent's date 1 consumption is given by $x_{sk}^i - \omega_s^i = \nu_{sk} \underline{N}_s z^i$ with $\nu_{sk} = w_s/M_{sk}$ for all $(s, k) \in \mathbf{S} \times \mathbf{K}$. $\square$

This proposition can be expressed more intuitively as follows: *when monetary policy introduces new shocks into an economy by creating fluctuations in the purchasing power of money ($\nu_{sk} \neq \nu_{sk'}$) against which agents do not have the facility to insure themselves, it adds to the risks in the private sector and makes agents worse off.* When the markets for the real risks are complete, monetary induced fluctuations in the purchasing power of money tamper with the effectiveness of the nominal contracts which, without such fluctuations, are well-adapted to the underlying real risks in the economy.

In making the distinction between real and monetary shocks (states), only two properties of the real states play a role as far as the proposition is concerned. First, these are the only states that affect the resources available in the economy. Second, these are states against which the financial markets provide insurance (risk sharing). Thus monetary shocks (states) can be included in the real-shock category if there are securities which provide insurance against these contingencies. If the economy had such a rich structure of financial markets that agents could insure themselves against all risks, both monetary and real, then once again monetary policy would be neutral—and irrelevant. Whatever new shocks the monetary policy might add to the economy could be traded out amongst the agents by suitable risk-sharing portfolios. Note that the assumption that the financial markets provide complete risk sharing against the real risks (rank $N = S$) implies that the choice of the monetary policy $M_1 = (M_s, \ s \in \mathbf{S})$ does not influence the equilibrium allocation. Thus while a monetary policy should not introduce new monetary risks, the exact way in which the policy is related to the underlying real risks is unimportant.

Incomplete Markets for Real Risks

When the financial markets provide only partial (i.e. incomplete) risk sharing against the real risks (rank $N < S$), then by Proposition 35.8 the choice of $M_1 = (M_s, \ s \in \mathbf{S})$ influences the equilibrium allocation i.e. M_1 is non-neutral. While the condition that a monetary policy should not add new monetary risks is still a necessary condition for optimality, it is no longer sufficient to characterize an optimal monetary policy.

When markets are incomplete, the appropriate criterion for judging the optimality of an allocation is the criterion of constrained Pareto optimality rather than Pareto optimality. Let us generalize Definitions 12.1 and 12.2 for the case of a two-period real economy to the case of a monetary economy. The planner can choose the date 0 consumption $x_0 = (x_0^1, \ldots, x_0^I)$ and portfolios $z = (z^1, \ldots, z^I)$ of the agents as well as the date 1 monetary policy $M_1 = (M_{sk}, (s, k) \in \mathbf{S} \times \mathbf{K})$ or equivalently the purchasing power of money

$\nu = (\nu_{sk}, (s,k) \in \mathbf{S} \times \mathbf{K})$. The set of constrained feasible allocations F_N of an economy $\mathscr{E}(u, \omega, N)$ satisfying assumptions (7)–(11) is defined by

$$F_N = \left\{ x \in \mathbb{R}_+^{(SK+1)I} \; \middle| \; \begin{array}{l} \exists \, z \in \mathbb{R}^{JI}, \; \nu \in \mathbb{R}_{++}^{SK} \\ \sum_{i=1}^{I}(x_0^i - \omega_0^i) = 0, \quad \sum_{i=1}^{I} z^i = 0 \\ x_{sk}^i - \omega_s^i = \nu_{sk} \underset{\sim}{N}_s z^i \\ \text{for } (s,k) \in \mathbf{S} \times \mathbf{K}, \quad i = 1, \ldots, I \end{array} \right\}$$

An allocation $\bar{x} = (\bar{x}^1, \ldots, \bar{x}^I)$ is *constrained Pareto optimal* (CPO) given the security structure N if (i) $\bar{x} \in F_N$ and (ii) there does not exist $x = (x^1, \ldots, x^I) \in F_N$ such that $u^i(x^i) \geq u^i(\bar{x}^i)$, $i = 1, \ldots, I$ with strict inequality for at least one i.

For an economy $\mathscr{E}(u, \omega, N)$ there are gains from trade using the incomplete market structure N if and only if the initial endowment ω is not constrained Pareto optimal. Let Ω^* denote the set of all such endowments

$$\Omega^* = \left\{ \omega \in \mathbb{R}_+^{(SK+1)I} \; \middle| \; \omega \text{ is not CPO given } N \right\}$$

36.5 Proposition (Necessary Condition for Optimal Monetary Policy): *Let $\mathscr{E}(u, \omega, N, M)$ be a monetary economy satisfying (7)–(12) in which there are gains from trade, $\omega \in \Omega^*$. If an equilibrium of $\mathscr{E}(u, \omega, N, M)$ is constrained Pareto optimal, then the monetary policy does not introduce additional uncertainty into the economy i.e. there exists $\underset{\sim}{M} = (\underset{\sim}{M}_s, \; s \in \mathbf{S})$ such that M satisfies $M_{sk} = \underset{\sim}{M}_s$ for all $(s,k) \in \mathbf{S} \times \mathbf{K}$.*

PROOF: Let $((\bar{x}, \bar{z}), (\bar{p}, \bar{q}))$ be a monetary equilibrium of $\mathscr{E}(u, \omega, N, M)$ such that $\bar{x}$ is CPO. The allocation x', defined by $x_0^{i\prime} = \bar{x}_0^i$, $x_{sk}^{i\prime} = \underset{\sim}{x}_s^i$ with $\underset{\sim}{x}_s^i = (1/\rho_s)\sum_{k \in \mathbf{K}} \rho_{sk} x_{sk}^i, (s,k) \in \mathbf{S} \times \mathbf{K}$, is constrained feasible with the portfolios $\bar{z}$ and the monetary policy M' such that $M_{sk}' = \underset{\sim}{M}_s, (s,k) \in \mathbf{S} \times \mathbf{K}$, where $\underset{\sim}{\nu}_s = (1/\rho_s)\sum_{k \in \mathbf{K}} \rho_{sk} \nu_{sk}$ and $\underset{\sim}{M}_s = \underset{\sim}{w}_s/\underset{\sim}{\nu}_s, \; s \in \mathbf{S}$. In view of the strict concavity of v^i in (10), $u^i(x^{i\prime}) \geq u^i(\bar{x}^i)$ with strict inequality if $\bar{x}^i \neq x^{i\prime}$. Since $\bar{x}$ is CPO, $\bar{x} = x'$. Since $\omega \in \Omega^*$, ω is not CPO, $\bar{x} \neq \omega$, and there is at least one agent i and one state s such that $\underset{\sim}{N}_s \bar{z}^i \neq 0$. Since $\bar{x}_{sk}^i - \underset{\sim}{\omega}_s^i = \nu_{sk} \underset{\sim}{N}_s \bar{z}^i$, $(s,k) \in \mathbf{S} \times \mathbf{K}$, $\bar{x}^i = x^{i\prime}$ only if $\nu_{sk} = \underset{\sim}{\nu}_s$ for all $(s,k) \in \mathbf{S} \times \mathbf{K} \iff M_{sk} = \underset{\sim}{M}_s$ for all $(s,k) \in \mathbf{S} \times \mathbf{K}$. $\square$

This proposition asserts that when financial markets for the underlying real risks are incomplete then an optimal monetary policy does not introduce monetary risks: this condition is necessary, but unlike the result in Propositions 36.2 and 36.4, it is not sufficient when markets are incomplete. Characterizing an optimal monetary policy, when markets are incomplete, requires maximizing the vector valued function $u = (u^1, \ldots, u^I)$ over the set of constrained feasible allocations F_N. By Proposition 36.5 it suffices to restrict attention to purchasing power vectors ν satisfying $\nu_{sk} = \underline{\nu}_s$ for all $(s, k) \in \mathbf{S} \times \mathbf{K}$ for some vector $\underline{\nu} = (\underline{\nu}_1, \ldots, \underline{\nu}_S) \in \mathbb{R}_{++}^S$. Solving this maximization problem leads however to misleading results. Typically there is no solution when $\underline{\nu}$ is required to be strictly positive; if instead $\underline{\nu}$ is taken to satisfy $\underline{\nu} \in \mathbb{R}_+^S$ and $\sum_{s \in \mathbf{S}} \underline{\nu}_s = 1$, then typically an optimal solution lies on the boundary of the simplex with $\underline{\nu}_{\bar{s}} = 0$ for some states $\bar{s}$, implying that in such states the quantity of money injected into the economy is infinite.

The intuition is roughly as follows: typically J securities are not well adapted to achieve income transfers across S states. A planner, seeking a constrained Pareto optimum, will be led to choose the purchasing power of money $\underline{\nu}$ so as to put weight on those states in which the securities permit socially beneficial income transfers ($\sum_{i=1}^I \pi_s^i \underline{N}_s z^i > 0$). Since the portfolios chosen to carry out these income transfers are not likely to lead to socially beneficial income transfers in the remaining states ($\sum_{i=1}^I \pi_{s'}^i \underline{N}_{s'} z^i < 0$), these non-beneficial effects can be cancelled by making money worthless in these states ($\underline{\nu}_{s'} = 0$): the planner (or monetary authority) thus effectively cancels all debts in these states, declaring universal bankruptcy for all debtors.

This result is far too extreme, and is indeed counterintuitive. It arises from the oversimplified way in which money can be inserted and withdrawn in each period from the economy: the function which is not being well modelled is the *medium of exchange* role of money and the way relative prices react to changes in the money supply. In practice, major increases in the money supply which lead to hyperinflation also create havoc for relative prices and thus introduce a new element of uncertainty which is not being captured by the model: no optimal monetary policy would ever involve extreme increases in the money supply.

Some readers might think that this counterintuitive result arises from the fact that the role of money as a *store of value* across periods has been factored out. This is not the case. Since money is not held as a store of value, the general level of prices at date 1 relative to date 0 does not influence the equilibrium allocation. In models where money performs the role of a store of value, it is generally found that the optimum quantity of money must be such that the nominal interest rate is zero, so that money is not dominated by the default-free bond as a store of value.[3] The result which is obtained in our model, which typically involves $\underline{\nu}_s = 0$ for some states, is perfectly compatible with a zero nominal interest rate. It is thus to the medium of exchange function of money that attention must be directed if a better economic model of money is to be obtained.

---

[3]This idea was introduced by Friedman (1969) and has given rise to an extensive literature. The most general formulation is due to Bewley (1980); an excellent presentation and discussion of the literature is given by Woodford (1990).

37.   INDEXING CONTRACTS

In the previous section the money supply process was taken to be under the control of the monetary authority which sought to stabilize fluctuations in the price level. In a more general analysis, the money supply process needs to be viewed as one of a broader array of government policies which include fiscal policy—government expenditure, taxation and debt—and in such a setting the money supply can perform the additional role of providing an important source of revenue for the government. Experience over many centuries, in many countries, has shown that institutional arrangements and political incentives, or extenuating circumstances such as war or (in more modern times) recession, often induce governments to use their power of controlling the money supply to change the objective of monetary policy from stabilizing the price level to providing a convenient method for financing government expenditure. Such behavior typically leads to substantial fluctuations in the price level: as a result, agents in the private sector are forced to find some way of isolating their contractual commitments from the significant risks induced by fluctuations in the purchasing power of money.

The natural way of isolating contractual commitments from fluctuations in the purchasing power of money is for agents to agree to switch from contracts whose payoffs are denominated in "units of money" to contracts whose payoffs are denominated in "units of purchasing power". If the purchasing power ν_s of a unit of money can be defined in a satisfactory way,[1] and if a contract pays N_s^j units of money, then the return on the contract in "units of purchasing power" is $\nu_s N_s^j$. The idea is to render the payoff $\nu_s N_s^j$ independent of ν_s or equivalently M_s. For this it is sufficient that the payoff on the contract instead of being N_s^j units of money be $\widetilde{N}_s^j = (1/\nu_s)N_s^j$ units of money. Then the (real) payoff of $\widetilde{N}_s^j$ in state s is $\nu_s(1/\nu_s)N_s^j$, that is, N_s^j "units of purchasing power."

In the idealized setting of a *one-good* economy it is clear how the purchasing power of money should be defined: since there is only one good that can be purchased with money, the *purchasing power of one unit of money in state s* is $\nu_s = 1/p_s$, the number of units of the good that can be bought with one unit of money. The transformation from the payoff N_s^j to the payoff $\widetilde{N}_s^j$, which amounts to multiplying N_s^j by the price of the good p_s (the price level)

$$N_s^j \longrightarrow \widetilde{N}_s^j = \frac{1}{\nu_s}N_s^j = p_s N_s^j$$

is called *indexing* contract j in state s. The payoff $\widetilde{N}_s^j = p_s N_s^j$ of the indexed contract in state s is the amount of money required to purchase N_s^j units of

---

[1] In this section the state space can be taken to be $\mathbf{S} \times \mathbf{K}$ i.e. to permit both real and monetary shocks. It is merely to simplify notation that we index states by $s \in \mathbf{S}$.

the single good (which provides the natural unit of purchasing power). If the return on the jth contract is indexed in every state, then it is said to be *fully indexed*: when the jth contract is fully indexed it is transformed from a nominal into a real contract.

Of course, in the real world there is a great diversity of goods, not to speak of the distinction between raw materials, intermediate goods, capital goods, consumption goods, and the like. As a result in a *multigood* economy it is far from clear how the purchasing power of money or equivalently the "unit of purchasing power" should be defined: there are many distinct goods and infinitely many composite commodities or bundles of goods that can be purchased with one unit of money. Even in the simplest exchange economy, in any given state, different agents are typically interested in using their money to purchase different bundles of goods, and the relative amounts of the commodities consumed by the same individual may well vary across the states. There is thus no reference bundle of commodities which is acceptable to all agents as the composite commodity or "unit of purchasing power" that they will seek to purchase in all circumstances with one unit of money. As Marshall (1923, p.28) put it: "An ideally perfect unit of general purchasing power is not merely unattainable: it is unthinkable." An element of arbitrariness and compromise is thus inevitable in defining the purchasing power of money in a multigood economy.

Suppose that there are L goods in the economy and that the reference bundle $y = (y_1, \ldots, y_L) \in \mathbb{R}_+^L$ is chosen as the "unit of purchasing power." If the (unit) prices of the L goods in terms of money are $p_s = (p_{s1}, \ldots, p_{sL}) \in \mathbb{R}_+^L$ in state s, then the *purchasing power of one unit of money in state s* is defined by

$$\nu_s = \nu_s(p_s; y) = \frac{1}{\sum_{\ell=1}^{L} p_{s\ell} y_\ell} = \frac{1}{p_s y}, \quad s \in \mathbf{S}$$

namely, the number of units of the reference bundle y that can be bought with one unit of money. $p_s y = 1/\nu_s$ is the *price index* (price level) in state s.

Since different nominal contracts typically involve different types of clientele, any attempt to widely index contracts is likely to lead to distinct reference bundles for distinct securities. For simplicity in the analysis that follows we assume that the same reference bundle is used to index all securities. Once agents have come to an agreement that contracts will be rewritten in terms of the new unit of purchasing power, each contract is indexed by dividing its payoff by the purchasing power of money or equivalently multiplying by the price index

$$N_s^j \longrightarrow \widetilde{N}_s^j = \frac{1}{\nu_s} N_s^j = p_s y N_s^j, \quad s \in \mathbf{S}$$

Once a contract becomes fully indexed, it becomes a real contract whose payoff in state s is the money price of N_s^j units of the reference bundle y.

If all nominal contracts are fully indexed, then there are only real contracts in the economy, and, with real contracts, the equilibrium allocation is invariant to monetary shocks—at least in the simplified framework of this chapter where agents do not carry cash balances across periods. The definition of a monetary equilibrium for an economy $\mathscr{E}(u, \omega, A, M)$ in which all contracts are real (their commodity payoff matrices being given by A) is obtained in the obvious way by replacing the budget set $\mathbb{B}(p, q, \omega^i, N)$ in Definition 34.1 by the budget set $\mathbb{B}(p, q, \omega^i, A)$ defined in equation (1) of Section 33.

37.1 Proposition (Neutrality of Monetary Policy with Real Contracts):   *If $\mathscr{E}(u, \omega, A, M)$ is a monetary economy in which all contracts are real, then monetary policy is neutral.*

PROOF: Let $((x, z), (p, q))$ be an equilibrium of the economy $\mathscr{E}(u, \omega, A, M)$ in which agent i's budget set is

$$\mathbb{B}(p, q, \omega^i, A) = \left\{ x^i \in \mathbb{R}_+^{L(S+1)} \ \middle| \ \begin{array}{l} p_0(x_0^i - \omega_0^i) = -qz^i, \ z^i \in \mathbb{R}^J \\ p_s(x_s^i - \omega_s^i) = p_s A_s z^i, \ s \in \mathbf{S} \end{array} \right\}$$

and the monetary equations are

$$p_s \sum_{i=1}^{I} x_s^i = M_s, \quad s = 0, 1, \dots, S \tag{1}$$

Suppose the current monetary policy M is changed to M'

$$M = (M_0, M_1, \dots, M_S) \longrightarrow M' = \beta \square M = (\beta_0 M_0, \beta_1 M_1, \dots, \beta_S M_S)$$

If the spot prices are scaled by the factor β_s in each state, then the monetary equation in each state becomes $\beta_s p_s \sum_{i=1}^{I} x_s^i = \beta_s M_s$, so that (1) continues to hold. Since under the change of prices

$$(p, q) = (p_0, p_1, \dots, p_S, q) \longrightarrow (\beta \square p, \beta_0 q) = (\beta_0 p_0, \beta_1 p_1, \dots, \beta_S p_S, \beta_0 q)$$

agent i's budget set remains unchanged

$$\mathbb{B}(\beta \square p, \beta_0 q, \omega^i, A) = \mathbb{B}(p, q, \omega^i, A)$$

it follows that (x^i, z^i) remains an optimal choice of agent i under the new prices $(\beta \square p, \beta_0 q)$. Thus $((x, z), \beta \square p, \beta_0 q)$ is an equilibrium of the economy $\mathscr{E}(u, \omega, A, \beta \square M)$. Conversely if $\widetilde{x}$ is an equilibrium allocation of the economy $\mathscr{E}(u, \omega, A, \beta \square M)$, then the same reasoning shows that $\widetilde{x}$ is an equilibrium allocation for $\mathscr{E}(u, \omega, A, M)$. Thus the equilibrium allocations are independent of the monetary policy M. $\square$

37.2 Corollary (Full Indexation Implies Neutrality of Monetary Policy): *In a monetary economy* $\mathscr{E}(u, \omega, \widetilde{N}, M)$ *in which all nominal contracts are fully indexed, monetary policy is neutral.*[2]

PROOF: The proof follows at once from the above proposition by noting that indexing replaces the nominal return N_s^j by $\widetilde{N}_s^j = p_s y N_s^j$, $s \in \mathbf{S}$, thereby converting the jth security into a real contract for $j = 1, \dots, J$. $\square$

In practice the indexing of contracts is made so as to keep the purchasing power of payoffs the same as it is at the time when the contract is signed (date 0 in our model): thus the payoff of a nominal contracts is expressed in units of date 0 purchasing power. In this case the indexation formula becomes

$$N_s^j \longrightarrow \widehat{N}_s^j = \frac{\nu_0}{\nu_s} N_s^j$$

For a one-good model the indexed contract is

$$\widehat{N}_s^j = \frac{p_s}{p_0} N_s^j = \eta_s N_s^j = (1 + i_s) N_s^j$$

where η_s is the inflation factor and i_s the inflation rate in state s. In the multi-good model, with base year reference bundle $y = (y_1, \dots, y_L)$, the indexing formula becomes

$$\widehat{N}_s^j = \frac{\nu_0}{\nu_s} N_s^j = \frac{p_s y}{p_0 y} N_s^j = \eta_s N_s^j$$

where the inflation factor is measured by the *Laspeyres index* $\eta_s = p_s y / p_0 y$. Many other indices can be used for measuring inflation, but every index necessarily involves an element of arbitrariness and suffers from some imperfections in measuring the purchasing power of money: for a systematic discussion see Irving Fisher's *The Making of Index Numbers* (1922) and Diewert (1987). The neutrality result in Corollary 37.2 is not affected by this modified form of indexation which seeks to keep the purchasing power of nominal contract payoffs at their date 0 value.

---

[2]This result extends to securities with both nominal and real components by appropriately indexing the nominal components of securities' returns.

Explaining Absence of Indexed Contracts

If nominal contracts are indexed, economic activity is isolated from the effects of monetary shocks: loosely speaking, indexing takes the monetariness out of a monetary economy. This has long been recognized. The substantial fluctuations in price levels experienced in England during the nineteenth century led classical economists—notably Jevons, Marshall and Fisher—to advocate the use of indexed contracts to isolate the economy from the vagaries of price fluctuations which, given the gold standard, were not easy to correct by government monetary policy.[3] At that time however any attempt to introduce indexing on a systematic basis faced the serious practical hurdle that there were no officially computed indices on which agents could write mutually acceptable and legally enforceable contracts. The plea by economists, particularly Marshall, to make available an official measure of the general purchasing power of money proved to be an important stimulus to the creation of official, regularly publicized indices such as the Consumer Price Index, now available in most Western economies. The lack of official indices is thus no longer (to all intents and purposes) a practical obstacle to the indexation of contracts.

If the practical and legal difficulties of instituting and enforcing indexed contracts have essentially been overcome, *how does one explain the presence of so many unindexed contracts in most Western economies?* Since the Second World War, despite periods of relatively variable rates of inflation in the seventies and early eighties, unindexed long-term contracts such as thirty year government and corporate bonds or thirty year mortgages for individuals are common; furthermore over half the wage and salary contracts whose terms typically stretch from one to three years are not indexed. On the other hand, during the same period most contracts (except those of the very shortest duration) were indexed in countries which experienced very high variability of inflation, such as the Argentine and Brazil. Thus the extent to which nominal contracts are indexed appears to be a function of the variability of inflation: *when the variability is sufficiently low, agents in the private sector seem to prefer unindexed contracts: when the variability exceeds a critical level then agents find it to their mutual advantage to make contractual commitments based on indexed contracts.*

The persistent reluctance of agents in the private sector to index nominal contracts has been viewed as somewhat of a paradox and has not confirmed the prediction of classical economists such as Jevons and Marshall who foresaw a completely indexed economy free from the effects of monetary disturbances as soon as official indices became available. The apparent paradox is largely resolved once it is recognized that indexing does not eliminate all risk—rather

---

[3]See Jevons (1875), Marshall (1887), Fisher (1911).

it substitutes one type of risk for another. The fluctuations of a price index py can be due either to fluctuations in the price level or to fluctuations in the relative prices of the goods in the reference bundle y. As a first approximation, *monetary* shocks change all prices by the same factor ($p_s = \alpha_s p$ for some $\alpha_s > 0$), while *real* shocks change relative prices ($p_s \neq \alpha p$ for any $\alpha > 0$). Typically both types of shocks are present, and both change the value of the index. Thus indexing on a reference bundle y, in an attempt to eliminate the monetary risks arising from fluctuations in the price level, unavoidably picks up the real risks arising from fluctuations in the relative prices of the goods in the reference bundle. If agents originally wanted to sign a nominal contract, it was presumably because they did not want to tie the contract to the variability of the relative prices of particular goods in the first place, and indexing inevitably introduces this type of risk.

It follows from this analysis that when monetary shocks are small relative to the real shocks, agents are likely to prefer nominal contracts, while when monetary shocks are significantly greater than the underlying real shocks, they will tend to prefer indexed contracts. Thus in periods where the underlying real shocks to the economy are fairly substantial, agents in the private sector may prefer to stick to nominal contracts even in the face of relatively severe fluctuations in the purchasing power of money.[4]

EXERCISES

1. *Positive nominal interest rate equilibria.*

> This exercise shows that if the monetary policy is suitably restricted, then there is no need to invoke the assumption that agents may not carry money balances from date 0 to date 1: when the nominal interest rate is positive no agent will carry over money balances even if permitted to do so.

Consider a one-good two-period monetary economy $\mathscr{E}(u, \omega, N, M)$ in which u^i satisfies Assumption $\mathscr{U}$, $\omega^i \in \mathbb{R}_{++}^{S+1}$ for $i = 1, \ldots, I$ and $M \in \mathbb{R}_{++}^{S+1}$. Suppose that transactions are carried out as explained in Section 34, with the sole difference that agents are now permitted to carry money balances from date 0 to date 1. Thus in the subperiod 0_2, agent i chooses not only the a portfolio $z^i \in \mathbb{R}^J$ of the J nominal

---

[4]A theoretical model establishing the results outlined in this subsection is given by Magill-Quinzii (1995).

securities, but also the amount of money $z_0^i \geq 0$ to be carried over for expenditure at date 1. The budget equations of agent i thus become

$$p_0 x_0^i = m_0^i - q z^i - z_0^i$$
$$p_s x_s^i = m_s^i + N_s z^i + z_0^i, \quad s = 1, \ldots, S$$

where m_0^i and m_s^i are the amounts of money received by agent i from the sale of his endowment. Let security 1 be the default-free bond: $N^1 = (1, \ldots, 1)$. Then the nominal interest rate r is defined by $q_1 = 1/(1+r)$.

(a) By studying the first-order conditions for the maximum problem of agent i, show that if the nominal interest rate is positive, then the agent will not carry money balances from date 0 to date 1 ($r > 0$ implies $z_0^i = 0$).

(b) For $\beta > 0$ consider the monetary policy $M_\beta = (M_0, \beta M_1, \ldots, \beta M_S)$ obtained by multiplying the date 1 component of the monetary policy $M = (M_0, M_1, \ldots, M_S)$ by the factor β. Show that there exists $\beta^* > 0$ such that if $\beta \geq \beta^*$ then the equilibrium nominal interest rate is positive in every monetary equilibrium (defined by Definition 34.1) of the economy $\mathscr{E}(u, \omega, N, M_\beta)$. Give an economic interpretation of this condition. Conclude that Definition 34.1 describes the equilibrium which would be obtained even if agents were permitted to carry money balances from date 0 to date 1, for all monetary policies M_β with $\beta \geq \beta^*$.

2. *Simplest example of non-neutrality of monetary policy.*

This exercise gives a proof of the non-neutrality of monetary policy under the simplifying assumption that there is only one security and that there is trade at the initial equilibrium.

Let $\mathscr{E}(u, \omega, N, M)$ be a monetary economy as in Exercise 1, in which the default-free bond is the only security. Suppose the economy has at least two consumers ($I \geq 2$) and has genuine uncertainty ($S \geq 2$).

(a) Let $((\bar{x}, \bar{z}), (\bar{p}, \bar{q}))$ be a monetary equilibrium of $\mathscr{E}(u, \omega, N, M)$ in which there is trade ($\bar{z} \neq 0$). Show that if

$$M' = (M_0, \alpha_1 M_1, \ldots, \alpha_S M_S) \quad \text{with} \quad \alpha_s \neq \alpha_\sigma \quad \text{for some} \quad s \neq \sigma$$

is an alternative monetary policy and if $((x', z'), (p', q'))$ is an equilibrium of $\mathscr{E}(u, \omega, N, M')$, then $x' \neq \bar{x}$.

(b) Give a geometric interpretation of the proof of the result in (a) when $S = 2$, showing that the market subspace spanned by the default-free bond tilts when the monetary policy is changed ($\langle [\nu']N \rangle \neq \langle [\nu]N \rangle$).

(c) Explain how the non-neutrality Proposition 35.8 (in the case $J = 1$) avoids the non-primitive assumption $\bar{z} \neq 0$.

3. *Realignment of portfolios to undo change in monetary policy.*

The object of this exercise is to explicitly derive the changes in prices associated with a change in monetary policy and the changes in portfolios which permit agents to "undo" what the monetary authorities "do", when markets are complete.

Let $\mathscr{E}(u, \omega, N, M)$ be a one-good two-period economy in which utility functions satisfy Assumption $\mathscr{U}$ and markets are complete, and let $((\bar{x}, \bar{z}), (\bar{p}, \bar{q}))$ denote a monetary equilibrium of this economy. Suppose the monetary policy changes to $M' \in \mathbb{R}_{++}^{S+1}$. Compute the portfolios and prices $(z', (p', q'))$ such that $((\bar{x}, z'), (p', q'))$ is a monetary equilibrium of the economy $\mathscr{E}(u, \omega, N, M')$. Check that $p_0'(\bar{x}_0^i - \omega_0^i) = -q' z'^i$, $i = 1, \ldots, I$.

4. *Nominal and real interest rates and anticipated inflation.*

The object of this exercise is to generalize the deterministic Fisher formula $1 + \hat{r} = (1+r)/(1+i)$ relating the nominal interest rate r, the real interest rate $\hat{r}$ and the rate of inflation i, to an economy with uncertainty.

Consider a one-good two-period economy $\mathscr{E}(u, \omega, N, \widehat{N}, M)$ in which the utility functions satisfy Assumption $\mathscr{U}$, in which the securities with payoff matrix N are nominal and those with payoff matrix $\widehat{N}$ are indexed. In particular the (default-free) nominal and indexed bond are traded: $N^1 = (1, \ldots, 1)$, $\widehat{N}^1 = (1 + i_1, \ldots, 1 + i_S)$ where $1 + i_s = p_s/p_0$. The price of the nominal and the indexed bond define the nominal and the real interest rate: $q_1 = 1/(1 + r)$ and $\hat{q}_1 = 1/(1 + \hat{r})$.

(a) Show that in an equilibrium of $\mathscr{E}(u, \omega, N, \widehat{N}, M)$

$$\frac{1}{1+r} = \frac{1}{1+\hat{r}} E\left(\frac{1}{1+i}\right) + \operatorname{cov}\left(\gamma, \frac{1}{1+i}\right)$$

where γ is the ideal security at the equilibrium (defined in Section 15).

(b) Interpret the inequality

$$\operatorname{cov}\left(\gamma, \frac{1}{1+i}\right) > 0 \Longrightarrow 1 + \hat{r} > (1+r)E\left(\frac{1}{1+i}\right)$$

Under what conditions does this serve to explain the fact that typically the nominal interest rate does not compensate for expected inflation?

(c) Give the explicit expression for the formula in (a) when the utility functions of all agents are linear-quadratic (Exercise 4, Ch. 3).

(d) Suppose $\omega^i \in \langle V \rangle$ for $i = 1, \ldots, I$, where V is the associated matrix of real returns in Proposition 35.1. Derive the explicit expression for the formula in (a) when agents utility functions are (i) logarithmic (Exercise 7, Ch. 3) and (ii) constant risk tolerance (Exercise 8, Ch. 3).

5. *Welfare loss from variable inflation.*

The object of this exercise is to calculate the welfare loss from monetary shocks in an economy with no real (fundamental) uncertainty, when the agents have linear-quadratic utility functions.

Consider the one-good two-period monetary economy $\mathscr{E}(u, \omega, N, M)$ introduced at the beginning of Section 36, in which the sole source of uncertainty comes from monetary shocks. The date 1 monetary policy is a function $M_1 : \mathbf{K} \longrightarrow \mathbb{R}_{++}$ defined on the space of monetary shocks $\mathbf{K} = \{1, \ldots, K\}$ with probabilities $\rho = (\rho_1, \ldots, \rho_K)$. Agents' endowments are given by $\omega^i = (\omega_0^i, \omega_1^i)$ where $\omega_1^i = \omega_1^i \mathbb{1}$ with $\omega_1^i > 0$ and $\mathbb{1} = (1, \ldots, 1) \in \mathbb{R}^K$ (no real uncertainty), and their utility functions are linear-quadratic (see Exercise 5 of Chapter 3)

$$u^i(x^i) = \lambda_0^i x_0^i - \frac{1}{2} \sum_{k=1}^{K} \rho_k (a^i - x_k^i)^2, \quad i = 1, \ldots, I$$

where $\lambda_0^i > 0$ and $a^i > w_1 = \sum_{i=1}^{I} \omega_1^i$. The only security $(J = 1)$ is the default-free nominal bond $N = \mathbb{1}$, and this contract is not indexed. Let $\nu_k = w_1/M_k$ denote the purchasing power of money in state k. Since for each agent the marginal utility of consumption λ_0^i at date 0 is constant, the social welfare function

$$\mathscr{W}(x) = \mathscr{W}(x^1, \ldots, x^I) = \sum_{i=1}^{I} \frac{1}{\lambda_0^i} u^i(x^i)$$

can be used to compare social welfare at different equilibria (see footnote 5 in Section 25).

(a) Suppose the monetary policy is non-random. Show that the social gain from trade at the (Pareto optimal) equilibrium $\bar{\bar{x}}$ is given by

$$\mathscr{W}(\bar{\bar{x}}) - \mathscr{W}(\omega) = G = \frac{1}{2} \sum_{i=1}^{I} \frac{(a^i - \omega_1^i)^2}{\lambda_0^i} - \frac{1}{2} \frac{(a - \omega_1)^2}{\lambda_0}$$

where $\lambda_0 = \sum_{i=1}^{I} \lambda_0^i, a = \sum_{i=1}^{I} a^i$.

(b) Prove that $G \geq 0$ and $G = 0$ if and only if the rates of impatience (Definition 15.3) of the agents at their initial endowments are equal $(r^1(\omega^1) = \cdots = r^I(\omega^I))$, in which case there is no trade at the equilibrium.

(c) Suppose the monetary policy is random. Let $\bar{x}$ denote the associated equilibrium. Show that the loss in social welfare relative to the equilibrium $\bar{\bar{x}}$ is given by

$$\mathscr{W}(\bar{\bar{x}}) - \mathscr{W}(\bar{x}) = \frac{\text{var}(\nu)}{E(\nu^2)} G$$

Check that the welfare loss is the same if the monetary policy M_1 is multiplied by a factor $\beta > 0$ $(M_1 \longrightarrow \beta M_1)$, so that $\text{var}(\nu)/E(\nu^2)$ measures the variability of the purchasing power ν of money at date 1, independent of its magnitude $(\|\nu\|_\rho^2 = E(\nu^2))$.

6. *Term structure of interest rates and inflation.*

The object of this exercise is to link the effects of anticipated monetary policy and inflation to the term structure of interest rates studied in Chapter 5.

Using the framework of Exercise 3 in Chapter 5, explore the relation between the term structure of interest rates and anticipated monetary policy (inflation). How would an anticipated increase in the variability of future inflation affect the term structure of interest rates?

HISTORICAL REMARKS

Early theory

This chapter brings together in a stylized way two branches of economic theory—the classical theory of money, known as the *quantity theory* and the modern theory of value as embodied in the theory of incomplete markets. The debate on the neutrality or non-neutrality of money has been one of the central debates of economics for the last four hundred years. The first theoretical discussions in economics emerged as disputes between pamphleteers, administrators, and politicians during the *mercantilist period* (1550–1750)—they stressed the important role of money in influencing economic activity, and their ideas had much in common with a central kernel of Keynes' *General Theory*.[1] The mercantilist theory advocated and led to extensive government interference with both domestic and foreign trade, with the objective of achieving a positive balance of trade. The mercantilist vision of an economy was based on an aggregated expenditure flow analysis in which money is non-neutral: they had however no theory of value.

As the reader knows, the theory of value was the contribution of the *classical period* (1750–1930). To appreciate the contribution of the classical economists, it is important to recognize the extraordinary degree to which mercantilism had pervaded economic thought

---

[1] In a nutshell their argument was that an increase in the money supply (achieved by an inflow of gold arising from a net excess of exports over imports) leads to a gradual increase in prices and a reduction in the rate of interest, which stimulates economic activity. Hence their well-known *balance of trade doctrine*, that the principal objective of government policy should be to achieve a positive balance of trade. Two articulate proponents of the non-neutrality of money were Law (1705) and Cantillon (1755). For an excellent discussion of the mercantilist period see Blaug (1985), Schumpeter (1954) and especially the famous Chapter 23 of the *General Theory* where Keynes spells out the close affinity between their arguments and his own, indicating clearly that there was a sound theoretical basis for the mercantilist doctrine which was so peremptorily dismissed by the classical economists. He concludes: "Regarded as the theory of the individual firm and of the distribution of the product resulting from the employment of a given quantity of resources, the classical theory has made a contribution to economic thinking which cannot be impugned. It is impossible to think clearly on the subject without this theory as a part of one's apparatus of thought. . . . Nevertheless, as a contribution to statecraft, which is concerned with the economic system as a whole and with securing the optimum employment of the system's entire resources, the methods of the early pioneers of economic thinking in the sixteenth and seventeenth centuries may have attained to fragments of practical wisdom which the unrealistic abstractions of Ricardo first forgot and then obliterated. There was wisdom in their intense preoccupation with keeping down the rate of interest. . . by maintaining the domestic stock of money. . . . In an economy subject to money contracts. . . where the quantity of domestic circulation and the domestic rate of interest are primarily determined by the balance of payments. . . there is no orthodox means open to the authorities for countering unemployment at home except by struggling for an export surplus and an import of the monetary metal at the expense of their neighbours."

for the previous two hundred years. Adam Smith's primary objective in writing the *Wealth of Nations* was to reveal the flawed thinking involved in the mercantilist doctrine, at least when looked at from the perspective of the theory of value. Hence his advocacy of the efficiency of markets, competition, and free trade. In his overwhelming desire to bring out this message, it was important that he silence the mercantilist argument showing that money is non-neutral—otherwise he would have been back where he began, with arguments showing how restrictions on trade could be used to beneficially affect domestic economic activity. This perhaps explains why the classical economists that followed were all very schizophrenic on the subject of money: when extolling the virtues of markets and free trade (the theory of value) they asserted that money is neutral—it is a veil which should not be confused with the fundamental forces which determine the direction and magnitude of economic activity.[2] The later classical economists, especially Jevons (1875), Fisher (1911) and Marshall (1923) realized that there was something faulty with their neutrality argument: the violent fluctuations in the purchasing power of money at the beginning and end of the nineteenth century had made it abundantly clear that money is definitely not neutral in an economy with nominal contracts such as bonds and unindexed salaries. They accepted this as an empirical fact, but their theoretical framework could not accommodate such an idea: their theory of money was the quantity theory, by which a change in the quantity of money leads to a change in the price level—but since the price level was irrelevant in their theory of value, money could not have real effects.

It was one of the main contributions of Keynes to have offered a way out of this *cul de sac*, although his contribution focused primarily on the way money affects economic activity in a production economy. A useful short-cut to Keynes' main message, which provides a way of linking the classical theory, the mercantilist theory, and his own vision of the functioning of the economy is contained in Chapter 21 of the *General Theory*:

> Thus if there is perfectly elastic supply so long as there is unemployment, and perfectly inelastic supply as soon as full employment is reached, and if effective demand changes in the same proportion as the quantity of money, the Quantity Theory of Money can be enunciated as follows: 'So long as there is unemployment, *employment* will change in the same proportion as the quantity of money; and when there is full employment, *prices* will change in the same proportion as the quantity of money.'

So everything reduces to whether there can be unemployment: the classical economists said no, Keynes said yes. Missing from this statement however are the redistributive effects of changes in prices: in an exchange economy, where production is taken as exogenously fixed, these are the only effects which are present. In essence what this chapter has attempted to provide is a generalization of the classical economists' theory of value which, when combined with their theory of money, permits the intuitions of Jevons, Fisher and Marshall to be

---

[2] The most outspoken statement of the classical view is that of Mill (1848, Book III, Chapter VII): "There cannot, in short, be intrinsically a more insignificant thing, in the economy of society, than money; except in the character of a contrivance for sparing time and labour. It is a machine for doing quickly and commodiously, what would be done, though less quickly and commodiously, without it: and like many other kinds of machinery, it only exerts a distinct and independent influence of its own when it gets out of order." He adds with characteristic self-confidence: "The introduction of money does not interfere with any of the Laws of Value . . . ".

formalized—namely that fluctuations in the money supply can have real (redistributive) effects in the setting of an exchange economy. For this initial analysis we have chosen to factor out the non-neutral effects of money on employment and output.

For excellent accounts of the quantity theory of money, we refer the reader to the following classics: Fisher's (1911) *The Purchasing Power of Money*, Marshall's (1923) deceptively condensed and astute *Money, Credit and Commerce*, Keynes' (1923a) lively *A Tract on Monetary Reform*, hot under the influence of the devastating post World War I hyperinflations, and, most penetrating of all, Wicksell (1898, 1906), whose systematic critique of the quantity theory lay at the basis of all subsequent developments in monetary theory. Friedman (1987) is the modern champion of the quantity theory, and his thoroughly enjoyable and thought provoking *Money Mischief* (1994) takes the reader on a rapid spin through 100 years of monetary history, showing how recent and uncharted is the world's experience with fiat monies.

Recent theory

The model of general equilibrium with spot and financial markets became the subject of intense research in the early 1980s. One group of researchers,[3] Magill-Shafer (1984/92, 1985/90), Duffie-Shafer (1985), Geanakoplos-Polemarchakis (1986), studied the model in which all financial securities are real, which evolved from the model originally proposed by Radner (1972). A second group, Cass (1984, 1985, 1989), Balasko-Cass (1985/89) and Geanakoplos-Mas-Colell (1986/89), studied the model with nominal securities generalizing the model originally proposed by Arrow (1953). In all these studies the concept of equilibrium used was that given by Definition 33.3. The striking phenomenon, first observed by Cass, was that with nominal securities such equilibria are seriously indeterminate: he presented this as a way of establishing that an economy typically has a host of sunspot equilibria and saw the phenomenon as presenting a threat to the viability of the concept of a rational expectations equilibrium. The indeterminacy property both puzzled and fascinated the general equilibrium school and several papers studying the dimension of the set of equilibrium allocations further elaborated on the basic results of Balasko-Cass and Geanakoplos-Mas-Colell (Werner (1986/1990), Polemarchakis (1988), Pietra (1992), Siconolfi-Villanacci (1991), Krasa-Werner (1991)). The results of this literature are systematically presented in the survey paper of Cass (1992). The technical side of the presentation in Section 35 draws heavily on the paper of Geanakoplos-Mas-Colell (1986/89), in particular the construction underlying Propositions 35.7 and 35.10.

Magill-Quinzii (1988/92) saw the introduction of nominal contracts as a natural point of departure for formulating a theory of monetary equilibrium within the framework of the theory of incomplete markets. When we originally (1988) presented the ideas of this chapter we encountered considerable resistance: how could something so simple-minded as a modified Clower constraint and a naive version of the quantity theory be reinstated in

---

[3]Since it has been rather typical of this literature that for some papers there was a lag of four or more years between the discussion paper and the published version, we sometimes indicate the date of the discussion paper in addition to the date of the published paper. Thus 1985/92 means that the working paper appeared in 1985 and it was published in 1992.

equilibrium theory? Our reaction was that nominal contracts will only ever be traded in an economy that is already using money as a medium of exchange; thus even if nominal securities were initially studied in a model without money (except as a unit of account), it seemed more reasonable to take the logical step of modifying the concept of equilibrium (Definition 34.1) so as to explicitly incorporate demand and supply equations for money just as for every other commodity and contract.

The idea that underlies Definition 34.1 is to explicitly assign a role for money as a medium of exchange by using the idea introduced by Clower (1967) of separating the moments in time when goods are sold for money from those at which the acquired money balances are used to purchase goods. The model outlined in Section 34 is thus close in spirit to the cash-in-advance models of Grandmont-Younes (1972) and Lucas (1980), which formalize in an infinite-horizon equilibrium framework the idea of the Clower constraint. Our model is essentially a two-period "slice" of an infinite-horizon cash-in-advance model in which the need to carry money balances across periods has been factored out by the device of the Central Exchange. The conversion to a two-period model loses some of the consistency of the infinite horizon model, but permits a more refined analysis of the effects of the variability of monetary policy on the income transfers achievable through nominal securities: our analysis depends crucially on the presence of heterogeneous agents and incomplete markets, two elements which are inevitably absent in the representative-agent, complete-market, cash-in-advance models currently used in macroeconomics.

The idea of introducing an explicit modelling of the role of money for transactions into the model by a Clower constraint was subsequently adopted by Dubey-Geanakoplos (1989, 1992) with a different way of injecting money into the economy: agents borrow money from the Central Exchange—which becomes the Central Bank—and must pay back their money balances at the end of the second period, unless they choose to default on their loan. Cass (1990) pointed out that putting money balances directly into the utility function is an alternative way of modelling the use of money for transactions and leads to a determinate concept of equilibrium. Villanacci (1991) observed that giving positive value to money by requiring that agents make tax payments in money at the end of the second period, without any transaction function for money, does not remove the indeterminacy.

An interesting extension of the analysis of this chapter has been provided by Neumeyer (1992). The analysis of Section 36 supports the classical prescription of avoiding monetary shocks. Neumeyer provides an alternative way of studying the welfare costs of inflation by showing that high and variable inflation reduces trade in nominal securities, thus cancelling mutually beneficial exchanges.

The model presented in this chapter is highly stylized—a compromise, as it were, imposed by the desire to restrict the analysis to a two-period framework. It is a well-accepted principle of macroeconomics that a satisfactory modelling of money requires an open-ended future. A second ingredient whose importance has been stressed by Hahn (1971a,b, 1973a,b) is that the modelling of money should take place in a sequence economy in which imperfections in the trading opportunities of agents provide a role for money. Two equilibrium models[4] with

---

[4]The proceedings of a conference sponsored by the Federal Reserve Bank of Minneapolis, published in the book *Models of Monetary Economies* (Kareken-Wallace (1980)) provide one of the best recent discussions of many of the issues surrounding the modelling of money. See in particular the

these properties that have been extensively used in macroeconomics are the overlapping generations model and the self-insurance model of Bewley (1980). However, since in these models money serves exclusively as a store of value, financial securities such as equity and bonds are not readily incorporated, since such securities typically dominate money as long-term stores of value.

An approach that simultaneously provides a role for financial securities and a role for money consists in extending the finite horizon model with incomplete markets to an infinite horizon, with a Clower constraint to capture the transactions role of money.[5] This amounts to generalizing the representative agent cash-in-advance model[6] to a true equilibrium setting with heterogeneous agents and incomplete markets, and seems to provide a promising alternative to the OLG and Bewley models for discussing questions of monetary theory and macroeconomics.

---

papers and discussion by Bewley (1980), Cass-Shell (1980), Brock-Scheinkman (1980), Scheinkman (1980), Hahn (1980), Tobin (1980), Lucas (1980), Townsend (1980) and Wallace (1980). Sargent (1987) and Blanchard-Fischer (1989) also provide a careful assessment of many of the models of money used in macroeconomics.

[5] A first step in this direction is provided by Magill-Quinzii (1993, 1994) which extend the model with real securities to an infinite horizon.

[6] As stressed by Hellwig (1993), to avoid the rigid timing of a cash-in-advance model which leads to a fixed velocity of circulation, it would be preferable to base agents' money holdings on an inventory theoretic approach in the Baumol-Tobin tradition, combined with an explicit modelling of the banking system. A model along these lines has been studied by Romer (1986).

References

Abreu, D. and A. Rubinstein (1988), "The Structure of Nash Equilibrium in Repeated Games with Finite Automata", *Econometrica*, 56, 1259–1282.

Akerlof, G. (1970), "The Market for Lemons: Qualitative Uncertainty and the Market Mechanism", *Quarterly Journal of Economics*, 84, 488–500.

Allen, F. and D. Gale (1988), "Optimal Security Design", *Review of Financial Studies*, 1, 229–264.

Arrow, K.J. (1951), "An Extension of the Basic Theorems of Classical Welfare Economics", *Proceedings of the Second Berkeley Symposium on Mathematical Statistics*, J. Neyman ed., 507–532, Berkeley: University of California Press.

Arrow, K.J. (1953), "Le Role des Valeurs Boursières pour la Répartition la Meilleure des Risques", in *Econométrie, Colloques Internationaux du Centre National de la Recherche Scientifique*, 40, 41–47; English version: "The Role of Securities in the Optimal Allocation of Risk Bearing", *Review of Economic Studies*, 31, 91–96, (1963).

Arrow, K.J. (1963), "Uncertainty and the Welfare Economics of Medical Care", *American Economic Review*, 53, 941–973.

Arrow, K.J. (1969), "The Organization of Economic Activity: Issues Pertinent to the Choice of Market versus Nonmarket Allocation" in *The Analysis and Evaluation of Public Expenditures: The PPB System*, Joint Economic Committee, United States Congress, vol 1, 47–64. Reprinted in *Collected Papers of Kenneth J. Arrow, Volume 2*, 133–155, (1983).

Arrow, K.J. (1971), *Essays in the Theory of Risk-Bearing*, Chicago: Markham.

Arrow, K.J. and G. Debreu (1954), "Existence of an Equilibrium for a Competitive Economy", *Econometrica*, 22, 265–292.

Arrow, K.J. and F.H. Hahn (1971), *General Competitive Analysis*, San Francisco: Holden Day.

Atiyah, P.S. (1989), *An Introduction to the Law of Contract*, Oxford: Clarendon Press.

Aumann, R.J. (1976), "Agreeing to Disagree", *Annals of Statistics*, 4, 1236–1239.

Azariadis, C. (1975), "Implicit Contracts and Unemployment Equilibria", *Journal of Political Economy*, 83, 1183–1202.

Azariadis, C. (1993), *Intertemporal Macroeconomics*, Oxford: Blackwell.

Bachelier, L. (1900), "Théorie de la Spéculation", *Annales Scientifiques de l'Ecole Normale Supérieure*, 3rd ser., 17, 21–88. Translated in *The Random Character of Stock Market Prices*, edited by Paul Cootner, Cambridge, Mass.: MIT Press, (1964).

Bailey, M.N. (1974), "Wages and Employment Under Uncertain Demand", *Review of Economic Studies*, 41, 37–50.

Balasko, Y. (1976), "L'Equilibre Economique du Point de Vue Différentiel", Thesis, Paris: Université de Paris IX - Dauphine.

Balasko, Y. (1988), *Foundations of the Theory of General Equilibrium*, Boston: Academic Press.

Balasko, Y. and D. Cass (1989), "The Structure of Financial Equilibrium with Exogenous Yields: The Case of Incomplete Markets", *Econometrica*, 57, 135–162; CARESS Working Paper, University of Pennsylvania, (1985).

Balasko, Y., D. Cass and P. Siconolfi, (1990), "The Structure of Finanical Equilibrium with Exogenous Yields: The Case of Restricted Participation", *Journal of Mathematical Economics*, 19, 195–216.

Banerjee, A. and E. Maskin (1992), "A Semi-Walrasian Theory of Money", Harvard University Discussion Paper.

Barnard, C. (1938), *The Functions of the Executive*, Cambridge, Mass.: Harvard University Press.

Barro, R.J. (1977a), "Unanticipated Money Growth and Unemployment in the United States", *American Economic Review*, 67, 101–115.

Barro, R.J. (1977b), "Long-term Contracting, Sticky Prices, and Monetary Policy", *Journal of Monetary Economics*, 3, 305–316.

Baumol, W.J. (1952), "The Transactions Demand for Cash: An Inventory-Theoretic Approach", *Journal of Economics*, 66, 545–556.

Benassy, J.P. (1990), "Non-Walrasian Equilibria, Money, and Macroeonomics", in *Handbook of Monetary Economics*, B. Friedman and F. Hahn eds., Amsterdam: North-Holland.

Berle, A.A. and G.C. Means (1932), *The Modern Corporation and Private Property*, New York: Harcourt, Brace and World.

Bernouilli, E. (1738), "Specimen Theoriae Novae de Mensura Sortis", in *Commentarii Academiae Scientiarum Imperialis Petropolitanae*. English Translation: "Exposition of a New Theory on the Measurement of Risk", *Econometrica*, 22, 23–36, (1954).

Bewley, T. (1980), "The Optimum Quantity of Money" in *Models of Monetary Economies*, J.H. Kareken and N. Wallace eds., Minneapolis: Federal Reserve Bank of Minneapolis.

Bewley, T. (1983), "A Difficulty With the Optimum Quantity of Money", *Econometrica*, 51, 1485–1504.

Bewley, T. (1986), "Knightian Decision Theory: Part I", Cowles Foundation Discussion Paper #807, Yale University.

Binmore, K.G. (1992), "Foundations of Game Theory" in *Advances in Economic Theory; Sixth World Congress, Volume I*, J.J. Laffont ed., Cambridge: Cambridge University Press.

Black, F. (1972), "Capital Market Equilibrium with Restricted Borrowing", *Journal of Business*, 45, 444–454.

Black, F. and M. Scholes (1973), "The Pricing of Options and Corporate Liabilities", *Journal of Political Economy*, 81, 637–654.

Blanchard, O.J. (1979), "Wage Indexing Rules and the Behavior of the Economy", *Journal of Political Economy*, 87, 798–815.

Blanchard, O.J. (1980), "The Monetary Mechanism in the Light of Rational Expectations", in *Rational Expectations and Economic Policy*, S. Fischer ed., Chicago: National Bureau of Economic Research.

Blanchard, O.J. (1981), "Output, the Stock Market, and Interest Rates", *American Economic Review*, 71, 132–143.

Blanchard, O.J. and S. Fischer (1989), *Lectures on Macroeconomics*, Cambridge, Mass.: MIT Press.

Blaug, M. (1985), *Economic Theory in Retrospect*, Homewood, Il.: R.D. Irwin.

Böhm-Bawerk, E. (1889), *Positive Theorie des Kapitales*, Jena: Fischer. English translation: *The Positive Theory of Capital*, South-Holland, Il: Libertarian Press, (1921).

Borch, K. (1960), "The Safety Loading of Reinsurance Premiums", *Skandinavisk Aktuarietidskrift*, 163–184.

Borch, K. (1962), "Equilibrium in a Reinsurance Market", *Econometrica*, 30, 424–444.

Borch, K. (1968), "General Equilibrium in the Economics of Uncertainty", in *Risk and Uncertainty*, K. Borch and J. Mossin eds., London: Macmillan.

Braudel, F. (1979), *Les Jeux de l'Echange*, Paris: Librairie Armand Colin. English translation: *The Wheels of Commerce*, New York: Harper and Row, (1982).

Brealey, R. and S. Myers (1989), *Principles of Corporate Finance (Third Edition)*, New York: McGraw-Hill.

Breeden, D. (1979), "An Intertemporal Asset Pricing Model with Stochastic Consumption and Investment Opportunities", *Journal of Financial Economics*, 7, 265–296.

Brock, W.A. (1975), "A Simple Perfect Foresight Monetary Model", *Journal of Monetary Economics*, 1, 133–150.

Brock, W.A. (1979), "An Integration of Stochatic Growth Theory and Theory of Finance, Part I: The Growth Model", in *General Equilibrium, Growth and Trade*, J. Green and J. Scheinkman eds., New York: Academic Press.

Brock, W.A. (1982), "Asset Prices in a Production Economy", in *The Economics of Information and Uncertainty*, J. McCall ed., Chicago: University of Chicago Press.

Brock, W.A. and L. Mirman (1972), "Optimal Economic Growth and Uncertainty: The Discounted Case", *Journal of Economic Theory*, 4, 479–513.

Brock, W.A. and J.A. Scheinkman (1980), "Some Remarks on Monetary Policy in an Overlapping Generations Model" in *Models of Monetary Economies*, J.H. Kareken and N. Wallace eds., Minneapolis: Federal Reserve Bank of Minneapolis.

Brouwer, L.E.J. (1912), "Über Abbildung von Mannigfaltigkeiten", *Mathematischen Annalen*, 71, 97–115.

Brunner, K. and A.M. Meltzer (1971), "The Uses of Money: Money in The Theory of an Exchange Economy", *American Economic Review*, 61, 784–805.

Cagan, P. (1956), "The Monetary Dynamics of Hyperinflation", in *Studies in the Quantity Theory of Money*, M. Friedman ed., Chicago: University of Chicago Press.

Cantillon, R. (1755), *Essai sur la Nature du Commerce en Général*, Reprinted by Augustus M. Kelley, New York, (1964).

Cass, D. (1984), "Competitive Equilibria in Incomplete Financial Markets", CARESS Working Paper, University of Pennsylvania.

Cass, D. (1985), "On the 'Number' of Equilibrium Allocations with Incomplete Financial Markets", CARESS Working Paper, University of Pennsylvania.

Cass, D. (1989), "Sunspots and Incomplete Financial Markets: The Leading Example", in *The Economics of Imperfect Competition: Joan Robinson and Beyond*, G. Feiwel ed., London: Macmillan.

Cass, D. (1990), "Real Indeterminacy from Imperfect Financial Markets: Two Addenda", CARESS Working Paper, University of Pennsylvania.

Cass, D. (1992), "Incomplete Financial Markets and Indeterminacy of Competitive Equilibrium", in *Advances in Economic Theory; Sixth World Congress, Volume II*, J.J. Laffont ed., Cambridge: Cambridge University Press.

Cass, D. and K. Shell (1980), "In Defense of a Basic Approach", in *Models of Monetary Economies*, J.H. Kareken and N. Wallace eds., Minneapolis: Federal Reserve Bank of Minneapolis.

Cass, D. and K. Shell (1983), "Do Sunspots Matter?", *Journal of Political Economy*, 91, 193–227.

Cass, D., P. Siconolfi and A. Villanacci (1991), "A Note on Generalizing the Model of Financial Equilibrium with Restricted Participation", CARESS Working Paper, University of Pennsylvania.

Cass, D. and J.E. Stiglitz (1970), "The Structure of Investor Preferences and Asset Returns, and Separability in Portfolio Allocation: A Contribution to the Pure Theory of Mutual Funds", *Journal of Economic Theory*, 2, 122–160.

Cassel, G. (1918), Theoretische Sozialökonomie. English translation: *The Theory of Social Economy*, London: T. Fisher Unwin (1923). Reprinted by Augustus M. Kelly, New York, (1967).

Chae, S. (1988), "Existence of Competitive Equilibrium with Incomplete Markets", *Journal of Economic Theory*, 44, 9–18.

Chamberlain, G. (1983), "Funds, Factors and Diversification in Arbitrage Pricing Models", *Econometrica*, 51, 1305–1323.

Chamberlain, G. and M. Rothschild (1983), "Arbitrage, Factor Structure and Mean-Variance Analysis in Large Asset Markets", *Econometrica*, 51, 1281–1304.

Chamley, C. and H. Polemarchakis (1984), "Assets, General Equilibrium and The Neutrality of Money", *Review of Economic Studies*, 51, 129–138.

Chandler, A.D. (1962), *Strategy and Structure*, Cambridge, Mass.: MIT Press.

Chandler, A.D. (1977), *The Visible Hand: The Managerial Revolution in American Business*, Cambridge, Mass.: Harvard University Press.

Chandler, A.D. (1990), *Scale and Scope: The Dynamics of Industrial Capitalism*, Cambridge, Mass.: Harvard University Press.

Clower, R.W. (1967), "A Reconsideration of the Microfoundations of Monetary Theory", *Western Economic Journal*, 6, 1–8.

Coase, R. (1937), "The Nature of the Firm", *Economica*, n.s. 4, 386–405.

Coase, R. (1960), "The Problem of Social Cost", *Journal of Law and Economics*, 3, 1–44.

Commons, J.R. (1934), *Institutional Economics*, Madison: University of Wisconsin Press.

Cooter, R. and T. Ulen (1988), *Law and Economics*, New York: Harper Collins.

Cootner, P. (1967), *The Random Character of Stock Market Prices*, Cambridge, Mass.: MIT Press.

Cournot, A. (1838), *Recherches sur les Principes Mathématiques de la Théorie des Richesses*, Paris: Hachette. English translation: *Researches into the Mathematical Principles of the Theory of Wealth*, London: Macmillan, (1897).

Cox, J., J. Ingersoll and S. Ross (1985a), "An Intertemporal General Equilibrium Model of Asset Prices", *Econometrica*, 53, 363–384.

Cox, J., J. Ingersoll and S. Ross (1985b), "A Theory of the Term Structure of Interest Rates", *Econometrica*, 53, 385–407.

Debreu, G. (1951), "The Coefficient of Resource Utilization", *Econometrica*, 19, 273–291.

Debreu, G. (1952), "A Social Equilibrium Existence Theorem", *Proceedings of the National Academy of Sciences*, 38, 886–893.

Debreu, G. (1959), *Theory of Value*, New York: Wiley.

Debreu, G. (1970), "Economies with a Finite Set of Equilibria", *Econometrica*, 38, 387–392.

Debreu, G. (1972), "Smooth Preferences", *Econometrica*, 40, 603–615.

DeMarzo, P. (1988), "An Extension of the Modigliani-Miller Theorem to Stochatic Economies with Incomplete Markets", *Journal of Economic Theory*, 45, 353–369.

Diamond, P.A. (1967), "The Role of a Stock Market in a General Equilibrium Model with Technological Uncertainty", *American Economic Review*, 57, 759–776.

Diamond, P.A. (1980), "Efficiency with Uncertain Supply", *Review of Economic Studies*, 47, 645–651.

Diamond, P.A. (1984a), "Money in Search Equilibrium", *Econometrica*, 52, 1–20.

Diamond, P.A. (1984b), *A Search-Equilibrium Approach to the Micro Foundations of Macroeconomics*, Cambridge, Mass.: MIT Press.

Diamond, P.A. (1994), *On Time*, Cambridge: Cambridge University Press.

Diamond, P.A. and J. Yellin (1990), "Inventories and Money Holdings in a Search Economy", *Econometrica*, 58, 929–950.

Dierker, E. (1974), *Topological Methods in Walrasian Economics*, Lecture Notes in Economics and Mathematical Systems, 92, Berlin: Springer.

Diewert, W.E. (1987), "Index Numbers", in *The New Palgrave: A Dictionary of Economics*, J. Eatwell, M. Milgate, and P. Newman eds., London: Macmillan.

Doob, J.L. (1953), *Stochastic Processes*, New York: Wiley.

Drèze, J.H. (1974), "Investment under Private Ownership: Optimality, Equilibrium and Stability", in *Allocation Under Uncertainty: Equilibrium and Optimality*, J.H. Drèze ed., New York: Wiley, 129–165.

Drèze, J.H. (1985), "(Uncertainty and) the Firm in General Equilibrium Theory", *Economic Journal*, 95, 1–20.

Drèze, J.H. (1987), *Essays on Economic Decisions under Uncertainty*, Cambridge: Cambridge University Press.

Drèze, J.H. (1989), *Labour Management, Contracts and Capital Markets*, Oxford: Blackwell.

Dubey, P. and J. Geanakoplos (1989), "Liquidity and Bankruptcy with Incomplete Markets: Pure Exchange", Cowles Foundation Discussion Paper 912.

Dubey, P. and J. Geanakoplos (1992), "The Value of Money in a Finite-Horizon Economy: A Role for Banks", in *Economic Analysis of Markets and Games: Essays in Honor of Frank Hahn*, P. Dasgupta et al. eds., Cambridge, Mass.: MIT Press.

Duffie, D. (1988), *Security Markets: Stochastic Models*, Boston: Academic Press.

Duffie, D. (1992), *Dynamic Asset Pricing Theory*, Princeton: Princeton University Press.

Duffie, D. and M. Jackson (1989), "Optimal Innovation of Futures Contracts", *Review of Financial Studies*, 2, 275–296.

Duffie, D. and W. Shafer (1985), "Equilibrium in Incomplete Markets I: Basic Model of Generic Existence", *Journal of Mathematical Economics*, 14: 285–300.

Duffie, D. and W. Shafer (1986a), "Equilibrium in Incomplete Markets II: Generic Existence in Stochastic Economies", *Journal of Mathematical Economics*, 15, 199–216.

Duffie, D. and W. Shafer (1986b), "Equilibrium and the Role of the Firm in Incomplete Markets", Research Paper No. 915, Graduate School of Business, Stanford University.

Edgeworth, F.Y. (1881), *Mathematical Psychics*, London: C. Kegan Paul.

Ekern, S. and R. Wilson (1974), "On The Theory of the Firm in an Economy with Incomplete Markets", *Bell Journal of Economics and Management Science*, 5, 171–180.

Epstein, L. and S. Zin (1989), "Substitution, Risk Aversion, and the Temporal Behavior of Consumption and Asset Returns", *Econometrica*, 57, 937–969.

Epstein, L. and T. Wang (1994), "Intertemporal Asset Pricing under Knightian Uncertainty", *Econometrica*, 62, 283–322.

Fair, R.C. (1979), "An Analysis of a Macro-Economic Model with Rational Expectations in the Bond and Stock Markets", *American Economic Review*, 69, 539–552.

Fama, E.F. (1970), "Efficient Capital Markets: A Review of Theory and Empirical Work", *Journal of Finance*, 25, 383–416.

Fama, E.F. (1980), "Agency Problems and the Theory of the Firm", *Journal of Political Economy*, 88, 288–307.

Fama, E.F. and M.C. Jensen (1983a), "Separation of Ownership and Control", *Journal of Law and Economics*, 26, 301–325.

Fama, E.F. and M.C. Jensen (1983b), "Agency Problems and Residual Claims", *Journal of Law and Economics*, 26, 326–343.

Fama, E.F. and M.M. Miller (1972), *The Theory of Finance*, Hinsdale, Il.: Dryden Press.

Farnsworth, E.A. (1990), *Contracts*, Boston: Little, Brown and Company.

Fischer, S. (1972), "Assets, Contingent Commodities, and the Slutsky Equation", *Econometrica*, 40, 371–386.

Fischer, S. (1977), "Long-term Contracts, Rational Expectations, and the Optimal Money Supply Rule", *Journal of Political Economy*, 85, 191–205.

Fischer, S. (1986), *Indexation, Inflation and Economic Policy*, Cambridge, Mass.: MIT Press.

Fisher, I. (1896), "Appreciation and Interest", *Publications of the American Economic Association*, 11. Reprinted by Augustus M. Kelley, New York, (1965).

Fisher, I. (1906), *The Nature of Capital and Income*, New York: Sentry Press. Reprinted by Augustus M. Kelley, New York, (1965).

Fisher, I. (1907), *The Rate of Interest*, New York: Macmillan.

Fisher, I. (1911), *The Purchasing Power of Money*, New York: Macmillan.

Fisher, I. (1922), *The Making of Index Numbers*, Boston: Houghton Mifflin.

Fisher, I. (1926), "A Statistical Relation Between Unemployment and Price Changes", *International Labour Review*, 13, 785–792; reprinted as "I Discovered the Phillips Curve", *Journal of Political Economy*, (1973).

Fisher, I. (1930), *The Theory of Interest*, New York: Macmillan. Reprinted by Augustus, M. Kelley, New York, (1960).

Fisher, I. (1933), "The Debt-Deflation Theory of Great Depressions", *Econometrica*, 1, 337–357.

Fleming, W. (1965), *Functions of Several Variables*, Reading, Mass.: Addison-Wesley.

Foley, D.K. (1970), "Economic Equilibrium with Costly Marketing", *Journal of Economic Theory*, 2, 276–291.

Foley, D.K. (1975), "On Two Specifications of Asset Equilibrium in Macroeconomic Models", *Journal of Political Economy*, 83, 303–324.

Friedman, M. (1968), "The Role of Monetary Policy", *American Economic Review*, 58, 1–17.

Friedman, M. (1969), "The Optimum Quantity of Money", in *The Optimum Quantity of Money and Other Essays*, Chicago: Aldine.

Friedman, M. (1987), "Quantity Theory of Money", in *The New Palgrave: A Dictionary of Economics*, J. Eatwell, M. Milgate and P. Newman eds., London: Macmillan.

Friedman, M. (1994), *Money Mischief, Episodes in Monetary History*, New York: Harcourt Brace and Company.

Frisch, R. (1933), "Propagation Problems and Impulse Problems in Dynamic Economics", in *Economic Essays in Honour of Gustav Cassel*, 171–205.

Galbraith, J.K. (1993), *A Short History of Financial Euphoria*, New York: Viking.

Gale, D. (1978), "The Core of a Monetary Economy without Trust", *Journal of Economic Theory*, 19, 456–491.

Gale, D. (1982), *Money: In Equilibrium*, Cambridge: Cambridge University Press.

Gale, D. and M. Hellwig (1984), "A General Equilibrium Model of the Transactions Demand for Money", London School of Economics, STICERD Discussion Paper No. 84/100.

Geanakoplos, J., M. Magill, M. Quinzii and J. Drèze (1990), "Generic Inefficiency of Stock Market Equilibrium When Markets are Incomplete", *Journal of Mathematical Economics*, 19, 113–151.

Geanakoplos, J. and A. Mas-Colell (1989), "Real Indeterminacy with Financial Assets", *Journal of Economic Theory*, 47, 22–38; Cowles Foundation Discussion Paper, Yale University, (1986).

Geanakoplos, J. and H. Polemarchakis (1986), "Existence, Regularity, and Constrained Suboptimality of Competitive Allocations when Markets are Incomplete" in *Uncertainty, Information and Communication: Essays in Honor of Kenneth Arrow, Volume 3*, W.P. Heller, R.M. Ross and D.A. Starrett eds., Cambridge: Cambridge University Press.

Geanakoplos, J. and W. Shafer (1990), "Solving Systems of Simultaneous Equations in Economics", *Journal of Mathematical Economics*, 19, 69–93.

Gould, B.G. (1973), *The Dow Jones-Irwin Guide to Commodities Trading*, Homewood, Il.: Dow Jones-Irwin.

Graham, B. and D.L. Dodd (1934), *Security Analysis*, New York: McGraw-Hill.

Grandmont, J.M. (1970), "On the Temporary Competitive Equilibrium", Ph.D. Dissertation, University of California, Berkeley.

Grandmont, J.M. (1974), "On the Short Run Equilibrium in a Monetary Economy", in *Allocation Under Uncertainty, Equilibrium and Optimality*, J.H. Drèze ed., London: Macmillan.

Grandmont, J.M. (1977), "Temporary General Equilibrium Theory", *Econometrica*, 45, 535–572.

Grandmont, J.M. (1983), *Money and Value*, Cambridge: Cambridge University Press.

Grandmont, J.M. and G. Laroque (1973), "Money in the Pure Consumption-Loan Model", *Journal of Economic Theory*, 6, 382–395.

Grandmont, J.M. and Y. Younes (1972), "On the Role of Money and the Existence of a Monetary Equilibrium", *Review of Economic Studies*, 39, 355–372.

Grandmont, J.M. and Y. Younes (1973), "On the Efficiency of a Monetary Equilibrium", *Review of Economic Studies*, 40, 149–165.

Granger, C.W.J. and O. Morgenstern (1963), "Spectral Analysis of New York Stock Market Prices", *Kyklos*, 16, 1–27.

Granger, C.W.J. and O. Morgenstern (1970), *Predictability of Stock Market Prices*, Lexington, Mass.: Health Lexington Books.

Gray, R. and D. Rutledge (1971), "The Economics of Commodity Futures Markets: A Survey", *Review of Marketing and Agricultural Economics*, 39, 57–108.

Green, J.R. (1972), "Temporary General Equilibrium in a Sequential Trading Model with Spot and Futures Transactions", *Econometrica*, 41, 1103–1123.

Grossman, S. (1977), "A Characterization of the Optimality of Equilibrium in Incomplete Markets", *Journal of Economic Theory*, 15, 1–15.

Grossman, S. and O. Hart (1979), "A Theory of Competitive Equilibrium in Stock Market Economies", *Econometrica*, 47, 293–330.

Grossman, S. and R.J. Shiller (1981), "The Determinants of the Variability of Stock Prices", *American Economic Review*, 71, 222–227.

Grossman, S. and L. Weiss (1983), "A Transactions-Based Model of the Monetary Transmission Mechanism", *American Economic Review*, 73, 871–880.

Grunberg, E. and F. Modigliani (1954), "The Predictability of Social Events", *Journal of Political Economy*, 62, 465–478.

Guesnerie R. and J.Y. Jaffray (1974), "Optimality of Equilibrium of Plans, Prices and Price Expectations" in *Allocation Under Uncertainty*, J. Drèze ed., New York: Wiley.

Hahn, F.H. (1965), "On Some Problems of Proving the Existence of an Equilibrium in a Monetary Economy" in *The Theory of Interest Rates*, 126–135, F.H. Hahn and F.P.R. Brechling eds., London: Macmillan.

Hahn, F.H. (1971a), "Professor Friedman's Views on Money", *Economica*, 38, 61–80.

Hahn, F.H. (1971b), "Equilibrium with Transaction Costs", *Econometrica*, 39, 417–439.

Hahn, F.H. (1973a), "On the Foundations of Monetary Theory", *Essays in Modern Economics*, 230–242, M. Parkin and A.R. Nobay eds., New York: Harper and Row.

Hahn, F.H. (1973b), "On Transaction Costs, Inessential Sequence Economies and Money", *Review of Economic Studies*, 40, 449–461.

Hahn, F.H. (1980), "Discussion" in *Models of Monetary Economies*, J.H. Kareken and N. Wallace eds., Minneapolis: Federal Reserve Bank of Minneapolis.

Hahn, F.H. (1982), *Money and Inflation*, Oxford: Blackwell.

Hakansson, N.H. (1969), "Risk Disposition and the Separation Property in Portfolio Selection", *Journal of Financial and Quantitative Analysis*, 4, 401–416.

Hammond, P.J. (1983), "Overlapping Expectations and Hart's Conditions for Equilibrium in a Securities Model", *Journal of Economic Theory*, 31, 170–175.

Hansen, L. and K. Singleton (1982), "Generalized Instrumental Variables Estimation of Nonlinear Rational Expectations Models", *Econometrica*, 50, 1269–1286.

Hansen, L. and K. Singleton (1983), 'Stochastic Consumption, Risk Aversion and the Temporal Behavior of Asset Returns", *Journal of Political Economy*, 91, 249–265.

Harris, M. and A. Raviv (1992), "Financial Contracting Theory", in *Advances in Economic Theory; Sixth World Congress, Volume II*, J.J. Laffont ed., Cambridge: Cambridge University Press.

Harrison, J.M. and D.M. Kreps (1979), "Martingales and Arbitrage in Multi-period Securities Markets", *Journal of Economic Theory*, 20, 381–408.

Hart, O.D. (1974), "On the Existence of Equilibrium in a Securities Model", *Journal of Economic Theory*, 9, 293–311.

Hart, O.D. (1975) "On the Optimality of Equilibrium when the Market Structure is Incomplete", *Journal of Economic Theory*, 11, 418–443.

Hart, O.D. (1987), "Incomplete Contracts", in *The New Palgrave: A Dictionary of Economics*, J. Eatwell, M. Milgate and P. Newman eds., London: Macmillan.

Hart, O.D. and B. Holmstrom, (1987), "The Theory of Contracts" in *Advances in Economic Theory; Fifth World Congress*, T. Bewley ed., Cambridge: Cambridge University Press.

Hayek, F.A. (1934), *Prices and Production*, 2d ed., London: Macmillan.

Hayek, F.A. (1945), "The Use of Knowledge in Society", *American Economic Review*, 35, 519–530.

Hayek, F.A. (1948), *Individualism and Economic Order*, Chicago: University of Chicago Press.

Hayek, F.A. (1988), *The Fatal Conceit: The Errors of Socialism*, Chicago: University of Chicago Press.

Heiner, R.A. (1983), "The Origin of Predictable Behavior", *American Economic Review*, 73, 560–595.

Hellwig, M.F. (1976), "A Model of Monetary Exchange", Princeton University, Econometric Research Program Memorandum.

Hellwig, M.F. (1981), "Bankruptcy, Limited Liability, and the Modigliani-Miller Theorem", *American Economic Review*, 71, 155–170.

Hellwig, M.F. (1993), "The Challenge of Monetary Theory", *European Economic Review*, 37, 215–242.

Hens, T. (1991), "Structure of General Equilibrium Models with Incomplete Markets", Doctoral Dissertation, University of Bonn.

Hicks, J.R. (1939), *Value and Capital*, Oxford: Clarendon Press.

Hildenbrand, W. (1974), *Core and Equilibria of a Large Economy*, Princeton: Princeton University Press.

Hildenbrand, W. and A.P. Kirman (1988), *Equilibrium Analysis*, Amsterdam: North-Holland.

Hirsch, M., M. Magill and A. Mas-Colell (1990), "A Geometric Approach to a Class of Equilibrium Existence Theorems", *Journal of Mathematical Economics*, 19, 95–106.

Hirsch, W. and S. Smale (1974), *Differential Equations, Dynamical Systems and Linear Algebra*, New York: Academic Press.

Holmstrom, B.R. and J. Tirole (1989), "The Theory of the Firm", in *Handbook of Industrial Organization*, R. Schmalensee and R. Willig eds., Amsterdam: North-Holland.

Huang, C. and R.H. Litzenberger (1988), *Fundamentals of Finance*, Amsterdam: North-Holland.

Husseini, S.Y., J.M. Lasry and M. Magill (1990), "Existence of Equilibrium with Incomplete Markets", *Journal of Mathematical Economics*, 19, 39–67.

Jensen, M. and W. Meckling (1976), "Theory of the Firm: Managerial Behavior, Agency Costs, and Capital Structure", *Journal of Financial Economics*, 3, 305–360.

Jevons, W.S. (1875), *Money and the Mechanism of Exchange*, London: Routledge and Kegan Paul.

Jovanovic, B. (1982), "Inflation and Welfare in the Steady State", *Journal of Political Economy*, 90, 561–577.

Justinian, C.F. (533), *Institutionum seu Elementorum divi Justiniani Sacratissimi Principis*. French translation and Latin original in: *Les Cinquantes Livres du Digeste ou des Pandectes de l'Empereur Justinien*, Paris: Rondonneau, (1806).

Justinian, C.F. (533), *Digesta Justiniani*. French translation and Latin original in: *Les Cinquantes Livres du Digeste ou des Pandectes de l'Empereur Justinien*, Paris: Rondonneau, (1803–1805).

Kakutani, S. (1941), "A Generalization of Brouwer's Fixed Point Theorem", *Duke Mathematical Journal*, 8, 457–459.

Kareken, J.H., and N. Wallace (1980), *Models of Monetary Economies*, Minneapolis: Federal Reserve Bank of Minneapolis.

Karni, E. and D. Schmeidler (1991), "Utility Theory with Uncertainty" in *Handbook of Mathematical Economics, Volume IV*, W. Hildenbrand and H. Sonnenschein eds., Amsterdam: North-Holland.

Kendall, M.G. (1953), "The Analysis of Economic Time-Series, Part I: Prices", *Journal of the Royal Statistical Society*, 96, 11–25.

Keynes, J.M. (1921), *A Treatise on Probability*, London: Macmillan.

Keynes, J.M. (1923a), *A Tract on Monetary Reform*, London: Macmillan.

Keynes, J.M. (1923b), "Some Aspects of Commodities Markets", *Manchester Guardian Commercial*, March 29, 1923. Reprinted in *The Collected Writings of John Maynard Keynes, Volume XII*, London: Macmillan, (1983).

Keynes, J.M. (1925), "An American Study of Shares Versus Bonds as Permanent Investments", *Nation and Athenoeum*, 2 May 1925. Reprinted in

The Collected Writings of John Maynard Keynes, Volume XII, London: Macmillan, (1983).

Keynes, J.M. (1930), *A Treatise on Money*, London: Macmillan.

Keynes, J.M. (1933), "A Monetary Theory of Production", in *Der Stand und die nächste Zukunft der Konjunkturforschung: Festschrift für Arthur Spiethoff*. Reprinted in *The Collected Writings of John Maynard Keynes, Volume XIII*, London: Macmillan, (1983).

Keynes, J.M. (1936), *The General Theory of Employment, Interest and Money*, London: Macmillan.

Keynes, J.M. (1937), "The General Theory of Employment", *Quarterly Journal of Economics*, 51, 209–223.

Kihlstrom, R. and J.J. Laffont (1982), "A Competitive Entrepreneurial Model of a Stock Market", in *The Economics of Information and Uncertainty*, J. McCall ed., Chicago: University of Chicago Press.

Kiyotaki, N. and R. Wright (1989), "On Money as a Medium of Exchange", *Journal of Political Economy*, 97, 927–954.

Knapp, G.F. (1905), *Die Staatliche Theorie des Geldes*, Munich: Duncker und Humblot. English translation: *The State Theory of Money*, London: Macmillan, (1924).

Knight, F. (1921), *Risk, Uncertainty and Profit*, Boston: Houghton Mifflin.

Koopmans, T.C. (1951), "Analysis of Production as an Efficient Combination of Activities", in *Activity Analysis of Production and Allocation*, T.C. Koopmans ed., Cowles Foundation Monograph, New York: Wiley.

Koopmans, T.C. (1957), *Three Essays on the State of Economic Science*, New York: McGraw-Hill.

Koopmans, T.C. (1960), "Stationary Ordinal Utility and Impatience", *Econometrica*, 28, 287–303.

Krasa, S. (1987), "Existence of Competitive Equilibrium for Option Markets", *Journal of Economic Theory*, 47, 413–431.

Krasa, S. and J. Werner (1991), "Equilibria with Options: Existence and Indeterminacy", *Journal of Economic Theory*, 54, 305–320.

Kreps, D. (1979), "Three Essays on Capital Markets", Technical Report 298, Institute for Mathematical Studies in The Social Sciences, Stanford University.

Kreps, D. (1982), "Multiperiod Securities and the Efficient Allocation of Risk: A Comment on the Black-Scholes Option Pricing Model", in *The Economics of Uncertainty and Information*, J. McCall ed., Chicago: University of Chicago Press.

Kreps, D.M. (1988), *Notes on the Theory of Choice*, Boulder, Co.: Westview Press.

Kreps, D.M. (1990), *A Course in Microeconomic Theory*, Princeton, NJ: Princeton University Press.

Kydland, F.E. and E.C. Prescott (1982), "Time to Build and Aggregate Fluctuations", *Econometrica*, 50, 1345–1370.

Laffont, J.J. (1988), *Economics of Uncertainty and Information*, Cambridge, Mass.: MIT Press.

Lange, O. and F.M. Taylor (1938), *On the Economic Theory of Socialism*, B.E. Lippincott ed., Minneapolis: University of Minneapolis Press.

Law, J. (1705), *Money and Trade Considered; with a Proposal for Supplying the Nation with Money*, London: Lewis. Reprinted by A.M. Kelley, New York, (1966).

Lehmann, E.L. (1966), "Some Concepts of Dependence", *Annals of Mathematical Statistics*, 37, 1137–1153.

Lerner, A.P. (1944), *The Economics of Control*, New York: Macmillan.

LeRoy, S.F. (1973), "Risk Aversion and the Martingale Property of Stock Prices", *International Economic Review*, 14, 675–684.

LeRoy, S.F. (1989), "Efficient Capital Markets and Martingales", *Journal of Economic Literature*, 27, 1583–1621.

LeRoy, S.F. and R.D. Porter (1981), "The Present-Value Relation: Tests Based on Implied Variance Bounds", *Econometrica*, 49, 555–574.

Lewis, D. (1969), *Convention*, Cambridge, Mass.: Harvard University Press.

Lintner, J. (1965), "The Valuation of Risky Assets and the Selection of Risky Investments in Stock Portfolios and Capital Budgets", *Review of Economics and Statistics*, 47, 13–37.

Long, J.B. and C.I. Plosser (1983), "Real Business Cycles", *Journal of Political Economy*, 91, 39–69.

Lucas, R.E. (1972), "Expectations and the Neutrality of Money", *Journal of Economic Theory*, 4, 103–124.

Lucas, R.E. (1976), "Econometric Policy Evaluation: A Critique", in *The Phillips Curve and Labor Markets*, K. Brunner and A.H. Meltzer eds., Amsterdam: North Holland.

Lucas, R.E. (1978), "Asset Prices in an Exchange Economy", *Econometrica*, 46, 1429–1445.

Lucas, R.E. (1980), Equilibrium in a Pure Currency Economy, *Economic Enquiry*, 18, 203–220, also in *Models of Monetary Economies*, J.H. Kareken and N. Wallace eds., Minneapolis: Federal Reserve Bank of Minneapolis.

Lucas, R.E. (1987), *Models of Business Cycles*, New York: Blackwell.

Lucas, R.E. and T.J. Sargent (1978), "After Keynesian Macroeconomics", in *After the Phillips Curve: Persistence of High Inflation and High Unemployment*, Federal Reserve Bank of Boston Conference, Boston: Federal Reserve Bank, 19, 49–72.

Lucas, R.E. and T.J. Sargent (1981), *Rational Expectations and Econometric Practice*, Minneapolis: The University of Minnesota Press.

Lucas R.E. and N. Stokey (1983), "Optimal Fiscal and Monetary Policy in an Economy without Capital", *Journal of Monetary Economics*, 12, 55–93.

Lucas, R.E. and N. Stokey (1987), "Money and Interest in a Cash-in-Advance Economy", *Econometrica*, 53, 491–514.

Mackay, C. (1841), *Memoirs of Extraordinary Popular Delusions and the Madness of Crowds*, London: Bentley.

Macneil, I.R. (1974), "The Many Futures of Contracts", *Southern California Law Review*, 47, 691–816.

Magill, M. (1977), "A Local Analysis of N-Sector Capital Accumulation under Uncertainty", *Journal of Economic Theory*, 15, 211–219.

Magill, M. and H. Cheng (1985), "Futures Markets, Production and Diversification of Risk", *Journal of Mathematical Analysis and Applications*, 107, 331–355.

Magill, M. and M. Nermuth (1986), "On the Qualitative Properties of Futures Market Equilibrium", *Journal of Economics*, 46, 233–252.

Magill, M. and M. Quinzii (1991), "The Non-neutrality of Money in a Production Economy with Nominal Assets", in *Equilibrium Theory and Applications*, W.A. Barnett et al. eds., Cambridge: Cambridge University Press.

Magill, M. and M. Quinzii (1992), "Real Effects of Money in General Equilibrium", *Journal of Mathematical Economics*, 21, 301–342; MRG Working Paper, University of Southern California, (1988).

Magill, M. and M. Quinzii (1993), "Incomplete Markets Over An Infinite Horizon: Long-Lived Securities and Speculative Bubbles", *Journal of Mathematical Economics*, forthcoming.

Magill, M. and M. Quinzii (1994), "Infinite Horizon Incomplete Markets", *Econometrica*, 62, 853–880.

Magill, M. and M. Quinzii (1995), "Which Improves Welfare More: Nominal or Indexed Bond?", Working Paper, University of Southern California.

Magill, M. and W. Shafer (1990), "Characterization of Generically Complete Real Asset Structures", *Journal of Mathematical Economics*, 19, 167–194; MRG Working Paper, University of Southern California, (1985).

Magill, M. and W. Shafer (1991), "Incomplete Markets", in *Handbook of Math-*

ematical Economics, Volume IV, 1523–1614, W. Hildenbrand and H. Sonnenschein eds., Amsterdam: North-Holland.

Magill, M. and W. Shafer (1992), "Allocation of Aggregate and Individual Risks through Futures and Insurance Markets", in *Equilibrium and Dynamics: Essays in Honor of David Gale*, M. Majumdar ed., London: Macmillan; MRG Working Paper, University of Southern California, (1984).

Makowski, L. (1980), "A Characterization of Perfectly Competitive Economies with Production", *Journal of Economic Theory*, 22, 208–221.

Malinvaud, E. (1977), *The Theory of Unemployment Reconsidered*, Oxford: Blackwell.

Malkiel, B.G. (1973), *A Random Walk Down Wall Street*, New York: Norton.

Mandeville, B. (1729), *The Fable of the Bees, Part II*, London: J. Roberts. Reprinted by Clarendon Press, Oxford, (1924).

Mankiw, N.G. (1986), "The Equity Premium and the Concentration of Aggregate Shocks", *Journal of Financial Economics*, 17, 211–219.

Mankiw, N.G. and D. Romer (1991), *New Keynesian Economics, Volumes 1 and 2*, Cambridge, Mass.: MIT Press.

Marimon, R. (1987), "Kreps' 'Three Essays on Capital Markets' Almost Ten Years Later", *Revista Espanola de Economia*, 4, 147–171.

Markowitz, H. (1952), "Portfolio Selection", *Journal of Finance*, 7, 77–91.

Markowitz, H. (1959), *Portfolio Selection: Efficient Diversification of Investments*, New York: Wiley.

Marshall, A. (1887), "Remedies for Fluctuations in General Prices", *Contemporary Review*, reprinted in *Memorials of Alfred Marshall*, A.C. Pigou ed., London: Macmillan, (1925).

Marshall, A. (1890), *Principles of Economics*, London: Macmillan.

Marshall, A. (1923), *Money, Credit and Commerce*, London: Macmillan.

Marx, K. (1867), *Das Kapital, Erster Band*, Hamburg: Otto Meissner. English translation: *Capital, Volume 1*, London: Swan Sonnenschein, Lowry and Co., (1887).

Mas-Colell, A. (1985), *The Theory of General Economic Equilibrium—A Differentiable Approach*, Cambridge: Cambridge University Press.

Mas-Colell, A., M.D. Whinston and J.R. Green (1995), *Microeconomic Theory*, Oxford: Oxford University Press.

McKenzie, L.W. (1954), "On Equilibrium in Graham's Model of World Trade and Other Competitive Systems", *Econometrica*, 22, 147–161.

McKenzie, L.W. (1955), "Competitive Equilibrium with Dependent Consumer Preferences", *Proceedings of the Second Symposium in Linear Program-*

ming, H.A. Antosiewicz ed., 277–294, Washington, D.C.: National Bureau of Standards.

McKenzie, L.W. (1959), "On the Existence of General Equilibrium for a Competitive Market", *Econometrica*, 27, 54–71.

Mehra, R. and E.C. Prescott (1985), "The Equity Premium: A Puzzle", *Journal of Monetary Economics*, 15, 145–161.

Menger, C. (1871), *Grundsätze der Volkswirtschaftslehre*. English translation: *Principles of Economics*, New York: New York University Press, (1950).

Merton, R.K. (1948), "The Self-Fulfilling Prophecy", *Antioch Review* , 193–211.

Mill, J.S. (1848), *Principles of Political Economy*, London: J.W. Parker. Reprinted by the University of Toronto Press, (1968).

Milgrom, P.R. and J. Roberts (1992), *Economics, Organizations and Management*, Englewood Cliffs, NJ: Prentice-Hall.

Minkowski, H. (1911), "Theorie der konvexen Körper, insbesondere Begründung ihres Oberflächenbegriffs", in *Gesammelte Abhandlungen von Herman Minkowski, Zweiter Band*, D. Hilbert ed., Leipzig: B.G. Teubner. Reprinted by Chelsea Publishing Company, New York, (1967).

von Mises, L. (1912), *Theorie des Geldes und der Umlaufsmittel*, Munich: Duncker und Humblot. English translation: *The Theory of Money and Credit*, Indianapolis: Liberty Classics, (1934).

von Mises, L. (1949), *Human Action: A Treatise on Economics*, New Haven: Yale University Press.

Mishkin, F.S. (1995), *The Economics of Money, Banking and Financial Markets*, 4th Edition, New-York: Harper Collins.

Modigliani, F. (1977), "The Monetarist Controversy or, Should We Forsake Stabilization Policies?", *American Economic Review*, 67, 1–19.

Modigliani, F. and M.H. Miller (1958), "The Cost of Capital, Corporate Finance, and the Theory of Investment", *American Economic Review*, 48, 261–297.

Moore, G.E. (1903), *Principia Ethica*, Cambridge: Cambridge University Press.

Mossin, T. (1966), "Equilibrium in Capital Asset Market", *Econometrica*, 34, 768–783.

Muth, J.F. (1961), "Rational Expectations and the Theory of Price Movements", *Econometrica*, 29, 315–335.

Myers, S. and N. Majluf (1984), "Corporate Financing and Investment Decisions when Firms Have Information that Investors do not Have", *Journal of Financial Economics*, 13, 187–221.

Nash, J.F. (1950), "Equilibrium Points in N-Person Games", *Proceedings of the National Academy of Sciences*, 36, 48–49.

von Neumann, J. (1937), "Über ein ökonomisches Gleichungssystem und eine Verallgemeinerung des Brouwerschen Fixpunktsatzes", *Ergebnisse eines mathematischen Kolloquiums*, 8, 73–83. English translation: "A Model of General Economic Equilibrium", *Review of Economic Studies*, 13, 1–9, (1945).

von Neumann, J. and O. Morgenstern (1944), *Theory of Games and Economic Behavior*, Princeton: Princeton University Press.

Neumeyer, P.A. (1992), "Nominal Financial Markets with High Inflation: A Welfare Analysis", Discussion Paper, University of Southern California.

Newberry, D.M.G. and J.E. Stiglitz (1982), "The Choice of Techniques and the Optimality of Market Equilibrium with Rational Expectations", *Journal of Political Economy*, 90, 223–246.

North, D. (1991), "Institutions", *Journal of Economic Perspectives*, 5, 97–112.

Okun, A.M. (1971), "The Mirage of Steady Inflation", *Brookings Papers on Economic Activity*, 2, 485–498.

Okun, A.M. (1975), "Inflation: Its Mechanics and Welfare Costs", *Brookings Papers on Economic Activity*, 2, 351–390.

Okun, A.M. (1980), "The Invisible Handshake and the Inflationary Process", *Challenge*, 22, 5–12.

Okun, A.M. (1980), "Rational-Expectations-with-Misperceptions as a Theory of the Business Cycle", *Journal of Money, Credit and Banking*, 12, 814–825.

Osborne, M.F. (1959), "Brownian Motion in the Stock Market", *Operations Research*, 7, 145–173.

Ostroy, J. and R.M. Starr (1974), "Money and the Decentralization of Exchange", *Econometrica*, 42, 1093–1113.

Pareto, W. (1896–1897), *Cours d'Economie Politique*, Lausanne: Rouge.

Pareto, V. (1909), *Manuel d'Economie Politique*, Genève: Librairie Droz. English translation: *Manual of Political Economy*, New York: Augustus M. Kelley, (1971).

Patinkin, D. (1965), *Money, Interest, and Prices; An Integration of Monetary and Value Theory*, 2nd ed., New York: Harper & Row.

Phelps, E.S. (1970), "The New Microeconomics in Employment and Inflation Theory", in *Microeconomic Foundations of Employment and Inflation Theory*, E.S. Phelps ed., New York: Norton.

Pietra, T. (1992), "Indeterminacy in General Equilibrium Models with Incomplete Financial Markets: Mixed Asset Returns", *Journal of Mathematical Economics*, 21, 155–172.

Pigou, A.C. (1920), *The Economics of Welfare*, London: Macmillan. .

Pigou, A.C. (1927), *Industrial Fluctuations*, London: Macmillan.

Polemarchakis, H.M. (1988), "Portfolio Choice, Exchange Rates and Indeterminacy", *Journal of Economic Theory*, 46, 414–421.

Posner, R.A. (1992), *Economic Analysis of Law*, Boston: Little, Brown and Company.

Prescott, E.C. and R. Mehra (1980), "Recursive Competitive Equilibrium: The Case of Homogeneous Households", *Econometrica*, 48, 1365–1379.

Radner, R. (1967), "Equilibre des Marchés à Terme et au Comptant en Cas d'Incertitude", *Cahiers d'Econométrie*, 17, 35–52.

Radner, R. (1968), "Competitive Equilibrium under Uncertainty", *Econometrica*, 36, 31–58.

Radner, R. (1972), "Existence of Equilibrium of Plans, Prices and Price Expectations in a Sequence of Markets", *Econometrica*, 40, 289–304.

Radner, R. (1974), "A Note on Unanimity of Stockholders' Preferences Among Alternative Production Plans: A Reformulation of the Ekern-Wilson Model", *Bell Journal of Economics and Management Science*, 5, 181–184.

Radner, R. (1979), "Rational Expectations Equilibrium: Generic Existence and the Information Revealed by Prices", *Econometrica*, 47, 655–678.

Rae, J. (1834), *Statement of Some New Principles on the Subject of Political Economy Exposing the Fallacies of the System of Free Trade and of Some Other Doctrines Maintained in the "Wealth of Nations"*, Boston: Hilliard, Gray and Company. Reprinted by Augustus M. Kelley, New York, (1964).

Ramsey, F.P. (1928), "A Mathematical Theory of Saving", *Economic Journal*, 38, 543–559.

Ricardo, D. (1816), "Proposals for an Economical and Secure Currency", reprinted in *The Works and Correspondence of David Ricardo, Volume IV*, Piero Sraffa ed., Cambridge: Cambridge University Press, (1962).

Ricardo, D. (1817), *On the Principles of Political Economy and Taxation*, London: John Murray. Reprinted by Cambridge University Press, Cambridge, (1970).

Romer, D. (1986), "A Simple General Equilibrium Version of the Baumol-Tobin Model", *Quarterly Journal of Economics*, 101, 663–686.

Ross, S.A. (1973), "The Economic Theory of Agency: The Principal's Problem", *American Economic Review*, 63, 134–139.

Ross, S.A. (1974), "Return, Risk and Arbitrage", in *Risk and Return in Finance*, I. Friend and J. Bicksler eds., New York: Health Lexington.

Ross, S.A. (1976), "The Arbitrage Theory of Capital Asset Pricing", *Journal of Economic Theory*, 3, 343–362.

Ross, S.A. (1978a), "A Simple Approach to the Valuation of Risky Streams", *Journal of Business*, 51, 453–475.

Ross, S.A. (1978b), "Mutual Fund Separation in Financial Theory: The Separating Distributions", *Journal of Economic Theory*, 17, 254–286.

Rothschild, M. and J. Stiglitz (1976), "Equilibrium in Competitive Insurance Markets: An Essay on the Economics of Imperfect Information", *Quarterly Journal of Economics*, 90, 629–650.

Rubinstein, A. (1986), "Finite Automata Play the Repeated Prisoners' Dilemma", *Journal of Economic Theory*, 39, 83–96.

Rubinstein, M. (1974), "An Aggregation Theory for Securities Markets", *Journal of Financial Economics*, 1, 225–244.

Rubinstein, M. (1976), "The Valuation of Uncertain Income Streams and The Pricing of Options", *Bell Journal of Economics*, 7, 407–425.

Samuelson, P.A. (1947), *Foundations of Economic Analysis*, Cambridge, Mass.: Harvard University Press.

Samuelson, P.A. (1957), "Intertemporal Price Equilibrium: A Prologue to the Theory of Speculation", *Weltwirtschaftliches Archiv*, 79, 181–219.

Samuelson, P.A. (1965), "Proof that Properly Anticipated Prices Fluctuate Randomly", *Industrial Management Review*, 6, 41–49.

Samuelson, P.A. (1973), "Proof that Properly Discounted Present Values of Assets Vibrate Randomly", *Bell Journal of Economics and Management Science*, 4, 369–374.

Santos, M.S. and M. Woodford (1993), "Rational Asset Pricing Bubbles", Discussion Paper 9304, Centro de Investigación Económica, ITAM, Mexico.

Sargent, T.J. (1979), *Macroeconomic Theory*, New York: Academic Press.

Sargent, T.J. (1987), *Dynamic Macroeconomic Theory*, Cambridge, Mass.: Harvard University Press.

Sargent, T.J. and N. Wallace (1975), "Rational Expectations, the Optimal Monetary Instrument and the Optimal Money Supply Rule", *Journal of Political Economy*, 83, 241–254.

Scheinkman, J.A. (1980), "Discussion" in *Models of Monetary Economies*, J.H. Kareken and N. Wallace eds., Minneapolis: Federal Reserve Bank of Minneapolis.

Scheinkman, J.A. (1989), "Market Incompleteness and the Equilibrium Valuation of Assets", in *Theory of Valuation, Frontiers of Financial Theory*,

S. Bhattacharya and G. Constantinides eds., Totowa, NJ: Rowman and Litttlefield, 45–51.

Schumpeter, J.A. (1912), *Theorie der wirtschaftlichen Entwicklung.* English translation: *The Theory of Economic Development: An Inquiry into Profits, Capital, Credit, Interest and the Business Cycle*, Cambridge, Mass.: Harvard University Press, (1934).

Schumpeter, J.A. (1942), *Capitalism, Socialism and Democracy*, New York: Harper and Row.

Schumpeter, J.A. (1954), *History of Economic Analysis*, New York: Oxford University Press.

Selten, R. (1990), "Bounded Rationality", *Journal of Institutional and Theoretical Economics*, 146, 649–658.

Selten, R. (1991), "Evolution, Learning and Economic Behavior", *Games and Economic Behavior*, 3, 3–24.

Sharpe, W.F. (1964), "Capital Asset Prices: A Theory of Market Equilibrium Under Conditions of Risk", *The Journal of Finance*, 19, 425–442.

Sheffrin, S.M. (1983), *Rational Expectations*, Cambridge: Cambridge University Press.

Shiller, R.J. (1978), "Rational Expectations and the Dynamic Structure of Macroeconomic Models", *Journal of Monetary Economics*, 4, 1–44.

Shiller, R.J. (1979), "The Volatility of Long-Term Interest Rates and Expectations Models of the Term Structure", *Journal of Political Economy*, 87, 1190–1209.

Shiller, R.J. (1981), "Do Stock Prices Move Too Much to Be Justified by Subsequent Changes in Dividends?", *American Economic Review*, 71, 421–436.

Shiller, R.J. (1989), *Market Volatility*, Cambridge, Mass.: MIT Press.

Shleifer, A. and R. Vishny (1986), "Large Shareholders and Corporate Control", *Journal of Political Economy*, 94, 461–488.

Siconolfi, P. (1991), "Sunspot Equilibria and Incomplete Markets", *Journal of Mathematical Economics*, 20, 327–339.

Siconolfi, P. and A. Villanacci (1991), "Real Indeterminacy in Incomplete Financial Market Economies Without Aggregate Risk", *Economic Theory*, 1, 265–276.

Sidrauski, M. (1967), "Rational Choice and Patterns of Growth in a Monetary Economy", *American Economic Review, Papers and Proceedings*, 57, 534–544.

Simon, C.P. and L. Blume (1994), *Mathematics for Economists*, New York: Norton.

Simon, H.A. (1947), *Administrative Behavior*, London: Macmillan.

Simon, H.A. (1951), "A Formal Theory of the Employment Relationship", *Econometrica*, 19, 293–305.

Simon, H.A. (1954), "Bandwagon and Underdog Effects of Election Predictions", *Public Opinion Quarterly*, 18.

Simon, H.A. (1957), *Models of Man*, New York: Wiley.

Simon, H.A. (1969), *The Sciences of the Artificial*, Cambridge, Mass.: MIT Press.

Simon, H.A. (1979a), *Models of Thought*, New Haven: Yale University Press.

Simon, H.A. (1979b), "Rational Decision Making in Business Organization", *American Economic Review*, 69, 493–513.

Simon, H.A. (1983), *Reason in Human Affairs*, Stanford: Stanford University Press.

Simon, H.A. and W.G. Chase (1973a), "Perception in Chess" *Cognitive Psychology*, 4, 55–81, reprinted in *Models of Thought*, New Haven: Yale University Press, (1979).

Simon, H.A. and W.G. Chase (1973b), "The Mind's Eye in Chess", in *Visual Information Processing*, W.G. Chase ed., 215–281, New York: Academic Press. Reprinted in *Models of Thought*, New Haven: Yale University Press, (1979).

Singleton, K. (1987), "Specification and Estimation of Intertemporal Asset Pricing Models", in *Handbook of Monetary Economics*, B.H. Friedman and F.H. Hahn eds., Amsterdam: North-Holland.

Slutsky, E.E. (1937), "The Summation of Random Causes as the Source of Cyclic Processes", *Econometrica*, 5, 105–146, translation of Russian original in *Problems of Economic Conditions*, vol. 3, edited by the Conjuncture Institute, Moscou, (1927).

Smith, A. (1776), *An Inquiry into the Nature and Causes of the Wealth of Nations*, London: W. Strahan and T. Cadell.

Smith, V.L., G.L. Suchanek and A.W. Williams (1988), "Bubbles, Crashes and Endogenous Expectations in Experimental Spot Asset Markets", *Econometrica*, 56, 1119–1151.

Smith, C.W. and J.B. Warner (1979), "On Financial Contracting: An Analysis of Bond Covenants", *Journal of Financial Economics*, 7, 117–161.

Spence, A.M. and R. Zeckhauser (1971), "Insurance, Information and Individual Action", *American Economic Review*, 61, 380–387.

Starr, R.M. (1972), "The Structure of Exchange in Money and Barter Economies", *Quarterly Journal of Economics*, 88, 290–302.

Stiglitz, J.E. (1969), "A Re-Examination of the Modigliani-Miller Theorem", *American Economic Review*, 59, 784–793.

Stiglitz, J.E. (1974), "On the Irrelevance of Corporate Financial Policy", *American Economic Review*, 64, 851–866.

Stiglitz, J.E. (1982), "The Inefficiency of Stock Market Equilibrium", *Review of Economic Studies*, 49, 241–261.

Stigum, B. (1969a), "Entrepreneurial Choice over Time under Conditions of Uncertainty", *International Economic Review*, 10, 426–442.

Stigum, B. (1969b), "Competitive Equilibria under Uncertainty", *Quarterly Journal of Economics*, 83, 533–561.

Svensson, L.O. (1985), "Money and Asset Prices in a Cash-in-Advance Economy", *Journal of Political Economy*, 93, 919–944.

Taylor, J.B. (1980), "Aggregate Dynamics and Staggered Contracts", *Journal of Political Economy*, 88, 1–23.

Tirole, J. (1988), *The Theory of Industrial Organization*, Cambridge, Mass.: MIT Press.

Tobin, J. (1956), "The Interest Elasticity of the Transaction Demand for Cash", *Review of Economics and Statistics*, 38, 241–247.

Tobin, J. (1958), "Liquidity Preference as Behavior Towards Risk", *The Review of Economic Studies*, 26, 65–86.

Tobin, J. (1980), "Discussion" in *Models of Monetary Economies*, J.H. Kareken and N. Wallace eds., Minneapolis: Federal Reserve Bank of Minneapolis.

Townsend, R.M. (1980), "Models of Money With Spatially Separated Agents", in *Models of Monetary Economies*, J.H. Kareken and N. Wallace eds., Minneapolis: Federal Reserve Bank of Minneapolis.

Turgot, A.R.J. (1769), *Réflexions sur la Formation et la Distribution des Richesses* in *Ephémérides du Citoyen*, 1769, vols. 1 and 12; 1770, vol. 1. English translation: *Reflections on the Formation and Distribution of Wealth*, London: Macmillan (1911). Reprinted by Augustus M. Kelley, New York, (1971).

Varian, H.R. (1987), "The Arbitrage Principle in Financial Economics", *Journal of Economic Perspectives*, 1, 55–72.

Varian, H.R. (1991), *Microeconomic Analysis*, 3rd Edition, New York: Norton.

Vickrey, W. (1961), "Counterspeculation, Auctions, and Competitive Sealed Tenders", *Journal of Finance*, 16, 8–37.

Villanacci, A. (1991), "Indeterminacy of Equilibria, Taxes and Outside Money in Exchange Economies with Incomplete Financial Markets", CARESS Working Paper, University of Pennsylvania.

Wald, A. (1933), "Über die eindeutige positive Lösbarkeit der neuen Produktionsgleichungen", *Ergebnisse eines mathematischen Kolloquiums*, 6, 12–20.

Wald, A. (1934), "Über die Produktionsgleichungen der ökonomischen Wertlehre", *Ergebnisse eines mathematischen Kolloquiums*, 7, 1–6.

Wald, A. (1936), "Über einige Gleichungsysteme der mathematischen Ökonomie", *Zeitschrift für Nationalökonomie*, 7, 637–670. English translation: "On Some Systems of Equations of Mathematical Economics", *Econometrica*, 19, 368–403, (1951).

Wallace, N. (1980), "The Overlapping Generations Model of Fiat Money" in *Models of Monetary Economies*, J.H. Kareken and N. Wallace eds., Minneapolis: Federal Reserve Bank of Minneapolis.

Walras, L. (1874), *Eléments d'Economie Pure*, Lausanne: Corbaz. English translation, *Elements of Pure Economics*, Homewood, Il.: R.D. Irwin, (1954).

Walras, L. (1886), "Théorie de la Monnaie", *Revue Scientifique*, 37, no 15, 449–457, no 16, 493–500, also in *Etudes d'Economie Politique Appliquée*, Lausanne: Rouge/Paris: Pichon, (1898).

Werner, J. (1985), "Equilibrium in Economies with Incomplete Financial Markets", *Journal of Economic Theory*, 36, 110–119.

Werner, J. (1987), "Arbitrage and the Existence of Competitive Equilibrium", *Econometrica*, 55, 1403–1418.

Werner, J. (1990), "Structure of Financial Markets and Real Indeterminacy of Equilibria", *Journal of Mathematical Economics*, 19, 217–232; Working Paper, University of Bonn, (1986).

Whitehead, A.N. (1925), *Science and the Modern World,* London: Macmillan.

Wicksell, K. (1898), *Geldzins und Güterpreise*. English translation: *Interest and Prices*, London: The Royal Economic Society, (1936). Reprinted by Augustus M. Kelley, New York, (1962).

Wicksell, K. (1906), *Vorlesungen über Nationalökonomie, Zweiter Band*. English translation: *Lectures on Political Economy, Volume II*, London: Routledge and Kegan Paul, (1935).

von Wieser, F. (1914), *Theorie der gesellschaftlichen Wirtschaft*. English translation, *Social Economics*, New York: Adelphi and Co., (1927). Reprinted by Augustus M. Kelley, New York, (1967).

Williams, J.B. (1938), *The Theory of Investment Value,* Amsterdam: North Holland.

Williamson, O. (1975), *Markets and Hierarchies: Analysis and Antitrust Implications*, New York: Free Press.

Williamson, O. (1985), *The Economic Institutions of Capitalism*, New York: Free Press.

Wilson, C.A. (1979), "An Infinite Horizon Model with Money" in *General Equilibrium, Growth and Trade: Essays in Honor of Lionel McKenzie*, J.R. Green and J.A. Scheinkman eds., New York: Academic Press.

Wilson, R. (1968), "The Theory of Syndicates", *Econometrica*, 36, 119–132.

Woodford, M. (1990), "The Optimum Quantity of Money", in *Handbook of Monetary Economics, Volume II*, B.M. Friedman and F.H. Hahn eds., Amsterdam: North-Holland.

Working, H. (1934), "A Random Difference Series for Use in the Analysis of Time Series", *Journal of American Statistical Association*, 29, 11–24.

Working, H. (1949), "The Investigation of Economic Expectations", *American Economic Review*, 39, 150–166.

Working, H. (1958), "A Theory of Anticipatory Prices", *American Economic Review*, 48, 188–199.

Zweigert, K. and H. Kötz (1992), *Introduction to Comparative Law*, Oxford: Clarendon Press.

Index